# A MUSE FOR HEROES
Nine Centuries of the Epic in France

Critics usually dismiss French epic poetry as generally of little consequence. Voltaire summed up this attitude with his famous statement: 'Les Français n'ont pas la tête épique.'

In this examination and re-evaluation of the epic genre in French literature from its origins in the Middle Ages to the present day, Calin analyzes eighteen major areas. He discusses three *chansons de geste* (*La Chanson de Roland*, *Raoul de Cambrai*, and *Huon de Bordeaux*); long narrative poems from the later Middle Ages, including the romances of Chrétien de Troyes, *Le Roman de la Rose*, and the *dits amoureux* of Guillaume de Machaut; Ronsard's *Les Hymnes* and *Les Discours*; epics from the baroque period such as *Les Tragiques*, *Moyse sauvé*, and *Saint Louis*; the mock-epics of Boileau (*Le Lutrin*) and Voltaire (*La Pucelle*); the work of Lamartine, Vigny, and Victor Hugo; and the recent epics of Saint-John Perse, Louis Aragon, and Pierre Emmanuel.

Calin considers shifts in tone and even in mode over the years, and examines the external literary factors that have helped determine the form of long poems: the influences of a growing didactic current in the Middle Ages, of Greco-Roman or Italian canon in the Renaissance, and of the lyric since 1820. He finds that, in spite of academic stricture, ignorance, and lack of interest, the epic has survived as a genre; its evolution is central to French literature as a whole; and it will, he predicts, thrive in the future.

This work was awarded the Gilbert Chinard First Literary Prize by the Institut Français de Washington in 1981.

WILLIAM CALIN is Professor of Romance Languages at the University of Oregon.

William Calin

# A MUSE FOR HEROES

Nine Centuries of the
Epic in France

UNIVERSITY OF TORONTO PRESS
Toronto Buffalo London

© University of Toronto Press 1983
Toronto Buffalo London
Printed in Canada
Reprinted 1986

ISBN 0-8020-5599-0

∞

Printed on acid-free paper

University of Toronto Romance Series 46

---

Canadian Cataloguing in Publication Data

Calin, William, 1936–
    A muse for heroes

(University of Toronto romance series,
ISSN 0082-5336; 46)
Bibliography: p.
ISBN 0-8020-5599-0

1. Epic poetry, French – History and criticism.
I. Title. II. Series.

PQ201.C35        841'.0309        C82-095127-7

---

Was der Alten Gesang von Kindern Gottes geweissagt,
  Siehe! wir sind es, wir ...

*Hölderlin*


             Make no more giants, God,
But elevate the race at once! We ask
To put forth just our strength, our human strength,
All starting fairly, all equipped alike,
Gifted alike, all eagle-eyed, true-hearted –
See if we cannot beat thine angels yet!

*Browning*


Mag traum und ferne uns als speise stärken –
Luft die wir atmen bringt nur der Lebendige.
So dank ich freunde euch die dort noch singen
Und väter die ich seit zur gruft geleitet.
Wie oft noch spät da ich schon grund gewonnen
In trüber heimat streitend und des sieges
Noch ungewiss lieh neue kraft dies flüstern:
RETURNENT FRANC EN FRANCE DULCE TERRE.

*George*

# Contents

# Acknowledgments

This book has been published with the help of a grant from the Canadian Federation for the Humanities, using funds provided by the Social Sciences and Humanities Research Council of Canada, a grant from the University of Oregon, and a grant from the Publications Fund of the University of Toronto Press. I am grateful to the Council, and to the Institut Français de Washington (Edouard Morot-Sir, President), which awarded the book in manuscript first prize in the 1981 Gilbert Chinard Literary Prize competition.

Françoise Calin provided encouragement, support, and inspiration for this project, from beginning to end: her counsel was always based upon a vast literary culture and the most solid common sense. My former student, Karen McPherson, and Judith Williams of the University of Toronto Press perused the text with unfailing patience, improving both its style and substance. So also did Professor Robert Finch of Massey College, University of Toronto, and Professor John R. Allen of the University of Manitoba, referees for the University of Toronto Press and the Canadian Federation for the Humanities respectively. Linda and William Clemente prepared the index. I thank them all.

Extracts from the poetry of Saint-John Perse are reproduced by permission of Editions Gallimard, Paris. Extracts from the poetry of Louis Aragon are reproduced by his permission. Extracts from the poetry of Pierre Emmanuel are reproduced by his permission (*Tombeau d'Orphée*) and by permission of Desclée De Brouwer, Paris (*Babel*).

# A Muse for Heroes

# Introduction

As a medievalist, I became aware that the major genres – *chanson de geste*, *roman courtois*, and *dit amoureux* – form a continuity of epos. In fact, the long poem dominates the first three centuries of French literary history, and it is from France that her neighbors (Spain, Italy, Germany, England) learned to sing of heroism and romance in the vernacular. From the vantage-point of the Middle Ages I then came to scrutinize more recent French literature; my research focused on romantic and heroic modes in general and on the long poem in particular. I perceived, of course, that whereas in the peroid extending from Ronsard to Chénier writers generally accepted the theoretical supremacy of the Virgilian *poëme heroïque*, it was never to dominate esthetically the literary production of that age or the subsequent one, yielding precedence to the lyric, the tragedy, and finally the novel. Nonetheless, I also noticed that some of the greatest masters of French literature have practiced the mode, in its serious and comic forms, with extraordinary success: d'Aubigné, Saint-Amant, Boileau, Voltaire, Lamartine, Hugo, Saint-John Perse, Aragon, and Pierre Emmanuel. Their work proves that epic seeds are solidly, fruitfully planted in Gaul, have flowered in the last four centuries, and need hardly dread comparison with Italy or the British Isles.

The generalization I make in the preceding paragraph has to be considered something of an original discovery. For the attitude manifest in volumes on literary history or student manuals, if they discuss the subject at all, can still be summed up by that statement attributed by Voltaire (on the last page of *Essai sur la poésie épique*) to the mathematician and gentleman of letters, Nicolas de Malézieu: 'Les Français n'ont pas la tête épique.'[1] This famous *boutade* launched or perhaps merely consecrated a myth: that French literature, in spite of its triumphs in other areas, nevertheless has to admit failure in one genre, perhaps the most prestigious of all: epic poetry. That such a myth could arise in the eighteenth century is understandable. The narrative poems of the Middle Ages had long since disappeared from purview, were almost totally unknown to the literary public; a new flowering of epic, which would not come into being until the Romantic era, could hardly have been predicted by anyone; and the epoch of the Enlightenment, governed by neoclassical taste in the image of Boileau, did not even appreciate what du Bartas, d'Aubigné, Saint-Amant, or Le Moyne had created in the preceding two centuries. The influence of foreign cultures, the pride that foreign countries manifested in their own poetry, would ensure a certain, sometimes begrudging respect for Ariosto, Tasso, and Milton that Frenchmen refused to their own Renaissance and baroque masters.

That the myth could have persisted to our own epoch is less justifiable. This state of affairs is to be especially regretted given the attention that epic poetry has received in recent years from specialists working within the traditional century time-periods. The *chanson de geste*, the Renaissance-baroque epic, and the nineteenth-century *épopée humanitaire* have been especially well treated, and the *roman courtois*, *dit amoureux*, and eighteenth-century epic have by no means been neglected. The problem is that excellent monographs have not enjoyed the influence that they deserve. Furthermore, the critical coverage and the theoretical concern with the long poem that we take for granted in English literary history are lacking in France. The few general studies devoted to the French epic as a whole, the majority quite old, favor the nineteenth century.[2] Lamartine, Vigny, Hugo, Leconte de Lisle, even Régnier and Samain are given adequate coverage, but *Roland* alone represents the Middle Ages, and d'Aubigné is forgotten in the shadow of *La Franciade* and *La Henriade*. Of a different stamp is the brilliantly provocative Freudian-Jungian synthesis attempted by Charles Baudouin.[3] This volume, whether or not we accept its sometimes excessive formulations, is worthy of our esteem. However, Baudouin treats the epic as a world-wide phenomenon, and his knowledge of French literary history is necessarily amateurish. As a result, Voltaire's *Henriade*, Lamartine's *La Chute d'un Ange*, and, of course, the long poems of Hugo alone represent France's contribution. Baudouin's volume, for all its acumen, could not possibly change attitudes toward the history of the epos in France; this was in no way its intention. Finally, I would like to mention two serious, extremely well-written books, by Thomas M. Greene and Leo Pollmann.[4] The former, which concentrates on the Renaissance throughout Western Europe, contains sensitive, acute analyses of d'Aubigné and Saint-Amant. The latter presents an overview of the epic in the four major Western Romance literatures. Since Greene's choice of topic and 'time-cut' inevitably differs from mine (he is a Renaissance comparatist), our studies prove to be complementary. The same is true for Pollmann, a scholar of range and erudition, who, nonetheless, in 187 pages can give us only a most schematic treatment of the French aspect of his subject and, in any case, concentrates on distinguishing 'horizontal' from 'vertical' epics. I respect Pollmann's formulation but am interested in other things.

For these reasons, I decided that a book studying the long poem from the Middle Ages to the twentieth century, à la Française, ought to be written, and that I should seek to write it. As a medievalist, I can provide sympathy for narrative in verse and tolerance for startling metaphor, non-mimetic characters and episodes, romantic archetypes, and plots not constructed with the rigor people are accustomed to find in Racine and Flaubert. And in an age of hyper-specialization it is perhaps desirable to traverse the centuries, to remind people that our Western literature is a continuum from the early Middle Ages to the present, that no major genre or mode is limited to one period alone. We are the bearers of a millenium-long heritage; it is our duty and our joy to carry the torch.

Were I to synthesize from a sampling of definitions of the term 'epic' in French and English reference works, I should be able, if not to define the genre, at least to formulate a number of typical characteristics: that it is normally in verse, of some length, in the narrative mode, fictional but based on history or legend; that it treats on a grand scale a martial, heroic subject, manifests artistic coherence because it concentrates on a single central hero or event of national significance, contains stylized 'episodes,' and is grounded in the supernatural.[5] Similarly, the most weighty, the most seminal scholarly books on the subject also list 'norms of epic': to adhere to the mode a poem ought to be a narrative, a good story well told; be based on history, the primary subject-matter 'real'; have a hero larger than life; treat martial feats; give a 'heroic impression' or 'epic awe'; manifest grandeur, largeness, high quality and seriousness, a sense of amplitude, breadth, inclusiveness, and general significance; testify to human achievement and the dignity of man; represent a 'choric voice,' a collective, community point of view; and, in strictly esthetic terms, be composed in the 'grand style,' benefit from the author's control, and perhaps use traditional stock motifs.[6] Despite some disparity, despite the difference in mode between dictionaries designed for the general reader and volumes written by scholars for other scholars, a consensus can be reached. I do not wish to contest specific traits or aspects of any one definition. On the contrary, I can agree with much of this theoretical material, especially Greene's formulation, which is both judicious and widely applicable, and, at the end of the book, shall myself state those features I find typical of French epic as a whole. Nonetheless, I prefer not to begin with such a list or definition, because I am convinced that, for a project such as mine, a priori formulations are inevitably based on too narrow or meagre a corpus of texts and, for this reason, restrictive and normative. To give an example: by the rigid, consistent application of his own principles, Tillyard arrives at a quite arbitrary ideal or model, which then enables him to exclude from the domain of epic Ovid, Lucan, the *Beowulf*-poet, Chaucer, Malory, Ariosto, and du Bartas, and to include Herodotus, Xenophon, Langland, Bunyan, Fénelon, and Gibbon – eventually, even novelists such as Defoe and Conrad.[7] Tillyard's quandary is perhaps inevitable in literary studies where the term 'epic,' like 'comedy,' 'tragedy,' 'allegory,' and 'satire,' can refer both to a specific genre located in space and time and to a more or less universal mode to be found throughout world literature. Nevertheless, his approach, valid in his own terms and for what he is trying to do, will not be of much help to me.

Specialists on epic, as well as compilers of dictionaries, at least those, like Tillyard, in the Anglo-Saxon world, usually have in mind a neoclassical model – 'from Virgil to Milton' – which works for the sixteenth and seventeenth centuries (hence the appropriateness of Greene's norms) but can present problems when applied to other periods. For Tillyard and some others, the epic died with the advent of Romanticism. However, a new generation of scholars has come to recognize and to acclaim its presence in the nineteenth and twentieth centuries: Wordsworth, Byron, Eliot, and Pound, Lamartine, Hugo, and Saint-John Perse are epic poets.[8] The problem appears to lie in the fact that the long poem has evolved rapidly since the time of Milton and Pope, and that a new golden age of epos has arisen that cannot be accounted for by the old rules. Only the limited, formalized, neoclassical *poëme heroïque* has disappeared, not epic in its broadest sense. It is obvious that modern writers who have been consciously aware of a tradition of neoclassical epos, who have either sought to compete with it or reacted against it, do not conform to or include in their own works all salient characteristics we find in Tasso and Milton. Three traits we can ascribe to modern epic are the lack of formal heroic activity or even a condemnation of it, the lack of a hero-leader superior in degree to other men, and the lack of a choric voice. Indeed, the romantic and post-romantic bard tells of the quest for such a voice by a poet-narrator-protagonist on behalf of himself or the people, which will give expression to a new, inner, non-martial heroism.

On the other end of the chronological scale, it is a commonplace in scholarly circles to include certain medieval texts – *Beowulf, La Chanson de Roland, El poema del Cid, Das Nibelungenlied* – under the category 'epic,' alongside the Homeric poems of Antiquity. However, it is also true that *chanson de geste* differs from classical precept at least as much as do *The Prelude* and *Anabase*. Not only does Turold not employ Homeric similes or stock classical motifs such as the voyage to the underworld; it is even debatable whether early medieval poems were composed in the sublime

style, whether their speech and diction were meant to be elevated in the
way that Virgil, Tasso, Camoens, and Milton certainly are. Yet, if we
include *chanson de geste* in our corpus, do we have the right to exclude
courtly romance and even medieval allegory? Medieval vernacular letters
exhibit much less genre-consciousness than is the case in the Renaissance
or the modern period; the boundaries between *chanson* and *roman*, between
*roman* and *dit*, are difficult to specify. According to some scholars, they
never did exist historically in the Middle Ages.[9] Furthermore, Chrétien de
Troyes, Guillaume de Lorris, Jean de Meun, and Guillaume de Machaut
all adored classical myth, were avid readers of Virgil and Ovid, in fact imitated them with more purposiveness than they did the singers of *geste*.
Indeed, Chrétien is as 'heroic,' as 'epic,' as Ariosto and Tasso. This is an
important point, for Pulci, Boiardo, Ariosto, even Tasso worked within a
tradition of 'romance' as well as of classical epic; that is, they benefited, in a
popular Italian format, from the heritage of medieval French narrative,
and are closer in spirit to late *chanson de geste*, Chrétien, and the *Lancelot-
Grail Prose Cycle* than to Antiquity. Their style of *poema*, whether *caval-
leresco* or *eroico*, has always been considered, and correctly so, *the* Italian
epic, with as much right to determine norms and values as that of any
nation. The same is true in England for Spenser, who has at least as many
affinities, historical and temperamental, with Arthurian romance and *Le
Roman de la Rose* as with Ariosto, not to speak of Virgil. Furthermore,
although English and French scholars distinguish between epic (*chanson de geste*) and romance or the novel (*roman*), for the Germans *die Epik*
traditionally designates all medieval genres of story-telling, subdivided
into categories such as *Heldenepik, vorhöfische Epik, frühöfische Epik,
höfische Epik, Tierepik, Kleinepik, Spielmannsepos*, etc.; hence books by
Schürr and Pollmann discuss Chrétien de Troyes as well as *La Chanson de
Roland* and *Le Charroi de Nîmes*.[10] This is the case, in part, because *Epos*,
one of Goethe's three *Naturformen der Poesie*, refers to the narrative mode
in general, as distinguished from the dramatic and the lyrical. This concept of the three "big genres" – *das Epische, das Dramatische, das Lyrische*
– which allegedly goes back to Plato and Aristotle (in fact, it was first
proposed by Minturno in 1559) had a tremendous influence on the Schlegel
brothers, Schelling, Hegel, Lukács, and the leading modern theoreticians
of literature in German-speaking countries. The influence remains strong,
even and especially when scholars propose two or four *Grundhaltungen*
(*Naturformen, Dichtweisen, Schreibweisen*) in place of the original three or
(as Goethe himself did) distinguish as carefully as they can the various
*Dichtarten* or *Gattungen*, such as epos, ballad, ode, or *Lied* that are derived
from *das Epische* or *das Lyrische*.[11]

From an historical perspective, a many-stranded yet precise, unified tradi-

tion includes *chansons de geste*; courtly romance; courtly allegory; the
Italian epics of the Renaissance, both romantic and neoclassical; later
romantic and classical epics in France, England, and Spain; and, still more
recently, romantic and modern epic throughout Western and Eastern
Europe. A prescriptive, normative definition of Epos which excludes from
consideration the *höfische Epik* and *poema romanzesco* (Chrétien, Ariosto,
Spenser) or modern *épopées humanitaires* (Shelley, Hugo, Spitteler) not
only impoverishes our critical perception of the topic but also is historically inaccurate. Outside the context of the West, we discover an even vaster
frame of reference and an even greater variety of mode, theme, form, and
tone. The medieval Persian epic (the most illustrious authors are Firdausī,
Nizāmī, 'Aṭṭār, Sa'dī, Rūmī and Jāmī) follows an evolution roughly parallel to that of the long poem in France over the same centuries: from national,
heroic texts to erotic romance to didactic allegory (primarily religious but
also erotic) and satire. The majority of these works recall Chrétien de
Troyes, Guillaume de Lorris, and Jean de Meun, not Virgil and Milton,
nor Turold and Hugo. The Japanese *Heike-monagatori*, on the other
hand, leans in the direction of chronicle, bringing to mind Tacitus and
Froissart. I can make comparable analogies for the Indian *Rāmāyana* and
*Mahābhārata*, the Near-Eastern *Gilgamesh*, and the oral tradition of Black
Africa or Central Asia.

Similarly, the generally accepted distinction between two sorts of epic –
primary, oral, authentic, popular, and primitive, on the one hand; secondary, literary, artificial, learned, and mature, on the other – will be of little
help in discussing the French tradition. First of all, along with such scholars
as Etiemble and Siciliano, I believe epic to be an aristocratic genre, that
it was never primitive or popular in conception, and that the notion of
*Volkstimmung* is a romantic myth no longer tenable.[12] In other words, the
*Iliad* and *La Chanson de Roland* are as complex, sophisticated, and purpos-
ive as the *Aeneid* and *Le Chevalier au lion* or *Le Roman de la Rose*: the
similarities between these five works of art are far more significant than their
differences. And secondly, because out of the eighteen authors or works
to be treated in this book, only the *Song of Roland*, only early *chanson de
geste*, can under the best of conditions be designated as 'primary,' and
even there we find controversy as to whether or not the Old French epic is
indeed 'oral' in any sense of the term other than that of oral delivery, true
for practically all medieval literature, sacred and secular, fictional and non-
fictional, in verse and in prose. Indeed, the fact that all medieval texts
were read, chanted, or sung aloud renders Aristotelian genre distinction
based upon the radical of presentation extremely precarious. Late *chansons* such as *Raoul de Cambrai* or *Huon de Bordeaux* are meant to be read
aloud, not chanted, and they imitate the early poems with as much con-

scious artistry, as much distance, as Chrétien de Troyes, Guillaume de Lorris, Jean de Meun, and Guillaume de Machaut refashion their sources, classical and modern. To base a major tenet of criticism upon the imitation of long-dead classics in foreign tongues as distinguished from all other imitation appears to me arbitrary. The 'primary-secondary' formulation is no doubt of use for Classicists who wish to compare Homer and Virgil but proves to be tangential for the discussion of nine centuries of French verse, so subtly and carefully intertwined.

Following some of the more recent proponents of the esthetics of reception, I submit that a genre such as epic (or novel or tragedy or satire) embodies not a fixed norm but a complex of directives for the reader. It is ever in a state of mutation, a shifting complex of shifting traditions, ever evolving in time. Theories based uniquely upon classical (or medieval) examples, clearly defined, will prove to be false or incomplete. No strict definition is possible, no set of necessary and sufficient properties can be ascertained, no one single trait found common to all texts examined, and no single work enshrined as a model for the genre taken in its entirety. Our notion of genre ought to be, as much as possible, tentative, inductive, and empirical – *in re* – rather than prescriptive, deductive, normative, and *ante rem*. Epic is all the poems, of all times and climes, that make it up. Such texts can be heroic, romantic, religious, philosophical, comic, satiric, idyllic, even lyrical.

In conclusion, for all these reasons I prefer to return to the Greeks, to the root-word for epic, *epopoiia, epopoiios*, defined, according to the *Grand Robert*, 'qui fait des récits en vers.'[13] We know that, in Homer, *'epikós* or *epos* meant an utterance, something said, and that, for Aristotle, *epopoiiai* was the 'metrical representation of heroic action,' a narrative in simple meter and unlimited in duration.[14] In other words, I shall adopt strictly formal criteria for deciding which works are to be included in this book: in general, poems of some length which, to a greater or lesser extent, tell stories. I agree only that epics are, for the most part, reasonably long and narrative. I am reminded of Albert B. Lord's formulation: 'A narrative poem is one that tells a story. The basic types are epic and ballad. Although metrical romance is often considered as a third basic type, it is probably rightly to be thought of as a kind of epic, because it shares important recurrent themes with epic and presents them in the same narrative manner'; also of the statement by a contemporary Scandinavian poet: 'I have defined an epic as a poetical narrative that is so extensive that one cannot read or recite it from the beginning to the end without pausing for repasts and sleep ...'[15] (Even here, some consideration has to be given the brief epic, in the line of Milton and Hugo.) Those works which partake of an epic tradition are the ones I wish, even if provisionally, to call epic. Only after considering the tradition of the long poem in its entirety – medieval, Renaissance, and modern; heroic, erotic, satirical, philosophical – shall I then, inductively, empirically, and *a posteriori*, propose conclusions concerning epic in France.

Perhaps the most interesting aspect pertaining to the conception of this volume was the choice of texts to be discussed. On the one hand, given the options discussed above – to cover all nine centuries of French literary history and to include poems of various styles and modes – it became imperative to write a book of some length. I simply could not allow *La Chanson de Roland* to stand for the Middle Ages or Saint-John Perse's *Anabase* alone to represent our century. On the other hand, since almost one hundred *chansons de geste* have survived in one form or another, since we have a comparable number of medieval verse romances and of seventeenth century *poëmes heroïques*, and some two hundred poems or collections of poems in the nineteenth century that can claim to be epic, any effort at totality would be physically impossible. Furthermore, to limit my interpretation of works as complex as *Le Roman de la Rose*, *Les Tragiques*, and *Jocelyn* to five or even ten pages would deny the purpose of these essays. Some concentration in depth (a limited, restricted depth, after all) on individual authors and texts was essential.

I elected to organize my work into eighteen chapters, each devoted to a single author or, for literature in Old French, a single opus. Equal attention is given to the three distinguishable periods of epic production in France: the Middle Ages; the Age of Classicism (taken in its broadest sense, the conscious, willful imitation of Greco-Roman antiquity that extends from the Renaissance to the Enlightenment); and the Modern Age, beginning with the Romantic revival.

For the medieval, I concentrate on the *chanson de geste*, the most obvious, most apparently 'epic' form France has produced, devoting chapters to three quite different but equally beautiful and original manifestations of the genre: *La Chanson de Roland*, *Raoul de Cambrai*, and *Huon de Bordeaux*. However, I consider it no less important to include chapters on the long narrative poems that perpetuated the epic spirit during the later Middle Ages and had so great an influence on the elaboration of sublime poetry in France and abroad. Therefore, I treat what I deem to be the leading masterpieces of this kind in the twelfth, thirteenth, and fourteenth centuries – that is, the romances of Chrétien de Troyes, *Le Roman de la Rose*, and the *dits amoureux* of Guillaume de Machaut.

The second period extends from 1500 to 1800, and since I agree with the traditional verdict that *La Franciade* and *La Henriade* are estimable failures, they receive only brief discussion in chapters devoted mainly to other works. Instead, I concentrate on the Baroque, devoting a chapter each to what I consider to be the three most beautiful epics of that age: d'Aubigné's *Les Tragiques*, Saint-Amant's *Moyse sauvé*, and Le Moyne's *Saint Louis*. These are preceded by a chapter on d'Aubigné's great predecessor, Ronsard – studied as the author of *Les Hymnes* and *Les Discours*. For the classical generation and the subsequent century I analyze what I believe to be the most successful form of the long poem in that period: the mock-epic – specifically, Boileau's *Le Lutrin* and Voltaire's *La Pucelle*.

The third and last portion of this book is divided equally between the nineteenth and twentieth centuries. For the earlier period I deal with Romanticism, with chapters allotted to Lamartine (the long epic), to Vigny (the brief epic), and to Victor Hugo, who carried both traditions to their ultimate perfection in *La Fin de Satan* and *La Légende des Siècles*. In the twentieth century I scrutinize the contemporary period, partly because I am convinced that some of the greatest poetry in French letters has been written since the Second World War and partly in order to show how vital the tradition of the long poem is in our own age. Therefore, I devote chapters to three moderns, each with a distinct voice, all of whom have produced masterpieces in recent years (although, of course, some of their texts date from an earlier period): Saint-John Perse (*Anabase, Amers*), Aragon (*Brocéliande, Le Fou d'Elsa*), and Pierre Emmanuel (*Tombeau d'Orphée, Babel*).

I regret not being able to discuss a host of beautiful *chansons de geste* (*La Chanson de Guillaume, Le Couronnement de Louis, Garin le Lorrain, Renaud de Montauban*, etc.) and *romans courtois* (*Floire et Blancheflor, Le Châtelain de Couci*, the *Tristan* romances, the works of Jean Renart and Beaumanoir, etc.). This book loses something because the philosophical-scientific poetry of the Renaissance (Peletier du Mans, du Bartas), the Parnassian continuation of the brief epic (Leconte de Lisle and his disciples), and the sublime Catholic verse of the early twentieth century (Claudel, Péguy) are referred to only in passing. Decisions were based upon what I consider to be the ultimate importance of certain figures in the history of literature but also, inevitably in some cases, upon my own personal bias. Such considerations also determined the choice of poems by an individual author, the fact that I neglect Lamartine's *La Chute d'un Ange* in favor of *Jocelyn*, for instance, and Aragon's *Les Poètes* in favor of *Le Fou d'Elsa*. For reasons of space, I largely rejected discussion of the 'brief epic,' making exceptions only for Ronsard, the master of the sublime style in the sixteenth century, and for Vigny and, of course, Hugo, who occupy a similar role in the first half of the nineteenth. These are *cas limites*, as are manifestations of medieval allegory. Finally, with the greatest regret, I also exclude long poems written in French by authors from other parts of the Francophone world (for example, Black poets such as Senghor, Glissant, and

Tchicaya U Tam'si, among others) and those written by Frenchmen in other languages, specifically Latin (Bernard Sylvester and Alan of Lille in the twelfth century) and Occitan (the medieval *Girard de Roussillon*, *Flamenca*, and *Jaufre*; Guillaume Ader in the Renaissance; and Mistral, Michel Camelat, and others during the last hundred years). These Latins, Occitanians, Bretons, Canadians, Black Africans, and men of the Caribbean have made a vital contribution in the long poem as in all other areas. Let us hope that one day they will receive the recognition and acceptance within the French community which they so magnificently deserve.

Now for a few words about methodology. I have elected to concentrate on modern critical analysis of individual texts, reserving less attention but still a reasonable amount, I hope, to the development of epic form and how the writer in question – a Ronsard, a Voltaire, a Hugo – turned to that mode. Observations on the nature of the French epic as a whole are then elaborated in a lengthy 'Conclusion,' where I also discuss, in a more synthetic manner, topics such as: the evolution of the long poem; its common traits; shifts in tone and mode over the years; external literary factors which help determine the form of long poems; the possibilities for a cyclical interpretation of literary history; sources; reception; and the future for epic.

The kinds of approaches I employ are varied: archetypal, Freudian, Jungian, phenomenological, structuralist, thematic – derived from the various schools of American modern criticism and the more recent French Nouvelle Critique; I hope that this pluralism will permit the text to 'choose' the methods appropriate to it and avoid the danger of forcing works of art onto a Procrustian bed arbitrarily designated in advance.

Modern criticism is the way of looking at literature in our time, as much a part of our age as philology and history were of the age of such men as Lanson and Bédier. It is true, medieval and Renaissance texts were created in a particular place and time: the trouvère earns a living under very different conditions than apply to Valéry and Eluard. However, once uniquely historical considerations have been taken into account, and providing that the critic makes use of whatever aid historical scholarship can give, he then has a right to approach a poem from within, seeking to determine what makes it a work of art – its structure, imagination, world, and tone. Although the external aspects of literary creation vary from age to age, internally the work of art remains essentially the same over the centuries. Furthermore, the insights of a Freud or a Marx are truly discoveries not inventions – that is, they concern truths of the human condition and are valid for men or poems of the past as well as of the present. They apply as well to *Huon de Bordeaux* and *Les Tragiques* as to the masterpieces of Aragon and Emmanuel.

I also believe that the insights of modern criticism, when applied with taste and discrimination, coincide with, and are reinforced by, the most recent trends in cultural history, for the best contemporary historians, people like Duby, Le Goff, Mandrou, Ariés, are returning to a study of imaginative literature and art in order to discover the symbolic and emotional mentalities of past ages; in the process, their insights correspond to those of modern criticism. A phenomenological approach – a study of the sexual and symbolic connotations of fire or water imagery in *Raoul de Cambrai* or *Moyse sauvé* – is eminently appropriate, since Bachelard, and Jung before him, took their notion of the four elements from scientific treatises of Antiquity and the Middle Ages. Similarly, a Freudian meditation on Eros and Thanatos is congruent in a tradition of lyric poets who knew exactly what they were doing when they proclaimed their desire to die for, with, and in their ladies – I am thinking specifically of Scève, Ronsard, and d'Aubigné. Prudish nineteenth- and early twentieth-century academics were perhaps unfamiliar with *la petite mort*; but we, thanks to Freud and more recent developments, can understand Renaissance poets on our terms, which also happen to be their own. Freud based some of his theories concerning the interpretation of dreams on the writings of the Ancients and on medieval dream books, and Jung was one of the greatest twentieth-century exponents of a renewed interest in alchemy and astrology. And the structuralist obsession with language and with such notions as a 'grammar of narrative,' practiced by Barthes, Genette, Todorov, and others, harks back to, and is directly influenced by, treatises of rhetoric, the school tradition so dominant in our culture until the time of the Third Republic. Literary criticism and literary history, properly employed, complement, indeed reinforce each other: the war between them that has divided literature departments in our universities for so many years may well be based upon a misunderstanding. And if our old literatures deserve to hold a place in the university curriculum and in our cultural heritage, they can no longer afford dispensation from the critical scrutiny that we apply to modern texts. To understand the past, one must be able to employ all the insights and approaches that the contemporary world offers us. If such literature is worth reading *as literature*, it can stand up under the most searching analysis. The past is no privileged domain, exempt from the rules of criticism, nor ought it to benefit from such exemption. The best French epic poetry, like all great poetry, is beautiful; no tools that can help us to explain it ought to be disdained. The final goal for our work is that we help render poetry more accessible and more vital to the reader of today.

## Chapter One

# 🙊 *LA CHANSON DE ROLAND*

Aside from Lives of Saints, the epic is the oldest vernacular genre to have flourished in the North of France. From the end of the eleventh to the end of the fourteenth century about one hundred *chansons de geste* (songs of deeds in arms) were written, most of which narrate exploits derived from early French history. Some, inspired by the crusades, tell of Charlemagne's victories over the Saracens (*La Chanson de Roland, La Chanson d'Aspremont*). Some exalt the concept of lineage, a family whose members struggle against villains at home and abroad, in support of a king who does nothing to help them (*La Chanson de Guillaume, Le Couronnement de Louis*). Some treat of civil war or a feud between two feudal dynasties (*Raoul de Cambrai, Garin le Lorrain*) or of a baron forced into rebellion by an unjust king (*Girard de Roussillon, Renaud de Montauban*). Still others, in particular the later *chansons*, under the influence of courtly romance, introduce elements of love and adventure in a romance cadre (*Huon de Bordeaux, Les Enfances Renier*). In the first half of the thirteenth century the various *chansons* were gathered into three great cycles: The Cycle of the King, the Cycle of Garin de Monglane (Guillaume d'Orange and his family), and the Cycle of Rebel Barons. However, a process of cyclical organization is also manifest in the early period. For example, *La Chanson de Guillaume* gave rise to sequels and these in turn to additional works, written to fill out Guillaume's epic biography, which tells the exploits of his youth and old age, and those of his father, his grandfather, and his nephews. In sum, from the oral legend concerning Guillaume d'Orange and the first *Chanson de Guillaume* were derived directly or indirectly all twenty-four poems that, in thirteenth-century manuscripts, make up the Cycle of Garin de Monglane.[1]

   *Chansons de geste* are composed in a largely paratactic, formulaic style, based on assonanced decasyllabic lines contained in strophes (*laisses*) of unequal length; in time epicists often shifted to twelve-syllable verse and rhyme. We know that the early texts were sung or chanted in public, as

opposed to later medieval narrative, which was read aloud. One of the
questions that has caused dissension among medievalists concerns whether
or not the Old French epic was actually *composed* orally, in a manner
comparable to that of popular bards or 'singers of tales' in twentieth-
century Yugoslavia, Bulgaria, and Central Asia. In my opinion, unlike oral
epic, the medieval *chansons de geste* (and the *Iliad* and the *Odyssey*) are
sophisticated, literary works of art that reveal mastery of psychology, of
political, social, and ideological questions, and of narrative structure.
However, the 'oral hypothesis' probably does explain the pre-literary origins of the genre and the particular stylistic form Turold and his successors gave to their creations in the twelfth and thirteenth centuries. Although
by no means primitive in any artistic sense, the medieval French epic,
especially in language, does appear static and compartmentalized, highly
lyrical as well as narrative, and with a monumental, almost sacral sense of
stylization and decorum. In this respect it is unique in the history of French
letters.[2]

Admittedly, the vast majority of these *chansons de geste* are mediocre,
indeed worse than mediocre. However, perhaps a dozen texts, including
the three studied in this book, can be considered of the very first quality.
Twelve masterpieces out of one hundred extant poems compares more
than favorably with the seventeenth-century theatre and nineteenth-century
novel, for example. In any age the vast majority of books do not withstand critical and esthetic scrutiny. But the masterpieces more than repay the
attention we lavish on them, stand out from the others, and mark the land
that give them birth. The heroic poetry of medieval France, in quantity and
quality, in variety and richness, surpasses comparable manifestations in
the other modern Western vernaculars and can only be compared with the
epic of ancient Greece and India.

*La Chanson de Roland*,[3] probably written between 1098 and 1100, perhaps by a certain Turold, otherwise unknown, is one of the oldest, best
French epics. It is certainly the most famous, the only *chanson de geste* to
have caught public fancy and become, in a sense, the national epic of France.
Critics have found in the *Roland* a fresh, martial exuberance, which recalls
similar works of the 'heroic age,' such as the *Iliad* or the Icelandic Sagas. In
comparison to the Renaissance epic and even to other *chansons de geste*,
*Roland* presents a static, relatively uncomplicated world, one of light without shadows, where ethical and moral lines are clearly drawn, and relatively non-problematic characters are at one with their universe. Life
and experience are felt as an immediate whole, grasped as a total process.
Authority and hierarchy are naturally inherent in social institutions considered in no sense external to man. At the center of a closed society, quasi-

invincible and superior to other men, Roland articulates the community experience, a collective consciousness, for he not only embodies the values of his age but also stands for his city or people, his destiny identical to theirs. Like Achilles, like Odysseus, he lives in an ideal world where men's highest spiritual values do not run counter to their physical capacities. The overall feeling is one of equilibrium, a heroic world in which men succeed in resembling the gods.[4] This equilibrium, however, does not prevent *La Chanson de Roland* from being a poem of violence, war, and death, containing perhaps the greatest massacre in French literature, a good one hundred of the dead mentioned expressly by name. The values of a shame, not a guilt, culture are grounded in external prestige, perceived by others, rather than an internalized sense of sin or remorse. Roland loves fighting for its own sake, for the sheer joy of wielding a trusty blow of sword or lance. He also fights for glory and honor, that men may never sing a *male cançun* about him or any member of his family. And his greatest exploit is to affront death, to brave the unknown even to the limits of his mortality, and to die nobly as the last expression of his manhood.

Nonetheless, *La Chanson de Roland* is a much more complex, even problematic work of art than many scholars have been willing to admit. More than the *Iliad* and the *Odyssey*, it is an ideological poem, in which questions of policy are treated with subtlety and penetration. For example, one reason why Roland and Ganelon quarrel and ultimately why Ganelon betrays his people derives from the fact that the two barons hold opposing political philosophies. When the Saracen ambassador Blancandrin proposes peace terms to the French, Roland urges Charles to refuse the offer and fight the Muslims to the bitter end, no matter how long it takes, whereas Ganelon counsels that the French go home on the conditions proposed by Blancandrin. Nor is this the first time that the two factions, or their leaders, have been at odds. Roland points out that when on a previous occasion the Saracens offered similar terms they executed the French ambassadors sent to conclude the treaty. Roland's allusion to those members of the Council who advised Charles madly ('alques de legerie,' 206) can apply only to Ganelon and his party, whereas Ganelon contrasts *bricun* and *fols*, e.g., Roland, who offer *cunseill d'orguill* to wise men such as himself:

> Ki ço vos lodet que cest plait degetuns,
> Ne li chalt, sire, de quel mort nus murjuns.
> Cunseill d'orguill n'est dreiz quë a plus munt;
> Laissun les fols, as sages nus tenuns! – AOI  (226–9)

Although the peace faction wins out (for Naimes and the others support

Ganelon), Turold makes it quite clear that his protagonist is in the right. Prior to this council-scene in the French camp we are told of a parallel colloquy in Saragossa. Thus the public benefits from information not available to the characters themselves. We realize that, as Roland suggests, the Saracens have fomented a plot. It is not true that they hope to assassinate the French ambassador and continue the war (as they did in Basin and Basile's day); on the contrary, their intention is to make peace, but, once Charles has returned to Aix-la-Chapelle, they will neither convert to Christianity nor become his men. Furthermore, when Roland designates Ganelon as the French ambassador to Saragossa, the latter is furious; his rage no doubt derives partly from the fact that even he recognizes that Saracens are capable of treachery. He knows that Roland is right. And each episode that follows corroborates this first impression: the Saracens come close to assassinating the French messenger (Ganelon), they betray the peace terms, and they ambush Roland and the rearguard, while time and time again God and his angels appear on the French side, to sanction Charles's crusade against the Infidel.

When, upon Charles's return to Aix, Ganelon is brought to trial for treason, he pleads innocent. He does not deny having brought about Roland's death but claims that since he publicly defied Roland, Oliver, and the Peers before setting out to Saragossa, it was his prerogative, as a feudal baron, to do them ill:

> Jo desfiai Rollant le poigneor
> E Oliver e tuiz lur cumpaignun:
> Carles l'oïd e si nob[l]e baron.
> Vengét m'en sui, mais n'i ad traïsun. –    (3775–8)

In other words, Ganelon was not Roland's vassal, nor was Roland his; therefore, acccording to feudal law, he had the right to declare war on his enemy. And Ganelon undoubtedly speaks sincerely. At the Saracen camp and elsewhere he always distinguishes between Charlemagne and Roland, praising the former enthusiastically even when he denigrates the latter. He perhaps even considers Roland's death to be in Charlemagne's best interests, since only then will these debilitating wars come to an end. Out of weakness, the court is ready to admit Ganelon's plea: because he has powerful kinsmen, because to execute him would deprive the empire of a by no means negligible unit of defense, because he is a great lord ('mult est gentilz hoem,' 3811), and because no decision of the court can bring Roland back to life: 'Morz est Rollant, ja mais nel revereiz' (3802). However, Tierri d'Anjou, the king's spokesman, points out that, whatever harm Roland did to Ganelon, Roland was Charles's vassal serving in Charles's army. By having him killed, Ganelon hurts his lord, and by implication, Charles's kingdom, and the Christian faith:

> Que que Rollant Guenelun forsfesist,
> Vostre servise l'en doüst bien guarir.
> Guenes est fels d'iço qu'il le traït;
> Vers vos s'en est parjurez e malmis.    (3827–30)

Significantly, during the judicial duel which eventually opposes Tierri and Ganelon's champion Pinabel, the latter speaks of the family bond whereas Tierri upholds God and the justness of his cause. Turold, of course, agrees, as presumably does God, for Tierri emerges the victor in this *judicium Dei.*[5]

Turold's 'political philosophy' can be analyzed in feudal terms. Roland and Ganelon are vassals of Charlemagne, who in turn owes fealty to the divinity. Since the Saracens, by the virtue of their 'Saracenness,' have rebelled against God, it is Charles's duty to avenge his Lord and decline all peace terms until the rebels have returned to the fold. By advising Charles to make peace with the Infidel and by destroying the rearguard, Ganelon commits an act of treachery against his lord Charlemagne, to whom he owes fidelity, aid, and counsel. Furthermore, Marsile, a vassal, betrays Roland, who is Charles's vassal. Charles exterminates Marsile's army but can totally avenge the affront only by fighting his equal, Marsile's overlord. Since Marsile and Roland have at various times invoked help, it is necessary for their calls to be answered and their quarrel resolved by higher powers. Thus Charles and Baligant fight in judicial combat for their vassals and to avenge harm inflicted on them. Baligant loses because he is in the wrong; his man had betrayed Charles's man. Furthermore, as Charles is vassal to God, Baligant belongs to Satan. Both sovereigns fight in lieu of their suzerains, masters over all. Roland, on the contrary, has been a good vassal – faithful to Charles and God – and can thus, at the moment of death, hand his glove, symbol of feudal service, directly to God's angel. Only when the bad vassals, Ganelon, Marsile, and Baligant, have been crushed will a harmonious, well-balanced feudal hierarchy be reestablished.

More likely, however, the author is setting off the values of feudal society, proclaimed by Ganelon, against an alternative, competing ethos embodied in Roland and Charlemagne. Ganelon's desire to go home after his service is over, his incredibly punctilious sense of personal honor, his readiness to declare war on other barons who have wronged him, his reliance on trial by battle and on his family – these are manifestations of the feudal ethos and clan solidarity. Significantly, Ganelon communicates perfectly with Blancandrin, for their values are identical. The pagan world is also grounded on a feudal ideology. Nonetheless, for the *Roland*-poet, this *saives hom* and his friends are in error, for other men have recognized a finer wisdom and more absolute standards: the community, the monarchy, France, and Christendom. A false concept of honor brings Ganelon to betray Roland; a false desire for peace, comfort, and domestic order brings him to betray Christ. Given that this lone individual divides the French army and Christianity itself, Turold counsels that the individual be subordinated to the group, anarchy to order and hierarchy, feudal or clan honor to Christian duty, and that God's sacred mission and the supremacy of the royal person take priority over other calls.

Roland too pays excessive heed to feudal and family honor when he declines reinforcements for the rearguard and refuses to call for help when ambushed. Roland endangers the sacred mission by needlessly placing his own life and those of Charles's twenty thousand crack troops in jeopardy. Indeed, he will fall in expiation for those errors. Yet his attitude of intransigence toward the Pagans was the right one, 'wiser' than Ganelon's prudent compromises, and before he dies Roland discovers what Ganelon never dreamed of: the preeminence of non-individualistic concerns. Roland's death puts the Christian army back onto its path. Charles and Naimes had been seduced by Ganelon's wise counsel; they also wanted to go home. But Roland's gesture of sacrifice to the cause, and the proof of Muslim perfidy made manifest by Roland's martyrdom, bring about a change of heart in the French high command. Charlemagne returns to the field and destroys the power of Islam.

It is probable that the socio-ideological content of *La Chanson de Roland* reflects, in a schematic way, real intracultural tensions manifest in late eleventh-century French society; that, like so many great epics, *Roland* reinterprets history and contemporary reality.[6] A council which chooses the wrong policy (peace) then designates and is about to exonerate the wrong ambassador (Ganelon) is shown to be flawed. Scholars have suggested that Turold supports the ascendancy of royal power against the quasi-autonomous great barons by having the king rely upon his closest advisers, the *curia regis* or *privés du roi*, upon the petty nobility, or upon young, unestablished *juvenes* free for a life of prowess. Those virtues presumed inherent in youth and in the late eleventh-century *bachelers* or the king's household – valor, generosity, abnegation – are then projected onto great barons, peers of the realm. Turold wishes that the vertical, anarchical traditions of feudalism and clan loyalty could be replaced by horizontal peerdom and a new aristocratic consciousness of community (*projektierte Gemeinschaft*), based upon chivalry, fidelity, and the total gift of self. The selfish individualism of a Ganelon is contrasted to the idealism, group

spirit, and order represented by Oliver and the dying Roland. No doubt the
poet and his public are also reacting against the slothful king of France
they know, Philip I, looking back nostalgically to a bygone golden age when
Charlemagne led his troops on fruitful campaigns. Roland and Charles
embody, each in his own way, those qualities of goodness, innocence,
power, and wisdom, non-existent in the age of King Philip, which Turold
finds so admirable in contrast to the feudalism of a Ganelon. Recognizing
the menace inherent in selfish, unruly barons and a weak king, La Chanson de Roland projects an idealized cultural pattern onto the past, compares
it implicitly with the present, and offers it as a program for the future. These
exemplary patterns of past conduct are presumed immanent for us here
and now.

For Turold, group solidarity and a more centralized royal power serve
a particular purpose: the Crusade, Gesta Dei per Francos. The hallmarks of
the primitive crusade mentality – the militia Christi, the via Hierosolymit-
ana considered as penance, the way to an eschatalogical experience in the
promised land, the consciousness of mission and sacrifice, and a cosmic
exaltation – flowered above all, for the great barons at least, in the eleventh
century, culminating in the First Crusade. Enthusiasm for war, hatred for
the foe, desire for vengeance – these sentiments are diverted onto an external
adversary. In the peremptory words of Roland:

> Paien unt tort e chrestïens unt dreit ...
> Nos avum dreit, mais cist glutun unt tort. –    (1015, 1212)

The king's most faithful servants, young heroes like Roland, possess the
will, the enthusiasm, to maintain the crusade to the utmost, in contrast to
older, established potentes in the style of Ganelon. And the chief justification for a strong, centralized, monarchical authority is that it alone can
provide the requisite control to prosecute the Holy War. France is conceived
as a community of free men who strive for cosmic justice under God and
his deputy, the French king-emperor.

The political forms one aspect of La Chanson de Roland, and an important one, but Turold is also a master of human psychology. In the famous
council-scene, political issues erect a façade that also serves to cover personal rancor, emotions hidden beneath the surface that never come directly
into view. Ganelon hates Roland because the latter is Charlemagne's
favorite, in spite of the fact that Ganelon is his senior and the king's brother-
in-law. The resentment felt by a mature man toward a youth more successful than he no doubt enters into Ganelon's psychological makeup. Also,
when Roland proposes Ganelon for the embassy to Saragossa, he refers to
the fact that the latter is his stepfather ('– Ço ert Guenes, mis parastre. –'

[277]), for Ganelon had married Charlemagne's sister, mother to Roland
by a previous marriage. Long before Freud we find throughout world literature and folklore the theme of enmity between stepfather or stepmother
and stepchild, based upon a form of sexual jealousy. It is also possible that
Turold knew of a legend whereby Roland was Charles's son by an incestuous union, a situation which could only add to Ganelon's resentment.[7]

However, the traitor loses his temper only after Roland both proposes
him for the Saragossa mission and then laughs at this discomfiture, that is,
his public display of anger (fear?) and impotent threats:

> Quant l'ot Rollant, si cumençat a rire.    AOI

> Quant ço veit Guenes que ore s'en rit Rollant,
> Dunc ad tel doel pur poi d'ire ne fent:
> A ben petit quë il ne pert le sens;
> E dit al cunte: – Jo ne vus aim nïent.    (302–6)

From Ganelon's point of view, since Roland believes that the Saracens are
likely to assassinate any Frenchman come to parley, he names Ganelon to
the post with the intent of having him killed. Ganelon is also furious that,
although Charlemagne has forbidden the twelve Peers to undertake this
mission, he agrees to his brother-in-law's nomination and thereby tacitly
avows that he is less important than the Peers, is in fact expendable. Nor
can Ganelon decline to go or accept Roland in his stead, for his honor
would be sullied and he would have to confess that the mission is indeed a
dangerous one and, therefore, that Roland was right and the Saracens are not
to be trusted. The traitor interprets Roland's laughter as a public humiliation and an insult to his honor as a baron, the last straw in a series of insults,
in sum a declaration of war.

Turold had the genial notion not only of endowing the antagonists of his
*chanson*, Roland and Ganelon, with diametrically opposed character traits,
but also of making the absence of communication between them in large
measure responsible for the tragedy which ensues. Each exists in his own
closed world, incapable of interpreting correctly the other's statements or
actions, just as Charlemagne cannot act upon the symbolic dreams he is
blessed with. Because Ganelon sees other people in his image – as cold,
intellectual, and lucidly treacherous – he thinks that Roland named him
to the rearguard as an act of vengeance. But, from all we subsequently discover about Roland, he could not have plotted against Ganelon. Roland's
first speech in council reveals him to be incapable of reflection and guile,
an exuberant warrior, boastful and fearless, and authentically impervious to compromise, hesitation, and fatigue. He is a man of impulse who

hunts rabbits one day and razes a city the next, loves war for its own sake, lives only for Charlemagne, and is married to his sword, his horse, and *dulce France*. Roland probably named his stepfather to the Saragossa mission as a mark of honor to his family and, therefore, to himself. On two occasions he offers to go, on his own, eager to give his life for the Cause and hardly aware that others lack his generosity, for he too mistakenly assumes that the rest of humanity resembles himself. For example, at Rencesvals he rejects out of hand Oliver's suggestion that Ganelon betrayed them:

> – Tais, Oliver! – li quens Rollant respunt
> – Mis parrastre est, ne voeill que mot en suns. –   (1026–7)

Incapable of treachery, Roland cannot imagine this trait in another, especially a relative. He also may well be playing a joke at Ganelon's expense, to embarrass the leader of the peace faction, who kept silent, failing to volunteer as the others do. And when Ganelon indeed manifests anger and perhaps a touch of cowardice, when he implicitly admits that the war policy is the correct one and, on top of it all, threatens the invincible Roland, the latter cannot help laughing in triumph and, perhaps, in contempt.

Thus Roland is guilty of a serious error in personal relations. He manifests equal tactlessness in his very first speech by boasting of his own accomplishments, brutally repulsing the Saracen peace overtures, and sniping at the peace party, who have not yet expressed an opinion. And when he himself volunteers to go to Saragossa, Oliver, who knows him better than other men, intervenes, crying: '– Vostre curages est mult pesmes e fiers; / Jo me crendreie que vos vos meslisez' (256–7). Indeed, Roland is not only sharp-tongued, impulsive, and quarrelsome; he manifests a pride in family and self that will be his undoing. For, as Ganelon could predict, Roland neither condescends to accept reinforcements for the rearguard nor, when the Saracens attack, calls for help. Roland refuses to blow the horn, lest his glory be tarnished and his family reproached:

> – Ne placet Deu – ço li respunt Rollant
> – Que ço seit dit [pur] nul hume vivant,
> Ne pur paien, que ja seie cornant!
> Ja n'en avrunt reproece mi parent.   (1073–6)

Thus is this simple man, all of one piece, easily manipulated by his more complex and subtle stepfather.

In the West, epic heroes partake of the ideals of strength and wisdom, courage and prudence, in Curtius's terms *fortitudo et sapientia*.[8] From the beginning of Western literature, courage and wisdom are considered the synthesis of manly virtue. They are to be found in Ulysses and the mature Aeneas, in Castiglione's Courtier, and in the ideal prince, master of 'armas y letras' in the Spanish Golden Age. But, from the beginning, poets realized that in real life men cannot live up to the ideal. Hence a splitting of the archetype, the painting of a tragic dichotomy: that the hero possessing *fortitudo* lacks *sapientia*, and vice versa. Supremely gifted but headstrong warriors appear as Gilgamesh in the Sumerian-Babylonian epic, wrathful Achilles, Turnus in the *Aeneid*, and, during part of his career, Roland. Like the others, Roland is guilty of hubris or *desmesure*, an excess of pride that brings about his fall.

The notion of *sapientia* is embodied in the person of Oliver, Roland's companion, who, lucid in a manner totally foreign to Roland's nature, judges his friend's hubris in the following terms:

> Kar vasselage par sens nen est folie:
> Mielz valt mesure que ne fait estultie.
> Franceis sunt morz par vostre legerie;
> Jamais Karlon de nus n'avrat servise.    (1724–7)

The man's very name, in contrast to the Germanic Roland, Charles, Turpin, and Ganelon, evokes a more clerical, Mediterranean world, where the olive plant is a symbol for peace and divine wisdom – the *sapientia* of Christ as well as of Minerva. Thus Roland and Oliver exemplify the dichotomy which is one of the basic themes of the poem:

> Rollant est proz e Oliver est sage;
> Ambedui unt me[r]veillus vasselage.    (1093–4)

Oliver exists as a reflection of, and foil to, Roland; he is Roland's double, his better conscience. It can even be said that these men represent the two poles of one divided, problematic consciousness: medieval heroism. It was a stroke of genius on Turold's part to elevate this Achates-figure – the image of the hero's faithful friend (cf. Gilgamesh and Enkidu, Achilles and Patroclus, Telemachus and Paisistratus, Orestes and Pylades, Aeneas and Achates or Pallas) – and make of him a hero in his own right. And his relationship to Roland is not just one of comradeship in arms or a military alliance; theirs is a warm, emotive philia, *amicitia* in the Virgilian and Ciceronian sense. Their friendship contributes a sense of pathos to the text since they disagree about fundamental matters through much of the action, almost coming to blows, and are finally separated by death.

But unlike many victims of excess, Roland is redeemed. Because he has

qualities of leadership and camaraderie, which endear him to his men, the
twelve Peers, Oliver, and Charles himself. Because he is a great fighter and
has taken many Saracens to death with him. But also because, to some
extent, he recognizes that he should have blown the horn, that he was
guilty of *legerie* and that, on account of him, many Frenchmen have been
killed. Roland comes to admit that the day is lost and that he, the *guarant*,
responsible for protecting his men, cannot save the rearguard, that they
die in his service, through his fault:

> – Seignors barons, de vos ait Deus mercit!
> Tutes voz anmes otreit il pareïs,
> En seintes flurs il les facet gesir!
> Meillors vassals de vos unkes ne vi:
> Si lungement tuz tens m'avez servit,
> A oés Carlon si granz païs cunquis!
> Li empereres tant mare vos nurrit!
> Tere de France, mult estes dulz païs,
> Oi desertét a tant rubost[e] exill!
> Barons franceis, pur mei vos vei murir;
> Jo ne vos pois tenser ne guarantir:
> Aït vos Deus, ki unkes ne mentit!    (1854–65)

Then he changes his mind and offers to call for help, even though presumably his family would receive as much *blasme* and *huntage* as before. He
replies humbly to Oliver's justified reproaches and no less humbly accepts
Turpin's compromise, manifests meekness inconceivable in the fierce paladin of the earlier episodes. He then expiates his folly, both by immolating
Saracens and by blowing the horn, thus denying his pride. Blowing the
horn 'par peine e par ahans ... A dulor e a peine' (1761, 1787) proves to be an
act of penance as well as of penitence, for it literally breaks his temples.
Roland perishes from this cause alone, his body untouched by Saracen
blade. Yet, before he dies, Oliver aims a blow at him by mistake. Blinded
physically, a sightless embodiment of justice, Oliver stands in opposition to
the morally blind Roland who refused to behold the invading Saracen
army and to recognize the truth that Oliver revealed to him. Oliver strikes
Roland physically as he has argued against him spiritually in the course of
the battle. And that Roland forgives his friend perhaps symbolizes an admis-
sion of personal guilt and his own desire for pardon.

He who had refused to climb Oliver's hill and gaze upon the Saracen army
now crawls up a different hill to die, this time facing Spain directly. The
martyr humbly says his *mea culpa*, misses the lands he has conquered,
regrets his home – *dulce France* – and his lord Charles, and offers his

glove to Saint Gabriel, an act of contrition, a sign that he is willing to make amends for having wronged his Lord.[9] Roland's greatest boon to others, his greatest act of prowess, is this sacrifice of pride and life. That his pride is so immense renders its sacrifice the more touching in human terms, and exalting as a lesson to men. Yet at the same time Roland dies a conqueror. Invulnerable like Galahad, at the extreme limits of Christendom, the *miles Christi* faces the enemy, master of the field, his sword and horn preserved from capture. Thus he maintains pride in king and country, and his soul is taken directly to heaven: 'L'anme del cunte portent en pareïs' (2396).

The tale of Roland, Oliver, Ganelon, and Charlemagne gives an impression of inevitability, of tragic destiny. As in Greek theater, the fall is derived from the protagonists' fundamental character traits and from the situation in which Turold places them at the beginning of the story. And, as with the Greeks, the impression of inevitability is reinforced by a perfectly ordered structure. It is perhaps no accident that the first masterpiece in French literature demonstrates mastery in the art of composition and a classical narrative pattern. *La Chanson de Roland* can be divided into four main blocks or 'acts': 1 / Ganelon's and the Saracens' treachery; 2 / First Battle of Rencesvals: the death of Roland; 3 / Second Battle of Rencesvals: Charlemagne's vengeance on the Saracens; 4 / Trial at Aix-la-Chapelle: Charlemagne's vengeance on Ganelon. The second battle of Rencesvals avenges the first, the trial avenges Ganelon's treason, and in the center of the poem is located Roland's death and the miracle of God's stopping the sun. The action of Acts 2 and 3 occurs on two successive days. Then, weeks later, another long day suffices to describe Ganelon's trial in France, concluding the story. Furthermore, the last three acts establish unity of place as well as of time: Rencesvals (2 and 3) and Aix-la-Chapelle (4). In the beginning (1) the forces of good and evil have not yet joined battle; Ganelon's plot is the decisive event which brings them together and unleashes 2, 3, and 4. Such relatively complicated machinations, requiring travel back and forth in space, occupy three days; the poem thus totals up to six in all not counting the return voyage. Finally, *Roland* tells of a treason plotted, committed, and avenged; it can lead only to crime followed by punishment of the crime and the application of justice.

Turold plunges the reader *in medium bellum*, beginning his account of the Spanish campaign seven years after Charlemagne first invaded the country. From time to time allusions are made to events which occurred during those seven years. And in the last lines of the *Chanson*, the emperor is about to set out on another expedition, to succor King Vivien at Imphe, in the land of Bire. Thus, it is possible to conceive of *La Chanson de Roland* as a poem with an 'open' structure, where characters possess an existence prior to the deeds recounted in the text, which then have repercussions in a later existence yet to take place. It is equally possible, however, to describe *Roland* as a 'closed' text where duration is radically different from that of normal human experience. Turold creates a 'scenic' rather than a 'panoramic' narrative; his use of time corresponds to that of Corneille, Balzac, and Dostoevsky, rather than to that of Shakespeare, Flaubert, and Tolstoy. This means, on the one hand, that the action is slowed down, that four thousand lines serve to recount only a limited number of events, that *Erzählzeit* and *Erzählte Zeit* converge. (The repetitive, lyrical quality of *laisses similaires*, retelling the same incident two or three times, also contributes to this effect.) But viewed from another perspective, action is speeded up, more events are compressed into a single day than could possibly happen to mere mortals, and the protagonists commit themselves to their major concerns with no time for eating or sleeping. Turold paints a picture of frenetic activity, of characters so dominated by their passions, so heroic, that their mode of existence differs from that of ordinary people and from their own lives in the previous seven years of campaigning or the return from Rencesvals to Aix-la-Chapelle. Roland, his friends, and his enemies live a privileged moment in time, concentrated, apocalyptic time, as if withdrawn from contemporary history. After seven years of indeterminate action (the cosmic number), for a few short days they participate in a struggle with cosmic overtones, in a kind of sacramental time, where past and future are manifest coequally in the present, *nunc stans*, where action is enacted as hieratic ritual. Only after these events have been played out do they return to the slow, grinding away of hours, days, and years that is the human condition; hence Charles's fatigue, his so human, non-Apocalyptic '– Deus! – dist li reis – si penuse est ma vie! –' (4000), which ends the *chanson*.

Precision with regard to geography is scarcely one of Turold's accomplishments. He tells us the names of Spanish cities (Saragossa, Cordoba, Seville, Toledo) and reveals features of the terrain (hill, slope, valley, pine, laurel, olive), in order to create an aura of verisimilitude. Scholars who assume that the author had a more precise knowledge of Spain, or that he visited the locale prior to writing his masterpiece, commit a grievous error. But these décors, by their very sparseness of description and remoteness in space, prove invaluable for literary purposes. *La Chanson de Roland* is unique among medieval epics in its power to evoke a landscape which not only situates the action but illuminates it at the same time.[10]

On one side lies Spain, '... clere Espaigne, la bele' (59), land of the Pagans, containing dazzling wealth and opulence. Charlemagne has conquered this vast, hostile empire, all but Saragossa, the capital, 'ki est en une muntaigne' (6), the one ostentatiously visible imperfection in the Christian scheme of things. In this archetypal city of evil, of Babelian pride, false peace overtures are conceived, treason is plotted, the ambush is launched, and Baligant takes over command, setting out to avenge Marsile's defeat. We soon discover, however, that beyond Spain lie seemingly infinite stretches of Pagan lands, whose inhabitants come to do battle with the army of the just. These are not only tribes from the far corners of the earth, from Cadiz to Kiev, from Ireland to Armenia. They also include exotic creatures: the Micenes, pig-people with spines down their backs; hordes from Occiant le desert, whose skin is as hard as iron, so that they fight without defensive armor; and the giants of Malprose. Their leaders' names sound with grating consonants that create an aura of mystery and horror: Corsablix, Malprimis de Brigal, Escremiz de Valterne, Chernubles de Muneigre, Aelroth, Malquiant, etc. And, in battle, 'Cil d'Ociant i braient e henissent, / [E cil d']Arguille si cume chen glatissent' (3526–7).

On the other side lies France, *Tere majur*, land of the ancestors, the homeland containing fiefs, wives, and family, to which the Franks are so eager to return. This is the country which literally quakes over Roland's death. The heroes dream nostalgically of *dulce France*, and the best battle-corps in the army, the equivalent of Achilles' Myrmidons, is formed of *Francs de France*. Such indications of patriotism, feeble as they are, anticipate the awakening of nationalism in late songs such as *Aymeri de Narbonne* or Chrétien de Troyes's triumphant declaration of *translatio imperii et studii* (*Cligès*, 28–42) on France's role as military and spiritual heir of the classical world.

It is obvious that the antithesis between France and Spain is not primarily feudal or nationalistic, nor is the battle of Rencesvals uniquely the fictional recreation of an historical event such as the confrontation of two feudal powers or an incident in the dynastic history of the French royal house. The mustering of the troops, an old Homeric and Virgilian convention, allows Turold to proclaim that the entire world, Pagan and Christian, converges to give battle in an apocalyptic struggle between absolute good and absolute evil. As in Homer, Virgil, and Lucan this is a decisive encounter between East and West, and the civilizations that each represents. France and Spain are separated geographically by the Pyrenees and morally by an unbridgeable chasm. On the map, France is placed topographically above Spain, Aix-la-Chapelle above Cairo-Babylon, just as, in moral and archetypal terms, France lies over Spain, heaven over hell, and good over evil.

France and Spain are divided by the Pyrenees, and close to the mountain chain lies the field of Rencesvals. Three distinct battles take place on or near it: between Roland and Marsile, Charles and Marsile, and Charles and Baligant. Although Turold could have changed the locale for his battle-scenes, each time the combatants join forces in the same general vicinity, an apocalyptic spot withdrawn from secular, realistic geography, where good and evil give battle and the fate of mankind is determined. How appropriate, then, the repeated, sinister evocations of the décor, which help create an aura of foreboding and anxiety:

> Halt sunt li pui e li val tenebrus,
> Les roches bises, les destreiz merveillus ...
> Halt sunt li pui e tenebrus e grant,
> Li val parfunt e les ewes curant ...
> Halt sunt li pui e mult [sunt] halt les arbres ...
> Passent cez puiz e cez roches plus haltes,
> Cez vals parfunz, cez destreiz anguisables,
> Issent des porz e de la tere guaste.
> (814–15, 1830–1, 2271, 3125–7)

A wild, mountainous country appropriate to sudden attack, Rencesvals recalls a masculine landscape à la Bachelard, the symbolic backdrop to a tale of treason and the clash of cosmic forces.

However, when Charles gives battle to Baligant the décor changes: Turold tells of a clear day, a shining sun, and broad plains:

> Clers est li jurz e li soleilz luisant ...
> Grant est la plaigne e large la cuntree ...
> Clers fut li jurz e li soleilz luisanz.   (2646, 3305, 3345)

And Roland dies not on the field of Rencesvals itself but under a pine tree, on top of a hill, recumbent on sweet green grass. In an example of pathetic fallacy, the landscape has been metamorphosed into a *locus amœnus*, an image of the earthly paradise which prefigures the celestial one to which Roland's soul will be carried. Rencesvals is situated below France and above Spain, also below heaven and above hell. The French battle-cry *Munjoie* is derived from *Mons Gaudii*, whereas Saracens dwell in places called Valpenuse, Valtenebre, etc. Thus the *puis* rise up to God, the *vals* descend to Satan; Rencesvals, to be associated with the *Vallis lachrymarum* of Psalm 83, is one location where Saracens have a chance to win. Oliver climbs a *pui halçur*, from which he perceives the Saracen host menacing the rearguard; his companion, of course, refuses to recognize the danger. Later, however, after Turpin also delivers his sermon from a slope, a much wiser Roland does climb a *pui agut* to die, at peace with God. His soul is borne to heaven, as Charlemagne's dream predicted it would, when the splinters of his broken lance were hurled into the sky. Nothing is permitted to undermine this vertical bond to the sacred. For Turold heights represent vision, salvation, and glory, whereas he imagines the Pagans dwelling in a very different sort of landscape.

A comparable antithesis can be established between image-patterns of light and darkness.[11] Admittedly, the sun shines as fixedly on the Pagan armies as on the French; their arms glitter as brightly as Roland's. And Baligant's fleet lights its way with shining carbuncles across the sea and up the Ebre so that, 'Par la noit la mer en est plus bele' (2635). However, this is artificial light, repugnant to God. And in the Pagan host are to be found Chernubles, who comes from Muneigre, a land without sun, wheat, rain, and dew, covered with black rocks, where people say demons live; Abisme, who does not believe in God, who never laughs and plays, and whose skin is as black as pitch; and fifty thousand soldiers from Ethiopia, 'une tere maldite' (1916). Roland takes one look at *La neire gent* (1917), with their broad noses and ears and cries, '– Ci recevrums ma[r]tyrie, / E or sai ben n'avons guaires a vivre' (1922–3). Turold's 'racism' can be explained by the fact that most Frenchmen had no acquaintance with sub-Saharan Africa in the eleventh century, and by the traditional connotations of the colors black and white in our culture. Well might Roland, upon seeing Ethiopians, assume that Marsile had summoned an army of demons against him! Chernubles, Abisme, and the Africans form a striking contrast to the barons from France, 'Les chefs fluriz e les barbes unt blanches' (3087), clad in shining armor, their swords, shields, helmets, breastplates, and pennons flashing in the sun, led by Charlemagne of the White Beard, whose blade, Joiuse, is encrusted with sacred relics and changes color thirty times a day. Nor should we forget that the sun, high in the heavens, lights the Christian army to victory, in contrast to Baligant's troops, who come by night, and that, as for Joshua, God stops the sun to give Charlemagne time to exterminate the enemy. Thus *splendor fidei*, imperial health and radiance, triumph over the enemies of all light and truth.

God blesses Charlemagne with visions and, at the end of the poem, Gabriel instructs him to succor King Vivien in the land of Bire. These dreams, corresponding to the four 'acts' of the drama, which inform the king in veiled terms of Ganelon's treachery, the two battles of Rencesvals, and Ganelon's trial, contribute a profusion of symbolic imagery not to be found in any other Old French epic.[12] The battle of Rencesvals is foreshadowed by an assault on Charlemagne's lance or right arm, in medieval terms an attack on his prowess. The enemy, from outside and from within, is represented by a wild boar (Marsile), a bear (Ganelon), a leopard (Marganice), and a lion (Baligant), animals which evoke Satan and the Capital Vices. In one splendid passage the Beasts of the Apocalypse assault him, and an Apocalyptic storm of thunder, wind, hail, and flames rains down on Charles, who stands helpless before the onslaught of Baligant-Antichrist:

> Carles guardat amunt envers le ciel,
> Veit les tuneires e les venz e les giels

E les orez, les merveillus tempe[rs],
E fous e flambes i est apareillez:
Isnelement sur tute sa gent chet.
Ardent cez hanstes de fraisne e de pumer
E cez escuz jesqu'as bucles d'or mier,
Fruise[nt] cez hanstes de cez trenchanz espiez,
Cruissent osbercs e cez helmes d'acer.
En grant dulor i veit ses chevalers.
Urs e leuparz les voelent puis manger,
Serpenz e guivres, dragun e averser;
Grifuns i ad plus de trente millers;
N'en i ad cel a Franceis ne s'agiét.
E Franceis crïent: – Carlemagne, aidez! –    (2532–46)

However, he receives succor from the mastiff, a friendly watch-dog
(Roland, Tierri) who helps give battle to the thirty thousand enemies or the
thirty bears (Judas betrayed Christ for thirty pieces of silver); and the
palace at Aix, image of right and order, the mastiff's home, is contrasted to
the Ardennes forest of anarchy, whence come the animals and tempest.
Man against beast, man against the elements, order against chaos – in these
terms Turold presents to Charles and to us his representation of the
*Reconquista.*

We can also interpret Charlemagne's dream in terms of modern
psychoanalysis, the beasts who assault the dreamer's lance or right arm
representing a symbolic castration threat and the dreamer suffering from
disturbance of the psyche which takes the form of veiled castration anxiety.
Without agreeing totally with Baudouin's assertion that the birth-trauma
and the Oedipal complex are central features in heroic literature everywhere,
I do believe that Turold reveals the classical Oedipal situation more overtly
than is done in other epics.[13] We never see Roland's father; his name, his
story, are left in the shadows. The father's place is taken by two older
authority-figures, father-surrogates: Ganelon and Charlemagne. The first,
who married his mother, plays the role of Terrible Father, the enemy
impeding his stepson's development. The second, a benefactor white like
the sun, who 'nourished' him and gave him Durendal, does all he can to
protect his surrogate son. All good is projected onto the one, all evil onto
the other. Because of this split in the father-imago, Roland suffers from less
anguish or conflict than, say, Tristan or Hamlet. But, to Roland's sorrow, the Terrible Father proves to be more immediate and efficacious than
the somewhat abstract ideal that Charlemagne embodies. Roland and
Ganelon are rivals for Charlemagne's favor and perhaps for the mother-
wife's favor also. Although Ganelon especially is threatened by Roland's
glory, Roland in turn finds that his quest for fulfillment, which includes

total extermination of the enemy, is impeded by the stepfather. In a sense, Roland refuses to yield to Ganelon's and the court's will; he strikes out against his surrogate father and, as a result, is punished unto death. At the same time, however, the youth's hatred for Ganelon is largely repressed, hence his refusal early in the battle even to consider that he was betrayed. Roland takes out his Oedipal aggression 'lawfully' on the Saracen enemy, whom he substitutes for the bad father, and, on the field of battle, with Charlemagne absent, becomes a father in turn to his men. Yet, since Ganelon trafficked with the enemy and they are doing his bidding, in a sense the Pagan hordes do attack Roland in his stead. In the end, of course, Roland recognizes that Ganelon is evil, defeats the evil father-surrogates, and expiates his own guilt; he dies with his thoughts on the Good Father (Charlemagne), having found still another Father (God) and a Good Mother (France) to cherish along with Charles, without guilt and remorse.

It can be said that Charlemagne, and the twelve peers, dwell in a strictly masculine universe. In spite of the matriarchal uncle-nephew bond, their society is patriarchal, ruled by a superhuman father-figure. Their energies are devoted to sport and war. The exemplary bishop is a man of violence, at least as much a *pugnator* as an *orator*. Their chief lines of affection are 'homosexual,' that is non-erotic philia between members of the same sex, whether young comrades (Roland and Oliver) or the young and old (Roland and Charlemagne). Roland does not think of his fiancée Aude when he dies, and Charlemagne cavalierly offers her his son Louis in exchange. The poem's ethos of *fortitudo* is reinforced by a 'masculine' pattern of imagery: the harsh landscape, the burning, dazzling light, and, above all, the bar-ons' swords. Each hero's sword has a name: Durendal (Roland), Joiuse (Charlemagne), Halteclere (Oliver), Almace (Turpin), Murgleis (Ganelon), Preciuse (Baligant). Each weapon belongs to its owner alone, is part of his being, his martial essence, and contributes to his prowess and glory. Furthermore, Joiuse and Durendal, encrusted with holy relics, are super-naturally luminous; these are *gladii Dei*, created for that masculine ideal – the crusade.

However, Turold's male society by no means exists in a vacuum. The French army itself is divided. It contains a faction, led by Ganelon, which stands in opposition to Roland's ethos. The traitor, a man of great beauty, who wears rich clothes, who thinks fondly of wife and son at home in France the Motherland, who lives by his wits not his strong right arm, is surely more 'feminine' than Roland and Charlemagne. His false values of peace and material comfort sap the Christian host's purpose; his false prudence undermines Roland's prowess. The Saracen enemy live in cities, travel by night, enjoy material gold and riches, recline on couches in the shade of exotic trees, are prone to bribery and treachery; they too represent the feminine, dark side of life in opposition to Durendal's light. Roland's simple, trusting belligerence alone does not suffice to vanquish the forces of darkness. Ganelon's *saveir*, turned to the wrong ends, is more than a match for him. Blancandrin and Ganelon, who converse so effectively on the ride to Saragossa, possess the same distorted *saveir*, uphold the same values of peace, personal honor, and chivalry. But in the hands of an Oliver or a Charlemagne, *sapientia* reinforces *fortitudo*. Roland's stance is pure actuality, whereas Oliver and Charlemagne represent also the potentiality for change, for adapting to new conditions in the world.

In the course of the *Chanson* Roland's sword gives way in importance to his horn, which, in Freudian terms, may be considered either a masculine or a feminine image. Like Durendal, the olifant belongs to Roland, but it is Oliver, a *sapientia*-figure, who urges him to blow it, whereupon Roland answers that he will wield his sword. Although the two great quarrels between Roland and Oliver concern the horn, it symbolizes reconciliation as well as opposition. The French army has been divided in two. Only Roland's sounding the horn will bring together the rearguard and the rest of the host, a physical reunion that corresponds to an analogous joining of minds. Isolation and individualism give way to a sense of common purpose in the community. Roland blows the olifant, and Charlemagne's trumpets sound a reply: the French will return to Spain! But too late to save Roland, who expires from the very act that proves his newly acquired wisdom. Before dying, however, Roland strikes one last blow. With the olifant he brains a Saracen who tried to seize Durendal. Thus the horn preserves and protects the sword; *sapientia* restores and fulfills *fortitudo*. This is the last exploit of the first Battle of Rencesvals (defeat) and the first exploit of the second one (victory). Fittingly, it is accomplished by the instrument which alone turns defeat into victory and which, symbolic of Roland's presence, inspires the army on the second day (the Baligant episode), long after Roland's passing.[14]

Roland dies in full possession of his sword and horn, master both of *fortitudo* and *sapientia*, his soul borne to heaven by Michael and Gabriel, God's warrior and messenger archangels. The harsh, rough Spanish landscape of Rencesvals gives way to a more feminine *locus amœnus*. Toward the end of the poem a new world, combining the best features of prowess and wisdom, replaces Roland's old one, as it has Ganelon's. The action shifts from the battlefield to the palace at Aix. Tierri d'Anjou succeeds Roland and defends his memory. Tierri is hardly in the champion's class physically: he is said to be slim of body, with dark hair and swarthy complexion, and of average height:

> Heingre out le cors e graisle e eschewid,
> Neirs les chevels e alques brun [le vis],
> N'est gueres granz, ne trop nen est petiz.    (3820–2)

Yet, because he is in the right, because he speaks the truth, because of his wisdom, God grants him victory over Ganelon's champion, the physically invincible Pinabel. Spiritual strength reinforces relative physical weakness, enabling this Frankish David to overcome his Goliath. It is perhaps not coincidental that only toward the end of *La Chanson de Roland* do we find, for the first time, a feminine element associated with the Franks: la belle Aude, Oliver's sister, who dies for love of Roland, and the Saracen queen Bramimunde, who is converted to Christianity, is renamed Juliane, and will find a place in the new *projektierte Gemeinschaft*. Her conversion symbolically parallels and negates the treason of Ganelon, who shifts in the opposite direction, not to apostasy but certainly from Christianity to 'non-Christianity.'

Before Christendom is transformed, Roland dies. It may be correct to say that for French society to be transformed, Roland has to die. Only when the Franks realize the terrible loss they have suffered can they appreciate Saracen treachery at its true value; only then will they be convinced how right Roland was, and know the meaning of the crusade. In a sense Roland's successor (yet no one can succeed him) is not Tierri but Charlemagne himself, who, for a short time, recovers the vigor of youth and prosecutes the crusade to the end, spurred on by *doel* and *irur*. Thus Roland is a kind of scapegoat, sacrificed that Christian truth may prevail. For although he is guilty of *desmesure* and lack of tact, we sense that the punishment he endures is greater than any crime he could have committed. *La Chanson de Roland* is a story of death and rebirth. But whereas so often in heroic literature an old king falls and a young king takes his place, here the archetype is reversed. A young man is replaced by an older, wiser one. The father is reinstated, becomes young again through the sacrifice of the son; through the son's freely offered sacrifice, the Good Father defeats the Bad Father, and society prevails.

The death and rebirth archetype is perhaps the most important the West has produced. In ritual, myth, and poetry, going back to the earliest texts, scholars observe a recurring pattern:

1 / Man's concern with the apparent mortality of all things. The sun will set, spring give way to winter, life and beauty disappear. The hero must die.

2 / Man's consciousness of renewal. Although one summer disappears, spring will come again; one day gone, the sun will rise tomorrow. And if a hero is lost to society, other men, perhaps the hero's own sons, will take his place. The individual may pass on but the race survives, proceeding to new heights.

Man imagines an arrangement whereby continuity is impossible without death (sacrifice), whereby seed must be thrown away before a crop is gathered or a son born. The old king has to fall for a new one to reign.

Cyclical patterns, in nature and society, are recognized to exist; both cycles are embodied in mythical archetypes. A hero, king, or god (Attis, Adonis, Osiris, Tammuz, Saturn, Proserpina, Orpheus) dies but is presumed to live anew, either literally himself or symbolically in the person of an heir. With the notion of a second birth, man seeks to overcome death and decay by giving expression to his deepest aspirations in a myth.

In our culture the death and rebirth archetype has been molded into a Christian pattern and imbued with Christian symbolism. According to the Church, faith in Christ is a victory over sin and death. Just as his savior perished on the Cross but was resurrected, the Christian will enjoy an afterlife in heaven. In order to live again, of course, one must first die (*Si le grain ne meurt ...*), but perishing gives promise of a new life more beautiful than the old.

It is obvious that Turold links his story to the Bible, uses scriptural analogies to give his poem resonance and depth. The twelve peers recall, of course, Christ's apostles. Ganelon, a 'vifs diables' (746), who betrays Roland with a kiss, who accepts rich gifts and is supported by thirty relatives, resembles Judas ('... elegit ... Judam Iscariotem qui fuit proditor,' Luke 6:16), and his extraordinary beauty reminds us of Lucifer's. God stops the sun for Charlemagne as he did for Joshua. Charlemagne's war against Baligant and his hordes parallels the wars of the Children of Israel in the Old Testament and anticipates the future cosmic duel between Christ and Antichrist. As the coming of Antichrist precedes Doomsday, Charles's victory over Baligant precedes his judgment of the sinner Ganelon. Thus Baligant, 'le viel d'antiquitét (2615), come from Babylon, perceived in a dream as a raging lion and with a dragon for his ensign, represents the *draco antiquus* of the Apocalypse, and Charlemagne, the anointed *rex sacerdos*, in his strength and weakness postfigures David and prefigures the Emperor of the Last Days as well as Christ himself. But, above all, the sacrifice of a son before his father-surrogate's eyes recalls the myths of Abraham and Isaac and, of course, of God the Father and God the Son. Like God the Father and Abraham, Charlemagne incarnates the principle of justice, and possesses patriarchal, sacramental dignity. Immolated alone, on a hill, near a lone tree, suffering from thirst, mocked by his enemies, Roland dies like Christ. Nature responds to both passions with earthquake, tempest, and darkness at noon. Since Roland is a Christ-figure, his triumphs also parallel those of the Son of God, Lord of Hosts, Christ the Conqueror who harrowed hell. To the extent that this *miles Christi* evokes our compassion, he recalls the Son of Man, the divine scapegoat beloved of the Mater Dolorosa who weeps over his clay as does Charlemagne over Roland's, and for whom the faithful weep on Good Friday, in temporary suspension of the knowledge that the Resurrection will occur two days later. Roland dies as Christ but is reborn in Charlemagne the warrior. And the six days of Rencesvals followed by the seventh day at Aix correspond to the seven ages of the world, culminating in Doomsday. From this perspective, the *Song of Roland* symbolically encompasses all of man's history, from the primeval treason (Satan-Ganelon) through the crucifixion (Christ-Roland) to the end of time (Antichrist-Baligant and Christ-Charlemagne).[15]

*La Chanson de Roland* does not end with Roland's immolation or Charlemagne's triumph. After Baligant and Ganelon have been punished, and the Pagan queen has been converted, a final episode rounds out the poem. Charlemagne goes to bed but is not permitted to sleep, for Gabriel comes to him once again, not with a foreboding dream but a command, not a *somnium* but an *oraculum*: 'Charles, summon the hosts of your empire! In force you will go to the land of Bire and succor King Vivien in Imphe, the city that the Pagans are besieging. Christians call unto you!' (3994–8). And Charlemagne, a weary old man alone in his bed, does not wish to go:

> Li emperere n'i volsist aler mie:
> – Deus! – dist li reis – si penuse est ma vie! –
> Pluret des oilz, sa barbe blanche tiret.
> Ci falt la geste que Turoldus declinet.   (3999–4002)

*La Chanson de Roland* is a poem of tragedy as well as of triumph. Tragic elements are contained in the elegiac tone of much of the poem, in the cries of anguish over the death of fine young men ('Tant bon Franceis i perdent lor juvente!' 1401); indeed, Turold's obsession with death and the foreboding of Charlemagne's dreams create an atmosphere of ineluctable fatality, as if the events recounted (and foreshadowed) are sacred, hieratic, and providential – with Charles powerless to forestall them. This sense of *lacrymae rerum* is centered on the father-figure of Charlemagne, who, unlike Virgil's Priam, Evander, and Mezentius, dominates his poem, which begins ('Carles li reis, nostre emper[er]e magnes,' 1) and ends ('Pluret des oilz, sa barbe blanche tiret,' 4001) with him. He mediates between Roland and the public, for we perceive Roland's superhuman prowess and his destiny filtered through Charles's human perspective. This almost priest-king, who enjoys a special relationship to God and receives prophetic dreams from heaven, whose age (two hundred years), dignity, and flowing white beard grant him a patriarchal aura as God's deputy on earth, appears at the same time to be a warm, human being, as tired and lonely as the weakest of mortals. Again and again we are given the impression that others, not Charlemagne, determine the course of events, against his wishes. And, like Ganelon, Charles does not belong to a peer group, does not enjoy the pleasures of a community; like Ganelon, he is alone. Roland's death is

felt most keenly by him, who loved his nephew, yet who has to live on and
defend the empire without him. For the victory over Baligant does not
end Charlemagne's career in a halo of glory. Although life goes on, and
campaign follows campaign, he is an old man, and his nephew can no
longer help him. He must face the Saracens alone. The crusade is not yet
over, for the struggle between good and evil will endure until Doomsday.
On the seventh day of Creation, the Lord of Hosts rested; but on his seventh day the Christian prince cannot rest, even after the most stupendous
victories, since for him existence implies eternal anguish and vigilance. Such
is the Christian life, for Charles and all men. It is this quality of Charlemagne's suffering, in an open universe, that appeals to the modern reader
and adds richness and depth to Turold's portrayal of the human condition.

More perhaps than any other French epic, *La Chanson de Roland* embodies the militant piety of the late eleventh century, the high Romanesque.
Turold's is a world of Christian exaltation, of typological splendor, of the
crusade. We are made aware of the absolute opposition between strong and
weak, high and low, near and far, light and dark. And, more perhaps than
any other French text, *Roland* is a poem of the aristocracy, treating kings,
heroes, and martyrs. The solemn, majestic, monumentally paratactic style,
austere but with an extraordinary expressivity, is an epic style, a *sermo
gravis* which evokes the dignity, the decorum, the pomp, the splendor,
the sense of tradition inherent in Turold's vision of man. Heroism makes
possible a feeling for the sacred, for rite and ritual. The author loves silk
and satin, gold and silver, bright colors, armor, swords, steeds, jewels, and
the bright light of day. He loves speeches and the ceremonial of a king's
court, deeds in arms and the sweat of battle. Yet he also weeps for youths
cut down before their time and old men compelled to survive them. He is
aware of the pathos in a knight's farewell to his men, in homesickness, in the
quarrel of friends, in a father's or a fiancée's bereavement. The old heroism is scrutinized with loving but lucid intensity; we perceive the paladin's
glory and his hubris. Yet great deeds, a hero's constancy against impossible odds and certain death, are performed to compensate for death, to assert
the best of the human condition in the face of mortality. People learn the
meaning of remorse, expiation, humility, generosity, sacrifice, and community. Men die and are reborn, but life and the community go on. And a
great story has been enacted, the first myth come from the Middle Ages
to enrich our cultural heritage.

Chapter Two

# ❧ *RAOUL DE CAMBRAI*

In the course of the twelfth century appear a number of *chansons de geste*, which follow upon the *Song of Roland* and are influenced by it, but turn away from Turold's idealism in order to treat the more sordid aspects of life:[1] such works as 1 / *La Chanson de Guillaume*, in which the hero has to struggle alone against Saracen invasions while the emperor dwells far off in Paris, indifferent to the fate of his knights, the concept of lineage having replaced that of empire as an ideal; 2 / *Le Couronnement de Louis*, in which the empire is floundering in anarchy, young King Louis incapable of coping with affairs, so that Guillaume himself must take command and spend his lifetime defending France against foreign and domestic enemies; and 3 / *Raoul de Cambrai* (c. 1180–1200), which describes a world in chaos, lacking all sense of honor, the barons driven to assault each other and the king in stupid battles where neither side can prevail. These poems, especially *La Chanson de Raoul*, treat in more conscious and 'realistic' a manner the problems that beset contemporary society and express to some extent the individualism that has become a hallmark of the twelfth century. They are more problematic, more introspective than *Roland*; they no longer exalt the myth of the central French monarchy, nor do they proclaim Turold's values in absolute terms. They exhibit an opening out of the epic genre to include new concerns, more recent socio-economic and intellectual currents, representing thus a most significant development in the evolution of the French epic.

Much of the action of *La Chanson de Roland* and *La Chanson de Guillaume* takes place on the fields of Rencesvals and L'Archamp, schematic, stylized landscapes, situated far from the poets' homeland, deprived of all but rudimentary local color. On the other hand, with the exception of occasional trips to Beauvais and Arras, and, of course, the court-scenes in Paris, *Raoul de Cambrai* recounts a story located in or near the towns of Cambrai, Origny, and Saint-Quentin, an area in the north of France contained today in the Departments of the Aisne and Nord.[2] The topography includes the church of Saint-Géri-de-Cambrai, which still existed in the twelfth century, and designated among the combatants are lords of the surrounding towns: Ribemont, Roye, Hirson, Laon, Douai, and Arras. Lacking Turold's exoticism and symbolism, *La Chanson de Raoul* is invested with a strong sense of local color; the public witnesses a drama enacted closer to home, a more immediate action with which they themselves can identify. *Raoul* gives a further impression of realism because the encounters take place with Frenchmen fighting on both sides; there are no wicked pagans on whom the hero tests his steel with impunity. And, although concentrated in a small part of France, the action is nevertheless diffused among four cities. Warfare is conceived in terms of several engagements separated in space, not the archetypal struggle of Rencesvals or l'Archamp.

These engagements are also separated in time. The plot begins with the death of Raoul Taillefer, Count of Cambrai, and birth of his son, young Raoul. Three years later King Louis seeks to give Taillefer's widow, Aalais, in marriage to Gibouin le Manceau. Aalais refuses but cannot prevent Gibouin from seizing the fief. Raoul is fifteen years old when Aalais sends him to Paris, accompanied by his squire, Bernier, bastard son of Ybert de Ribemont. An indefinite period ('une grant piece,' 538), perhaps several years, goes by until the Easter when Ernaut de Douai's two sons are accidentally slain in fencing practice. The following Pentecost, when Raoul, urged on by his uncle, Guerri le Sor, demands his patrimony, King Louis offers him instead the first fief to become vacant. One year and fifteen days later Herbert de Vermandois dies, leaving four grown sons, one of whom is Bernier's father. The following Lenten season, invested with the fief, Raoul invades the Vermandois and razes the Convent of Origny, where Bernier's mother perishes in the flames. After a violent quarrel Bernier takes refuge with his father at Saint-Quentin. The ensuing battle culminates in Raoul's death at the hands of Bernier and Ernaut. From five to seven years then elapse until Guerri's wounds heal and Raoul's nephew, Gautier, comes of age. War flares up a second time, with one battle at Saint-Quentin, a second at Cambrai, and several individual combats. Exactly one year later, during a royal banquet in Paris, Guerri strikes Bernier without warning, and another single combat is arranged between Bernier and Gautier. However, the day ends with a general reconciliation. The former enemies then unite against the king, burn Paris, and go home in anger.

The *Erzählte Zeit* extends over a period of from twenty-five to thirty years. With a story projected over the lives of three generations, the unfolding of the narrative appears less concentrated than in *La Chanson de Roland* and *La Chanson de Guillaume*. Furthermore, the pattern of war in *Raoul de Cambrai* or *Garin le Lorrain* – a continuity of engagements –

resembles more closely the reality of medieval warfare than do the single, decisive battles that Turold evokes. In this sense, the later epics bear witness to a more accurate portrayal of life, a striving toward a more complete vision: of total war, and the hero's entire lifespan. This duration has an important symbolic function as well. We are made aware of the passing of time, the futility of war, and man's suffering when exposed to it. The motif: 'Iceste guere dur[r]a ele toudis?' (5183; also 5257, 5271, 5307, 5380–1) recurs repeatedly toward the end of the song, recalling not only Charlemagne's lament in the *Roland* ('si penuse est ma vie') but also Ulysses' and Aeneas's melancholia and the *lacrymae rerum* of people everywhere who discover too late the ravages of strife. Ultimately the trouvère is concerned not with who is in the right (Raoul's family or Bernier's clan) but rather with the fact that an armed feud fails to resolve any issue.

In *La Chanson de Roland* immense hosts battle on an open plain. The first engagement at Rencesvals tells how 20,000 Frenchmen stand off first 100,000 Saracens, then many more. In the second battle the main Frankish host (350,000) defeats at least 1,500,000 Pagans. Roland, Oliver, Turpin, and Charlemagne overcome hundreds of enemies single-handed, and the first conquers an entire army before he falls. The *Raoul*-poet paints a different picture. On the field of Origny 10,000 Cambresians give battle to 11,000 from the Vermandois. The armies are reduced to 5,700 and 7,000 soldiers respectively at Raoul's death, and to 140 and 300 when Guerri finally quits the fray. Extraordinarily precise as to the number of combatants on either side, the author wishes to indicate that Origny is the meeting ground of two French counts, both powerful and well-equipped but neither a superman. The allies from Vermandois slightly outnumber their adversaries, and the two forces are whittled down in proportion, the Cambrai-Artois contingent losing in the end because of its initial quantitative and qualitative inferiority. More credible still are later engagements between the clans when 1,000 Cambresians attack 500 of Ybert's men, or when the Vermandois-Brabant-Hainaut alliance replies by invading the Cambrésis with a total of 3,000 troops. After the disaster of Origny neither side can muster anything like the hosts of yesteryear! And in real life the most exciting battles are not always chronologically the last.

Furthermore, war does not always occur in a general melee. As in the *Aeneid*, the author describes mass encounters, single combats, sieges, ambushes, forage and pillaging operations, and impromptu brawls, in which non-knightly soldiers ('fraipaille ... sergant et pietaille,' 1064, 1066) participate and where civilians are involved against their will. Raoul begins his campaign by laying siege to a town and destroying a convent of nuns. The city-dwellers struggle in vain to defend their *borc*; a quarrel between these burghers and three of Raoul's men sets off the explosion. Later the inhabitants of Saint-Quentin (archers and arbalesters) come out from behind their walls to help Bernier repulse Gautier's assault:

> Eis les borgois de S. Quentin issus,
> .D. archiers qi ont les ars tendus,
> Des arbalestes n'iert ja conte tenus.
> 'Diex!' dist B., 'li cuers m'est revenus:
> Par ceste gent serai je secorus.'   (3907–11)

Even in open battle, on occasion heroes prove to be cowardly (Bernier, Guerri, Ernaut), not to speak of their men (2387, 2400), and in place of the splendid landscape of Rencesvals they fight on a swamp, rendered slippery by rain and the blood of the fallen:

> La terre est mole, si ot .j. poi pleü;
> Li brai espoisse del sanc et de[l] palu.   (2774–5)

The mood is one of cruelty and violence; the maimed live on to be wounded again, emphasizing the sordidness rather than the glory of feudal war.

   Even though the *Raoul*-poet adheres to the same elevated, even rigid style as Turold's, the protagonist and his friends are no less capable of invective in *sermo humilis*. I cite Raoul's almost maniacal threat of reprisal if the men of Arouaise do not respond to his summons:

> 'Se Dex se done qe je vis en repaire,
> Tant en ferai essorber et desfaire,
> Et pendre en haut as forches comme laire,
> Qe tuit li vif aront assez que braire.'   (1024–7)

After having wounded two of his enemies, severed an arm from one and a leg from the other, Raoul assures them they will not have to look for work, for he has given them new jobs; one can be a sentinel, the other a gatekeeper (2930)! And he insults the Abbess Marsent, gratuitously accusing her of prostitution:

> – Voir! dist R. vos estes losengiere.
> Je ne sai rien de putain chanberiere
> Qi ait esté corsaus ne maaillere,
> A toute gent communax garsoniere.
> Au conte Y. vos vi je soldoiere,
> La vostre chars ne fu onques trop chiere;
> Se nus en vost, par le baron s. Piere!
> Por poi d'avoir en fustes traite ariere.   (1328–35)

Finally, although Raoul and Bernier resemble the heroes of *La Chanson de Roland*, they live in a different world from Turold's. Instead of crusading against foreign infidels, French barons fight each other or the king; rather than harmony in the body politic, we see bitter feuding and the seeds of revolt. High moral purpose and a devotion to the crusade or to the motherland give way to egotistical squabbling over fiefs, gruelling wars arising out of personal insult, and the end of respect for authority, God's or man's. The Rolandian framework has been corroded, and traditional norms of society are found no longer conducive to existence.[3]

In a poem such as *Raoul de Cambrai* the hero is placed in an ambiguous position. He strives for himself yet relies on others, is self-reliant and dependent at the same time. He manifests loyalty to his family, obeys his feudal lord, serves the best interests of his king, and, above all, acts to preserve his own honor and the peace of the realm. When these duties come into conflict, he is forced to choose between them, but since they carry approximately equal weight, he cannot do so and remains in a state of perpetual anguish. Of course, the hero finally does cast the die one way or another but against his will and only to be haunted afterwards by feelings of remorse.

Whereas a good king, the Charlemagne of *La Chanson de Roland*, will find a way to resolve the hero's problems, in the revolt epics the king cuts a different stripe, oscillating between the indifference of Pontius Pilate and the conscious tyranny of Herod or Nero. This type of monarch acts out of motivation for his own power and expediency, not for the good of the realm. King Louis in *Raoul de Cambrai* commits a first act of injustice by seizing the Cambrésis and giving it to Gibouin, a second by disinheriting Herbert of Vermandois's sons in order to mollify Raoul, a third by seeking to disinherit Bernier for his own pleasure. We discover that Louis is not only weak but vicious, for, first, he is directly responsible for the feud, having consciously instilled civil war among his men in order to profit from the ensuing anarchy, and, second, once the war begins, he does nothing to help Raoul in his travails. The *Raoul*-poet openly condemns Louis early in the poem, as Guerri does at the end, leaving no doubt in the public's mind:

> R. ot droit, trés bien le vos dison:
> Mais l'emperere ot trop le quer felon
> Qi de tel terre fist a son neveu don
> Dont maint baron widierent puis arçon ...
> R. ot droit, si con je ai apris;
> Le tort en ot li rois de S. Denis;
> Par malvais roi est mains frans hom honnis ...
> 'Cis rois est fel, gel taing a sousduiant.

Iceste guere, par le cors s. Amant,
Commença il, se sevent li auquant ...
Cest coart roi doit on bien essillier,
Car ceste guere nos fist il commencier,
Et mon neveu ocire et detranchier.'
      (777–80, 823–5, 5369–71, 5425–7)

Like Ganelon, he is a felon and traitor, for he has broken the family and feudal bonds, as demanding on the lord as on his vassal.

With such a king, the foundations of society crumble. For without a strong, just ruler, who keeps his responsibilities as law-giver and judge, authority, honor, and peace all become meaningless. Tyranny and remissness are equally blamable in a well-ordered, natural universe. Forced by the emperor into revolt, barons sacrifice public to private morality and set themselves against the feudal hierarchy, no matter what the consequences. The anguish of proud souls torn by contradictory duties and by unending war is evoked in a series of tragic episodes, in which the public's sympathy is drawn to the hero whichever way he turns, and to more than one hero. Needless to say, in direct opposition to Turold, the *Raoul*-poet's sympathies lie decidedly with the nobility against the royal house.

Like the other epics of revolt, *Raoul de Cambrai* reflects intracultural tensions within medieval society, based upon a highly stylized view of the late Carolingian world (*La Chanson de Raoul* recounts historical events purported to have occurred in 943 and, perhaps also, in 896) molded by conscious archaization, for the author also refers to strife in the twelfth century when he lived and wrote. It is a commonplace of sociological criticism that, in the words of Lukács: 'The division between the personal individual and the class individual, the accidental nature of the conditions of life for the individual, appears only with the emergence of class, which is itself a product of the bourgeoisie.'[4] I suggest that the consciousness of class first appeared in vernacular literature earlier than Lukács imagines and that its concrete manifestation, although brought about partially by the emergence of a middle class, occurred within the aristocracy and was given expression in a literature reflecting the aristocracy's views. In the course of the twelfth century the Capetian monarch, always suzerain and ultimate master of his realm *de jure*, began to establish *de facto* control as well. He seized the land of feuding barons, imposed the king's justice in regional disputes, and sent his *familiares* throughout the realm. For the nobility, the increase in royal power was a hated innovation and violation of long-standing rights, a misuse of authority placing society in jeopardy. Meanwhile, the rising bourgeoisie for the first time strove for a measure of sovereignty in its affairs. Most important towns in Northern France were declared independent communes in the twelfth and thirteenth centuries. Quite often the king and burghers worked together, allies in their common struggle against the great barons.

The nobility's influence went into a relative eclipse. This second feudal period represents a moment of crisis in the ranks of the aristocracy, a time when they consciously or unconsciously sensed that for the first time since Charlemagne they were no longer the dominant force in society. One form of reaction, the most important no doubt, was to claim status on the basis of a highly ornate code of chivalry founded on artificial distinctions of birth and breeding, enforced by law, and nourished by a literature of escape and wish-fulfillment (see chapter four). This 'exclusive club' mentality, which brought about a resurgence of the knightly ideal and contributed to the elaboration of great literary genres, the *chanson de geste* and *roman courtois*, is for the social historian a symptom of decay. It is the attitude of the master in fear of change: social conservatism coupled with nostalgia for a bygone golden age.

However, I am convinced that certain poets, those who composed the epics of revolt, strove to come to grips with the malaise of their society. They portray a situation in which a king is weak, cowardly, tyrannical, and readily swayed by traitors. He prefers his favorites, for example the *palazin* Gibouin, to the barons of the realm. Disinherited, insulted, with no place to go, no crusade to distract their energies, the nobles are forced into rebellion or civil war. Although the author takes the side of the aristocracy, in *Raoul de Cambrai* as in *Garin le Lorrain* selfish, vindictive barons are criticized as much as the king, whereas Bernier, the bastard, who in the end wins prerogatives and land, may well be a projection of the landless petty nobility, the *povres bachelers*, whose aspirations are different from those of the great barons.[5] This is because the enthusiasm, the spontaneity which it was possible to idealize in a late eleventh-century epic (*La Chanson de Roland*) become dangerous if not irresponsible in the context of a more complex national society. The valor, so prized in older texts, here can only be exercised against one's own people. And good in the individual becomes a social curse. Turold idealized a utopian fusion of individual spontaneity and group interest, but the poets of revolt had far too 'realistic' a vision of their times to copy him. For them, individual and group interests lead inevitably to conflict.

The solutions arrived at by the late trouvères, therefore, are often more than a trifle ambiguous. In some epics (*Girard de Roussillon*, *Renaud de Montauban*) the rebel yields to the king even though he is in the right, then sets out on a crusade or pilgrimage to the Holy Land. He fails because the ultimate lesson of the *chanson de geste* is one of order and harmony, an all-inclusive peace that goes beyond individual, family, and feudal honor to preach submission to authority. In *Raoul de Cambrai*, on the other hand, the two warring families, recognizing in the end that their feud has been a mistake, that Louis was originally responsible for so much bloodshed, and that he had manoeuvred Raoul into invading the Vermandois for his own purposes, make peace and then unite against the son of Charlemagne, insult him, wound him, and burn Paris. The only means of neutralizing their quarrel is to render it subservient to, and part of, a vaster conflict between feudal and royal authority. Their deeds make a vivid protest against the old social order. Yet, although the emperor is mocked and his city destroyed, his life and office remain sacrosanct. None of the rebels could have dreamed of abolishing the kingship, assassinating Louis, or even forcing him to abdicate, in spite of Guerri's one remark, 'Cest coart roi doit on bien essillier' (5425), and Bernier's blow at the king's person (5432–5). The barons' revolt results in no program for reform. Raoul ultimately falls because, first, he too is a rebel, acting against the peace of the realm and his ultimate suzerain, God in heaven, and, second, he is not the emperor. If Bernier succeeds in defeating Raoul, it is because the latter proves to be an even greater menace to society than Bernier. The king remains relatively untouched since he is the king. The *Raoul*-poet breaks off his story when the revolt turns against Louis, for he was no doubt unwilling, perhaps incapable, of punishing Louis or exonerating him. This open ending provides only a provisional solution to the problems raised in the narrative. We are told neither whether Guerri's or Ybert's side is in the right nor how far the king should be punished. And the alliance between the two feuding houses is fragile, to say the least. We see that the rebel's alienation is stated as a fact. The trouvère provides no easy answers because there are none.

The protagonist of *La Chanson de Raoul* is a Roland-figure patterned after the hero of Turold's masterpiece. Like Roland, he embodies *fortitudo* not *sapientia*, joys in the thrill of fighting for its own sake, and possesses a worthy comrade in arms, Bernier. As was the case for Roland, his loved ones, including a radiant fiancée, deliver laments over his corpse. Raoul has the dash, sparkle, and generosity which endear the rough-hewn adventurer to the masses. His tragedy derives from the fact that, possessing Roland's virtues, those considered necessary to the warrior caste – and only one vice, Roland's *desmesure* – he cannot lead the paladin's glorious life. Raoul's hubris is formally condemned by the author:

> Biax fu R. et de gente faiture;
> S'en lui n'eüst .j. poi de desmesure,
> Mieudres vasals ne tint onques droiture.

Mais de ce fu molt pesans l'aventure;
Hom desreez a molt grant painne dure.    (494–8)

and by Ybert de Ribemont:

'Hom orguillous, qe qe nus vos en die,
N'ara ja bien, fox est qi le chastie.
Qant q'il conquiert en .vij. ans par voisdie
Pert en .j. jor par sa large folie.'    (1869–72)

Raoul de Cambrai is inherently a great man, whose life is twisted by an act of injustice committed when he was three years old. Because of the disinheriting and the subsequent loss of status, a blow to his right to exist in society, he becomes enslaved to a form of paranoia, a feeling that the community conspires against him and, consequently, that he is entitled to employ any means to obtain his rights. He then reacts to the world around him with orgies of cruelty, which lead him down the path of hubris to a violent end. The hero archetype of *Roland* disintegrates, losing its original cohesiveness as it absorbs other views of man. Because Raoul is not permitted to use his talents in the normal (idealized) way, but is persecuted by a malevolent king who incarnates a demonic rather than a celestial world order, his character partakes of the Prometheus-figure, a victim of universal madness. Nor is it surprising, since he becomes a rebel and shares traits with Ganelon as well as Roland, to find Raoul assimilated to the Satan archetype, depicted as an enemy of the group, undermining society's most sacred values. And, because harmony can only be restored after the rebel has been defeated, like Roland he performs the role of *pharmakos* or sacrificial victim, whose immolation is necessary to the fulfillment of the tragic ritual. The rebel holds as much to tradition as any other hero but, because he partakes of several types, appears more complex and lifelike. Perhaps because of this ambivalence of perspective, the medieval public admired Raoul in spite of his guilt, even because of it, for the same reasons that their descendants have cherished Stavrogin, Vautrin, Rodogune, and Roxane, because Lucifer too was once the noblest of angels.

Like Oliver in *La Chanson de Roland*, Bernier embodies the virtues of widsom, prudence, and restraint that Roland and Raoul lack. Like Oliver, he is the hero's comrade, bears witness to his honor, counsels against *desmesure*, and does his utmost (generally without success) to ward off trouble. He functions as a projection of Raoul. Just as Guerri is Raoul's double, an evil genius urging him to crime (in terms of twentieth-century allegory, his id), Bernier serves as the hero's conscience or superego. His imago is to be found in Marsent, the only figure of parental authority on whom he can rely. It is she who counsels him to remain faithful to Raoul, and to the feudal bond, even though she and the family suffer for it:

> Et dist B.: '...
> R. mesires est plus fel que Judas:
> Il est mesires ...
> Ne li fauroie por l'onnor de Damas,
> Tant que tuit dient: 'B., droit en as.'
> – Fix,' dist la mere, 'par ma foi, droit en as.
> Ser ton signor, Dieu en gaaingneras.'
>                              (1379, 1381–2, 1384–7)

Ironically, Raoul himself destroys the restraining influence (superego), and almost immediately thereafter Bernier breaks with his master. Yet this Achates-figure is an orphan, he also lacks land. As a bastard, he can never fit into the social hierarchy. An outsider, he is 'lower' than his master, vulnerable to insult (the others call him *bastars* or *fix a putain* throughout), and bears within him a lifelong inferiority complex. Differing from Gilgamesh, Hector, Aeneas, Beowulf, the Cid, Roland, and even Raoul, he is not the protector of his people, for he has no people, and he must work out his problems alone. Because he is Ybert's son, the youth finds himself personally involved in Raoul's war, torn between loyalty to his father and uncles and his feudal bond to the lord of Cambrai, who dubbed him a knight. Although throughout the poem he is prey to conflicting emotions, ever seeking a just solution to his dilemma, in reality he cannot make a final decision. To employ reason in dealing with the passions of others serves no purpose in a community inhabited by Raoul, Guerri, and Louis. Bernier oscillates between careful statements of reason, based on wisdom, and passionate outcries of protest. His tragedy is that of a gentle man forced to act in a violent world yet unable to make up his mind.

Bernier is better than Raoul, but his character, like Raoul's, disintegrates in the course of time, under the pressure of combat and passion. For he also is a rebel and, accused of being *outrequidiés* (2223), shares some characteristics of the rebel type. This split in his character – he is an epic hero and a wise counselor, possesses both courage and prudence – endows Bernier with an aura of complexity unusual in medieval literature. Like many a modern 'problematic' hero, he stands as a figure of the divided self, containing within him the good and evil that struggle to dominate mankind. Differing from the majority of great rebels, however, Ybert's son does not end his days in a monastery or on a crusade. Just as his career was devoted to a search for truth, a slow groping for some principle on which to base existence, so in the end, although he humbly makes peace with

Raoul's family, he will continue to live in the world and manage his hereditary fief. In fact, it is to defend Bernier's right to inherit the Vermandois
that the former enemies unite against King Louis. The poet's message
is one of harmony and forgiveness but even more an appeal to the integrity
of the self. If feudal law is no longer sufficient for guidance, man must
turn within. Bernier's life is an example of such a quest, for after decades of
struggle he continues to search. Living has become a sufficient end in
itself.

   Like Racine's *Andromaque*, *La Chanson de Raoul* depicts a universe
inhabited by children born too late, incapable of emulating the deeds of
their parents. Charlemagne's, Raoul Taillefer's, and Ybert's sons live only
one generation after Roland and Oliver, yet the contrast between the world
of the elders and their own weighs heavily on them. On the one hand,
Raoul, Bernier, and Gautier partake of an epic tradition (especially *Gui de
Bourgogne* and *Aspremont*) that exalts the young hero, who alone possesses the enthusiasm and purity necessary for the prosecution of great deeds,
those qualities of *jovens* as essential to the crusade mentality as to *fin'
amor*. On the other hand, the poet condemns childlike behavior on the part
of an *enfes* such as Raoul, which can lead to disaster in war and feudal
politics. Guerri correctly prefers a more adult conduct, in which *chevalerie*
and *vaselaige* are allied to *sens* (4029–32). This is presumably the forte of
a Bernier or Gautier, who embody the topos of *puer senex*, the youth who
possesses the wisdom of an old man.[6]

   Be this as it may, human relationships in *Raoul de Cambrai* are significant in the following respect: although Raoul and his companion are both
children, their elders partake of the same traits. These secondary characters
have one quality in common: they are all related to Raoul or Bernier by
blood. One development in late *chansons de geste*, particularly manifest in
*Raoul de Cambrai*, is the importance allotted to the clan. The *Raoul*-poet
elaborates a complex drama with many actors, in which conflict occurs not
between two or three epic heroes but between families. The individual is
dependent upon others for existence; his autonomy recedes before that of
the group, and the 'story' concerns entire families and provinces. On the
one hand, members of the clan may be considered 'extensions' of a protagonist: Guerri, for instance, is Raoul's alter ego, and Marsent stands for
Bernier's conscience. Furthermore, each family, homogeneous from a
psychological and moral point of view, is set off against the other. The
Cambrai-Artois invaders are wild and impulsive, full of *desmesure*, manifesting an excess of *fortitudo*, whereas their adversaries embody the gentle,
reasoning side of man's nature: in a word, *sapientia*. The heroism exemplified by Raoul and his clan contrasts with the more humble, martyrdom-
oriented, often indecisive acceptance of life in Bernier and Marsent. Raoul's

people are masters who indulge in a sadistic will to power, while some of
Ybert's clan consent to be victims with a touch of masochism. Yet Vermandois physical weakness is offset by a comparable spiritual strength, which far
surpasses the others' prowess.

The Cambresian allies, often blind to reality, react to their existential
predicament in an inauthentic fashion. Such are Raoul and Guerri, who
use purported insults to their honor as pretexts for satisfying blood lust, and
Aalais, who, even though she castigates Raoul for his bellicose activities
and reproaches herself for his death, nonetheless pursues Bernier with savagery as fanatical as Raoul's, projecting her sense of guilt onto him. These
people not only lie to themselves; they also fail to communicate with others.
Raoul deceives Marsent as to Bernier's involvement in the war, accusing
him of having incited the venture, then breaks his promise not to attack the
monastery because one of his men lies to him about a quarrel with the
burghers and Raoul doesn't take the trouble to investigate before screaming
for revenge. Like Ganelon, he also wrongly imputes the most dastardly
intentions to his comrades and relatives. Raoul, Guerri,and Aalais continually insult each other, working at cross-purposes, each one instinctively
rejecting any suggestion offered by the others. Pride and susceptibility prevent them from making the constructive decisions they really believe in.
Whenever Raoul proposes peace, Guerri insists on war, and vice versa. A
striking example of their failure to communicate is the fact that, assur-
ances to the contrary, Raoul and Guerri become separated in the final battle,
which entails the former's death. And Gautier can only speak to Bernier
with his sword, delivering a speech or singing a song with blows:

> 'S'or n'avoit ci de ta gent tel fuison,
> A ceste espée qi me pent au geron
> T'aprenderoie ici pesme leçon
> C'onques n'oïs si dolereus sermon:
> Ja par provoire n'ariés confession ...
> Au branc d'acier vos noterai tel lai
> Donc ja n'arez a nul jor le cuer gai.'    (3982–6, 5037–8)

This in contrast to the Vermandois people, who, but for one episode, the
Aliaume-Guerri duel, communicate well with each other and work together as a team. For the most part they are free from bad faith. They
recognize the problems they face and the alternatives available to resolve
them. Bernier declines to resort to ruse or ambush, a favorite tactic of his
enemies (4188–90). Significantly, during the Battle of Origny marvels of
prowess are performed on the Cambrai-Artois side but only by Raoul and
Guerri; they are the only two heroes worthy of mention. None of their

adversaries, not even Bernier, can match them, yet the Vermandois feats
are ascribed to many combatants. Added up, they win the day. Although
Bernier is a bastard, he has many blood relatives; Raoul is an orphan. The
assembly of the Vermandois-Brabant-Hainaut troops is more impressive
(2026–94); in contrast the only 'muster' associated with Raoul is the list of
his forty hostages (751–90), men who help him win a legal point with the
king but never serve under his colors where they could be of real value. The
Vermandois clan as a whole is superior to Raoul and Guerri or to Guerri
and Gautier; working together as a group, it surpasses the divided,
anarchistic rebels from Cambrai.

Paradoxically, the individual's dependence on family bonds serves only to
isolate him. Raoul and Bernier, the one an orphan, the other a bastard,
grow up without fathers or land. Raoul's surrogate father, King Louis,
having disinherited him, launches him into an unjust, losing war. His
other surrogate father, Guerri the Red, is an impulsive, violent man, who,
for all his loyalty, seldom acts in the youth's best interest and forgets his
own sons on the field of Origny. These men are a far cry from the good
father-surrogates to be found in earlier epic: Phoenix, Mentor, even Hroth-
gar and Hildebrand. Significantly, the immature Raoul, blamed for the
death of Ernaut's sons, becomes a paternal figure to Bernier, proving to
be as inadequate a father to his friend as Louis and Guerri are to him. The
*enfes* thinks of Aalais as a Terrible Mother. When she appeals to him from
her advanced years, like Hecuba in the *Iliad* warning her son not to fight, he
spurns her because she is elderly. He has no confidence in her, acts like a
spoiled adolescent who refuses to do what he is told. He sends her to her
own quarters, ordering her, a mere woman, to tend to the refectory:

> 'Maldehait ait, je le taing por lanier,
> Le gentil homme, qant il doit tornoier,
> A gentil dame qant se va consellier!
> Dedens vos chambres vos alez aasier:
> Beveiz puison por vo pance encraissier,
> Et si pensez de boivre et de mengier;
> Car d'autre chose ne devez mais plaidier.'    (1100–6)

And Bernier suffers the archetypal Oedipal nightmare, witnessing his
mother perish before his eyes (rendered immobile, he drops his sword and
faints away), struck down by his father-surrogate. Whereas Aalais accuses
Raoul of wounding her breasts, that gave him milk ('Je te norri del lait de ma
mamele; / Por quoi me fais dolor soz ma forcele?' 1002–3), Bernier watches
his mother's breasts burn in the flames of Origny: 'Celes mameles dont
ele me norri / Vi je ardoir, par le cors S. Geri!' (1527–8). Both young men

rebel against evil parents or parent-surrogates and enter into a quest for good ones. Raoul fails and dies. Only after his death will there appear a spiritual son worthy of succeeding him: the 'young hero' Gautier. Although Bernier atones with his good father, Ybert de Ribemont, first he has to witness his mother's death and reject and kill his evil surrogate father, Raoul. As a result, in a sense he takes Raoul's sin unto himself, for, like Gautier, Bernier becomes as violent as Raoul used to be. The latter's penance is swift death, Bernier's a lifetime of struggle.

The *Raoul*-poet underscores what can be called, without excessive anachronism, his heroes' alienation. No less important than the orphan-bastard motif is a pattern of reification that runs through the epic. King Louis considers his vassals' land as an object, property to be distributed at his fancy, and thus refuses to take into account the human factors inherent in the bond between an individual and his fief and a man's right to bequeath it to his sons. The king deprives his barons of their human dignity and their place in the hierarchy, merely to reward others who lack dignity and status. Louis treats Aalais as well as her fief, the Cambrésis, as properties, bestowing the two of them onto Gibouin, Aalais's body considered less important than her land, possession of the former serving as a pretext to enjoy the latter. People continually offer to exchange one fief or promise of a fief for another, or to barter reparation (either wealth or acts of self-humiliation or both) for an insult or a wound. Normally knights expect a *don* in exchange for feudal service. Because their affairs go wrong, Bernier complains that Raoul rewards (pays) him badly for services rendered:

> 'Je sui vostre hom, a celer nel vos qier,
> De mon service m'as rendu mal loier ...
> – Diex!' dist Bernier, 'con riche gueredon!
> De mon service m'ofr'on ci molt bel don ...
> Je t'ai servi, amé et sozhaucié,
> De bel service reçoif malvais loier.'    (1644–5, 1663–4, 1704–5)

And later, the surviving members of the Cambrai clan declare that Raoul in turn has been badly paid for the real services he did render to Bernier, but that the latter will be made to 'pay for it' in the end. For example:

> 'Oncles,' dist l'enfes, 'ci a male soldée
> Qe B. li bastars t'a donnée,
> Qe nouresis en ta sale pavée.
> Se Dex se done q'aie tant de durée
> Qe je eüse la ventaille fermée,
> L'iaume lacié, enpoignie l'espée,

Ne seroit pas si en pais la contrée.
La vostre mort seroit chier comparée.'    (3638-45)

The worst insult one knight can hurl at another is a variation on: 'I will
deal you a blow such that never again will you hold land!' or 'Your land will
go to another!' (4502-4, 4984, 5005), and the strongest of threats: 'If I
cannot avenge my shame, I am not worth a red cent' or 'I will not have one
cent's worth of pleasure if I do not succeed in killing you' (1515-6, 3325-6,
3888, 4384-5, 4472).[7] In the course of the war the characters gradually
lose their sense of decorum, their capacity to interrelate following generally accepted norms. Raoul strikes Bernier on the head with the staff of
a lance. Later, Aalais, a woman, tries to wound him with a stake. And at
King Louis's banquet the two families quarrel like savages, hitting each
other with knives, sticks, and a leg of venison.

    Alienation is perhaps most strongly expressed in spatial terms. Too far
from Spain or southern Italy, no outside-oriented crusades are provided
for these people. And no vertical vistas, leading up to God. Indeed, the
barons act like invading Saracens, ravaging *dulce France* for their own
purposes. In this limited, too sharply defined space where there is not
enough land for all, they impede each other and cannot escape. Raoul has
energy and spontaneity but no fief. He either travels fruitlessly from
Cambrai to Paris and back or is launched in the wrong direction (toward
Saint-Quentin) on the bad impulse of a Guerri and a Louis. In battle he
flings himself about, chasing Ernaut de Douai in undirected, jerky movements which separate him from his own men. At Origny, too, the burghers
agitate themselves but are massacred inside the palisade they were unable
to defend. Marsent walks out from the town to placate Raoul, but she too is
immolated between walls. Although, like his mother, Bernier is relatively
passive, he finally does ride from Origny to Ribemont, exercising freedom
to change sides. And, before the Battle of Origny, the Vermandois people
send two representatives to Raoul, with peace offers, which the invaders,
rigid in their fanatical belligerence, reject. In the second half of the poem,
disintegration of character is depicted through a progressive restriction of
the environment. The conflict proceeds from invasions and battles on a
plain to a pillaging expedition, to duels between two or four individuals, to
insult at a banquet table or in a closed room. This reduction of external
space is not entirely negative, however. Chaotic, precipitous movement
early in the poem closed off any possibility for debate. After Bernier's
invasion of the Cambrésis, a change in locus brings in its wake confrontation
between the opposing sides; at first physical violence is transposed to the
verbal sphere: Gautier and Bernier insult each other, on the field or when
lying wounded in the same room; then this pattern of verbal abuse gives

way to genuine communicating and an effort, ultimately successful, at accommodation. Bernier, who lost a mother, appeals to Aalais, who lost a son; both suffer, both are responsible. And, in the end, the opposing sides leave Paris together, mobile and in harmony, forming a community, while King Louis, the man of crafty immobility, will be forced to move also – to suppress their rebellion.

For the characters in this epic, Raoul especially, land is the most important possession a man can own, since it alone grants him status in the feudal world, it alone mediates for happiness and prestige. The fief is Raoul's goal in life, his only reason for living. His greatest shame derives from permitting someone else to enjoy his land (661–4, 695–708). Bernier, who embodies wisdom, even though he is as landless as his master, offers on more than one occasion to give up his own heritage in order to make peace. It can be said that Raoul abandons Aalais in favor of the Vermandois land, which takes the place of mother and fiancée. The monastery of Origny, an enclosed space associated with Marsent, contains green grass, fresh fields, and clear flowing water:

> Car bele est l'erbe et fresche par les prez,
> Et si est clere la riviere ...'    (1279–80)

Although it is a *locus amœnus*, Raoul insults Marsent and devastates her convent, resulting in its total loss, to him as well as to its rightful lord, Ybert. In the ensuing war the region of Origny is transformed into a muddy swamp by rain and the blood and brains of fallen soldiers. Raoul desecrates the 'treasure' epic heroes ought to win and preserve: the sacred temple, the garden is metamorphosed into a Waste Land. Whereas the landscape of *Roland* has a particularly masculine heroic quality about it, the slippery water-soaked marsh of Origny (plus the church) adheres to the 'feminine' décor evoked by Bachelard, G. Durand, and J.-P. Richard. For medieval man, the earth, one of the four elements that make up the universe, is 'feminine.' Raoul has succeeded in ravaging his enemies' church and land slaying their consecrated women, but they will be avenged. Ybert wonders (1913–14) why God doesn't suffer grass and earth to part, swallowing up the rebel. Later, during the battle, Raoul cries out to Ernaut that neither grass nor earth nor God nor his saints can deliver him from death:

> 'Terre ne erbe ne te puet atenir,
> Ne Diex ne hom ne t'en puet garantir,
> Ne tout li saint qi Dieu doivent servir.'    (3017–19)

However, Ernaut is spared, and Raoul falls in his stead, struck down by

Bernier, the 'son' he cast off. He does lift himself up and strikes out with his sword, but missing Bernier it cuts into the earth and can be drawn out only with a great effort (3115–21). Raoul has violated Mother Earth for the last time. Only thus does he show love and mastery of the land. Thus will he enjoy his fief, which, cursed by him, possesses his sword in turn and drinks his life's blood.

Against his enemies Raoul employs fire and sword. Ultimately both fail. In the stanzas describing the burning of Origny, the poet alludes repeatedly to the flames, which plunge and sparkle, climb towers, and penetrate walls. They have a life of their own.

> Dieu en jura et la soie pitié
> Q'il ne laroit por Rains l'arseveschié,
> Qe toz nes arde ainz q'il soit anuitié.
> Le fu cria: esquier l'ont touchié;
> Ardent ces sales et fonde[n]t cil planchier.
> Tounel esprene[n]t, li sercle sont trenchié.
> Li effant ardent a duel et a pechié ...
> Li quens R., qui le coraige ot fier,
> A fait le feu par les rues fichier.
> Ardent ces loges, ci fondent li planchier;
> Li vin espandent, s'en flotent li celie[r];
> Li bacon ardent, si chiéent li lardie[r];
> Li saïns fait le grant feu esforcier,
> Fiert soi es tors et el maistre cloichier.
> Les covretures covint jus trebuchier;
> Entre .ij. murs ot si grant charbonier,
> Les nonains ardent: trop i ot grant brasier;
> Totes .c. ardent par molt grant encombrier;
> Art i Marsens qui fu mere B. ...'    (1464–70, 1481–92)

According to medieval lore, fire is masculine, in contrast to the feminine elements, earth and water. It is associated with the planet Mars and with choler in the body, the humor attributed to the Mediterranean peoples. The flames of Origny evoke Raoul's will to power, his anger, passion, and hubris. And *Guerris li sors*, Guerri the Red, an even more choleric individual, is Raoul's evil genius. Burning and killing are the only ways they can express their virility and overcome the feminine principle inherent in Marsent and, to a lesser extent, Bernier. Whereas Marsent ought to radiate in the sunlight, symbol of God's wisdom, she perishes from the flames of martyrdom, unleashed by a rebel, in his own way an Antichrist or Satan-figure. Yet, fire deserts Raoul on the soggy, swampy field of battle where

he is cut down: before dying he can only pitifully evoke the intercession of
the last, greatest of Mothers: 'Secorés moi, douce dame del ciel!' (3131).
In the end, the Cambrai and Vermandois leaders, realizing how they had
been duped by the emperor, their real enemy, defy him and leave Paris
together, but not before burning the city (5482–8). Just as the action begins
in Paris, it ends in Paris; as Louis was responsible for the war, he pays for
it. And the flames of Paris, the royal city, prove the only just expiation for
the flames of Origny.

To what extent is this pattern of expiation and retribution religious in
nature? When Raoul is born, Aalais sends him at once to be baptized by
their relative, the Bishop of Beauvais. She does so in order that Raoul may
be recognized as his father's heir, but, perhaps unbeknownst to herself,
her act places Raoul in the community of God-fearing people and launches
his career under religious auspices. Years later, after cursing her son,
Aalais runs to the church of Saint-Géri-de-Cambrai to ask God's pardon,
invoking Longinus who pierced Christ's flesh on Good Friday (1141–9).
In the midst of his campaign, Raoul proposes to pitch his tent in a convent
church, use the crypt for his canteen, perch his hunting birds on the
crosses, sleep before the altar, leaning on the crucifix, and hand over the
nuns to be enjoyed by his squires (1231–43). Although dissuaded from
these acts, he burns the convent anyway. Marsent, a nun and a saintly
woman, immolated during Holy Week, perhaps Good Friday, on consecrated ground, within the walls of her church, recalls Mary Magdalene,
innumerable martyrs of the Church, the Virgin Mary, and even Christ.
Furthermore, a psalter that dates from the time of Solomon the Wise burns
with her on her breast (1308, 1506). Since, for the medievals, the Bible is
the word of God, written by the Holy Spirit, an insult to the Book is an
insult to God himself. Then, on the same day, after having 'grilled' the
nuns, Raoul orders meat, drinks, plays chess,and strikes Bernier in the head.
The gloom of the Lenten season in Raoul's camp contrasts with the joy of
Easter in Ribemont when Bernier and Ybert are reunited (as were Christ and
the Father in heaven). However, the Easter feast is dampened by Bernier's suffering and the fact that he has not been avenged. Although his
flowing blood recalls Christ's, unlike Christ he does not turn the other
cheek. On the battlefield itself Ernaut thrice prays to the Virgin, twice
promising to rebuild Origny if his life is spared (2596–7, 2832–3, 2995–7).
He does survive, whereas by blaspheming against God and his saints Raoul
in effect renounces God ('Q'a celui mot ot il Dieu renoié,' 3023), becomes
like a mad dog, and, possessed by the devil, is slain without mercy. Most of
the other principals have at one time or another broken feudal law; Raoul
alone defies the rule of God. Therefore, *Diex* and *drois* help Bernier win
(3101); he grieves over having killed his lord but knows he has been

spared by divine grace, that *drois* is for, not against him. Ybert's son invokes God more than any of the other characters. When his peace overtures are spurned, he turns to the divinity ('Tot est en Dieu,' 5202); at the very end of the poem he begs for peace, stretched out in the form of a cross, and the Abbot of Saint-Germain threatens Guerri with damnation if he refuses to accept Bernier's terms.

It is true that the *Raoul*-poet does not provide for Bernier's dilemma or for the socio-juridical problems posed by the text a Christian resolution such as pilgrimage, crusade, or an eschatological experience. An exclusively religious interpretation of the epic as a whole would be false. But Raoul has sinned against God as well as against man; as Bernier says, the real bastard is the man who denies God ('Q'il n'est bastars c'il n'a Dieu renoié,' 1709), who is our only true Father and Creator; and in a war between David and Goliath, David will never be totally vanquished. In contrast to *La Chanson de Roland*, God is largely absent from *Raoul de Cambrai*. Yet, as in the novels of Bernanos, Mauriac, Julien Green, and Cayrol, is not his absence a commentary on the way people live, on the 'world' of *Raoul*, which can only enrich our understanding of the epic?

Structurally, I find three crises in the poem around which the action turns, which may properly be called peripetias: 1 / the burning of Origny; 2 / Raoul's death; 3 / the final reconciliation. The first part of the epic is focused on Raoul's criminal act against society, and the quarrel with Bernier, his criminal act against the individual. From this point the action leads to his death at Bernier's hands, God's and man's vengeance, a just punishment for both crimes. The remainder of the epic deals with the passions unleashed by Bernier's retribution, culminating in reconciliation and a second punishment, this time of King Louis, responsible even more than Raoul for the evil that has occurred. Before Origny, the narrative is dominated by the lord of Cambrai, whose folly brings France to the brink of destruction. After the quarrel, attention is centered on Bernier, Raoul's most tragic victim and the instrument of divine vengeance. Once Raoul falls, we turn again to the Cambresians and to Gautier, who will walk in his uncle's footsteps, become his uncle, thus prolonging the feud until the story is worked out at Court where it had begun. The plot as a whole conforms to the outline of tragedy: a hero commits a crime against society or the gods, setting up an antithetical or counterbalancing movement which leads to revenge on himself and on the figure who impelled him in the first place, to expiation, and to the restoration of order. Just before the burning of Paris Ybert declares Bernier to be his heir. For the first time the bastard is integrated into society, becomes one with his world. Hence it is appropriate for the action to come to a halt. Yet, in spite of the fact that certain characters do grow over the years, that Gautier proves to be wiser than Raoul, that he and Bernier succeed in finding parent-figures and learn to accept each other as equals, the author has articulated a circular rather than a linear structure. He presents us a double reversal of fortune in Raoul's and the king's punishments, and on both occasions the restoration of order implies a return to the situation in which the characters found themselves in the beginning.

There is a tradition of *chanson de geste* in which stable, archetypal characters (hero, traitor, king) adhere to conventional roles, and conflict between them is clearly defined; in which exemplary individuals embody the ideals of feudal society, continuity maintained from the past to the present and between epic narrative and its public. *Raoul de Cambrai* diverges from the pattern, indicates how far a late epic can evolve in other directions, be concerned with other issues. Compared to *Roland* and even to most poems of the Guillaume Cycle, *La Chanson de Raoul* gives expression to crises in identity, a questioning attitude toward the old heroic values, concern for socio-political problems, and multiple perspectives on reality. The treatment of warfare, of language, even of space and time, is mimetic, is relatively close to our own perception of reality. The old archetypes are twisted; indeed, the traditional epic protagonist is deemed to be so villanous that a new hero (derived from the Achates-figure) comes to replace him.[8] The trouvère explores questions of feudal law and the varied occasions for strife that can occur between king and subject, lord and vassal, friend and friend. He also investigates the role of the family, that is, both the conflict of individuals within a kin group and problems that ensue when family groups as a whole declare war on each other. Alienated young men (an orphan; a bastard) desperately seek land, a father, and a place in society. As likely as not, they fail, because the old heroic code can no longer be of help and because the new ways based on money, exchange, social standing, manipulation, and fraud are seen to be all-pervasive. The result is not only a masterpiece of unusual power but also a lucid, disillusioned commentary on the twelfth century from the inside. Given the implicit Christian faith which serves as a backdrop for the *Raoul*-universe, we ought not to be surprised. When faith encounters its opposite, the esthetic outcome can be either lyrical exaltation (*Roland*) or a version of high tragedy (*Raoul de Cambrai*). Both are authentic medieval attitudes, both manifest the epic spirit in early French literature.

Chapter Three

# 🌺 *HUON DE BORDEAUX*

Although *Huon de Bordeaux*,[1] probably written between 1212 and 1229, gave rise to a tradition that includes five major sequels within the *chanson de geste* convention, plus versions in Alexandrines and in prose, in the popular format of the Bibliothèque Bleue and the 'troubadour genre' of the Comte de Tressan, not to speak of Shakespeare's *Midsummer Night's Dream* and *Oberons* by Wieland, Weber, and Carducci, this extraordinary poem stands apart from most other Old French epics. It cannot be fitted easily into one of the three traditional cycles: the Cycle of the King, the Guillaume Cycle, the Cycle of Rebel Barons. On the one hand, the trouvère promises to sing a 'Boine canchon estraite del lignaige / De Charlemaine ...' (3–4). On the other hand, the beginning and end of his story recall themes that form the doctrinal core of *Raoul de Cambrai* and the epics of revolt: disinheriting, divided loyalties, *desmesure*, and treason. However, these opening and closing scenes frame central episodes which serve an entirely different purpose. Whereas *Raoul de Cambrai* or *Renaud de Montauban* plunges directly into the most anguishing juridical questions of the day, this epic reacts to contemporary issues by escaping from them, establishing an ideal world where such problems are resolved through wish-fulfillment, where we judge things by how they ought to be rather than by how they are.

Exiled from France, accompanied by a small troop of supporters, Huon travels to Rome and Jerusalem, then is aided by an old hermit, Gériaume, who advises against traversing a forest inhabited by Auberon, king of the fairies. Contrary to expectations, Auberon befriends Huon. Although forbidden to do so by his new benefactor, Huon visits the French renegade Oede at Tormont and the giant Orgueilleux at Dunostre. He defeats both monsters and at Dunostre liberates a beautiful girl, Sebile. Upon arrival at Babylon, however, he is imprisoned. Fortunately, Esclarmonde, the daughter of the emir Gaudisse, has fallen in love with the youth and comes to his aid. Huon defeats Orgueilleux's brother Agrapart on the emir's behalf.

Then, with the help of Auberon's army, he takes command in Babylon and brings Esclarmonde home to be his bride. During their return journey, however, a storm casts the lovers onto a desert island. Esclarmonde, captured by pirates, falls into the hands of the emir Galafre in Aufalerne. Huon eventually finds his way to the court of Gaudisse's brother, Yvorin. War having broken out between Yvorin and Galafre, Huon and Gériaume join forces, seize Aufalerne, and escape to France with a treasure and Esclarmonde; whereupon they undergo further acts of treachery that give rise to further adventures, before the inevitable happy ending.

   *Huon de Bordeaux* illustrates, perhaps more than any other French epic, the archetypes of romance, by which I refer not to any one specific medieval literary genre, such as the Arthurian tale, but to Northrop Frye's much broader concept of romance as mode or mythos. He defines it as the 'mythos of literature concerned primarily with an idealized world' and writes: 'The mode of romance presents an idealized world: in romance heroes are brave, heroines beautiful, villains villainous, and the frustrations, ambiguities, and embarrassments of ordinary life are made little of.'[2] The archetypal structure of romance often resembles that of the folk tale, fairy story, or popular ballad. Above all, the general outline of the protagonist's life will adhere to that pattern analyzed by Rank, Raglan, Campbell, and De Vries, traditional to heroic-romantic literature everywhere. True, Huon de Bordeaux does not partake of all characteristics of the popular hero. He is not endowed with supernatural parents; he is not born in striking fashion; he is not separated from family during infancy or given an unusual upbringing. Faithful to the tradition of the *chanson de geste*, the poet says nothing of his protagonist's life before early manhood. But from this point on, from the moment the great adventure begins, his career corresponds to that of the typical hero of romance. Joseph Campbell has summarized it in the following terms: 'A hero ventures forth from the world of common day into a region of supernatural wonder: fabulous forces are there encountered and a decisive victory is won; the hero comes back from this mysterious adventure with the power to bestow boons on his fellow man.'[3]

   In most such literature he must first be separated from his environment, compelled to lead a life of adventure. Our poet provides a structural catalyst to this effect in the hero's disinheriting. Borrowing a series of motifs to be found in epics of revolt (including *Raoul de Cambrai*), he devotes the first and last parts of the poem to elaborating a pattern of royal injustice, the king associated with nefarious villains, including the protagonist's brother, Gérard. *Malvais iretier* are contrasted with Huon, the exemplar of a good son and heir. Although these political episodes are of interest in their own right and the poet is concerned with such issues,[4] the unique quality of *Huon de Bordeaux* is to be found elsewhere, in the adventure-quest to the Orient. The disinheriting-treason section serves as a frame for the quest.

Driven into exile, Huon commits a transgression and suffers a fall but will one day be permitted to return. Before doing so, however, according to Charles, he must proceed to the court of Emir Gaudisse in Babylon (Cairo). There he must slay the first knight he finds at the imperial table, kiss the emir's daughter three times, and bring back a hoard of treasure:

> 'De moie part l'amiral rouverés
> Que il m'envoit mil espreviers mués,
> Mil ours, mil viautres tres bien encaenés,
> Et mil vallés, tous jovenes bacelers,
> Et mil puceles qui aient grant biautés,
> Et de sa barbe les blans grenons mellés,
> Et de sa geule quatre dens maiselers.'    (2364–70)

This ordeal recalls the many heroes of myth who conquer an ogre and win a bride, or Malraux's character in *La Condition humaine* who declares that one must both kill and make love in order to arrive at adulthood. Throughout the ages, conquest in love and war is considered a necessary attribute of the heroic life. Slaying symbolizes valor, is a tangible sign of Huon's martial accomplishments, and the kiss is an act of possession, which marks his conquest of the woman. In our text, interaction of the two motifs occurs, since Huon's victim turns out to be Escalarmonde's fiancé and Esclarmonde the emir's daughter. Thus by killing the man he runs greater risks in love, and by kissing the girl he will face far greater dangers in war.

Discovering or capturing a treasure is a standard motif of the folk tale as is the accomplishment of impossible tasks set by a hostile king (the myths of Perseus, Bellerophon, Jason, Theseus, and Hercules). Gold, silver, youths and maidens, exotic birds and beasts – these are tokens of victory. One of the greatest medieval epics, the *Nibelungenlied*, makes conquered treasure a symbol of the hero's glory. Paris of Troy is associated with the golden apple of discord as well as with golden Helen of Sparta, Theseus with the Golden Fleece as well as with Medea. Not only do great men possess treasure: he who is master of a hoard becomes a powerful, feared leader.

In the last analysis, Charles's conditions serve above all as an excuse for adventure. On several occasions Huon rejects the suggestion that he adhere strictly to his mission. Rather, he says, he has come to the Orient for the sake of adventure, and it will have priority.

> 'Sire, dist Hues …
> Jou ne lairoie por vo grant disnité

Que jou ne voise le gaiant visiter;
Car por çou vin ge de France le rené,
Por aventures et enquerre et trover ...'
– 'Sire Geriaumes, dist Huelins li frans,
Por l'amor Dieu, c'alés vous dementant?
Tres puis cele eure de France fui tornant,
Si m'aït Dix, n'aloië el querant
Fors aventures, ce saciés vraiemant.'    (4617, 4619–22, 4716–20)

(See also vv. 2634, 3827, 8513, and 9025.) Huon certainly lives up to his
claim. He enjoys life for the sake of living, leaps from one crisis to another,
truly a picaresque hero in his own time.

Quest and adventure imply a departure. The hero leaves home, family,
friends, the world of ordinary mortals behind. He is exalted by the concept
of travel and movement, a search for the unknown. Through the voyage
he penetrates to the limits of his world and himself. Jason and the Argonauts, Odysseus, the Israelites seeking the Promised Land – these are the
most famous embodiments of the archetype. Northrop Frye has pointed out
three stages in the action of romance – journey, struggle, and exaltation –
which correspond to the stages of classical tragedy: agon, pathos, anagnor-
isis. Of these, the journey is the most distinctive for medieval man.

The other phases are also important, however. For all the hero's greatness, for all our faith in his capacities, he must work hard for victory.
Struggle against opposition forms one of the principal aspects of romantic
narrative, indispensable for keeping the public's interest aroused and creating sympathy for the protagonist. Huon de Bordeaux will encounter obstacles on the path to the object he seeks; he too will struggle to accomplish
his quest.

Although his most immediate adversaries are Saracens, opposition to
the hero must be seen as more than the hostility between two empires or
religions. Once the protagonist leaves Jerusalem he enters an exotic, magical realm which, despite a few realistic details added for the sake of verisimilitude, bears little resemblance to the real world of the thirteenth century. Great cities, vast armies, uncountable riches, wonders of all kinds fall
upon Huon's route. The poet creates a stylized yet highly evocative portrait of the East, a pagan world which indeed is replete with aspects of the
supernatural. It has been said that in *Huon de Bordeaux* the marvelous is
so important that, if it were suppressed, the narrative would have to be
conceived in radically different terms. It is the author's great innovation,
his contribution to the *chanson de geste* as a genre, and a determining reason
for the poem's success with the medieval public and modern reader. In
fact, the way in which *Huon* is bathed in the marvelous, the supernatural
becoming natural, appearing to be the only possible way of life, places the

text in direct association with courtly romance. The fabulous Orient in
*Huon de Bordeaux* may well reflect the Celtic Other World, that mythological realm containing supernatural beings which is from time to time open
to select members of the human race.[5]

Since the Other World is denied to the vast majority of humans, insurmountable barriers, physical and spiritual, separate it from our own.
Only a chosen elite are permitted to cross the threshold. In *Huon de Bordeaux* the Orient is separated from the West by a series of exotic *sauvages
teres* (2908) surrounded by the desert. Voyaging from Jerusalem to Babylon,
Huon must traverse Femenie, a country of great poverty where the sun
never shines, women do not bear children, dogs do not bark nor cocks
crow; the territory of the Kumans, a tribe who eat raw meat, live like the
beasts, and are covered by their own long ears; and Foi, land of milk and
honey, where grain is free and all men good.

Having crossed the desert, Huon now stands in enemy territory, Babylon
directly before him. The hero's mentor, Gériaume, informs him that two
routes lie at his disposition. He may choose a route containing dangers from
which no man can escape, which, however, will bring him to his goal in
only fifteen days; or he may take an easy road through populous cities, but
the trip will last a year:

> 'L'unne des voies fait tant a redoter
> Qu'il n'est nus hom qui en puisse escaper;
> Et si te di, por voir et sans fauser,
> Qui i peüst aler a sauveté
> En quinse jours i venroit, en non Dé.
> Et se tu veus autre cemin aler,
> Un an tout plain a tordre vous metrés,
> Mais boins osteus i troverés asés,
> Et bours et viles et castiaus et chités.'    (3155–63)

The motif of the two roads is not uncommon in folklore and romance.
Among the most famous examples are the two bridges to the land of
Gorre in Chrétien's *Lancelot* and the *Lancelot-Grail Prose Cycle*. Like Lancelot, Huon chooses the more dangerous route. The hero's success depends
not only on inherent spiritual and physical resources but also on his actual
presence in the Other World. The two roads are such a test and the only
way of attaining the inner sanctum.

In *La Chanson de Huon* the short road leads through a *bos* (3171). It is
Auberon's realm, where he practices magic, a region from which no man
who has answered the fairy's greeting escapes. Between Tormont and
Dunostre are situated other wooded areas containing wild beasts. And we
know that, near Paris and near Bordeaux, at the beginning and end of the

story, traitors launch their ambush from a *bruellet* or *bos* or *selve foillie*. In medieval literature the forest stood traditionally as a place of mystery and adventure, a *locus* apart from society where the hero undergoes supernatural ordeals. The forest may be idealized as a refuge for lovers (Tristan and Iseut), prophets (Merlin), or good outlaws (Girard de Roussillon, Renaud de Montauban). It may equally well be deemed a setting for evil. To medieval man it appeared an enemy, an implacable opponent to be withstood at every turn. In addition, the wood retains demonic overtones of a more poetic nature. Throughout world literature the *selva oscura*, dark, menacing, impenetrable, image of the maze or labyrinth, evokes connotations of mystery and is conceived as an ante-region to the inferno or an extension of hell.[6]

More ways of proceeding to the Other World are to be found than exclusively by land. The barrier will often be conceived in terms of a river or sea, such as the Mediterranean, which gives rise to a tempest that capsizes Huon's boat; the Red Sea, by which lies Dunostre, monstrous keep of the ogre Orgueilleux, who can be assimilated to the guardian of a ford in Arthurian romance; and the four levels of river or moat that protect the inner recesses of Babylon. Like the forest, the ocean stands for the mystery of primeval nature, those elements of the universe untamed by man, hence ever a threat. Like the forest, it remains a barrier to man's enterprises. Such is the role the English Channel plays in Thomas's *Tristan*. A storm, plus subsequent calm, prevents Tristan and Iseut from being reunited; then a willed misinterpretation of naval signals, the white and black sails, results in the hero's death. A tempest at sea also provides obstacles to Huon's union with Esclarmonde. Huon consummates his love and, as if in immediate response, a storm brings him to the edge of death:

> U lit se coucent sans point de l'arester;
> De le pucele a fait se volenté.
> Onqes si tost n'ot son deduit pasé
> Une tempeste commence par le mer.    (6825–8)

The difference between these two poems is that, despite his certainty of perishing like Tristan, Huon will live to recast his existence.

The Duke of Bordeaux succeeds in traversing strange lands and difficult routes, in conquering forest, river and sea. He arrives at the goals set for him by the emperor, which generally take the form of a castle or tower. One after the other he conquers Auberon's castle in the forest, Oede's city of Tormont, the tower of Dunostre, and the emir's palace in Babylon. Each of these structures, redolent with mystery, is reserved for an elite. Christian typology has traditionally associated Babylon with hell and the Antichrist, an association reinforced here by the custom of the four bridges,

which declares that if a visitor to the city admits to be French (Christian)
he will have a hand severed at the first bridge, another at the second, a foot at
the third, and his remaining limb at the fourth. Guards will then carry
him before the emir to de decapitated. At Dunostre, Sebile explains to Huon
how he must proceed to confront Orgueilleux: he is to traverse four
chambers, the first containing provisions, the second treasure, the third four
idols, the fourth the redoubtable master of the keep himself, whose bed-
stead is adorned with magic birds (singing automatons) at the four corners.
Once again we find progressive initiation to an inner sanctum, fraught
with danger and consecrated by the number four – image of worldly power.
We also see Orgueilleux's fortress designated a tower. The tower has
always been conceived as a particularly romantic structure, in Northrop
Frye's terms a 'point of epiphany' joining heaven and earth, a place of
confrontation between the human and the supernatural. A conventional
demonic motif ('Childe Roland to the dark tower came,' 'Le Prince d'Aquitaine à la Tour abolie'), it has had great vogue in modern as well as medieval
romance.

If no other evidence were forthcoming, we should be convinced of the
tower's demonic overtones by the fact that for the hero it becomes a trap:
he is imprisoned as in a cage. Three castles (Tormont, Dunostre, Babylon)
serve as jails; all three contain dungeons where good people languish.
Along with the desert island, where Huon is abandoned, and Galafre's
harem, in which Esclarmonde is detained, they embody the infernal aspects
of Huon's quest. This is menacing, demonic, enclosed space, twice in form
of a maze or labyrinth, once associated with a serpent, which complements the vast open regions associated with the Orient.

For each prison a guardian serpent of one kind or another is provided.
Danger to the hero lies less in topography (forest, desert, tower) than in the
monsters who block his path: Oede the renegade, who disregards the
laws of hospitality and family; the giant Orgueilleux, a cannibal related by
blood to devils in hell; and his brother Agrapart. In addition to the two
giants, the metallic automatons that defend Dunostre, the serpent guarding
the Babylon fountain of youth, and the custom of the four bridges evoke
a supernatural horror reserved in our day to the prose of science fiction. The
*Huon*-poet emphasizes Agrapart's frightful personal traits:

> Dis et set piés ot de grant li maufés;
> Les ex ot rouges com carbons embrasés;
> Demi piet ot entre l'uel et le nés;
> Entre sorciex, un grant pié mesuré.   (6322–5)

Huon is tiny in comparison; their duel recalls that of David and Goliath. A
'little man,' hero of light, triumphs over a shadow-monster, as in the

myths of Theseus, Perseus, Jason, Odysseus, Gilgamesh, Michael, David, and Christ.

Our hero will vanquish the ogre. In spite of insurmountable obstacles, in spite of persecution by pagan enemies, an unjust king, and a traitor in his own family, Huon penetrates to the heart of his symbolic Other World and succeeds in the quest. Success is due in part to the young man's personal qualities, the marks of a hero. He is strong and brave, a warrior without peer, especially adept at fencing, a skillful pleader at court, with a sense of justice and fair play. Most of all, Huon is the archetype of innocence, for he is absolved of guilt – his purity is confirmed – by a series of physical and spiritual ordeals. Passing these tests proves the boy's good character, his right to sovereignty in the feudal world. He thus becomes a *vas electionis*, '... net et pur et sans pecié mortel' (3731), who succeeds where others have failed and alone deserves the privilege of the quest. In capacity and performance, he adheres to Frye's characterization of the romantic hero: one 'superior in degree to other men and to his environment ... whose actions are marvellous but who is himself identified as a human being.'[7]

It is a typical romance motif that the protagonist, a relatively colorless figure, triumphs less from his own exertions than as a result of the help he receives from other beings. Our trouvère in no way diverges from the convention. However, a case can be made that even when Huon does receive aid (without which he could not have fulfilled the quest), he is to some extent responsible for it himself. Not the least of his powers is the ability to inspire loyalty in others. This most certainly is the case with regard to women. Seduced no doubt by the youth's skill in arms, even more by his beauty ('Biax fu li enfes de membres et de vis, / Plus bel enfant n'avoit ens el païs,' 1763–4) and his kiss, Sebile, Esclarmonde, and Yvorin's daughter deliver him from more than one crisis. All three resemble the Ariadne figure in myth: the medieval variants of the maiden who helps the hero defeat the Minotaur are the Saracen princess in *chanson de geste* who makes advances to a paladin, releases him from prison, converts to Christianity, and marries him, and the damsel in distress of Arthurian legend rescued by a gallant knight. Of course, the girl may be portrayed as a comrade or squire-surrogate (Sebile), a bride (Esclarmonde), or a temptress (Yvorin's daughter). But in all three cases a young man does accept favors from a maiden subjugated by his youth and beauty. It is a male wish-fulfillment situation where an anima-figure helps him defeat an ogre and then offers herself as his prize for victory. In traditional epic the hero saves the damsel, but often in romance the situation is reversed: the protagonist becomes a man by and through women.

Similarly, though obviously not for the same motives, Huon is succored by other men. Although he sets out in life an orphan, it can be said that his deceased father, Duke Seguin of Bordeaux, plays a significant role in the narrative. Because of him, a large number of people scattered through the world all rush to Huon's side. Most of these are also blood relatives of the Bordeaux clan. Thus, like Diomedes, Telemachus, and Pallas in classical epic, Huon is associated with his father in people's eyes and expected to uphold the glory of his lineage. Yet non-relatives will aid him, including the ten knights who, along with some others, make up his band and follow the young duke to the ends of the earth. Abandoning everything for him, giving themselves to *aversité* (2797), they all perish in the Orient or at Bordeaux.

I refer to the paladin's followers as a band intentionally. The author demonstrates concern for numerical precision. Often he refers to these men by number, whether twelve, thirteen, or fourteen. Our poet is affirming the integrity of the group. Huon's band remains a self-sufficient, purposeful social unit. Although the contingent's identity does not depend on its retaining a given number of men, the poet probably did not wish to increase its size indefinitely; fourteen, including Huon, most likely provided the ideal number. Such it will remain, except for one moment when Esclarmonde herself, firmly installed in her husband's good graces, is admitted as number fifteen. In this exaltation of the homogeneous, autonomous group, we observe a trend in certain late epics away from the ideal of the individual to a concept of man as a member of society. Roland befriends Oliver, Ami and Amile each other, Renaud de Montauban is served by his three brothers, but Huon de Bordeaux has behind him a team of men. The hero as captain replaces the hero as individual; leadership replaces the more strictly individual exploits of the early *chanson de geste* and *roman courtois*.

For all his personal virtues and help from other men, Huon would have failed but for aid from other-worldly beings and things. From Orgueilleux Huon seizes a hauberk that provides its wearer with immunity against fire, water, and the sword, and a ring that guarantees safe conduct within Gaudisse's empire. Auberon gives his protégé magic presents: a goblet, which can never be drained and which will pour only for those pure in heart; a horn, which, when blown, will cause listeners to sing and dance and/or cure their ills, and which can summon a banquet and/or Auberon himself with a hundred-thousand-man army. Scholars have pointed out analogues for these objects in Celtic folklore (the Grail) and in early epic (Roland's olifant). Joshua's triumph at the Battle of Jericho could also be cited. Whatever the source, it is significant that, although one of the objects serves largely to provide a moral test, the other to summon reinforcements, both may be considered, at least symbolically, sources of abundance. They supply the hero with riches in the guise of food, wine, or men. Wine from the goblet is said to resemble a fountain (4171-2). This vessel is recognized by Freudian analysis to be a feminine image; the horn can be either masculine or feminine. In our text they indicate that the hero has successfully taken command of nature and has at his fingertips the bounty, grace, and energy which nature, depicted as the Eternal Feminine, bestows on men.

Participating in both the human and animal world stands Malabron. A fairy knight and vassal of Auberon, he has been transformed into a sea creature (*luiton*) for having offended his master. Twice he intercedes with Auberon on Huon's behalf, then comes to the youth's aid; in each case travel by water is involved. With Malabron, who partakes of an Old Man of the Sea tradition (Proteus, Triton, Nereus, and Neptune; in Ovid, Horace, the Arabian Nights, etc.),[8] even the water barrier can be rendered amicable. Huon's tears, the wine of innocence poured by the magic goblet, and Malabron's intervention from the depths contribute to a pattern of water-imagery symbolizing Huon's goodness that stands in opposition to, and serves to mollify, the sunlight of Auberon's justice. Malabron claims to love the paladin as a mother loves her child:

> Je sui uns hom qui moult vous a amé;
> Autant vous aim, se Dix me puist sauver,
> Com fait la mere l'enfant qu'ele a porté.    (7110–12)

The representative of Mother Nature, of our mother the sea, this savage creature is eager to help mankind. Huon needs a supernatural help and, more than help, sympathy, intercession, expiation. Malabron provides the superhuman atonement essential to the completion of the quest.

Little indeed, however, is his contribution compared to Auberon's. The king of the fairies is without doubt the chief factor in Huon's success and, esthetically speaking, the most striking character in the epic, destined to acquire greater fame than the duke himself. In the first laisse we are told his father was Julius Caesar, his mother Morgain la Fée (8–18; also 3513–17); he partakes of the classical and Arthurian world, inheriting the power and wisdom of both. Despite his claims to the contrary, Auberon appears to be freed from mortal limits (as we all would be but for the Fall), a practitioner of white magic assimilated to Moses and even Christ, an oracle who serves God's will, possesses the secrets of heaven, and is assured of one day sitting next to God:

> 'De paradis sai jou tous les secrés
> Et oi les angles la sus u ciel canter,
> Nen viellirai ja mais en mon aé,
> Et ens la fin, quant je vaurai finer,
> Aveuqes Dieu est mes sieges posés.'    (3579–83)

Scholars have interpreted this figure in various ways. Auberon goes back, it is claimed, to a pagan god of light, a Germanic god of the underworld or dwarf with supernatural powers, or a Celtic Merlin Sylvester or dwarf king of the antipodes.[9] With more cogency, we can point to the analogy between *La Chanson de Huon* and folk tales where an unfriendly demon is forced to give the hero assistance. The adversary has posed the young man questions and, because of his refusal to answer, is compelled to pay a high price for compliance. The defeated god then becomes the protagonist's servant and helps him in the pursuit of his quest. Literary examples of this pattern are Jacob and the angel in the Old Testament, Menelaus and Proteus in Greek mythology, and Sigfried and Alberich in medieval German literature. The poet may have taken some such tradition as a source for his poem, transforming it in the process.

Rather than embody hostile forces, Auberon may represent the traditional non-hostile divine agent acting on the hero's behalf. He stands as a protective figure, a catalytic character, not unlike Athena, Venus, or for that matter Loki and Merlin. He is an outside dispenser of justice, a *deus ex machina* who rectifies the evil perpetrated by false judges, Charles the Great and Gaudisse. In the words of Northrop Frye (not referring to *Huon de Bordeaux*): 'In the analogy of innocence the divine or spiritual figures are usually parental, wise old men with magical powers.' Or Joseph Campbell: 'In fairy lore it may be some little fellow of the wood, some wizard, hermit, shepherd, or smith, who appears, to supply the amulets and advice that the hero will require.'[10] Thus is to be explained Auberon's association with the forest. He is a nature figure who controls storms and rivers, an outsider to society, symbolizing the benign, protective power of destiny. His physical deformities (he is a *nains bocerés*) are equally traditional, to be found in all literature. Archetypally, the gifts of power and wisdom are accompanied by a corresponding mutilation: Samson was blinded, Tiresias was blinded and/or made into a woman, Vulcan had a club foot. Poets teach us that perfection is denied the human race, and any man who achieves distinction in one facet of life must pay a penalty in others. Finally, if the poet likens Auberon's beauty to the sun (3177, 3239, 3532, etc.) it is because, archetypally, he manifests the light of day, his presence in the story is that of the sun, blessing and fecundating all it touches. A pattern of oppositions runs through the poem: good and bad, heaven and hell, life and death, light and darkness. The darkness of the forest and of Saracen prisons implies a static, deathlike state; in contrast stands a world of dazzling movement and radiance symbolized by Auberon, the sun-figure. Light plays almost an anagogic role in this epic, and the *Huon*-poet anticipates the archetypal patterns of imagery we find in such Renaissance masters as Ronsard, Tasso, Spenser, and d'Aubigné.

A problem which has puzzled scholars for generations is why the fairy
king and sun-figure feels tenderness for Huon, a perfect stranger, why he
works so thanklessly on the youth's behalf. Although the theory – that in
the trouvère's hypothetical source, derived from Germanic legend, Auberon was indeed Huon's father and aided his son in a bride-quest – has been
discredited, we can retain the notion of Auberon as a father-surrogate,
i.e. a friend, magician, or old, wise man who acts as father to the hero (often
an actual or presumed orphan). This tradition is widespread in literature;
it provides the inspiration for Dante's *Commedia*, Corneille's *Illusion comique*, and Balzac's *Père Goriot*. As we have seen, the Old French epic as a
whole is grounded on a symbolic paternal cult, in which seasoned warriors
such as Charlemagne, the older Guillaume and Aymeri de Narbonne,
Ybert de Ribemont and Guerri le Sor assist their actual or surrogate sons. In
*La Chanson de Huon*, as in *Raoul de Cambrai*, the hero has lost his real
father. He is, symbolically at least, searching for a father-substitute and has
not been able to find one in Charlemagne, the traditional father of his
people. Betrayed by his brother, in the end he has no family at all. Since
Auberon, presumably unmarried, has equal need of a son and heir, it
should not surprise us when, at the poem's close, Huon, who is the most
handsome of mortals, whose beauty corresponds to Auberon's, 'becomes' his child, joins his family, inherits his fairy kingdom. He will replace
his new father and presumably become one in turn. Huon chooses Auberon, a 'good father,' over Charlemagne, a 'bad father.' Auberon, the judge
of Gaudisse and Charlemagne, turns out to be the supernatural paternal
guide his predestined child has been seeking. Huon's story becomes one of
initiation and the succession of male generations, of role-transference
from father to son. Furthermore, Auberon is depicted not only as a king but
as a kind of solar deity. We are aware of the long-standing tradition that
ascribes characteristics of the sun to the divinity and, conversely, of a father
to the sun. This conception, central to the elaboration of some of the
most striking Indo-European myths, gives rise to poetic overtones in our
text. This masculine sunlight then is complemented by the more feminine
water-imagery (tears, wine, the sea) associated with Huon.

Huon's most dangerous adventure, the sea voyage, partakes of an archetype we have seen in *Roland* and *Raoul*, also to be found in *Gilgamesh*, the
*Odyssey*, and the *Aeneid*: death and rebirth. We behold the young man
buffeted by a storm, set adrift on a plank, and left naked and abandoned on a
desert isle; we are told how pirates tie the hero's hands and feet and bind
his eyes, leaving him blind and naked, how even when rescued by Malabron
and placed on shore, he remains penniless and naked. Huon has become a
*sauvages hom* (7196), an outcast from society, exposed, alienated, and
alone, so degraded that he is pitied by Estrument, the lowest of the low, a

mere jongleur. An Adam figure, he has sinned and been properly punished by the fairy-god of the Other World. Yet, expelled from Eden, fallen to the bottom of the knightly hierarchy, he assumes the right to call into question both the hierarchy and the values it upholds.[11] Why should Huon obey one father-figure (Auberon) when another (Charlemagne) has been so cruel to him? And since Auberon chooses to abandon him, does not the youth have the right to abandon Auberon in turn?

> 'Cis nains boçus m'a honni et tué,
> Mais, par Celui qui en crois fu penez,
> Puis qu'il m'i laise en si grant povreté,
> Se mestiers est, je mentirai asés,
> Ja mais por lui ne sera trestorné.
> A cinq cens diables soit ses cors commandés!'    (7168–73)

Cut off from Charles's authority and releasing himself from Auberon's, he becomes free to tell lies, to fornicate, and to force his way back up the hierarchy with his strong right arm and ready wits, not with Auberon's gifts. However, the episode is significant in an archetypal as well as existential context. Since the ocean receives ships and men's bodies into its depths, it evokes the notion of death, but as a fount of nature it also evokes life, the eternal mother. Huon's nakedness at sea implies, in Freudian and Jungian terms, a return to the mother's womb, a movement to the center of nature and existence. Set down naked but whole on the island (a point of epiphany), 'Tout aussi nus comme au jor que fu nés' (6841, 6868, 6909, 7176, 7192, 7405, 7984), Huon experiences a symbolic death and rebirth. The young hero risks dying through immersion, expects to perish, but survives to participate in a new life. He has lost what status he possessed in the old world but has been cleansed of the dross, inauthenticity, and less-than-perfect attainment implied in it. The abandoned child and chosen savior defeats monsters, escapes from prison and the threat of death, and, with the gift of Auberon's kingdom, new talismans of identity, and a new family, attains symbolic immortality. This episode contributes an important link in the pattern of Huon's initiation. Victory in Paris was not sufficient to prove his exceptional heroic qualities. Victory at Babylon also does not suffice. Huon must come to grips with the most elemental forces of nature and be cleansed of the past before his initiation is completed.

The young man's return establishes his sovereignty. He is acclaimed as Duke of Bordeaux, rightful heir to his father's land: the orphan is no longer disinherited, his birthright no longer denied. Huon finds a place in the community in much the same way as Chrétien de Troyes's heroes or Guillaume d'Orange and Aymeri de Narbonne. Winning a fief and a bride

constitutes acceptance into the feudal hierarchy; the woman and the city
are symbols of the hero's achievements and witnesses to his glory, a pattern
derived from Homer and Virgil that flourished in medieval France, as
such poems as *La Prise d'Orange, Aymeri de Narbonne, Le Siège de
Barbastre, Guibert d'Andrenas,* and *Foucon de Candie* show.[12] Yet the
story does not end here; the problems raised in the narrative cannot be
disposed of quite so easily. Huon, a feudal baron mistreated by the king,
a spiritual cousin of Raoul, Bernier, Girard de Roussillon, Ogier the Dane,
and Garin le Lorrain, will never be left in peace. The king remains weak
and unjust. His court is rotten to the core. In spite of the youth's performance, order is not, cannot be restored to France; Charles the Great
abides, a permanent lord of misrule, and Huon, for all his glory, remains
independent of and dependent on Charlemagne at the same time. At the
beginning and at the end of *La Chanson de Huon,* we see that the hero
cannot survive in Charlemagne's evil world; he has to get out. Indeed, it
can be claimed that the Saracen Orient proves paradoxically to be safer for
Huon than his own country: the Pagans are more predictable than Frenchmen, less intelligent, and not subject to outrageous treachery. And in the
East one is free from the political and moral constraints that operate at
home. A way exists, nonetheless, for the poet to alleviate his hero's predicament. Huon has achieved status in two realms – the supposedly real domain
of the *chanson de geste,* and the patently fictional one where Auberon
holds sway. The Carolingian world serves as a frame for Auberon's. In
the end the two are first juxtaposed (Auberon's and Charles's dinner
tables placed side by side), when Auberon invades Bordeaux and proves
his moral as well as physical superiority. Then, Huon, who wished to transform his duchy into a kingdom, is offered sovereignty in the realm of the
fairies – and accepts. By returning to the symbolic Other World, he chooses
to abandon Carolingian France altogether. He will dwell where people
are predictably all good or evil, where good father-surrogates replace evil
ones and freedom replaces constraint. The only flaw in Auberon's kingdom is that it is unreal. Like so many heroes of later medieval narrative,
Huon resolves the problems of his day by escaping to a utopian paradise,
a realm of fantasy.

   *La Chanson de Huon de Bordeaux* is for the modern reader, also, a poem of
escape, where he may participate in a domain of fantasy, a 'primitive,' childlike world where heroes are rewarded, villains punished, and the anguishing
problems of secular life forgotten. This is a realm of melodrama where the
hero stands untouched by moral constraints and physical opposition, free to
choose adventure in a never-never land where good people are supremely
good and the wicked absolutely evil, a land of treason and ambush, of foster
parents, pirates, and narrow escapes, of dark and light ladies, of super-

natural guides who appear like magic in order to serve the paladin, whose victory is given him less because of his own virtues and exertions than because fate, chance, and a benevolent supernatural always serve the true and the pure. This is a world in which the persecuted popular hero is temporarily impeded by fraud or his own folly but never defeated in the end. Given that archetypal patterns will often reveal, in man's unconscious, the desire for a life of adventure based upon wish-fulfillment, it can be posited that the *Huon*-poet evokes a world of dreams. The lure of romance, so powerful in the Middle Ages, has persisted to our own day: that may explain why the paladin and his great mentor caught the fancy of a Shakespeare and a Wieland, why they have survived the silence of the centuries.

More than one scholar has compared *La Chanson de Huon* to Ariosto's *Orlando furioso*, a comparison more valid than such analogies usually are. Both the trouvère and Ariosto draw from a variety of literary and folkloric sources to create a synthesis of the previous tradition. Both *Huon* and the *Furioso* are works of art, written in premeditated fashion. And, for all its sincere exaltation of the ethos of chivalry, there is much comedy in Ariosto's poem. Such also is the case with *Huon de Bordeaux*. Quite a few specialists have made the error of ignoring the poem's humor, treating it in much the same way as they do *Raoul de Cambrai* or *La Mort le roi Artu*. Their failure to recognize that romantic and comic elements are expressed simultaneously in the epic's fabric has led to misunderstanding.

It is often said that the highest, most subtle form of the comic is comedy of character, a truism as valid for the Middle Ages as for the centuries of Molière and Proust. Humorous traits are to be seen here in the protagonist. Although we are made only too aware of Huon's virtues, he is often forgetful or unaware, acts in error and out of folly. In my opinion these examples of *foleté* or *desmesure* are not tragic in nature. They provide a counterpoint to the protagonist's heroic deeds, a comic rhythm which contributes to the elaboration of a very complex psycho-narrative pattern.

One incongruous trait in so great a hero is physical weakness: specifically, his inability to withstand hunger. Certain forms of debility are typical of the very young hero, *puer senex*, who nonetheless possesses the enthusiasm necessary for the realization of great deeds. However, Auberon uses the fact that Huon has not eaten for three days as a weapon against him, bribing him with the promise of nourishment. But once the offer is made, Huon will talk of nothing else. He interrupts the sorcerer or answers his questions by calling for dinner. It has become a fixation, blocking out all other concerns. Similarly, later in the poem, in order to eat, the young man yields to Esclarmonde's seductions, even at the price of damnation (5930–3), and, constrained by hunger, becomes the servant of a minstrel after having committed apostasy. Huon is driven to further excess because of his appetite for wine as well as meat. After having imbibed, he will sound Auberon's horn without need and will deflower Esclarmonde. Charles too makes an inebriated fool of himself at Bordeaux and is given a tongue-lashing by Naimes. The theme of folly through drink occurs in *Le Pèlerinage de Charlemagne* and *Gaydon* as well as in many other epics. It under-scores the Bergsonian contrast between the ideal and the actual, between man's intellectual pretensions and those physical elements which also make up the human condition. We are reminded of his dictum: 'Est comique tout incident qui appelle notre attention sur le physique d'une personne alors que le moral est en cause.'[13] Furthermore, as Curtius has shown, the Medievals considered the acts of preparing and devouring food somehow incongruous with the heroic or contemplative life, hence the presence of so much *Küchenhumor* in medieval literature.[14] There can be no doubt that, for Huon, a banquet with the fairy king Auberon is both totem and tabu, forbidden and, therefore, sought after all the more. On the one hand, Huon's transgression recalls the sin of Adam, an act of *Superbia* and *Gula*; on the other hand, Auberon's providing a banquet to the skeptical youth out of nowhere resembles miracles in the Bible (Moses, Christ) and the *Vitae Sanctorum*. Finally, Charlemagne is confounded when Auberon's dinner table appears by magic in Charles's own hall, and the king of the elves partakes of his own food and wine, seated above the King of France.

Bound to the physical, perhaps to some extent derived from it, is a 'spiritual' characteristic: cowardice. Huon, *puer non senex*, is unduly afraid. He fears the Kumans ('Por nient les crient,' says the poet, 'car il ne font nul mel,' 2921) and Auberon; he fears to enter Dunostre and Babylon; once inside both fortresses he wishes he could leave; at one time or another he lacks faith in the magic horn, hauberk, and ring and either dreads to use them or tries them out on the wrong occasions. Huon is also prone to tears. He weeps throughout the poem, at every moment of crisis. We know to what extent weeping, symptomatic of a passionately, even violently emotive life, was typical of the feudal period. Nonetheless, Huon cries more than other protagonists of epic. Fear, so natural to an ordinary mortal, is unfitting in a hero of his grandeur.

*Foleté* or comic hubris is most concretely manifest in the young man's relations with his benefactor. Auberon orders Huon not to summon him with the magic horn except in an emergency; Huon blows the horn to test it. He commands Huon not to visit Tormont; the youth goes there inten-tionally. Once again Huon sends for Auberon when not in mortal danger. Auberon begs his disciple not to seek a fight with Orgueilleux; Huon visits Dunostre that he may challenge him. The fairy king tells him never to lie; in Babylon Huon declares he is a Saracen. He forbids the youth to sleep with Esclarmonde before their marriage; Huon violates her on the ship returning to France. The paladin once again lies, this time to Estrument.

On seven distinct occasions Huon consciously, willfully defies his master. He reacts like an automaton opposing whatever counsel Auberon offers, however logical it may be. A humorous effect is created by the element of repetition, central to the notion of *raideur mécanique*. Bergson's image of the jack-in-the-box is appropriate in this context. Even more comic is Huon's state of mind after he has been punished for defiance. Whenever, in accordance with everyday human justice, Auberon corrects his pupil, the latter responds with outrage, infuriated that anyone should have dared to rebuke him, and then insults his erstwhile benefactor in no uncertain terms. 'He! Auberons, pullens nains bocerés, / Cil te maudie qui en crois fu penés!' (5910–1) he cries in a Babylonian prison; on Moÿsant Island he uses much the same language, in spite of the fact that Malabron has just come to liberate him. In fact, Huon threatens to defy Auberon again, by telling another falsehood, if ever he falls into difficult straits (7168–73). And in Estrument's presence he does just that! He will punish his benefactor by committing additional faults which cannot but place him in a still worse predicament, materially and in Auberon's eyes.

At the same time, Huon's attitude is not entirely without reason, nor do we cease to sympathize with him. The author leads us to believe that his protagonist's lapses are not as serious as Auberon would have them. For one thing, Huon himself does not condemn his lying, nor does he consider it to be of great import. He claims that Auberon takes anger 'Por poi de cose' (7238). In spite of some formal regrets, he never really admits the error of his ways. 'What I did was not important,' he says; 'I forgot or was enchanted by the devil. Auberon won't notice a thing, and if he does and is at all a *preudom*, he will forgive me' (5505–9, 5565–7, 5638–42). The implied public is forced to accept, at least in part, the hero's own interpretation of his deeds: after all, forgetfulness is less blameworthy than inherent evil, and Western justice, especially in the last few centuries, does emphasize one's intent at least as much as the concrete outcome of one's acts; furthermore, in spite of imprudence, in spite of being punished by Auberon, Huon always wins in the end. He succeeds in the quest, regardless of the obstacles placed in his path, perhaps because of them. Indeed, his lying, his very breach of fidelity, grant him the ruse or disguise that permits victory on his own and our human terms.

In certain kinds of literature the protagonist can do no wrong; those who oppose him are in error. His goodness is an absolute, a given of the story, not open to discussion. Although he commits acts repugnant to

society's commonly accepted standards, the very notion of ethics is transformed. Rather than that the hero be considered favorably because he conforms to given standards, his actions prove to be good because it is he who
commits them. In other words, right and wrong are determined not with
reference to a moral code but by the hero himself, who embodies the desires
and aspirations of society. A protagonist of romance, leading a life of
adventure and glory, a fictional character in a fictional world, Huon claims
the right not to be mistreated or punished. Since the standards applied to
ordinary mortals are not applicable to him, he may disregard Auberon's
imperatives. Since his ethos is the only one relevant to the epic structure,
in the long run the public will agree with him.

Yet he also defends the world's point of view. One of the reasons the
young duke will not obey Auberon's rules is that by so doing he would place
himself in situations normal for a hero of romance but in conflict with
everyday common sense. When Huon and Gériaume wander through
Auberon's forest, the boy is famished. Gériaume counsels him to live on
roots, as he himself did for thirty years. Huon replies: 'I'm not at all used
to it; so help me God, I can't eat such things' (3234–5). Another time,
beleaguered by Oede's men, Huon is about to summon Auberon; Gériaume
objects that his friend has not yet been wounded, is not in mortal danger,
and thus would be breaking Auberon's command. Huon replies:

> 'Q'esse? dist il, ore i soient maufé!
> Atendrai tant qe je serai tués?
> Je cornerai, qui k'en doie peser.'    (4506–8)

One of Auberon's vassals points out that the magician should not be more
strict in meting out justice than God himself, who forgave Adam. Although
*foleté* gives rise to sin, these sins are 'temporary' and deserve in Christian
terms to be forgiven, since we are all sons of Adam and guilty of the same
fault. Starvation as inner discipline, risking death as proof of heroism – these
mean nothing to Huon. No man must be forced by ethical or moral
doctrine beyond the normal powers of human nature. The youth is guilty of
refusing to adhere to traditional standards of conduct. The exigencies of a
stylized, artificial heroic life are placed in opposition to the demands of
common sense, and this opposition indeed arouses laughter in the public.

By refusing to obey Gériaume and Auberon, by frustrating their will to
master him, Huon acts far more authentically than his entourage. He
denies Oedipal guilt and any form of predetermined ethical conduct. In a
sense, he is more free, more open to dialogue with the outside world
(magicians, kings, renegades, Saracens, princesses) than the wise, fearful old
men who surround him. Condemned to symbolic blindness by pirates or

his faithless brother, Huon's greatest act of freedom is to go see new people and places; condemned to immobility in prison, he seeks to escape to wherever his fancy takes him. His is a victory of animal vitality and quick wits over custom and inertia. Whenever a conventional response is expected, Huon gives the opposite. His nature as a literary character is fundamentally ambivalent. Huon chooses the hard road, through the fairy king's forest, then regrets his decision. He ardently desires Auberon's hospitality but wishes to leave immediately, even when offered gifts. He claims to have no fear of Auberon but trembles whenever the mighty dwarf appears on the scene. He agrees to whatever request is made but almost immediately thereafter refuses to obey. Huon displays heroism and weakness, prudence and folly, conformity and independence. Each state follows directly the one that has gone before, is structurally and psychologically dependent on it. These sudden changes in attitude lack the resilience of human nature at its best, appear rigid and mechanical, yet the public also finds Huon's changeableness sympathetic, because the eternal conflict of words and deeds, of theory and practice, of intellectual construct and empirical reality, is set into relief; and because most human beings do, at one time or another, act in a humorous, that is, unnatural, manner. Bergson would have us believe that comedy requires distance, a lack of emotional involvement on the part of the public. Often this is so. But no less often the public, while recognizing a man's foibles and laughing at them, will also sympathize, even identify with him in his incongruous situation. We identify to some extent with the comic hero, seeing ourselves and all of humanity in him.

Although the comic aspect of Huon's *persona* is brought out most clearly in his rapport with Auberon, the latter does not exist merely as a foil. He also fluctuates, changes, manifests a spirit of contradiction. How many times he is obstructed and baffled by Huon! Yet, though blustering with rage and righteous indignation, each time he forgives the prodigal son. He comes to his rescue personally (at Tormont, Babylon, Bordeaux) or through an associate (on the Red Sea, in the desert). The only valid explanation for Auberon's conduct is the deep, lasting affection he has conceived for the boy. Although he first appears as a dreaded, even monstrous figure, he is somehow taken with the young duke's personal qualities, offers him magic gifts, and remains true to him ever after. He demonstrates sorrow for Huon's errors and the trouble they involve him in, going so far as to praise his *loiauté* (3509, 4519, 4521, 10298). Now, although Huon has perhaps been a faithful enough vassal of Charlemagne (though he threatens more than once that in the future he will hold his hereditary lands as a kingdom, that is, renounce his feudal bond), he certainly does not manifest loyalty to Auberon.[15] For the Medievals, *loiauté* meant, above all, keeping one's word. Granted that Huon is incapable of the treachery perpetrated by his enemies, he lies and tricks his way from city to city and tower to tower. He is at times 'faus et trop desmesurés' (6813) and 'trop legier d'asés' (6677). I suggest we interpret Auberon's praise in part ironically, as an instance of his being blinded by love for Huon and often incapable of seeing him as he really is. I use the word 'often' because, of course, Auberon is lucid part of the time. The comic element in his nature springs from a tension between fierceness and good nature, between blindness and lucidity, between the righteous condemnation of a judge and the loving pardon of a friend. He too acts and reacts, back and forth, like a jack-in-the-box.

Auberon and Huon, each a comic character in his own right, interact to form a comic pair. Repeatedly Auberon will be angry at his protégé. He will rage against the paladin's folly, in his presence or from a distance. Huon, fully aware of Auberon's wrath and his own guilt, becomes terribly afraid. Then, moved by the pitiful condition into which the young man has fallen, Auberon will take pity on him, restoring him to favor, giving him another chance. But as Huon gains confidence in himself he ceases to dread Auberon. In response to the latter's affection he will demonstrate indifference and a stronger chafing at his master's domination. When in order to assert independence Huon defies the magician, this act unleashes Auberon's rage and his own misfortune. Both men return to the point whence they began, and the action is unleashed once more. The narrative's internal pattern is thus circular in nature; each humorous interlude, having run its course, drives the characters to a point where the same or a similar episode logically follows. Tormont, Dunostre, Babylon, the ship, Aufalerne, are structurally the same. They form what we may call the fundamental comic increment of the poem; repeated and extended, they make up *Huon*'s comic pattern.

The pattern is rendered so inevitable, so apparently natural, because it flows directly from the two main characters' given personality traits and the initial situation in which the author has placed them. Neither can exist without the other. Auberon is a great ruler but childless and seemingly friendless. He seeks affection, an heir, someone on whom to bestow his favors. He chooses Huon largely by chance, without the latter's deserving such fortune. Huon, on the other hand, is an orphan, a rightful heir who has been disinherited. He has already been mistreated by one father-surrogate (the king) and must defy and conquer another (the emir). He is proud and independent, a young rebel lacking in altruism, concerned only with his personal quest for glory. Auberon should be the master, the dominant figure, in their relationship, since he possesses the riches, wisdom, and power without which Huon cannot survive. But the king of the fairies is rendered impotent by the very extent of his emotional involve-

ment with a youth, who, indifferent to his patron, defies him, knowing he
will be forgiven in the end. In fact, Huon is the master, he knows it and
acts on it. Our author has constructed a parody on the traditional paternal
relationship in which the father suffers at his son's hands, is held up to
ridicule by the son. The insolence with which Huon treats his benefactor is
different in style, but not in kind, from that found in the earthiest of
medieval *fabliaux*.

A parody of the father-son relationship is a variation on the old theme
of youth versus age. There is a tradition in late *chanson de geste* of the type
of adventure Huon undergoes forming the *enfances*, the first exploits of
the young hero.[16] The author refers to Huon from first to last as *Huelin* or
*Huon l'enfant*, the *enfes*, the *baceler*, the *petit orfenin*, a youth who has
yet to prove his credentials, whereas such villains as Amauri, Gaudisse, and
even Charlemagne are shown to be venerable patriarchs. The duel between
Amauri and Huon is set in terms of the following contrasts: great versus
small, strong versus weak, *senex* versus *puer*:

> Or sont el camp li doi baron entré.
> D'unne part fu Amauris de Viés Mes:
> Grans fu et fors et ricement armés,
> De Huon graindres un grant pié mesuré,
> S'ot cinquante ans par eaige pasé.
> Et Huelins fu jovenes baceler,
> N'avoit encore vint et deus ans pasé ...    (1765-71)

Of course, we find examples of kindly greybeards, including Gériaume,
Naimes, and Auberon. Despite appearances, even though he enjoys the
freshness and beauty of a child, Huon's mentor was born before Christ:

> 'Cis petis enfes ki vous a salué,
> Que vous avés enfanchon apelé,
> Nasqui ançois que Jhesucris fust nés.'    (3445-7)

For all his power and wisdom, Auberon is a weak old man, weak in that
he needs Huon as much as, if not more than, the paladin needs him. He
cannot or will not recapture his hauberk from Orgueilleux or destroy the
pagan kingdoms existing in his part of the world, without first being
goaded into it by Huon. Even more important, Auberon is weakened by
affection, a burning desire that Huon become his son and heir. He must
dominate him, impose his wisdom on the audacious free spirit inherent in
the Duke of Bordeaux. He lives vicariously through Huon, is rejuvenated
by contact with him. Huon is his mediator to life. Yet by impinging on the

hero's freedom, he blocks his development, acts against the rules of romance, and thus has to be condemned. And Huon's failings – his dependence on physical comfort, his impetuosity, foolhardy courage, forgetfulness, naïve boasting, even his weeping – are all manifestations of *grant enfanche* (2671), traits generally ascribed to the young and forgiven all the more readily because so often in literature, and even in some historical periods including our own, *jovens* sets the standards for society as a whole, because good traits ascribed to the child – purity, generosity, enthusiasm – more than offset his liabilities.

One conflict between old and young centers on the issue of love. Auberon and Gériaume each take a conservative, puritanical stand toward Huon's affair with Esclarmonde. Auberon forbids the couple to make love before they are married; Gériaume, after having warned Huon in like manner, abandons ship, leaving the sinners to their fate. We are also told that Emir Galafre permits Gériaume to speak with Esclarmonde because he is so old that a maiden would never seek his love (7952–7). In these episodes Huon thinks of sex quite differently. Desiring Esclarmonde on the boat, he enjoys her in spite of the greybeards, exulting in his passion and its fulfillment. On the desert island he encourages his fiancée to make love again:

> – 'Dame, dist Hues, or laisiés çou ester;
> Foi que doi vous, n'i valt riens dementers.
> Acolons nous, se morrons plus soef;
> Tristrans morut por bele Iseut amer,
> Si ferons nous, moi et vous, en non Dé.'    (6846–50)

Then, after they have been reunited, Huon must be separated from Esclarmonde for the one night they spend in the Abbey of Saint-Maurice. If they slept together, says the poet, Huon would surely have had his will of her and profaned the convent, 'Car Hues ot trop legier cuer d'asés' (9113).

Thus does he oppose Auberon and Gériaume. Thus does his joy vanquish their scruples; thus does the symbolic id triumph over a series of figures that embody the superego. But if, after having won Esclarmonde, the youth indulges in sensuality, he steadfastly refuses to do so on other occasions. At Babylon he kisses the princess only out of duty. Having fallen passionately in love with him, she makes advances that he has the strength to resist. Out of regard for him, she suggests murdering her father, an offer which he also declines. Later he will spurn Yvorin's daughter, who lusts for him no less forthrightly and comically than Esclarmonde does. This temptation motif is common to some thirty *chansons de geste*, to courtly romance, and to the epic of Antiquity: *Gilgamesh*, the *Odyssey*, the *Aeneid*. Thus Huon stands in contradiction to himself; from a youth of inflexible principles he is transformed into a bold skirt-chaser, returns to his principles, then once more is tempted by lust. His transformation, comic in and of itself, corresponds to and complements a change on Esclarmonde's part. Although the princess defends her virginity, regretting the sin she and her fiancé commit, in Babylon she has made no less sensuous and brutal advances to Huon (with the exception of physical assault) than he makes to her on the ship. Inflamed by his kisses to the point of fainting, she declares:

> 'Sa douce alaine m'a si le cuer emblé,
> Se jou ne l'ai anuit a mon costé,
> G'istrai dou sens ains qu'il soit ajorné.'    (5728–30)

We cannot justify these transformations on psychological grounds alone. They exist, structurally, for the sake of comedy. On two distinct occasions, in Babylon and on the open sea, a lover desires his mate but his advances are repulsed. We know from Ovid that frustrated love is laughable in its own right. We know from Old French epic that the Saracen princess as 'forthputting damsel' is inherently a comic figure, as is the somewhat innocent French paladin.[17] Indeed, the enamored female, proud or timid, plays a comic role, especially when she resorts to ruse, either to seduce her man or to preserve him from harm at the hands of her Saracen relatives. But when a chaste hero of the old school yields to his senses and a Saracen passion-flower is overcome with scruples, the poet satirizes literary conventions, the way in which literary characters are supposed to act. The Huon-Esclarmonde affair attains comic heights by means of a mechanical, artificial reversal of roles, a 'switch on a switch.' When one gives in to lust, the other is overcome with scruples; both characters change brusquely and symmetrically but in opposite directions. As a result both are seen to act in humorous fashion, their way of loving held up to gently benevolent laughter. Yet Esclarmonde and Yvorin's daughter partake of the same type: the Saracen princess who makes advances to the hero and helps him out of dire straits. One is portrayed as a faithful virgin bride, the other as a vengeful temptress. Splitting the archetype contributes to the tone of humor.

In love, as in war, Huon defeats old men. He wins the affection or pity of beautiful maidens (Sebile, Esclarmonde, Yvorin's daughter) and survives. To do so he must defy the Saracen potentates (Orgueilleux, Gaudisse, Galafre, Yvorin) who guard them. Despite their jailers, however, the young women aid Huon in fulfilling his quest. The four greybeards, whatever their roles in the story, are father- or husband-surrogates; Huon then plays the role of a young lover who defies their will and wins the maiden(s) for himself. He deceives them nonchalantly, in spite of themselves. Denying the

sexual repression promulgated by the Fathers in a male world, he successfully harmonizes the demands of the pleasure and reality principles. The
id frees itself from the superego, sons from fathers, the weak from the
strong, and freedom from restraint. Huon comes into his own in the
more feminine world of the East (forest, ocean, prison, maze), dies and is
reborn to beautiful women whom he rightly prefers over the stern *duri
patres* (Charles, Auberon, Gériaume) in his life. Youth triumphs over age,
nature will have its way – as in so much of medieval and modern literature, from *Floire et Blancheflor* to the theater of Jean Anouilh.

In the last analysis, Huon's quest anticipates the career of the *pícaro*
besides paralleling the voyage of the Arthurian knight. These French pilgrims are aided by supernatural beings from a fairy land; they also get out
of more than one scrape by their quick wits and ready tongue. As Gaudisse
is forced to confess: 'C'est fine verités / Que de François ne se puet nus
garder' (6614–15). Huon exploits Auberon's magic gifts and undermines
them at the same time. Failing to heed his mentor's advice, he achieves a
victory all the more spectacular. And his *foleté* adds salt to the recital of his
exploits. Perhaps he is a 'fool,' but an invincible one committed to festivity
and the affirmation of life, sacred to the extent that he is protected by
supernatural forces and that he serves as a moral barometer through whom
the entire world can be judged.

I have discussed *Huon de Bordeaux* as romance and as comedy. More than
one critic has declared that laughter is incompatible with true epic or the
romantic spirit. My reply is that humor and romance do coexist in *La
Chanson de Huon*, simultaneously and in a state of tension; the tone is
serious and willfully comic at the same time. Some of the motifs were taken
from contemporary folklore. There is a difference, however, between the
world of folk tales and the fairy-tale atmosphere of a poem of the court
(Chrétien de Troyes, Ariosto, Spenser, La Fontaine). *Huon de Bordeaux*
is a highly sophisticated text. Its romantic material, of whatever provenance,
is treated in a sophisticated, artistic manner and with courtly detachment.

From the point of view of comedy, although conventional literary forms
are being laughed at, although traditional institutions are held up to ridicule, the humor in this poem is by no means bitter. Comic catharsis, it has
often been said, is achieved by sympathy and ridicule rather than by pity
or terror, and sympathy plays at least as great a role here as its companion.
The protagonist is a heroic, Christian adolescent. Although he is guilty of
*foleté* and *desmesure*, we laugh at these faults. We find them funny, neither
wicked nor seriously blamable; we continue to sympathize, even to identify, with the young duke. He triumphs over his world, and the public
triumphs with him. In no way do Huon's failings interfere with his heroic

stature. The comedy in *Huon de Bordeaux* is that of rapidity, enthusiasm, and love. It expresses, as so often in the Middle Ages, a sense of the richness and beauty of life, the closeness of poet and public to the realities of existence. In this sense, humor complements rather than conflicts with the element of romance. Both contribute to an esthetic of joy, triumph through laughter and adventure. Sin and death are discomfited; man endures.

The *Huon*-poet draws from many sources. He straddles different worlds (epic, Oriental, Arthurian, folkloric, bourgeois), bringing them into his text. As in the *Orlando furioso*, epic is combined with romance, comedy with the supernatural, satire with sentiment, fantasy with burlesque. *Huon de Bordeaux* opens up widening circles of experience, manifests breadth, includes much of the variety and inclusiveness of life. It is a culmination of the genre, perhaps the last great 'heroic' masterpiece in France before d'Aubigné. More than most works of French literature, it exhibits a cosmic view of life and embodies a vision all to rare, even in the Middle Ages.

Ernst Robert Curtius has written that the Golden Age of the Old French epic coincides with the turn of the twelfth century – with the reign of Philip Augustus.[18] Without in any way denigrating *La Chanson de Roland* or other early texts – *La Chanson de Guillaume*, *Gormond et Isembard*, *Le Couronnement de Louis*, *Le Pèlerinage de Charlemagne* – I hope that these two brief essays on *Raoul de Cambrai* and *Huon de Bordeaux* can serve to substantiate Curtius's statement. The period extending approximately from 1190 to 1230 saw the creation of many fine *chansons de geste*; the same period gave rise to the novels of Jean Renart and the flowering of the courtly lyric. At least a generation after Chrétien de Troyes, Marie de France, Béroul, and Thomas had written their masterpieces, the extraordinary vitality of epic production continued, in spite of the evolution of new literary standards and genres.

The tradition of heroism exemplified by *La Chanson de Roland*, even by *Le Couronnement de Louis*, was modified in the course of the twelfth century. These are but two examples of what amounts to a radical change in taste. In other *chansons* of the period also we are made aware of the refinements in life open to a nobility that appreciates fine clothes, food and drink, sheen, and luxury. The trouvères indulge in more elaborate descriptions, exult in precision and the mastery of insignificant detail. Class distinctions come into prominence; the peasant or lout is set off against a new kind of aristocrat, a man of elegance and extraordinary personal beauty, capable of acts of chivalry, of delivering speeches, paying court to ladies, and obeying rules of etiquette. The supernatural, both Christian and non-Christian, helps shape the narrative line. Most important of all, the author has his hero participate in erotic relationships, often

using a courtly vocabulary and the outward signs of courtly ritual; he may
even parody *fin' amor* by fusing it with the older poetic tradition, with
which it is incompatible. The protagonist often sets out on a quest, participates in adventures, is concerned with his growth as an individual. In more
than one late *chanson* the trouvère indulges in the ironic mode, regarding
with a smile the antecedent tradition and his own creation. The late poets
are often concerned with contemporary reality, the vital problems of existence that men face in the real world. There is no doubt too that the epic
has opened out in ideological terms, its representation of life expanded, that
it includes greater reaches of space and time and is concerned with the
development of characters over many years, emphasizing differences as well
as similarities between men, and that it testifies to the shattering of the old
world-view and the old 'romanesque' idealism. Perhaps theirs is a 'gothic'
mentality in which the body, empirical reality, and man's conscience find
a place.

The *chanson de geste* develops in time; poetry is created and esthetic
precedents set, only to be transformed; old patterns are corroded and new
ones evolve in their place, not necessarily inferior or superior to the old,
simply different. A great literary tradition presumes richness and purity,
tradition and innovation, coherence and diversity. Such is the evolution
of the French epic from the *Song of Roland* to *Huon de Bordeaux*.

Chapter Four

# CHRÉTIEN DE TROYES

In the second half of the twelfth century a new genre of narrative poetry came into being: the courtly romance. Romance differs from *chanson de geste* in several ways. Whereas the *chansons* retain a concern for religion and the crusade, and epic heroes devote part of their careers to a struggle against the Saracens, except in the tales of Perceval and Galahad Christ is largely absent from the *romans.* The epic gravitates around Carolingian emperors established in Paris or Aix-la-Chapelle; the romance often deals with King Arthur and his knights in a mythical realm, Logres, corresponding geographically to the Angevin kingdom of Henry II. *Chansons de geste* presume to recount history; the novel is more readily accepted as fiction. Whereas the epic hero is united with his people or city and performs exploits at the head of a great army, the protagonist of romance sets out on a solitary quest, undergoing adventures of a more personal nature. War and feudal honor, the dominant motivating forces in epic, yield the center stage to the urgings of love. Woman plays a much more important role; indeed the novelistic action can be viewed from her perspective. In addition to the qualities we find in a Roland or a Bernier, the new hero exemplifies virtues of refinement and elegance – the distinction of a leisurely, aristocratic community. Although medieval poets created masterpieces in both epic and romance, the latter genre benefited from more conscious, artistic premeditation, the work of clerics; we know the names of many authors of romance, few of epic. Finally, epic and romance differ with regard to form, since, in contrast to the decasyllabic *laisses* of *chanson de geste*, the *roman* is usually composed of octosyllabic rhyming couplets. And the monumental, paratactic syntax and hieratic structure of the earlier genre gives way to a more supple, elegant, flowing, hypotactic style based upon rhetorical *amplificatio* and the desire to interpret, to explain, to symbolize – for a romance treats *matiere* but also contains *san* in a total *conjointure.*

Three major currents, in addition to the Old French epic itself, contributed to the elaboration of romance: the Occitan love-lyric, Celtic legend,

and the literature of Greco-Roman Antiquity. From the troubadours
Chrétien de Troyes and his contemporaries derived a revolutionary notion
of Eros and the role that both love and woman ought to play in man's life:
Chrétien himself composed at least two of the earliest courtly lyrics extant in
Northern France. In Geoffrey of Monmouth's *Historia regum Britanniae*
(1136) and its French adaptation, Wace's *Roman de Brut* (1155), as well as in
a vigorous oral tradition in Welsh, they found a treasure house of themes
and motifs, characters and episodes, the building blocks with which to construct palaces of wonder. A case can be made that the Anglo-Norman
court gave romancers a sense of history, and that chronicles (by Dares,
Dictys, Gaimar, Geoffrey), available in Latin or French, served as the
models for new, innovative writing. And in the Latin classics these children
of the Twelfth-Century Renaissance, of the *aetas ovidiana*, discovered in
addition to history a sense of form, a concern for art, and exemplary tools of
rhetoric. Thus *clergie* joined *chevalerie* to form the knightly ideal, and
poets were as proud of the *translatio studii* from Greece and Rome to France
as of the *translatio imperii*.

A first group of romancers adapted the classics, that is, retold in French
the stories of Alexander, Narcissus, and Pyramus, of Oedipus and the
Seven against Thebes, of the *Aeneid*, and the Wars of Troy. They are
responsible for the *Roman de Thèbes*, *Eneas*, *Roman de Troie*, fragments
of several Alexander romances, and a much shorter *Piramus et Tisbé* and
*Narcisus*. The extraordinarily productive second generation, which to
some extent overlaps chronologically with the first one (1165–90), then
created original works of art based on classical or Celtic themes. The
masters of this group include Marie de France, who wrote twelve Breton
*lais*, Béroul and Thomas, authors of *Tristan* romances, Gautier d'Arras,
and Chrétien de Troyes. Chrétien is without any doubt the greatest, most
prolific writer of his century. His extant works include a translation of
the Philomela episode of the *Metamorphoses*, conserved in the fourteenth-
century *Ovide moralisé*, two or more courtly lyrics, and five romances:
*Erec et Enide*, *Cligès*, *Lancelot*, *Yvain*, and *Perceval*. Due to limitations of
space, I can consider only two of Chrétien's long narratives. I have
chosen *Lancelot* and *Yvain*, which, along with the incomplete and highly
controversial *Perceval*, are perhaps his masterpieces and present the most
rounded picture of his achievement.[1]

More than any other medieval verse romance, with the possible exception of
the Occitan *Flamenca*, Chrétien's *Lancelot* or *Le Chevalier de la
Charrete* (1170–81),[2] completed by Godefroi de Lagny, exemplifies the
code of *fin' amor*. Guinevere has been abducted from Arthur's court by a
dark knight from the land of Gorre, Meleagant. Lancelot leaps onto a

Shameful Cart (thereby destroying his reputation) in order to follow the queen and performs a series of heroic deeds, culminating in a victorious duel with the ravisher. As a result Guinevere and the other prisoners from Logres are free to go home and, after a misunderstanding, she and her savior make love. However, Meleagant tricks Lancelot and succeeds in imprisoning him. The hero's passion for Guinevere then sustains him during well over a year's captivity. In the end, after a sequence of adventures, Meleagant's sister liberates the hero, who returns to Logres and slays his enemy in a final *judicium Dei.*

In *Lancelot,* then, we find a totally authentic relationship, where the woman has the option whether to love or not, and to grant to the suitor her favors only when she chooses. One of the first rules of *fin' amor* is loyalty: Lancelot has to remain faithful to his lady. Indeed, one of his ordeals is a chastity test, in which he declines the advances of a maiden with whom he must lie naked in bed. Chrétien exploits love conventions to be found in the troubadours: loving a woman from afar (the *amor de lonh*), and the separation of heart and body. These motifs underscore one of the most important themes in the narrative, also an integral aspect of *fin' amor*: the notion of obstacle. The troubadours and trouvères discovered that often the best of Eros is to be found in longing, rather than in static, humdrum, conjugal satisfaction. Frustrated desire arouses lovesickness that, in extreme cases, can lead to death, the ultimate obstacle. The relationship in the Occitan lyric and in many Northern romances (the Tristan and Isolt story; Marie de France's *Guigemar, Yonec, Laüstic,* and *Eliduc*; Gautier's *Eracle* and *Ille et Galeron*; and Chrétien's own *Cligès*) is an adulterous one. Such is the case in *Le Chevalier de la Charrete,* since Guinevere is King Arthur's consort and Lancelot is therefore breaking the Seventh Commandment during their stay in Gorre. Although Meleagant also lusts after Guinevere, because he keeps the latter captive and scrutinizes her every move he plays the role of *gilos*; and by denouncing to his father a purported adultery between Guinevere and Kay, Meleagant also acts as a *losengier,* the spy, tattle-tale, and sower of discord, one of the most reprehensible characters in the world of *fin' amor.* Because of the adulterous nature of their affair and because of the presence of spies and jealous guardians, the lovers are obliged to practice the courtly virtue of discretion. Following in the footsteps of Isolt, Guinevere does not hesitate to swear a casuistical oath, the *juramentum dolosum,* to disculpate herself from Meleagant's charges, and she indicates in the most inconspicuous manner, with a glance of her eye, how Lancelot shall communicate with her that evening: 'Et la reïne une fenestre / li mostre, a l'uel, non mie au doi ...' (4506–7).

*Le Chevalier de la Charrete* is remarkable for the exceptional value bestowed upon woman. In a prologue the author praises his patroness, the

Countess of Champagne (1–29). Chrétien's exaltation of, and humility before, his countess (clerkly service) parallels Lancelot's deference before Guinevere (the service of chivalry); the one claims to receive intellectual, the other, erotic guidance from the *domna*. Guinevere is a lady of much higher social status than her lover, proud, aloof, domineering, a queen who deigns to accept only the best. Lancelot remains in a state of absolute submission to her. On four distinct occasions he falls into a kind of ecstasy (anticipating Perceval's trance in *Le Conte du Graal*) which shuts him off from the world around him. He forgets himself and all others for love, even at the risk of his life. The episode in which Lancelot falls into oblivion upon beholding some of Guinevere's golden hairs in a comb reminds us not only that *fin' amor* came into existence in imitation, and parody, of the Christian faith, but also to what an extent it was a new, secular 'religion.' For he worships Guinevere's comb and hair like a sacred relic, prays before the shrine of Guinevere's chamber, and adores her body.

> si l'aore et se li ancline,
> car an nul cors saint ne croit tant ...
> Au departir a soploié
> a la chanbre, et fet tot autel
> con s'il fust devant un autel.    (4652–3, 4716–18)

Furthermore, he confesses his sins to her, his love-confessor, manifesting penitence, and she absolves him. Adultery is purified by the rites that accompany it; as with Abelard and Heloise, desire is conceived in religious terms and exalted by religious awe. Like the true Christian, Lancelot serves his divinity with fervor, ever in a state of anguish and uncertain that he merits grace, ever seeking to embody the virtues of faith, hope, and love. Thus in literary history Lancelot becomes for all time the exemplar and archetypal protagonist, the saint, of the passion cult. He is the absolute, predestined lover, who willfully sacrifices *mesure* and *reison*, who submits joyfully to a force, *fin' amor*, and a person, Guinevere, alone capable of granting meaning to his life, absolute mediators between himself and the world.

When epic is transformed into romance, the center of gravity, narrative and thematic, shifts from war to love, from the battlefield to the bower, from sword to fountain, from day to night, from male to female. Eros is a jealous God: he will not permit his chosen people to bow down unto other divinities. To recover Guinevere Lancelot has to climb onto the Shameful Cart (a punishment for criminals), an act that Gawain, the embodiment of traditional chivalric honor, declines to perform, as does Lancelot's adversary, the Proud Knight, even at the cost of his life. As a result Lancelot's shame is broadcast throughout the land of Gorre; he becomes a figure of *desenor, let, blasme,* and *honte.* Finally, Guinevere herself castigates her lover – not because he climbed onto the cart but because he hesitated for a few seconds before doing so, because he permitted Reason to debate with Amor in his heart. Later in the narrative Lancelot 'does his worst' (*au noauz*) in a tournament on two successive days, plays the fool, and is again subject to public humiliation – to satisfy Guinevere's whim. I consider it significant that the queen and her knight are not joined as equals, nor in a legitimate feudal bond, lady to lover as lord to vassal, with mutual rights and responsibilities, but in that cruel parody of vassalage: the master-slave relationship, in which the latter has no rights and his social role in the community is negated.[3] Of course, this slave is content with his state, asking only to maintain it forever, without having to share it with others. Perhaps in the *Charrete fin'amor* stands for the symbolic denial of feudalism, as it refutes no less vigorously the traditional, medieval view of man as a rational being in full mastery of the flesh. Significantly, whereas the Arthurian world embodies a system of exchange, of ritualized, highly specific promises or *covenanz* based upon service, payment, reciprocity, mutual interest, or threat of force, Lancelot, on the contrary, serves Guinevere gratuitously, with total, absolute self-abnegation. Any rewards he may receive occur as a result of service but never as a reason or cause of it.

However, in the end, the opposition between love and honor is more apparent than real. Because of his exemplary passion, his total gift of self to *fin' amor,* Lancelot is sought after by a host of ladies eager to love him even though he declines their advances, willing to serve him gratuitously. In addition to Guinevere, ten others help the knight, guide him, pray for him, and deliver him from prison.[4] He serves ladies, in Guinevere's name, and they serve him in the name of love. They mediate between him and Guinevere or between him and Amor. In addition, Lancelot's passion spurs him on to perform great deeds. Because of it he is ever in haste, ever forward, to rescue the Lady, and to rescue damsels in distress. And each time he triumphs. Each time shame turns to glory, *desenor* and *let* to *enor* and *pris.* At the tournament in Logres Lancelot wears red armor, symbolic of courage, passion, and victory. For in battle he is as agile as the flame of love that burns within him. He does what he has set out to do.

On the one hand, love's tyranny is a privilege for those of gentle heart who willingly accept public shame in the eyes of the profane, those outside the pale of *fin' amor.* Even so, Lancelot is recognized for the man he is by the discerning few. The herald cries: *Or est venuz qui l'aunera! Veez celui qui l'aunera!* On the other hand, the protagonist's shame is also quickly dispelled, for in the end his prowess silences mockers, and his honor is restored. Thus, although Lancelot is as a slave to Guinevere, he is, to all intents and purposes, master over every one else in the world. And he is master because of love. He proves to be the best knight because he loves the best, for *fin' amor* is not only superior to all other values but also the source of all good in the world, in Andreas Capellanus's terms: 'Omnis ergo boni erit amor origo et causa.'[5] Thus, whereas Meleagant, seeking enjoyment of Guinevere's body and a reputation for prowess, loses the queen, his life, and his reputation, Lancelot, who is content to sacrifice worldly honor, is exalted in it and wins Guinevere as well. Instead of contradicting prowess and chivalry, love enhances them. *Militia* and *amor*, the dominant calls in medieval secular life, are bound one to the other. Guinevere could not esteem Lancelot if he were a weakling in arms, and he could not triumph in war without the spur of her affection. Although the two forces often undermine each other, neither can survive alone, and both are indispensable for attainment of perfection in Chrétien's ideal world.

It must never be forgotten that Lancelot's adventures have a social function as well as an erotic one, that his private life contributes to, rather than diminishes, his public life. Although the Knight of the Cart sets out on a quest to Gorre because Guinevere has been abducted, on the road he does good deeds, rescuing damsels in distress, for her sake. Even more, by saving Guinevere this prisoner of love also delivers the other prisoners, captive peoples from Logres who were detained in Gorre all these years. Lancelot thinks of the queen but saves the community. His triumph is collective as well as individual: he is a savior, one who succeeds in delivering his comrades.

As the story progresses, as Lancelot comes closer to his goal, he is joined by others who contribute to or benefit from his victory. Their presence bears witness to his growing commitment to society. Some of these people are hostile to Lancelot; others pray for his success. The first community we perceive is King Arthur's in Logres, where Guinevere is lost. Significantly, Lancelot, absent from the court, cannot be held responsible for what happens. Then, following Guinevere, he encounters a group of people in a field, who castigate his shame yet learn to respect him. Later, the Knight of the Cart wins the allegiance, first of a vavassor and his sons, then of the prisoners from Logres, of King Bademagu and the people of Gorre, and finally of King Arthur's court. Joy was originally interrupted at court, and important members separated from the community. Meleagant had innovated a wicked *costume* in much the following terms:

> Maleoite soit tex costume
> et cil avoec, qui la maintiennent,
> que nul estrange ça ne vienent
> qu'a remenoir ne lor covaingne

et que la terre nes detaigne;
car qui se vialt antrer i puet,
mes a remenoir li estuet ...
Tel costume el païs avoit
que, puis que li uns s'an issoit
que tuit li autre s'an issoient.    (2096–102, 3899–901)

Society itself was placed in jeopardy. Lancelot's quest serves to reintegrate
the separated members by slaying the intruder. Thus the original *ordo* is
restored, and Lancelot's mission, as defender of the community, accomplished. Even Bademagu and his people are paradoxically content when
Meleagant is defeated, his *costume* overturned, and the prisoners permitted to leave. However, the greatest manifestation of joy takes place at Logres
upon Lancelot's return. There he joins with Meleagant in a sort of ritual
combat ending in ritual execution, in the grassy field beneath an old syca-
more tree near a fountain. There he and the community are reconciled in
joy – the last word in the poem before the Epilogue:

Li rois et tuit cil qui i sont
grant joie an demainnent et font.
Lancelot desarment adonques
cil qui plus lié an furent onques,
si l'en ont mené a grant joie.    (7093–7)

*Le Chevalier de la Charrete*, like *Erec et Enide*, culminates in a Joy of the
Court. Lancelot's, Gawain's, and Guinevere's careers are of withdrawal
and return. Disruption, which begins in Logres, can only be set right there.
Court scenes inevitably frame the more poetic, miraculous adventures of
the open road.[6]

Up to now I have reserved comment on what is perhaps Chrétien's
greatest contribution to Western literature: the poetry, mystery, and myth
which emanate from his romances. The reader is caught up, 'enchanted'
by the world of Logres and Gorre, lands reminiscent of twelfth-century
Britain yet projected onto a distant past, where the solitary knight, devoted
uniquely to love and arms, sets out on a quest and undergoes adventures,
which come to him (*ad-venire*) because he is a chosen hero, a member of
that elite destined for a life of adventure. Chrétien cultivates an aura of
suspense and magic. We cannot but wonder at the hidden identities of
characters, including Lancelot, at the significance of marvelous people,
places, or events, and at the bizarre system of communication whereby
the inhabitants of the Other World are automatically aware of the Knight of
the Cart's presence and shame. And the reader takes pleasure in elucidat-

ing these mysteries. Chrétien de Troyes is the first great master of a genre, the ancestor not only of the Gothic Romance but also the modern detective story.

The central narrative increment can probably be traced to a Celtic myth concerning Queen Gwenhwyvar, who was kidnapped by Melwas, a king from the Other World, but later restored to Arthur. And a host of subsidiary motifs are to be found in early Irish and Welsh texts.[7] However, as with *Huon de Bordeaux*, the plot and images of *Le Chevalier de la Charrete* recall the archetypes of romance, not limited to Celtic legend but found throughout world literature. The abduction of a lady by a Shadow-figure resembles the stories of Eurydice and Persephone. And the earliest myths of the West recount how a divinity representing peace and order is threatened by a Dark God. This latter captures the Light God or his champion, but a new champion (a younger god) defeats the usurper and restores order.[8] In *Lancelot* the Shadow-figure himself serves as a Herald of Adventure: by coming to Arthur's court and seizing Guinevere, he forces the queen into a life of adventure and, at the same time, compels a tiny elite, consisting of Lancelot and Gawain, to follow her. As in *Erec et Enide*, *Perceval*, and, to a lesser extent, *Yvain*, the Call to Adventure takes the form of an outrage, a public insult to the protagonist or the court by a wicked outsider or by Kay the Seneschal, a no less wicked 'insider.' At the risk of his life, Gawain crosses the threshold to the Other World in the form of a subaqueous bridge (*li Ponz Evages*); Lancelot has to ford a river, cross a narrow land-passage (*li Passages des Pierres*), and finally traverse the sword-bridge with naked hands and feet (a 'molt estrange mervoille,' 3096) over black, treacherous, demonic waters and a narrow ravine:

> l'eve felenesse,
> noire et bruiant, roide et espesse,
> tant leide et tant espoantable
> con se fust li fluns au deable,
> et tant perilleuse et parfonde
> qu'il n'est riens nule an tot le monde,
> s'ele i cheoit, ne fust alee
> ausi com an la mer betee.    (3009–16)

Again and again he must struggle through narrow passages, across water, *ab aspra ad astra*. His trip in the Shameful Cart may also be considered an element in crossing the frontier. The ford and dangerous passage are defended by adversary-knights, guardians of the Other World, whom Lancelot defeats before proceeding farther, while the sword-bridge appears to be protected by lions, and the Cart by a dwarf. In fact, Lancelot's quest to

enter the Other World and, once inside, to penetrate to the inner sanctum
and deliver the prisoners, consists of a series of nine ordeals: the Cart of
Infamy, the Bed Perilous, duelling the Knight of the Ford, defending a
damsel from purported rape, resisting her blandishments, lifting the stone
of his own tomb, crossing the Stone Passage, duelling the Proud Knight, and
crossing the sword-bridge. It is obvious that these adventures, some of
which are undertaken against human antagonists, others against natural or
supernatural forces, prove Lancelot's physical and spiritual prowess, his
right to be in the Other World. Chrétien's Knight of the Cart is indeed the
popular hero of folklore, unknown to and despised by the crowd, who
ultimately convinces them and us of his greatness. Invincible in arms, he can
be defeated only through fraud, and it is through fraud, through the guile
of loving women, that he reattains liberty.

At the very center of the Other World Lancelot engages in sacred
combat with Meleagant, the archetypal foe, the ogre who guards the fairy
queen inside the labyrinth. This dark hero is as thoroughly evil as Lancelot is good. The presence of both Guinevere and Meleagant in the inner
sanctum testifies to the ambivalent perspective from which Chrétien de
Troyes views the Other World, a realm containing a happy community
playing games in the fields and a tower-prison on an island, peopled
by helpful fays, a benevolent old king, and ferocious ogres, where girls are
threatened by rape and men by death, but the highest glory awaits the
pure and steadfast in heart. Lancelot's final ordeals, which mark a provisional end to his Road of Trials, are two judicial combats with Meleagant,
which frame a night of love with the queen. In opposition to the Shadow-
figure, who embodies negative elements in the hero's personality that
threaten his identity, Guinevere embodies the best of his self and his society.
In the Other World she plays a regal role, triumphing before Lancelot
and Meleagant, in striking contrast to her humiliation at the court of Logres.
She unites in herself divergent archetypes of woman. Mistress, lady, temptress, queen, and goddess all in one, she leads man to happiness or salvation.
A secular Dame Fortuna, she determines the outcome of duels and tourneys, and when she frowns on her devotee he is captured. This archetype,
the Jungian anima, is found throughout world literature: some manifestations, in addition to the troubadour *domna* and Guinevere herself, are
Dante's Beatrice, Rousseau's Julie, Stendhal's Mme de Rênal, and Proust's
Duchesse de Guermantes. Lancelot's quest is crowned by initiation with the
greatest of ladies, a goddess of the cult of love:

> Tant li est ses jeus dolz et buens,
> et del beiser, et del santir,
> que il lor avint sanz mantir

une joie et une mervoille
tel c'onques ancor sa paroille
ne fu oïe ne seüe ...   (4674–9)

Chrétien's imagery can be interpreted in more immediately erotic terms:
the Other World renders otherwise tabu expressions of the libido possible. Guinevere's comb and hair serve as fetish-objects that mediate between
herself and Lancelot. The ordeals of the flaming lance (endured while
lying in bed) and of the sword-bridge, over which Lancelot crawls with
naked hands and feet, threaten him with metaphoric castration, as do the
dwarfs, lions, guardians of the Other World, the alleged rapists in another
damsel's bed, and Meleagant himself, who embodies the Shadow, the
Terrible Father, and libido anxiety. But it is not Lancelot who is mutilated;
on the contrary, he symbolically mutilates the enemy when, at Logres, he
severs the latter's right arm, cuts out his entrails, breaks his teeth, and,
finally, beheads him. To the extent that Lancelot's quest represents a
forcing of narrow apertures, passages, and beds, of crawling on a sword-
bridge (of all the *portas angustas* the most terrible), it can be interpreted as
a form of sexual initiation. And Lancelot proceeds steadily to the heart of
the Other World, represented by Guinevere. Chrétien's knight-errant
bends open the bars of the window to Guinevere's chamber, tearing his
hands, causing his battle wounds to reopen and blood to flow. He then
penetrates into the chamber, into Guinevere's bed (his third 'perilous bed'),
and into Guinevere. Symbolically, he has triumphed over the enemy and
over his own unconscious libidinal anxiety. Although traces of blood are
found on the sheets, a symbol of guilt – Lancelot's blood, not the queen's
– the couple succeed in evading punishment for their 'sin.' Just as the lions
disappear from behind the sword-bridge when Lancelot dares to cross, so
too the *vagina dentata* of Guinevere's chamber welcomes him, for she
proves to be a loving, kind, gentle, mother goddess, when he dares to push
aside the bars.

Scholars have pointed out that *fin' amor* in the Middle Ages reflects to a
striking degree symptoms of the Oedipal relationship. Often in courtly
literature the lady appears as a mother-figure: she is older than the lover,
married to someone else, of higher social class, and, from his perspective,
the source of all good. He submits masochistically to her will. Although the
lover yearns for fulfillment in her arms, seldom or never is his passion
consummated. Naturally, when the lady treats him harshly he falls into a fit
of depression. He suffers from guilt, pines for forbidden pleasures, yet is
sworn to secrecy, and his greatest fear is that she may reject or forget him.[9]
It is significant that Lancelot, more than any other medieval romance
hero, more even than Tristan, conforms to this Oedipal pattern also to be

found in the lyrics of the troubadours and trouvères. His story throughout is based upon the play of prohibition and transgression. However, I
believe that, in *Le Chevalier de la Charrete*, guilt is diminished through a
process of displacement and transference. By seizing Guinevere, Meleagant
replaces King Arthur, becomes a husband and father-surrogate to her.
Hence, when Lancelot makes love to the queen, he cuckolds Meleagant, not
the king. It is Meleagant, not Arthur, who denounces the presumed adultery and who indulges in a fit of jealousy; and it is Meleagant, not Arthur,
whom Lancelot slays as the final step of his initiation into manhood. In
this fantasy world, his id indeed becomes liberated, he commits the Oedipal
incest, discovers his self and the mysteries of death and rebirth; his ego
awakens, and the castrating father is slain. Yet, at the same time, to the
extent that Meleagant, like Lancelot, is a young warrior who has committed a symbolic rape of Arthur's consort, the two heroes are rivals for their
surrogate mother's affections, and their mutual hatred can be assimilated
to post-Oedipal sibling rivalry. Thus Meleagant, and Kay the seneschal for
that matter, can be conceived as doubles of Lancelot, threatening paternal
or sibling-figures, embodying respectively coarse desire and superficial chivalry. Chrétien projects guilt and anxiety onto the bad son, which enables
him to exorcise Lancelot's sexual guilt. Under these conditions, Lancelot is
assimilated to the good son, who punishes the bad, adulterous, incestuous son and restores his mother to the paternal home. He therefore enjoys
Guinevere almost righteously as a legitimate substitute for her husband
the king, uniquely in the Other World, a wish-fulfillment, fantasy realm.
Significantly, Arthur receives Guinevere after her stay in the Other World
without question or reproach; and the old King of Gorre, Bademagu, who
corresponds to King Arthur of Logres, respects Guinevere's chastity and
disapproves of his son Meleagant's actions. Both he and Arthur appear as
kindly, hospitable judges, with no designs on Guinevere, friendly to her
and especially to Lancelot. Indeed, throughout the *Charrete*, wise, old but
weak fathers are contrasted to their evil sons.[10] The good son, the good
ego-principle, rejects the id inherent in Meleagant by siding with the paternal superego (Arthur and Bademagu). As a result, the father also sides
with him, his shame is dissipated, he succeeds to the father without punishment, and he wins the mother's love as a gift of grace.

Lancelot's adventures correspond to the ultimate rite of passage; the
experience of death and rebirth. At one point Guinevere and Lancelot
each think the other has perished; Guinevere contemplates, and Lancelot
attempts, suicide, the latter delivering plaints to *Morz* (4263–83, 4318–96)
before and after his attempt. They are brought together by the threat of
annihilation, the 'obstacle' serving to reinforce their passion and leading to
communication, just as death in each other's arms precedes awakening.

Although Guinevere and Lancelot do not perish separated from each other –
indeed, resurrected from the false rumor of annihilation, they are happy
to pass away and be renewed in bed – Eros and Thanatos are intimately
bound in this land of the Mothers (beds, tombs, narrow passages, flowing
water), the Other World.

According to Chrétien, the Cart of Infamy, used in those days as a
pillory, a sort of tumbril to punish criminals, casts shame on the man who
climbs inside (321–38); it can also be assimilated to a cart of death. Chrétien
points out that when people saw it they made the sign of the cross:

> Por ce qu'a cel tens furent tex
> les charretes, et si cruex,
> fu premiers dit: 'Quant tu verras
> charrete et tu l'ancontreras,
> fei croiz sor toi, et te sovaigne
> de Deu, que max ne t'an avaigne.'    (339–44)

The cart is guided by a dwarf, a conventionally negative figure from the
Other World. And it is most plausible that the land of Gorre, 'el rëaume ... /
don nus estranges ne retorne ... el rëaume don nus n'eschape' (640–1, 1936),
the *de facto* ruler of which is a dark knight whose only function appears
to be the capture of prisoners and who takes Guinevere into exile accompanied by a bier, corresponds to a kingdom of the dead. This is an appropriate location for a story treating the death-rebirth archetype. Significantly,
Lancelot not only is sorely wounded in the course of his adventures and
risks the fires of hell in the Bed Perilous, but also comes across his own
burial place in the Cemetery of the Future. He then raises the tombstone,
anticipating his eventual victory and proving he is the greatest knight in the
world, a Messiah. Lancelot's transgression against death (here and in his
duel with Meleagant) parallels his breaking the feudal-Oedipal tabu of
Guinevere's body. Presumably, only a knight capable of facing such an
obstacle and incapable of suicide is deemed worthy to rescue others from the
land of the dead. This Christ-Orpheus of *fin' amor* opens his own tomb
and harrows Meleagant's inferno. Subjected to mockery and shame, to
*blasme* and *let*, he mounts the Calvary of the Shameful Cart and endures
wounds on his hands and feet. Then he is honored as a Messiah by the
prisoners he has come to free. He follows his lady to the Underworld and
resurrects himself, his lady, and his friends. Reborn in love and in war, he
surpasses the human condition, attains a kind of immortality for his own
sake and for the community. Indeed, a case can be made that he is a Christ-
figure and that his quest symbolizes the historical regeneration of mankind, humanity's collective quest for salvation.[11]

One of the boons that Lancelot and Guinevere, benefiting from increased consciousness and individuation in this land of the Mothers, receive from the Other World is a form of understanding, a greater, more refined knowledge of love and of their own celestially oriented destiny, that is often expressed in terms of visual imagery. Meleagant accuses his father, Bademagu, of blindness because the latter wishes to treat Lancelot honorably, but, of course, it is Meleagant who is morally blind, and his obsession with killing Lancelot will result in his own death. Although he correctly observes marks of blood on Guinevere's sheets (she fails to notice these clues), he misinterprets them, falsely accusing Kay of adultery (Kay was sleeping in the queen's chamber; he also had fresh wounds that could have opened), as others accused Lancelot of dishonor. On the other hand, Lancelot's failure to see the Knight of the Ford or even to look at Meleagant in battle, which temporarily diminishes his honor as a knight, enhances his standing as a lover (he was in a state of ecstasy), and he triumphs. After all, the Knight of the Cart has no trouble perceiving golden hairs in Guinevere's comb, a relic in the cult of *fin' amor*, and he succeeds in the ordeal of the Perilous Bed even though he is not aware of the burning lance before it strikes him. Bademagu's daughter rescues Lancelot, locked up in a tower, in spite of the fact that at first neither one lays eyes on the other. Gazing at the departing Guinevere out of a window is enough to make Lancelot set out after her, and he is rewarded when, at Gorre, for the first time he and Guinevere cast eyes on each other; this time she is looking down on him from a window: he defeats Meleagant by keeping his eyes fixed on the queen. And Guinevere shows Lancelot the window through which he will enter her chamber by a glance of the eyes. They find windows in walls, they communicate in a secret language of vision, the source of courtly passion, see without being seen, and make love without being heard.

I agree with those scholars who posit a two-part structure to Chrétien de Troyes's romances.[12] In *Lancelot*, as in *Erec et Enide*, *Cligès*, and *Yvain*, the hero wins a provisional victory, arrives at an apparently happy ending which is then placed in jeopardy; only after a long series of adventures is the threat removed and an ultimate denouement assured. In both Parts 1 and 2 Lancelot undertakes a quest and endures humiliation, and his glory is restored. At the time of the first humiliation, the shame of the cart, he hesitates; the second occasion, the shame of the tourney, is a triumph of the will freely undertaken which redeems the first one. In the beginning he bears no name, is insultingly labeled 'The Knight of the Cart'; later he wins the right to call himself both 'Lancelot' and 'The Knight of the Cart.' In Part 1 he liberates the prisoners but has not delivered society from the threat of the outsider; he will only do so at the end of Part 2. Thus 2 crowns and completes the achievements of 1. However, Chrétien de Troyes varies the tone and texture of Lancelot's exploits, and the circumstances under which they occur. The action of Part 1 fills a period of approximately one week, in which Lancelot undergoes ten ordeals; he even triumphs at night (the Bed Perilous, the forthputting damsel). This mobile, questing knight gives a display of frenetic energy, of feverish activity, rushing precipitously to his goal, refusing to be sidetracked under any circumstances. In contrast, Part 2 takes up almost a full year and a half; during most of this period, although still under time pressure, Lancelot is imprisoned at the seneschal's domain or in the tower. Compelled to wait passively, immobile, to be patient in opposition to his inherent nature, the hero's triumph is all the more striking. At first Lancelot is free yet a willing prisoner of love who delivers Guinevere from bondage; he then becomes Meleagant's captive, remains in love's bonds, and is even more spiritually free than before. In between the two parts Chrétien has placed Lancelot's initiation and erotic rite of passage, a moment of joy which rewards his feats in 1, sanctions those of 2, and anticipates the joy of reunion at Logres in the end: just as, spatially, inside Gorre we find Bademagu's palace containing Guinevere's chamber, containing Guinevere's bed, containing Guinevere. *Le Chevalier de la Charrete* has been shaped both in a linear and a circular pattern. The narrative begins with a scene at Arthur's court. Guinevere, followed by Lancelot, proceeds to Gorre; then, followed by Lancelot, she returns to Logres. The coming together of the lovers, a spiritual, intellectual, and erotic union, is placed at the very center of the romance, at the center of the Other World. But the story is not brought to a close until both return to Arthur's seat. Lancelot's triumph in Bademagu's realm at his 'surrogate court' is considerable but not sufficient to establish his greatness as a knight or to reestablish the chivalric *ordo*. He still has to cross the return threshold and recover his place in our world. The action began at Arthur's court and can only properly end there, once again in the spring, sanctioned by society in all its splendor. Only then can the Knight of the Cart be recognized as a messianic hero, mysterious and all-virtuous, predestined for great deeds, his preeminence sanctioned by the inscription on his tomb and by the victories he attains in the course of his adventures. Thus has Chrétien de Troyes created a unified, complex and at the same time subtle work of art, the first version of what was to become one of the greatest legends of all time.

*Le Chevalier au Lion* or *Yvain*[13] was written at about the same time or shortly after *La Charrete*. Although in several important respects the new romance contrasts sharply with the preceding one, both were written by the same author and adhere to the same literary kind. Like *Lancelot*, *Yvain* recounts a hero's road of trials in an Other World setting. Calogrenant ostentatiously, explicitly describes how he set out alone in quest of adventures:

> Il m'avint plus a de set anz
> que je, seus come païsanz,
> aloie querant aventures,
> armez de totes armeüres
> si come chevaliers doit estre ...
> – Et que voldroies tu trover?
> – Avanture, por esprover
> ma proesce et mon hardemant.   (173–7, 361–3)

The narrative then amplifies how Yvain continues in his cousin's footsteps and succeeds where the latter fails. Indeed, as in *Lancelot*, the reader is immersed in a stylized, poetic world where knights exist in order to submit to ordeals which test their valor, the other classes in society (vavassors, peasants, women) living only to serve brave warriors or to be rescued by them. Adventures come as if miraculously to a tiny elite, and events in the external world are interpreted symbolically, as a representation of inner struggle and initiation. The adventure, extra-historical, above mundane contingencies, gives meaning to life, is the essence of the knightly world; only the chivalric-courtly society is worthy of such an experience.[14]

On at least two occasions Yvain finds himself in predicaments which can only occur in the Other World. First Calogrenant, then seven years later his cousin, undergo the ordeal of the fountain. A knight traverses a Waste Land of woods, nettles, and heath (the barrier to the Other World), encounters a Hospitable Host and a Giant Herdsman (guardians of the threshold), and finally arrives at a *locus amœnus*, containing a fountain near a tree and a chapel, a place where, when one pours water from a gold cup onto a basin of emerald and rubies, the fluid boils, a tempest is unleashed, and birds sing for joy. The custom demands that the intruder give battle to the master of the place, Esclados the Red. And when Yvain succeeds in slaying the Red Knight, he marries Laudine, his widow. This episode probably results from a contamination of three Celtic myths: one describes a testing of the warriors of Ulster by Curoi, god of the tempest and the sun; another recounts how Modron, an aquatic fay, summons or lures a mortal to the Other World and constrains him to defend her realm; the third focuses on a rain-making cult at the fountain of Berenton in the forest of Brocéliande.[15]

Sir Gawain then convinces Yvain to leave his bride and join him in quest of martial exploits. When the knight overstays his leave, Laudine repudiates him, causing him to go insane. However, through a long process of struggle Yvain regains a sense of respectability: by defending the

Lady of Norison from a predator, Count Alier; by rescuing Lunette, Laudine's servant (who had previously helped him to win her mistress's affections), from slanderous assault; by defeating a giant, Harpin de la Montagne, who threatened members of Gawain's family. Finally, there is the ordeal of Pesme Aventure. Upon arrival, Yvain receives sinister forebodings and, after having entered the castle, is obliged to accept the hospitality of the place but also, as dictated by the *costume*, to pay for it in barbarous fashion. Maidens from an 'Isle as Puceles' (an additional Other World motif) are sent as tribute to a pair of gruesome creatures, sons of *netuns* or sea-monsters, who hold them in captivity. Only the elected knight is capable of freeing them and breaking the *costume*. Yvain succeeds in these battles with the aid of a lion, who befriends him and becomes his pet after Yvain took his side in a fight with a serpent. Then, following upon a trial by battle with Gawain at court, Yvain returns to the fountain in order to recover Laudine.

In *Lancelot* the realm of mortals and the Other World are clearly distinguished: the one is called Logres and ruled by King Arthur, the other is known as Gorre, under the sway of Bademagu and Meleagant. Even so, the boundary between the two remains vague. The situation is still more complex in *Yvain*. Here, as in *Erec et Enide*, manifestations of the Other World – Laudine's fountain, the Lady of Norison's castle, Pesme Aventure – surge up within the confines of Arthur's universe. Furthermore, humans have no difficulty entering into contact with Other World characters, although at their risk and peril, and a Harpin de la Montagne regularly terrorizes Gawain's own relatives.

Yvain's story, which includes a solitary journey, adventures, rites of passage, withdrawal and return, marriage, and attainment of sovereignty, corresponds to the traditional structure of quest romance. We find the same pattern of prohibition and transgression, of adversaries and helpers (*opposants* and *adjuvants*) as in *La Charrete*. Chrétien has given an original direction to the romance plot, however, for the fairy bride is a widow not a maiden, and the hero, before winning her, slays her husband. In other words, the basic increment in *Le Chevalier au Lion* corresponds not only to Celtic myth but to the death and rebirth archetype I discussed in the chapter on *Roland*. Frazer (in *The Golden Bough*) and others have associated this archetype with the dying god motif of the Rex Nemorensis, a priest-king who defends the sanctuary of Artemis at Nemi and is succeeded only by a newcomer who slays him in battle. The priest-king of the grove or the knight of the fountain, regularly replaced and as regularly married to a goddess-fay who abides, who each spring takes a new husband to fertilize the soil, recalls cycles of the day, the month, the year, and human life. However, Yvain refuses to become like Esclados, to perish and be replaced by another Yvain. Instead, protected by Lunette, by a 'little moon,' he succeeds himself, that is, the Knight of the Lion succeeds Yvain. Yvain dies and is reborn as the Knight of the Lion in order to win back ('remarry') the divine lady. But before so doing or because he desires to do so, he violates a tabu, falls from grace, and is expelled from her presence, another form of death. His experience in the woods, naked, mad, devouring the raw flesh of beasts, is a spiritual degradation, which can be considered the death of Yvain's rational faculty and of his social being. During this part of the narrative he has disappeared from the court, indeed from the known Arthurian world, and no one can say whether he is still alive. Yvain's fall corresponds to Adam's, both men driven naked from their paradise. Then the Lady of Norison and her maidens cure the man with an ointment, a motif perhaps derived from the *Roman de Troie*, but also symbolizing baptism and the anointment of Christ by the three Marys, or prevenient grace from the three cardinal virtues.[16] And he is given new clothes, *nova vestimenta* for a *homo novus*, and soon acquires a new name: the Knight of the Lion. Although Yvain talks of dying at the fountain, and claims he will perish if Laudine does not take him back, and although his lion attempts suicide, neither he nor his pet dies. After the symbolic death-rebirth experience he proceeds to live in the world with his new name and to conquer the supernatural bride a second time.

Ever since the time of Frazer and Freud people have recognized that the dying god archetype and the Oedipus complex are profound, though inevitably imperfect, interpretations of the same phenomenon: the pattern of replacement and continuity in the race. I have no doubt that Yvain's battle with the Red Knight, whom he slays, and his subsequent marriage to the semi-divine Lady of the Fountain, are a version of unconscious Oedipal wish-fulfillment, especially since one source for *Yvain* was probably the Oedipus-Jocasta story in the twelfth-century *Roman de Thèbes*. Although the young knight's virility is threatened by the Giant Herdsman, tamer of bulls, and the giant Esclados, a sun-figure whose spear and horse are larger than Yvain's, he nonetheless succeeds in defeating the father-figure and penetrating into an enclosed, feminine Other World, where to some extent the id rebels and the ego is awakened. Youth wins out over age and creates a new, festively congenial society in its image, successfully enacting the Oedipal fantasy. Now, although Chrétien presents the Oedipal fantasy in a more forthright, authentic fashion here than he does in *Le Chevalier de la Charrete*, nonetheless the protagonist endures symbolic guilt: he slays Esclados but is himself wounded in the process. Laudine proves to be a Terrible Mother as well as a good one. The water produces a tempest and a bird-concert, and Laudine's palace, with its falling portcullis, is a castrating trap as well as a paradise. Within, the victor of the fountain is rendered timid and passive, whereas the active role is taken over by Laudine. And, for whatever conscious reasons, Yvain desires to escape the fountain and its mistress as soon as he can. This is the opposition between *tornoiier* and *donoiier* in *Erec et Enide*, between male participation in tournaments and other martial activities and a more feminine orientation toward immobility and repose within a castle near a paradise-like source. Only with the denouement does Chrétien depict a mature, socially acceptable male desire which breaks the curse and brings about reconciliation.

In addition to symbol and myth, Chrétien de Troyes treats other matters in terms of 'realism' (although of a far different kind, of course, than we saw in *Raoul de Cambrai*). Whereas *Le Chevalier de la Charrete* portrays love and chivalry that can exist only in a fantasy-realm, *Le Chevalier au Lion*, like *Erec et Enide*, strives to relate *fin' amor* to everyday reality, to adapt the new love-ethos to the universe in which we live. The Other World is amalgamated with the real one, becomes a place for resolving ethical and psychological problems. The individual and his concerns become a central focus for the narrative. In some respects at least, Yvain and Laudine's relationship corresponds to those of the troubadour and his *domna* and of Lancelot and Guinevere. Courtly conventions abound. The problem is that this exemplary tone is corroded from the beginning. It is absurd, truly 'mad,' for Yvain to adore his greatest enemy in the world, the widow of the man he has just slain, and for him, in his courtly position as a prisoner of love, to take hope from the misogynistic proposition that Laudine, being only a fickle woman, can change heart and come to accept him. Chrétien then mocks the courtly world even more by having Laudine, on her side, not merely cherish but agree to wed the murderer. And he does this, in a most delicious way, by having Lunette, the Ovidian *ancilla*, convince her, according to the 'logic' of *fin' amor*, that she has no choice but to marry him. For, as Lunette points out, laying down a courtly syllogism: 1 / Laudine can love only the best of knights, for indeed Esclados was the best; 2 / but now there is a better one than he, Yvain, the individual who 'bested' him in combat; 3 / therefore, Laudine has to love Yvain. Ideally, *fin' amor* is based upon a free choice of the will. But in this case Lunette's logic is a brutal imposition of the rigid and the mechanical on natural human emotions. Nonetheless, Laudine not only accepts Lunette's reasoning but pleads Yvain's case in her own mind, in a daydream, and thus grants him the victory before she lays eyes upon him, indulging all the while in flagrantly precious casuistry. This is the same Laudine who wept so passionately over Esclados's corpse, who berated so virulently his assassin. Now our courtly Widow of Ephesus cannot wait the full five days it will purportedly take for Lunette's messenger to fetch the new husband:

– Et quant le porrons nos avoir?
– Jusqu'a quint jor. – Trop tarderoit,
que, mon vuel, ja venuz seroit.
Veigne enuit ou demain, seviax.
– Dame, ne cuit pas c'uns oisiax
poïst tant en un jor voler ...
– Cist termes est trop lons assez:
li jor sont lonc.   (1822–7, 1834–5)

Although she is equally impatient, equally headstrong, both times, the objects of her passion are not the same. As a result, this sudden erotic displacement from one man to another, from love to indifference vis-à-vis the first and from hatred to love vis-à-vis the second, generates laughter. We cannot but smile when Yvain's big wedding so abruptly cancels Esclados's big funeral. In the words of the author:

Mes or est mes sire Yvains sire,
et li morz est toz oblïez;
cil qui l'ocist est marïez;
sa fame a, et ensanble gisent;
et les genz ainment plus et prisent
le vif c'onques le mort ne firent.   (2166–71)

Then too, although the great warrior Yvain falls passionately in love with Laudine on first sight and courts her the way people do in books, on his knees ('Hinc amor, hinc timor est; ipsum timor auget amorem,' *Heroides*, 12: 61; 'amorosus est semper timorosus,' *Tractatus de Amore*, Rule 20), Laudine reacts in a very different way. He lives the courtly code; she plays at it. He is lyrical, she reflective. He acts like an adolescent, she like an experienced, Machiavellian plotter. Thus, even though the lady accepts Yvain's suit in a courtly framework, she does so for the most uncourtly reasons. She only agrees to love him after Lunette points out that King Arthur is coming to challenge the fountain and after Yvain commits himself to defending it for her (2035–9). This latter point is far more important to Laudine than her suitor's hyperbolic declarations of love. For she recognizes the necessity for a noble widow to remarry that she may defend her lands against predatory neighbors or rival inheritors. For her, the feudal interests of her caste take precedence over esteem and passion. Thus a factor of twelfth-century profane reality encourages Yvain's courtly suit and nullifies Laudine's no less passionate courtly sentiments toward Esclados the Red. All of which does not prevent Laudine from acting the hypocrite by arranging for her seneschal to propose Yvain as her husband and for the court to 'compel' her to marry the man as if he were a total stranger. Once again the ideal is set off against reality, an artificial code juxtaposed to the immediate, practical necessities of twelfth-century life. Both characters inauthentically play a role, a ritualized, selfish game, fitting their lives into preconceived romantic or feudal contexts, the forms of love and honor substituted for the real things.

This brings us to another incongruous point, the fact that Laudine engaged in one very courtly relationship with her husband, Esclados, and now launches a second one with Yvain, whom she also weds. To some extent the troubadours, Béroul, Thomas, and, most certainly, Andreas Capellanus, considered love between husband and wife impossible. Andreas has the Countess of Champagne pass judgment on the question. She declares, in the *Tractatus de honeste amandi*: 'Dicimus enim et stabilito tenore firmamus, amorem non posse suas inter duos jugales extendere vires.'[17] This is the same Countess Marie who allegedly supplied Chrétien with the adulterous *matiere* and *san* for *Le Chevalier de la Charrete*. Other northern romances, where youth and maiden are permitted to marry, usually treat only their pre-nuptial adventures. In *Erec et Enide* and *Le Chevalier au Lion*, on the other hand, Chrétien proposes marriage as a solution to the courtly dilemma, a legitimate compromise between Reason and Amor, for it can be envisaged both as love-match and marriage of convenience. He pairs off his hero and heroine relatively early in the narrative, then investigates the problems that Eros faces in marriage; that is, scrutinizes what happens to people after the traditional happy ending of romance. One week after the wedding Gawain convinces Yvain to leave his bride for a round of tourneys. Only in this way, says Gawain, can the youth maintain his reputation for prowess and avoid losing *pris* and *enor*, becoming *recreant*, the jealous husband of courtly tradition. Chrétien here is reconsidering a theme he treated in *Erec et Enide*, where people reproach Erec with having spent too much time with his wife to the detriment of his knightly responsibilities. Unlike Erec, Yvain rushes to the opposite extreme, forgets Laudine, overstays the year's leave she accorded, and, as a result, is banished from her presence. It is obvious that in both poems Chrétien is investigating the relationship between *militia* and *amor*, between prowess and love. These two elements give meaning to existence and are spurs to perfection in courtly man: a knight cannot expect to attain preeminence in the hierarchy until he performs deeds in arms and is loved by a great lady. Furthermore, the two forces depend one on the other, each reinforcing the other. A hero achieves the greatest feats only at the goading of Eros, and he will be rewarded only because he has succeeded in martial pursuits. However, love can also undermine war, as war can undermine love, because, in a paradoxical world similar to Corneille's, neither passion nor prowess is determined once and for all as essence. Each must be reaffirmed within a state of existential contingency, in the flux of temporal duration. Laudine will cease to cherish Yvain if his reputation for valor decreases; he can avoid such diminution only by leaving her to renew his status, but, by so doing, he risks losing her through absence and forgetfulness. Contrariwise, although he does deeds of prowess only for love of her, in desiring her he is tempted to remain by her side and abandon the call to arms. The tension between *militia* and *amor* can be resolved in a wish-fulfillment world of adultery, where a not overly dangerous husband and his retinue provide a convenient obstacle that reinforces *fin' amor* and, for a variety of extraneous reasons, the lover is compelled to absent himself from the court, thereby winning martial renown (the Lancelot and Tristan stories). But when Erec and Enide or Yvain and Laudine are married to each other, such built-in obstacles cease to function; the couple must invent new ones in order, through their own will, to surpass themselves. The conflict Chrétien strives to resolve is an eternal one: indeed, in its way it corresponds to one problem of twentieth-century man, his desire for happiness and fulfillment, for family or pleasure and a career, and his anguish at not being able to satisfy both longings equally and at the same time.

Not only the public but Yvain himself comes to understand the truths Chrétien wishes him (and us) to learn. In a very real sense, like Telemachus and Aeneas, he grows in the course of the narrative, and *Erec et Enide*, *Le Chevalier au Lion*, and *Perceval* can be considered the first *Entwicklungsromane* in French literature. The *Lion* plot begins with Yvain brave, impetuous, and enthusiastic, full of romantic brio, but not yet arrived at a state of perfection. His comportment in the Other World, his attitudes toward Esclados and Laudine especially, mark him as a vain, self-centered human being who has far to progress on the road to maturity. He lacks measure in love and in war. He is guilty of *nonsavoir* (6772) and a form of *acedia*, that is, neglect of marital and professional obligations, slothful *oblianz* that leads to *tristitia* and *melancholia*, an insane, frenetic despair. Ironically, when Calogrenant refers to his own madness on the quest, Yvain accuses his cousin of being *fol* (584, 586) because the latter kept silent over his adventures, and, of course, the protagonist refuses to commit the folly of arguing with Kay. Lunette counsels against *folie* on Yvain's part; he should keep still in the castle. Laudine, guilty of acting *folemant* in mourning Esclados, accuses Lunette of *desreison* when the latter offers her good advice. And the implied author accuses Laudine of typically feminine folly in these terms:

> La dame set molt bien et pansse
> que cele la consoille an foi;

mes une folie a en soi
que les autres fames i ont:
trestotes, a bien pres, le font,
que de lor folie s'ancusent
et ce qu'eles voelent refusent.    (1642–8)

Furthermore, surely Yvain was *fol* to love his enemy's widow in the first
place. But these are mere words. Our hero literally goes insane after having
committed a crime against his lady, the God of Love, and the code of
chivalry. He hates himself, wishes to perish, and, bereft of reason, wanders
naked in a *salvage terre*, himself an *hom forsenez et salvage* (2830), hunting wild animals and devouring their flesh. Yvain has become a beast,
punishment for the beastly way he treated Laudine, his failure to respect
her as a human being; yet also a state endemic to good lovers and, therefore,
to be pitied and regarded with wonder. And his madness serves as a
purgatory for past mistakes and a way of avoiding comparable excess in the
future.

Yvain returns to a semblance of social intercourse through the mediation
of a hermit, who, in exchange for raw venison and pelts, supplies him
with bread and cooked meat. This first human contact is based upon barter
and upon direct contact of nature and culture. As Yvain was formerly
served by Lunette, again it is three ladies who cure him, the Lady of Norison and her handmaidens, images of the beneficent feminine principle
inherent in nature and in *fin' amor*. For the rest of his career, the Knight of
the Lion will struggle to deserve reconciliation with Laudine, not by
proving himself in frivolous, contrived, 'show' tournaments but by serving
others, by ridding the community of ogres who threaten the public weal.
And in each case he serves women, he rescues damsels in distress: the Lady
of Norison, Gawain's niece, Lunette herself (known for her generosity to
*povres dames*, 4353), the three hundred prisoners of Pesme Aventure, and
the Maiden of Noire Espine. This madman who formerly was assisted by
ladies and then scorned his wife is redeemed only by climbing a Calvary of
service to womankind. Thus he integrates the feminine principle, the
anima, without which he and his society prove to be imperfect; thus he
becomes a whole, adult human being.

Directly after his victory over the Lady of Norison's pursuer, the first
altruistic act, Yvain, having acted like a lion, encounters a lion giving
battle to a serpent, takes the lion's side, and, as a result, wins him as pet and
ally. In this adventure the lion chooses of his own free will to follow
Yvain. He hunts for his master (like Husdent in Béroul's *Tristan*) and also
serves him three times in battle. Thus, at the very center of the narrative,
Yvain earns a friend. The lion is derived from the folk-tradition of the

grateful beast, who repays the hero for having saved its life. Works of literature such as the Book of Daniel and versions of the Androcles and Jerome legends may also have contributed to the motif. Whatever symbolic interpretation we give the animal, there is no doubt that he represents natural or supernatural forces that grant Yvain special aid, prove his heroic virtue and his election to greatness, and sanction his quest.

Significantly, Calogrenant and Yvain both encounter a Giant Herdsman, assimilated to the *vilain*-figure found in several Old French romances, including *Eracle* and *Aucassin et Nicolette*, a caricature of the medieval peasant viewed from a courtly perspective:

> Uns vileins, qui resanbloit Mor,
> leiz et hideus a desmesure,
> einsi tres leide criature
> qu'an ne porroit dire de boche ...    (286–9)

This man resembles in various ways elephant, cat, owl, wolf, and boar (292–305). Hideous, naïve, sloppy, and ill-mannered, he has no idea what the word *aventure* means. He is truly an *agroikos* in Frye's sense of the term, the rustic refuser of festivity in a romance context. In the same register, Harpin de la Montagne and the two ogres of Pesme Aventure are depicted as *vilains*, who possess unknightly weapons and armor. Presumably they appear ridiculous to Chrétien's courtly public in part because of their peasant-like 'absurdity' and their no less absurd desire to measure arms with Yvain, son of King Urien. However, in contrast to the eager but inept Calogrenant, the Herdsman holds lordship over bulls, bears, and leopards. Indeed, Calogrenant's incapacity to communicate with the man may well be more subject to laughter than the despised peasant himself, especially when we realize how badly Yvain's cousin will be discomfited by Esclados the Red. In the end it is perhaps the rustic who triumphs, for although he does not comprehend courtly niceties, he supplies accurate information to Calogrenant and, in his own way, confounds him; when King Arthur's knight asks him what sort of created being he is, the Herdsman responds, 'I am a man!' and, further on, does not hesitate to question Calogrenant as to his identity and reason for being in the area. Should not the latter heed Terence's dictum, 'Humani nihil a me alienum puto'? Now, Yvain, who at various points in the narrative is compared favorably to a dove, falcon, and lion, after he goes insane descends to an animal level, lower than that of the Herdsman and Harpin. Then, on the way to recovery, he who hunted Esclados, hunter of men, tracks wild game for a hermit (a parody of his former knightly prowess), is thus transformed into a grateful beast himself, and, in his adventures with the lion, respects a grateful animal in turn, masters a creature like the Herdsman, and is aided by a lion far more loyal and loving to him than he himself used to be to Laudine. Distinctions between social classes, even between the human and bestial states, are rendered ambiguous. A man must struggle to retain his place in the cosmic hierarchy, which he can lose at any time.

A humorous element develops when the lion becomes Yvain's faithful friend, vassal, and servant. We may or may not smile at an attempted suicide (a subject for laughter in ages less sentimental than our own), but such behavior from a doting lion cannot be taken seriously. A comic tension is set up between the human and the animal in that human behavior is depicted in animal terms and a wild beast succeeds in acting like a person. Whenever we think of this knightly, efficacious warrior in battle, we are also reminded of his feline exterior. Furthermore, the lion is not only depicted as the king of beasts but also a pet dog or cat, who hunts for Yvain in the woods. The qualities of a lion and of a house-pet are juxtaposed, as are those of an animal and a human. As a pet, it is ridiculous for him to give battle to giants, to kneel and weep, offering homage, or to attempt suicide with a sword which he dragged along with his teeth. As a human or a lion, it is absurd for him to sleep at his master's feet, to burrow under a doorway, or to tremble with anger like a cat ('se herice et creste,' 5525) and beat the earth with his tail, manifesting traits incongruous in a *miles dominans*. A Bergsonian analysis is as valid for Yvain's lion as for the two leading characters in *Huon de Bordeaux*.[18]

Finally, the lion gives Chrétien's protagonist his name, helps resolve his identity crisis. Yvain's name is an honored one, announced with pride by him to Lunette and by Lunette to Laudine. In fact, Laudine is especially eager to marry him when she discovers he is Yvain, son of King Urien. However, between lines 3629 and 6277 the name is not mentioned, by Yvain or by anyone else. In his dishonor, Yvain, like Lancelot, has lost the right to bear this sign of his personality. As evidence of his newly acquired humility, he insists on fighting incognito. However, almost in spite of himself, Yvain soon becomes known as 'li Chevaliers au Lÿon.' In itself the new identity reveals to us the break in Yvain's consciousness, an integral step in his initiation experience, and his own recognition of the dual nature of his career. And the lion, become part of Yvain's title, also shares his identity. The lion sanctions Yvain's quest, lends him his name and his honor – as king of the beasts – until the *homo novus* has won enough glory that he can, first at Arthur's court, later in Laudine's castle, unlace his helmet and reveal that the Knight of the Lion and Yvain are identical.

The young man's growth is intimately connected with problems of human interaction and illusion and reality. To begin with, Yvain and Laudine are out of touch with each other, each incapable of divining the other's intentions. They fail to relate properly, they play at courtly conventions. Temporarily united by Lunette, they are quickly driven apart and Yvain is condemned to solitude in the woods. Then he succeeds in communicating first with the hermit, secondly with his lion, even though in both situations no words are spoken. The Lady of Norison and her maidens recognize Yvain, although he is naked and unconscious, and manipulate him for their own purposes, although he is mad. These scenes form a striking contrast to episodes where Laudine's helpless servants are driven to frenzy, and Laudine with them, because Yvain has been rendered invisible; where Yvain and Gawain, inside their respective suits of armor, almost kill each other by mistake; where, reliving the episode of Odysseus and Nausicaa, for all his eloquence Yvain cannot convince the lord of Pesme Aventure that he has good reasons for not marrying the latter's daughter; or where, for all his eloquence, he is rendered speechless and a coward in the presence of Laudine. Because communication is interrupted despite elaborate efforts to interrelate, people take appearance for reality and are deceived. A variation on the same theme occurs when, although characters do succeed in communicating, nonetheless, by twisting the truth, one of them manipulates the others through language. This is the case when King Arthur tricks Gawain's protégée into admitting that she disinherited her sister, and when Lunette first manoeuvres Laudine into marrying Yvain then manoeuvres her into taking him back. Here the equivocal use of words succeeds where justice, ethics, mercy in the abstract, and prowess itself fail. Lying brings out the truth, and illusion serves the cause of reality.

Derived from the Ovidian confidante and go-between (Dipsas, Cyprasis, Nape), Anna in the *Eneas*, Brangien in the Tristan romances, and a variety of fays in Arthurian legend, Lunette has lost all traces of witch-craft to be found in Chrétien's sources. Instead, she deceives her mistress and her benefactor, manipulating them with brio. It is not an easy task to play Cupid for the conqueror become a snivelling adolescent and the impet-uous, vain widow who bursts into rage at untoward moments. Yet this *dolosa serva* worthy of Molière, Marivaux, and Beaumarchais speaks when she has been ordered to keep still, intervenes where she is not wanted, and succeeds three times in furthering love, marriage, and a happy ending. One of Chrétien's finest moments as an artist, and as the father of the modern novel, occurs when he recounts the sprightly, witty dialogue between ser-vant and mistress, manipulator and manipulated, by which this *sapientia*-figure on the distaff side triumphs over all obstacles.

It is also true that Laudine is tricked not only by Lunette but also by herself. Her elegant self-deception, her charming 'bad faith' are worthy of a Louis XIV salon or a Louis XV drawing-room. Although this Gothic Célimène mourns her dead husband passionately, in fact she is obsessed with her own wounded pride; she believes she hates Yvain but at all times is ready to love him; and she pities the Knight of the Lion, never dreaming that his pitiless lady could be herself. Yvain also at one time deceived himself with false promises of chivalry; as soon as the mask of untruth is removed, he goes mad, but then learns to accept reality. And once this is accomplished he puts a new mask on his face, the literal armor (and fictional identity) of the Knight of the Lion. The deceived man learns to deceive in turn. Along with Lunette, he manipulates Laudine the way Odysseus tricked Penelope and only pulls off his mask when, because of Lunette's ruse, she is forced to renounce her own bad faith and restore their love.

For Chrétien's public one manifestation of paradise lost is the Arthurian world itself, specifically King Arthur's court at Camelot in the Kingdom of Logres. To some extent, as in *La Charrete*, the court represents an ideal of social decorum and moral judgment, a norm against which Yvain must be measured. However, Chrétien's attitude toward the institution is more than a little ambivalent. It contains witty, gracious people – Guinevere, Gawain, and Calogrenant – but also Kay the Seneschal,[19] a *miles gloriosus*, an impulsive, choleric Thersites who acts in as inconsequential a fashion as he did in *Lancelot* and is referred to by the queen as *envieus*, *vilains*, and *forssenez*, whereas Calogrenant remarks on Kay's unchangeability in more concrete terms: 'Toz jorz doit puïr li fumiers, / et toons poindre ...' (116–17).

Even Sir Gawain, the 'observed of all the observers,' the norm against which knights who aspire to chivalry are measured, is guilty of having seduced Yvain into quitting his bride immediately after their honeymoon. Gawain promised Lunette to be her knight, to defend her whenever she needs him. But when the seneschal accuses her of treason, King Arthur's nephew is away somewhere else, looking for Guinevere, and, as we know from *La Charrete*, not making a good job of it. It is Yvain who protects Lunette and delivers members of Gawain's own family, during the sun-figure's eclipse. Finally, when the latter does return from his fruitless quest, he promises to support the older maiden of Noire Espine, without enquiring into the justness of her cause, and thus finds himself on the wrong side in a *judicium Dei*. Yvain does not physically defeat Gawain; their duel ends in a draw. But morally he has surpassed his friend, this flawed embodiment of *sapientia*, has gone beyond him in service to the community, and, so doing, has learned to cope with the person, symbolically that part of himself, responsible for his *oblianz*. Indeed, halfway through the story he changes companions. In Gawain's stead he substitutes the lion –

'de ce, s'il vos plest, me creez,
qu'il est a moi, et je a lui;
si somes conpaignon andui.' (6460–2)

– who proves to be of more help to him than Gawain or any other man. For the norms of the court he substitutes a more elemental, more spiritual force.

The court represents the world that judges Yvain, embodies the essence which Yvain struggles to partake of. However, he does not win his 'essence' there. He acts, becomes, his ordeals take place, in other locations, especially the fountain. The fountain-scene contains a juxtaposition of the tree and the flowing water and basin, of tempest and the peaceful, joyful song of birds. A typological interpretation can be applied to the pine tree (*arbor vitae* or Tree of Jesse), the spring (*fons vitae*), and the baptism of love that takes place there. Three times Yvain undergoes an adventure at the source; three times he rescues or conquers a fair lady (Laudine, Lunette, Laudine). The first ordeal brings Yvain status, the second grants him inner worth, responsibility, and self-awareness, the third consecrates his worth and restores status. In the end, driven by Amor, Yvain leaves the king and queen to return (alone, with the lion) to his wife. The climax of his career is symbolized not in acceptance at court but reconciliation at home. And he will devote the rest of his active life to defending the fountain, maintaining a reputation for prowess away from King Arthur. Thus the public and private worlds of action are dissociated, and, to some extent, the private is given value over the public. Yvain decides in favor of existence over essence, of an eternal becoming over stasis. The structure of *Le Chevalier au Lion* is thus in large measure determined by the opposition of these two symbolic locations, the court and the fountain, and voyages by the hero and other characters from one to the other. Significantly, in between them presumably lies the *gaste terre* where Yvain goes mad, rejected by both Arthur and Laudine. Yet also, in between the two poles, he encounters the lion, his chosen companion, the super-Gawain, and by rescuing the lion performs his first selfless act. His upward climb is embodied in a series of adventures, graded in order of significance. At first Yvain rescues creatures in return for services rendered or that will be rendered (the Lady of Norison, the lion, Gawain's family, Lunette); he then assists the maidens of Pesme Aventure and the Maiden of Noire Espine gratuitously, out of pure altruism. In Bezzola's terms (who referred to *Erec et Enide*), from *aventure subie* (frivolous jousting in tourneys) Yvain shifts to *aventure acceptée* (repayment of debts) and finally willingly, joyfully undergoes *aventure recherchée* (service and charity).[20]

As in *La Chanson de Raoul*, it is possible to speak of competing masculine and feminine 'worlds' in *Le Chevalier au Lion*. The masculine universe
is embodied in King Arthur's court and its most brilliant representative,
the sun-figure Gawain. The feminine, of course, is manifest in the fountain
of storms and fertility, and the labyrinthine castle with its secret chambers, this strange, magical realm under the sway of the passionate, capricious
Laudine and her servant, Yvain's second friend, the dark-haired moon-
figure Lunette. The sun- and moon-figures compete for Yvain's loyalty:
Lunette is the embodiment of ruse as opposed to Gawain's force, of love
as opposed to his comradeship and honor. Only by integrating both of
them, the masculine and feminine aspects of his self and of the universe
(mind and heart, reason and passion, the conscious and the unconscious,
responsibility and self-indulgence, animus and anima, reality and faerie,
the real and the supernatural) can Yvain become a total adult being, capable
of serving others and of sovereignty – in marriage and in the state.

In *Raoul de Cambrai* we saw a trouvère cope directly with the class
struggle, disruption, and violence inherent in late twelfth-century society.
The *Raoul*-poet depicts without flinching the disintegration of his world.
Chrétien de Troyes also portrays, in stylized form, aspects of contemporary
twelfth-century reality, the most noteworthy in *Yvain* being the Giant
Herdsman (the 'peasant problem') and the three hundred maidens of Pesme
Aventure, whose situation evokes the reality of female exploitation in the
spinning trade and can be interpreted as an urban sweat shop or a manorial
*gynécée*, unless it is simply a stylized, mythical projection of feudal ideology. It is equally true that, taken as a whole, Chrétien's is a world of romance, of escape, of wish-fulfillment, different from that of *chanson de
geste*. However, Chrétien, Béroul, Thomas, and their followers wrote for
approximately the same public as did the epic trouvères, and they provide
a no less significant perspective on the problems of the age. Arthurian romance quite possibly expressed the aspirations of Angevin kings of England, was meant to serve as a counterweight to epics which proclaimed the
glory of the reigning Capetian House of France. And we have reason to
believe that the *roman* also supported the petty nobility, young, landless
knights and squires (*bachelers*) alienated from the feudal world. In these
poems we find a kind, generous, but inactive King Arthur who, bursting
with largesse, willingly delegates power and glory to the barons of his
court. These are relatively poor but gently born knights-errant who set out
alone on quests, right wrongs, and triumph over obstacles. In this fundamentally reactionary vision of life, the knights destroy wicked new *costumes*, replacing them by good old *costumes*, marry heiresses, and become
kings or princes in turn. Owing to the young men, to them and them alone,

the realm achieves spiritual and moral splendor. They create, are responsible for, and are integrated into a new aristocratic class closed to outsiders, an *ordo* created by God in which all knights, rich and poor, participate as equals. Chrétien glorifies the Arthurian myth, projecting onto it the aspirations of a threatened social class in his own day, resolving intracultural tensions by the creation of a world of fantasy; ritualized action and popular myth are co-opted by poets who exalt the feudal nobility.

Calogrenant prefixes his story with an appeal to the courtiers: may they listen to him with their hearts as well as their ears, 'car parole est tote perdue / s'ele n'est de cuer entandue' (151–2). His words serve as a warning, not only from Calogrenant to Arthur's court but from Chrétien de Troyes to his public in the twelfth century and in ours. A civilized reader is presumed for such tales of adventure that create distance and also demand reflection and ironic insight, that withdraw from life and strive to capture empirical reality at the same time. This conscious artist, this master of *matiere*, of *san*, and of *conjointure*, has created a complex opus, rich with *senefiance*, containing sundry tones juxtaposed, capable of interpretation on more than one level. His romances tell exciting stories, evoke a splendid world of adventure and feats in arms. They portray in strikingly accurate terms the manners of a newly elegant secular world obsessed with decorum and the most refined conduct: food, clothing, architecture, domestic and exotic beasts, ceremony, amusement, and war. They delve deeply into the psychology of people in love and that of the personal interactions of small groups and turn inward to the more private, individual concerns of man, his growing self-awareness and quest for self-realization. They tell of the problems inherent in love and marriage, of the tensions that develop between happiness and fulfillment, of the crisis within twelfth-century feudal society. They emphasize the importance of order, harmony, and inner discipline in response to a brutal outside world. And in them we perceive the poetry of forests, castles, and enchantments, the magic of the Other World. This is the eternal quest of heroes to save themselves and their society, to rediscover a lost paradise, the image of feminine bliss beyond the flux of time. In Chrétien we find a combination of mystery, psychological analysis, and sophisticated elegance, given form in a *sermo mediocris* containing both wit and the poetry of the heart, tension and the relaxation of tension, romance and anti-romance. Chrétien believes in the possibility of joy and of equilibrium. He affirms that man can triumph over himself, and his world can grow. He is a man of the twelfth-century Renaissance committed to the beauty of the secular world, of chivalry, of woman's integrity, and of the exaltation of life and love. Thus *chevalerie* and *clergie* are allied, indeed fused in a unique cultural synthesis.

That the synthesis was not destined to endure in no way diminishes its value. Chrétien sought to transfer the art of Virgil and Ovid to France through his version of *translatio studii*; in so doing, he renewed and transformed the long narrative in verse. His opus provides one of the great moments in literature and a unique response (*höfische Epik*) to the evolving epic needs of medieval France. Other solutions to the same problems, other answers to the same needs, will be explored in my next chapter.

## Chapter Five

# 🐾 *LE ROMAN DE LA ROSE*

Although courtly romance flourishes in the period after Chrétien de Troyes, the complex synthesis, the delicate balance of forces embodied in Chrétien's work are lost to his successors. His themes are elaborated on divergent planes by a host of narrators. Some concentrate on tales of questing and mystery in an Arthurian décor (*Le bel Inconnu*, *L'Atre perilleux*, sundry Grail romances). Others, imitating *Cligès*, project adventures onto an exotic, pseudo-Byzantine world (*Partonopeus de Blois*, *Florimont*) where wish-fulfillment is attained in a strictly secular ambiance. Still others treat of *fin' amor* in elegant, worldly surroundings in a more or less contemporary environment. The greatest of these romancers is Jean Renart, whose masterpieces, *Guillaume de Dole* and *Le Lai de l'Ombre*, shine with wit and a delicate, refined, oblique sensuousness. And two of the most fecund developments in romance stand free from Chrétien's influence. The first portrays the idyllic love, separation, and reunion of two childhood sweethearts (*Floire et Blancheflor*, Jean Renart's *L'Escoufle*, *Aucassin et Nicolette*). The other, which appears in the second half of the thirteenth century, recalls the twelfth-century stories of Tristan, Pyramus, and Dido and tells of the tragedy of love, ending in death. *La Châtelaine de Vergi* and *Le Châtelain de Couci* are perhaps the last great verse romances in French literature.

However, just as the prestige of the *chanson de geste* recedes before that of verse romance, the *roman* gives way to other genres in turn. The greatest narratives of the thirteenth century are written in prose (therefore, as I explained in the Introduction, out of the purview of this book): the *Lancelot-Grail Prose Cycle*, a masterpiece of the stature of Dante's *Commedia*. And in its wake appear other cycles, the *Prose Tristan* and *Guiron le Courtois*, for example. Such works bear witness to a growing concern on the part of author and public alike for realism, credibility, and seriousness (the prose) and for completeness, a total, systematic world-picture (the cycle). These concerns are also manifest in the rise to favor of a new poetic genre – the allegory of love.

Like comedy and tragedy, the baroque and the classical, 'allegory' is an elusive, ambiguous term. On one level it designates a technique of writing, that is, a structure of extended metaphors or personifications that functions as a trope on at least two levels of meaning or that includes a pattern of relationship in both tenor and vehicle. Vaguer, no doubt, yet referring to the same phenomenon, are the medieval formulations – Isidore of Seville: 'Allegoria est alieniloquium. Aliud enim sonat, et aliud intellegitur'; Augustine: 'Allegoria dicitur, cum aliquid aliud videtur sonare in verbis, et aliud in intellectu significare'; Aquinas: 'Allegoria est tropus seu modus loquendi quo aliquid dicitur et aliud intellegitur.' Perhaps the vagueness of such definitions has led some modern scholars to confuse allegory with symbolism or to extend the term to include symbolism; thus, for example, to define allegory as any 'twice-told tale written in rhetorical, or figurative, language and expressing a vital belief.'[1] As a result, it is then conceived as a mode to be found throughout world literature, corresponding to the comic or the tragic, evidenced in writers as disparate as Virgil, Dante, Spenser, Swift, Hawthorne, Melville, Zola, Kafka, Orwell, Camus, Michaux, and detective and Western novelists. Although such grandiose conceptions can be defended, most scholars distinguish between allegorical and symbolical expression as they distinguish between the personification-allegory we find in the *Romance of the Rose* and the allegorical or typological interpretation of Scripture or of classical myth, no less prevalent in the Middle Ages. The allegorist begins with abstract concepts which he then conveys in concrete terms, whereas the symbolist sets out from the concrete world of sense impression to seek deeper reality beyond it. Allegory and symbolism both exist on two levels, literal and figurative, vehicle and tenor, signifier and signified, but the interpretation of allegory is primarily an intellectual process, that of symbolism an imaginative one. That is, in allegory the relationship between tenor and vehicle is precise, logical, fixed, and univocal, whereas symbolic expression encourages varied, shifting, intuitive readings. Although it has been fashionable since the time of Goethe, Coleridge, and De Sanctis to denigrate allegory in favor of symbolism, the most sophisticated contemporary critics recognize that the two techniques or modes each fulfill a separate function. There are great allegorists in world literature as well as great symbolists, mediocre symbolists as well as mediocre allegorists. And, as we shall see, nothing prevents both modes from coexisting in the same work of art.

Finally, just as scholars consider romance and tragedy to designate universal aspects of world literature and also specific literary kinds historically determined, I do not hesitate to designate as 'allegory' a particular literary genre or subgenre of the late Middle Ages, comparable to, and no less important than, the *chanson de geste* and the romance. Around the year

1190 or 1200 it ceased to be a mere ornament or didactic element and became the fictional cadre for an entire work of art. Medieval allegory can be defined as a pseudo-autobiographical narrative poem, often in the form of a dream or vision, the subject of which is often love or religion and the majority of whose characters are personified abstractions. Late twelfth- and early thirteenth-century philosophical or religious allegorists are represented by Raoul de Houdenc, *Le Songe d'Enfer*; an anonymous *Voie de Paradis*; Huon de Méry, *Le Tournoiement Antéchrist*; and Robert Grosseteste, *Le Château d'Amour*. However, the master of the genre is Guillaume de Degulleville, author of *Le Pèlerinage de la Vie humaine* (1330–1) and *Le Pèlerinage de l'Ame* (1355–8). The first great vernacular love-allegory is *Le Roman de la Rose*, written by Guillaume de Lorris and Jean de Meun, followed in the fourteenth and early fifteenth centuries by the works of Guillaume de Machaut, Jean Froissart, and Christine de Pisan. Given the importance of allegory in France and abroad (Dante, Petrarch, Chaucer, Pero López de Ayala, and Juan de Mena), it is no exaggeration to say that it became the dominant literary mode of the late Middle Ages.[2]

In the early 1220s Guillaume de Lorris wrote his incomplete masterpiece *Le Roman de la Rose*.[3] The poem contains two levels, the literal and the allegorical. Guillaume tells the following story. On a spring morning the Narrator wakes up and takes a stroll; his path leads to the Garden of Delight. On the outside wall he contemplates paintings of individuals named Haine, Felonie, Vilenie, Convoitise, Avarice, Envie, Tristesse, Vieillesse, Papelardie, and Pauvreté. He enters the garden through a narrow wicket guarded by a lovely young girl called Oiseuse. Within, he talks and dances with, in addition to Deduit and Oiseuse, Leece, Beauté, Richesse, Largesse, Franchise, Courtoisie, and Jeunesse. Strolling toward the center of the garden the Narrator looks down into the Fountain of Narcissus, also called the Fountain of Love, and perceives, reflected in two crystal stones, a rose-patch containing a particularly beautiful rose. He proceeds toward the rose-patch but is wounded by the God of Love, who orders the Narrator to surrender, upon which the latter offers homage. Amor then instructs the youth in the nature of the feudal service that will be required of him and delivers to him the Ten Commandments of Love. The Narrator approaches the Rose, accompanied by a young man called Bel Accueil, who encourages him to caress it and even gives him a leaf. But when he asks Bel Accueil to pluck the Rose for him, its guardian, Danger, leaps forth, urged on by Honte and Peur, reproaches Bel Accueil, and chases the Narrator away. Plunged into despair, the suitor consults with Raison, who urges him to give up the adventure, and with Ami, who advises him to continue, but employing greater stealth and cunning in the future. The Narrator follows Ami's advice and, with the help of Franchise and Pitié, is once again authorized to enter the rose-patch. He asks Bel Accueil's permission to kiss the Rose. Bel Accueil objects, but is convinced by Venus, who speaks on the young man's behalf. As soon as the kiss is granted, however, a certain Male Bouche informs Jalousie. As a result of these and other discussions, the Narrator is chased away a second time and Jalousie builds a castle around the Rose, to be defended by Danger, Honte, Peur, and Male Bouche, with Bel Accueil locked in the keep under the surveillance of la Vieille. The *Roman* breaks off with plaints of despair from the Narrator.

This is the *sensus litteralis*. In quest of a *sensus allegoricus*, we can interpret the romance in the following terms. Although the Narrator stands partly for a fictional representation of one young man, the mock-author Guillaume de Lorris, the 'I' who tells the story, he also represents anyone twenty years old, a kind of Every Man, or, to be more precise, the ideal potential courtly lover – if you will, Every Lover or Any Lover. In the course of time, strolling along the River of Life or Time, he experiences love in adolescence, the spring of life, the period during which the psyche awakens.

But it is of a very special kind, the *fin' amor* of the troubadours and trouvères, of Chrétien de Troyes and Thomas, a love which can occur only under ideal conditions, in a world of elegance, refinement, and good taste, people living together at court. Guillaume tells us that away from this social world *fin' amor* is impossible. Yet the world of the court is not open to everyone. The high walls, the narrow wicket, the guardian, indicate that only an elite, only young people of the highest possible character and attainments, are authorized to partake of the mysteries within. The vast majority of mortals presumably never enter the garden. The paintings depict qualities incompatible with *fin' amor*, which render a person unfit to love; as with the *Stilnovisti* love repairs only to a gentle heart, and determination of nobility of character (the gentle heart) precedes becoming amorous. If you cannot prevent these traits from entering the garden and thus from corrupting your own character, then you shall not be a good lover. Guillaume's prohibitions against poverty and *vileinie* (the state of being a peasant as well as a villain) and the presence of Oiseuse as gatekeeper ('Deus nobis haec otia fecit,' Virgil, *Eclogue* 1) indicate to how great an extent *fin' amor* was a class characteristic: for the Medievals, only people of birth and breeding were considered capable of indulging in the good life. Guillaume's world-view reveals the following *senefiance*: that delicate, romantic love, or any other sentiment of an esthetic nature, is a luxury which the poor can ill afford and which requires a concentration of libido and expenditure of time that leave little room for other concerns.

This Virgilian, Ciceronian *otium* stands for the active life devoted to esthetics and play, for total commitment, and for that leisure indispensable to feeling deep sentiments and writing poems about them. The God of Love's secrets are to be revealed only to an elite; the doctrine and its way of life are blatantly aristocratic: this is an ideal of the best for the best. Inside the gate the Narrator meets people who represent traits which a lover must possess in order to be initiated into the mysteries. These virtues are the exact opposites of the vices painted on the outside wall. Guillaume de Lorris has imagined two opposing intellectual systems and two naturally exclusive worlds: those who love and those who do not. And he expresses an indisputable preference for love over non-love, in that the love-virtues are admirable traits embodied in attractive young women, whereas the non-love-vices are incarnate in old hags. In addition, the virtues are 'real people,' alive, vocal, participating in harmonious group activities (song and dance) – that is, they contribute to the narrative – whereas the vices are not alive, they are silent, isolated images, mere descriptions. In a daring parody of standard Christian doctrine Guillaume tells us that, from the perspective of *fin' amor*, non-love is merely love distorted or the absence of love – it has no existence in and of itself; just as, throughout history, young people in the throes of passion are oblivious to anything but themselves, for in their own minds, in terms of amorous psychology, only they exist.

With 'la fontaine au bel Narcisus' (1511) Guillaume de Lorris no less daringly represents, in a manneristic, playful conceit, the Ovidian and courtly convention that man falls in love after gazing into a lady's eyes, thus permitting a flame or Cupid's arrow to pass from her eyes to his and to his heart. Although whether the fountain refers to the Narrator's eyes or to those of his lady is open to question, it cannot be denied that the two sparkling, many-hued, reflecting crystals inside the fountain signify pupils, the water flowing from two ducts equals tears, and the thick grass around the fountain stands for eyelashes. That the crystals are mirrors, that they reflect one-half of the entire garden, and that they presumably also reflect the individual gazing into them (hence the Fall of Narcissus) also exemplify the courtly doctrine that beholding beauty in woman opens up a new world to the lover and leads him to a greater knowledge of himself. From a Jungian perspective, the anima projected onto a girl in a dream is an aspect of the protagonist's self. Of course, the Rose refers to the girl, or perhaps to her love.

The Narrator yearns after the Rose but is prevented from plucking it by Amor. Lorris tells us that perception precedes sensation, that physical acquaintance with the loved one precedes desire, which in turn precedes love, and that *fin' amor*, in its finest, most delicate manifestation, restrains brute desire and renders the lover timid, not aggressive. It is just at this moment, when the Narrator has become enamored for the first time, when *novel rage* is transformed into *fin' amor*, that he assumes responsibility for his state: he commits himself to the erotic life, placing love foremost in his thoughts and actions (the act of vassalage) and is ready to comprehend it intellectually (Amor's instruction).

We are informed of two allegorical efforts to seduce the Rose, two occasions when the Narrator makes physical advances to his beloved. On each occasion he expresses a desire to go beyond erotic foreplay to the sexual act itself. Although the girl recoils and he is forced to withdraw, the second time she becomes angry at a later stage, further along the path of surrender. It is probable that Guillaume's poem in its extant form is patterned after a well-known motif in classical and medieval literature, the *gradus amoris* or stages in courtship. The *quinque lineae amoris* (four in Andreas Capellanus) are the following: *visus, alloquium, tactus, osculum* or *basium*, and *factum*. Guillaume takes the Narrator through the first four steps; presumably the 'deed' (*factum*) would have crowned the final episode, which the author did not write.

At this point Bel Accueil is sequestered. Both internal psychological and external social forces – specifically, scandal-mongers who blacken a suitor's reputation in his lady's eyes, and his and her reputations to her entourage (the *lauzengiers* of the troubadours); the Rose's father or mother; and an old servant, loyal to the parents – exert pressure on the lady. From the lover's perspective, their effects are the same. And the Narrator, in a moment of despair, also seeks help from an inner trait, his Reason (she is part of his personality, she echoes thoughts in his psyche), and from a person in the outside world, Ami, the friend or confidant Andreas Capellanus authorizes every lover to have.

*Le Roman de la Rose* treats the psychology of young people in love. Every step of the action, every speech and episode, refers to an inner crisis, debate, resolution, or act on the part of one or both lovers. Human motivations are never pure, stable, and univocal, nor do they appear so in the eyes of an outside observer. One can forget the Other's appearance but not her humors, her basic character traits, which, to the Medievals as to many Moderns, make up her essence as a person, regardless of whether her hair is blond or dark, her eyes blue or brown.

Although Guillaume de Lorris is one of the first writers in modern literature to pay attention to the beloved as well as the lover, to characterize her psychological processes as well as his, it is no less a fact that the story is a pseudo-autobiography; therefore told from one point of view, the I-Narrator's, and reflected through one prism, his. The Rose's psychology appears in the romance for the first time only when he makes contact with her, and her psychological forces are described as they appear to him, with his value-judgments attached to them. Thus any changes in her 'character' – for example, the appearance of new allegories – means not that her psyche has indeed metamorphosed but that, in the flux of time, the Narrator perceives her to be different. Furthermore, Bel Accueil is conceived as a handsome youth and Danger as a disgusting wretch precisely because this is how the suitor reacts to them.

*Le Roman de la Rose* is concerned with the progress of a total love affair. According to the traditions of *fin' amor*, love begins with the man, not the woman, but once he recognizes that he has fallen in love, he seeks to attain the *ultimum solatium* or *totius personae concessio* of which Andreas Capellanus speaks. Therefore, once he sets out to win tangible favors from the Rose, she must inevitably play a more active role. As long as the Narrator merely gazes upon her from afar, she appears to him as a vision of beauty and goodness, but now he becomes aware of contradictory trends in her comportment toward him, and of divergent traits within her. Another self enters into the plot, and the play back and forth between her psyche and his constitutes the action. Her processes are given voice, we perceive her reactions to the Narrator and to the people around her, her swinging from 'no' to 'yes' and from 'yes' to 'no.' Indeed, the poem's décor is transposed from life in general (the river-bank) to the court (the garden) to the girl's psyche (the rose-patch). The ultimate drama of the poem takes place inside her, her heart is the stage on which the lover's fate will be determined.

Following upon Ovid, Guillaume de Lorris also attempts to differentiate between male and female psychology. The youth attacks, the maiden defends. The former accepts love readily, and in him anguish comes only from frustrated desire, whereas the maiden is torn between whether to love or not. However, both male and female exist only for Eros, the one absolute force that rules the universe. He lives to pluck the Rose or to despair, she to yield or to refuse being plucked. Neither has any other function in life. Furthermore, each treats the other uniquely as a thing, a love-object. For neither lover nor beloved, though each is capable of communication within himself or with outside persons, ever succeeds in establishing a meaningful relationship.

A solitary figure at the beginning of the poem, the Narrator joins a group, the dancers of the garden, and later interacts with a host of beings around the rose-patch. From passive observation of pictures on a wall, he participates in a dance, undertakes social obligations (becoming the God of Love's vassal), and finally seeks to alter the garden by plucking one of the roses. Not only is this *bellum intestinum* within the psyche depicted in terms of human quarrels, blandishments, and alliances; we also find that the Narrator and the Rose do not live in a vacuum. They are surrounded by real people – the Narrator's friend, the Rose's father or mother, an old servant, a gossipy neighbor – who influence the course of their affair. All of which proves that, for Guillaume de Lorris and his medieval public, love cannot exist as a private relationship between two elect souls in the manner of Victor Hugo. People live in society, have social responsibilities. Love takes place in the world, where lovers must cope with the concrete reality which surrounds them. Indeed, the pleasure principle of desiring the Rose is immediately counterbalanced by the reality principle embodied in the girl's reticence and the conventions that society has evolved to soften brute lust and gratuitous copulation. The privileged irresponsibility of childhood, the play and self-absorption represented by Oiseuse and Deduit, have to be surpassed before the Narrator can become a loving, adult individual. *Fin' amor*, by its very nature, takes place at the court. Although the love affair must be conducted with the utmost discretion, it is a social act and, as in the case of Lancelot and Guinevere, contributes to the spiritual and physical well-being of an aristocratic caste. Indeed, a case can be made that all the knowledge the Narrator obtains is to be used in society, that his every act is directed as much toward its acceptance by society as toward winning the Rose. He creates his own identity in the community and, integrated in it, helps contribute to the ordering of a true *curialitas*.

Up to now I have discussed *Le Roman de la Rose* as allegory. However, Guillaume de Lorris's poem contains a 'symbolic' texture as well.[4] Indeed, in my opinion, the unique quality of *Le Roman de la Rose* is accounted for by a synthesis of intellectual balance and precision (the allegory) and a rich, sensuous pattern of imagery (the symbolism). Guillaume takes the basic stuff of Arthurian romance and turns it inward; the adventures, the quest, the marvels of *Lancelot* and *Yvain*, the battle of *opposants* and *adjuvants*, are taken from the outside world and applied uniquely to representing the hero's inner state as he learns to love. Nonetheless, the lover undertakes a quest as numinous and all-consuming as that of any of King Arthur's knights. And there can be no doubt that the Garden of Delight, with its river-barrier, walls, narrow entrance, pleasance, fountain, and castle within, is a legitimate manifestation of the Other World.

This grove partakes of Curtius's *locus amœnus*, a topos which can be traced back to Homer, to Virgil (Elysium, the Golden Age), and to the earthly paradise of Genesis and the gardens of the Canticles and the Apocalypse.[5] The *locus amœnus*, containing birds, flowers, shady trees, grass, flowing water, and little animals, is conceived as a place of perpetual spring and eternal joy, a 'dignus amore locus' which encourages the growth of love, is in fact the only décor where it can properly flourish. The action also takes place in springtime, according to medieval science the sanguine period, favorable to the young, warm and moist, the season evoked in courtly lyric. Most of May falls under the astrological sign of

Taurus in the House of Venus, again a time appropriate to the flowering of Eros. Spring is also the season of renewal in Nature, of the New Year, and, in religious terms, of the Annunciation and Easter, of the conception and resurrection of Christ. For all these reasons we are moved by the spatial and temporal archetypes that Guillaume de Lorris so carefully introduces into his work.

Penetrating through a normally locked, narrow wicket into this luxuriant, enclosed flower-garden, the Narrator compares the earth to a woman putting on new clothes in spring:

> lors devient la terre si gobe
> qu'el velt avoir novele robe,
> si set si cointe robe feire
> que de colors i a .c. peire;
> l'erbe et les flors blanches et perses
> et de maintes colors diverses,
> c'est la robe que je devise,
> por quoi la terre mielz se prise.   (59–66)

Catalogues of birds, trees, and flowers indicate a profusion of riches and fecundity. The squirrels and rabbits contained in the garden are associated with Venus and female sensuality, as are the roses. We have a right to consider the *locus amœnus* in general, and Guillaume de Lorris's Garden of Delight in particular, as a feminine landscape. This is the soft earth, the dream of repose, of sensuous well-being, which evokes in male poets nostalgia for the Mother. *Le Roman de la Rose* thus consecrates that evolution in the long narrative poem (see chapter three), from epic to romance and idyll, from war to love. Light, open fields, and the sword give way to shade, intimacy, and flowing water. Male gives way to female. This décor consecrates woman and love. The Narrator, who revels in his new-found labyrinth, gives himself utterly to a world of dreams and yearning for lost innocence. And as he penetrates to the center of the *hortus conclusus*, it is as if he returns to the womb; he masters the labyrinth of enclosed intimacy which is the nature of the *Ewig-Weibliche* and, for man, the only path to fulfillment. As for the Rose, it is the dominant image of the poem. Flowers (the rose or the lily in the West, the lotus blossom in the East) contain qualities men dream of finding in their mates: youth, beauty, freshness, purity; and the shape of the blossom arouses sensuous, erotic feelings. The woman and the rose both live for but a short space; both are evanescent and subject to decay; and as the rose is surrounded by thorns, resists conquest, the lady is an ambiguous love-object embodying joy and misery, desire and repulsion. The woman-flower archetype is one of the richest in world literature, manifest in Sappho, Catullus, Horace, Ovid, Ausonius, Poliziano, Garcilaso, Ronsard, d'Aubigné, Malherbe, Goethe, Heine, Apollinaire, Jouve, and Aragon, as well as in medieval allegory.

The Fountain of Narcissus provides an aura of classical myth. It is true, Guillaume de Lorris minimizes the fatalistic, tragic quality of Ovid's story, drawing from it the trivial moral that ladies ought to yield to their suitors, lest they be punished the way Narcissus was. However, as *la Fontaine d'Amors* brought death to Ovid's hero, here it is the occasion for the Narrator's falling into the nets and traps of Amor:

> car Cupido, li filz Venus ...
> fist ses laz environ tendre
> et ses engins i mist por prendre
> demoiseilles et demoisiaus,
> qu'Amors si ne velt autre oisiaus ...
> que maintenant ou laz cheï
> qui maint home a pris et traï.   (1586, 1589–92, 1611–12)

Also designated as 'li miroërs perilleus' (1569), containing 'cristaus merveilleus' (1547), it recalls that other Fountain Perilous, where Yvain worked out his destiny. Thus the fountain appears as a magic, numinous spot redolent with the supernatural, open to adventures. Bachelard refers to the Narcissus Complex in connection with the imagery of fresh water, which he assimilates both to a mirror and to the eyes, envisaging it thus as a vehicle for knowledge of the self and of the cosmos. Indeed, in *Le Roman de la Rose* these magic crystals, a synthesis of light and water, help the lover to know his beloved and himself, and as a result of active meditation on her, to perceive himself and the world (the rest of the garden) through her eyes. They reflect a superior world and, as a *speculum*, contain or reveal wisdom, an esoteric doctrine that the Narrator attains through a long initiation process including rites of passage. However, the fountain, image of Nature's renewal through water, is a symbol of birth as well as of knowledge, of the feminine element (cold and moist), source of life, instrument of nourishment and baptism, healing and purification. As such, it is as much a feminine image as the rose, and, along with the rose, contributes to harmony, while also serving to represent psychic forces and the unconscious, a bursting forth of life and mystery in the hearts of young people.

While the Narrator is gazing into Narcissus's fountain, the God of Love stalks him unseen. Then, wounded by five arrows, the youth surrenders, awarding the mastery of his heart to Amor:

> Ja savez vos de verité
> que mon cuer m'avez si toloit

et si pris que, s'il bien vouloit,
ne puet il fere rien por moi,
se ce n'estoit par vostre ostroi.
Li cuers est vostres, non pas miens,
car il covient, soit maus soit biens,
que il face vostre pleisir,
nus ne vos en puet desaisir.    (1978–86)

From this moment on, in the tradition of the *Amores* and the *Ars Amatoria*, the Narrator is depicted as a *miles Amoris*, a soldier in Love's army, and the remainder of the *Roman* tells of a struggle between forces favorable to his suit and those against it. Venus's torch and Danger's club – these images underscore the martial quality of Guillaume's psychomachia. In Bachelardian terms, Jalousie's castle is constructed from hard earth of the will, a masculine rock that stands in opposition to the maternal, feminine landscape of the outer garden. It is also true, I believe, that the assault on a fortress is a fundamental image of love-conquest. The war of the sexes, courtship conceived as a battle between man the aggressor and woman the defender, even the physical act of intercourse depicted as the pricking of a lance or the cutting of a sword – these are to be found in Ovid and in any number of writers on love, including the troubadours. Furthermore, as I said with reference to *Huon de Bordeaux*, poets often associate triumph in love and in war, deem conquest of a woman and city to be hallmarks of the active life, evidence that the hero deserves a place in the community. For without a city a youth cannot participate fully in martial life; without a woman he cannot partake of the social life. In *Le Roman de la Rose* the Narrator, if and when he triumphs, will obtain the Rose and her castle, and he cannot win one without the other.

Within the world is to be found a wall, within the wall a garden, within the garden a fountain, and within the fountain circular crystals. Near the fountain lies a rose-patch and within the rose-patch a rose or, encompassing it, a fortress, within the fortress a keep, within the keep Bel Accueil. The Narrator penetrates from without to within, from outside to inside, living with greater and greater intensity. He gives himself utterly to a quest which leads through a labyrinth to the sacred place, the *Rosa rosae*, the goal for Every Lover, a paradise surrounded by magical defenses and repellent guards, containing warmth, intimacy, festivity, song, and dance. The woman is the garden, and the garden a woman; she, circle and center of the circle, in this quasi-anagogical realm, can only be known and enjoyed from within.

In *Le Roman de la Rose* the Narrator finds himself in a décor of pathetic fallacy, where the external world gives expression to his inner state. It is a world of perpetual spring, of tenderness and ecstasy, which corresponds perfectly to the troubadour ideal of *jovens*. The lover's dream embodies a nostalgia for a better life, for Eden or a lost Golden Age and, in the form of wish-fulfillment, consecrates his return to innocence, idyllic peace, and the green world. And it reflects a spiritual journey, his initiation into a state of grace, of absolute beauty. The first and last impression the reader takes away from Guillaume's *Roman* is an esthetic vision – of song, harmony, brightness, light, and truly 'beautiful people' dancing in the sun. The God of Love chooses a lady:

> cele dame avoit non Biautez ...
> el ne fu oscure ne brune,
> mes reluisant come la lune
> envers qui les autres estoilles
> resemblent petites chandailles.
> Tendre ot la char come rosee ...   (992, 995–9)

She, more than all others, incarnates the Garden of Delight.

Guillaume de Lorris's section of *Le Roman de la Rose* is a complex, ambiguous work of art. You will not find in it the shadowy or artificial abstractions, the moral platitudes some readers presume to be typical of allegory. Although Guillaume is eager to teach us, the didactic element is most subtle, and enriches rather than impoverishes the fabric of his poem. The characters represent moral identities, but they have a life of their own; they are made 'real,' embodied in 'real people,' and at the same time partake of the aura of mythological gods and universal archetypes. The effect is created by an extraordinarily delicate balance of tensions, a synthesis of convention and human experience, of instinct and conscience, of psychology and symbolism, of the everyday and the universal, of the intellectual and the numinous. *Le Roman de la Rose* is an *Ars amandi*, the story of a love affair, a psychological case study of two individuals, a poem of seduction, a confession, and an evocation of cosmic forces and eternal, universal beauty. We observe love's progress in the Narrator, in the story of his growing up, as he progresses from spectator or listener to actor, and as the poem evolves from tableau to mask to dance to drama. Guillaume tells of the youth's slow but sure initiation into the community, his mastery of the ritual of courtly living, of love as art and as social gesture. The mood is one of joy yet also of tender melancholy, the poetry of *jovens* written by one who is perhaps no longer young. Hence the juxtaposition of credulity and naïve astonishment, on the one hand, and refined sophistication on the other; hence the nostalgic yearning for the green world of lost happiness, for the Eternal Woman.

The romances of Chrétien de Troyes bear witness to a crisis in feudal society and represent an effort to resolve the crisis by creating a utopian world of chivalry. Two generations later the Arthurian solution was recognized to be a failure. People saw that it was no longer relevant to contemporary life. Once again the public turned away from reality (a literary reality, this time) in favor of new utopias. The writers of the time offered them two such worlds of wish-fulfillment. One is the quest for the Holy Grail, the other the inner life of a youth and his Rose.

In the decade that extends roughly from 1264 to 1274 Jean de Meun brought to a conclusion *Le Roman de la Rose*, the allegory left unfinished some forty years earlier by Guillaume de Lorris. Guillaume's and Jean's combined work has survived to our own century in some three hundred extant manuscripts. *Le Roman* was partially translated by Chaucer, was modernized and edited by Marot; it influenced Dante, Boccaccio, Machaut, Froissart, Chaucer, and a host of lesser writers. It was the subject of the first great French literary quarrel, which occurred at the turn of the fourteenth century. Thus Jean proved to be the first recognized 'author' and 'authority' in French literary history, his work glossed, explicated, quoted, indexed, and quarreled over, that is, treated as if it were a Latin classic. And, praised by Lemaire de Belges, Marot, du Bellay, Ronsard, Baïf, and Pasquier, Jean's text was one of the few masterpieces of the Middle Ages to have been neither condemned nor forgotten at the time of the Renaissance. The total *Roman de la Rose*, containing some 21,750 lines, is historically and perhaps esthetically the most important single work of literature produced during the medieval period.[6]

The length of the final product, 17,722 lines added to Guillaume's text, gives us some idea of Jean's intentions and character, of his scope, willpower, and vision. In reality, of course, Jean de Meun does not merely 'complete' the earlier poem; he grafts a totally original sequel onto it. Indeed, it is more accurate to say, he uses Guillaume's *Roman* as a jumping-off point, a foundation on which he builds his own house. To begin with, the action slows down considerably. The God of Love with his army comes to succor the forlorn Narrator. In a first sequence Faux Semblant and Abstinence Contrainte slay Male Bouche, permitting the Narrator direct contact with Bel Accueil. A pitched battle between the attackers and defenders of the castle ends in a truce. Finally Venus leads a victorious assault, tossing her torch into the sanctuary, so that the Narrator wins the Rose before waking up from his dream. However, by far the greater portion of Jean's *Roman* is devoted to speeches: exhortations from Raison and Ami to the Narrator, Faux Semblant's avowal of his nature to the God of Love, la Vieille's exhortation to Bel Accueil, Nature's confession to Genius, and Genius's pastoral letter to the army. Jean's philosophy, art, and vision of the world are totally different from Guillaume's. His speeches are longer, the style more varied (more sublime on the one hand, more earthy on the other). Jean is concerned with 'problems' – ethics, economics, cosmology, astrology, optics, alchemy, the University – foreign to Guillaume's universe. The latter's delicate allegories give way to virulent satire and sublime invective, his sentimentality to burning sensuous instinct and high intellectual wit. As a result, the combined *Roman de la Rose* is unique in world literature. To find its equivalent one would have to imagine Rabelais expropriating Charles d'Orléans's *Ballades* for *Gargantua et Pantagruel*, Saint-Simon grafting his *Mémoires* onto *Le Songe de Vaux*, or Hugo completing Chénier's *Bucoliques* with *La Légende des Siècles*.

Compared to his predecessor, Jean de Meun is a master of truculent vulgar speech, material detail, and picaresque naturalism. Throughout *Le Roman de la Rose* he shifts our perspective from top to bottom, from rose petals to what is underneath, to what Bakhtin, referring to Rabelais, calls the material bodily lower stratum.[7] A generation before Dante, Jean de Meun, along with his contemporary Adam de la Halle, juxtaposes *sermo gravis* and *sermo humilis*. Scenes, images, and speech at one time reserved to the *fabliau* are included here in a serious work of art, next to the sublime. The Jealous Husband and la Vieille walk side by side with Dame Raison and Dame Nature. The 'communities' of Chaucer and Juan Ruiz are already present in Jean de Meun's rose garden.

The presence of the Jealous Husband and la Vieille underscores the role of money in the erotic life. Richesse, a virtue in Guillaume de Lorris, is now condemned as a vice. However, whereas Guillaume praised riches and then more or less forgot about them, Jean de Meun admits their importance in the real world. Richesse declines to help the Narrator in his quest, but not before the latter has attempted to take the path of Trop Donner. Furthermore, Ami urges the youth to bribe the Rose's defenders. There was no money in the Golden Age, he says, but since that time we have both gold and kings; nowadays, ladies listen to the jingle of coin, not to the roll of fine verses. The Jealous Husband is a miser, who chastises his wife as much for spending his earnings as for deceiving him, and he is convinced that her lovers sniff around his doorstep for her gold as well as for her body.

Faux Semblant is one of a band of evil friars, who amass ill-gotten wealth by begging; they take false vows of poverty, giving spiritual succor only to the rich, who succor them in turn. And la Vieille urges Bel Accueil to prostitute himself, to 'give himself' only to rich men for money and to fleece his lovers and their families as well.

The Jealous Husband regards his wife as a thing, as property to be enjoyed and defended against all comers. So, too, for Ami and La Vieille the opposite sex is an object to be purchased, bartered, or exchanged for money or for other commodities. The Narrator also thinks of the Rose only as a sex-object; and when telling the story of her defloration, he discourses on his other conquests, contrasting the relative merits of young and old roses.

Indeed, the process of reification is symbolized by Jean de Meun's transformation of the woman-rose into a piece of lifeless architecture (the sanctuary) which the Narrator pries open with his pilgrim's staff. In the end he refers to his conquests in gastronomic terms (the assorted courses of a meal) or as wide and narrow roads that constitute female geography. In certain *chansons de geste*, *Raoul de Cambrai* and *Garin le Lorrain*, the feudal crisis of the twelfth-century French nobility was expressed in concrete terms. Here, a century later, the superstructure of *Le Roman de la Rose* reflects a quite different infrastructure. The old concerns for land and feudal honor no longer exist. Jean de Meun depicts a universe in which tensions are partly of economic origin, and gold plays an overt role. His view of socio-economic conditions is much more 'progressive' than is that of *Le Jeu de Robin et Marion*, for example, or *La Châtelaine de Vergi*.[8] In sum, Jean evokes a world populated by different social classes, all of whom are motivated by the same forces: lust for flesh and for money. These two lusts are conceived in identical terms. And both men and women are victims of the process of reification to which the entire society is subjected. It also goes without saying that Jean does not remain impassive before this state of affairs. In his own voice, in the voice of his characters, he deplores the fall of the Golden Age because of possession and exchange; he castigates a way of life in which property, the profit motive, and the hoarding of riches give men *mestrise*, in which things take precedence over persons.

Even more striking, perhaps, is the role the author ascribes to manipulation and duplicity. To cite the most illustrious example, Faux Semblant is the archetype of duplicity, and his presence at the center of the romance is evidence of Jean de Meun's concern for this facet of the human condition. He delivers a diatribe against the hypocrisy of the friars, who are compared to Isengrin in the *Roman de Renard* and to the scriptural wolf in sheep's clothing. Since Faux Semblant is the most honest of Jean de Meun's tricksters, because of his virulent condemnation of cheating, he is inconsistent with his given nature and thus commits a further act of deception. Then, after the speech is over, he returns to a position of integrity, that is, non-integrity, and tricks Male Bouche. Although Male Bouche is warned by Abstinence Contrainte not to judge people (the Narrator) by appearances only, he continues to do so – that is, to accept Faux Semblant's and Abstinence Contrainte's appearance: their disguise as pilgrims! His naïveté leads to quick death. Thus the most communicative creature in Jean's poem slays the figural representation of communication: Male Bouche.

And, for all their proclamations of distaste, the Narrator and the God of Love welcome Faux Semblant, realizing that his is a necessary force on their side in the war of the sexes.

Communication serves two purposes: to instruct, and to trick. All the world's people can be divided into two classes: knaves and fools, masters and slaves, the deceivers and the deceived. Ami, the Jealous Husband, la Vieille, Faux Semblant, even Raison, seek to be masters, not slaves, to exploit rather than to be exploited. Each is an embodiment of will-to-power, his every word and action directed toward triumphing over the Other. The fact that some of them fail – that the Jealous Husband is manipulated in turn, that la Vieille is fleeced by one man even more resourceful than herself – in no way modifies the situation. In this world of lust and money, people live only to pluck and be plucked, the Other is always an object, and the individual's prime concern becomes not to be treated like an object in turn.

Finally, the human beings who inhabit Jean's world create illusion by hiding behind masks: they disguise themselves. Faux Semblant dresses as a pilgrim, and Abstinence Contrainte as a Béguine, in order to deceive Male Bouche. Genius plays the role of bishop to exhort Love's army. And the Narrator becomes a Pilgrim when he is about to force the Rose's sanctuary. La Vieille advises a whole repertory of disguises – changes in dress and the use of cosmetics – to seduce men. The Jealous Husband points out that clothes ought to contribute to a woman's modesty, but such is not the case with his wife; he really prefers her naked in bed!

> Mes, por le filz seinte Marie,
> que me vaut ceste cointerie,
> cele robe couteuse et chiere ... ?
> Que me fet ele de profit?
> Conbien qu'el aus autres profit,
> a moi ne fet ele for nuire;
> car quant me veill a vos deduire,
> je la treuve si encombreuse,
> si grevaigne et si ennuieuse
> que je n'en puis a chief venir ...    (8813–15, 8821–27)

Clothes do not make the monk, says Faux Semblant, and the Jealous Husband declares that they are silk and flowers on top of manure (8877–83). Yet, between a clothed wife and a naked one, which is reality and which is illusion? Pygmalion is perhaps wiser than the Husband when he dresses up his statue, creating an illusion later transformed into reality. It is not easy for people to distinguish appearance from truth, the mask from flesh, the literal bark from an allegorical kernel. Jean's characters discover this, and so do his readers.

Although the author does not personally favor dissimulation, violence, and evil, he tells us that they are part of the human condition and that we must learn to cope with them. Throughout the *Roman* he urges the Narrator and his public to be lucid, to go beyond appearances and seek the truth. Thus he holds up to scrutiny commonly accepted ideas about love, money, fortune, the kingship, dreams, alchemy, and clerical celibacy. Raison, Nature, Genius, Ami, la Vieille, even Faux Semblant speak to open our eyes and rip aside the mask of falsehood.

Jean de Meun favors light, not darkness – he wants us to raise up the mask, to open the garden, and to peel off clothes and petals, or at least to unblind ourselves to the fact that masks exist and are as real as the faces they cover. Thus, although some mirrors distort the truth (such as Guillaume de Lorris's *miroërs perilleus*), others offer an image of, and the way of arriving at, truth.[9] Jean de Meun's *Roman de la Rose* is, itself, a *miroër aus Amoreus*, a *speculum* which not only contains a vast amount of information about the cosmos but also, anticipating a much later notion of enlightenment, tells us how to seek truth and avoid appearance and illusion.

At the very beginning of Jean's section of the *Roman* we find the Narrator reduced to despair, ready to abandon the rose quest, faithful to the God of Love only out of a sense of honor, all because he is a prisoner of the false, artificial conventions of *fin' amor*. By repressing what the author considers to be natural human responses, by willfully adhering to a false code of chastity and gentility when he truly desires to penetrate into the Rose's sanctuary, the young man proves himself to be acting in Sartrean bad faith. No less inauthentic are Raison, who attacks love and then asks the Narrator to be her lover, and the Jealous Husband, who repudiates the slavery of marriage and recalls with longing the freedom of his celibate state when what he really wants is to render his wife a slave, himself the master, within marriage. The Husband, in particular, is incapable of facing reality, of forming any sort of relationship with a woman, for he never listens to her or even is aware of her side of the story. In contrast, however, by the end of the romance the Narrator liberates himself. He joins those in Love's army who are lucid, open to reality, and capable of dealing with it, sufficiently adaptable to cope with life's problems. He recognizes his lustful nature and commits himself to satisfying it. Thus he attains to a measure of freedom and participation in the vital forces of the universe. He becomes a master not a slave, a free man not a prisoner, an adult not a boy. Having discovered the reality of life, he is able to use deceit for his purposes, not be used by it.

These disparities between appearance and reality, between a person's ideals and his acts, can be expressed in either the tragic or the comic mode. Jean de Meun chooses the world of comedy. Humorous elements crop up in the most unexpected places; for example, in Reason's oh-so-serious lecture to the Narrator.[10] And various characters in the *Roman* adhere to a tradition of archetypes that has flourished in Western literature from Menander to Feydeau.

The faithful friend is not usually a comic figure in medieval letters, though he may indeed be so; witness Gériaume (*Huon de Bordeaux*), the Lion (*Yvain*), and Gawain and Galehaut in certain sections of the *Lancelot-Grail Cycle*. In *Le Roman de la Rose*, Ami plays the role of *dolosus servus*, rendered immortal by Plautus, Terence, and, later, Molière. The tactics of seduction he counsels are funny in themselves (as was the case for Ovid), especially when we consider that Ami claims to be a faithful disciple of the God of Love, whose teachings, however, he distorts, interpreting them for his own purposes. We also find in him the humorous juxtaposition of high-sounding phrases and low sentiments. Although he counsels the Narrator to suffer patiently his beloved's faults, indeed chastises the Jealous Husband for misogyny, Ami also insults ladies. He condemns husbands for trying to hold on to their wives, indeed blasts monogamy generally, but then, in the tradition of the *Ars Amatoria*, 2: 13: 'nec minor est virtus, quam quaerere, parta tueri,' gives the Narrator advice on how to retain his Rose after she has yielded to him. And he praises the *tempus aureum* while urging the Narrator to use every trick in the trade practiced since.

The Jealous Husband also corresponds as closely to a character-type in New Comedy as to his predecessors in courtly lyric and romance, not to speak of *fabliau*: the *senex iratus*, an old husband or father, who impedes the young hero in his quest for the girl. Jean's *alazon* has the same fixations as analogous figures in Plautus or Terence: jealousy and avarice, an obsessive desire to possess money and women. In an extraordinarily Bergsonian performance, he proclaims over and over again his wife's unchastity, her frivolousness, and her prodigality. Hence his extreme statements, that all women are whores, that a good one is rarer than a phoenix or a white crow. Hence his incapacity to separate the significant from the trivial, when he chastises his wife as much for putting a new dress into her wardrobe as for bringing a new lover into her bed. This worthy repeatedly, mechanically berates the lady, his tirades serving only one purpose – to goad her on to do the very thing he abhors: spend more money and take more lovers.

La Vieille partakes of still another type dating back to Antiquity, the *vetula* or old whore who acts as go-between, a character immortalized by Ovid in the *Amores*, *Ars Amatoria*, and the *Remedia Amoris*. She also borrows traits from the old servant or duenna in medieval Latin elegiac comedy, early *fabliaux*, the *Eneas*, *Eracle*, and *Cligès*. Later embodiments of the archetype are to be found especially in Spanish literature, in *El Libro de buen amor*, *La Celestina*, and Lope de Vega's *Dorotea*. Like the Jealous Husband, la Vieille goes to extremes, driven by obsessions comparable to his: money, material comfort, and vengeance. It is humorous when an ignorant woman of the people declares herself a *doctor amoris* and presumes to lecture the young; it is even more comic when she cites classical sources and uses scholastic reasoning to make her points. (La Vieille's speech is by no means unbelievable, however; her many years of intimacy with the clergy no doubt sufficed to provide her with a patina of culture.) Finally, like the others, the bawd makes us laugh because of her contradictions, because, so committed to the defense of woman, she makes anti-feminist statements and, unable to live up to her own precepts, she has succumbed to an exploiting male.

Nature manifests humorous traits presumed typical of woman, which appear more ridiculous still in a numinous, semi-divine allegorical personification. Genius consoles her with a misogynistic tirade, accusing females of becoming easily upset, of losing their tempers, and of talking too much; then he assures Nature that his remarks do not concern her. However, the comedy of the situation derives from the fact that his diatribe does indeed apply directly to her. Her oft-expressed fury at mankind, her repeated fits of anger, her tears, the fact that though she has been given no leave to stop working she steps out of the forge, her hands free, to protest at length about her work – these are perfect examples of Bergsonian rigidity. Furthermore, a distraught, melancholy hypochondriac, Nature complains and complains and complains, for almost three thousand lines. Later, she digresses to say she won't tell about dreams and visions, for it would take too long; then she tells it all.

If, however, on the one hand, Jean de Meun lashes out at his characters, proclaiming their foibles without mercy, he also, on the other, depicts them with such gusto and breathes the breath of life into them with such joy that we cannot help being overawed by them and sympathizing with them too. The Jealous Husband is a fool, yet we are carried along by his rhetoric; although la Vieille is a knave, we respect her courage, persistence, and indomitable will to power. How can we resist these Faux Semblant, these Renard the Foxes, so intelligent and always victorious? Humanity breaks through the mask. We have the right to admire and even love such magnificent satirical types, vibrant with life and so true to the human condition.

The common distinction between comedy and satire, between love and hatred, between Horace and Juvenal, is misplaced when we read works like *Le Roman de Renard* and *Le Roman de la Rose*. Although Jean sets forth a doctrine, indeed an ideology, in my opinion his ultimate purpose is to evoke a comic world. He laughs at everyone and everything, at the

ineptness, foolishness, cruelty, stupidity, and ruse that make up our lives.
He also tells a story in which, owing to quick wit, vitality, and an uncon-
querable will-to-power, the army of Eros (made up of comic tricksters)
triumphs over the old world of opposition. Defiant instinct, celebration, the
victory of youth and of man's healthy animal nature are affirmed in an
erotically happy ending in which a festive, almost cosmic transformation of
society takes place.

To create this comic world requires a narrative technique, a control of
voice and point of view quite different from that employed by earlier
writers, including Guillaume de Lorris.[11] The 'I' of Guillaume's section of
Le Roman de la Rose is a dramatized, active participant in the story, a
reliable commentator who succeeds in moulding our beliefs. We sympathize
with him because the story is filtered uniquely through his consciousness,
because he has full control over the inside vision, because his is the central
intelligence and, except for the God of Love, the only intelligence capable
of establishing norms by which to judge the other characters.

In Jean's portion of the romance, Amor informs his troops that the
young man whom they have come to support is Guillaume de Lorris, a loyal
servant of Eros, who will begin Le Roman de la Rose but will leave it
incomplete, to be taken up more than forty years later by Jean de Meun:

> Puis vendra Johans Chopinel,
> au cuer jolif, au cors inel,
> qui nestra seur Laire a Meün,
> qui a saoul et a geün
> me servira toute sa vie,
> sanz avarice et sanz envie,
> et sera si tres sages hon
> qu'il n'avra cure de Reson,
> qui mes oignemenz het et blasme ...
> Cist avra le romanz si chier
> qu'il le voudra tout parfenir,
> se tens et leus l'en peut venir,
> car quant Guillaumes cessera,
> Jehans le continuera,
> enprés sa mort, que je ne mante,
> anz trespassez plus de .XL. ...    (10535–43, 10554–60)

And the God of Love urges that Lucina preside over this great poet's
birth, and Jupiter over his upbringing. Needless to say, it is physically
impossible that Guillaume de Lorris dreamed of his own death and of the
book he had not yet conceived of writing being continued by someone else;

it is no less impossible that Jean could have discovered the outcome of Guillaume's dream forty years after the latter's demise. On the contrary, Amor is fully conscious that he and his army are characters in a book, and that the events they 'live' occur years before the author's birth. Thus, in an extraordinarily modern use of point of view, Jean undermines with comic brio the privileged voice of Guillaume's I-Narrator and establishes distance between himself (as implied author) and that personage. He also willfully undermines the illusion of reality, the temporary suspension of disbelief, which is the hallmark of traditional mimetic fiction. The Narrator is still an active agent in the story, and his participation contributes drama and immediacy, as in all first-person tales. But, since he lacks the author's support, we are expected neither to identify with him nor to espouse his views. He is reliable enough as a Narrator (*erzählendes Ich*), but not at all as a character (*erlebendes Ich*). He tells the story accurately but does not control our judgment or mould our beliefs. We see beyond him (as a character), gain insights into the plot and the doctrinal strife that he consciously does not have. Furthermore, a host of other characters deliver speeches which, although filtered through the Narrator's consciousness and recounted to us as they were purportedly told to him, are so long that we forget the filtering process and imagine that the Jealous Husband, Faux Semblant, or Genius addresses us directly. For certain episodes which occur during the protagonist's absence (la Vieille's lecture to Bel Accueil, Nature's confession to Genius), the presence of the original I-narrator is so unobtrusive that we can fall into the illusion that he is or has become an objective, omniscient third person. Narrative voice and point of view vary continually. Jean de Meun's *Roman* can be considered an excellent early example of polymodality: a story told by an I-narrator, who is at various times hero, witness, or quasi-omniscient outsider (mock-author), and also delegated to a series of secondary I-narrators, sometimes focalized through their consciousnesses, sometimes not. Yet the poem contains so much dialogue that no real internal focalization is possible. In fact, these insertions, these delegated voices, provide such immediacy and drama that the protagonist's own point of view can appear objective, indeed omniscient, in contrast. Furthermore, since each of the other narrators speaks in his own voice, and with equal vehemence and authority, we cannot assume that Jean de Meun necessarily agrees with any one over the others. Indeed, if by chance we have yielded to the rhetoric, he creates distance by undermining them once their speeches are over. As in real life, no commentator leads us by the hand through *Le Roman de la Rose*, although the reader eventually knows more than any of the characters, including the Narrator (as lover). Jean fails neither to establish norms nor to affirm his own beliefs, but he does so indirectly, by showing his 'villains' to be even more ridiculous than his 'heroes.' It is up to the reader to judge each character in turn, as he involuntarily, unconsciously reveals his own shortcomings, blatantly holds forth logical inconsistencies, and sophistically misinterprets the very classical *auctores* he cites so badly. It is his job to analyze facts and motivations, cause and effect, mind and rhetoric, whether he wants to or not.

These shifts in perspective, the presence of multiple points of view, and the fact that each character speaks in his own person, expressing his own opinions, make it difficult for the reader to identify Jean de Meun's stand on any given issue. The 'ideological content' of *Le Roman de la Rose* is a more complex matter than generally realized.[12]

Are we then to conclude that no dominant idea pervades the work, aside from Jean's quest for lucidity and truth, his distaste for exploitation, his horror of romantic masks? This, in my opinion, is not the case.[13] The God of Love refers to Jean's book as the *Miroër aus Amoreus* (10621), a text that continues Guillaume de Lorris's '*Romanz de la Rose*, / ou l'art d'Amors est tote enclose' (37–8). Romance has been metamorphosed into a *speculum*! Although Jean has a very different notion of love from Guillaume, he nonetheless writes an *Ars amandi* in his own way.

It can be maintained that every line of the *Roman* refers directly or indirectly to love, taken in its broadest sense. Jean de Meun's text expounds on all facets of the subject – good longing (for sex and reproduction; also friendship, justice, humanity, reason, and God) and bad passions (for Fortune and money; also hypocrisy, clerical celibacy, and the insincere affection of false friends). He treats the *theoretica* (Amor, Nature, Genius) and the *practica* (Ami, Faux Semblant, la Vieille) of his science. All love, human and divine, is contained in the *Roman*.

Although in this grand *conflictus*, this *disputatio amoris*, each character disagrees with the others and seeks to refute their views, it is possible to find one common ground on which all or most of them can agree. All favor some kind of sexual intercourse; all but Ami and la Vieille favor it for the specific purpose of reproduction, love considered not as an end in itself but a means to an end, the preservation of the race. Nature, who assumes the role of *vicaria Dei*, and her priest, Genius, a Dionysian fertility-figure, both derived from Alan of Lille's *De planctu Naturae*, proclaim a doctrine of plenitude, 'la diffinitive santance' (19474) that insists upon the constant, perpetual regeneration of the species. In the words of Scripture, 'Crescite, et multiplicamini, et replete terram' (Genesis 1:28). Then argument gives way to action, being to becoming. The Narrator not only deflowers his Rose, the first of many such acts with her and with other flowers, young and old; he also becomes obscene, learns to accept the scurrilousness he had earlier refused in his dialogue with Raison. Furthermore, he scatters pollen inside the petals, mixing the 'seeds' in such a way that they cannot be parted, and the bud is stretched and widened:

> A la parfin, tant vos an di,
> un po de greine i espandi,
> quant j'oi le bouton elloichié ...
> Si fis lors si meller les greines
> qu'el se desmellassent a peines,
> si que tout le boutonet tandre
> an fis ellargir et estandre.    (21689–91, 21697–700)

This may be a way of saying, *allegorice*, that the Narrator answers the call of Nature by impregnating the Rose, that, having lost his own virginity, he also becomes a father. At the beginning of the courtship Faux Semblant and Abstinence Contrainte were needed to further the youth's campaign, but in the end Genius's words and Venus's torch suffice. Nature wins, to the satisfaction of the Narrator and, presumably, also of Jean de Meun and his readers. This Human Comedy ends as comedies must, in joy and laughter, with the couple packed off to bed.[14]

The specifically pastoral aspect of Guillaume's *Roman* (innocence, goodness, the *hortus deliciarum*) is either repudiated or projected onto the Golden Age in the past or the Park of the Lamb in the future, the latter a Christian bucolic setting reserved ironically for active reproducers. However, other aspects of the classical idyll, of Ovidian rather than Virgilian flavor, abide with Jean: the free irresponsibility of amorous pleasure (Tasso's 'S'ei piace, ei lice') and the critical, judgmental quality of political pastoral. Thus Jean's message of fecundity is allied to pleasure in sex and joins his unmasking of manipulation, lordship, inauthenticity, and financial exploitation. Christian asceticism inhibits freedom, desire, and the dynamic struggle against extinction of the race. Love and life in nature are good; non-love and non-life, inflicted on us by historical institutions, are evil. Jean's ideal is to be free, to live one's existence with fervid authenticity, in contrast to the slavery and alienation men bring onto their fellows when they disobey the precepts of Nature. Sovereignty is as much an issue as desire, and the solution to both is liberty in joy.

Oiseuse was Guillaume de Lorris's gatekeeper. In Jean de Meun's section, she is replaced, so to speak, by Nature, who labors incessantly, running a never-ending race with Death. She embodies an ideal of activity that contrasts with Guillaume's static Garden of Delight. In his turn Genius urges the soldiers in Amor's host to work at it:

Saiez es euvres naturex
plus vistes que nus escurex
et plus legiers et plus movanz
que ne peut estre oiseaus ou vanz! ...
Remuez vos, tripez, sailliez,
ne vos lessiez pas refredir
par trop voz mambres antedir!
Metez touz voz ostiz en euvre:
assez s'eschaufe qui bien euvre.
   Arez, por Dieu, baron, arez,
et voz lignages reparez.   (19659–62, 19666–72)

Love as ecstasy gives way to love in action, the perfection of an eternal spring to a universe in perpetual creation – in other words, being to becoming. We can thus understand Jean's condemnation of lazy, shiftless friars, and his contrast of the dynamism of the God of Love's army outside the castle to the static, lifeless figures who defend chastity within.

   The poet's vision is elaborated through a pattern of archetypal imagery. Nature reproduces the species by hammering out individuals in her forge. Genius urges the host to make love in terms of phallic metaphor: they are to hammer on anvils, plow fields, and scrape their quills on parchment. These soldiers swear in turn their fealty on 'relics,' their arrows, and other pointed, cutting implements, whereupon the Narrator breaks into the 'sanctuary' with his pilgrim's staff. Such blatantly Freudian motifs underscore Jean de Meun's view that the reproductive organs were created by God for the most important function in the universe. No less masculine is the image of the torch: the soldiers swear on torches as well as on the arrows, and it is by tossing her firebrand into the fortress, by setting it aflame, that Venus brings victory. This is not the choleric, Satanic fire of *Raoul de Cambrai*, but, in Jean de Meun's cult of fecundity, an analogue to the Holy Spirit, become a weapon for the secular Prometheus. An image of sexual creation, its spark symbolizes the male seed, striking out against the feminine images of fountain, *hortus conclusus*, and enclosed castle. From this torch comes the light that pierces the darkness of courtly obscurantism, that enlightens a garden immune to the rays of the sun. Nature and Venus both assume masculine characteristics, as if the notion of sexual and intellectual liberation forms part of a male world view. Thus can be explained Jean's elaboration of the images of the hunt and of the siege, the assault on a fortress, whereby Guillaume de Lorris's *bellum intestinum* is transformed into a battle of cosmic proportions. The epic quality of Jean's *Roman* is one of its most notable features, in the line of Virgil, Ovid, Bernard Sylvester, and Alan of Lille – and as a parody and pastiche of *chan-*

*son de geste.* The war of the sexes is one of Jean's basic motifs, both as reality and as archetype: he has created in la Vieille the most notable devouring, castrating woman in medieval French letters. Finally, even though Guillaume's garden of delight has more or less disappeared from Jean de Meun's poem, the Rose remains. On the one hand, as in Guillaume de Lorris it is an image of Nature's bounty and of God's benevolence, of the good life. But Jean also interprets it blatantly as the female sexual organ, literally and figuratively deflowered by the Narrator's purse and staff.

Jean de Meun's world, partially inherited from Guillaume de Lorris, is one of enclosed, compartmentalized space: the Rose in her sanctuary, Bel Accueil in la Vieille's tower, Male Bouche and the others guarding the exits, Nature and Genius holding a dialogue indoors in her chapel, Fortune's island and the Garden of the Lamb separated by barriers from our direct purview. However, in the course of the poem the walls are broken in, enclosed space opened, the sanctuary door shattered. The end of the *Roman* is a humorous yet profound representation of the sexual act; male and female libido (the God of Love and Venus) unite to help fecundity triumph. In this wish-fulfillment world Amor, Ami, Faux Semblant, la Vieille, Nature, and Genius are all manifestations of the id. Only Raison embodies the restraining force of the superego, and she is vanquished. Although one Terrible Mother, one castrating shrew (la Vieille) does appear, she embodies a triumphantly aggressive pleasure principle and sides with the young against their obstructive society. The Father-enemy does not exist at all or appears only as a shadowy, ridiculous *gilos*, playing no active role in the allegory. The superego figures are females, whereas the male authorities, Amor and Genius, take the Narrator's side. Those who decline to reproduce are threatened with castration, a fate which indeed overcomes Adonis, Abelard, Origen, and the Greek god Saturn, from whose *coilles* Venus is born. And when Faux Semblant cuts out Male Bouche's tongue, he too pays the price for opposing the vital force of the universe.

Although, on a surface level, the youth's psychomachia is less an ecstatic initiation, a rite of passage, than in Guillaume de Lorris, the metaphysics of plenitude, the Dionysian cosmos, the pansexualism that permeate Jean's universe provide an aura no less redolent of the Mysteries. In both authors the Narrator dreams, undergoes ordeals, and is instructed by semi-divine guides. However, in Jean alone he succeeds totally, is initiated and reborn and, in the end, becomes an adult and a father. Guillaume de Lorris had Amor reveal the Ten Commandments of Love to the Narrator in a sacred space much as Jehovah delivers the Tables of the Law to Moses. However, Jean de Meun carries religious pastiche much farther. The entire army is given the call as apostles to preach the good word and evangelize the world. Faux Semblant is a friar, and Genius an ordained priest; both hear confession, the latter excommunicates and delivers a pastoral letter. The Narrator adores at a shrine, then his pilgrim's staff pries open the sanctuary door, and, with his account of the action, Raison's metaphor is taken seriously: *coilles*, *viz*, and *con* are in fact transformed into sacred relics, and from the contact of these entities a miracle will burst forth, the birth of a child and the symbolic regeneration of the race. The *iter salutis* and *via stricta* of Christian salvation are pastiched with a quite different narrow passage, for the rose of a girl's virginity to be deflowered has replaced the *flos florum* of the Virgin Mary, and the flames and dove of 'sainte Venus' (10797) the Holy Spirit of God. Of course, Jean's 'blasphemy' is delivered in good humor, is one among many comic devices in his arsenal. Yet the 'new religion,' this natural mysticism, for all its scholastic foundations and its profound differences from Guillaume's, is, like *fin' amor*, a doctrine not entirely compatible with Albertus Magnus and Thomas Aquinas, not to speak of the geniune Christian mysticism of Bernard of Clairvaux and Bonaventura. Alongside them Jean has his own priests, chaplains, dogmas, relics, and sacred army of *milites crucis*.

One aspect of Jean's comic vision, and of his philosophy of plenitude, is a relative denigration of the intellectual and artistic pursuits that the Goddess Raison embodies. Thus, early in his career, the Narrator declines her invitation to gloss the poets: he will put aside studies until after he has conquered the Rose! And just before the conquest an older, wiser Narrator proclaims joyfully that he prefers his sexual organs to his harp and guitar. On the other hand, since several times in the *Roman* Jean insists that he as author and the lover-narrator are not identical personages, he invites us to view with a more critical eye what the latter does and says, including the remarks cited above. After all, the *Roman* is a story of language; that is, it is made up of long speeches, of discourses replacing action, in which the various characters seek to communicate to each other intellectual truth, in which they often recommend rhetoric or sophistry as an arm in the war of seduction; and Jean's work is conceived not only as a sequel but also a gloss on the text of his predecessor, Guillaume de Lorris. The famous comic dispute between Raison and the Narrator over *coilles*, itself an implied critique of Guillaume's notion of courtesy, concerns the functioning of language, more specifically literary language, in society. Furthermore, even though art is proclaimed inferior to nature and nature given clear precedence over culture, by having Amor designate him as the favorite of Jupiter and prophesy that he will become the finest poet of France, one who will preach love's commandments throughout the kingdom, Jean de Meun exalts himself as an artist, the creator of *Le Roman de la Rose*, and even claims the title of erotic Moses or Joshua. Thus the God of Love delivers a battle-speech on writing! In another passage (15105–272), Jean obtrusively intervenes in the story to defend himself against possible charges of misogyny and anticlericalism. He appears humble enough on the surface ('I only quote the Ancients; I only criticize bad monks'), but, in reality, his apology, a *captatio benevolentiae*, an example of ironic 'affected modesty,' serves as a counter-offensive against his enemies, reaffirming his position as poet and satirist, proclaiming his right to seek the truth and tell it as he sees it. Elsewhere in the *Roman*, Ami, imitating Ovid, regrets the fact that, although in distant times poetry was appreciated, and Ennius and Virgil honored though not of gentle birth, nowadays only money brings respect. Similarly, the God of Love confesses that he broke his arrows in grief over Tibullus's death, and praises Gallus, Catullus, and Ovid, as well as Guillaume de Lorris and, of course, Jean de Meun. Jean is the first narrative writer in a modern vernacular to introduce himself in his own story obtrusively and to emphasize the role of the book, his creation, in the plot. God, creator of the universe, is absent, but not Jean de Meun, creator of the book which imitates Nature, who carries out God's work. The book serves to vindicate the Narrator's career and prove that his waking up is not an end but a beginning. There are only two entirely successful lovers and men in *Le Roman de la Rose*: one is Pygmalion, the creative sculptor, who shapes his loved one with his own hands and from her has a son, Paphus; the other is the Narrator, who first obeys Genius's order to reproduce himself by striking quill on parchment, then, after he wakes up, presumably begins to set down his dream in verse, with quill on parchment. Pygmalion and the Narrator both create new life (the statue, the child, the Rose's offspring) and works of art (the statue, *Le Roman de la Rose*). Chastity in speech and in life are condemned and the guilty ones punished by castration or having their tongues cut out, for artistic creation is a mirror of sexual reproduction. In Jean's world, the father and the artist are one.[15]

Jean de Meun's *Roman de la Rose* is one of the most extraordinary works in the history of French literature, in Northrop Frye's sense of the term an anatomy that contains the best of its age. With it the long poem and the epic spirit enter into a new domain: the world of ideas, of philosophical analysis and dissemination (of learning and militancy).

The creation of such a book marks a major shift in medieval literary taste. However, Jean is by no means a spokesman for the rising middle classes, as some scholars would have us believe. He flails at merchants as much as at courtiers, kings, and friars. His ideology is partly bourgeois, partly clerical, and, of course, he writes for an aristocratic public. This translator of Boethius, Vegetius, Abelard, Giraldus Cambrensis, and Ethelred of Rievaulx, who lived most of his life in the shadow of the Sorbonne, was one of the most cultured men of his day and, in a real sense, the first great philosophical poet in modern letters. More than any other Medieval he contributed to the raft of translations from Latin, to the dissemination of lay wisdom, to the development of a more philosophical, rhetorical use of the vernacular. He also helped vulgarize classical myth and a certain Greco-Roman attitude toward life, death, and nature. More than romancers like Chrétien de Troyes and Guillaume de Lorris, more than encyclopedists like Alard de Cambrai and Brunetto Latini, Jean de Meun embodies that awakening of humanism, that rebirth of interest in classical Antiquity, that joyful lust for life which mark so much of the twelfth and thirteenth centuries and which helped lay the foundation for an independent, viable culture for those people of varied social estate who did not read Latin but wished to learn and to know.

A reader of the Ancients, Jean was nonetheless a *modernus* in his rebellion against authority, his freedom from servile imitation, his exaltation of liberty in all its forms, and his acceptance of life. By repudiating *fin' amor* and clerical celibacy, by questioning the prevalent 'establishment views' of his age, Jean de Meun in his way is a rebel. He is the first serious writer in the vernacular to portray the role of money, exchange, and reification in human affairs. He is the first to make a place for low speech and bodily functions. A 'medieval naturalist,'[16] perhaps a Latin Averroist, he urges common sense and moderation (*soffisance*) in a world marked by ideals of religious or courtly asceticism; he corrodes these ideals, breaks the old patterns, substituting new ones in their place. No wonder then that in 1277 Etienne Tempier, Bishop of Paris, condemned as heresy 219 propositions, some of which are to be found in Andreas Capellanus and in *Le Roman de la Rose*. Jean thus forms one link in another Golden Chain, the chain of writers condemned for their ideas. Indeed, he anticipates Rabelais and Voltaire, those two masters who, along with Jean, believed in God yet even more in mankind. Like them, he attacks infamy, rips off the mask, and defies death. Like them, he creates an eternal Comedy in praise of life and light.

## Chapter Six

# 🏵 GUILLAUME DE MACHAUT

The fourteenth and fifteenth centuries, a period known as the Waning of the Middle Ages,[1] bear witness to a transformation in the world of letters. The literary kinds in vogue in the early period decline or disappear and are replaced by new ones. The most successful genres of the later age are the lyric, the mystery play, the farce, and the *sottie*, in verse; and the chronicle, the short story, and the novel, in prose. Although in the 1300s verse epics and romances continue to be written, they have little value. A century later vast compilations of Carolingian or Arthurian material, which correspond to *Le Morte Darthur* in England, are composed, but exclusively in prose. As it turns out, the tradition of *Le Roman de la Rose* proved to be more durable than those of epic and romance, more in keeping with the spirit of the times. Thibaut (*Romanz de la Poire*), Baudouin de Condé (*Prisons d'Amours*), Nicole de Margival (*Dit de la Panthère d'Amours*), Watriquet de Couvin, Jean Acart de Hesdin (*Prise amoreuse*), Mahieu le Poirier (*La Cour d'Amour*), and several anonymous rhymesters composed a series of love-allegories in the style of Guillaume de Lorris. However, the only author who succeeded in renewing the genre, illustrating it in a major capacity, was Guillaume de Machaut (1300–77).[2]

Machaut is best known as France's leading composer of the fourteenth century. He wrote innumerable *ballades*, *rondeaux*, *virelais*, and *lais*, many of which he set to music, and a variety of sacred compositions, including the *Messe de Nostre Dame*, the first complete version of the Ordinary of the Mass by one person. In the period of his full maturity, extending approximately from 1330 to 1370, Machaut also wrote ten long narrative poems or *dits*. Two of the most important of these are *Le Jugement dou Roy de Navarre* and *Le Voir Dit*. In examining them I wish to show how this partially neglected master of French literature harmonized the disparate voices of Guillaume de Lorris and Jean de Meun and how, particularly in the realm of narrative technique, he made contributions to the history of fiction which can only be appreciated today. Machaut was a great lyric poet and musician; he also was the last Medieval who attained supremacy in the long narrative poem.[3]

In the 1330s Guillaume de Machaut wrote *Le Jugement dou Roy de Behaingne*. This work recounts a debate over a point of love casuistry: who suffers more, a lady whose lover died or a knight whose mistress left him for another man. Machaut has King John of Bohemia decide in favor of the knight. It appears that over the years *Le Roy de Behaingne* stirred up controversy, that Machaut's verdict was criticized by certain members of the court, especially the ladies. At any rate, some time after 1349 he wrote *Le Jugement dou Roy de Navarre*,[4] a sequel and palinode to the *Behaingne*.

According to *Le Jugement dou Roy de Navarre* the Narrator spends the winter locked in his room for fear of the plague, meditating on the calamities of the age. With the advent of spring, he goes out hunting, whereupon he is noticed by Lady Bonneürté, an allegorical figure representing Happiness or Good Fortune, who reproaches him for the decision he made in *Le Jugement dou Roy de Behaingne*. The two agree on a new trial, to be held before Charles the Bad, King of Navarre. As plaintiff, Bonneürté is assisted by allegorical attendants: Franchise, Honnêteté, Charité, and others. The Narrator conducts his own defense. Both parties narrate *exempla* taken mostly from the *Ovide moralisé*, modern vernacular romance, or contemporary hearsay. Finally, King Charles and his councillors (Avis, Raison, Mesure, and Connaissance) decide in favor of Bonneürté. The Narrator is condemned to write a *lai*, a *chanson*, and a *ballade*.

The generally accepted opinion on *Le Jugement dou Roy de Navarre* assumes that Machaut pretends to uphold his original decision but in fact reverses it, taking the exactly opposite stance. One could equally well maintain the contrary: that the poet, while he gives the impression of renouncing his first judgment, in fact defends it with wit and courage. I suggest, however, that, even more than Jean de Meun, Machaut was interested in literature rather than ideas, that is, in creating literary characters and a world of comedy.[5]

The world is centered upon the fiction of a trial. Machaut follows the workings of the law closely. His realistic parody of judicial proceedings contributes a sense of authenticity to *Le Roy de Navarre* but also generates humor because we can never forget that the proceedings are so preposterously and obviously a figment of the author's imagination. The subject at issue concerns whether a lover suffers more from his beloved's death or her infidelity, but from Bonneürté's first speech the trial degenerates into a war of the sexes in the tradition of Jean de Meun, a debate on the respective virtues of men and women. At no time do the judges correct this travesty of justice; nor do they reprimand the litigants for indulging in irrelevant casuistry: arguments over who suffers more, Pyramus or Thisbe, Hero or Leander; over who loves more deeply, a person dying from a broken heart or one who has gone insane for the same reason; over whether the insane lover remains perpetually in excruciating torture or suffers only the instant he went mad. The allegorical ladies attack the Narrator one after the other; the arguments they use and the stories they tell are roughly the same. For all the importance of tradition in medieval law, and reverence for *auctores* throughout medieval culture, the fourteenth-century public could not but recognize the absurdity of attempting to prove universal judgments by means of a few contemporary or historical anecdotes. Indeed, they knew the law well enough to appreciate a mock-trial when it was presented to them. At one point Honnêteté interrupts Charité, who had opened her mouth to speak, because she herself wishes to take the floor:

> Charitez vout après parler,
> Et pour apointier son parler,
> Elle avoit ja la bouche ouverte.
> Mais Honnesté fu si aperte
> Que tantost fu aparillie
> Et dist ...   (2561–6)

Then, after the Narrator has delivered an unusually sharp misogynistic remark, the ladies lose their collective tempers and begin to murmur; upon which the misogynist requests that his adversaries be permitted to continue their pleading in unison, to have done more quickly! And they do speak all at once, whereupon King Charles smiles and the Narrator rejoices:

> Si firent elles, ce me samble;
> Qu'elles parloient tout ensamble,
> Dont li juges prist a sousrire
> Qui vit que chascune s'aïre.
> Et certes, j'en eus moult grant joie,
> Quant en tel estat les vëoie.   (3157–62)

We cannot take seriously a trial where a fear-stricken defendant proclaims it will be good to hear the fine arguments on both sides, at which Bonneürté laughs:

> 'Mes cuers y est ja tous entiers,
> Car ce sera uns biaus mestiers
> D'oïr les raisons repeter

Et les parties desputer
Soutilment, par biaus argumens,
Qui vaurront auques jugemens.'
A ces moz prist la dame a rire
Et en riant tantost a dire ...   (1083–90)

We cannot take seriously a trial where the verdict and sentencing also provoke laughter. An absurdly minor point of love casuistry, discussed in a poem at least ten years old, unleashes a full-fledged legal confrontation before the King of Navarre; the result of this massive trial machinery is to condemn the defendant, a poet, to write more poetry.

Although the plot of *Le Jugement dou Roy de Navarre* is not based on the romance pattern, the themes of adventure and the chase do contribute to the narrative, in a comic register. When the Narrator goes hunting, he is so engrossed that he fails to notice Bonneürté ride by. Hurt by the Narrator's discourtesy, she summons him into her presence. From this interview the trial follows directly. The hunt brings the Narrator and Bonneürté into contact but, because of his distraction, it keeps them apart. Bonneürté accuses the Narrator of having failed to show respect to her as a lady and thus having insulted ladies in general. His action parallels in humorous fashion the more serious affronts he made as a poet in *Le Jugement dou Roy de Behaingne* and will make in the trial scene to come.

How should we interpret the hunt? Medieval man often considered the chase a symbol of idolatry and riding on horseback an image of vanity. To pursue a little furry animal, a rabbit or hare (505), is an erotic situation which evokes the sin of lust and was condemned in moral and satirical treatises as were 'bad hunters' in Scripture (Nimrod, Esau). The Narrator's horse, Grisart, can be assimilated to the call of the flesh; whether or not the poet, who ought to embody reason, is capable of properly directing him is another matter. On the other hand, imagery of the chase, as of falconry, was assimilated to the noblest impulses of *fin' amor*. I am thinking of troubadour and trouvère poetry, *Eneas*, *Erec et Enide*, *Aucassin et Nicolette*, and the passage where the God of Love tracks the Narrator in Guillaume de Lorris's *Roman de la Rose*. Machaut undoubtedly knew either from Jean de Meun or *l'Ovide moralisé* that Venus advised Adonis to hunt rabbits and hares (*Amor*), not fierce beasts (*Militia*). The 'chase of love' then became a familiar theme in late medieval allegory, in *La Prise amoreuse* by Jean Acart de Hesdin, *Li Dis dou cerf amoreus*, *Le dit du cerf blanc*, and *Die Jagd* by Hadamar von Laber.[6]

It is possible to interpret the Narrator's pastime as lustful, non-courtly amorous pleasure, insulting to Bonneürté, or as an effort on his part to be a courtly lover in the grand style. I wish to suggest still another hypothesis. In courtly literature as in the *Remedia Amoris* the hunt also stood for an alternative way of life, in opposition to, or in competition with, the erotic. Such is the case in *Guigemar*, *Partonopeus de Blois*, *Guillaume de Dole*, *Durmart le Galois*, and so many episodes of *l'Ovide moralisé*, where a youth or maiden in the service of Diana will not submit to erotic advances, even from a god. The examples of Daphne, Actaeon, Narcissus, and Arethusa point to a fundamental opposition between love and the chase, as representing totally irreconcilable attitudes toward life. When a mythological personage (Meleager or Adonis) seeks to combine the two or to pursue them at the same time, he is doomed. In *Le Jugement dou Roy de Navarre* then the Narrator's participation in the chase is anathema to Bonneürté, for by so doing he partakes of a pleasure different from love. He remains ignorant of love and of Bonneürté's presence, enjoying himself fully in a parody of the only true joy a priestess of *fin' amor* will admit. And finally, he dares partake of a court pastime; he, a non-noble, a coward, and a poet, a clerkly narrator opposed to *fin' amor*, presumes to act like a knight, even to defend rabbit-hunting as a sport in which he can attain honor. Instead of bagging the rabbit for a stew, he will discover that he is the hunted not the hunter in a quite different game.

The Narrator excuses his discourtesy by claiming to have been seized or ravished (*ravis*, 795) out of his senses, hence his failure to recognize the ladies. He refers to the rabbit hunt as a *queste* (553) for *honneur* (502, 508, 510, 516), and to an encounter with Bonneürté's messenger as an *aventure* (536). If tale-bearers had spoken against him, that would have been an *aventure* also (835). Later, he is accused of being *forfais* (811, 860) to ladies. His fear of the trial is compared to enchantment (1340), his *onneur* (1064) again at stake, and Bonneürté refers to the whole affair as a *merveille* unique in its kind (1477–8). Machaut places his protagonist in a situation which recalls Arthurian romance. He encounters Bonneürté and her messenger as by accident or in some miraculous way and is observed by her, unaware of her presence. For a much longer time Bonneürté's identity remains hidden from the Narrator and the reader; like so many figures in Chrétien de Troyes, including Lancelot and Laudine, her name is revealed only at her moment of triumph (3851). She resembles the fairy queen of the Other World, potentially a dangerous enemy. After having endured threats and insults, the hero metaphorically undergoes an ordeal, a parody of sacred combat, expiates his sins, and is delivered from enchantment. The court is free to revel in joy.

These romance motifs have been introduced in *Le Roy de Navarre* paradoxically for the sake of laughter. In fact, the Narrator takes no risks, fights no battles, has engaged upon no covenant. A mighty hunter of rabbits, his only prowess is verbal. His closest approximation to martial activities is to participate in solitary sport (the hunt) and courtly games (the trial): both are ironically substituted for real war. Our hero defends the

wrong side (from the courtly point of view) and loses in the end. Fair
ladies harm rather than help him, benevolent authority-figures with supernatural aura prove hostile, and his ordeal turns out to be a joke. In the
adventure motif, as in the trial and love casuistry, we see the hand of a
master of comedy. Machaut demonstrates that men are foolish because
they cannot live up to the courtly ideal and that they are naïve in seeking to
live up to an ideal which itself is untrue to life. The Narrator is a foil to
the ladies, just as they are foils to him.

What I have said up to now is based on the assumption that the Narrator is not a self-portrait of Guillaume de Machaut the poet and that a trial
scene with allegorical adversaries must be interpreted as fiction not autobiography. It is certain that by obtrusively identifying the Narrator as Guillaume, author of *Le Jugement dou Roy de Behaingne*, by having him
named as such by the other characters (573, 601, 651, 686, 695, 726, 746,
760, 779, 802, 862, 915, 974, and so forth) and by himself (4199–200),
Machaut individualizes this traditional *persona* more than did either Guillaume de Lorris or Jean de Meun. For all that, in works of fiction the
semi-autobiographical 'I' is not and cannot be strictly identified with the
author. (Rubrics in the text distinguish what 'Guillaume' says at trial
from plot material told by 'L'Acteur.') The *Roy de Navarre* Narrator still
manifests conventional traits, and whether or not the real Guillaume de
Machaut was a saucy but inept pleader at court is as difficult for us to
ascertain as whether Guillaume de Lorris was a timid, virtuous, and immature wooer when he wrote *Le Roman de la Rose*. No doubt some of the
humor, in *Le Roy de Navarre* as in Froissart and Chaucer, derives from
both similarity and dissimilarity between the author as narrator and the
author as poet, from the irony generated when Machaut tells a fictional
tale in his own voice, quite probably reciting it himself before Charles of
Navarre, a story in which both men play roles.

The dominant tradition in medieval letters was that of a 'poetic' or universal 'I,' an Everyman representative of mankind.[7] As a reliable Narrator
with a valid claim to authenticity, he would generally be objective, unobtrusive, and unself-conscious. However, in the late Middle Ages the
naïve, blundering, comic hero also became a literary convention, largely
developed by Machaut himself (though it existed already with Jean de
Meun), then imitated by Froissart, Christine de Pisan, and Chaucer. Such
a figure may also serve as a witness, and as non-hero or non-lover provide
comic relief or act as a foil to the protagonist (Machaut's *Roy de Behaingne*, *Dit dou Lÿon*, and *Fonteinne amoureuse*; Chaucer's *Book of the
Duchess*). In *Le Jugement dou Roy de Navarre* the 'I' is still the center of
consciousness and single focus for the plot. What he says is to be given
credence; he participates actively in the tale as hero. Indeed, since the
mode of the *dit* is highly dramatic – the Narrator shows rather than tells, his

technique is scenic rather than panoramic; and there is interference from other, delegated voices, the defendant's adversaries in the trial – Machaut succeeds in creating the illusion of objective truth. On the other hand, for this very reason the focalization is external to the Narrator's deepest feelings and sentiments. Like Jean de Meun's protagonist, we recognize him to be obtuse and naïve, not aware of many comic overtones in his story. Machaut, even though he may identify with the Narrator, erects a barrier between himself and his all too human literary creation. He is more sophisticated than his Narrator, and his attitude toward the events recounted in *Le Roy de Navarre* may be quite different.

Machaut the author appears inside and outside the plot: as a literary character, a defendant at court; as the same character, telling the story later; and as himself, the master pulling the strings. From this situation emerges distance and control – the unself-conscious, unobtrusive Narrator separated from the only too self-conscious, obtrusive litigant and from the author hiding behind the scenes. Machaut the author provides both support and correction, sympathy for and criticism of, the Narrator as hero.

I have not yet discussed at all the first part of *Le Roy de Navarre*, those five hundred or so lines which describe the Narrator's experiences during the plague winter of 1349.[8] This section of the poem not only constitutes a semi-realistic frame set in contrast to the central episode, so that, by displacement, the archetypal structure of allegory can be adjusted to a credible context; it also contributes thematically and structurally to the narrative as a whole. The calamities striking France in the winter of 1349 – flame, tempest, earthquake, war, plague – are manifestations of contemporary reality that conform to a traditional medieval motif, the universe upside-down (Curtius's notion of *verkehrte Welt*).[9] The world is rife with corruption and decay; humanity has wasted God-given bounty. The Narrator flails at the abuses of his time, then demonstrates how God punishes mankind for its sins. All four elements that man corrupted are now used by the Almighty to scourge him: earthquake, the flame of war, water poisoned by Jews and air by the plague. If the universe has decayed (*mundus senescit*), in an earlier, happier age people lived at peace with God and themselves. When I was young, says the Narrator, no such calamities befell (*Laudatio temporis acti*):

> Car il a plus grant difference
> Dou temps que je vi en m'enfance
> A cestui qui trop est divers,
> Qu'il n'ait des estez aus yvers.    (95–8)

The *Mundus senescens* reflects a comparable state within the Narrator. Examples of 'pathetic fallacy' were by no means rare in the Middle Ages.

The outer and inner worlds were united by a bond; the microcosm of man's individual destiny and the macrocosm of world history were as one. Humankind is guilty of sins against God and Nature, the Narrator in his paltry way of a sin against polite society, embodied in Bonneürté. The trial before King Charles parodies a more serious judgment and punishment of humanity by the divinity, for both episodes comment on the difficulty of life in a *verkehrte Welt*. We hear repeatedly that the Narrator suffers from melancholia (37, 106, 109, 115, 142, 454, 543, 591, 715, 1336, 1429), a condition linked to an excess of black bile in the body, under the influence of the Greater Infortune, the planet Saturn, matching autumn or winter in the cycle of the year and old age in man's life.[10] It is no coincidence, then, that the Narrator becomes melancholic in autumn; meditates on the calamities of an old, decaying world set against the times of his youth; evokes the historical personage Guillaume de Machaut, who was about forty-nine years old when the action of the poem supposedly took place; and later in the story opposes the doctrine of young love espoused by Bonneürté. Let us not forget that Guillaume de Lorris banished both Tristesse and Vieillesse from the Garden of Delight. A melancholic man is presumed antisocial and prone to cowardice and the sin of *acedia* (especially rampant in those who practice the contemplative life), as much a state of sadness as of sloth. Therefore, the Narrator spends all winter alone, hiding in his cold, gloomy room, dreading the plague and, later on, the prospect of defending himself in court.

Another theme common to both parts of *Le Roy de Navarre* is that of madness. In Part 1 the world has gone insane. The Flagellants are the most notorious example of unreason, though no doubt Machaut ranged makers of war and the miscreant Jews under the same heading. Earthquake, tempest, and landslide signify that the rational order of the universe has been undermined. We know that the Medievals considered a tendency to insanity proper to the melancholic man and unhappy love. The Narrator's actions during that winter, his sudden changes in temper and enforced isolation, hardly reinforce our confidence in his mental equilibrium. Although in Part 2 he shows no symptoms of rage other than having contradicted Bonneürté, insanity (generally related to Eros) crops up during the trial. The Narrator tells of a clerk of Orléans who went mad for twenty years, a dog whose rabies was cured by removing a worm in his tongue, and a knight who cut off his finger out of gallantry. Although they do not wish to denigrate *fin' amor*, the ladies cite examples of famous people who, in *l'Ovide moralisé*, are driven mad by love: Dido, Ariadne, and Medea, among others.

Melancholy and insanity are linked to a sense of mortality. According to the Narrator, God has unleashed Death upon the world. Nine of every ten people perish from the plague, still others from wars, natural disaster, or conspiracy. Fear of dying impels the Narrator to remain in seclusion all winter. Later, during the trial, we are told one story after another in which a lover dies or commits suicide. Then, at the end of the poem, for a bereaved lady the Narrator composes *Le Lay de Plour*, which contains the traditional imagery associated with this theme: rivers of tears, a great tree pulled out by its roots, and the lady sobbing over her lover's coffin.

Although the fundamental question of *Le Jugement dou Roy de Behaingne* – whether infidelity or death is a greater obstacle to love – is pushed aside, the theme of mortality contributes to *Le Roy de Navarre* nonetheless. On the one hand, the tangible, recorded calamities in Part 1 anticipate ironically the somewhat artificial *Liebestöde* of Part 2, derived from romance and *l'Ovide moralisé*. The excessive love-grief of individuals pales before the horror of the plague, just as the Narrator's personal predicament (he is accused of a literary sin) appears trivial in the light of historical reality. For this very reason, we are made aware that death remains a terrifying force in the universe. The Narrator is wrong to denigrate its power. Eros and Thanatos are bound together, in the literary tradition (Virgil, Ovid, *Tristan*) and in everyday life. Not only, as the Freudians have demonstrated, is the sexual act both a refusal to die and an anticipation of the end, but Western man has also converted Eros itself into a death-wish. For all the humor in *Le Roy de Navarre*, Machaut never lets us forget that love is accompanied by pain and mortality, and can never escape from either of them.

The Narrator's answer to his predicament is an attempt to avoid love and death. He seeks refuge from the plague and contests the rules of courtly orthodoxy. In fact, however, although he compares aspects of the amorous life to imprisonment (1992–3, 2045–62), it is he who has spent the winter in a kind of jail (485). Remaining in his home for months on end is a sort of punishment, which the Narrator shares with all of humanity, but is also a symbolic return to the self in a sanctuary closed to outsiders where he can contemplate the human condition. This is an intimate, enclosed, feminine refuge, appropriate to a hunter of rabbits meditating on death but not to an insulter of ladies! Then, with the coming of spring, season of love and sunshine, he breaks out of his cell. From the immobility of containment within four walls, he proceeds to ride to the chase. But he succeeds no better in the world of life than he had in the world of death. Lady Bonneürté summons the Narrator to court where, terrified, he again is 'enclosed' and overcome by melancholia and must defend himself in hostile surroundings. This second captivity is, to be sure, presented ironically, in the comic vein. Because the refuser of festivity remained by himself in winter, then in springtime went hunting alone with no concern for others, he is now forced to share human company. From the author's viewpoint, the court is a good prison, beneficial to the social order. A contrast is drawn between savage, dreary, cold, wintry solitude and the elegant, sunny, warm, springlike court of love in which song, happiness (Bonneürté), and the work of art (*Le Roy de Navarre*) find a place. Machaut evokes the community in laudatory if ironic terms, as a possible refuge in a world upside-down.

Opposition to *fin' amor* is presented as both valid and invalid. Love is a powerful force; we may eschew the excesses of love-madness and the clichés of an artificial code, but we should not reject Eros altogether. Common sense (*mesure* and *souffissance*) requires some form of accommodation to so vital a force in nature and polite society. The poet, more than other men, must avoid hubris, learning to accept the best the world has to offer, since his place ultimately lies in the world and at the court.

From Parts 1 to 2 winter gives way to spring, isolation to the community, Saturn to Venus, and death to rebirth. With an end to the plague the Narrator hears a fanfare of musical instruments, for men are no longer dying. People celebrate the return of spring with games and pastimes, the hunt – and a mock trial, which reflects the archetypal struggle between the old and the new, dying winter and the birth of spring. In this combat the mature, antisocial, melancholic Narrator represents, against his will perhaps, the old. His aristocratic patrons permit him to enter their society. He serves as a scapegoat, the intruder or killjoy whose presence contributes to the festivities, since he must lose and his views be defeated. Death and the calamities of a *mundus senescens* are overcome at King Charles's court. Spring wins out; the rebel is converted or, at any rate, subdued; and his sentence delivered with laughter and joy.

Although Guillaume de Machaut pretends to recount a trial scene in all seriousness, in fact he regards the proceedings with more than a little skepticism. Evidence can be twisted by either side; both plaintiff and defendant lose their tempers. But what difference does it make, once we realize that the author is not primarily interested in an ideological war of the sexes but in the experiences of human beings and their ludicrous interrelations in society? On the contrary, he exploits the game of the chase and the play of the trial, for love itself proves to be but a game and the Narrator's chief crime is to have broken the rules. *Le Jugement dou Roy de Navarre* radiates wit, charm, good humor, and the smile of a man of the world. Behind *Le Lay de Plour*, behind the trial, behind the Narrator's *persona* stands a master of irony who pulls the strings and creates a dynamic, believable, richly comic world.

In the title of *Le Voir Dit* (*The True Story*) (1363–5),[11] Machaut makes an unusual claim for authenticity: he invites comparison with other romances of the day and with his own previous *dits*, presumed less 'true' than the new one. The author justifies his choice of title, which may have appeared pretentious, in the following words:

> Le *Voir-dit* vueil-je qu'on appelle
> Ce traictié que je fais pour elle,
> Pour ce que jà n'i mentiray.    (p. 17)

(Cf. also letter 35, p. 263: 'Et aussi, vostre livre avera nom le *Livre dou Voir dit*; si, ne vueil ne ne doy mentir.') He declares that the *Voir Dit* narrative occurred in real life, that he has told of his amours with Toute-belle at her command. She wants everyone to know their story, even if her reputation suffers because of it. And to support his claim to authenticity, Machaut includes in the text of his tale the lyric poems and prose letters which he and Toute-belle are purported to have exchanged.

The Narrator recounts the following story. Tout-belle sends him a *rondeau*, in which she says that she offers him her heart. The Narrator replies in kind. Soon the aging poet and his youthful admirer are involved in an amorous correspondence. He visits her several times, and they indulge in physical intimacies. Some time after his return home, the Narrator dreams that Toute-belle's sentiments toward him have changed. The lovers continue to write to each other. However, a harsh winter, the plague, fear of highwaymen, and reports against the lady cause the Narrator to postpone further meetings. Finally Toute-belle convinces him of her good will, and the book ends as they swear eternal love and plan once more a reunion.

The majority of scholars identify the Narrator with Guillaume de Machaut the poet and Toute-belle with Peronne or Peronnelle d'Unchair, Dame d'Armentières, whose stepfather was Jean de Conflans, Vidame of Châlons and Lord of Vielmaisons in Brie. They proclaim that *Le Voir Dit* is autobiographical and that in this quality of truth resides one of the poem's chief merits, that Machaut invented the *roman vécu* or *mémoires intimes* and that, a Romantic in advance of his time, he anticipates Rousseau, Goethe, Chateaubriand, and Stendhal.

However, following Georg Hanf,[12] I believe that *Le Voir Dit* in its entirety is a work of the imagination. Leaving aside the matter of internal contradictions, chronological errors, etc., my main point is the following: the Narrator's correspondence and Toute-belle's are indistinguishable. Their letters are constructed in the same manner and written in the same style. They contain identical motifs. Similarly, the lyrics ascribed to Toute-belle employ rhyme, meter, imagery, and diction identical with the Narrator's. Her poems are of the same high quality as his. So extraordinary a talent as Toute-belle's, bursting forth at the age of twenty, making her the equal of the leading French writer of the age, would have been noticed by her contemporaries. But they say nothing of Peronne d'Armentières or any other lady poet until Christine de Pisan. Quite the contrary: several of the songs ascribed to Toute-belle are included by Machaut in his own canon, in the complete collections of lyrics or of music in manuscripts prepared under his personal supervision. And, whether attributed to the Narrator or his beloved, quite a few of the *Voir Dit* lyrics, purportedly composed in the early 1360s for an allegedly 'real' love affair, in fact appear in manuscript collections where they can be dated much earlier. Only one conclusion is plausible: the brilliant young poetess existed in Guillaume de Machaut's imagination. A fictional character, she is not to be identified with Peronne d'Armentières or anyone else who actually lived in the fourteenth century. She has as much historical reality as those other frenetic letter-writers, Marivaux's Marianne and Rousseau's Julie.

The letters and poems are central to the plot of *Le Voir Dit*, the skeleton on which the story itself hangs. In a sense, the story exists to set them off, to explain why they were composed.[13] Once they are admitted to be fictional, not much is left to the domain of reality. It is quite possible that the prototype for Toute-belle was a certain Peronne; perhaps she can be identified with Machaut's young contemporary, Jean de Conflans's stepdaughter. But we will never know the exact relationship between this Peronne and the author of *Le Voir Dit*, whether or not they exchanged a poetic correspondence, whether or not they were in love. At the very most, the details of Machaut's private life gave him inspiration. Just as Proust drew upon his experience to create *A la recherche du temps perdu*, so too Guillaume de Machaut's creative imagination has transferred autobiographical elements into a work of art, the world of his *dit*.

Indeed, it is likely that Machaut partakes of a medieval tradition, a genre we can call the erotic pseudo-autobiography, that is, an account by a poet of his purported love life, containing his own interpolated lyrics and presuming to explain their composition. Examples of works in this tradition are Ulrich von Lichtenstein's *Frauendienst*, Dante's *Vita Nuova*, Juan Ruiz's *Libro de buen amor*, Machaut's own *Remède de Fortune* and *Fonteinne amoureuse*, and several long poems by Froissart.[14]

Like Jean de Meun, Machaut exposes traditional courtly artifice, indulges in a parody of *fin' amor*. The courtly and the non-courtly, the romantic and the down-to-earth, are juxtaposed, one convention played off against another for literary purposes, to create a mood of laughter and sophisticated, ironic detachment. For example, when Toute-belle has not written for a long time, the Narrator falls into melancholia ('Si pris à merencolier ... Si devins merencolieus,' p. 24), turns pale, changes color, loses sleep, and cannot eat. In a *ballade* he swears he will die unless God and ladies help him:

Vestés-vous de noir pour mi,
Car j'ay cuer taint & viaire palli,
Et si me voy de mort en aventure,
Se dieus & vous ne me prenés en cure.    (p. 25)

Although in fact someone or something always turns up to cure him, no matter how often the protagonist recovers he shortly reverts to melancholia and, as often as not, is put to bed within an inch of his life.

The Narrator has not been felled by lovesickness alone. He was ill in bed before ever having heard of Toute-belle, even though at that time he had not been enamored for a good ten or twelve years. He suffers from the gout, several times is physically incapacitated, and bewails the fact that he is neither handsome nor worthy enough to appear before his beloved, a reference perhaps to the fact that he has lost the sight of an eye, for he refers to himself as 'vostre borgne vallet' (letter 13, p. 118). These plaints represent not the conventional humility of a well-read courtly lover but an inferiority complex deriving from concrete, physical infirmity. Machaut's poem recounts a love story between a young girl and an old man. Toute-belle declares, and the Narrator agrees, that their passion has come too late. The Narrator also compares his lady to Hebe, who, in *l'Ovide moralisé*, rejuvenated Iolaus; in similar fashion, he says, Toute-belle restores my youth and cures my ills (pp. 210–11).

In his interpretation of the portrait of Amor, Machaut repeatedly tells us that a lover must be brave. Like Lancelot or Yvain, he may be timid before his lady, but must show courage to other men, be willing to earn her favor with love-service. However, although in this *aventure* (p. 2) the Narrator is offered two occasions to test his prowess, he fails lamentably both times. Returning from Toute-belle's residence, he dreads an encounter with brigands. Real bandits do catch sight of him, but he is taken prisoner by an allegorical figure, a woman. Angry at him because he has neglected to mention her in his book, Espérance demands as 'ransom' that a *lai* be composed in her honor. Once he has indeed been ransomed, the Narrator rides home and hides in his chamber. Machaut has created an amusing parody of courtly adventure. The episode is patently fictitious, an excuse for inserting in *Le Voir Dit* the poet's elegant, technically sophisticated *lai*, yet it also tells us something about the Narrator's character, his inability to conform to Arthurian romance in a post-Jean de Meun world. Toute-belle goes along with the joke. She pretends to be overjoyed that the Narrator survived these 'aventures vous avés eu en chemin' (letter 22, p. 182). Her use of the term *aventure* indicates that she also is aware of the tradition which her lover can follow only in jest.

The second occasion occurs when the Narrator permits his secretary and others to dissuade him from visiting Toute-belle. The weather is bad, says the secretary, and bandits prowl the land. And they are extremely dangerous:

> 'Trop sont faus & mauvais leur tour;
> S'il vous tiennent en une tour
> .III. jours ou .IIII. durement,
> Vous serez mors certeinnement;
> Car vous estes un tenres homs ...'    (p. 285)

The times are too harsh even for a young man, not to speak of one suffering from gout; in any case Toute-belle would not want her suitor to risk his life. Indeed she does not but cannot help reproaching him for not having come to see her (letter 43). For, as the girl points out, the Narrator not only stayed at home in winter and when mercenaries were ravaging the land, but also in summertime when the roads were open and his health improved. Toute-belle says that if she had been in his shoes, she would have acted differently. All this implies, of course, that, judged from a courtly perspective, he fails as a lover and as a man.

As in *Le Jugement dou Roy de Navarre*, Machaut's protagonist is measured against the traditional hero of romance. By comparing himself to Gawain, Lancelot, and Tristan, the Narrator reveals how his conduct differs from theirs, that in fact he resembles more closely King Arthur and Mark. His innocence and naïvety correspond to those of the *Dümmling* Perceval, except that Perceval is young and can develop in the course of his career, whereas the Narrator has had his chance and lost it. In any case, the latter's adventures are psychological, his ordeal merely to face a lady. Normally in the world of romance a youth desires a beautiful maiden but is separated from her by a husband or husband-surrogate. The hero's victory implies defying the obstructive authority-figure and winning the girl for himself. In *Le Voir Dit* no father or husband prevents the Narrator from loving Toute-belle, and the chief opposition he must overcome is not the plague, bandits, or cold weather, but his own fear. He himself is old enough to be her father or grandfather; he is the *durus pater*, a superego arousing anxiety in himself, bearing within his own psyche the obstacle to fulfillment. And Toute-belle, pleasure principle incarnate, fails to break down this greybeard's scruples. On the contrary, conscious of violating tabus, the Narrator entertains ambivalent feelings toward his mistress and pupil, lady and surrogate daughter. At his age he still cannot integrate the anima.

Finally, this ridiculous suitor, who compares himself to Christ betrayed by Judas, adores Toute-belle like a goddess. He sends her a verse epistle of some fifty-one lines, in which the refrain, 'Mon cuer, ma suer, ma douce amour' (pp. 184–5), recurs twenty-four times, creating an effect

not unlike the mock litanies in Baudelaire, Verlaine, and Carducci. Twice
the Narrator proclaims that Toute-belle has cured his illness by miracle.
He also adores the poems, letters, and love-tokens she sends him; he kneels
before her portrait as if it were an icon; and we are told that the image
heals him and appears in his dreams. It is obvious that Toute-belle has been
assimilated to Mary, and that the Narrator venerates her as he would the
Holy Virgin. This does not prevent our clerical hero from worshiping Venus
also, or from transforming Toute-belle into a pagan deity, higher in sta-
tion than Pallas, Juno, and Venus, who after she dies will become a star to
illumine the world. The Narrator's immediate ecclesiastical superior would,
however, be more concerned to discover that his canon undertakes a novena
as an excuse to visit Toute-belle, and every day in church thinks only of
her; that he reads the Hours while waiting for her at a rendezvous or, worse
still, composes lyrics in her honor instead of performing his devotions.
And they go on a pilgrimage to Saint-Denis, where they snuggle in bed.

Although Machaut's contemporaries would not have been shocked by
his narrative, they could have responded to it as comedy. Unlike Lancelot,
Guilhem de Nevers, and other heroes of romance, the *Voir Dit* Narrator
is not a knight parodying or temporarily masquerading as a cleric, but the
contrary: a cleric aping a knight. Profane love is ennobled by contact with
the divine in the *Lancelot-Grail Cycle* and in Dante. In Machaut the opposite takes place: Toute-belle and Venus replace the Virgin, and flesh
triumphs over spirit. The man of the cloth is tempted from the true path and
willfully whores after strange gods. A scholar and poet, he takes himself
seriously as a lover, abandons Reason for Love, and fails miserably. We
discover that the knight-lover and poet-scholar are distinct entities. Any
effort to play both roles at the same time results in disaster.

In *Le Voir Dit* the functions of lover and beloved, knight and lady, are
reversed. The Narrator manifests cowardice, prudishness, vacillation, and a
quick temper, and is compared to Dame Fortune. Toute-belle, on the
contrary, makes the advances and gives evidence of pluck and courage. For
all her innocence, she appears more experienced in the code of *fin' amor*
than the Narrator himself. He teaches her poetry and music, but she
instructs him in love. Wisdom is to be found in the girl, a *puella senex*, not
in the distinguished writer who, despite his advanced years, acts like a
child. The Narrator functions as a woman, while Toute-belle assumes the
man's role; their attributes have been exchanged or, at least, merged. In
sum, three centuries after its inception, *fin' amor* is recognized to be a social
game, a mask which hides and at the same time reveals.

The total effect is a corrosion of romance by what may be called the ironic
vision. Machaut's lyrics contribute a courtly tone, a representation of
love in the abstract, which is then belied by rhyming couplets and prose

epistles that tell of an affair between two people in the world. The exalted language of the *ballade* and *complainte* does not fit the day-to-day existence of Toute-belle and her suitor. Sentimental, inauthentic rhetoric is deflated when characters who try to live up to the romance ideal are forced into a situation where their code proves worthless. The public discovers that people cannot live up to it, and that the code itself is invalid because it no longer relates to everyday reality.

The plot line of *Le Voir Dit* is subject to more than one ambiguity. When the Narrator comes to say goodbye to Toute-belle (pp. 153–63), we do not know whether their love is consummated or not. Nor does Machaut ever give a satisfactory explanation for the estrangement that develops between them in the second half of the *Dit*. There must be some physical or psychological reason to explain why the lovers, so close to consummation (or already there), do not meet again for over two years. But should we ascribe their estrangement to Toute-belle's fickleness or to the Narrator's cowardice and jealousy? Who is 'in the right' – the man or the woman? Venus's cloud, the 'miracle' that keeps their tryst hidden from public gaze, serves as an image for the poem as a whole, for a veil of mystery that both the Narrator and the reader seek to pierce.

Ascertaining the truth is rendered difficult by space and time. The story begins at summer's end, 1362, when Toute-belle first sends a *rondeau* to the Narrator, and ends with the forty-sixth letter, which can be dated not long after 1 May 1365. It covers almost three years, a greater duration than any of Machaut's previous tales, with the possible exception of *Le Dit de l'Alerion*. We are made aware of the passing of time, of the change of seasons, of a lover's frustration without word from the beloved. People evolve over so long a period, and their sentiments change also. Although the Narrator insists too much on the theme of metamorphosis in Ovid and the Bible not to be conscious of metamorphosis in his own life, he is never certain of who and what have been transformed at any particular moment, whether at a given instant Toute-belle does indeed cherish him or, on the contrary, his suspicions are justified.

He would have little difficulty in discovering Toute-belle's feelings but for the fact that communication between them is precarious. He and the girl are separated for almost the entire plot. Much of the external décor of *Le Voir Dit* and secondary characters as well – bandits, storms, winter, the plague, allegorical figures such as *Malebouche* and *Danger* – serve one function only, to keep the lovers apart. Although the Narrator sets forth more than once to find his beloved, his quest is never realized; the lovers attain neither permanence nor total commitment. Space stands between them, preventing understanding. Each remains in solitude or surrounded by people who cannot help, unaware of or hostile to his longing.

They are eager to behold each other, for sight nourishes love and truth. Toute-belle's eyes possess curative powers; even in a dream, she heals the Narrator by gazing at him. On the other hand, he dreads appearing in the girl's presence, lest his physical unattractiveness should dampen her ardor. Dazzled from afar by her beauty, he doubts whether he can dazzle her in return. The first time they lie together in bed he cannot perceive her, for they are in the dark; he touches her gropingly, is paralyzed by fear, and she must make the advances. The second time he enters through an open window (phallic imagery) and contemplates her in the nude. Venus's cloud covers them from the gaze of outsiders while their passion triumphs; they see each other without being seen. He does enjoy a kind of possession:

> Et là fist miracles ouvertes,
> Si clerement & si appertes
> Que de joie fui raemplis,
> Et mes desirs fu acomplis:
> Si bien que plus ne demandoie
> Ne riens plus je ne desiroie.   (p. 157)

Yet the Narrator's victory is short-lived, since he is not permitted to behold Toute-belle again. How well did he ever see her, this one-eyed old man? The bad lover, Polyphemus, also one-eyed, never discovered the truth about Galatea; he was later blinded by Odysseus, as perhaps the Narrator has been all along by the God of Love. After all, the elderly suitor's obsession with being discreet, with masking their relationship, for all its conformity with courtly orthodoxy, may well be erotically destructive. Is he punishing himself for violating a tabu, for curiosity sinful in a man of his age and estate? or for inability to satisfy his curiosity?

Toute-belle and the Narrator do communicate by letter, although their correspondence is hindered by a variety of material considerations and Toute-belle's limited freedom of action as an unmarried young lady of the gentry. A person's letters are an artificial, semi-literary projection of himself, not necessarily more authentic than a novel he is writing. The Narrator can never be certain that the girl's missives are sincere, nor can she count on his. In fact, he informs us that in one epistle he intentionally tampers with the truth:

> Toutevoie je m'avisay,
> Et moult y pensay & visay,
> Qu'unes lettres li escriroie,
> Et que riens ne li manderoie
> De ce qu'on dit tout en appert,
> Qu'elle vest, en lieu de bleu, vert.   (p. 313)

Furthermore, by the time one of them reads the other's letter, it no longer necessarily reflects the writer's sentiments or how their situation has evolved in the interval. The lovers also communicate in their sleep, but the Narrator does not believe dreaming to be an infallible source of truth, for he declares: 'Car clerement vi que mon songe / N'avoit riens de vray fors mensonge' (p. 233). Dreams, letters, lyric poetry, even the portrait, are mediators; they help the lovers to maintain contact but, objects or external happenings, they contain no guarantee of validity. The Narrator and Toute-belle each are aware of their own sentiments but can never 'prehend' the other's. And the reader cannot arrive at objective truth either.

Machaut tells his story in the first person, through a narrator who, as in *Le Roman de la Rose* and *El Libro de buen amor*, is also the protagonist and a lover. Except for the letters and poems ascribed to Toute-belle, *Le Voir Dit* is filtered through the Narrator's consciousness, whether he recounts events as participant or observer. His is the central focus; the action is seen almost exclusively through his prism. Although an I-narrator will often elicit from the reader sympathy and a heightened emotional reaction, he cannot create the illusion of omniscience we find in most third-person fiction. Machaut is aware that the reader places limits on how much an 'I' can reasonably be expected to know outside his own purview: hence the protagonist's explanations that he was informed of certain events by Toute-belle's confidante or by the girl herself.

For the first time in the history of French fiction the Narrator's limited perspective has an important function in the plot. If we believe his truth-claim, accept his norms, and allow his point of view and ours to coincide, we must then agree with his version of the story. However, the *erzählendes Ich* is not necessarily reliable, nor are we obliged to accept without question his interpretation of events. We have the right to disagree with him. We know the Narrator's opinion but not that of Guillaume de Machaut the poet, for whom the *erlebendes Ich* is a literary character the same as Toute-belle. This blurring of focus is the key to the tale's structure. Illusion is taken for reality, and reality for illusion. Truth can be revealed through appearance (a dream), or perhaps a lie is told in seemingly truthful terms and given the authenticity of a dream-vision. Narrative omniscience is out of place in a story that reveals the Narrator-hero's lack of omniscience. Ironically, in *Le Voir Dit, The True Story*, neither the protagonist nor the reader ever succeeds in unravelling the *Voir Dit* mystery.

One thing is certain, however: as in the case of Jean de Meun, knowing no more than the Narrator, we perceive his weakness and vacillation. We do not see the reality behind Toute-belle's mask (her portrait, letters, and dream appearances), but we do recognize that it is a mask and realize that the poor fellow is incapable of distinguishing between it and reality. Regardless of the true state of affairs, the Narrator demonstrates a crushing lack of trust. His tragedy lies not in the Other but in himself, and the ultimate truth of *The True Story* concerns not his external relations to another (over which he agonizes) but his inner self, of which he is almost totally oblivious. For a master of *fin' amor*, a specialist in the ways of the heart, he is an unaware, unlucid, inauthentic individual. In this sense surely the reader discovers a 'truth' the Narrator never dreamed of and arrives at a point of knowledge far beyond his.

The Toute-belle perceived by the Narrator, in part a product of his imagination, differs from the real one whom neither he nor the public ever gets to know. She is his inspiration, his muse, but as such takes on a universal, not a particular, aura. He conceives of her as the *domna* of tradition, not a living fourteenth-century girl less than twenty years old. He writes his best poetry when they are separated, perhaps unconsciously seeks obstacles to keep them apart, in order to live up to the *amor de lonh* convention and because the reality of Toute-belle's presence cannot but interfere with his idealized picture of her and silence him. He does not want her to grow into a real woman, prefers her arrested sexual development. Significantly, in the second half of *Le Voir Dit* her portrait comes to replace the real girl. Just as Toute-belle is dehumanized in the relationship, so also in the Narrator's mind she is metamorphosed into an object (the portrait) and a spirit (who comes to him when he dreams), onto whom he projects fantasies at will. Perhaps he loves only himself or the idea of love and projects his self onto the Other, finds himself reflected in her, is eager to be loved in order to proclaim his personal value, to write and then be reflected in his reader. At any rate, the 'I' and the 'Thou' as present entities, potentially capable of an authentic, total relationship, are here separated; as a result, communicating by letter, they relate to each other as 'I-It,' as subject to object, person to non-person, in a quite reified sense.

For the elderly poet-lover of *Le Voir Dit*, the *erlebendes Ich* is a fictional character once removed, a narrated self who exists in words not historical fact; he has been created not only by Guillaume de Machaut the author but by his own other half, the *erzählendes Ich* who composes their story. By sending her portions of the book as they are completed, the Narrator seeks to mold Toute-belle's and the reader's interpretation of the events he has just lived through. Curiously enough, the same is true for Toute-belle and the Narrator as poets and correspondents: the various lyrics and prose epistles are written specifically for their 'narratees' and for the public at large, to create a calculated effect on others. The entire book and all it contains assume the existence of implied readers called upon to witness the fictional selves of the purported authors (Toute-belle, the Narrator as *actant*, the Narrator as *scripteur*). Each seeking to impose his own vision of the self on the Other and on the public, they are inevitably guilty of bad faith.

As we have seen, one mode of communication in *Le Voir Dit* is the written word, embodied in songs, prose letters, and the book itself, a True Story, which the Narrator is supposed to be composing. The theme of art is more fully developed in this poem than in any other medieval French narrative. In spite of his age, ill health, and loss of an eye, Machaut's protagonist attracts Toute-belle because of his reputation as a writer. Throughout the story she sends to him for lyrics, declares she adores reading them and will learn them by heart. He then goes along with her pretensions by composing songs solely in her praise. These texts crystallize the love-experience and function to advance the plot; they show us and the characters how to write and how to love; and, because of their very artistic perfection, they create an illusion of authenticity, 'proving' that the *Dit* is indeed *Voir*. The Narrator also agrees, though with misgivings, to transcribe the whole of their affair in his book. Toute-belle not only sacrifices her honor and defies convention for the sake of fame: she succeeds in her objective! Within the context of the story, she becomes known in society as the Narrator's muse. And, in a larger sense, like Beatrice, Laura, Délie, Cassandre, Marie, and Hélène, she is known today because she was a character in a work of art.

The Narrator is a lover and a poet, a lover because he is a poet and vice versa. In *Floris et Lyriopé*, *Cléomadès*, *La Divina Commedia*, *Il Filocolo*, and *Le Voir Dit*, a book causes two people to meditate on Eros and on each other. Poems, letters, and the tale itself, viewed as their story in the making, bring the Narrator and his beloved together; they are perhaps the only mediators in an affair which would never otherwise have come into being and which is kept alive only by poetry.

Machaut's hero does not finally succeed as a lover. As a poet, he depends for inspiration on sources, on authorities, weighing down his tale with mythological or allegorical lore. He tells stories and draws conclusions but does not act to win his lady, as a young suitor must. A learned man, the Narrator is afraid to experience the world directly, yet without concrete activity he cannot succeed in love. Significantly, he flees Toute-belle at all costs, prefers the world of books and his bookish vision of the *domna* to the real girl, ensures that his only knowledge of her is derived from the act of reading (her poems, her letters). In a sense he creates her as a work of art, whether it be the fetish of her portrait or her 'real' presence as a literary character. For good or ill, both lovers envisage the Other exclusively as writer and reader: for them, the book truly replaces the bed. Like *Le Roman de la Rose*, *Le Voir Dit* is a tale of language – speech, poetry, prose correspondence – in which words and the art of verse impede rather than encourage physical action. An educated poet is as much a fool as other men *sub specie Veneris*, and his knowledge turns out to be useless. The Narrator would never have had a chance with Toute-belle if he had not been a great poet, but the absence of concrete human experience implicit in the clerical life also condemns him to failure.

However, whatever his success or failure as a lover, the Narrator's status as an artist is never left in doubt. He takes pride in his work, is conscious of his pre-eminence as a poet, and on more than one occasion brings off a tour de force – answering Toute-belle's songs in their own rhyme scheme and composing impromptu *rondeaux*, *ballades* and *virelais* to illustrate intense emotional states as they occur, the most extraordinary being the *virelai* he creates at the very moment he enjoys Toute-belle in bed.

Likewise, his beloved, said to be an excellent singer even before she met the Narrator ('la mieulz chantans / Qui fust née depuis .c. ans,' p..4), develops into a poetess herself. She learns to answer his poems following his own rhyme scheme and, like him, to compose *rondeaux* spontaneously in moments of intense emotion. Approximately one-half of the *Voir Dit* lyrics form 'duets,' companion pieces in which one of the lovers answers and imitates the other. There is a direct analogy, indeed a bond, between love and art: instruction in the one (from a *maistre* or a *dame*) should accompany the other. Unfortunately, in the comic world of *Le Voir Dit* the two calls become disjunct, from a pedagogical perspective as well as others. Thus, it can be said that Toute-belle turns out better as a poet than the Narrator as a lover. She improves in the one realm, while he falters in the other, and, to give him his due, he is a more successful teacher of letters than she is an instructress in the ways of Eros.

The protagonists collaborate on their story, *Le Voir Dit*; the writing of *Le Voir Dit* becomes the subject of *Le Voir Dit*, the poem making itself. For the Narrator, as for Toute-belle, their secular opus partakes of much of the symbolism the Medievals ascribed to the Book of God and the Book of Nature: it is a world to them and comes to make up their world. This book is purportedly written by the Narrator more or less as the story takes place, from July 1363 to May 1365. Toute-belle declares that her greatest pleasure lies in reading parts of it as it comes into being; she is urged to assume some editorial control in its elaboration; and surely her love is nourished by the book and by her own role in its elaboration. Then, at the end, although the Narrator's passion has not been consummated and the future of his relationship with Toute-belle remains uncertain, he has the book to fall back on: he will complete the history of their amours. It exists, when all else proves to be illusion. In a sense, this man, who loves his craft more than his lady, sublimates an impossible yearning for her by creating *Le Voir Dit*. As Apollo kills Coronis but their son, Aesculapius, is saved, so too the Narrator's love eventually dies, but his creation, the Book, will live on. The writer becomes truly educated, first, by experiencing life and, second, by creating out of his failure in life a successful poem. Poetry (the lyrics) fails to bring about happy love but succeeds (*Le Voir Dit* as a whole) in creating a *Gesamtkunstwerk* of the most daring proportions. Ultimately, art triumphs over existence because the latter, as Machaut's protagonists live it, has no meaning or permanence apart from art: literature creates life, not the opposite, and the Narrator creates the characters of his story, including himself. It is not coincidental that the book itself appears in the title, is the archimage which dominates a poem that refers to and is justified only by itself.

*Le Voir Dit* is the most complex of Machaut's tales. His ending especially is ambiguous because, although the lovers do reconcile, we are never made aware of the exact relationship between them and to what extent either one loves the other or is capable of a mature relationship. The Narrator believes in their reconciliation, but he and the reader are ignorant of Toute-belle's sentiments in the matter. Whether he will caress the maiden again is open to question. As in the very best contemporary fiction, the reader has to divine the 'situation' at any given moment without help from the author. Furthermore, this incomplete ending gives the poem an aura of truth, for tensions are left unresolved, as is so often the case in real life. The plot is open, not closed; the characters live on; and their problems persist, not to be resolved by a fortuitous marriage or death. Machaut also anticipates the novel of our age by creating the illusion that his book takes shape as the characters live it, that they create their own story, and that the work of art itself becomes a living organism, free from convention and an author's will. Yet, as we know, such is not the case in Machaut's world any more than in Gide's and Sartre's. An author does shape his characters; he adheres to or rebels against literary conventions; he constructs a narrative. The contrast between the authenticity of artistic creation and the illusion of realism, as well as between the ideal of *fin' amor* and the reality of two people living on our planet, is central to the ironic vision of Machaut's True Story.

Machaut's greatest triumph as a poet may well be the new literary type he made his own: the inept, blundering narrator, who is also an inept, blundering lover. This pseudo-autobiographical character is prone to cowardice, sloth, snobbery, misogyny, and pedantry. Guilty of excess, unable to cope with everyday social life, obsessed by his failings, he acts in a delightfully comic manner, in contrast to the elegant gentlemen and ladies of the court. For the first time in French literature the fool has become a protagonist in a serious work of art; Machaut's development of the *Roman de la Rose* tradition was to have a profound influence upon his most gifted successors, Froissart and Chaucer.

Sometimes in Machaut a lover recounts his experiences directly; sometimes they are told by a witness-observer. As in the great eighteenth-century novels, the narrator may participate actively in the story or withdraw from it; he can be reliable or unreliable, omniscient or in error. By playing with point of view and illusion-reality, Guillaume pioneered the development of a more sophisticated narrative technique. These themes enter into the structure of his finest tales, giving them a complexity seldom to be equalled in early fiction.

Furthermore, he manifests extraordinary self-consciousness and pride in his own function as a poet: by introducing a version of himself as the major character in several *dits*; by claiming mastery in his art and exploiting the myth of the artist; by making the craft of writing, indeed the writing of a book, the subject of a book; by arranging his *Œuvres complètes* in manuscript form, supervising his manuscript collections, ensuring their correct order, and making us conscious of his opus as a totality. For the first time we find a *poëte* in the modern sense (the term is used by Eustache Deschamps with reference to Machaut) replacing the trouvère, one who combines the roles of narrator-hero of lyric and romance, clerkly narrator, and scribal editor organizing codices, one who resembles the classical *auctores*. Not until du Bellay and Ronsard will the dignity and importance of the poetic vocation again be so exalted.[15]

It is well known that Guillaume de Machaut enjoyed a high reputation in his day and over the next two or three generations. There can be no doubt that the major developments in late medieval verse narrative, in the lyric, and in sacred and profane music are due in part to his influence. He set a pattern which lasted a good hundred years. However, the literary kinds Machaut brought to perfection (the *dit amoureux*, the lyric *lai*, the *virelai*, the motet, and the polyphonic *ballade* and *rondeau*) fell into decline after his death. (Other genres – particularly the non-musical *ballade* and *rondeau* – were perfected by Charles d'Orléans, Villon, and Marot.) The Master, often imitated, at his best was inimitable. In spite of his influence as a narrative poet, Machaut had no true successors, none in France at least, although Chaucer, Gower, and the Scottish Makars perpetuated his ideal abroad. He proves to be the last master of the long poem before the Renaissance.

For most of the medieval age epos flourished in France. As was to be expected, a shift occurred in esthetic taste and mentality over the centuries, as *chanson de geste* gave way to the *roman*, which in turn yielded precedence to allegory and the *dit amoureux*. On the other hand, the various genres also coexisted in time; overlapping the same chronological periods, they competed for the public's favor, at times divided the public between them according to its education or social standing. The decline of one genre vis-à-vis another in no way implies decadence; on the contrary, such evolution not only is inherent in the notion of literary history but also, at least for medieval France, testifies to an extraordinary variety of forms and quantity and quality of output. After 1400 the long poem does fall into relative decline only, as we shall see in the next few chapters, to be renewed in a new guise and with much of its old splendor in the Renaissance and Baroque.

## Chapter Seven

# 🐝 RONSARD

The differences between the Middle Ages and the Renaissance have been grossly exaggerated. Traits presumed to be hallmarks of the new times – a passion for classical letters; the desire to embellish contemporary writing with Greco-Roman myth; a rich, lusty enjoyment of love, life, and nature; the exaltation of man in his secular destiny – all these are amply manifest in the works of Chrétien de Troyes, Guillaume de Lorris, Jean de Meun, and Guillaume de Machaut. Similarly, quite a few so-called medieval practices – alchemy, astrology, allegory, and typology – extended well into the seventeenth century. Distinctions between the two periods can be made, however, and for our purposes perhaps the most significant are a sense of history and of literary self-consciousness.

The French Middle Ages were strikingly autonomous. French and Occitan literature reigned triumphant throughout Europe. Native authors were influenced by Celtic legends and, of course, by writings in classical and medieval Latin; thus the twelfth century has been rightly called an *aetas ovidiana*, and Virgil was a supreme authority during the entire era. But Frenchmen created their own vernacular poetry largely without adhering to foreign models. *Chansons de geste*, courtly romance, the allegorical *dit amoureux* evolved 'naturally,' each author aware of his predecessors' work but creating on his own, the 'rules' derived from within. And from where else could they come? In the early period *artes poeticae* were devoted uniquely to general problems of rhetoric and to works in Latin. When a *Razos de trobar* and *Art de seconde rhétorique* tradition evolved oriented toward the vernacular, first in Occitan, later in French, only the lyric genres were considered appropriate for normative scrutiny.

In the sixteenth century, on the other hand, men sensed differences between themselves and preceding ages, whether the medieval or the Greco-Roman. It has been said that this epoch marks the beginnings of French literary history, with Renaissance humanists (dating back, it is true, to the end of the fourteenth century) for the first time becoming aware of period divisions.[1] Suffering from an inferiority complex in the face of Antiquity, envisaging the Ancients in a new light, Ronsard and his successors sought to imitate classical genres, not just to incorporate myths, themes, or rhetorical figures: that is, to revitalize form as well as content. In this, they partook of an international, European concern: for the first time in centuries France underwent a major foreign cultural influence – that of Italy – and learned to share the Italian obsession with Greece and Rome. Following in the wake of Petrarch, Boccaccio, Ariosto, Sannazaro, and Vida, Frenchmen conceived of a genre – the *grand œuvre* (Sebillet), *long poëme* (du Bellay), *grand poëme* (Ronsard), or *œuvre heroïque* (Peletier) – which could recreate classical epic, approximating and even rivalling Homer and Virgil. This reorientation in the conception of literature was the product of the 1540s and 1550s, of a new school (Ronsard's *Brigade*) that called for a literary revolution. Significantly, whereas Sebillet's *Art poétique françoys* (1548) only devotes a few words to epic, an entire chapter in du Bellay's *Deffence et Illustration de la Langue Françoyse* (1549) concentrates on the *long poëme Françoys* (Book II, chapter v). And, in contrast to Jean Lemaire de Belges, Sebillet, and others, du Bellay's esthetic is based entirely upon a conscious, willful repudiation of the past national heritage as he knew it in favor of imitating Antiquity:

> Se compose donq' celuy qui voudra enrichir sa Langue, à l'immitation des meilleurs aucteurs Grez & Latins: & à toutes leurs plus grandes vertuz, comme à un certain but, dirrige la pointe de son style … Et certes, comme ce n'est point chose vicieuse, mais grandement louable, emprunter d'une Langue estrangere les sentences & les motz, & les approprier à la sienne: aussi est ce chose grandement à reprendre, voyre odieuse à tout lecteur de liberale nature, voir en une mesme Langue une telle immitation …
>
> Ly donques & rely premierement (ò Poëte futur), fueillete de main nocturne & journelle les exemplaires Grecz & Latins: puis me laisse toutes ces vieilles poësies Francoyses aux Jeux Floraux de Thoulouze & au Puy de Rouan … (1: viii; 2: iv)[2]

Several causes can be adduced to explain the rise of French Renaissance epic. One of the most important is a revival of classical scholarship, especially Hellenic studies: in the 1540s Hugues Salel translated Homer, Richard Le Blanc translated Plato and Hesiod, Jacques Peletier du Mans translated Horace's *Ars Poetica*, Homer was edited in the text, and Aristotle's *Poetics* was translated in Italy. The Italian influence was indeed paramount, both with regard to original creations and in the area of criticism. Among heroic poems from beyond the Alps, composed in Latin or the

vernacular, the following had the greatest impact: Petrarch's *Africa*
(1338–43–74), Boccaccio's *Teseida* (1340), Pulci's *Morgante* (1483),
Boiardo's *Orlando innamorato* (1494), Ariosto's *Orlando furioso* (1516,
1532), Sannazaro's *De partu Virginis* (1526), Vida's *Christias* (1535), and
Trissino's *Italia liberata dai Goti* (1547–8). The rules for epic were decreed
in *Artes poeticae*, in prefaces to epics, or in independent treatises. Also to be
considered are the factors of patronage (the poet flatters his patron by glorifying the latter's ancestors), of Christianity (he adopts a prestigious pagan
apparatus to propagate the true faith), and of French patriotism (he seeks to
vie with the best produced by ancient Rome and modern Italy). Renaissance
authors, obsessed with a newly discovered artistic self-consciousness,
yearning to display both encyclopedic knowledge and philosophical depth,
and aware of the esthetic as an essential element in literature, strove to
create works of high art planned according to rules – in Ronsard's own
words, 'Les conceptions grandes & hautes ... une bouche sonnant plus
hautement que les autres.'[3] The Pléiade regarded epic highly because it enabled people to take the vernacular seriously, it required learning from the
poet, it bestowed immortality upon him, and it enabled him to demonstrate
the full richness of his native language.

The neoclassical epic reigned supreme in France, as in the rest of Western
Europe, for three centuries, for the period which extends from Ronsard
to Chénier and beyond. The 1650s and 1660s mark a high point in its
production, but the sixteenth and eighteenth centuries produced their full
share. Throughout this era the heroic poem was considered by all to be the
noblest of literary kinds, the only one capable of granting utter glory to a
writer, a nation, and a language. However, it would be an error to assume
stereotyped uniformity over all three centuries. Within a general Virgilian
framework, room for variety was to be found. Ovid, Lucan, Tasso, and
Marino, even medieval epic and romance, served as models. In terms of
subject-matter, we can classify epics as pagan neoclassical, Italianate romance, Biblical, hagiographical, idyllic and pastoral, historical, contemporary, encyclopedic and philosophical, or burlesque and comic. And
they could be derived from sacred or profane history or be works of pure
imagination.

As is to be expected, the kinds of epic in vogue shifted over the years,
as did the particular models held up for imitation. In the age of Scève and du
Bartas the scientific epic (*Lehrepos*) proved to be more important than
heroic poems. Then, for a good fifty years *La Franciade* dominated the scene,
and most poetasters prior to 1623 sought to write historical or neoclassical texts in the style of Ronsard. The seventeenth century in general, and the
epics of the 1650s in particular, were more romantic in conception, subject to the influence of Torquato Tasso. The same period also witnessed a

flowering of Christian Biblical and hagiographic poems. Then, after 1660, for another fifty years or so epicists sought to captivate their audience with shorter, more credible and 'rational' performances. The eighteenth century continued this trend but, after 1730, with a new model in vogue, Voltaire's *Henriade*, and with a politically militant Voltairean orientation. Other no less significant trends in Enlightenment epic are to be traced to the influence of Milton and Fénelon, and to contemporary explorations or the march of scientific progress. From the 1640s on we also find a development of Italian origin: comic epic – first burlesque travesty (Scarron, Dassoucy) then the heroi-comic poem in all its splendor (Boileau, Gresset, Voltaire, Parny).

Poets and theoreticians were divided over several issues: can an epic treat a contemporary or near-contemporary subject? should it be historically accurate or largely a work of the imagination? should the action be simple and coherent or contain a plethora of episodes? should the subject be taken from national (for example, medieval) history, from classical Antiquity, or from the Bible? and should it be embellished by the Christian supernatural, pagan myth, or allegories? Nonetheless, the vast majority of these men agreed on the basic characteristics of epic, its nature and function. They conceived it as a narrative in verse of illustrious actions – illustrious because they treat of prowess in war and because their 'actors' are of noble rank: cf. Horace's *Ars Poetica*, 73: 'Res gestae regumque ducumque et tristia bella.' An epic is ample in scope, contains vast practical and theoretical knowledge, 'une forme et image d'Univers' (Peletier), 'quasi un piccolo mondo' (Tasso), and is worthy of being interpreted on one or more allegorical levels. Therefore, it has to be morally exemplary, with admirable protagonists, capable of serving as a model to princes. And in order to convince princes to follow the path of virtue, the plot has to be credible. The heroic poem will also be permeated with the supernatural, borrow themes, motifs, and conventions from Greco-Roman Antiquity, and be composed in the sublime style.

The most significant fact about the neoclassical epic in France, from Ronsard to Chénier, is its alleged failure. Histories of literature, student manuals, studies by eminent scholars, are, for once, in agreement. The richness of the French epic in the Middle Ages as well as in the modern period renders the phenomenon all the more striking. It is certainly true that this most illustrious of genres did not produce a work of art generally considered to be a masterpiece, one of the monuments of world literature: the official, academic literary canon in France makes no claim to a *Lusiads* or a *Paradise Lost*; and none of the neoclassical epicists is presumed to be on a par with Corneille, Molière, and Racine. On the contrary, two of the greatest writers in French letters, each a titan in his age, attempted a heroic poem in the style of Virgil which proved, in the eyes of posterity, to be mediocre: Ronsard's *Franciade* and Voltaire's *Henriade* were sufficient in and of themselves to launch the notion 'Les Français n'ont pas la tête épique.'

Reasons given for this state of affairs are many. Renaissance and neoclassical authors suffered from having to vie with Homer and Virgil on their own terrain: the genre was defined too precisely from classical models, leaving the modern poet insufficient scope for his own genius. He felt obliged to imitate in an artificial, mechanical way the structure, themes, and motifs of his models and as a result captured only the externals of the *Iliad* and the *Aeneid*, never their essence. He simply adhered too strictly to the rules. And he often chose Greco-Roman subjects not appropriate for his own time, with no relationship to the modern world. The imposed supernatural, the incoherent juxtaposition of a more or less authentic *merveilleux chrétien* and a totally conventional *merveilleux payen* contributed to disparity in tone. Because the characters, especially the hero, were expected to illustrate virtues and vices, to be all good or all bad, they generally succeeded in having no personality at all, lacking the modicum of mimetic, credible psychology. Finally, it is a fact that only great writers produce masterpieces, and far too many French epicists – including the highly touted Chapelain – lacked the talent for the job. For whatever reasons, they did not make their creations live.

My preceding two paragraphs summarize the generally accepted view. However, I should like to make the following observations. Although the neoclassical Renaissance heroic poem turned out to be a relative failure, this failure, like the conception of the genre in the first place, was a European phenomenon, not strictly a French one. Spain, with her *siglo de oro*, perhaps the richest literature in the world between 1500 and 1700, did not succeed in the epic any better than France. Nor did Germany. Nor, with the lone exceptions of Camoens and Milton, did Portugal and England. Ronsard and Voltaire were very great writers who ruined themselves at epic – as did Petrarch with the *Africa*, Boccaccio with the *Teseida*, Sannazaro with the *De partu Virginis*, and Lope de Vega with the *Jerusalén conquistada*. Then, too, just as the French Middle Ages produced innumerable masterpieces in late *chanson de geste*, romance, and allegory, which do not resemble the *Song of Roland*, the Renaissance succeeded in other genres, among which are sublime short poems and long ones in various styles worthy of being considered masterpieces even though they do not resemble the *Aeneid*. This phenomenon has long been recognized by critical circles in Italy and England concerning their own national literatures. With all due respect to Tasso's genius, Pulci, Boiardo, Ariosto, even Marino and Tassoni have found a place in the Italian critical canon on an equal footing. In England (a nation less rich in the long poem) Spenser has never been presumed inferior to Milton simply because he was influenced by medieval romances and Ariosto rather than by Virgil. I submit that a comparable situation occurred in France, one largely unknown to the general reading public and to many specialists in the field. Several major writers, including paradoxically the two mentioned above, succeeded brilliantly in other kinds of elevated verse or in mock epic: I refer to Ronsard's passionately sublime *Hymnes* and *Discours*; d'Aubigné's militant satirical poem against the Catholics, *Les Tragiques*; Saint-Amant's Biblical *idyle heroïque*, *Moyse sauvé*; and Boileau's and Voltaire's riotously funny *Le Lutrin* and *La Pucelle*. And I believe that one unknown, forgotten writer of the seventeenth century, Pierre Le Moyne, SJ, wrote a splendid *poëme heroïque* in the style of Tasso, *Saint Louis, ou la Sainte Couronne reconquise*, which deserves rehabilitation. In other words, when writers in France, between 1500 and 1800, tried to redo Homer and Virgil, the results were unfortunate. However, the *artes poeticae* did not stifle all talent. Indeed, we discover a striking discrepancy between theoretical precept and the practice of living, creative artists, for the creative impulse in many cases simply did not surrender to the law of pedants. Although epicists rarely challenged the authority of the Ancients, they were adept at ignoring or shaping the rules to suit their own convenience and thus did produce masterworks, 'irregular' indeed, but no more so than *chansons de geste*, which perpetuated the greatness, the spirit even, of *chanson de geste* and of Virgil also. This is one of the very real triumphs of the French Renaissance and of French classicism.[4]

Following the counsel promulgated in the *Deffence et Illustration de la Langue Françoyse*, Pierre de Ronsard (1524–85) decided, by imitating Homer and Virgil, to render French literature illustrious through the creation of a heroic epic. As leader of the *Brigade*, it was up to him to master the leading genre encompassed within the new program. Indeed, he worked on *La Franciade*, off and on, for some twenty-five years. There is no need to retell the long story of the poem's genesis, the ups and downs of Ronsard's quest for subsidy; suffice it to say that in 1572 the Prince of Poets published the first four books of his epic, out of a projected twenty-four. Although the poem was moderately successful and although Ronsard returned to these four books, revising them in the course of subsequent editions of his *Œuvres*, he never attempted to bring the work to completion. However, whatever his, or our own, opinion of its ultimate merits, we must not forget that *La Franciade* had a tremendous influence on two generations of poets, indeed that most French epics written in the period 1572–1623 were patterned after it. The poem even solicited a variety of sequels and pastiches: Jean Godard's proposed *Franciade* (1594), Pierre Delaudun d'Aigaliers's *Franciade* (1603), Claude Garnier's Book 5 of the *Franciade* (1604), Jacques Guillot's Books 5 and 6 of the *Franciade* (1606, 1615), and Geuffrin's *Franciade* (1623).

*La Franciade*[5] seeks to reproduce the structure and the thematic material of the *Aeneid*. From Virgil's masterpiece Ronsard takes the Trojan context of the plot, the storm-shipwreck-recital pattern, a love affair à la Dido and Aeneas, and the rough equivalent of a trip to Hades. Thus Francus leaves his home to found a new Troy; he is shipwrecked on the isle of Crete, delivers his host from a redoubtable adversary, and becomes involved with the king's daughters, one of whom commits suicide while the other foretells her beloved's progeny. Ronsard's poem amplifies the dynastic aspect of the *Aeneid*. Since Francus is said to be the founder of the French royal house, praise of him redounds to the credit of Ronsard's sixteenth-century patron, King Charles IX. A lengthy prophecy occurs in Book 4 because the protagonist expresses interest in the future of his race, especially his most renowned descendant – Charles IX! Thus a nine-hundred-line section on Merovingian kings fits into Ronsard's design. It also serves a moral aim, as a *speculum principum* or lesson in governance to King Charles himself. Furthermore, the notion that France and Rome developed from the same Trojan stock is crucial to our understanding of the text. Ronsard tells us that both Francus and Aeneas are at the origin of the *translatio imperii et studii* central to Valois ideology and his own claims as an artist. Thus the poet seeks to instill in his readers loyalty to the prince and a sense of national, civic purpose. Book 4 concerns France not Francus, a nation not a mere individual; *La Franciade* fuses chronicle and epic.

Another Virgilian theme is the triumph of reason over passion, order over chaos, war over love, duty over desire – of male over female values. Indeed, Ronsard goes beyond the *Aeneid*, moralizing and Christianizing Virgil in Book 3 of his epic. From Dido (and from Apollonius of Rhodes's Medea) he creates two women, sisters: Clymène and Hyante. Clymène is given Dido's evil, passionate nature; she and Francus never enjoy a tête-à-tête nor does physical intimacy occur between them. Hyante serves a prophetic purpose: she reveals to Francus (and to the reader) the future of the French royal line. These innovations are introduced in order to render the protagonist guiltless, so that he can in no way be blamed for actions committed at the Cretan court. Reinforcing this thrust, we find a profusion of religious observances: rites, prayers, auguries, prophecies. Ronsard's poem exalts active, martial energy (the young Francus and Merovingian *rois fainéants* are condemned for laziness) and an upright family life, whether in Epirus or Crete, both under the aegis of all-powerful Jove.

It has been said that a sheaf of pages extracted from *La Franciade* would establish the glory of any poet.[6] Critics agree that certain set-pieces, specific scenes or episodes, are quite successful. Of these, we can cite the storm at sea and a splendid duel between Francus and Phovère in the spirit of David and Goliath (Book 2). Clymène's fierce, masochistically passionate outburst of jealousy in Book 3 is most convincing, as is the satirical portrait-gallery of wicked kings in Book 4. Ronsard the author of *Hymne des Daimons* creates a convincingly 'dark,' demonic atmosphere for Hyante's prophecy as well as Clymène's suicide.

Nonetheless, despite the fact that *La Franciade* contains splendid episodes, beautiful individual pages written in powerful, exquisite verse, it does not hold together as a work of art. The poem simply lacks unity and cohesion. Ronsard imitated Virgil, Homer, Apollonius, Ovid, and others in all the externals but, unlike Tasso and Camoens, failed to give the poem his own stamp, its unique voice and tone. In addition, his choice of hero was unfortunate. Instead of following du Bellay's advice in the *Deffence et Illustration* and glorifying a genuinely national, popular figure, a Tristan or Lancelot, Ronsard decided upon an artificial, humanist, scholarly Francus, whose legend by the 1570s no longer commanded popular belief. His poem thus lacks the genuine historical foundation that might have encouraged him to exploit Virgilian topics creatively in a new context. However, what Ronsard did with Francus was even less fortunate. Hector's legendary son lacked both mythical aura and historical credibility; Ronsard then dealt him the final blow by rendering him, as Diderot would have said, perfect, that is, lifeless. He and the other characters do not manifest depth, a tragic flaw, or genuine, active heroism. They are listless, one-dimensional stereotypes. In other words, the writer of a long narrative poem must possess the ability to create living, believable individuals, that novelistic talent also required for long narratives in prose. Ronsard, superb in all aspects of creative verse, was simply not a story-teller. Therefore, *La Franciade* became the first of a series of highly acclaimed, long-awaited epics that turned out not to be bad but to be mediocre, to miss the very first rank that their authors and public presumed they had a right to attain.

Although *La Franciade* is one of the failures in the history of French literature, by an extraordinary turn of irony Ronsard nonetheless proved to be the first great master of the sublime style since Jean de Meun.[7] He did this with a series of shorter texts, the best of which are to be found in two volumes of *Hymnes* published in 1555 and 1556 and in *Discours des Misères de ce temps*, written for the most part in the early 1560s. Some of these poems were conceived as sketches for *La Franciade*; others bear no direct relation to the incomplete masterwork and adhere to literary kinds other than the Virgilian epic. Nonetheless, it is there, as in *Gargantua et*

*Pantagruel*, that the reader will find the true epic spirit of the French Renaissance. I believe that these pieces are as essential to the history of the sublime style in France as the 'petites épopées' of Vigny and Hugo and, for that reason in addition to their intrinsic esthetic worth, they merit scrutiny.

Scholars generally have divided *Les Hymnes* into the following categories: encomiastic; didactic (scientific, moral, philosophical, religious); and heroic or mythological. In reality, each and every hymn contains all three elements, though in varying proportions. Conceived in the panegyric mode and connected to the 'demonstrative' genre in rhetoric, each was written with a particular dedicatee in mind, conceived as a prayer to God for the dedicatee and as a gift that will grant him immortality. Each hymn purports to contain learning, having come into existence by a special act of grace from the Muses to a poet in ecstasy, a *poeta doctus* who transmits their message to his public (the dedicatee) in lyrical, ecstatic tones. And this wisdom is generally accompanied by, and embodied in the telling of, classical myths, which in epic style sing the deeds of ancient gods or heroes in order to celebrate their power and, by so doing, exalt the dedicatee, himself associated with the hero-gods. The Ronsardian hymn then is epic, didactic, and lyrical; it is extrinsically bound to a flesh-and-blood patron of the arts in sixteenth-century France; and it seeks, in the Orphic tradition, to discover and reveal the secrets of the universe through a form of ritual incantation. These are sacred poems, celebrating, glorifying, raising up to the divine; indeed, they partake of, or invoke, a ritual of sacrifice and initiation.[8] I propose to examine two of the more strictly narrative of these 'naturae rerum cantica docta,' as Dorat called them in his liminary poem to the 1555 edition: *Hymne des Astres*, and *Hymne de Calaïs et de Zethes*.[9]

In *Hymne des Astres* Ronsard concentrates on telling a myth, partly taken from Hesiod's *Works and Days*, partly of his own invention. When the giants rebelled against Olympus, they would have seized the citadel by night but for the stars, who warn Jupiter and help him defeat the adversary. As a reward, the king of the gods fixes the stars and grants them astrological power. This story obviously appealed to Ronsard, since he had already treated it in the famous *Ode à Michel de l'Hospital*. For him, the cosmic battle between gods and giants symbolizes a never-ending struggle between forces of harmony and order and the powers of chaotic darkness. *Allegorice*, the Olympians stand for God and his angels, the court of France, Pléiade learning, virtues, and the harmony of the spheres; their terrestrial adversaries for Satan's armies, Huguenot rebels against the French crown, the ignorant Sorbonne, vices, and cosmic anarchy. Other poets, perhaps Ronsard also, meant the giants to represent human beings who, guilty of hubris, forget their origin and their mortal limits, men who by denying

the human condition refuse God's law.[10] Regardless of the specific allegories
we impose on the poem, the author's position is clear. Like Claudel, he
supports order over disorder, legitimacy over rebellion, Jupiter over the
Satyr. In the class struggle, whether on a secular or cosmic scale, he will
remain loyal to the masters and will condemn the upstart who, choosing to
go beyond his given, natural bounds, threatens the stability of the universe.

To go beyond one's bounds implies motion, hence Ronsard's ideological
preference for immobility over movement. He tells us of fishermen, hunters, and merchants, who voyage over the earth, and of the heroes of the
*Iliad* and the *Argonautica*; these men are not condemned as such, but
their pursuits are deemed no better than others. Since all mortals are subject
to the will of the stars, it makes little difference whether they cross the
seas or remain at home. Indeed, the only professions to receive special
adulation are the philosophers, astrologers, and poets, presumably a sed-
entary folk. Similarly, in early times the stars wandered about the heavens
like a flock of sheep. Their activity, though decorative, was of no particular use and, like that of the mortal wanderers, merits neither praise nor
criticism. After the battle is over, Jupiter nails the stars in place. Symbolic
of divine power, knowledge, and beauty, they form a perfect circle of light,
a circumference whose center is God himself. They are pure, immutable
fire; their world will no longer be subject to change as ours is.

Some types of motion are entirely physical (sailors at sea, the dance of
the early stars), while others bear spiritual overtones. The giants' effort
to rise vertically to heaven and dethrone the gods belongs to the second
category. Although it results in a physical movement upward, symbolically
it represents a descent, for the giants seek to bring down the gods ('à fin
de debouter / Jupiter de son regne, & vaincu, le donter,' 43–4), and their
power of reason is subjected to passion and lust. Ronsard elaborates the
conventional antitheses of height and depth, heaven and hell, good stars and
evil earth. Not all vertical motion is evil, however. The stars look down
on us, influencing our destinies while, paradoxically, man, who is most
subject to astrological power, is the only creature who names the stars
and seeks to comprehend them:

> Mais l'homme, par sur tout, eut sa vie sujette
> Aux destins que le Ciel par les Astres luy jette,
> L'homme, qui le premier comprendre les osa,
> Et telz noms qu'il voulut au Ciel leur composa.    (105–8)

The Narrator of *Les Astres* also rises to heaven. His is a true spiritual
ascent, for his purpose is understanding not fighting, he loves the divinity,
and he will undergo enlightenment during the voyage. It is wrong for

man's soul to be imprisoned on earth, says Ronsard; instead it should contemplate divine mysteries:

> C'est trop long temps, Mellin, demeuré sur la terre
> Dans l'humaine prison, qui l'Esprit nous enserre,
> Le tenant engourdy d'un sommeil ocieux
> Il faut le delïer, & l'envoyer aux cieux ...   (1–4)

In contrast to the giants' trudging up mountains, the poet's soul truly flies, an act which brings exaltation and joy, the soaring of the imagination, feelings of liberty, harmony, and transcendence, and conquest over both space and time.

As a result of the battle between giants and Olympians, the cosmos is transformed. The stars are fixed, from 'un bel ornement' (23) they become functional, mobility gives way to immutability, and, before the poem is over, the Narrator is illumined, becoming a nobler, wiser man. Thus the movement of *Les Astres* is forward, one of progress. A good cosmos becomes better. In that process, the stars grant us duration and measure, help us tell the future and predict tempests and plagues. Time is shown to be good, and mastery over time good also. The one unhappy note derives from the fact that the constellations are eternal and we are not. Included in their stasis is immortality; although our souls are permanent, on earth we are neither static nor perfect; and our imperfection prevents even philosophers from comprehending the stellar mysteries or making use of astrological information.

In a certain sense, the giants have been guilty of sedition against the father of the gods, Immortal Jupiter, and thus of a variation on the Oedipal rebellion that includes the breaking of a tabu and exercising forbidden curiosity. Their punishment is Oedipus's, a symbolic mutilation. The stars, who side with the superego Father against the passion-ridden, chaos-oriented giants, are rewarded with power, while the Narrator, who also supports the Father, is rewarded with knowledge. His flight to the stars is an acceptable quest for divine protection. Anticipating Milton, he tells us that real heroes, like Abdiel, Enoch, and Lot, remain faithful to authority.

The cosmic battle between gods and giants is expressed as a confrontation between light and darkness. The giants climb up from the nether world in darkness. Their purpose is to fall upon the Olympians at night and to imprison them in Hades. In a splendid passage, these creatures of hell are blinded by the stars and brained by Jupiter:

> Ja desja s'ataquoit l'escharmouche odieuse,
> Quant des Astres flambans la troupe radieuse

Pour esbloüir la veüe aux Geantz furieux,
Se vint droicte planter vis-à-vis de leurs yeux,
Et alors Jupiter du traict de sa tempeste
Aux Geantz aveuglez ecarbouilla la teste,
Leur faisant distiller l'humeur de leurs cerveaux
Par les yeux, par la bouche, & par les deux naseaux,
Comme un fromage mol, qui surpendu s'égoute
Par les trous d'un pannier, à terre goute à goute.    (69–78)

Their state can be represented as absence of good, absence of sight, and absence of light. The stars, on the contrary, made up of pure fire, are the source of light. Their vision is perfect, for they look down on us and also perceive the giants' assault early enough to warn Jupiter. Then they blind the giants with their light (divine spiritual power), while Jupiter brains them with his lightning (divine physical power). Night-time is appropriate for crime, illumination for its disclosure and proper punishment. The stars and Olympians are able to see without being seen, and by seeing they conquer. Furthermore, like the stars, the Narrator is gifted with spiritual insight. Renouncing the slumber of earthly affairs, he is vouchsafed a vision of the heavens, he unravels the secrets of the cosmos, and he permits us, his public, to envisage the entire event. His colleague and dedicatee, Mellin de Saint-Gelais, a specialist in astrology, is associated with gold-colored honey (12) and also considered to be a child of heaven. In this hymn fire plays a dual role: as punishment for the giants, and as initiation for the Narrator. The fundamental element that makes up the stars, fire represents purgation and chastisement, divine power, the source of life, and, finally, a subject for philosophical and poetic revery. It is the masculine force contained within this masculine location, the skies, the true home for man's soul and his intellectual spirit.

In this poem, as so often in Ronsard's works, the Narrator undergoes an Orphic experience, a divine voyage where he is wafted to the heavens and, through the intervention of his *daimons* or guardian Muse, enjoys a vision of the cosmos. As the Gallic Apollo or his priest, Ronsard is granted a special vocation because of his relationship to the gods, is even permitted to enhance Jupiter's (Henry II's) glory by celebrating it in his verse. Like the stars whom he resembles, whom he consciously emulates, the poet serves his lord morally and spiritually. He is blessed with *furor poeticus*, which gives him both knowledge and the mastery of verse. He becomes a teacher, an enlightener, a master. By discovering some of these secrets, by passing them on to us, the Narrator mediates between us and the gods. Spiritually as well as spatially, he occupies a middle realm between heaven and earth, thus rendering himself half divine and the equal of the King of France or his ministers.

It is appropriate that a poet should become the chosen mediator. In the Renaissance sense of the term, he is a philosopher and a magus, capable of dealing with astrological mysteries; as a singer and a philosopher, he is also capable of appreciating the mathematical harmony of the spheres, the *musica mundana* of the macrocosm that corresponds to the *musica humana* of man's body (the microcosm) and the *musica instrumentalis* Ronsard indulges in each time he sings his own lyrical works.

Pierre de Ronsard writes in an optimistic vein. In spite of certain mortal limits, the Narrator-poet-philosopher's vision is a tribute to man's conquest of nature, his freedom and lordship in the universe. According to the Renaissance notion of *dignitas hominis*, some humans are eager to know, capable of effort and enthusiasm, superior because they are erect and can watch the stars, in Ovid's phrase 'erectos ad sidera vultus.' The stars assist men to become great by instilling in them fundamental character traits and by their mere existence, for philosophers fulfill their destiny seeking to read the astral message, to fathom its truth. These individuals use their heads, in contrast to merchants and adventurers who travel the earth horizontally, oblivious to spiritual concerns. God's power over mankind can never be wholly understood. We all exist under his sway, subject to external fate and to our own bodily humors, but some people, especially those, like Ronsard, born under the sign of Saturn, can partially escape their destiny through poetic furor. Even though God's dominion is inscrutable to us, he is all-good and all-knowing, the benevolent first principle of existence. Those 'brainless' enough to rebel against him or to question his rule deserve the eternal punishment meted out to the giants. *Hymne des Astres*, which exalts the grandeur of the universe, also paints a moving contrast between cosmic fate and its human response, between the serene, eternal stars and men on earth, fragile in their mortality yet endowed with hope, insight, and lyrical faith.

*Hymne de Calaïs et de Zethes* is one of two poems in the second book of hymns (1556) – the other being *Hymne de Pollux et de Castor* – written specifically with *La Franciade* in mind. The two fragments, narrating episodes in the saga of the Argonauts, were meant to demonstrate to prospective patrons, such as the King of France, his sister the Duchess of Savoy, and the Cardinal of Lorraine, that they should subsidize the poet's endeavors to endow France with a national epic. Ronsard consciously adapted the versions of Apollonius of Rhodes and Valerius Flaccus and introduced into his hymn motifs from Virgil and Ovid, elaborating what Renaissance men considered a fitting monument of *sermo gravis*. It is perhaps a pity that the Vendômois did not continue his cycle of 'petites épopées' illustrating the life of Jason (a third fragment, entitled *Orphée*, was to be published in 1578), his own *Argonautica*, for it is in these hymns, not in *La Franciade*, that he recaptures the spirit of Greek myth.

For the first time since the *chansons de geste* and *romans d'aventures*, we find truly monstrous adversaries, shadow-figures depicted with the panoply of archetypal demonic imagery. Ronsard paints in glowing colors the suffering of Phineus, who has been blinded by Jupiter and is prevented from feeding himself by harpies. The story is told from Phineus's point of view. We sense the impenetrable darkness which enwraps the old man and how his only contact with the outside world – rendered all the more poignant in the case of a sightless person – is the birds' sharp-cutting talons, the snapping of their jaws, and their filthy, disgusting odor:

> Vomissant de leur gorge une odeur si mauvaise
> Que toute la viande en devenoit punaise.
> Tousjours d'un craquetis leur machoire cliquoit,
> Tousjours de palle fein leur bec s'entrechoquoit
> Comme la dent d'un loup, quand la fein l'epoinçonne
> De courre apres un cerf : la machoire luy sonne
> L'une sur l'aultre en vain, & par l'air d'un grand bruict
> Faict craqueter sa gueule apres le cerf qui fuit.    (185–92)

Ronsard develops a pattern of rot-filth-stench imagery worthy of Baudelaire or Sartre. Furthermore, the harpies reign over a desolate country, truly a Waste Land, in which the blessed function of nourishment has been thwarted. And since these demonic creatures, half-bird, half-woman, were placed under Jupiter's special protection (shedding one drop of their blood is tabu), they instill supernatural awe. We should remember that, according to Phineus's prophecy, the Argonauts have to escape or overcome obstacles no less threatening than the harpies: the Cyanean Rocks, the Amazons, the Stymphalian Birds, Prometheus's eagle, and the fiery bulls, the Cadmean army, and Argus, who guard the Golden Fleece. Their voyage is made up of a series of encounters with one supernatural adversary after another, a trek to the Other World in quest of treasure and a woman, the eternal tradition of romance.

However, Phineus proclaims that the Argonauts will succeed in their endeavors. In this particular episode, to give battle to the flying harpies come two splendid flying youths, sons of the wind. Calaïs and Zethe chase the harpies away, vaulting through the air like cranes, hawks, and falcons. Their wings are of gold and blue, their gold-blond hair flows in the wind,

they wield a 'flamboyante espée' (362), and Jason himself, who shines like
the planet Venus at night (54–5), has the beginnings of a golden beard.
Ronsard also praises the brightness of Marguerite of France, the poem's
dedicatee, who shines for her people. Thus the blind Phineus, a prisoner of
the night who swears oaths by the sun he can no longer see, is rescued by
a pair of light-heroes, members of a golden band led by a golden chief in
quest of the Golden Fleece, narrated in a poem dedicated to a princess of
the day. In the end Phineus is permitted to eat meat again and is honored by
the young people who surround him. In return, he enlightens them. For,
if they can defeat harpies beyond the blind man's ken, with his inner light he
perceives and predicts the future, beyond theirs. The two modes of vision
assist each other, and, as in *Hymne des Astres*, brightness triumphs over the
dark; thus the poet expresses through a pattern of day-night imagery the
ultimate victory of good over evil, of heroes over monsters.

Ronsard himself suggests a symbolic or allegorical reading of the myth:

> Or' adieu Chevalliers, fils des Dieux excellants,
> Adieu noble Jason, adieu freres vollans.
> Ou soit que vous soyez gens de tresbones vies,
> Philosophes constans, qui chassés les harpies
> De la table des Rois, les flateurs, les menteurs
> Qui devorent leur bien, & de leurs serviteurs,
> Ou soit que vous ayez la plante si legere
> Que l'on ait faint de vous la fable mensongere
> Que vous passéz les vents (car la viste Aëllon,
> Cellenon, & sa sœur ne denottent sinon
> Les sofflets ravissants des vents & des orages),
> Voguez heureusement aux Colchides rivages.    (707–18)

These two interpretations, the physical and the moral, conform to the
medieval traditions of the *Ovide moralisé* and the *Genealogia Deorum* or
to Ronsard's own *Hercule chrestien*.[11] The moral one especially is worthy of
scrutiny. *Hymne de Calaïs et de Zethes* is dedicated to Marguerite of
France, Duchess of Savoy, who, according to Ronsard, despises flatterers
and sycophants (9–42) and who, in addition, granted him a favorable
reception. We know that in the early 1550s, Marguerite defended the Pléiade
poets in general, and Ronsard in particular, against influential people at
court who preferred the older Marotic school of Mellin de Saint-Gelais. It is
appropriate, therefore, that Ronsard should refer to 'gens de tresbones
vies' who defend kings and kings' servants against evil courtiers. He thus
fuses the mythological, didactic, and encomiastic threads in his narrative.
If my interpretation is correct, Calaïs and Zethe correspond to Marguerite,

the harpies to the Marotic poets and their protectors, and Phineus to Ronsard himself. Fittingly, the dedicatee is assimilated to the mythical heroes, the ostensible subject of the hymn. In addition, Phineus has the power of prophecy and is punished for having revealed the truth, as Ronsard was criticized for excessive furor in his Pindaric odes. Like the immortal Homer, Phineus is blind, and Ronsard is partially deaf. Just as the mythical Greek prophet mediates between mortals and the gods, so does the author of *La Philosophie*, *Les Daimons*, *Les Astres*, and *L'Eternité*. Furthermore, although Marguerite and others help Ronsard to become the Prince of Poets and nourish him, his former enemies, powerful, distinguished men, continue their own court-careers; so Calaïs and Zethe are forbidden to kill the harpies or even to shed their blood. Significantly, at the end of *Calaïs et Zethes* Ronsard delivers a diatribe against great lords who do not reward poets. Phineus's position may now be secure but such is not yet the case for his sixteenth-century French spiritual progeny.

Another interpretation of the allegory-passage is the following: the 'gens de tresbones vies,' who are also 'philosophes constans,' refer to the Pléiade poets, du Bellay (author of *Le Poëte courtisan*) and Ronsard, who in their verse flailed out pitilessly at the venal muse and evils of the court. Calaïs and Zethe as falcons attack the flying harpies; so, *allegorice*, Ronsard is pitted against evil doubles, bad court poets or aristocratic court parasites. Members of an elite band of warriors that includes Jason, Orpheus, Peleus, Castor, and Pollux, the twins correspond to the Prince of Poets and his friends, creators of verse for an elite! In the end, the implied author offers his hymn to the heroes themselves, perhaps as an arm to be wielded by fellow fighters; once again he emulates the subject of his own poem. If I am correct, Ronsard imagines the Argonauts in Ancient Greece and the *Brigade* in sixteenth-century France as having attained that synthesis of *fortitudo et sapientia*, of *armas y letras*, which was the ideal of both Ancient and Renaissance Man; not prowess coming to the aid of wisdom but courage and wisdom fused in the same heroes, who wield their quills like swords and go singing into battle. Calaïs and Zethe, children of the wind (the Word), who wear Apollo's gold, prudently insist on guarantees, lest, by helping Phineus, they offend the gods. They are truly *pueri senes*, young boys with the wisdom of age that Phineus himself lacks. However, nothing prevents us from accepting both interpretations, perhaps symbolically rather than as fixed allegories. The poet as savior, the poet as victim, Ronsard as winged youth and as an infirm greybeard – are not these the two poles of his own psyche that represent his ambivalent feelings toward the court and his calling as a writer? This poem, in praise of a patron, takes as its subject the relationship between poet and prince, poet and patron, poet and public.

The theme of the artist is central to *Calaïs et Zethes*. Among the Argonauts, whose voyage benefits from the protection of Juno and of Pallas, goddess of wisdom, we find the poet-seer Orpheus, who partakes of the company but is not required to row. It is with verbal encouragement, through singing and the telling of stories, that he performs distinguished service. In a sense, he is the heart and soul of the expedition, the upholder of a sacred vocation, allotted a place of honor apart from the others. This is the Orpheus so often designated in Ronsard's verse as the first poet to receive the divine flame, a mediator between gods and men.[12] Also on the quest is Mopsus, a prophet of Apollo, who wears laurel on his helmet. Both Orpheus and Mopsus are, to some extent, conquerors, for, like Jason, Calaïs, Zethe, Pollux, and Castor, they explore strange new realms and are the first humans to cross the seas. Phineus also is a prophet beloved of Apollo, although cursed by Jupiter. Like Tiresias and Homer he is blind and reduced to misery; we know that Orpheus will die in wretchedness, torn apart by Maenads; and Mopsus is incapable of predicting his own end. Prophets, like poets, suffer alienation from the gods. Their gifts bring deformity and pain. Nonetheless, Phineus utters finer sounds than Jupiter's harpies, who make cruel noise with their beaks, furies who indulge in *furor non poeticus*. He has hope, is saved by the Argonauts, and then predicts their future. Divine inspiration and the power to communicate through language have never abandoned him. Nor presumably will they abandon the Vendômois hymn-maker, Pierre de Ronsard, who possesses a prophetic as well as poetic fury, who, like Orpheus and Mopsus, claims to explore the secrets of the cosmos and to mediate between gods and men. The poet, the artist, and the prophet have a role in epic, to encourage great heroes, to share their tribulations, to contribute, if possible, to their victory, and, singing their glory, to render them immortal. This is true in ancient times and in the Renaissance. Ronsard has found more than one alter ego among the bard-prophets of Greek myth, figures on whom he projects his own anxieties and his aspirations to grandeur.

Finally, *Calaïs et Zethes* tells a traditional tale of romance. Because of Phineus's prophecy and Ronsard's earlier muster of the Argonauts, the entire *Argonautica* is brought inside the frame of this one hymn. Like *romans d'aventures* in the Middle Ages, the Quest of the Golden Fleece concerns a hero who, having accepted a Call to Adventure, sets off with his friends on a long journey in order to win a precious object. We see him brave the unknown, undergo adventures and ordeals in an Other World setting, overcome monsters and natural or supernatural forces, with the help of supernatural guides succeed in winning the treasure and a fairy bride, then cross the Return Threshold to his own realm. In the tradition of Gilgamesh, Achilles, and Aeneas, he and his band are a chosen race of demigods ('O troupe genereuse, enfans des Dieus issus ...' 235), engaged in an expedition to savage lands. The number of possible adventures between the starting point and their ultimate triumph is practically infinite; *Hymne de Calaïs et de Zethes* recounts but one of these adventures.

Indeed, part of the story's charm, of its appeal to the Renaissance public, derives from the fact that, resembling the medieval *Chevrefoil* or *Folie Tristan*, it tells of one episode in the life of an already famous hero. Calaïs and Zethe appear as world-saviors, sacred because they are *dioscuri*, who, owing to their supernatural origins, benefit from a divine nimbus and divine protection. In addition to helping others, however, the youths also help themselves. Like Lancelot's and Yvain's, their voyage is one of growth, of initiation in the ways of man and of the gods. Their wings appeared at the time of puberty, and their hair and wings are the color of the sun, of flame (the masculine element), and of procreative power. In Jungian terms, to fly is to proclaim one's freedom, imagination, spirituality, and deliverance from the gross material cares of the world, an inner dynamism and triumph over obstacle. In Freudian dream-interpretation, flight is an image of sexual stimulation, if not the sexual act itself. Now these youths chase away with their swords disgusting female adversaries, creatures of filth who threaten Phineus with their beaks and devour his food. The harpies represent the Terrible Mother, woman conceived as a murderous, castrating adversary. And Phineus, related to the sons of the Wind (he is their brother-in-law), whom they rescue and restore to his previous honor, is depicted as a decrepit old man:

> Il s'esleva du lict, ainsy qu'un songe vain,
> Apuyant d'un baton sa miserable main,
> Et tatonnant les murs sortit hors de la porte
> D'un pied foible & recreu, qui à peine supporte
> Son corps qui tramblotoit de vieillesse ...
> Ore un estourdiment tout le cerveau luy serre,
> Ore tout à lentour il pensoit que la terre
> Chancelloit dessoubs luy, & ores il dormoit
> Acablé d'un sommeil qui son chef assommoit.    (207–11, 217–20)

Does he not act as a father-surrogate to the youths? In my opinion, the *Hymne* recounts a symbolic sexual-puberty initiation, in which the young ego rejects his id and supports his superego, takes the father's side against the mother, atones with the father, then continues his route with an all-male band. However, the ego also projects onto the father his weakness and guilt (Phineus's rebellion against Father Jupiter and punishment for it by Jupiter's own harpies, blindness as wages for the Promethean and Oedipal sin of knowledge), while retaining for himself both innocence and strength. In the end day triumphs over night, male over female, life over death, rite, ritual, and sacrifice over despair, and a decent respect for age and property is restored as is food to a Waste Land, in an all-male, heroic fantasy world.

Of course, this interpretation applies primarily to the original myth and to its first great literary embodiment in Apollonius of Rhodes, secondarily to Ronsard. Homoerotic overtones in the myth especially are more appropriate to an ancient than to a modern society. Yet the story was recounted with enthusiasm by the same conservative, conformist, elitist Prince of Poets who exalted the cosmic 'power structure' in his other *Hymnes* and who would take the Catholic, royalist side with no less gusto in the *Discours*. In *Calaïs et Zethes* the tragic old world of Phineus gives way to the brighter, more optimistic one of the youthful Argonauts. Phineus's self-assertiveness is beaten out of him for his own good and that of society. He then expiates and is redeemed. Light triumphs over darkness. Yet the forces of night have not been destroyed. Their blood cannot be shed either; they have simply moved away. Both Apollo and Jupiter are satisfied, the *pueri* and the *senex* offer sacrifice to the gods, their sacrifices are accepted and their *pietas* recorded. The rebellious individual is restored to the community, and seemingly disparate elements subsumed under a cosmic, Olympian order. And the function of nurture is restored to mortals.

In the 1560s Ronsard wrote a series of poems concerned with the disputes between Catholics and Protestants then dividing France. These *Discours*, published singly, appearing as propaganda in the heat of battle, were gathered together in the 1567 edition of *Les Œuvres*; still others were added to the 1578 edition. The first three discourses are statements from a moderate, loyal Catholic who deplores violence and rebellion but sees good in both parties. However, with the Massacre of Vassy in 1562, Ronsard found himself drawn into the war on the Catholic side as the official literary spokesman for the court. For a year he wrote polemic after polemic, each more passionate and partisan than the last. Then, obeying Catherine de' Medici's orders, he silenced his committed muse, but for an occasional outburst, such as those following upon Catholic victories at Jarnac and Moncontour in 1569. And it is to Ronsard's honor that he was one of the very few Catholic writers who did not applaud the Saint Bartholomew's Day Massacre. Because of their exceptional literary worth, I shall restrict my study of the *Discours* to four poems written between May 1562 and April 1563, the most powerful of his early satires: *Discours des misères de ce temps*, *Continuation du Discours des misères*, *Remonstrance au peuple de France*, and *Responce aux injures et calomnies*.[13]

Ronsard is normally a poet of concord and harmony, the singer of light's victory over darkness. He was certainly capable of creating patterns of 'demonic imagery' in *Hymne des Daimons, Calaïs et Zethes, Pollux et Castor,* and *Hymne de l'Hyver.* But nowhere in his opus, nowhere in all of sixteenth-century literature prior to d'Aubigné, do we find so powerful an evocation of those dark, chaotic forces that threaten our sanity as in *Discours.* Protestants are compared to hail, rain, and wind, hostile Nature assaulting man. They wield knives and swords against France and shed her blood, aided by foreign invaders, the northern Goth with his cold wind or the Englishman from the Thames. The merchant is robbed and killed by brigands –

> Elle semble au marchant, helas! qui par malheur
> En faisant son chemin rencontre le volleur,
> Qui contre l'estomaq luy tend la main armée
> D'avarice cruelle & de sang affamée:
> Il n'est pas seullement content de luy piller
> La bourse & le cheval, il le fait despouiller,
> Le bat et le tourmente, & d'une dague essaye
> De luy chasser du corps l'ame par une playe:
> Puis en le voyant mort il se rit de ses coups,
> Et le laisse manger aux mâtins & aux loups.    (*Continuation,* 9–18)

– who also resemble the army of monsters born from a dragon's teeth in the myth of Cadmus. And God is threatened by the same unreasoning titans as in *Hymne des Astres.* Leagued against the forces of good are Calvinist vipers, serpents, and locusts of the Apocalypse with the potency of scorpions. A serpent has injected poison into Luther's body. The Reformers are caterpillars who, if permitted to survive one winter, ruin an orchard in the spring. These are the prelates who hide in sheep's clothing but are truly wolves. They are Circe's pigs, Cerberus, a werewolf, a donkey, a bull, tigers, lions, foxes, frogs, hornets, and wild bees. Their humanity has been reduced to the level of savage, unreasoning beasts, to creatures of the flesh unworthy of heaven. And Ronsard evokes in their wake figures of rot and garbage reminiscent of the harpies in *Calaïs et Zethes,* of nauseous disgust that reduces them beyond the pale of life.

As a result of this demonic assault, embodied in imagery of war, storm, and illness, mankind in general and France in particular are shown to be unstable. In *Remonstrance* Ronsard points out that men swing back and forth like weathercocks. Using what was to become a standard baroque motif, he compares people to bubbles, smoke, and leaves. The honors of the court are a torch soon snuffed out. Given this state of mutability, how can we expect to unite against the Turk? How will Jews and Saracens convert, seeing us as we are?

In our present state, says Ronsard, we have lost proper hierarchy and authority. In *Misères* he creates a pattern of imagery that can be ranged under the category of *verkehrte Welt*. Children struggle against their parents, brother against brother, servants against their masters, wives against husbands. People abandon their rightful pursuits to become soldiers or preachers, plowshares are bent into swords, and churches become pigsties. France is a horse out of control, refusing to obey her rider; the ship of state is abandoned; the rock of France and of Peter's Church has fallen; the tree is cut down. While inferiors defy natural order and seek sinful equality or even more sinful tyranny over their betters, the latter are remiss in allowing proper authority to slip from their grasp. In every way Nature is defied, and, in Ronsard's own words,

> Morte est l'autorité: chacun vit à sa guise
> Au vice desreiglé la licence est permise,
> Le desir, l'avarice, & l'erreur incensé
> Ont sans-dessus-dessoubs le monde renversé.    (*Misères*, 175–8)

The end result is the most unnatural act of all, suicides of Ajax, of the Roman Empire, and of France also.

One motif in Ronsard's world upside-down was to find striking favor in later writers, especially Agrippa d'Aubigné: the image of the Mother. In *Elégie à Des Autels* he compared France to a mother, and in *Hymne de Henry II* Germany was depicted as a woman in chains begging her son, the descendant of Francus, to help liberate her. Ronsard takes up the notion again in *Continuation*. Here we are told of Théodore de Bèze, who, nourished by his mother in Vézelay, yet turns against France, and of France herself, a poor matron insulted in her person and beaten to death by her children. She is like the viper whose young open her belly, killing her as they are born. The Narrator addresses France, a queen in pain, gaunt, her glory gone, poor, and in rags, who then delivers a plaint to him. By creating a mother-child relationship between the state, the church, or the queen, on the one hand, and the Narrator and his public, on the other, Ronsard establishes still another hierarchy that ought not to be broken, still another appeal for obedience.

In *Misères* and *Remonstrance* we find a different maternal figure, a Terrible Mother, the ogre who brought Protestantism into the world and who stands in opposition to destitute France: the allegorical monster 'Opinion,' derived from Fama in the *Aeneid*, from the Monster of the Fountain of Merlin, and from Heresy in the *Orlando furioso*. She is a light, winged creature (instability, mutability), her feet made of cotton and wool (deception) or of the wind. Her wings and her hundred tongues seduce the people. Daughter of Jupiter and Presumption, she represents dogmatic, constraining belief, the intellectual form taken by pride, that leads to hated innovation. This evil personage then gives birth to Luther, who will be possessed by a serpent. Indeed, she delivers the venom to Luther herself, for, instead of nourishing her child, she poisons him, in order that his disciples will in turn poison their mother, Catholic France.

One remarkable aspect of the *Discours* is the direct, personal, obtrusive intervention of a militant Narrator, which becomes more pronounced with each poem. He assumes the role of prophet and witness, in the Biblical and modern senses, of an upright man outraged by the iniquity of his times and moved to write for posterity's sake, 'D'une plume de fer sur un papier d'acier' (*Continuation*, 6). France herself orders him to record her speech and to publish it abroad in the world:

> Ce pendant pren la plume, & d'un stile endurci
> Contre le trait des ans, engrave tout ceci,
> A fin que nos nepveux puissent un jour cognoistre
> Que l'homme est malheureux qui se prend à son maistre.
>
> (*Continuation*, 441–4)

Yet, of course, the Narrator speaks not only for future generations but also for his own. Sometimes he condemns Huguenots for preaching a gospel armed with pistol and cutlass, and urges Frenchmen to wage war on the heretics with the pen, not the sword. He attacks the Protestants for being false artists, that is, players and mountebanks who deceive the people, mere tragic actors, inauthentic creatures dreading genuine martyrdom. But more often, in response to Calvinist accusation, he claims his pen is indeed a sword and he himself a soldier engaged in a holy war, in which he takes up the arms of his profession to defend the Church. He will tell God's truth, firm like a wall and rampart. His is peaceable good fighting, in contrast to that of bandits who shed blood. In *Continuation* and *Responce*, his chosen adversary, his poetic alter ego, is Théodore de Bèze, the greatest Huguenot divine and man of letters of his generation, whom Ronsard recognized to be the only poet in the enemy camp capable of matching steel with him. The Narrator asks why Bèze does not translate Homer or continue his neo-pagan Latin verse (the *Poemata*) instead of sowing religious discord. He and Bèze will struggle like Greek gladiators in a Roman circus. He will confound his rival as the furies confounded Orestes, and gadflies confound a bull, for he is a true poet-hero, and Bèze a false one. The very telling of the poem is not only a creative act but a heroic one in the good fight:

> Quand à mourir, Paschal, je suis tout resolu,
> Et mourray par leurs mains si le ciel l'a voulu,
> Si ne veux je pourtant me retenir d'escrire,
> D'aymer la verité, la prescher & la dire.    (*Remonstrance*, 541–4)

Ronsard compares himself to Hercules giving battle to Cerberus, and offers to vanquish the Protestant monster. This man, who proudly recounts how he defended his church, sword in hand, against a heretical contingent, realizes in his own person the ideals of *fortitudo* and *sapientia* to be found separately in Jason and Orpheus. He fulfills himself as the warrior-poet struggling in defense of one Faith, one Law, one King.

The Calvinists had accused Ronsard of being an ordained priest. He is not, says the Narrator-poet of *Responce*, although he ought to be, for poets used to be pontiffs, even kings in Egypt and Greece. However, he is willing to exorcise the Protestant werewolf and cast demons out of his body. We know how seriously he assimilates the frenzy of poets, prophets, and priests, for all three mediate between the gods and men, are semi-divine; how he confesses, indeed proclaims, his own star-caused melancholia. The Narrator compares real Huguenot madness (they are as insane as Circe's pigs; his verses drive them to frenzy) with his own *furor poeticus*, his 'gentille & docte frenaisie' (*Responce*, 896), their spiritual blindness and deafness with the strictly external physical ailments he and du Bellay share with Homer and Tiresias. He is deaf to Bèze's preaching, says the Narrator, and that is a good thing; in any case, God alone restores sight and hearing. And as a healer, a spiritual exorcist, despite the bodily frailty that the Calvinists denounce in him, Ronsard declares that he is in good health and that through art he will help cure the illness of his nation.

Mother Opinion urged Luther to speak from the Chair in order to corrupt the people. The Protestants use language in the worst possible ways. Their poisoned honey almost killed the Narrator in his youth, but a good *daimon* pulled it out of his mouth in time. Indeed, the Huguenots are like dogs, for they only dare to howl now that François de Guise has been murdered. People of discord, they utter mere noise. They can fool men but not God. When Christ, the Good Preacher (in contrast to Bèze), speaks, he tells simple truth to his disciples, arguing with words not arms. When he says, 'C'est cy mon corps & sang' (*Remonstrance*, 114), we should believe him, not Reformist lies. Ronsard too uses speech, singing in church, speaking to France, to the royal family, to Protestants, and to God. His will

be the language of truth and justice. Whether his subject be religious wars
or details of his private life, the poet will refute Calvinist falsehood. It is
through language, through discourse, that he hopes in these *Discours* to
turn the tide against disorder and rebellion. Just as in the past he argued with
Huguenots publicly (*Continuation*), now, in a didactic literary genre, like
a teacher he will mold the beliefs of his public, turning them away from
heretics through the force of his words. The Protestants fail to communicate, whereas Ronsard communicates in order to persuade the people,
nobles, prelates, other poets, judges, Catherine, God, and, if possible, even
Théodore de Bèze and the Prince de Condé.

Hope does not lie only in the soldier-poet, however. In *Misères* the
Narrator appeals to Catherine de' Medici to take over the helm of the ship
of state and to save wild bees by tossing powder on them (an image taken
from *Georgics* 4). As the captain of a ship and a husbandman, she will
resemble Christ; as a mother to her king and her people, the Virgin Mary.
She alone can save the floundering nation, the other good mother France,
and, like rain, revive the wilting flower (fleur-de-lis). She will defeat Opinion, as her son Charles ix will defeat Opinion's son, the heretic Luther,
and as, in later discourses, her other son the Duc d'Anjou will defeat the
Calvinist Hydra. God's truth, the light of the Eucharist, will triumph
over evil. And the divinity, who permits people to walk on the sea if he
chooses, and who saved Noah's Ark, will save our ark; he will spare the
Church and deliver us from the tempests that beset us.

In *Responce* the Narrator is obliged to defend the *Discours* as art. His
poetic 'discours' reveals his theory and practice of poetry. Reproached for
alleged disorder, he distinguishes between the strict, classical composition
appropriate for prose (rhetoric) and the *frenaisie* to be found in verse. Yet he
also proclaims that this disorder, this *fureur*, is an *artifice à part* (873), an
*art caché* (874), itself determined by a higher form of order, unrecognizable
to mortals, comparable to the seemingly capricious wanderings of the bee
in search of pollen. It is appropriate for Ronsard the aristocrat, con-
temptuous of his uncouth, low-class adversaries, exulting in the esthetics of
negligence, to despise the inhibiting restrictions of pedants; he will remain a
free man, guided only by his genius![14] He claims to regret having illustrated
the French language if it is to be used by *valets de boutique* and heretics.
Yet, in fact, he exults in his alleged superiority over the Calvinist versifiers:
he is learned, whereas heresy is derived from ignorance; and, in contrast
to himself, they are bad writers suffering from bad fury, writing in a bad
language. Indeed, he proclaims, I wear the crown of poetry. I am the
fountain and you the stream; all your verse is derived from me! a daring
claim of primacy which corresponds to that of the Catholic Church itself
in its relation to the Reformers:

Tu ne le puis nyer! car de ma plenitude
Vous estes tous remplis: je suis seul vostre estude,
Vous estes tous yssus de la grandeur de moy,
Vous estes mes sujets, & je suis vostre loy.
Vous estes mes ruisseaux, je suis vostre fonteine,
Et plus vous m'espuisés, plus ma fertile veine
Repoussant le sablon, jette une source d'eaux
D'un surjon eternel pour vous autres ruisseaux.    (*Responce*, 1035–42)

In his work, form corresponds to content, willed rhetorical disorder to the disorder of the times, a crude, violent style to the violence of the wars. These *Discours* are the first native genre to appear in France since the Middle Ages. They are also perhaps the first manifestation north of the Alps of a new style in literature: the Baroque. The proud, confident humanism of the early Renaissance, of which Rabelais and the young Ronsard are France's greatest spokesmen, receives its first setback. For the first time humanism is found wanting, and another esthetic, another attitude toward life, takes its place.

In the *Hymnes* and *Discours*, as in *La Franciade*, Ronsard is a didactic poet, busy constructing a Mirror for Princes, teaching us secrets of the universe and urging us how to live. He is also fascinated by the reaches of cosmic space and time, by the fecundity of nature, and by the marvels of the world-spectacle. Furthermore, a son of soldiers, a page to kings, the Vendômois never forgets his own martial vocation: he sings of heroes from ancient myth (*Astres, Calaïs, Pollux, Hyver*) and himself becomes a warrior, whether against phantoms in the night (*Daimons*), foreign enemies of his prince (*Mort*), or the Protestant werewolves and Théodore de Bèze (*Discours*). Ronsard is a poet of Christ as well as of arms, of God as well as of heroes. He conceives his inspiration in Christian terms, as being of divine origin and linked to the gift of Grace. This is not surprising in the *Discours* – a committed, militant polemic against heretics – but is also to be found in the *Hymnes*, dedicated to Odet Cardinal de Chastillon and Charles Cardinal de Lorraine, where the future Canon of Saint-Julien du Mans and Saint-Martin de Tours, disciple of Pico, Ficino, and Dorat, 'recuperates' pagan myth by Christianizing it, reveals the secrets of a syncretic Christian cosmos. In all of these spheres, cosmological, heroic, and religious, Ronsard favors order over chaos, hierarchy and authority over rebellion, high over low, light over darkness, and life over death. No one understands as well as he the terrors of the medieval night – with serpents, *daimons*, dark grottos, and the powers of a melancholic Saturn. Yet he always insists that they are redeemed by the brightness of the fixed stars, by

Jupiter's power and Apollo's wisdom, by the eternity of philosophy and the gifts of an inspired poet. The myth he sings over and over again is the same: the celestial forces of order and harmony are attacked by the powers of darkness but succeed in retaining their prerogatives and maintaining the cosmos as it is. And in a quite modern sense, much of Ronsard's poetry tells of poetry, the epic hero representing a poet who struggles to make his way against adversaries and to mediate between men and the gods. Thus he gives expression to high ideals, to a quasi-religious sense of his vocation as an artist. Although Ronsard did not write a consecutive, unified narrative telling of one hero's struggle with his mortality, imposing his glory onto the world, he did create an initiatic, incantatory poetry dealing with great themes, opening out in ever-widening circles, evoking that epic awe or astonishment (Tasso's *meraviglia*) which France knew in the days of the trouvères but had since lost. It is this truly sublime subject-matter and style of his verse, its martial quality and militancy, which grant these texts epic stature. Despite the failure of *La Franciade*, in the sublime as in other modes, Ronsard was the first writer in Europe to come to grips with the whole classical tradition, including the heroic, and to make it and its spirit live for future generations.

## Chapter Eight

# 🕸 D'AUBIGNÉ

Ronsard's *Hymnes* are among the first manifestations of a significant current in the development of sixteenth-century verse: what has been called 'philosophical' or 'scientific' poetry, a genre derived from Antiquity and from contemporary Neo-Latin practice.[1] The most notable works in this domain, in addition to the *Hymnes* and Ronsard's own *Les quatre saisons de l'an* (1563), are Jacques Peletier du Mans, *L'Amour des Amours* (1555); Maurice Scève, *Le Microcosme* (1562); Guy Lefèvre de la Boderie, *L'Encyclie* (1571) and *La Galliade* (1578); Guillaume de Salluste du Bartas, *L'Uranie* (1574), *La premiere Sepmaine* (1578), and *La seconde Sepmaine* (1585); François Beroalde de Verville, *Les Apprehensions spirituelles* (1583); and Isaac Habert, *Œuvres poétiques* (1582) and *Les Trois Livres des Meteores* (1585). In these texts science, philosophy, and magic are fused; the poet-narrator is presumed to be a magus, a visionary as well as an artistic creator and teacher. He aspires to an intellectual synthesis, for unity of all that can be known, in the lyric, narrative, or gnomic modes. Given the encyclopedic character of such works and their supreme claim to greatness, the scientific current approximates Renaissance notions of epic. Indeed, *La premiere Sepmaine* and *La seconde Sepmaine* were considered for generations, outside of France, as the Protestant long poem par excellence, and du Bartas had a lasting influence on the development of epic in Northern Europe, specifically on the works of Vondel and Milton. He also began his career with a brief religious heroic poem, the first of its kind in France: *La Judit* (1574), treating the Judith-Holofernes story.

However, by a strange twist of fate, the leading inheritor of Ronsard's genius turned out to be not du Bartas but, instead, another provincial Huguenot, one of the bravest captains on the Protestant side during the Wars of Religion: Théodore Agrippa d'Aubigné (1552–1630). The first flights of d'Aubigné's muse, at age sixteen, are dedicated to Ronsard. Four years later, in 1572, he sent verses to the Prince of Poets, who deigned to reply. The youth proceeded to fall in love with Diane de Talcy, Cassandre

Salviati's niece. In *Le Printemps* he consciously plays on this connection, the erotic as well as literary analogy between himself and his famous predecessor. I do not doubt that Agrippa loved Diane partly because of Ronsard and that the inspiration for these impassioned, corrosive lyrics comes largely from the latter's *Amours*. Later, again following in the footsteps of the Vendômois, d'Aubigné rejects the erotic, lascivious verses from his own past and the prevailing 'light' court poetry of the age in favor of *rude poésie*, a vision of virtue and glory expressed in the sublime style. In this he conforms to a specifically Protestant, provincial, anti-Parisian current also represented by du Bartas and Lefèvre de la Boderie. However, the young Huguenot does not attempt to redo *La Franciade* or *Les Hymnes*. Instead, inspired by *Discours des Misères* (in addition to Greco-Roman and Biblical sources), in his own voice he tells of contemporary events in France, the misery of the people, the horror of civil war, and his hatred of injustice and evil. *Les Tragiques*,[2] written largely from 1577 to 1589, published in 1616 with a much enlarged edition around 1623, are an anti-*Discours* or a super-*Discours*. Not only does the Calvinist poet depict the Wars from the opposite perspective; he goes beyond Ronsard, surpassing him both in satire and heroic narrative. He writes a 'long poem,' a truly unified, extended masterpiece in place of Ronsard's fragmented discourses and unfinished saga of Trojan Francus. The true epic of the Wars of Religion was written for the eventual losers, not the winners.[3]

As in *Discours*, but more so, the prevailing tone of d'Aubigné's masterpiece is one of violence and horror. We read of the torture and execution of Huguenot martyrs: in one case, an individual's hands are cut off, he is then racked, and his feet burned; in another, a man's cheeks and tongue are flamed and his eyes gouged out. We witness the murder-starvation of Périgord peasants and see how, during the Saint Bartholomew's Day Massacre, Catholics slaughtered Protestants from sadistic and sexual motivations. And we behold, with the Last Judgment, the ultimate horror of damnation for multitudes. France is a battlefield, on which a reign of terror has been unleashed, by war, religious fanaticism, and the homicidal fad of duelling. Everyone slays or is slain. And these people kill with passion, with hatred for life and a thirst for blood. Their furor is embodied in a series of *chocs destructifs*, explosions, and plunging to death.[4] Cutting, piercing, breaking, striking, hard knives, rocks, castles, and mountains are masculine images of the will, of war and aggression. Freud has demonstrated how sexual aggression coincides with a death-instinct turned toward the external world, marked by sadism and a will to destruction. And we discover, as in Ronsard, a demonic pattern of cannibalism, sodomy, incest, ogres, harlots, witches, wolves, serpents, fire, towers, infernal cities, and the Waste Land.

The fifth book of *Les Tragiques* is called *Les Fers*, the fourth one *Les Feux*. For d'Aubigné, the fire of the stake is as dreadful as the daggers of civil war. He contrasts the metaphoric flames and blood of his own early love poetry with the physically real burning that devastates the countryside in wartime. This fire symbolizes, from a Christian perspective, evil passions, especially choler and lust, that unleash violence – the lechery, adultery, incest, and perversion, the libido of the court that finds an outlet only in destruction. And we discover behind the Cardinal of Lorraine and the Pope of Rome that most august of nether Princes, who brings with him his own hell-fire wherever he goes.

Catholics are said to be lions and wolves that suck the blood of lambs, mad curs that devour human corpses, wild boars trampling grain in the field, crows feasting on carrion, and monkeys that indulge in disguise and mimicry at court. Catherine de' Medici herself is a serpent and a hydra, with vipers in her hair, whereas Satan, transformed into a snake before God's eyes, enters Catherine's body in his authentic form (a motif taken from Ronsard's *Remonstrance*, where it refers to Martin Luther!). Nor should we forget the Beast of the Apocalypse, image for the entire line of Roman Popes. Against this mass of predators stands the Protestant Church, represented by flocks of sheep and cattle, and an occasional tracked stag. There is little hope for the victims, dismembered by their stronger, more numerous adversaries. In this brutal world of the chase, the strong hunt the weak, carnivores devour their prey, and the pastoral world of innocence is defiled by the reality of blood and gore.

D'Aubigné gives renewed vigor to traditional Christian imagery of the wolf in sheep's clothing, the lion, tiger, and bear as figures of the vices, and the serpent and the wolf as images of Satan, who deceived Eve in the Garden of Eden and devoured Christ the Lamb on Good Friday. The Protestant lambs also evoke the Children of Israel and the early Church by reference to their shepherd, be he Moses, David, or Christ the *Agnus Dei*. D'Aubigné enriches the world of *Les Tragiques* with the wolf-lamb antithesis, which, whether it be found in classical fable or medieval beast epic, in Christian Scripture or baroque poetry, embodies one of the most powerful archetypes in our literature.

In addition, d'Aubigné tells us something about men degraded by fanaticism and war. The Catholics, dehumanized, reduced to the level of animals, cannot communicate in a normal manner. Catherine de' Medici bays like a dog; Charles ix wakes up at night moaning. Howling, crying, hissing, and gnashing of teeth are standard attributes of these bestial tormentors, whom d'Aubigné assimilates to those who constructed the Tower of Babel. Furthermore, although the lambs are morally superior to the wolves, they too manifest negative traits: witness the passage in *Jugement* where d'Aubigné excoriates Huguenot apostates to Catholicism, the plagued sheep of the fold who lick blood off the feet of their sires' murderers. Because of the Wars, all men, Protestant and Catholic, have been dehumanized. Devouring their own dogs and horses, people become beasts, more savage than their pets. Meanwhile, a comparable degradation takes place in the animal world, where domesticated creatures turn wild, devour men, and replace humans in the towns. It is evident that wolves and lambs are complementary. The former cannot survive without meat. Although they can indeed live without wolves, lambs depend on them to affirm their spiritual identity. The bestial world unites torturer and victim in a hideous bond that degrades both.

I have hitherto not mentioned one of the most important facets of d'Aubigné's world: the 'little animals,' vermin that destroy men's bodies and endanger their souls. The Huguenot poet develops a pattern of rot, stench, and filth imagery, of feminine earth-symbolism no less striking than his masculine evocation of lions and daggers: for example, Catherine de' Medici releases the plague from her nostrils and is associated with decay, excrement, famine, and poison. When d'Aubigné depicts the life of the court, we see flatterers cast up from the garbage heap, and soft, insinuating, pus-like hypocrites; princes swimming on whores' breasts, they, their mistresses, and their procurers endowed with leprous bodies and still more leprous souls; rotten corpses in whited sepulchres; and artificial perfumes that strive in vain to cover the stench of secret accouchements and abortions.

D'Aubigné's rot-imagery is assimilated to the bodily functions, especially eating. Hence the striking portrait of France as a sick, dying giant, whose viscous organs no longer function; he suffers from the dropsy, excrement fills his stomach, and his brain is transformed into a 'champignon pourri' (*Misères*, 156). This Body Politic topos appears again, when an insane king orders members of his own person to be amputated. The Périgord peasant family dies in part from hunger and thirst; German knights sought flesh to eat and, when their demands go unanswered, destroy the flesh of those poor folk. Now, if good people perish from hunger, the wicked indulge in blood-lust and cannibalism. We find a mother devouring her own baby, the judges of *La Chambre dorée* sucking the blood of lambs, and the murderers of Saint Bartholomew's Day tasting a Huguenot martyr's heart. For d'Aubigné, from a strictly literary perspective, digestive and excremental functions contribute as metaphor to a sense of the demonic. Furthermore, an imbalance in the humors associated with food, ordure, and sex is shown to be symptomatic of illness and/or insanity. Filth and decay are physical signs of an inner, spiritual defilement with Biblical overtones that is of Satanic origin.

Several castles are located in this tragic, monstrous realm. The first, and most important, is the Palace of Justice in Paris. Proud, splendid, standing so high, it ought to represent the best in human endeavor. Unfortunately, the dome is of gilt not true gold, recalling the Tower of Babel instead of a legitimate Christian edifice. And, behind the façade, beneath the dome, God discovers that its foundations are made of bones and skulls, its mortar of ashes and blood, and its quicklime of marrow.

> Mais Dieu trouva l'estoffe et les durs fondemens
> Et la pierre commune à ces fiers bastimens
> D'os, de testes de morts; au mortier execrable
> Les cendres des bruslez avoyent servi de sable,
> L'eau qui les destrempoit estoit du sang versé;
> La chaux vive dont fut l'edifice enlacé,
> Qui blanchit ces tombeaux et les salles si belles,
> C'est le meslange cher de nos tristes moëlles.
>
> (*La Chambre dorée*, 179–86)

This bright, projecting, 'masculine' building parallels a no less demonic 'feminine' one, the prison of the Holy Inquisition in Spain, a place of stench, darkness, starvation, smothering, and secret death. Later in the poem, Satan inspires Catherine de' Medici to build a house for demons, the epitome of false art and false pride: the Palace of the Tuileries. Whole cities – Paris, Rome, the Iberian centers of the Inquisition – are assimilated to Babel, Babylon, Nineveh, Sodom and Gomorrah, and, of course, the Capital where Satan dwells. Whether conceived as 'hard earth' (the rock, the tower) or 'soft earth' (the dungeon, the tomb), castle, prison, evil machinery, and the infernal lie at the center of d'Aubigné's demonic kingdom. Ideally, such edifices should be sacred temples, located in an isolated, holy space, *loci amœni* tended by guardians of the cult, devoted to enlightenment. They should be 'points of epiphany,' reserved for communion with God, intersecting heaven and earth. In d'Aubigné's world they stand in a Waste Land of disorder, hideous caricatures, the Tower of Babel substituted for the Garden of Eden, the Temple of Baal replacing the Temple of Jerusalem, Peter's Catholic rock crushing down the true Church, made of human beings not stone.

In *Le Printemps* d'Aubigné criticizes cities, courts, money, and the decadent manners of his age; the theme will appear again in *Les Avantures du baron de Faeneste*. This Renaissance commonplace is derived from a variety of classical writings, especially Virgil's *Bucolics* and *Georgics*. For d'Aubigné the court is subject to criticism because it is the stronghold of the Catholic faction, therefore a den of falsehood and illusion. He continually lashes out at *faussaires* and their *feintise*. Catherine de' Medici and Henry III both wear makeup; the latter's mask is associated with his per-

verted sexual proclivities, for he dresses as a female prostitute in a mas-
querade ball, and, in the affairs of state, he and Catherine change roles:

> L'autre fut mieux instruit à juger des atours
> Des putains de sa cour, et, plus propre aux amours,
> Avoir ras le menton, garder la face pasle,
> Le geste effeminé, l'œil d'un Sardanapale:
> Si bien qu'un jour des Rois ce douteux animal,
> Sans cervelle, sans front, parut tel en son bal.
> ... son menton pinceté,
> Son visage de blanc et de rouge empasté,
> Son chef tout empoudré nous monstrerent ridee,
> En la place d'un Roy, une putain fardee ...
> Pour nouveau parement il porta tout ce jour
> Cet habit monstrueux, pareil à son amour:
> Si qu'au premier abord chacun estoit en peine
> S'il voyoit un Roy femme ou bien un homme Reyne.
>                     (*Princes*, 773–8, 781–4, 793–6)

The Louvre Palace is perceived to be a mask hiding the cemetery of bastard
babies slain there, just as the palace of justice veils the horrors of its
foundations, while servants dash about seeking a midwife for masked,
pregnant princesses. That the court dons costumes for elaborate religious
processions proves to be a lie, a mask, since the Catholic Church itself is
the Whore of Babylon, made up and in disguise. In the Spanish *auto-da-fé*
symbols of Christ's passion (the robe, the crown of thorns, the cross) are
used to torture living Protestant Christs: in this hideous pastiche of the Last
Judgment martyrs are dressed like devils, and their torturers like the
lowest of gladiators.

Yet worse remains: the ultimate horror is to be found in d'Aubigné's
portrayal of woman. Book 1 of *Les Tragiques* contains great maternal figures: the captive Church in chains; Melpomene the tragic muse, transformed
into a hag, who curses the earth, tossing her spilt blood to the skies;
France, whose two babies tear at each other and at her breast; the dying
mother in Poitou; and the cities of Old France who used to give themselves
and their milk to their kings but now are sterile, ravished corpses. The
*Mater nutrix* ought to be an image of refuge, warm and intimate. Her
breasts should evoke fertility and the good things of life. But in d'Aubigné's universe milk turns to blood and poison, infants expire at their
mothers' side, birth is transformed into abortion, and bounty into sterility.
Phallic sadism and rape are committed against the female, while she, like her
children, suffers violent death.

Not only are good mothers ravished and murdered; they are also replaced
by terrible, perverted ones, especially Catherine de' Medici, perhaps the
most striking villainess in all of French literature. Catherine ('impure
Florentine,' *Misères*, 802) is Italian, foreign, corrupt, an evil mother associated with Jezebel and Agrippina, her viper children with Nebuchadnezzar and Nero. She brings to France Florentine poison and Vatican intrigue.
At her passage, Nature shrinks in horror: she breathes the plague, fire,
and smoke; she is a priestess of Astarte, a sorceress who resembles the
Medusa, who sacrifices babies to Satan, who turns water into blood and
resurrects zombies from the grave:

> La nuict elle se veautre aux hideux cimetieres ...
> Desterre sans effroi les effroyables corps,
> Puis, remplissant les os de la force des diables,
> Les fait saillir en pieds, terreux, espouvantables,
> Oit leur voix enroüee, et des obscurs propos
> Des demons imagine un travail sans repos;
> Idolatrant Sathan et sa theologie,
> Interrogue en tramblant sur le fil de sa vie
> Ces organes hideux; lors mesle de leurs tais
> La poudre avec du laict, pour les conduire en paix.
> Les enfans innocens ont presté leurs moëlles,
> Leurs graisses et leur suc à fournir des chandelles,
> Et, pour faire trotter les esprits aux tombeaux,
> On offre à Belzebub leurs innocentes peaux.    (*Misères*, 902, 908–20)

Other monstrous females are the twenty-eight wicked allegories inside
the Palace of Justice (*La Chambre dorée*); while *Princes* depicts a terrifying
nocturnal visit: the goddess Fortuna, painted like a whore, comes to a
young man's bedside claiming to be his mother, but, 'mere aux estranges
amours' (1189), voluptuously tries to seduce him. Just as in d'Aubigné's
love poetry the dominant female-figure is an incarnation of Diana-Hecate,
huntress of beasts and men, patroness of witches, in *Les Tragiques* we find
versions of the Terrible Mother or Fatal Woman as temptress, sorceress,
and fiend. In the wake of Ishtar, Delilah, and Circe, she may shine with
beauty, or like Scylla, Charybdis, and Grendel's Dam, be a creature of
horror. In either case she is a virile, aggressive, castrating figure, accompanied by and associated with serpents, who destroys the men who cross her
path. In d'Aubigné's secular realm fathers scarcely appear: rulers (Henry
III) are transformed into half-women. The male has abdicated in favor of
the female, reason in favor of unbridled violence and lust, and the Fatal
Woman triumphs alone. For a Catherine to rule France, in defiance of

the Salic Law, is as unnatural as for passion to unseat reason and for the idolatrous Church of Rome to persecute Huguenots. In all three cases the evil woman triumphs over the good or over man. For the Calvinist poet, as for Isaiah and Ezekiel, the reign of the Whore of Babylon over the Judge of Israel marks the end of time and the ultimate in earthly horror.

In the *Anatomy of Criticism* Northrop Frye designates *sparagmos* or dismembering to be an image of the ironic vision of life. More than any singer of *geste*, more than any baroque playwright, d'Aubigné expresses this notion of dislocation, disintegration, and destruction. Babies tearing at each other, mutiny on shipboard, Bellona the goddess of war or the body politic of France ripping itself apart are the most striking examples. Man, political order, nature herself disintegrate under the strain. Not that evil exists alone in the world. In his 'dramatic alignment' of forces, d'Aubigné sets princes, evil judges, wolves, Catherine, and the Catholics against the people, good judges, lambs, Elizabeth of England, and the Protestants.[5] Unfortunately, in the secular sphere evil persistently wins. In this upside-down world nature has lost her proper function: confusion and disorder reign, nature gives way to non-nature and justice to non-justice. D'Aubigné's favorite Biblical story is neither the Creation nor Exodus; it is the unnatural murder of Abel by Cain, the image of civil war (brother against brother), the triumph in a fallen world of evil over good.

Evil triumphs, yes, but on one level only. We discover another dimension, which in the course of the poem gains in importance. God's presence increases steadily until, at the end of *Jugement*, he is all-pervasive, he alone exists. The first two books treat profane concerns exclusively. With *La Chambre dorée* and *Les Feux* God is introduced as a spectator who witnesses but does not participate in the 'tragedy.' Then, in *Les Fers*, the divinity grants Satan permission to tempt mankind (a theme taken from the Book of Job), which he proceeds to do with the Wars of Religion and the Saint Bartholomew's Day Massacre. However, although Satan's might is apparent, our Lord's is greater. At the end of *Les Tragiques*, in *Vengeances* and *Jugement*, d'Aubigné shows us how God reverses the various forms of injustice that the devil has perpetrated in the world, for, absolute in power, Christus Pantocrator levels the Palace of Justice in Paris and the Holy Office in Spain, and Themis in her chariot will ride over the bodies of tyrants.

On earth God's justice is manifest in two ways. First of all, because the Covenanted People falter in their ways, the Almighty punishes them with his scourge, their Catholic enemy, the modern Babylon. Secondly, following the epic tradition of Homer, Virgil, Camoens, Tasso, and Spenser, the divinity does protect some good people against persecution. He also brings victory to outnumbered, outmanned Huguenot armies, in the battles of

Saint-Denis, Arques, Ivry, Navarrin, and Saint-Gilles. Most of all, however, the author tells how God directly punishes evil-doers in the course of
human history (*Vengeances*). D'Aubigné adopts Mosaic law ('an eye for
an eye, a tooth for a tooth, a life for a life') in a striking way, establishing the
convergence of crime and punishment, and here Satan's demonic weapons
are used by God against evil-doers. The plagues of Egypt, the fire of Sodom,
the stench and rot of Paris occupied by the League are fitting punishments
for crimes committed in days of prosperity. Charles ix and François de
Valois shed others' blood in their lifetime; they perish from consumption,
spitting out their own. The two Herods, Maximian, Philip ii of Spain, and
Pope Paul iv sent vast hosts to massacre the faithful. They are then invaded
in turn by God's *petits soldats* and left to die lingering deaths from leprosy
and vermin. Most pitiful of all, no doubt, are those who, like Charles
Cardinal of Lorraine, blasphemed God directly and are punished by demonic possession, leading to insanity. In Lorraine's case all of nature is
perturbed, and Satan's realm exults when his soul can at last be carried
off:

> L'air, noirci de demons ainsi que de nuages,
> Creva des quatre parts d'impetueux orages;
> Les vents, les postillons de l'ire du grand Dieu,
> Troublés de cet esprit retroublerent tout lieu;
> Les desluges espais des larmes de la France
> Rendirent l'air tout eau de leur noire abondance.
> Cet esprit boutefeu, au bondir de ces lieux,
> De foudres et d'esclairs mit le feu dans les cieux.
> De l'enfer tout fumeux la porte desserree
> A celui qui l'emplit prepara cette entree ...
> L'enfer en triompha, l'air et la terre et l'onde
> Refaisant le cahos qui fut avant le monde.
>                     (*Vengeances*, 1045–54, 1061–2)

God's final justice takes place on Doomsday, as recounted in the seventh
and last book of *Les Tragiques*. Here time becomes eternity, and poetry
and theology are fused. The entire created universe dies, and all creatures are
fixed for eternity. In this ultimate reversal of judgment in the last appeals
court, those who tortured will suffer, and those who submitted will know
joy. There will be no more fleeing, for the good or the wicked. Although
the latter try one last time to escape from God's sight, they are forced to
strip off their raiment and deposit their tiaras, mitres, keys, and slippers
in a pile on his left hand. Naked they stand, and in naked truth they will be
returned to hell for torment. In total despair, these reprobates cannot

even hope for death, suffering instead 'l'eternelle soif de l'impossible mort' (*Jugement*, 1022). Hell is their destruction in non-destroying, for, like Cain, they must ever live, enduring, in a state of non-life, full knowledge of the bliss enjoyed by the Elect. These latter, having suffered in the body, now reap absolute pleasure with all five corporeal senses. Their joy is physical and spiritual at the same time, inexpressibly superior to comparable phenomena in the world. *Jugement* gives *Les Tragiques* meaning. Only here do we find expressed fully God's triumph, the revelation of truth, and d'Aubigné's hope.

Since the greatest danger to the Huguenots comes from diabolic seduction, from becoming like their tormentors, it is apparent that ill fortune serves rather than imperils their quest for salvation. In a variation of *felix culpa*, d'Aubigné creates a *felix tragœdia* where, in an atmosphere of cosmic irony, the devil casts good people into God's arms. The true hero resists temptation, in contrast to Satan's rebels. Passive will and endurance are to be preferred to martial conquest. The traditional epic warrior is repudiated in favor of a new hero inspired by Grace who conquers himself, whose exploits are of the Holy Spirit. Thus martyrdom becomes a positive act and a statement of identity; significantly, the listing of martyrs occupies structurally the central canto (*Lex Feux*) of the poem. Martyrs become Protestant soldiers, and vice versa. These little people, the humble of the earth, triumph by remaining little, by refusing false secular glory. In a version of Christian pastoral, like Saul and David they are chosen by God to be his kings and judges. They imitate Christ, himself a carpenter by trade and a shepherd of souls, son of Abel and of David, his coming prophesied in Virgil's *Fourth Eclogue*, who was tortured by kings, priests, and judges, yet who becomes King and Judge in heaven. In the 'Préface' Vaudois shepherds win against armies. In *Vengeances* the Narrator himself, as a humble shepherd, one who adored the Christ child, brings milk not myrrh to the Lamb:

> Si je n'ay or ne myrrhe à faire mon offrande
> Je t'apporte du laict: ta douceur est si grande
> Que de mesme œil et cœur tu vois et tu reçois
> Des bergers le doux laict et la myrrhe des Rois.    (*Vengeances*, 5–8)

The protagonist of *Les Tragiques* is the Church – a community of Hebrews, early Christians, and sixteenth-century Protestants – a large flock of lambs. These people of the lower classes find a sense of brotherhood, of communion, and of abnegation that kings lack: their exploits, a *gesta Dei per pauperos*, will lead to a true *pax christiana* in an earthly Utopia or in Christ's own kingdom.

Similarly, the Calvinists' physical weakness – the fact that their greatest martyrs are women, children, and old men – brings them closer to God. The death of a child by starvation, or the cannibalistic devouring of an infant by its mother, is perhaps the ultimate in horror in this *verkehrte Welt*, this monstrous, deranged universe where the baby's cradle or the mother's breast serves as a bier. Nonetheless, in *Vengeances* the Narrator wishes that he had the purity and innocence of a babe or that, like an old prophet, his spirit could leave the body and soar to heaven. The weakness of the child, which permits physical defeat, also contributes to spiritual victory in a universe where, at Doomsday, lambs are spared and wolves condemned. As in the old *chansons de geste*, the *puer senex*, though physically weak, possesses purity, courage, and enthusiasm that adults lack. Hence the fact that in the 'Préface' the Narrator refers to *Les Tragiques*, his poem, as his offspring, born in a tomb but sent out into the world with a mission to perpetuate life, even though its father dies. Hence the particularly glorious fate reserved for young martyrs, beloved of Christ, who lay in a manger and confounded Elders in a temple. These dying children ensure the renewal of the Church.

One technique employed by d'Aubigné is to replace demonic imagery with the pastoral or apocalyptic, or to endow the original demonic pattern with apocalyptic overtones. God's truth and d'Aubigné's verse are swords that pierce the enemy or hammers that beat on an anvil. Huguenot martyrs joyfully walk on thorns in memory of the straight and narrow path that leads to the kingdom of heaven and because Christ, King of the Jews, wore a crown of thorns. They offer a bloody severed hand to God or raise on high the stumps where their hands used to be, in order to imitate the Savior, who was pierced by nails on the cross. The author tells us that a Huguenot lady weeps the last drops of blood from her heart, so that nothing moist will remain inside her, only fire to rise to her bridegroom, Christ. Sentenced to be burned at the stake by sacrilegious, idolatrous Catholic fire, first she delivers a sermon; although they sever her tongue, it is to no avail, for she has received the Pentecostal gift, Tongues of Fire, from the Holy Spirit.

Thus the demonic flame of lust and choler associated with Catholics can be redeemed by divine inspiration, poetry, prophecy, Christian faith, ecstasy, martyrdom, purification, eternal life, the cosmic power of creation, and God's truth and love – all embodied in fire. In the 'Préface' the Narrator refers to *Les Tragiques* as a poem that is inspired by divine flame but that will be cast into fire by its enemies. And in 'Aux lecteurs' a mock-editor claims to have stolen the poem from its author the way Prometheus stole fire from Zeus for the benefit of mortals. No wonder then that the Narrator assimilates himself to Moses guided in the desert by a pillar of

fire or that the martyrs are inspired by the very flames that bring them to
God.

In *Jugement* we are told that the carnivores will be tormented as they
tormented others. Wolves will be muzzled, bears' noses pierced, lions
tracked down, and the Serpent defeated. Meanwhile, on earth God uses
beasts either to undo men's crimes or as instruments of vengeance. Thus
gods feast on Jezebel's corpse; an army of vermin torture evil kings; with an
animal howl the earth rejects Satan and Cain; and hell itself appears as a
devouring beast. As to the Huguenots, the people of the New Covenant
can learn to rebel; after 1560 these lambs, transformed into lions, defend
themselves valiantly (*Les Fers*). From a different perspective, in *Jugement*
we behold the triumph of the Lamb, his shed blood having redeemed ours,
metamorphosed into the Lion of Judah, symbolic of Christ's majesty,
strength, courage, and resurrection. Finally, although François de Valois
changes feathers like a pigeon, birds generally play an admirable role in *Les
Tragiques*. A hen nourishes with her eggs a Huguenot fugitive. Protestants
are slaughtered like sheep or cattle, but their souls fly up to a better world.
The publication of *Les Tragiques* is also compared to the soaring of a
bird. Birth, death, and rebirth in Christ take on the figure of flying birds,
image of freedom and renewal in spring, of spiritual man released from
the fetters of earth and, in traditional Christian typology, of the Church, the
baptized Christian soul, the dove of the Ark, and the Holy Ghost, that is,
God's Word and Love made flesh.

The green world also contributes a 'good' pattern of imagery, negates or
rectifies the more savage, demonic animal and mineral worlds; thus the *locus
amœnus*, whether in Savoy or Paradise, contrasts with the city, the prison,
and the sterile Waste Land of central France. It is true, d'Aubigné refers
more than once to flowers masking Catholic carrion, to snakes hidden
underneath the blooms of Dame Fortune, to the smell of roses mixed with
the stench of blood. He also resolves to abandon the profane flowers
(poetry) of his youth, tramples through the underbrush, stomping down
useless greenery, and warns his readers that when God casts down great
cedars the flowers that grow beneath them are crushed also. However, in
*Les Tragiques* the green world generally evokes divine not courtly love,
for the Protestant martyrs cut down by Catholics will be reborn in God. *Les
Fers* (721–44) tells of wheat in the field destroyed by horses, wild boars,
wind, and hail; only a few grains are spared, to survive in the forest and
become God's harvest. This image is derived from the Psalms and the
Book of Matthew. In another passage, moved by Psalm 91, 'Plantati in
domo Domini, in atriis domus Dei nostri florebunt,' and exploiting a
theme from the Church Fathers, d'Aubigné sings of the ashes of the martyrs
returning to the earth and giving birth to new flowers. The ashes are seed,

the martyrs' blood is water, and their sighs are zephyr winds. Winter has yielded to spring, and our worst travails are behind us! Reacting against Ronsard's *carpe diem* poetry, he declares that the roses of autumn are the most beautiful, referring to martyrs of the Church in this the autumn of human history:

> Le printemps de l'Eglise et l'esté sont passés,
> Si serez vous par moi, vers bouttons, amassés,
> Encor esclorrez-vous, fleurs si franches, si vives,
> Bien que vous paroissiez dernieres et tardives;
> On ne vous lairra pas, simples, de si grand pris,
> Sans vous voir et flairer au celeste pourpris.
> Une rose d'automne est plus qu'une autre exquise:
> Vous avez esjouï l'automne de l'Eglise.    (*Les Feux*, 1227–34)

For him, the only true flowers are Christian martyrs, whose purity and love (white and red) bloom in the apocalyptic garden of the Lamb. The imagery of fecundity is applied to conversions in the world (new crops of martyrs) and to the final resurrection harvest in God. As in Guillaume de Lorris's *Romance of the Rose*, but from a strictly religious perspective, d'Aubigné's garden is assimilated to all that is beautiful, good, and true, to our dreams of a lost Eden and to our hopes for eternal rebirth in a new one.

The four elements defiled by Catholic fanatics do not accept their degradation. In one of the most powerful scenes in the epic, in their own voice they accuse Catholics before God's judgment seat: that fire was employed to burn people alive, that the air was infested by the stench of carrion and transmitted pestilence, that martyrs were tossed from precipices and hanged from trees, and that the waters were sullied by blood of the dead:

> 'Pourquoy, dira le feu, avez-vous de mes feux
> Qui n'estoyent ordonnez qu'à l'usage de vie
> Fait des bourreaux, valets de vostre tyrannie?'
> L'air encor une fois contr'eux se troublera,
> Justice au Juge sainct, trouble, demandera,
> Disant: 'Pourquoi, tyrans et furieuses bestes,
> M'empoisonnastes-vous de charongnes, de pestes,
> Des corps de vos meurtris?' – 'Pourquoi, diront les eaux,
> Changeastes-vous en sang l'argent de nos ruisseaux?'
> Les monts qui ont ridé le front à vos supplices:
> 'Pourquoi nous avez-vous rendus vos precipices?'
> 'Pourquoi nous avez-vous, diront les arbres, faits
> D'arbres delicieux execrables gibets?'    (*Jugement*, 770–82)

Furthermore, nature serves as God's instrument of vengeance against the wicked. All four elements destroy Sodom (a rain of fire, the earth opens to form a muddy lake, and black vapors kill flying birds) and Egypt (Moses' ten miracles). In more recent times tyrants are undone by worms engendered from the earth, by drowning, by winds that topple buildings or spread the plague, and by a subtle fire that destroys bodies from within. And Ocean's judgment in favor of the Protestants at the end of *Les Fers* is ratified by God's at Doomsday. In spite of persecution, the elements protect Huguenots in life and contribute to their rebirth after death: fire as purgation, purification, and a creative male force; water as purification, fecundity, and a creative female force; air as liberation and transcendence; and earth as an intimate refuge. According to d'Aubigné's Calvinist theology, all that makes up the universe – people, animals, plants, inanimate objects, the four elements, the humors and organs within our bodies – were created by God. They all suffer from original sin, that is, they were tainted by man's first transgression, and, therefore, are eagerly concerned with the future of humankind. They await deliverance just as we do. Because they never participated directly in the Fall, they are furious at being perverted by humans, and, fighting for their own salvation, they redeem themselves by accusing us before God and taking his side against Satan. Their participation in the 'tragedy' bears witness to the inherent goodness of nature and to God's supreme benevolence, intelligence, and power.

The triumph of the green world requires the feminine principles of fertility, growth, and a natural organic hierarchy to prevail over flame and stone. Although the Catholics are sterile, Protestants partake of, and participate in, nature; as God's chosen people, they are close to the forces that bring life and order, and are assimilated to them. However, d'Aubigné's 'good mothers' (Mother Earth, the Woman of the Apocalypse, Themis, Queen Elizabeth of England) fail to counterbalance the terrifying vision of woman that for the most part pervades *Les Tragiques*. In d'Aubigné's universe, it is the good father, a beneficent, all-powerful male principle, that ensures the ultimate triumph of justice. One of his most beautiful scenes, imitated from Book 21 of the *Iliad*, tells how the god Ocean awakens, his white beard sullied by the blood of Protestant martyrs, their corpses borne by the rivers of France to the sea. Having been informed of the situation, the old one is eager to collect these relics himself and grant them the purest of burials in his waters:

> 'Je garderay ceux-ci, tant que Dieu me commande
> Que les fils du bon heur à leur bon heur je rende.
> Il n'y a rien d'infect, ils sont purs, ils sont nets:
> Voici les paremens de mes beaux cabinets.

Terre qui les trahis, tu estois trop impure
Pour des saincts et des purs estre la sepulture.'    (*Les Fers*, 1525–30)

Thus Father Ocean provides succor for Protestant martyrs too pure to be buried in Mother Earth.

Although in the 'Préface' the implied author, d'Aubigné, refers to himself as the sire of his poem, *Les Tragiques*, as of its older brother, *Le Printemps*, nonetheless he acts like a child before the greatest progenitor of all, God, who, in the last book of the epic, mounts his throne and dispenses justice to the cosmos. A father in the sky fulfills the prophecy made by a father in the waters and a father-poet on earth. Throughout *Les Tragiques* the Narrator repudiates his early woman-oriented love poetry and seeks to be united with God. At the end of *La Chambre dorée* he joins David in calling upon God as the bride calls for her groom:

Comme elle nous crions: 'Vien Seigneur et te haste,
Car l'homme de peché ton Eglise degaste.'
'Vien, dit l'esprit, acours pour defendre le tien.'
'Vien,' dit l'espouse, et nous avec l'espouse: 'Vien!'
(*La Chambre dorée*, 1059–62)

A similar pattern of imagery taken from the Song of Songs pervades the second half of *Jugement*, where we are told that the Blessed will taste heavenly viands and enjoy Christ's own kisses. The Narrator himself, who can neither see nor speak, faints away in ecstasy. His moment of mystical, amorous release is associated not with a mother's womb but the father's lap. Many great poets – Teresa of Avila, Juan de la Cruz, and, more recently, Pierre Jean Jouve and Pierre Emmanuel – have followed the Canticles in associating the erotic with the religious and expressing their yearning for the Godhead as a woman's longing to be possessed by a man, to die with love in his embrace and be impregnated by him with the breath of eternal life. The end of *Les Tragiques* is one of the most powerful of these erotic exaltations of the superego. In this patriarchal world of the spirit the Narrator is content to become a woman or a small child; having repudiated his desire for the mother (Diane Salviati, the Whore of Babylon), he replaces her as the father's beloved and is absorbed into him. More than other religious writers, d'Aubigné creates in his text a symbolic paternal incest transference which leads to atonement with the father-imago. The male superego destroys the female id-temptress and the soft, corrupt, sex-filled world of the court, establishing virile austerity in their place. Good sons (Protestants) are preferred over wicked sons (Catholics), and the latter punished for phallic sadism against the good mother (France).[6]

The struggle between good and evil necessarily takes place in a space-time continuum. To some extent, d'Aubigné depicts France as a gentle, gracious land, corrupted by outside forces: Catherine de' Medici, from Florence; the Guise family, from Lorraine; the Jesuits, from Spain; cruel *reistres*, from Germany; and the Pope, from Rome. Like the *Roland*-poet, Chrétien de Troyes, and Ronsard, d'Aubigné is a patriot, manifesting pride in his native land and a belief that she was, is, and should ever be associated with liberty, equity, and justice. On the other hand, in *Les Feux* especially, he breaks away from national lines, speaks of Wyclif and John Huss, of Jane Grey and Montalcino. Good versus evil is interpreted as poor versus rich or Protestant versus Catholic rather than as Frenchmen versus foreigners. Worthy Reformers are to be found throughout the world, especially in England, but also in the city of Rome, 'nid de Satan' (*Les Feux*, 1112), while in *Misères* and *Jugement* d'Aubigné assumes the mantle of a Biblical prophet to denounce France, a proud, wicked country justly punished by God for her sins. One can conceive d'Aubigné's map of Europe in the following terms: good, Protestant England and Germany in the North versus evil, Catholic Italy and Spain in the South, with France in the center, the battleground and prey of these opposing forces.[7]

In the beginning of *Misères* we find the Narrator marching eastward, like Hannibal or Moses, a conqueror about to pierce the Alps. This is the quest-hero, the leader of men engaged in an active life of movement and adventure. As in the Bible, the *Iliad*, Herodotus, and Xenophon, also *chansons de geste* and the *Poema del Cid*, a trek to the East evokes a struggle for truth and justice against decadent barbarism. On other occasions, the Narrator's career is assimilated to traditional Christian imagery of sea-voyage, storm, and port, or he is compared to the prophet Jonah, who underwent a death-rebirth experience in the belly of a whale. More often, however, the persecuted Huguenot minority flee into exile, like the Children of Israel crossing a Red Sea of their own blood, on a holy quest into the wilderness to found their own New Jerusalem, spiritually superior to Francus's New Troy. Following a topic which dates back to Antiquity (Horace's *Beatus ille* ...), evil culture is contrasted to good nature, dallying at court to a finer life in hills and valleys. Enclosed space, buildings, rooms, and beds, traps for young courtiers and Huguenot princes, are set off against the open, innocent holy places where a chosen elite, the covenanted people, aspire to enlightenment, to an existence beyond the senses, where man can know God. Thus the Albigensians find a refuge in obscure, rocky mountains, where Truth has a home; or poor people hide in the woods, under Nature's skirts. Truth, who dwells in the desert, summons and welcomes the Narrator, a second John the Baptist ('Vox clamantis in deserto') who calls himself 'Le bouc du désert.' This return to nature, a

Renaissance-classical motif, is given renewed vigor when we realize that d'Aubigné refers to real wilds, not the Arcadia of a Theocritus, a Virgil, and a Sannazaro.

If wolves appear to be the masters on this horizontal plane, the additional dimension permitting the lambs to triumph is portrayed also in spatial terms, as a vertical (as in Ronsard's *Hymne des Astres*). It is true, d'Aubigné compares wicked princes to craggy mountains (*Les Princes*) and exclaims over the height of the Palace of Justice, whereas he finds truth in humble, sweet valleys. The attempt to rise above others, in a purely secular way, is condemned. Pride goeth before a fall, and the Narrator prays God to descend to his level. On the other hand, little people, because they remain lowly, are enabled to climb above the mountains, to redeem the primeval Fall of Man. God in heaven looks down as a spectator on the iniquities of the Palace of Justice and the Inquisition, while the souls of Protestant martyrs soar to their new home. Indeed, the Narrator himself is blessed by a divine miracle that permits his spirit, like Ronsard's, to view celestial doings. In cosmic terms, Satan commands the nether world, in combat with God, master of celestial space. Up is good, down is evil. Lucifer and Adam fell; Christ descended but then rose to heaven on the third day; and in the course of the poem God comes down to inspect the world then removes himself in horror. The planet earth, although often under Satan's sway, is a battleground between the two, comparable to France the battleground between Protestant England and Catholic Spain. However, God is master of the entire universe, with the result that, although out of false pride Satan flew up to heaven, he fails to deceive the divinity, and at Doomsday everyone, good and evil, is dragged up to the heavenly throne where God decrees the death of nature and the transcendence of space as we know it. The wicked will be cast down forever to hell, and the good remain on high in a stasis of bliss.

*Les Tragiques*, like the *Odyssey* and the *Aeneid*, the *Lusiads* and the *Gerusalemme liberata*, begins *in medias res*. That is to say, d'Aubigné depicts the present miseries of France before recounting stories of past persecution and vengeance (*Les Feux*, *Vengeances*) or predicting the future of mankind and the end of the world (*Les Fers*, *Jugement*). In the tradition of Lucan, of the medieval French and Occitan crusade epic, and of Camoens and Ercilla, d'Aubigné's poem is one of a minority of epics that specifically treat contemporary events. Unlike Ronsard, d'Aubigné is resolutely a *modernus*. For him, the present re-enacts the past and anticipates the future; it is as vital as the story of Troy and the life of Charlemagne because all of history, including the here and now, reflects divine will and is included in God's divine plan, because the Church, as the central protagonist in history, abides in the past, present, and future.

Thus d'Aubigné, while concentrating on the present, on the events of his own time, includes in *Les Tragiques* all the past and future of the race. His sixteenth-century characters are associated with historical personalities, and, as in the *Lusiads* (but from a different perspective), d'Aubigné evokes the glory of old kings and warriors. *Les Tragiques* establishes a contrast between the Capetian kings of France and their Valois descendants. Even periods the author hated, such as the Roman empire, compare favorably with the present. The lowest trash of Rome, paid gladiators, are braver than Henry III's fops; there are few good magistrates today compared to Greece and Rome; and so on. Like Ronsard, d'Aubigné propounds a version of political philosophy we found in *La Chanson de Roland* and *Raoul de Cambrai*, rejection of the present in favor of an idealized past; and those innovations he favors are presumed to have existed a long time ago. Accused of advocating democracy, the poet defends himself with vigor ('Aux lecteurs'). Like Ronsard and most of the great spirits of his age, whether Protestant or Catholic, he is a royalist reactionary, not a reformer.

The Christian notion of history is neither cyclical, like that of the Greeks and certain primitive societies, nor linear, based upon the premise of continued progress, like that of the modern period. Christian time is both linear and cyclical: it begins with Creation, ends with Doomsday, and is organized according to a pattern, with key moments such as the Fall, the Flood, Exodus, the Crucifixion and Resurrection, and the Second Coming playing an essential role, dominating the flow of history, giving it sense and structure. Because certain events resemble each other, and the consequences they unleash are in direct correspondence or antithesis to other events, the Christian exegete envisages a pattern of recurrence, similar to that evoked by Mircea Eliade and given meaning by symbolism rather than by pragmatic cause and effect. Actions are significant because they participate in transcendant being and because each act imitates a divine archetype. In our Christian world this 'mentality' is represented by such figural and allegorical interpretations of Scripture, that is, of sacred history, as were prevalent in the early Christian period, in the Middle Ages, and on into the modern world, a tradition that ceased only in the nineteenth century. The typological method, which Ronsard consciously practiced in certain of his hymns, *Hercule chrestien*, for example, and *Hymne de la Justice*, and which was used by both Luther and Calvin, will also help us to understand *Les Tragiques*.[8]

The analogies d'Aubigné establishes between Charles IX and Esau or Herod, between Henry IV and Gideon or Moses, between himself and Jonah or David, are not mere literary metaphors. Esau's hostility to Jacob in the Old Testament prefigures, foreshadows Herod's tracking down the infant Christ in the New Testament, an event which fulfills the type or figure.

And (here d'Aubigné extends the method to post-Biblical secular history, a less common but by no means unknown practice) both episodes are post-figured by Charles IX's massacre of the Protestants in the sixteenth century. All three are united in a symbolic nexus, each existing historically in time but none receiving its full significance until the others are also taken into account. D'Aubigné's pattern includes male leaders, female leaders, cities, and countries, good and evil. History is dominated by three great periods, three ordeals in the life of the Church, which witness crimes against the Father, the Son, and the Holy Spirit: persecution of the Children of Israel by Babel, Sodom, Egypt, Canaan, Babylon, and Nineveh, under the reigns of Nebuchadnezzar, Sardanapolis, Esau, Achitophel, Holofernes, Achab, Jezebel, Athaliah, and Semiramis; persecution of Christ and the early Christians by Jerusalem and Rome, under the dominion of Herod, Nero, Messalina, and Agrippina; persecution of the Protestant Reformers by Paris, Florence, Rome, and the Spanish Houses of the Inquisition, under the leadership of Henry II, Charles IX, Henry III, Catherine de' Medici, Marguerite de Valois, the Duke of Guise, the Cardinal of Lorraine, and the Pope. Meanwhile, the Church is defended by Jacob, Gideon, Samson, Moses, Deborah, Esther, Jonah, and David; by Christ; and by Henry IV, Elizabeth, and the author himself. However, if we take into account d'Aubigné's references to the four seasons, to the roses of autumn being the most beautiful, to his claim that mankind has arrived at the end of time, with the worst behind, and if we remember that, for sixteenth-century Calvinists, contemporary Rome was the Antichrist and that the Day of Wrath was indeed nigh – then we realize that one more stage in history remains, a fourth level of recurrence, the Last Judgment, when the Church faces its final ordeal and the persecutors are defeated by Christus Pantocrator in all his majesty. Here the grapes of wrath are harvested, the Pregnant Woman in the desert triumphs in a New Jerusalem, city of the blessed, and the Elect partake of their wedding feast to the Lamb. Adam, Moses, and Christ all fled from the Temple to the wilderness, and then returned to the Promised Land. So too will the Huguenots, the covenanted people, God's last remnant, children of Adam, Moses, and Christ, on Judgment Day. Spring refers to early chronicles of the Church in the Old Testament, summer to Christ and primitive Christianity, autumn to the last flowering of the Church in the Protestant Reformation, and winter to the Second Coming and the end of the cosmic year. These four levels of history correspond to the pattern of a fourfold interpretation of Scripture: spring, to the literal level (Old Testament), summer to the typological or allegorical level (New Testament), autumn to the tropological or moral level (the life of the Christian here and now, for example the late sixteenth century), and winter to the anagogical level (Doomsday). The Huguenot armies live in an intense, almost sacral present, yet also participate in the past and future. They march in the steps of their ancestors, spiritual as well as physical. And Agrippa d'Aubigné refuses traditional distinctions between sacred and secular or between pre- and post-advent history. For him, time includes all of history, all moments of which contain the past and future consubstantial with the present, for all are imbued with the divine. Long before Lamartine and Hugo, he tells the epic of humanity, for mankind's voyage on the planet, meaningless in itself, becomes intelligible and is given value in anticipation of divine justice at Doomsday. With Doomsday, space is abolished, time merges into eternity, and, at this point, now outside of duration, the Narrator faints. God acts in history and out of it, both through the temporal dimension of the chronicle (*Vengeances*) and the symbolic one of Apocalypse (*Jugement*).

These preceding remarks indicate how great a role the Narrator plays in *Les Tragiques*. Scholars have proposed quite a few 'heroes' for the epic: the Protestant community, France, God, and d'Aubigné himself, the figure of the poet. From beginning to end, the latter intrudes, plays a role, serves as intermediary between the public and the events he recounts.[9]

The Narrator of *Les Tragiques* is a literary creation, embodying conventional literary *personae*: the observer or eyewitness, the chronicler, the party spokesman, the preacher, the prophet, the active fighter, and the poet. Although he speaks in the traditionally omniscient voice of classical epic that grants divine sanction to the events recounted, at the same time his purported reminiscences, his participation, give an air of authenticity to the story, helping to integrate the public into his own experiential world. D'Aubigné thus combines features of what Stanzel calls the *auktoriale Erzählsituation* and the *Ich-Erzählsituation*.[10] This *Ich-Erzählsituation* partakes of modes to be found both in Roman satire and in Scripture. In the tradition of Juvenal, the illusion of the poet's own involvement permits heightened exuberance and indignation, hence a series of splendid invectives against leaders of the Catholic party. And, as Biblical prophet, like Jonah chosen by God and spared from death as part of the divine plan, the Narrator has visions, curses his enemies, predicts the future, and cries out for vengeance. He becomes himself an instrument of revenge and the purveyor of God's innermost thoughts; he is both a mortal man and a divinely inspired bard. It is even possible to plot the evolution of the Narrator's psyche in the course of the poem: from exile to witness, from fighter and rebel to prophet and mystic.

I consider especially important the epic quality that pervades the Narrator's career. This individual who pierces through the Alps and crosses the Rubicon, who kills a python and slings stones at Goliath, is portrayed in terms of the traditional romance hero. The fact that he is primarily an artist and is urged by God's angel to fight with his pen by no means belies the heroic aspects of his task. David and Caesar, to whom he is assimilated, were writers as well as warriors, Odysseus and Aeneas told their stories with professional skill, and the historical d'Aubigné was a captain as well as a poet. The author is developing the traditional topic of *fortitudo et sapientia*, so important, we saw, in the elaboration of *La Chanson de Roland*, *Raoul de Cambrai*, and the militant verse of Ronsard. When the mock-editor tells us that the mock-author composed *Les Tragiques* on the field of battle, he feigns to apologize for the poem's rough exterior. In reality he establishes a bond with the implied reader, positing the author-narrator as an exemplar of the ideal epic hero, master of *fortitudo* and *sapientia*. Like Ercilla in *La Araucana*, he is proud to be 'Armado siempre y siempre en ordenanza, / La pluma ora en la mano, ora la lanza' (20:24). The poet himself struggles against the outside world and becomes one of the heroes of his own story. And the creation of the poem, d'Aubigné's fathering it and bequeathing it to the world ('Préface'), is a tangible sign of God's power and victory, that good fathers shall triumph in the end and that the Huguenot soldier shall be one of them.

For all this, the Narrator's drama is primarily an inner one. His adversaries – witch, ogre, serpent – are representations of falsehood, dissimulation, vanity, and corruption, court vices which assail him at all times. Nor ought we to forget that the Narrator's career, his scruples and his anguish, reflect Calvinist notions of conversion and vocation in the Christian life.[11] Having once converted, the Huguenot is nonetheless tortured by uncertainty, for he is still a sinner, 'simil peccator et justus,' and must struggle with the ontological ambiguity of a provisory, temporary state of grace. He oscillates between hope and near-despair, ever in a state of tension, torn by anxiety. Hence the man's humility, his yearning for and dreading the *frui Deo*, the final ecstasy in God.

Nonetheless, although the Narrator fails to change the external world, metamorphosis does occur in his soul. The soldier is transformed into a warrior-poet and a mystic; his spiritual journey becomes an active conquest of the secret of the tabernacle, of truth, faith, and being. He himself seizes the reality of creation. We read of a new kind of prophet, of his alienation, followed by progressive reintegration and self-affirmation. In the course of the poem he repudiates his youth, struggles to find himself, to go beyond appearances. He liberates himself from vice and fear of vice; he turns from darkness to light; and in the end, a *homo novus*, he attains self-realization, freedom, and mastery of a new language. He has transgressed, has, like all men, been guilty of Original Sin. Expelled from the terrestrial paradise, he undergoes the long journey of the dark night of the soul only to know in the end authentic transcendance. In Jungian terms the heroic-religious experience implies transference of affection from earthly objects to the heavenly Father. The Elect gives expression to his longing for sun, stars, and the deity. Renouncing all earthly father- and mother-figures (Henry IV, France), he communicates with the deity, becomes one with him, undergoing a death-rebirth experience similar to those of the mythical Osiris, Tammuz, Attis, Adonis, Mithra, the legendary phoenix, and, of course, Christ.

The Narrator recounts his story not out of pleasure or egotism but in his chosen role of 'protest-ant' or witness. It is his responsibility, as a Christian and a poet, to use his 'talent,' to 'sacrifice' his poem to God. From these religious, apocalyptic concerns derives d'Aubigné's esthetic. Following in Ronsard's footsteps, inspired by *furor poeticus*, he becomes a prophet and seer. However, he claims to go beyond Ronsard: a member of the true Church, his is an authentic experience, and he is inspired by the true God. His furor comes as a gift of divine grace, from the breath of the Holy Spirit, for his soul has been purified by fire, not water, and his genius is of Biblical not pagan-classical provenance. Hence the traditional epic repudiation of youthful amorous or bucolic verse (in Virgil, Dante, Ronsard, and Tasso: cf. Propertius, 'Aetas prima canat veneres, postrema tumultus') takes on a new aura. D'Aubigné defends the low, crass outer crust of *Les Tragiques* because he seeks to describe reality authentically and thus create an equivalence between form and content, but even more because the very lowness of the style brings it closer to the Bible.

He assimilates his poem to the tradition of *sermo humilis* in the Old and New Testaments, and the specifically Calvinist esthetic of *sermo rudis et plebeius*: that is, a text of immense Christian significance yet written for all mankind in a language people can understand. He rejects his own pseudo-Greek style for a natural, Biblical one: *vif, aspre, hardi, inconnu*. He also adheres to the Renaissance 'esthetics of negligence' which we find in Rabelais, Montaigne, La Fontaine, and the Ronsard of the *Responce*.[12] According to this conception, the aristocrat partakes of life and creates in a spirit of divine enthusiasm, in contrast to the dull, low-class, pedantic court poetaster, whose work can only be the result of hard labor and adherence to rigid, artificial codes. The 'negligent poet' is spontaneous (he breaks the rules), consubstantial (form matches content), and irresponsible. D'Aubigné accepts the first two facets of the code but modifies the third. He will be responsible not to court moralists or law-givers but to God.

As the pseudo-editor declares in 'Aux lecteurs,' excusing himself for having 'stolen' *Les Tragiques*, the talent buried in the earth, and fire without air, are useless. So too is an epic without an audience. No other Western epic is as directed toward an implied audience; in none do we find so great an emphasis on the persuading, cajoling narrative voice. D'Aubigné seeks a direct, personal, I-Thou relationship to the public. He speaks to his characters, and to his readers, in the present tense, concerning immediately vital matters. He writes not for an elite but for all men, Protestant and Catholic, to console the former and to terrorize the latter, for language is a weapon in his hands, as it is a dagger in Christ's mouth, the only arm that remains to the silent ones who, by 1616, had lost everything else. D'Aubigné is a prophet in a book-centered, sacramental universe. His vocation, that of a modern oracle, inspired by the one and only Book, Scripture, is to translate his vision into human speech, God's Word into the vernacular of men, and through his judicial rhetoric make us also pass judgment on these cosmic trial proceedings. Having received the Word, he transmits it to the people. God's book and word are open to those who have eyes to see and ears to hear. Agrippa d'Aubigné, who twice calls his poem *discours*, like Ronsard but on the opposite side, writes as a mediator between God and men, to bring to his fellows the faith, hope, and love he himself has come to possess.

What kind of poem is *Les Tragiques*? There can be no doubt that d'Aubigné's masterpiece partakes of a variety of literary conventions and adheres to more than one genre. It contains elements of epic, satire, chronicle, history, confession, lyricism, polemic, diatribe, pamphlet, martyrology, meditation, allegory, and prophecy.[13] To what extent the poem is a 'true epic' is open to question. On the one hand, it does not recount the adventures of a single great hero, in the tradition of Homer and Virgil, or, for that matter, of the *chanson de geste* and *roman courtois*. The author certainly ignores or defies Ronsard's advice (in *l'Art poëtique*) to avoid partisanship, exact history, and events of his own time. On the other hand, however, he consciously introduces into *Les Tragiques* traits, themes, motifs – especially the supernatural – associated in his day with heroic poetry, which would direct the public toward epic. His text is a song of battle with political orientation that claims to be historically authentic and ethically of the highest, most exemplary validity. It tells of illustrious deeds, is 'choric,' that is, expresses the ethos of its society, sustains the rhetorical strategies of epic, and is composed in the grand style, festal, energetic, evoking in the reader a sense of *meraviglia*.

In my opinion, d'Aubigné, like Spenser and Milton, chose to refurbish the traditional epic so that it could embody a contemporary, Protestant vision of man. He breaks with some classical conventions, uses others (the example of Lucan's *Pharsalia*, for instance) for his own purposes, to establish his personal claim for originality as an artist. He tells a story, but the story of the Church, of the entire human race, not just one Odysseus or

Aeneas. He plunges *in medias res*, that is with the events that make up his
own times, then sweeps back to the beginning of the world and forward to
Doomsday. From his vantage-point, it is God and the poet as witness
who embody traditional heroic virtues and the new consciousness. D'Aubigné's modern epic world is shown indeed to be historical and true in the
same sense that the Bible is more authentic than classical myth. And it is in
this essence of the universal that Christian epic is to be found, in contrast
to its pagan forebears. For *Les Tragiques* is an 'anatomy,' a world-mirror
containing within itself the entire cosmos and all of mankind's history.
Like Milton, d'Aubigné sensed a gulf between traditional heroic artistry and
the theme he wished to illustrate. Unlike Milton, he chose to innovate
both in form and content, to create a Christian epic form, *le stile saint*, to
match his Christian epic content.

Agrippa d'Aubigné was one of the most extraordinary men in an extraordinary epoch. A prodigy at the age of six, an orphan at fifteen, an officer
and hero at eighteen, a courtier and Petrarchan love-poet at twenty-one,
an *uomo universale* who read Latin, Greek, and Hebrew and was learned in
science and occultism, he became one of the great soldiers of his age, a
councillor and spiritual guide to princes. And, literally in his spare time,
d'Aubigné composed the greatest poem of his age, the great Protestant
epic of martyrdom and resistance. In its realism, passion, violence, and
Dionysian archetypal power, *Les Tragiques* recalls the more powerful
medieval epics, *Raoul de Cambrai* and *Les Lorrains*, for example, and
anticipates some of the most exciting, tortured writings of modern times.
It manifests the power, the emotion, the cosmic vision and scale we find in
Hugo, Claudel, Saint-John Perse, and Aragon. Indeed, it is most appropriate that the poets of the Resistance, like Aragon and Pierre Emmanuel, were
influenced by d'Aubigné, and that a recent issue of *Europe* was devoted
to him. This collection of essays emphasizes his central place in a tradition of
protest that includes Victor Hugo and extends to our day, a viable cultural
alternative to the 'Corneille, Racine, Molière' beloved of French lycées and
Alliance Française lecturers. It is also true, *Les Tragiques* tells the story of
losers. In 1628 La Rochelle, the last Huguenot citadel in the kingdom of
France, fell, and, less than two years later, d'Aubigné, the old fanatic, fell
also. But his poem lives on, as an eternal witness to an age and a man, the
masterpiece of the French Baroque. Thierry Maulnier was perhaps not
mistaken when he wrote in 1939, 'D'Aubigné est notre Hugo, il est celui que
Hugo crut être, et réussit à faire croire qu'il était.'[14]

## Chapter Nine

# 🌺 SAINT-AMANT

Quantitatively, if not qualitatively, the seventeenth century is one of the great periods in the history of the French epic. One scholar provides us with over a hundred titles of heroic poems; another insists that only fifty of these can be considered true epics.[1] Whether 46, 118, or a compromise figure in between, the number of long poems corresponds favorably to the production of the early Middle Ages and was surpassed only in the time of Lamartine and Hugo. Within the century the flowering of epic can be assigned to two main periods. Between 1600 and 1610, eleven such texts were written, several of these composed at the court of Marguerite de Valois. They include four imitations of, or sequels to, *La Franciade*. Unfortunately, all eleven are failures. Of more interest are the heroic poems composed between 1653 and 1671. In the 1650s, six highly regarded men of letters published epics: these are Saint-Amant's *Moyse sauvé* (1653); Scudéry's *Alaric* (1654); Godeau's *Saint Paul* (1654); Chapelain's *La Pucelle* (1656); Desmarets de Saint-Sorlin's *Clovis* (1657); and Le Moyne's *Saint Louis* (1658). Another thirteen or so came to life in the succeeding decade, including four Biblical narratives by Jacques de Coras, and a *Marie-Madeleine* (1669) and an *Esther* (1670) also by Desmarets. However, they are relatively modest, sober, and, above all, short, and thus manifest a reaction against the long heroic poem; they bear witness to decline in the genre.

The epics of the 1650s appeared on the literary scene at the same time as the madrigal. Do they embody the typically 'baroque' heroism of the age? or a nostalgic yearning for absent heroism? or are they a literary phenomenon, come into being from strictly literary causes? It is certain that the writers of epic gave expression to a nostalgia for power and glory, for honor, martial living, and knightly doings, but also that the nobility tried to live up to such models in their own lives. In this period, as in the twelfth century, heroic literature reflects and helps create wish-fulfillment on the part of a threatened aristocratic class. So also do comparable artistic manifestations: the great prose romances, *Le Grand Cyrus* and *Clélie*, and the last heroic plays of Corneille: *Andromède* (1650), *Don Sanche d'Aragon* (1650), *Nicomède* (1651), and *Pertharite* (1651). To some extent, *Alaric* and *Clovis* as well as *Cyrus* and *Andromède* bridge the gap between epic and romance, between heroism and gallantry, as did, four and one-half centuries earlier, late *chansons de geste* such as *Huon de Bordeaux* and *Renaud de Montauban*. Since, however, the majority of the Homers and Tassos of the 1650s began to write during the reign of Louis XIII, under the sway of Richelieu, this particular current ought to be associated with the age as a whole, not the specific, highly localized incidents of the Fronde (1648–53). We might also consider literary forces that encouraged epic production: Jesuit instruction in the colleges; the example of Italy – of Tasso's *Gerusalemme liberata* (1581) and a host of *seicento* imitations – as well as of Ronsard, du Bartas, and the abortive epics of Henry IV's reign; and, finally, a reaction on the part of certain social classes, literary circles, and individual writers against the frivolous court-lyrics of Voiture and his circle, and the esthetics of gallantry and licentiousness they represent.

With the succeeding generation the *poëme heroïque* ceased to be in vogue, due in part to the striking failure of *La Pucelle* (the purported masterpiece that people had been awaiting for years), in part to the attack on the French epic school contained in Boileau's *Art poétique* (1674), in part to a far-reaching shift in taste, from what we now call the baroque to the classical age. It is also true that most of these texts are pompous, rigid, tediously correct, and sterile. Their creators sought to instruct rather than please, to inspire virtue at all costs, always a dangerous wish in art. And they were guilty of a mechanical adherence to the 'rules' of epic production as laid down by Tasso, Castelveltro, Piccolòmini, Scaliger, Vida, and Vossius. These poems all contain armed, casked maidens, seductive sorceresses, enchanted islands or palaces, Satanic magicians, council-scenes in hell and heaven, lengthy foretelling of the patron's genealogy, and so on. A distinguished scholar echoes the generally accepted opinion when he states: 'En fait, aucune de ces œuvres n'est encore lisible. Aucune ne mérite même le plus timide effort de réhabilitation.'[2] Although, on the whole, I agree with this formulation, I wish to make two exceptions. These are Saint-Amant's *Moyse sauvé* and Le Moyne's *Saint Louis*, in my opinion literary works of the highest quality, deserving careful, loving scrutiny. Their only fault is to have come into the world during a time of transition, surrounded by a host of mediocre brothers and sisters. They will form the subject of my next two chapters.

Antoine Gérard, sieur de Saint-Amant (1594–1661),[3] was one of the most important, perhaps *the* most important poet of his generation. He is best

known for meditations on solitude in nature ('La Solitude' and 'Le Contemplateur') and for a number of burlesque poems on food, drink, and bad
lodgings. However, his first collection, *Les Œuvres* (1629), contains three
heroic idylls in the tradition of Marino's *La Sampogna*: *Andromède*, *Arion*,
and *La Métamorphose de Lyrian et de Sylvie*. In the 'Avertissement' to
*Les Œuvres*, Saint-Amant speaks of having begun a 'grand Poëme heroïque'
on Samson in honor of Louis XIII. Four or five hundred lines were written
but subsequently lost, and the piece was never published. Also in the 1620s,
Saint-Amant worked on a poem telling the Joseph story. Part of this
composition, after revision, was later incorporated into *Moyse sauvé*, part
published as a separate fragment in *Le Dernier Recueil* (1658). Although
as early as 1638 Chapelain, in a letter to Balzac, describes the outline for the
*Moyse*, it appears that Saint-Amant worked most intensively on the epic
from 1638 to 1642 and revised it from 1645 to 1648. He took a copy of it
with him when in 1649–51 he visited his patroness, Louise-Marie de
Gonzague, Queen of Poland, and published the final, polished version after
his return to France, in 1653.[4]

Saint-Amant calls his poem an *idyle heroïque*, and in a letter to his friend,
the scholar Samuel Bochart, he writes: 'Vous me direz peut-estre, Monsieur, que mon ouvrage n'en porte pas tout à fait le titre [that of *poëme
heroïque*]; mais estant à peu près de mesme nature, je le luy aurois bien pû
faire porter, si j'en eusse voulu croire quelques-uns des plus capables'
(p. 255). From the author's point of view, his work adheres, at least in part,
to the Renaissance notion of what an epic is and should be.

The central action deals with Moses' adventures as a baby, that is, when
his parents, Amram and Jocabel, expose him to the Nile to escape Pharaoh's
massacre of newborn Hebrews. The infant is threatened by a crocodile,
flies, a storm, and a vulture; he is defended by his sister, Marie; a shepherd,
Elisaph; and the latter's uncle, Mérary. Pharaoh's daughter, Termuth,
eventually discovers and adopts this living, abandoned treasure. A series
of secondary actions, presented as 'episodes' or *tiroirs*, recount the heroic
careers of Jacob and Joseph, and prophesy the future exploits of the adult
Moses.

Careers of various Old Testament figures, including specifically Jacob,
Joseph, and Moses, have contributed to our modern conception of the
hero: indeed, the notion of the hero in archetypal or myth criticism is based
as much upon Hebrew as upon Greek and medieval models. Therefore,
merely the telling of Biblical stories grants Saint-Amant's text an epic aura.
In terms of battle, adventure, the quest, withdrawal and return, initiation, death-rebirth, and similar patterns, the author has preserved all the
motifs in his source and added a few of his own.

The adversaries of the Children of Israel appear as Shadow-figures, rebels against God, demons of the night. Such are to some extent Jacob's choleric brother Esau, a hunter and killer, from whom he flees, and the whorish Potiphar's wife, responsible for Joseph's imprisonment. Such also are the forces that seek to destroy the infant Moses in his cradle: the crocodile from hell, compared to the Monster of Lerna, weeping deceptive tears like Satan; flies and wasps, compared to harpies, in league with the devil; the infernal storm that unleashes winds, waves, and a hundred crocodiles; and the vulture, a demon in the form of a bird, that assaults Moses with its beak and talons. In addition, Pharaoh's army indulges in a blood-curdling Massacre of the Innocents far more effective than the machinations of all the crocodiles on the Nile. His descendant, the Pharaoh of Moses' adult life, pursues the Hebrews to the Red Sea, the giant Nimrod (a symbol for pride) painted on his breastplate and the crest on his helmet shaped like a dragon (a symbol for Satanic evil). Engulfed by the Red Sea, he persists to the end, defying God and the death God administers, with a grandeur in evil worthy of the most splendid villains in Corneille's middle period and of the great adversaries in Renaissance epic: Rodomonte, Argante, Solimano, Braggadochio, and Turpine.

The Shadow-figures are masters who force the Children of Israel to be their slaves. For a while Joseph suffers from Egyptian bondage. Pharaoh then persecutes his descendants, enslaves them, compelling them to build pyramids and canals on the Nile. Indeed, it is because an Egyptian master whips an Israelite that Moses intervenes on his countryman's behalf, duels with the Egyptian, and slays him. The master-servant conflict also exists within the Hebrew world. Jacob and Esau struggle each for power over the other. Jacob then serves Laban for fourteen years (Saint-Amant here follows Flavius Josephus) before earning his right to marry Rachel and, eventually, to return to his homeland in peace. A variation on this theme appears in the erotic sphere: Saint-Amant tells us that, although Jacob is Laban's servant, the latter's daughter, Leah, becomes a love-slave to him, and that through love the bondsman Joseph renders his mistress, Potiphar's wife, a captive in turn.

The master is depicted as one who encloses, the slave as one who is enclosed. Hebrews are compelled to build structures in stone, and Joseph is locked up in a prison following upon Potiphar's wife's slander. Mérary ironically comments on his and his friends' bucolic occupations: themselves captives, they are busy constructing cages for birds (2: 93–104). In baroque conceits the day is imprisoned by night, and Elisaph breaks some of Marie's love-chains (her hair) when he liberates her from the Nile. These images are taken up again when the Children of Israel escape from bondage like birds from a cage. Their liberation, of course, parallels that of Jacob and Joseph at other times in the poem.

Saint-Amant, who painted in such vivid terms imminent death by water or from a sea-monster (*Andromède, Arion*), evokes similar perils in his *Moyse sauvé*. Among those who fall in this manner are the Israelites in the time of Noah and the Egyptians in the age of Moses; Moses himself as a child and his sister Marie face drowning in the Nile. Both physical and metaphorical storms threaten the baby's life and tear apart Jocabel's inner peace. And Hebrew blood, shed during the years of bondage, is avenged by Moses' miracle, one of the plagues on Egypt – transformation of the Nile into blood; by the lamb's blood smeared onto the doors of Israelite households, so that only Egyptian first-born perish; and by the waters of the Red Sea, literally colored in this version of the story, that destroy Pharaoh's army.

In the end, good triumphs over evil, and the holy over the demonic, a course of events attributable to the deeds of great men. As is to be expected, aspects of war are formulated in a pattern of 'masculine' imagery: that of the sword and the flame. Sometimes swords are used for evil purposes, symbolize pride, anger, cruelty, and the power of the will; witness Pharaoh who, even in the face of God's wrath, will not drop his blade, glittering in the sun (5: 333–40). Sometimes the weapon is wielded in God's own cause by his kings and judges. Fire, on the other hand, normally stands for the divinity and his Chosen People. Thus the infant's eyes flame while Aaron's head is covered with a fiery nimbus; in addition, Pharaoh is crushed by God's lightning, a pillar of fire leads through the desert, and God appears to Moses as flame in the Burning Bush and on Mount Sinai. Well then might Saint-Amant himself invoke sparks from Moses' bush to save his poem, *Moyse sauvé*, from the waters of neglect.

It is true, the hero of *Moyse sauvé* is an infant, totally passive but for his quasi-miraculous feat of warding off flies, in the tradition of the baby Hercules. It is also true that other characters wage martial deeds in Moses' stead; Elisaph and Mérary, for instance. The recital of past and future events also allows for heroism on the part of Jacob, Joseph, and the adult Moses, 'ange liberateur,' for a pattern of heroic 'episodes' to set off and balance the more idyllic central narrative. However, even the infant Moses does not differ strikingly from those other relatively passive heroes, the Huguenot martyrs in *Les Tragiques*. One feature of baroque epic is for the protagonist to remain passive, without growth or inner conflict, and with little direct participation in the action, which is performed in his stead by other humans or by divine intervention (cf. Sannazaro, Tasso, and Camoens).[5] Saint-Amant simply takes a baroque motif and, in typical baroque fashion, pushes it to its extreme point.

Given this peculiar notion of heroism, it is appropriate that the author call his poem an *idyle heroïque*. Perhaps because, by the seventeenth cen-

tury, the rules for epic had been carefully formulated and were well
known, perhaps because the word *idyle* was almost a neologism, in his
prefaces Saint-Amant pays more attention to the idyllic than the heroic.
In 1629 he describes the idyll as 'des Descriptions de quelques avantures
celebres dans la Fable ancienne';[6] in 1653, as 'de petites Matieres narratives
& fabuleuses' (p. 7). He goes on to designate the non-heroic aspects of
his poem: 1 / in *Moyse sauvé* we do not find battles, sieges, and a single
dominating protagonist; 2 / the action occurs over a period of one day only,
instead of a year, the custom in epic; and 3 / lyrical passages make up the
largest part of the text: 'Le Luth y éclatte plus que la Trompette' (p. 8). This
is by no means clear; and in any case, for knowledge of classical letters
Saint-Amant was inferior to Ronsard and d'Aubigné as well as to Chénier.
He may even have coined the term *idyle heroïque* as a gesture of bravado.
Nonetheless, I think we can deduce from his critical remarks and from the
text itself that the idyllic in *Moyse sauvé* refers more to the central action
than to the episodes; that is, to the largely fictitious story of Moses' adventures as an infant rather than to the Biblically inspired careers of Jacob,
Joseph, and the adult protagonist. In contrast to the subplots, the narrative
kernel treats intimate family concerns and is, at least in part, concerned
with evoking the life and manners of the Hebrew people, depicted in the
pastoral mode.[7]

I propose that the word 'idyllic' in Saint-Amant can be roughly translated
by 'pastoral,' that Saint-Amant's contribution to the development of the
long poem in France, following nonetheless in the traces of Marino (the
*Adone*, 1623),[8] is to combine Virgilian *sermo gravis* and *sermo humilis* or,
at least, *sermo mediocris*, that is, the *Aeneid* and the *Bucolics*, by creating a
new genre, the pastoral epic. Like Chapelain, he was surely impressed by
Marino's achievement in the 'modern style' and sought to emulate the Italian
master's epic of peace, or, rather, to fuse it with the more traditional,
ancient notion of heroism. Although in *Moyse sauvé* rustic characters do
give battle, employing rustic arms, it is hardly an epic feat for a shepherd
and a fisherman to fight off a vulture or a swarm of wasps. And, whenever
Moses or his family find the opposition to be beyond their powers, a
helpful angel steps in. Good always prevails in this narrative of the arts of
peace. The setting is limited to Amram's house; the banks of the Nile,
covered with bullrushes and gladioli; Termuth's palace; and her grotto on
the river, where we find roses, tulips, carnations, and anemones. Saint-
Amant exults in a festival of flowers. Elisaph and Marie are shepherds;
Mérary is a fisherman; Amram chooses the Nile as a refuge for Moses
because he has fished there often, he who also works as Termuth's gardener.
The characters guard their flocks (losing one lamb to the vulture), capture
birds and fish, construct birdcages, and partake of a rustic meal, dining on

figs, dates, black bread, fish, almonds, raisins, and palm milk. Finally, as in the modern romantic idyll (*Jocelyn*, *Hermann und Dorothea*), we find serious, 'rural' poetry devoted to family life: Amram and Jocabel at home, discussing domestic problems in the intimacy of the bed; Jacob's warm reception into Laban's household; or the touching family reunion when Termuth rescues the infant: a kind of intimate *kreatürlich* reality that Auerbach noticed in French prose of the fifteenth century and which recurs from time to time since then.[9]

Occupying a central place in Saint-Amant's pattern of idyllic imagery are trees. Elisaph climbs a palm tree to provide lunch for Marie, and Joshua's enemy, armed with a cedar, falls like a pine. More significant for our purposes, Jacob is a trunk that will give birth to famous fruits, and his departure with Nebur is compared to a farmer transplanting a tree. Although, according to Pharaoh's oracle, Moses is a branch on a plant that will overshadow and smother Egypt, because of Termuth he will indeed be grafted onto the Egyptian branch. And in his adult life Aaron's rod is metamorphosed into an almond tree in full bloom, with flourishing limbs and leaves. The tree is an image of vertical power, of fertility, serenity, and harmony, a refuge in the green world. The Children of Israel are close to nature. And theirs is a family, a line of descendants, the genealogical Tree of Jesse, that extends from Adam to Christ, who restores the Tree of Life with his Cross. Through the image of the tree this sacred line is assimilated to the innocence of the pastoral in nature.

Evil flying creatures, specifically the vulture, flies, and hornets that attack Moses, serve as antagonists. Yet birds can also figure God's justice: Joseph's prison-mate dreams of being devoured by birds; the winged angel wrestles with Jacob; and an eagle finally slays the attacking vulture. Less ferocious are the tiny birds placed in cages by Marie, happily imprisoned, or Marie herself, joyful as a mother swallow returning to her nest when she discovers Moses alive and well after the storm. Although the Hebrews also resemble caged birds, they are eager to escape their Egyptian masters and do so. Since Termuth is not assimilated to the other Egyptians, however, it is appropriate for swans to feed from her hand. And the poem ends at sundown with fireflies and nightingales contributing to a vision of peace on earth and good will toward men (12: 445–60). The good mothers in the poem – Marie and Termuth – are associated with birds, just as good fathers are associated with trees. The bird is a spiritual, liberated creature symbolizing the finest aspirations in the universe. A dispenser of nourishment, the image of grace, charm, and transcendance, and of the maternal breast, like the tree the bird is closely assimilated to the pastoral world, to good love and the security of the nest.

In Theocritus and Virgil, in Sannazaro, Ronsard, Montemayor, and

Honoré d'Urfé, a rural setting and flocks of sheep serve as adornments to chaste love. Saint-Amant, who had composed a series of pieces in the neo-Petrarchan style ('Le Bel Œil malade,' 'Madrigal,' 'Amarante,' 'Plainte sur la mort de Sylvie') and in 1629 published a long mythological erotic-pastoral, *La Métamorphose de Lyrian et de Sylvie*, did not let the occasion go by. Hence into *Moyse sauvé* he inserts a strictly non-Biblical love interest between Elisaph and Marie. In contrast to Potiphar's wife, herself or her lust designated as *lascive, indiscrette, molle, sale, infames, languissans*, and *lubrique* (11: 1–116), with regard to Elisaph and Marie Saint-Amant employs the terms *une discrette flâme, une coustume et licite et fidelle*, and *flames secrettes* (2: 82, 85; 7: 133). The shepherd fights in his beloved's name, even saves her life when she falls into the Nile. This latter scene gives rise to charming baroque conceits. Elisaph declares he regrets having broken his love-chains (Marie's hairs) by pulling her to shore; he did so not out of insolence but to spare her life:

> Ce penser odieux me donne mille gesnes;
> Il reproche à mes doigts d'avoir tiré mes chaisnes,
> D'en avoir rompu mesme afin de te sauver,
> Et le rude service il n'en peut approuver.
> Mais, excusez leur faute, ô Liens desirables;
> S'ils n'estoyent criminels vous seriez miserables ...    (Part 7: 149–54)

Otherwise, he would have preferred himself to perish in the water. Marie replies that her outrage is sweet, for his fingers did indeed rescue her:

> Tu n'as point fait d'outrage aux honneurs de ma teste,
> Ou si tu m'en-as fait, le mal en est si dous,
> Que tes doigts, de tout crime en demeurent absous.    (Part 7: 170–2)

The same convention extends to the 'episodes,' where the adult Moses weds Zipporah of the Midianites, whose family are shepherds, and in exile keeps flocks; and where Jacob the shepherd, contrasted to Esau the hunter, woos the chaste shepherdess Rachel, carves his beloved's name on trees and stone, and offers her shepherd's crooks as gifts.

Finally, consider Pharaoh's daughter, Termuth. She is not a shepherdess; she is married but childless, and, as far as we can tell, neither in love nor beloved by anyone. For all that, Saint-Amant depicts her in scarcely veiled tones of baroque sensuousness. Chaste like Diana, Termuth is more beautiful than the sun. Her relationship to her swans is revealing:

> Un Estang precieux dont seulement les Cygnes
> Entre tous les Oyseaux s'osoyent reputer dignes,

> Pour la belle raison de la conformité
> Qu'avoit leur innocence avec sa pureté ...
> Ces Nageurs blancs et doux luy venoyent rendre hommage;
> Mais, si-tost que dans l'Onde ils voyoyent son Image,
> Ils n'osoyent l'approcher de peur de troubler l'Eau,
> Et de faire perir un si rare Tableau.   (Part 10: 261–4, 277–80)

Later, as she walks into the Nile, the stone steps kiss her feet. The river then receives her in its embrace. Waters jump about her lovely body, and when she thrusts them away from her while swimming, they express disappointment. Then towels drink her bath-water and a comb bites into her hair. In the tradition of Tristan l'Hermite and of Voiture, love is elaborated in terms of compliment, game, spectacle, and art – as a court ritual. Saint-Amant's Marie recalls a hundred chaste shepherdess maidens, his Termuth a hundred unapproachable courtly ladies (and her prototype, Saint-Amant's patroness, the very real Queen of Poland). The erotic motifs in *Moyse sauvé* anchor the poem in a literary tradition, a set of conventions, and a feeling for decorum typical of the age.

I have already spoken of family life and intimacy in *Moyse sauvé*. It is significant that this poem contains, more than any other long narrative in French, a concerted, sustained pattern of relationships between mothers and children. Although the infant Moses is the protagonist, he is far from being the only child in the epic. Jacob and Esau fight in Rebecca's womb, and are raised together. In a scene original to Saint-Amant, when Jacob flees from Laban, Rachel absconds with the father's pagan idols in order to give them as toys to her children. Moses' brother Aaron, the future Levite, is depicted as a lovely three-year-old boy-prophet, his blond hair flowing in a heavenly nimbus, but also a child who is reprimanded by his mother for prattling while adults hold serious conversation. Termuth would not have adopted Moses were she not sterile, for she yearned passionately for a baby, to the extent of painting the portrait of one in her leisure time. And we must not forget the child who gathers shells during the crossing of the Red Sea, a scene which provoked Boileau's ire but is, indeed, one of the most charming of the entire poem:

> Là l'Enfant esveillé courant sous la licence
> Que permet à son âge une libre innocence,
> Va, revient, tourne, saute, et par maint cry joyeux
> Témoignant le plaisir que reçoivent ses yeux,
> D'un estrange Caillou qu'à ses pieds il rencontre
> Fait au premier venu la precieuse montre,
> Ramasse une Cocquille, et d'aise transporté,
> La presente à sa Mere avec naïveté;

Là, quelque juste effroy qui ses pas solicite,
S'oublie à chaque objet le fidelle Exercite;
Et là, prés des rempars que l'œil peut transpercer,
Les Poissons esbahis le regardent passer.    (Part 5: 241–52)

In *Moyse sauvé* the Biblical confrontation of Messiah and Monster is fused with a romance tradition of opposition between young and old, of child and greybeard, in which the weak and innocent are menaced by stronger Terrible Father adversaries. The child-god, the *puer senex*, is conceived as weak and abandoned but destined to be the savior of mankind.

Good fathers exist in the epic: Isaac, Jacob himself, and Amram. But we largely forget them in favor of the more emotionally charged mother-figures. Significantly, the male-oriented hunter, Esau, 'De son humeur farouche, insolente, et nuisible' (2: 178), who brings game to Isaac, is discomfited by his female-oriented shepherd brother, who gives presents to Rebecca. The extremes of maternal sentiment are manifest in Jocabel, compared to a mother ewe and a doe; Marie, assimilated to a mother swallow; and Termuth. Yet, beyond these, the most impressive *mater nutrix* of all is the Nile. Although the river once threatens Moses' cradle (urged on by Satanic forces), in general it plays a maternal, protective role and is portrayed more in pastoral, even erotic, terms than in demonic ones.

Termuth's palace and grotto are constructed on the Nile. They are *loci amœni*, an oasis of freshness and peace in a hot land. Calypso's grotto in the *Odyssey* and Armida's garden in the *Gerusalemme liberata* are here transformed into a morally admirable décor, sensual indeed but lacking overt sex. The chaste Termuth, a Diana among women, a married Nausicaa, bathes without feeling the need to avenge herself on an Actaeon. The waters consecrate her purity, play with her body, even bring the baby she has been yearning for. Does she not herself symbolize the Nile, and do not she and the river together 'save Moses,' the main action of the poem as indicated by its title?

At the beginning of *Moyse sauvé*, in the morning, Jocabel plays an active role defending her son. At the end of the poem, at dusk, although Jocabel will continue to nurse the infant, Termuth assumes the role of surrogate mother. For most of that fateful day the baby has been entrusted to the Nile. Moses' cradle is hidden in a labyrinthine shadow of reeds, bullrushes, and water-irises; there, in the Green World, in mystery, he finds a refuge from sea-monsters and from Egyptian soldiers who range over the countryside. He is as safe in water as is Aaron in God's fire. Aaron's nimbus is a masculine image of God's power and the Word, the Nile a feminine image of maternal bounty. Furthermore, placing anyone, but especially an infant, in a bark and releasing him to the waters symbolize a return to the mother's womb. Later in the hero's life, with the crossing of the Red Sea, waters again protect the Israelites and are again associated with a Hebrew child. Just as the Nile preserved the baby Moses from Pharaoh's search party, the Red Sea preserves all the Children of Israel from another Pharaoh's army. This latter individual manifests masculine will to power. He is then defeated by the Red Sea, temporarily transformed into a hard labyrinth (of crystal and rock) for the Hebrews' benefit but returned to feminine water in order to destroy Pharaoh.

I submit that Saint-Amant has created in this poem a pattern of relationships that evokes one manifestation of the Oedipal situation: a world in which the Father is evil or non-existent but the threatened child finds solace and protection in his all-powerful Mother. The Mother defends the child against, and helps him overcome, the Father-enemy. Thus fire and the sword yield to water, and war yields to a vision of pastoral. The poem is crowned by a happy ending, occurring near a grotto, on the waters, in which a couple agrees to marry and the foundling acquires two mothers, his own and a princess.

Of all epic themes, the most important for Saint-Amant's poem is perhaps the death-rebirth experience. Leaving aside the symbolic initiations of Jacob, Joseph, or for that matter the Children of Israel as a whole, let us consider Moses' own career. As an adult he is reborn after his encounter with the Burning Bush and the voice on Mount Sinai. The mature Moses is saved from waters when the Red Sea separates; the baby is spared because, in spite of death-wielding monsters, his cradle, a *fresle Vaisseau* (1: 8), does not sink or stray, does not become his coffin. The predestined child is threatened by death (Bachelard's 'Charon Complex') but is born for a second time from an ark on the waters and is taken into the royal palace of Egypt with a princess for his surrogate mother. Withdrawal and return are associated with one of Van Gennep's most important rites of passage: birth itself; and Baudouin's notion of the epic as a form linked closely to the birth-trauma is exemplified perhaps more closely in *Moyse sauvé* than in any other work of literature.

As in d'Aubigné, good people are portrayed as shepherds, carpenters, and fishermen. No doubt Saint-Amant wished to avoid the pretentious, artificial heroism that mars the poems of his rivals Chapelain, Scudéry, and Desmarets. Furthermore, it is appropriate, in a Christian epic, that emphasis be placed on pastoral virtues – innocence and humility – in place of the arts of war. Although the goal of Christian life and Christian history is a city, the Celestial Jerusalem, the foreshadowing of this millenium and even its actual symbolic representation are always in terms of a garden: Eden, or the gardens of the Canticles and the Apocalypse. In the Biblical tradition, Abel and David tended flocks. Christ's nativity was heralded by shepherds in the field, and Christ himself, the Agnus Dei, became a pastor to us all. He who walked on the water chose a fisherman to be his chief disciple and, along with Peter and Andrew, became a fisher of men. The fish and the lamb are symbols of Christ's body, consumed in the Eucharist, and of his message. Just as d'Aubigné's humble Protestants are the spiritual descendants of Christ and the Apostles, so also Saint-Amant's no less humble Israelites are their ancestors. These low-class people, shepherds and fishermen, stand at the antipodes of Greco-Roman heroism: Moses differs from Achilles as Christ differs from Aeneas. Yet, in spite of their humility, they are more heroic, and their deeds of greater cosmic significance, than anything told in the *Iliad* or the *Aeneid*. Although the Bible lacks the stylistic splendor of Greco-Roman rhetoric, its scriptural *sermo humilis* is also *gravissimus*: all men are destined to receive the Word of God because of its lowliness and because of the sublime subject-matter it treats.

For a writer treating subject-matter located in the distant past yet presumed by everyone in his century to be literally true, Saint-Amant does have an acute sense of history, is aware of other cultures in time and space differing from his own. He revels in the exotic ways of pre-Christian Egypt, is concerned in his 'Préface' and in the 'Lettre à Samuel Bochart' to prove the accuracy of what he has written, commenting, among other things, on Levantine flora and fauna, the artistic media available to Egyptians, topography, mores, and the state of the Hebrew religion before the Tables of the Law. Within the text itself, although the central action of *Moyse sauvé* covers less than twenty-four hours (the author is proud of his innovation – adherence in a long poem to all three classical unities: 'Préface,' pp. 13–14), it is obvious that, like Corneille and Racine, Saint-Amant makes his public aware of a temporal past and future. Extensive passages of the narrative treat matters that occurred before Moses' birth (the Flood, the stories of Jacob and Joseph) or will take place later during his adult life. In a yet more striking manner, indulging in an authentic baroque paradox, the poet establishes impossible cause-and-effect relationships between events widely separated in time. That is, he tells us how the winds and the river, conscious because of Jocabel's dream that Moses one day will debase them, unleash their fury on the infant in his cradle now. And, as Narrator, he berates the wasps and flies for attacking the baby in the present, since in the future he will grant them miraculous powers to plague Egypt. Saint-Amant revels in a world as young and innocent as the baby Moses himself, a world that will mature just as the protagonist himself grows into heroism. If *Moyse sauvé* had been written in the twelfth or thirteenth century, it would have been entitled *Les Enfances Moyse*. As in epics by Ronsard and Camoens, we are told of the past deeds and future glory of the hero's people, of the perils of Moses' early days and of the splendor of his future mission.

Finally, Saint-Amant conforms to the sense of Christian history we find in *La Chanson de Roland*, in *Les Tragiques*, and in modern Christian epic also. Temporal unity reminds us that we all live in sacred time, an eternal present, that each moment of our lives is crucial to our own salvation and to the future of mankind. The day Moses spends on the Nile is a symbolic day in the life of mankind, not fourteen or fifteen hours to be counted out as in a naturalist novel. However, just as this duration recounts textually the past of Jacob and Joseph and Moses' own future, the Christian eternal present contains past and future within itself. The quarrel between Jacob and Esau is important because it has been foreordained that Jacob's, not Esau's, descendants will bear the flame of the chosen race. So also the victorious brother is tricked into marrying Leah as well as Rachel, for the sake of their children, in accordance with God's plan. Jacob's son Joseph brings the Hebrews to Egypt and builds the palace where Termuth now spends her days. Amram refers to his ancestors Abraham and Isaac, and to God's pact with the family; Mérary, Elisaph, and Marie, all cousins, speak of Jacob, their forefather. It is clear that Saint-Amant has written a family story. Although Moses the infant does not 'evolve,' all of history, past and future, is centered in him. This is because he descends from Abraham, Isaac, Jacob, and Joseph, and he will give birth to kings and judges in turn, a line that will end in Christ. Saint-Amant's fruit and plant imagery refers to the Tree of Jesse, extending from Abraham to Jesus. Termuth is sterile, but the Hebrews are not, and their fruition in history gives unity and significance to otherwise disparate events. Thus the true story of *Moyse sauvé* concerns less the baby Moses than the Tree of Jesse, and its hero is 'Jacob,' not the man but the people, all the Children of Israel.

Since, in my opinion, Saint-Amant's notion of Christian time resembles d'Aubigné's, *Moyse sauvé* can perhaps bear a figural or allegorical reading similar to the one I proposed for *Les Tragiques*. Indeed, in his 'Préface,' the author refers to Tasso, who wrote one half of the *Gerusalemme liberata* unaware of allegory and the second half with such interpretations in mind; Saint-Amant then claims that he himself thought of allegory 'en la pluspart de [s]es inventions,' and that these inventions 'contiennent encore quelque chose de misterieux,' for there is a sense hidden 'dessous leur escorce' (p. 20). Although he also warns us that critics will perhaps see in *Moyse sauvé* more than the author intended to put there, 'des choses à quoy je ne pensay jamais,' I believe modern scholars to be in error when they assume that he wrote this paragraph of the 'Préface' ironically. Guilty of late nineteenth- and early twentieth-century prejudice, they fail to appreciate the historical importance typology still held in the seventeenth century and the rich esthetic possibilities open to this mode.

A. Marni suggests an allegorical interpretation of *Moyse sauvé* consistent with ones given to *la Gerusalemme liberata*, *la Gerusalemme conquistata*, *Alaric*, *La Pucelle*, *Jonas*, and *Josué* by their authors. According to Marni, the infant Moses represents the endangered human soul; the four obstacles (crocodile, storm, flies, and vulture) stand for threats from Satan in the form of vices and the temptation to sin. The baby is then protected by divine aid (the angels) and earthly powers (Mérary, Elisaph) and saved by divine grace (Termuth). S. Noehte proposes a more elaborate critique that associates *Moyse sauvé* with pro-Jansenist religious activity in the middle of the century; according to her, the ordeal of the crocodile depicts the Fall of Man in Genesis; and the episode of the vulture the redemption of man through Christ in the New Testament; while the other two adventures treat the problem of grace, of *gratia gratis* and *gratia actualis*.[10]

Marni's and Noehte's hypotheses are plausible: either one may be correct. Of the three levels of 'spiritual' exegesis of Scripture, Marni's interpretation corresponds to the tropological or moral level, Noehte's to the moral and to the typological or allegorical levels. I would like to suggest a different reading, one which would take into account the entire narrative structure of *Moyse sauvé*, not just the baby's four ordeals. I believe that if Saint-Amant included the stories of Jacob, Joseph, and the adult Moses in his epic, he did so not only to fill out a thin narrative line and to develop the Tree of Jesse motif, but also because for centuries, in fact throughout the history of the Church, Biblical exegetes were in the habit of juxtaposing these stories with the life of Christ in terms of prefiguration and fulfillment. D'Aubigné, Pascal, Bossuet, Godeau, Le Moyne, Desmarets, Marolles, and a host of baroque lyric poets all favored or practiced figurative readings of the Bible; typological symbolism is to be found in the *Josué* and *Samson* by Coras and in a Latin Moses epic which Saint-Amant may have known, the *Moyses Viator seu imago militantis Ecclesiae* (1636–9) by Antoine Millieu, sj. In addition, there are three specific figurative allusions in Saint-Amant's text: the Narrator draws an analogy between Moses the baby and the infant Jesus, both hunted by a wicked Pharaoh-Herod but, finding a refuge at the Nile, spared in Egypt (1: 161–72); Marie's prophecy, when the vulture seizes one of her lambs, that the sacrifice of a Lamb shall one day save us all:

> Ainsy faut-il qu'un jour, Jour grand, cruel et dous,
> Un innocent Agneau paye et meure pour tous. –    (Part 10: 147–8)

and Moses' rod transformed into a tree, with allusions to the Holy Rood:

> Dieu veut qu'en son Parvis il rende tesmoignage
> De la Charge attachée à son noble Lignage,

Jusqu'à tant qu'au vray Prestre, au Messie attendu,
Sur un Arbre plus saint l'honneur en soit rendu.   (Part 6: 241–4)

A standard topic in Biblical exegesis is the analogy between Christ and
Moses, a coupling that dates back to the New Testament and even to the
prophets of the Old Testament, if we remember that the coming Messiah
is invoked as a Second Moses, who will again lead the Children of Israel out
of bondage into the *terra repromissionis*. All events in Moses' adult life, as
told in the Book of Exodus, were assigned a function prefiguring or foreshadowing comparable events in the life of Christ. Thus, and I cite only the
most noteworthy examples, both men were shepherds and leaders of their
people. The scene of Moses and the Burning Bush anticipates Christ's communion with his Father in the desert. Moses' miracles (the plagues on
Egypt) correspond to Christ's. The first-born of the Jews spared by a lamb's
blood on the door prefigure Christ, the first-born of the New Law,
spared by his own blood, that of the *Agnus Dei*. Moses crosses the Red Sea,
and Christ walks on Galilee. Corresponding to, and fulfilling, Passover
are the Last Supper (a Passover feast), the Crucifixion, and the Resurrection.
And, as Pharaoh was slaughtered by God on Moses' behalf, Christ harrows hell and destroys the power of Satan. The community of the Just in the
Sinai Desert is fulfilled by the first Christian community: manna from
heaven promises the bread of the Last Supper, and the water from the rock,
wine. The Tables of the Old Law received by Moses on Mount Sinai are
then fulfilled and superseded by the New Law, the Sermon on the Mount,
the New Covenant replacing the Old Covenant of Israel, for only Christ
can redeem mankind exiled in a spiritual Egypt.

We can posit a comparable typological pattern for Saint-Amant's own
story of the infant Moses. Jocabel and Marie both prefigure the Virgin
Mary; Saint-Amant's use of the French form 'Marie' for the Biblical
Miriam underscores the analogy, and Moses comes into the world without
birth pangs. Still another Virgin-figure is the chaste, sterile princess Termuth, whose chariot is borne by three unicorns, a traditional symbol for the
Trinity, the Annunciation, and the Incarnation. Although the heavenly
messenger who heralds Moses' birth is to be found in Flavius Josephus, in
Saint-Amant the scene also can be said to foreshadow the Annunciation,
while Amram and Mérary play roles analogous to that of Joseph. Indeed,
the old fisherman, who serves Moses, recalls those other fishers of men,
Peter and Andrew. As Saint-Amant himself points out, Moses and Christ
both escape a Massacre of the Innocents by fleeing to the Nile. The shooting star on the river obviously corresponds to the Star of Bethlehem, and the
good shepherds of Memphis to those who came to adore Jesus in the
manger. Aaron's prophecy as a child recalls Christ's feats with the Elders of

the Temple, and Jocabel's tears are literally transformed into nectar for
the infant just as Christ's blood is transformed into the wine of the Eucharist
for all mankind. The baby conquers his fiendish opponents – crocodile,
flies, vulture – as Christ resists the temptations of Satan and the tortures of
Pontius Pilate and, finally, defeats the Serpent himself in hell.

Questions of space prevent me from developing comparable analogies
between the stories of Noah, Jacob, and Joseph, on the one hand, and the
life of Christ, on the other. However, the flood-motif is of crucial importance to our interpretation of Saint-Amant's poem. In Prophets and Psalms
it is said that since God, in the time of Noah, punished the mass and saved
the remnant, he will do so again. And in *Moyse sauvé* evil-doers are twice
punished by water – by the Flood and by the closing of the Red Sea. Good
people, the chosen race, are saved from stormy waters three times: from
the Flood, from the Nile in Moses' infancy, and from the Red Sea in his
adulthood. Whereas Noah and Moses delivered mankind from death by
water, Christ will deliver us from fire in hell with the water of baptism.
Analogies are established between Noah's ark, Moses' cradle, the ark of
the covenant, the infant Jesus' manger, and the Holy Sepulchre or the Holy
Rood. And, of course, victory over the Flood also signifies Christ harrow-
ing hell, defeating Leviathan in his own element.

For a figural pattern to function efficaciously, the implied reader has
to be aware of both the foreshadowing and fulfilling material. More than a
little didactic and esthetic self-consciousness on the author's part is obliga-
tory. Therefore, the telling of tales is important in *Moyse sauvé*. Mérary
recounts the story of Jacob, and Amram the tale of Joseph; both men
serve as poets, as delegated narrators. Indeed, Amram's narrative elicits
from Termuth pity for the Hebrews, and thus prepares the way for her
adoption of Moses. Art is not limited to the spoken word, however. Amram
carves and sculpts in Termuth's garden, thus earning the right to talk to
her about his people. Furthermore, one of the Biblical stories (the Flood) is
'told' on a tapestry, the other (Joseph) on a painting. With this motif
Saint-Amant partakes of the epic convention of ecphrasis as exemplified by
Achilles' shield, Jason's cloak (in the *Argonautica*), Aeneas's shield, and
their more recent imitations in Ariosto, Camoens, Tasso, Spenser, Marino,
and writers of French Biblical epics such as Marie de Pech and Montchres-
tien.[11] More important, I think, is the praise the poet lavishes on Jocabel and
Marie, masters in the art of tapestry. Elisaph carves Marie's portrait on
the bark of a tree; it is a miracle of love, we are told, that he can do so well
without training! Finally, Termuth, who listens to Amram's commentary
on an old painted scroll of the Joseph story, is an artist in her own right. She
paints, weaves tapestries, and, like Arion and Lyrian, sings, plays the
lute, or meditates in her grotto. Birds keep silent, her song is so beautiful,

and although Termuth's body is sterile, her hand is not, since she paints the portrait of a child from imagination before ever laying eyes on Moses (10: 349–56). For the lovely Egyptian princess, art is inspiration and consolation. Saint-Amant projects onto her and onto his patroness, the Queen of Poland, his ideal of the poet-artist-musician, a creative person inspired by beauty and faith.

I only refer in passing to the frequently discussed passage where the Narrator declares that even Poussin would not have been able to paint the scene of Marie's joy:

> Quel Esprit merveilleux auroit assez d'adresse
> Pour faire en un Tableau flamboyer l'allegresse
> Qui parut en Marie ... ?
> Je doute si Poussin, ce Roy de la Peinture,
> Cét Homme qui dans l'Art fait vivre la Nature,
> Oseroit se promettre, avec tous ses efforts,
> D'en exprimer à l'œil les aymables transports.    (Part 7: 41–3, 45–8)

The 'painter in words' is a common baroque motif, to be found in Théophile de Viau and Tristan l'Hermite as well as in Saint-Amant.[12] More important, I suspect, is the theme of Moses the writer. We sometimes forget that for the readers of Bossuet's century as well as Thomas Aquinas's, he was presumed to be the author of the Pentateuch. Saint-Amant certainly did not contest the tradition; in his 'Préface' he notices that some people also ascribe to the protagonist the Book of Job. In the text of *Moyse sauvé* the leader of the Israelites composes hymns to glorify the Creator. And we find Saint-Amant appealing to Moses *grand Escrivain*, with the hope that Moses will lend him a spark from the Burning Bush, a spark of his own genius:

> Et toy, grand Escrivain, dont la celeste Plume
> Forma d'une Encre d'or l'Honneur du saint Volume,
> Fay qu'on voye en ces Vers, d'une riche façon,
> Briller l'auguste Feu que tu vis au Buisson:
> Impetres-en du moins quelque vive estincelle
> Qui m'embraze, et m'excite au soin de ta Nacelle;
> Sois mon Guide toy mesme, et fay qu'en ce Tableau
> Ce Feu me serve enfin à te sauver de l'Eau.    (Part 1: 25–32)

Related to the theme of art is the elaboration of a pattern of artificial, elegant, shining surfaces in the style of Marino, a hard, mineral world of jewelry. *Moyse sauvé*, a poem of light as of water, radiates baroque splendor. Termuth dreams of finding a diamond, but the baby she does acquire possesses two eyes brighter than suns, analogous perhaps to the shining stones on Jacob's Ladder, a Saint-Amant amplification not to be found in the Bible. When Termuth bathes, the steps of her pool shine with joy; her hair, all gold, shimmers in the silver Nile, and the sun takes her body for supple ivory and floating marble:

> Un precieux Degré, fait de Nacre et d'Agathe,
> N'eut pas si-tost senty sa plante delicate
> Qu'il redoubla son lustre, et par ce vif honneur
> Prouva de ses baisers l'indicible bonheur.
>                     ... qu'un aymable Zephire,
> Desnoüant de son chef le mobile tresor,
> Sembloit faire descendre un noble ruisseau d'or
> Sur le flüide argent des flamboyantes Ondes
> Où brilloyent à l'envy ses graces vagabondes;
> Et que l'Astre du Jour la prit en mesme instant
> Pour de l'Yvoire souple et du Marbre flotant.
>                               (Part 12: 33–6, 42–8)

Her breasts of snow distill pearls (water-drops); an ivory comb bites into her golden hair. In the grotto nature is tamed and brought under the control of geometric order; man reduces, solidifies, masters the external world. The same is true for the Crossing of the Red Sea, except that here it is God's work, not man's. A seascape is transformed into a landscape, the waters dominated by God and metamorphosed into a classical French garden.[13] And, as with Termuth's pool, the Israelites pass through a lapidary world of sheen and decoration. This motif takes the form of hard earth bathed in light, a synthesis of earth and air or of water and fire, a masculine phenomenon which contrasts to the more feminine flowing water. It is as if aspects of the intimate, maternal paradise are alchemically transformed into jewelry and gold.

These manifestations appeal to the visual sense of characters within *Moyse sauvé*, and to the public outside it. True, the Hebrews wish to hide Moses from Pharaoh's sight, and they succeed in blinding a crocodile who metaphorically evokes the tyrant. On the other hand, Elisaph declares to Marie that he must behold her eyes with his own, and Queen Louise-Marie is said to slay demigods with her glance. This is the power of the gaze that so dazzles lover and beloved in the troubadour-Petrarchan tradition and in the early plays of Corneille. However, physical sight also serves as an image for spiritual or moral insight granted the Chosen People, in contrast to Egyptian blindness. Hence the Israelites see a shooting star that indicates where Moses is to be hidden. Jacob sees a ladder shining with light and splendor (2: 469–84) and the angel with whom he will wrestle. Aaron literally witnesses the future. God also casts his gaze upon the world and is moved by what he sees: the long travails of the Israelites. In addition, the implied author, in his own voice, intervenes repeatedly in the narrative to tell us he recognizes certain things and wishes us to do so as well. Saint-Amant underscores the visual orientation of his characters and at the same time seeks to engender in the reader, through the illusion of seeing, a quality approaching Marino's *ammirazione* and *meraviglia*.

Upon crossing the Red Sea, the Children of Israel, and we the implied readers, are astonished by a typically baroque spectacle: people crossing a land area which is also the sea. For the 'trees' are in reality bunches of coral; the ruby walls are made up of ocean; and animals tread where fishes ought to dwell. In other words, reality proves to be illusion, and illusion reality. A still more extraordinary instance of blurred frontiers between appearance and truth is to be found in Jocabel's tapestry and Termuth's old painting. Saint-Amant never permits us to forget that the violence of the Flood is a concrete human phenomenon and, at the same time, the subject of a work of art. It is real in spite of its being contained within the borders of a tapestry, which also paradoxically prevent the rains from causing even greater damage. The Deluge is an artifice, yet one could almost hear the groans of the dying:

> les Portraits lamentables,
> Donnant, quoy que menteurs, des touches veritables ...
> Ceux qui de ce Travail avoyent veu les merveilles,
> Avoyent veu par leurs yeux suborner leurs oreilles,
> Car on croyoit oüyr les cris et les sanglots
> Des Nageurs vains et nus, qu'on voyoit sur les flots:
> Et sans le beau rempart d'une riche bordure
> De fruits, de papillons, de fleurs et de verdure,
> Qui sembloit s'opposer au Deluge dépeint,
> Un plus ample ravage on en eust presque craint ...
> (Part 3: 381–2, 393–400)

It is through such works of art, and Saint-Amant's poem, that man attains mastery over illusion and inconstancy, or, at least, understanding of how these universals function in our life.

God approves of deception as he approves of artifice. *Moyse sauvé* treats the efforts of Moses' family to lie to the Egyptians and mask the baby from their gaze. Jocabel and Marie conceal their joy when the infant is adopted by Termuth; God himself caused him to be born without birth pangs lest Egyptian suspicions be aroused. The theme is underscored in the 'episodes.' Rebecca plots to substitute Jacob for Esau, so that Isaac may be tricked into giving his blessing to the younger son. God himself transforms Leah, so that she may replace Rachel in Jacob's bed. On both occasions an angel justifies these *ruses discretes*, examples of *douce Imposture* and *agreable ruse*, which brings about an *infidelle Delit* due to *legitime excuse* (9: 45; 2: 245, 261; 8: 420; 2: 262). And Jacob tricks Laban with the spotted calves, making away with the majority of his master's livestock. On the pastoral level, well might Elisaph and Marie rejoice in the small birds they capture, an 'innocente Chasse' resulting in 'liberté ... noblement reduite' (10: 14, 38).

Such trickery, although subject to blame from a strictly modern secular point of view, can be justified in a sacred epic treating a subject taken from sacred history: 1 / God's ends justify his means, the ends being to preserve the Chosen People and the Tree of Jesse that will flower in Christ the Savior; if Machiavellian policy can be employed for the good of the state, *raison d'état*, how can one condemn it for *raison de salut*? 2 / events which appear unjust on the literal Old Testament level bear spiritual, figurative value for the New Covenant; 3 / in any case, all human behavior must ultimately be considered from God's perspective, as part of the divine plan and, therefore, incommensurate with our imperfect notion of right and wrong. Paradoxically, God's justice and truth are brought about through acts of deception and ruse, just as, in a variation of *felix culpa*, from the Israelites' distress comes success, from evil comes good. The Hebrews suffer then rise to greater heights because of their suffering. Considering literary genre and mode, in this idyllic epic in which woman plays so dominant a role, fraud is employed as *the* weapon enabling the weak to vanquish the strong, the sons the fathers, the slaves their masters. How appropriate it is that the very notions of illusion and deception central to the baroque world-view should be incorporated into a Christian epic, should form a cornerstone for the author's baroque Christian faith!

Despite scholarly findings to the contrary, Saint-Amant still has the reputation of ignorance and debauchery, of having written in the fumes of wine, of performing splendidly in the descriptive, bacchic, or grotesque genres but being incapable of high seriousness. I submit, on the contrary, that the *goinfre*, the *bon gros*, is a *persona*, a literary convention that the young provincial from Rouen assumed for a specifically literary purpose when speaking of food and drink; he then adopted other *personae*, other conventions in order to write about nature, love, God, and war. He did so in order to prove his originality, proclaim himself resolutely a Modern, and, practicing the esthetics of negligence, be recognized as an *honnête homme* free from pedantry, with a legitimate right to frequent the most aristocratic circles in Europe.

We know that Saint-Amant did serious research prior to writing *Moyse sauvé*, consulting a raft of sources in at least three languages; that, one of the finest, most vigorous minds of his generation, he was conscious of his art and had a high opinion of it. He read the theoreticians and justified his own practice at length: a poet of reason, he knew the rules especially when he chose to break them, and his poetic achievement, whether in high or low style, manifests an awareness of esthetic decorum and of the hierarchy of literary kinds.[14]

Nor should it surprise us to find a genuinely Christian inspiration in his work. This member of the Académie was never truly a *libertin* or *esprit fort*, even in his youth, despite his attachment to Théophile de Viau and the latter's circle. His opus contains important poems that are largely religious: 'Le Contemplateur' and the *Joseph*-fragment, composed in his youth, and four other works dating from his maturity: *La Généreuse*, 'Stances à M. Corneille sur son Imitation de Jésus-Christ,' 'Fragment d'une méditation sur le crucifix,' and, of course, *Moyse sauvé*. From the devotional tradition he adopts both composition of place and figural abstraction, even for strictly secular texts.[15] It is true that conversion in one's later years to religion or to a more pronounced Christian stance is a convention in the baroque period, that to be the singer of God is a poetic *persona* no more and no less genuine than that of the *goinfre* or the *mélancolique*. Whatever Saint-Amant's personal feelings, he worked assiduously on his Biblical epic and on other important religious verse, and he succeeded in infusing in these works a power and intensity, a grace and elegance, comparable to that of the best Catholic poetry of his time. This is all we can ask of a writer.

Be this as it may, it is true that *Moyse sauvé* proved to be not sufficiently classical to find favor with Boileau's generation. The author of the *Satires* and the *Art poétique* ridiculed Saint-Amant the epicist, stating that 'Le Moïse commence à moisir par les bords' and depicting him as follows:

> Mais souvent un Esprit qui se flatte, et qui s'aime,
> Méconnoist son genie, et s'ignore soy-même.
> Ainsi Tel autrefois, qu'on vit avec Faret
> Charbonner de ses vers les murs d'un cabaret,
> S'en va mal à propos, d'une voix insolente,
> Chanter du peuple Hebreu la fuitte triomphante;
> Et poursuivant Moïse au travers des deserts,
> Court avec Pharaon se noyer dans les mers.[16]

It was natural for Despréaux and his friends to unseat the leading poet of
the preceding age and for the Ancients of the 1670s to attack the Moderns of
the 1650s. Less forgivable is the fact that generations of scholars, extending to our own day, persist in seeing the Baroque with Boileau's eyes as
they see the Middle Ages with Ronsard's. Going beyond neoclassical
prejudice, judging *Moyse sauvé* on its own terms, we find a good story well
told, tight construction, symmetry, and a true sense of composition; a
complex narrative with subplots and episodes, tales within tales; visual
imagination, fantasy, the exotic and bizarre, and a rich, meaningful poetry
of light and darkness. Saint-Amant demonstrates unusual powers in working within neoclassical canons yet maintaining his personal authenticity
and freedom as an artist, his right to variety and pleasure. He creates a new
sub-genre, the heroic idyll or pastoral epic, combining the martial and
bucolic modes. Potential tragedy is transformed into romance, parable, and
fairy-tale. Conflict ends in reconciliation and peace, in the restoration of
the family and the flow of a mother's milk. Perhaps for the first time in
French verse we perceive the heroic softened and domesticated, the universe reduced to little things, and the unalloyed joy and tenderness of childhood. In this manner the author recaptures something of the old Homeric
unproblematic *Weltanschauung*, a primitive, childlike, distant world projected onto the Bible not Greco-Roman mythology.

Wonder in beauty – of dawn, noon, and dusk – wonder in the youth of
the cosmos and in God's presence – these create the 'tone' of *Moyse
sauvé*. Like all great works of art, it manifests richness and diversity, partakes of tradition and is new. And his synthesis of the heroic and bucolic,
of the male and female, contributes to the elaboration of a Christian epic that
is both sublime and humble, that treats of one day in the life of shepherds
and of the history of mankind, for in its juxtaposition of elements is to be
found the objective correlative of typological, Biblical truth. *Moyse sauvé*
is a story of celebration, of splendor, of ritual play, of joy without fear, of a
calm, serene, replete tranquility. It tells of the release of a sacred person,
the child-savior, from persecution, and of the release of the Hebrew people
by the savior and his line. Saint-Amant resembles Marino and La Fontaine in the elaboration of his elegant, sophisticated, eminently civilized
poem. As in Marino's *Adone* (1623) or La Fontaine's *Adonis* (1658),
artifice is brought to bear on and support a relatively meagre plot. In his use
of sheen, sparkle, and verbal brio, Saint-Amant resembles his Italian
predecessor and classical French follower. Like them he invests every ounce
of his talent in the revitalization of a beautiful story from the past. In all
three we observe a European phenomenon: the shift within the epic itself
from heroism to a more elegiac, idyllic, lyrical stance, and from pure
narrative to a greater reliance on the descriptive.[17] It is appropriate that this

extraordinarily varied singer of myth, nature, erotic love, Petrarchan love, food and drink, the burlesque, the fantastic, the macabre, personal lyricism, impersonal realism, and religion should have introduced the pastoral epic into France and have composed perhaps the finest long poem of the Splendid Century in the entire Romance world, the only one, except for *Adone* and *Saint Louis*, worthy of occupying a place alongside *Paradise Lost*.

Chapter Ten

# ❧ LE MOYNE

Among serious, 'important' writers of the seventeenth century, Pierre Le
Moyne, sj (1602–71) is one of the most obscure. He is among the few
whose works we have to consult in the original editions,[1] a man totally
unknown to the general reading public in France and even to the majority
of professors. The baroque period, more even than the Middle Ages, suffered from neglect on the part of scholars that has only recently been
corrected. Indeed, it is in the last generation or so that specialists have
rediscovered a number of poets – Sponde, La Ceppède, and Chassignet in
the first rank, Fiefmelin, Poupo, Labadie, Auvray, Hopil, du Bois Hus, and
Drelincourt in the second – so that the age extending from Ronsard to La
Fontaine can now be revalued as one of the richest in the history of French
verse. No man has contributed more to this revaluation than Jean Rousset, who quotes from Pierre Le Moyne and refers to him as an extraordinarily gifted writer, the Victor Hugo of his century. (It is also true that
Rousset limits his praise to Le Moyne the lyricist and considers *Saint Louis*
to be his worst book.)[2]

   This Jesuit father composed a vast quantity of religious verse and prose.
Among his works largely or exclusively in prose are *Les Peintures morales*
(1640 and 1643); *La Gallerie des femmes fortes* (1647), his most popular
work, translated into English, Italian, and German; *La Devotion aisée*
(1652), a treatise in the line of François de Sales' *Introduction à la Vie
dévote*; and *De l'Art de regner* (1665). In my opinion, Le Moyne's most
notable successes in verse, those texts which most deserve a twentieth-
century reading, are the following: *Hymnes de la Sagesse divine, et de
l'Amour divin* (1639 and 1641); the verse portraits of Lais, Actaeon, Hannibal, Andromeda, and Semiramis included in *Les Peintures morales*; his
epic, *Saint Louis, ou la Sainte Couronne reconquise* (1658); and *Entretiens et
Lettres poëtiques* (1665).

   Le Moyne cultivated the heroic, encomiastic vein early in his career. To
celebrate the feats of Louis XIII he wrote a non-extant ballet produced for

the Jesuit College of Reims (1628) and a series of odes in the style of Malherbe: *Les Triomphes de Louys le Juste* (1629, renamed *Hydre deffaite*, 1650) and a 600-line *Portrait du Roy passant les Alpes* (1629, renamed *Les Alpes humiliées*, 1650). These poems, martial in theme, are not epics. However, by 1641 Le Moyne conceived a project for a heroic poem on the subject of King Louis IX's Egyptian crusade. And from 1650 on he dwelt in the professed House of the Jesuit Order on the Ile-Saint-Louis. The newly constructed house and church were dedicated to Saint Louis. Over the façade was placed a statue of Louis IX beneath the arms of France; inside were paintings by Simon Vouet, one celebrating the Saint's apotheosis, another depicting King Louis XIII as he offers the plans of the church to his ancestor in heaven. It was in this atmosphere that Father Le Moyne worked away on his nationalistic, dynastic, and religious poem. Although a first draft of seven books, containing some 7,200 lines, was published in 1653, he revised this fragment extensively, transforming the underlying themes, the plot, and the style, before offering to the world the final version of eighteen books and 17,880 lines in 1658.[3]

Scholars have claimed that Le Moyne lacks originality, that, like his contemporaries Scudéry, Chapelain, and Desmarets, he follows the rules too closely. It is true that *Saint Louis* contains an enormous number of conventions, themes, and motifs, all of which are derived from Homer, Virgil, Lucan, Ronsard, and Tasso. In his approach to the problem of genre, Le Moyne is less spontaneous than d'Aubigné and Saint-Amant; *Saint Louis* is a heroic epic pure and simple, its narrative structure based entirely upon classical and Italian models. Although Le Moyne speaks highly of Virgil, he owes the most to Tasso, to *la Gerusalemme liberata* and *la Gerusalemme conquistata* (1593).[4] His plot-line follows closely those of his great predecessor. Thus the Christians undertake a victorious crusade against Saracens, in this case an expedition to Egypt in order to seize the Holy Crown of Thorns. An older hero in command, Louis IX, is assisted by a vigorous young warrior, his nephew Bourbon; from both men will descend a glorious line. The youth loves but gives up a Saracen princess, Almasonte, who is later mistakenly killed in battle by a suitor. Bourbon's great exploit is to slay a dragon and thus dispel enchantments in a forest where the crusaders were cutting trees. The Christians are aided by recruits from Palestine: a married couple, Raymond and Belinde; and Lisamante, a widow born in romantic circumstances and suckled by a tigress. On the other side stand an indomitable old man, the sultan Mélédin; an indomitable younger warrior, Forcadin; and a wily old sorcerer, Mirème, all of whom perish in the end. It is through Mirème's offices that Mélédin decides to sacrifice his daughter, Zahide, to the Nile, in return for which the waters rise, causing a flood. The Saracens indulge in a night sortie, attack with the help of elephants, Greek fire, and demons from hell. However, the Franks are defended by angels, and God performs miracles on their behalf, including the opening of a passage across the Nile and Louis's voyage to heaven on a throne of fire, where he observes the orders of the blessed, speaks to his late father, King Louis VIII, and beholds Christ in majesty. Zahide, no mean *bellatrix* herself, is captured, converted, and married, and Louis wins the war and brings home his sacred relic.

Among the strongest impressions the reader receives from *Saint Louis* is one of splendor and magnificence. 'La valeur est pompeuse, et la pompe est vaillante,' (p. 224A) says Le Moyne of the Christian host before its ultimate ordeal. Grandiose speeches and battle-scenes serve as backdrops to a martial saint-king whose every word and deed is solemn, heroic, and hierarchical. The faith of the crusaders is embodied in ceremonial and liturgy, in color and pageantry. The technical skill of the duels, the ostentatious rhetoric of speeches, the spectacle of religious events – funeral, baptism, marriage, Corpus Christi procession – fulfill the demands of an age. Le Moyne caters to, and recreates in his epic, the decorum of courtly civility. His poem celebrates the external forms of grandiose living, for in his world reality manifests itself immediately in appearance. Like the plays of Rotrou, Mairet, Tristan, du Ryer, and, above all, Corneille, *Saint Louis* proclaims a glorious chivalric-Christian ideal that perhaps has never existed but in men's minds. Indeed, in contrast to Tasso, whose characters, greater than life, often appear downcast and alone, Le Moyne's people (at least the Franks) work together for the common good, in harmony, contributing to social order.

Perhaps the most striking festivity recounted in the epic is a tournament (Book 4), which corresponds to the 'games' of the *Iliad* and the *Aeneid* and to the courtly festivities of medieval romance. However, as the four contingents march onto the field, each clad in special colors and proclaiming allegiance to a particular form of love, with a page singing or declaiming a cartel, we realize that Pierre Le Moyne's carrousel does not correspond to the reality of a thirteenth-century tourney. The historical Louis IX never witnessed a gigantic artificial rock that opens to display a grotto inside, or an elephant with a globe on its back that also opens before our eyes. Le Moyne's tourney is fully in the spirit of his own epoch. The most famous comparable spectacles in the seventeenth century continued the medieval tradition of martial games (tilting at a ring, tilting at the quintain, or real jousting) but also gave rise to pageantry and spectacular displays of luxury in clothing, armor, and pavilions, to sparkle and a riot of colors. Le Moyne's elephant and the fireworks 'invented' for the occasion are taken directly from the carrousel of 1612, celebrating the double royal wedding of Louis XIII and his sister to the Infantes of Spain. It is surely not coinci-

dental that the seventeenth-century public presumed the tourney, with its
martial aura and cartels on old romance subjects, to be a peculiarly medieval institution, which both symbolized and contributed to a sense of
harmony in the community.[5]

In an age in which the topic *mundus theatrum* was in its greatest vogue,
exploited by writers as varied as Ronsard, Shakespeare, Marvell, Calde-
rón, Gracián, Corneille, Rotrou, and d'Aubigné, it is not surprising that
Pierre Le Moyne should have written a long didactic poem entitled *Le
Theatre du sage*. Similarly, in his epic the tourney takes place as if in a
gigantic theater, with King Louis and the old knights as spectators;
Zahide is sacrificed on an altar dating from pagan times, constructed in the
form of a theater (Book 6); Saracens arrive on boats to attack the Franks,
as if they were participating in a Roman circus, providing a spectacle for
their adversaries (Book 7); and God, his angels, and Saint Louis look
down from heaven on a world stage where glory and ambition seek to
dominate the scene but end in the grave:

> Cette boule flotante et demi-submergée,
> De son poids soustenuë, et de son poids plongée,
> Est l'espace, dit-il, où le mortel orgueil,
> Croit avoir un Theatre, et n'a qu'un vain cercueil ...
> Sur ce Point cependant les Passions humaines,
> Font leurs tragiques Jeux, ont leurs sanglantes Scenes.
>                                         (Book 9: p. 101B)

The play, like the tournament, stands somewhere on the frontier between
the sacred and the profane. Its gratuitous, ludic quality softens the reality of
warfare, interposing distance and decorum between the public and the
events recounted. The 'reality' of the plot is in the author's mind. We are
expected to accept it, however absurd it may appear, for he presents us
with art, that is, artifice, not life. It is equally true, however, that, as in
d'Aubigné, beleaguered Christians and King Louis wafted to heaven do
participate in the action – they become players on the world stage, and their
positive ostentation, their monumental will to impress others contributes
to God's glory as well as to their own.

If life is a play, and the theater an image for the world, life is based
upon play, that is, wit and jest, and its reality embodied in artistic illusion.
The Nile flood (Books 6 and 7) gives rise to some extraordinary effects of
illusion through metamorphosis, and of paradox through illusion. Thus, at
night, the waters rise in the darkness, and one cannot distinguish between
land and river. With the coming of dawn, however, before our eyes a floating desert comes into view, with fishes and boats in place of plowmen; the

crusaders are astonished by this desert of water, a floating tomb where trees have drowned and boats cut into the land like plows. Earlier in the story, when the crusaders left Cyprus for Egypt, their fleet appeared to be a forest floating in the air or an armed camp rolling on the seas:

> Jamais un Camp plus beau ne roula sur la Mer;
> Ni plus belles forests ne volerent en l'Air.
> L'Aurore à son lever en parut étonnée;
> Le Soleil pour la voir avança la journée;
> Et sembla de rayons plus clairs et mieux dorez,
> Vouloir peindre les Lys sur nos masts arborez.    (Book 2: p. 21B)

This is the same *verkehrte Welt* we have seen before, but Le Moyne develops it in greater detail than others do. In his upside-down world nature has lost her proper function, and the unnatural triumphs over the natural. Confusion and disorder reign. Yet, for Le Moyne, *impossibilia*, even if of demonic origin, make a fascinating spectacle. And in several *Peintures morales* ('Laïs,' 'Andromede,' 'Acteon'), he celebrates monstrous yet electrifying myths of metamorphosis.

As can be observed from my last quote, a comparable phenomenon occurs in pathetic fallacy, with aspects of nature participating in the lives of men. When the Corpus Christi is rolled into Damietta, the sun withdraws and palm trees bow down (Book 3). God permits Lisamante to walk on the Nile; therefore, the moon stops her course in astonishment, and stars come closer to light her way (Book 13). Saint Louis or Belinde dying, stars, flags, and banners beam less brightly, rubies, gold, and torches go pale; Saint Louis cured, tents, flags, trumpets, equipment, and armor shine and sound with joy (Books 16 and 17). Furthermore, like his fellow epicists, Pierre Le Moyne relishes verbal play on the theme of violent death. A host of warriors perish 'appropriately,' according to their state in life or dominant trait. Thus a Greek musician is pierced through the ears, a swimmer's arms are cut off, a singer's vocal chord is severed, a fencer dies, his arms outstretched, fencing with the sea. And, in an extraordinary scene, after having shot his mistress Zahide in the neck by mistake with an arrow, the Saracen Alfasel commits suicide, strangling himself in the neck with his own bowstring, so that his heart, which ever loved her, will remain intact even in death (Book 15).

Whenever the Saracens take the field, Frenchmen are offered a spectacle of exotic banners, accoutrements, and musical instruments, of vast foreign hordes who 'Mesloient l'affreux au riche, et la pompe d'horreur' (p. 224B). In contrast, on the march the crusaders are compared to a Virgilian beehive (Book 5). That is, their monarch, Louis IX, through speech, action, and his mere presence, controls the army, ranging it within the bounds of order. A figure of *sapientia* as well as of *fortitudo*, he raises the spirits of his men. He is at the center of his host, the troops marshalled around him under his command. His is the image of the impassible, serene Christian monarch, who, like Goffredo in the *Conquistata*, never hesitates and never doubts. This is Counter-Reformation militancy in its strongest form.

Ethically, *Saint Louis* resembles that other great crusade epic, *La Chanson de Roland*. Although Le Moyne has no sense whatsoever of class struggle or of the intracultural tensions that render the political context of the *Roland* so problematic, he and Turold share one fundamental postulate: that *Paien unt tort e Chrestien unt dreit* (1015). They share a classical-Judaeo-Christian tradition of *bellum pium*: Cicero's notion of *pietas* as *iustitia adversum deos* and the Hebrew intransigence of Exodus 22: 18: 'Maleficos non patieris vivere.' They proclaim it is the Prince's right and duty to exterminate his enemies, whether Pagans or rebellious vassals.[6] It is only after having recognized and accepted this basis of Le Moyne's universe that we can come to grips with the more striking manifestations of 'religious injustice' in his religious melodrama. For example, in Book 3 Alcinde, a Christian inhabitant of Damietta, 'émeuë et de zele et de foy' (p. 33B), willfully and without warning kills a crocodile, the tutelary deity of her city; the Saracens then slaughter two hundred Christians in retaliation, including the murderess. In Book 13, although Lisamante, a prisoner of the Saracens, yields to the Sultan's proposal of marriage, on their wedding night she murders the bridegroom in his drunken slumber, upon which the Saracens execute still more Christians. A modern reader might well excuse the Moslem retaliations and condemn Alcinde and Lisamante both for fanaticism and an absence of fair play. Yet it is clear that Le Moyne sides one hundred per cent with his *femmes fortes*. According to his crusading Jesuit ethos, a Christian can do no wrong. He is always right, those who oppose him in error. Although both Alcinde and Lisamante commit acts repugnant to society's commonly accepted standards, the notion of ethics, as we moderns know it, is transformed. Rather than that a Christian hero be considered 'good' because he conforms to given standards, his actions are proved good simply because he is the man who commits them. In other words, right and wrong are determined not with reference to a pre-established moral code but by the hero himself, who has a particular end in view, and the means always justify the end.

A second point is that, although conflict appears in several guises, it proves to be illusory. The divinity's free gift of grace is ever available to his servants. Le Moyne's universe has no place for tragedy. Under God's eternally vigilant eye, the world is ever good (cf. *Hymnes, et Eloges poetiques*, including 'La Sagesse divine' and 'L'Amour divin'). When heroes die, we know for certain that they proceed directly to their respective thrones in heaven. However, as Louis informs his army in more than one speech, the crusaders can also count on victory. The Lord of Hosts who performed miracles in the past – who made the Flood recede, destroyed Sodom and Gomorrah, helped David vanquish Goliath, and preserved Joseph and Moses from the wrath of Pharaoh – shall succor his Chosen People of the New Covenant. And so he does. God continually intervenes in the world. Through intermediaries – guardian angels or Saint Michael – or from his own fire and thunder, miracle after miracle occurs, sparing individual heroes and the army as a whole. The Nile in rage, demons from hell, monstrous dragons, Saracen armies are impotent against the will of God.

Le Moyne's characters do not grow, do not develop in the course of the narrative. In contrast to Tasso's, his people display little or no weakness, withdrawing neither from the battlefield nor from their Christian duty. Bourbon is much less impulsive than Rinaldo and Tancredi; although the French knight Brenne loves Zahide passionately, their amours are irrelevant to the plot-line until after she becomes Lisamante's prisoner and is about to convert. Indeed, the only change a Zahide, a Muratan, or a Bourbon undergoes is sudden conversion, brought about by divine miracle, whereas Louis himself and the majority of his men are steadfast in their devotion to the Cause. Driven by *ardeur* or *vertu*, they commit acts beyond the ordinary in a mood of ecstasy. No hesitation, no waiting, separate an impulse from the act it gives rise to. The idea comes first, character second, determined by the idea. What he says he does and is. Furthermore, this kind of hero does not become great but is slowly and surely recognized to be so. And he performs great deeds because he is born to perform them. His virtues are present from the beginning, are part of him, since he is French, Christian, and the ancestor of Le Moyne's seventeenth-century patrons. As in the plays of Corneille, he inspires admiration rather than pity or terror. He is the magnanimous man, an archetype of manly virtue, a social ideal as well as an individual one. The hero does not stand alone: he is the delegate of a fictional society in the epic and the ideal of a real one in seventeenth-century France. This is not description but celebration, supreme personal splendor, and ritual play, in an essentialist universe.

It is true, more than one scene is characterized by will to power in the style of Corneille. Following the precepts of Plato and Cicero, the Le Moyne hero is also an orator. Fortune can destroy me, cries Mélédin, but my heart and will stand firm. Since heaven will not help me, I invoke hell!

> Meledin par le sort peut estre combatu,
> Mais le sort ne sçauroit abatre sa vertu:

Et tant que sa vertu conservera sa place,
La Fortune à son gré, peut bien changer de face;
Elle peut tout mesler, elle peut perdre tout;
Le cœur de Meledin demeurera debout:
Et c'est contre ce cœur, plus haut que mes ruïnes,
Que le Corsaire Franc doit dresser ses machines.    (Book 1: p. 3B)

Si le Ciel ne m'y sert, l'Enfer m'y servira:
Ce que le droit ne peut, le crime le pourra:
Et le crime se change, et cesse d'estre crime,
Quand la necessité l'a rendu legitime.    (Book 5: p. 57B)

Olgan and Forcadin scorn the enchantments Mirème has marshalled on their side; relying on brute force, they defy both God and the world (Books 7, 13, and 18). Like Nicomède, Cléopâtre, Rodogune, Auguste, and Horace, these men apply to themselves and others the law they freely choose. Repudiating common morality, anguish, and despair, they make a decision and live up to it at any cost. Their lives are their creation. They are masters, never slaves. However, Le Moyne differs from Corneille in that such speeches are reserved to Saracens and, therefore, are not meant to be taken as models for conduct. Louis IX once indulges in a comparable tirade, proclaiming his *vertu*, but he is rebuked by God's lightning (Book 10). Zahide and Muratan are converted and turn their indomitable will (which had been broken by God) to good purposes. Indeed, throughout the poem Le Moyne speaks out against man's presumption; he attacks the illusions of worldly grandeur (cf. *Le Palais de la Fortune*, *Le Theatre du sage*, and *De la Paix du sage*) in favor of asceticism and a quite different, truly Christian grandeur.

On one occasion, Forcadin declares his independence from all contingent forces, human and divine, yet also permits Mirème to execute Christian captives, in order to appease the populace and the dead Sultan's shade (Book 13). This is perhaps his only moment of bad faith. However, Forcadin, a worthy descendant of Virgil's Turnus and Tasso's Argante, even though he becomes generalissimo, is never truly in command of the Saracen camp. Those who are – Mélédin and Mirème – woo Fortune in any way they can. They are as Machiavellian as any of Corneille's villains, and, far more than in Tasso, particularly prone to deception, to fighting the Christians not by force of arms or will but through deceit.[7]

Le Moyne proposes as models for conduct neither the hero of will-to-power (Forcadin) nor the practitioner of Machiavellian cunning (Mélédin). On the contrary, Saint Louis discovers (Book 8) that the highest places in heaven are awarded to ascetics who have conquered the world in their own flesh (battles more glorious than on the field) and to martyrs who have submitted patiently to their fate. The prince of martyrs and, by extension, of ascetics as well is Christ: it is our highest duty to imitate him. Le Moyne's protagonists fight inner battles, learning to renounce physical passion and false worldly honors in favor of a more sublime religious life. King Louis and his princes follow the Corpus Christi into Damietta, bareheaded and with bare feet, weeping. And they are eager to die for God, to seek death in God. The crusader's true role is martyrdom, King Louis says, and the most glorious life is the shortest. We have seen that in the baroque period religious heroism often takes on a passive, not active, stance, is based on endurance, not achievement, and manifests itself in resisting temptation rather than military conquest. Yet Le Moyne resembles Corneille rather than d'Aubigné in that, for him, renunciation is triumphant, never tragic, and death proves to be an instrument of realizing human potentiality, chosen not endured, allied to reason and not separated from it. Renunciation and death are man's greatest achievements, opening the portals to heavenly bliss. There is only one crime possible in Le Moyne's world, though it may take sundry forms – apostasy; and only one virtue, from which all others derive – faith.

Up to now, I have spoken largely of *Saint Louis* as a poem of convention, decorum, spectacle, and almost ritual high seriousness. In addition, it is many other things, being, like Tasso's *Gerusalemme liberata*, a complex work of art. Pierre Le Moyne shares with Tasso a predilection for romance. Knights resist monsters, dragons, and fiends from hell. Sundry enchantments occur, in the tradition of late *chansons de geste* and Pulci, Boiardo, Ariosto, and Tasso. These include poisoned armor and a poisoned crown of thorns, the Nile flood, an attack by fire-demons, walking on or passing through the Nile, magic water that heals wounds or saves souls, God's fire that destroys the aforesaid venomous objects, and a host of illusory monster-demon obstacles. We must not forget that magic, whether white or black, was accepted as a natural facet of life in the seventeenth century. Thus conceived, the supernatural is not an adornment but an intrinsic part of the action, for, as in d'Aubigné, the entire universe takes sides for or against the crusaders, and, on the outcome of their battle, much of the future course of history depends. Magic stood somewhere on the frontier between science and religion, between mysticism and technology. In literary terms, to dominate occult forces with enchantments was useful for arousing *meraviglia* as well as a sense of mystery in the cosmos; it rendered *meraviglia* credible and allowed man's fascination with the occult to manifest itself freely.

This spectacular epic contains most of the archetypes of romance, and much of its plot (although in a complex and fragmented way) is based upon the quest pattern found in late *chanson de geste*, Arthurian romance, Homer, Virgil, and Tasso. Thus the crusade is envisaged as a quest for a sacred object, Christ's crown of thorns. Mirème and Mélédin invoke creatures from hell. Louis IX voyages to heaven, and Bourbon twice struggles with supernatural powers in a symbolic Other World. Louis, Bourbon, and the warrior-maidens submit to ordeals, defeat monsters, deliver captives, and commune with symbolic or real parent-figures. Saint Louis, a sun-figure with a holy nimbus, the ancestor of the sun-king Louis XIV, gives battle to the forces of darkness. Once Artois, the king's younger brother, is sacrificed, the others proceed to victory, for he is a good scapegoat, sacrificed in Christ's name so that Christ's army shall live. After these trials, the poem closes with total victory over the enemy, celebrated in three acts: conversion (Zahide and Muratan), marriage (Zahide and Brenne), and the coronation of Saint Louis with the Crown of Thorns, the greatest, most holy of treasures brought back to the homeland. And death-rebirth experiences – whether they take the form of a supernatural voyage, a battle with a dragon in dark woods, crossing the Nile, being wounded in battle and restored by miracle, or dying while one's soul is wafted to heaven – occur in almost every book of the epic.

Unlike the one in *La Chanson de Roland*, Le Moyne's crusader host contains no old men of note (with the exception of the blind Commander of the Templars, mentioned in passing). No Nestor or Naimes stands by Louis's side; he is his own best adviser, or he takes counsel from the archangel Michael. In heaven Louis does speak to his father and is guided by him, yet, being the son of a great king, still in his youth, he is succored by God the Son, as if the *puer senex* quality of the Christian army is to be maintained on all levels, including the celestial. Add to this that the good hermit, Tasso's vecchio d'Ascalona, has been transformed into a lady two hundred years old but eternally young and beautiful, and that, even though the enemy are depicted partially in terms of feminine imagery (subterranean halls, the Nile, and so on,) Egyptian women are all young and benevolent. Evil is to be found only in their men. On the other hand, the most memorable of the Saracens, their leaders and guiding spirits, are two horrifying greybeards, the Sultan and his sorcerer. Significantly, much of the poem recounts how youths and maidens, pagan and Christian, seek to escape from their clutches. It would appear that Le Moyne has unconsciously elaborated a pattern of Oedipal wish-fulfillment in which good young men and women defeat old men with the help of supernatural sons and good mothers. And they mark their triumph over the fathers with either physical marriage on earth (Zahide and Brenne), spiritual marriage in heaven (Lisamante and Béthunes), or a coronation and the assumption of a father's role in turn, on earth (Louis) or in heaven (Artois). From King

Louis, father of his people, from Bourbon, and from others will sprout many a fair flower of France.

Although Le Moyne has the crusaders triumph over their hoary adversaries, he does not permit many happy love affairs. The Jesuit father holds a most ambiguous attitude toward sexual passion. On the one hand, *fin' amor*, in its baroque, post-Petrarchan, precious form, runs through the epic. On several occasions, heroes indulge in acts of gallantry. Again and again, youths and maidens tread on fire or ice, pierced by arrows, floods of tears bursting from their eyes. Zahide's suitors, princes and sultans all, are reduced to slavery by her eyes:

> Son nom estoit Zahide; et depuis le rivage,
> Où la Mer divisée à l'Hebreu fit passage,
> Jusqu'à cette autre rive, où le flot trémoussant,
> Se colore aux rayons du Soleil renaissant;
> Il n'estoit point de Cour soit barbare ou galante,
> D'où, des plus braves cœurs Zahide conquerante,
> N'attirast à Memphis, par bandes enchaisnez,
> Des Esclaves regnans, des Captifs couronnez.    (Book 1: p. 3B)

On the other hand, throughout his works, the author condemns patently evil effects of lust. And in the *Dissertation du poëme heroïque* he criticizes Virgil, Ariosto, Tasso, and Marino, all for having gone too far in the sympathetic depiction of Eros. Le Moyne will accept love as a convention in heroic poetry, but only in secondary episodes; furthermore, it shall be depicted in pure, noble colors, and shall exist not as an end in itself but a means to an end, to inspire martial glory.[8] From both an ethical and an esthetic perspective, *amor* is deemed hierarchically inferior to *militia* and *caritas*.

Therefore, even though Le Moyne yields to convention, even though in certain episodes he follows the example of Tasso, on the whole Eros plays a sorry role in his epic. Four illustrious Moslems – Mélédor, Olgan, Alfasel, and Sultan Mélédin himself – commit cruel acts, in defiance of moral law, and are reduced to the level of beasts, all in the name of love. Dominated by lust and jealousy, they become anti-heroes. Significantly, all four fail in their endeavors, indeed pay with their lives. God is not merciful to wooers in this poem; they fall in battle, dreaming of their ladies, their charms and erotic vows unable to save them. Although Brenne is dazzled by Zahide, and Bourbon by Almasonte, in somewhat the way Rinaldo was by Armida, and Tancredi by Clorinda, at no time does either man become a love-slave in an equivalent of Armida's garden. Alégonde speaks out splendidly against passion. She says that Bourbon cannot pluck laurels on the soft, decadent plain of love, but only on the mount of labor, glory and virtue:

> Mais, Seigneur, ces Lauriers ne sont pas de ces plaines,
> Où se cueille la fleur des delices humaines.
> On ne les void point naistre en ces lieux enchantez,
> Où le Luxe nourrit les molles Voluptez:
> Où l'Amour, cette Abeille agreable et funeste,
> D'une courte douceur, fait une longue peste.
> Ils se doivent cueillir sur ces Monts escarpez,
> D'honorables sueurs, de sang noble trempez,
> Où bien loin du repos, bien plus loin des delices,
> Entre de hauts rochers, et de bas precipices,
> Par un sentier qu'on void de peu de gens battu,
> On arrive à la Gloire, en suivant la Vertu.    (Book 11: p. 130A)

Man cannot be a slave and a master at the same time, for the chain of love leaves no place for a crown. Begin, she tells Bourbon, by conquering yourself! A child, Cupid vanquished you; you expect to slay a dragon yet you cannot even withstand this insect! Indeed, it is only by renouncing Almasonte that Bourbon wins the right to wear Aymon's armor and conquer the serpent.

In place of Eros, the poet proposes another sort of relationship between the sexes, and in place of Armida other models for womankind. Raymond and Belinde, Aymon and Alégonde, Lisamante and her late husband are exemplars of chaste Christian wedlock. Father Le Moyne places as much emphasis on continence as on nuptial vows: these couples are evoked in terms that apply to a Josephine marriage. Indeed, in Book 8 a special place in heaven is reserved for the chaste (Susanna, Judith, three *femmes fortes*) and for Josephine spouses, including Saint Crispus and Saint Joseph.

That three great ladies are mentioned in the same terms as Susanna and Judith, that Judith is shown to be the first and greatest scriptural *mulier fortis*, indicate both the extent to which sexual purity and martial vigor are associated in Le Moyne's mind and the fact that his condemnation of *luxuria*, unlike that of many clerics, is not misogynistic. On the contrary, he joyfully exploits the warrior-maiden tradition in Virgil (Camilla), Ariosto (Marfisa, Bradamante), and Tasso (Clorinda, Armida). In *Saint Louis* we find two eminent *bellatrices* in the Christian camp and two (plus a hundred others in the ranks) among the Saracens, all treated sympathetically. Belinde claims the right to fight in battle side by side with Raymond, for, a free person, she submits only to the laws of love and honor. Since love has taught her where lie the paths of glory, she and her husband will be immortalized together in history. King Louis grants her request, proclaiming that no sex is forbidden honor:

> Qu'elle vienne, dit-il, que cette Ame heroïque,
> Nous preste en ce combat, son exemple et sa pique:
> Qu'elle nous fasse voir, que la force est du cœur,
> Et qu'il n'est point de sexe éloigné de l'Honneur ...
> (Book 10: p. 119A)

Then Judith, cutlass in hand, descends from heaven and convinces Lisamante to behead Mélédin, crying 'Je viens à ton secours, Femme forte' (p. 162B). Le Moyne echoes a literary current prevalent in his day, especially in the 1640s – exaltation of the strong, domineering woman, active and continent, as a feminine ideal. This current, to which the author himself contributed directly (cf. *La Gallerie des Femmes fortes*, 1647), was partly responsible for the fashion of Judith, Esther, and Susanna as literary and artistic subjects and for a tradition of martial ladies in seventeenth-century epic.[9]

As does Tasso, Le Moyne expresses in vivid terms the fate of lovers separated by death, instilling in the reader an intimate, truly Virgilian sense of *lacrymae rerum*. Tasso's idyllic-elegiac figures – Olindo, Sofronia, Erminia, Clorinda, Tancredi, even Armida – live again in the pages of his French disciple, who feels pity for all unhappy lovers, even Saracens, for longing undeclared or unrequited, forbidden or renounced, and for happy affection cut short in its prime. This lyrical, subjective mood of pathos extends to non-amatory martyrdom, to the Christian children used as shields by the Egyptians and then burned at the stake, to Robert of Artois cut down inside Mansourah, flinging his blood in the air, a sacrifice to God. An atmosphere of foreboding pervades the epic. Like Tasso, Le Moyne is moved by the heroism of failure, the poetry of darkness and ruins, and man's anguish in the face of cosmic mysteries.

Thus, for all its beauty, life is full of illusion and deception: *Omnia vincit Mors*. All the more reason, cries the Jesuit poet, for man to renounce secular glory and secular desire! In the last analysis, there is only one love: that of man for God, and of God, principle of power, wisdom, and love, for man. God's *caritas* radiates from the center of his essence out to man, and man's rises up to God. Le Moyne shares a neo-Augustinian, anti-Stoical doctrine rife in the seventeenth century (shared by the Dominican Coëffeteau and the Oratorian Senault) that love, illuminating reason and the will, directs our passions toward the Good.[10] These passions, the sources of virtue and vice, are in themselves neutral. Their source and goal is love. They are surmounted not by reason and will but by love, a stimulus to glory. And, although Le Moyne is aware of mystical ecstasy (for example, the ecstatic hermitess Alégonde), he is most attracted to Christian heroism, that is, to earthly love purified and transformed by the divine, by a celestial fire that is God (*Hymnes de l'amour divin*).

The opposition of forces, in Le Moyne's works as in those of d'Aubigné, is given expression in a pattern of antithetical demonic and apocalyptic imagery. The analogies are so striking between these two baroque writers that, to avoid repetition, I shall not analyze Le Moyne's imagery at length. Suffice it to say, in the line of d'Aubigné (and, for that matter, Ronsard and Saint-Amant), this Jesuit father specializes in scenes of battle horror, in the grisly and the macabre, in depicting decadent, grotesque architecture in terms of ruins, stench, excrement, decay, and pestilence; the enemy are assimilated to serpents, dragons, and demons; they assault the Christian host with poison, blood, flooding water or storm, and varied sorts of fire. Zahide's blood is to be spilled, in order that the Nile waters rise; Muratan, Mélédin's son, mockingly, pathetically requests that the sultan fell Zahide himself, washing his crown in his daughter's blood:

> Que Zahide perisse, et que des Ombres vaines,
> Viennent boire à tes yeux le beau sang de tes veines:
> Assouvis t'en toy-mesme, et join Pere inhumain,
> Le crime de la langue à celuy de la main.
> De ta main, de ton sang ta Couronne lavée,
> Sans tache et sans déchet, te sera conservée ...    (Book 6: p. 67A)

The Moslem dragon, ultimately vanquished by Bourbon, kills with his blood as well as his venom; he is also a fire-creature, with flaming eyes and tongue. Finally, Mirème creates for Bourbon a vision of the pit, a river of fire and blood that torments a thousand souls:

> L'épouvantable gouffre à rez-de bord est plein,
> D'un fleuve limonneux, rouge de sang humain:
> Le feu s'y mesle à l'onde, et l'onde fugitive,
> Roule sans intervalle alentour de sa rive.
> Là mille malheureux haut et bas agitez,
> Et des vagues, du feu, du limon tourmentez,
> Flottent, comme l'on void le debris d'un naufrage,
> Sur la mer en courroux, flotter durant l'orage.    (Book 16: p. 204B)

In *la Gerusalemme liberata* night-time can evoke a mood of nostalgia and elegy, of repose in the quiet of a friendly, intimate cosmos. Such is

practically never the case in *Saint Louis*. For Le Moyne, the setting of the
sun is an invitation for Satan to act. After dark Mirème invokes the dead and
performs a black mass; Mélédin sacrifices his daughter; the Nile rises;
Forcadin and Zahide invade the crusaders' camp; Bourbon faces a phantom
attack; and fire-spirits burn the invaders' bridge. And it is at night that the
Frenchmen hear cries of horror and behold flames in the sky, discovering
only the next day that the Christian minority in Damietta has been
massacred!

> La Lune s'avançoit ...
> Quand des cris de frayeur, et des voix de menace,
> Telles qu'on les entend au sac de quelque Place,
> De leurs tristes accens rompent nostre repos,
> Et réveillent au loin les Vents et les Echos.
> Les Echos et les Vents en trouble leur répondent:
> Du rivage prochain les vagues les secondent:
> Et les vagues, les Vents, les Echos et la Nuit,
> Font un concert d'horreur, de tumulte et de bruit.    (Book 3: p. 31B)

These muffled, foreboding sounds contribute as much to a mood of terror
as do flames and darkness. So in the midst of a night sortie the reader is
struck by an echo of exotic Saracen musical instruments, tumult, the neigh-
ing of horses, and howls of the dying. And people hear the dragon hiss
and the noise of falling trees and rocks before the monster comes into view.
Darkness and noise are two factors that accompany the enchantments
unleashed upon Saint Louis's men; they help invoke a vision of chaos and
evil, of the world upside-down, in all its terrifying cosmic finality. And,
of course, this darkness symbolizes a spiritual blindness on the part of
Saracens, who fail to see God.

Satan tricks us with worldly honors, then destroys us through war and
black magic. He commits crimes against nature, against man, and against
God. However, the authors of *verkehrte Welt* are not victorious; in this
cosmic struggle of good versus evil, God ever maintains a *concordia discors*,
against which their disruptive efforts prove futile. Demonic imagery is
nullified or transformed from evil to good. Sacred water (tears of repentance, a martyr's blood, the miraculously curative Matariya fountain),
sacred fire (the flame of love, the burning sparks of the stake, God's own
lightning), and sacred light (the saint king, Louis ix, assimilated to his
descendant, the sun-king Louis xiv) neutralize or destroy the power of
Satan. Although Mélédin will do anything to defend his throne, including
murdering his daughter, he will perish, his dynasty with him, and Saracen
thrones and altars will be transformed into pedestals for the Cross. On

the other hand, Louis's and Bourbon's families will rule France forever. A flying machine, in the form of a throne, cleansed in fire, takes Louis to heaven where he beholds Christ's seat of majesty and the chair he himself will occupy one day. Similarly, the pagan altar, used to sacrifice Zahide, fails in its function, is nullified by the throne that she also is promised in heaven (Book 17) and by good Christian altars: the holy altar with the Eucharist rolled into Damietta (Book 3); the spectacular tournament altar with a burning phoenix drawn by unicorns and guided by a virgin (Book 4); and the altar of heaven, to which an angel brings Saint Louis's tears (Book 8).

Pierre Le Moyne also contrasts lifeless pagan stone to manifestations of nature in the green world. Earthly power and the chains of mortal sin yield to Christ's crown of thorns. Offered the crowns of the Holy Roman and Byzantine-Oriental empires (emblems of power and riches), Louis chooses the symbol of Christ's passion, kisses it, and places it on his head (Book 8). This holy diadem protected the Saracen throne as long as it was housed in Cairo; with its capture, Mélédin's house falls, and the thorns will protect the Capetian and Bourbon crowns of France. The poem ends with Louis's coronation, when the relic miraculously places itself on his head (Book 18).

This crown is associated with the Holy Cross. When, in heaven, King Louis chooses Christ's thorns over the empires of Rome and the Orient, he also requests his cross and nails:

> Aux épines, Seigneur, si vous joignez vos cloux,
> Les liens en seront plus fermes et plus doux:
> Et vostre Croix pour comble, à vos cloux ajoustée,
> Tiendra d'un poids plus fort mon amour arrestée.
> Heureux si prés de vous à la Croix attaché,
> Je puis de vostre sang nettoyer mon peché!
> Et plus heureux encor, si vos flames divines,
> S'allument dans mon cœur, sous ces saintes épines!
> (Book 8: pp. 91B, 92A)

In Book 1 Le Moyne invokes Christ's crown of thorns on the altar of the crucifix, and in Book 9 he tells how Christ, stretched on wood, killed the Serpent and with bloody nails forged keys to the kingdom of heaven. It is appropriate, then, that Bourbon place his trophy, the head of the slain dragon, under the Rood, Christ's tree, that redeems Adam's Tree of the Knowledge of Good and Evil (Book 12).

Finally, Le Moyne speaks of the laurel as a symbol of heroism, of the palm branch as a symbol of martyrdom, and, above all, of the French

*fleur-de-lis.* He declares that King Louis's victory will result in a grafting of
the crown of thorns onto the crown of lilies, ensuring that Louis's descendants will sprout on the royal tree and that future kings and kingdoms will
place their names beneath the names of Louis's and Bourbon's descendants
(Books 1 and 8). And he praises Julie de Montausier, daughter of his patrons, the Marquis and Marquise of Rambouillet, who will bloom on the
family tree and, crowned by myrtle, be allied with the *fleur-de-lis.* Christ
and the French royal House are assimilated: the lily, the emblem chosen by
Clovis for his purification through baptism, stands for the Virgin Mary
and the annunciation of Christ's coming as well as for the Capetian-Bour-
bon dynasty.

As with d'Aubigné, the triumph posited by Pierre Le Moyne – of fire
over fire, of water over water, and of flowers over stone – can be explained
only in terms of Christian paradox. Louis ix's tears suffice to dam the flood
of the Nile in the same way that a few drops of Christ's spilt blood broke
the doors of hell and drowned Satan's demons. The only riches that Louis
seeks in Egypt are a handful of miserable thorns. If he had sought more,
he would have been defeated a hundred times, but since he covets thorns, he
will win the treasures of the Orient and, because of this pitiful, ironic
crown, the crown of France will remain in his family forever. A uniquely
spiritual prize ensures material as well as spiritual rewards. And dead,
sterile thorns alone provide fertility, both in the Egyptian wasteland and in
France's blessed garden. Similarly, this glorious conqueror walks humbly, barefooted, behind God's altar, ready for defeat whenever God wills it.
Since he welcomes martyrdom, Louis always triumphs; because he proclaims that the greatest victory is to suffer, he never fails. In Book 9 Michael
tells Louis that because of Christ's death all deaths died:

> Voy tirant vers le Nord cette seche colline,
> Qui se montre de haut à la Cité voisine.
> C'est le sacré Theatre, où la Vie à la Mort,
> S'unit par un fatal et solennel accord:
> Où de la mort d'un seul tous les Morts revescurent;
> Et d'une seule mort toutes les morts moururent.
> C'est là que l'homme-Dieu sur le bois attaché,
> Ecrasa le Serpent, étouffa le Peché;
> Et que des cloux sanglans, qui les mains luy percerent,
> Les clefs des Cieux fermez, par l'Amour se forgerent.
> 
> (Book 9: p. 104B)

Louis undergoes symbolic death more than once, and, therefore, he is
reborn. He imitates Christ, chooses his master's crown, and thus becomes
worthy of being Christ's deputy in the world.

*Saint Louis, ou la Sainte Couronne reconquise* is an uneven work. The modern reader will be repelled by the more conventional or topical scenes in Le Moyne's poem: Lisamante's romantic childhood, the tournament, and the lengthy foreshadowing of modern French history. However, where Le Moyne is at his best – and this turns out to be a surprisingly high proportion of the total work – he is magnificent. In descriptions of a storm at sea, of naval and land battles, of demonic landscapes, in the psychology of jealousy and will to power, in scenes of martyrdom and love-death melodrama – he surpasses all but the greatest of his contemporaries. No less impressive is the richness and complexity of a poem containing such extraordinary juxtapositions of style, theme, and tone. Pierre Le Moyne includes in his masterwork epic, lyric, war, romance, horror, extravagance, melodrama, and mystical ecstasy. A mixture of Tassian *mirabile* and *patetico*, of *furore* and *concetti*, could hardly please Boileau's generation, but it corresponds admirably to a more recent romantic and even surrealist esthetic. A public capable of appreciating this Jesuit father only has come into being centuries after his death.

In many respects, Le Moyne's is a typically Cornelian world. *Saint Louis* is composed in the grand manner, in solemn, sublime language, using the classical figures of rhetoric. Le Moyne's vocabulary is rich but never descends to the low, nor does he mix high, middle, and low styles. Like Corneille, he believes in the values of duty, sacrifice, and chivalry; like Corneille's, his characters shine with glory. These aristocrats are profoundly *généreux* in the Cornelian sense, that is, of noble blood and caste. Their *vertu* can be defined as manliness, grandeur of heart, and the resolution to become and remain a master. They possess a vivid desire to resist the inconstancy of the times, to remain true to the ideals they hold dear. They prove to themselves and to others the law they freely choose. Nothing can prevent a Le Moyne or a Corneille hero from acting – neither memory, prudence, scruples, nor adverse counsel. Totally free, such a man wins our admiration by exercising his will to the utmost. And we admire him for his ardor, for manifesting an almost prelapsarian strength and joy.

I believe that Father Le Moyne reacts against an amorous *galant* current in the 1650s, a preciosity that had infected contemporary French epic and romance and even Corneille's theater. Curiously, Le Moyne's revulsion from this current parallels that of Boileau. Repudiating Scudéry and Tasso, he seeks to restore an earlier heroic vision of life, now lost. In his poem order triumphs over passion, and the crusade over sexual love. Instead of an Alaric or Clovis or Rinaldo feminized within a shady garden, his Lisamante and Belinde are transformed into men. Unlike the author of the *Song of Roland*, Le Moyne does not remove women from his epic; on the contrary, he rehabilitates them by granting them the same martial heroism

embodied in their suitors and husbands. Comrades in arms, they join battle
side by side in a world of glory.

It is in the nature of his ideals that Le Moyne diverges most from Corneille. The dramatist from Rouen illustrates the last flowering of a feudal
mentality, the striving of great aristocrats to defy fate, to exalt their egos at
the expense of others, to express their pride, authority, and even rebellion
in the face of central authority. In his best-known plays, Eros is joined to
reason and harmonized with the will; as in courtly romance, love and
honor stand together, each impossible without the other. In *La Sainte
Couronne reconquise*, on the other hand, purified love is rendered subservient to war and religion; if it cannot inspire noble sentiments, it has to be
uprooted. Meanwhile, the political and personal ambitions of the great barons are directed against a foreign adversary. Within France, King Louis is
an absolute monarch reigning over all, and the greatest of his men, Anjou,
Artois, Poitiers, even Bourbon, live only to serve him, to be his sword
and shield. Differing from the tradition of epic in Homer and Tasso, Le
Moyne suppresses any conflict of authority between the king and his
captains.[11] For all their will-power, his French, Christian heroes do not act
independently from the community or from a higher moral law. Although
their lives are their own creation, they fashion them for the purpose of
aiding their king and their God.

Above all, Le Moyne's work always contains a supernatural, metaphysical
dimension. The interests of the state transcend those of the individual,
but God's interests transcend those of the state, and if Louis rules as an
absolute king, he does so as God's deputy on earth and in imitation of a
divine order in the heavens, his task to bring about the secular betterment of
his subjects and to lead them on the path of salvation. The ultimate in Le
Moyne's world is the afterlife. Kings live and rule justly, in order to be
seated on an eternal throne in heaven, a crown of laurel or roses on their
brows. Since life is threatened by death, permanence by mutability, and
reality by appearance, the only truth, being, and constancy are to be
found beyond the grave. God is the only register of life, action, energy, and
will. Thus, in what he considers to be decadent times, Pierre Le Moyne
seeks to restore values in a new heroic synthesis that will combine *virtus* and
*pietas*, the beauty of roses and of the stars, that will reconcile the Church
and the secular world of Louis xiv's court.

We must never forget that Le Moyne's century represents one of the
most fruitful periods of religious activity in all of French history, that the
*grand siècle* brought about reform in religious orders, the introduction
into France of the discalced Carmelites and the founding of the Oratoire and
Saint-Sulpice. This is the age of saints and theologians as well as of the
classical theater and Louis xiv's wars. Pierre Le Moyne belongs to the last

generation of baroque religious poets, including Bussières, Martial de Brives, du Bois Hus, and the Protestant Drelincourt. His is one of the last voices of the Catholic Renaissance. The great themes of the Counter-Reformation and of the Jesuit Order are to be found in his work. Indeed, Le Moyne is a fine poet *because* he belonged to the Society of Jesus and was inspired by the ideals of his order, one of many Jesuit humanists and mystical writers. His *Saint Louis* reflects the ostentatious, ornamental, sensuous, and mystically intolerant Catholicism of his age. He and Tasso are the Western Catholic counterparts of d'Aubigné and Milton. They represent the sublime militant spirit of the Catholic Renaissance which has made a significant moral and esthetic contribution to our civilization.

It is no accident that the leading baroque epicists are given to one form or another of Christian commitment. This is true both inside France, with du Bartas, d'Aubigné, Saint-Amant, and Le Moyne, and in a broader European context: Tasso, the Marino of *La Strage degli Innocenti*, Hojeda, Milton, and Vondel, not to speak of the literatures of Poland, Hungary, and Croatia.[12] The Baroque is a peculiarly sacral age, perhaps more so even than the medieval era. This may help to explain not only the fervor with which Christian heroic poetry was cultivated in the 1650s but also why, in subsequent increasingly secularized periods, epic fell out of fashion, perhaps even why, to this day, the French canon will include, say, La Rochefoucauld, La Bruyère, and Madame de La Fayette, while finding d'Aubigné and his Catholic adversaries a trifle foreign or 'excentric.' Nonetheless, the latter are truly French and baroque, representative of a great culture and numbering among its most significant esthetic triumphs.

## Chapter Eleven

# ✤ BOILEAU

A grave, sublime manner is generally considered to be the hallmark of epic, and not without reason. Several of the greatest practitioners of the mode were unendowed with a sense of humor or, if they had one, sedulously avoided cultivating it. Virgil, Tasso, Spenser, Le Moyne, Milton, and, in more recent times, Wordsworth, Lamartine, Vigny, Tennyson, and Saint-John Perse are examples. However, some epics present comic scenes which in no way undermine the gravity of the work as a whole. Such is the case in Homer and in the *chanson de geste*. Still other heroic poems, especially those in the romance mode, contain humorous and serious traits in about equal proportions, mocking chivalry or *fin' amor*, for example, and treating them with reverence at the same time. Under this heading we can range *Huon de Bordeaux*, Chrétien's *Yvain*, the romances of Jean Renart, Machaut's *Le Dit dou Lÿon*, Chaucer's *Troilus and Criseyde*, Boiardo's *Orlando innamorato*, and Ariosto's *Orlando furioso*. Earlier in the book I studied *La Chanson de Huon de Bordeaux* and long poems by Jean de Meun and Guillaume de Machaut, emphasizing that so early in the French tradition sophisticated poets were capable of elaborating a fundamentally comic or satirical vision of the universe. In this chapter I am concerned with a different kind of humor and a different subgenre of epos; here I wish to treat the mock or burlesque poem, uniquely comic in tone, conceived specifically as a parody of classical masterpieces from Greece and Rome or the modern *poëme heroïque*.

The ancient Greek *Batrachomyomachia* mocks the *Iliad*, and the medieval French *Roman de Renard* undermines both *chansons de geste* and *romans courtois*. However, a full flowering of the burlesque epic occurs for the first time in Renaissance Italy. Our words for 'heroi-comic,' 'burlesque,' 'grotesque,' and 'pastiche' are of Italian origin; in no other country has there been so great a fusion of the sublime and its comic parody. The first major long poem of the High Renaissance was Pulci's *Morgante* (1483), and contemporary with Boiardo and Ariosto we find the works of Teofilo

Folengo. The sixteenth century was the age of Berni's *Rime*; his style
then became a vogue in the hands of Allegri, Allori, Bellincioni, Capitoli,
Caporali, Doni, Franzesi, Lasca, Mauro, Nelli, and Tansillo. Finally, the
baroque period gave rise to two important mock-epics, Bracciolini's *Lo
Scherno degli Dei* (1618) and Tassoni's *La Secchia rapita* (1622), and to
the first burlesque travesty of a Greco-Roman classic, Lalli's *Eneide traves-
tita* (1633).

This Italian current influenced du Bellay and Ronsard as well as Régnier
and the *satyriques* Sigogne, Motin, and Berthelot. Sorel introduced par-
odic elements into *Francion* (1622) and *Le Berger extravagant* (1627). However, the greatest French disciple of Berni was the author of *Moyse sauvé*,
Saint-Amant, who was familiar with recent Italian and Spanish trends. From
1629 on he included in his works a series of mock *encomia* of cheese,
wine, beer, tobacco, bad lodgings, cities (Rome), and countries (England).
Of particular importance for the development of light epic is an absurd
banquet of the Gods in his *Le Melon* (1631) and his half-serious, half-playful
heroic poem *Le Passage de Gibraltar* (1640). In the preface to the latter
text, Saint-Amant praised Tassoni and claimed to have introduced into
France the Mediterranean word 'burlesque.'

If Saint-Amant can be considered a great precursor, the master of the
burlesque style is Paul Scarron, who launched a veritable movement in
the arts by publishing his *Recueil de quelques vers burlesques* (1643) followed by a *Suite* in three parts (1644, 1647, 1656), the first complete long
narrative poem in burlesque, *Typhon* (1644), and the first formal classical
travesty north of the Alps, *Virgile travesty* (Books 1–7, 1648–52; Book 8,
1659). Charles Dassoucy, second only to Scarron in fame and talent, published *Le Jugement de Pâris* in 1648, *l'Ovide en belle humeur*, based on
Book 1 of the *Metamorphoses*, in 1650, and *Le Ravissement de Proserpine*,
from Claudian, in 1653. The vogue extended for several years, with travesties of Virgil by Furetière, Brébeuf, Dufresnoy, and Charles Perrault (unpublished), of Ovid by Richer, of Homer by the Perrault brothers and H. de
Picon, of Lucan by Brébeuf, and of Horace, Juvenal, Claudian, and
Ariosto. We find three parodies of Virgil in Occitan, four in 'Burgundian.'
However, by 1649 Scarron himself denigrated the mode, as did later on
his friend Pellisson, Mlle de Scudéry, and the Jesuit Vavasseur, author of *De
ludicra dictione* (1658). Brébeuf pointed out that people were unable to
distinguish good from bad burlesque, therefore condemned it all as 'une
maladie de l'expression.' In spite of these attacks, in spite of Boileau's
strictures in *L'Art poétique* (1674), the genre persisted into the eighteenth
century, with Marivaux's *Iliade travestie* (1716) and *Télémaque travesti*
(1736), a *Henriade travestie en vers burlesques* by Fougeret de Monbron
(1745), and a *Henriade mise en vers burlesques auvergnats* by Amable

Faucon (1784). Meanwhile, Scarron had an extraordinary influence between 1664 and 1680 in England, and in the eighteenth century he was imitated in the German-speaking world, by Hölty, Bürger, and, above all, Aloys Blumauer, author of *Abenteuer des frommen Helden Aeneas* (1783).

A great deal of research has been devoted to the burlesque movement.[1] One school of thought claims that it does not represent a reaction against Classicism or the Greco-Roman masters; on the contrary, the travesties of the 1640s and 1650s are an offering of love to Virgil and Ovid, even serve to renew interest in them. The burlesque poets bear no relation to the Fronde, nor do they attack the *Précieux* or other contemporary writers. Their verse represents a rehabilitation of Marot and the introduction into France of a current from south of the Alps. Theirs is a legitimate artistic manifestation treating in the comic mode what others treat in the sublime, which mocks the gods but in no way undermines poetry, is the work of respectable men of letters, such as Saint-Amant, Sarasin, Ménage, Scarron, Dassoucy, and Brébeuf, and, at least in the early years, was praised by Guez de Balzac and Corneille.

The other school points out that Dassoucy and his circle, a group of irreverent young poets, had ties to the *libertin* movement, and that the Perrault brothers were already rebelling against the Ancients. The burlesque practitioners were men of the Baroque, consciously imitating Saint-Amant, reacting against the effete court verse of the time and against Malherbe and the more recent neoclassical affectation of a post-Louis XIII age. Their works manifest a spirit of independence and a refusal of pompous literary convention; they implicitly undermine classical simile, metaphor, and plot development. Like other baroque writers, like the *Précieux*, they scorn measure and constraint, they seek to amuse and astound with their wit. Indeed, burlesque and *préciosité*, committed to deformation of language and creating a sense of amazement in the reader, can be considered the last two baroque currents before the triumph of Classicism.

Both positions contain truth. Above all, however, I urge us to accept the artistic claims of the burlesque-travesty movement. Scarron and Dassoucy are not realists but masters of fantasy and the grotesque. Their language is not at all low-class but an intentionally stylized art form, their texts are based upon other texts, and their chosen mode adheres to strictly literary norms. An artificial genre, epic travesty was written not for the masses but for a public of connoisseurs, for educated people familiar with the classics and with neoclassical rules. In fact, these poets consciously illustrated *sermo humilis*, a *style bas et plaisant*. Dassoucy, especially, but also Scarron and Brébeuf were proud of what they wrote and manifest as much vanity as any composer of lyrics or tragedy. In 1677 Dassoucy replied to Boileau, attempting to define burlesque as an art form. And Fontenelle, in his 'Description de l'empire de la poésie,' in the *Mercure Galant*, January 1678, designated the epic as capital of the 'province de la haute poésie' and burlesque as capital of the 'province de la basse poésie.'[2] If in his own lifetime Dassoucy never received the recognition I believe he deserved, Scarron at least was praised by many a contemporary, his work considered inimitable and an honorable tribute to the immortal Virgil.

The burlesque epics are known for their striking literary style. The language of *Virgile travesty* or *Ovide en belle humeur* is a motley affair, a mixture of 'high' and 'low' expressions plus archaic, technical, invented, and foreign terms. Whatever writers normally exclude from refined poetic diction – the familiar, the vulgar, the obscene, and all forms of slang – here finds a place. Scarron agrees with Malherbe that the style of Ronsard and du Bartas is ridiculous – that is why he introduces 'neo-Pléiade' speech for comic effect. Classical *proprietas* is broken and the new standard grounded in dissonance and discrepancy. This rhetoric of the burlesque is in part the result of gratuitous verbal fantasy: it is vigorous, dynamic, and can create the illusion of natural utterance.

By having Aeneas and Apollo speak such a language, the *Burlesques* succeed in pulling the old gods down to the level of most unheroic, undivine mortals living in the seventeenth century. In the process not only speech is undermined but character and situation as well. The reality of modern life is substituted for handsome lies in the past. Among the techniques employed to create this effect are temporal anachronism and social leveling. The old gods wear Louis xiv clothes and wigs, hold offices appropriate only in France. They move in a bourgeois salon, or they swear, drink, and fight like the Parisian rabble. Virgil's characters are transformed into comic stereotypes worthy of Molière: Mars is depicted as a *miles gloriosus*, Minerva as a pedant, Venus as a whore, Mercury as a pander, Cassandra as a *précieuse*, Calchas as a *bigot*. Burlesque poets also emphasize concrete physical detail no less anachronistic, realistic trivia forming a part of everyday life that poets with a taste for the sublime carefully avoid. Thus we hear of Priam's binoculars, Aeneas's tobacco, and Venus's makeup. Even the sexual aspect of the old stories – Dido's lust for Aeneas, or Apollo's for Daphne – is brought into sharper focus. Andromache's story of her life with Pyrrhus (*Virgile travesty*, Book 3) is replete with wife-beating, cuckoldry, and bottom-farce. Finally, and in this Scarron and Dassoucy improve upon Lalli, an I-narrator, the mock-author, constantly and obtrusively intrudes in the story, breaking the fluidity of Virgil's or Ovid's style, undercutting in his own voice the *pietas*, *lacrymae rerum*, and *bienséances* to be found in the original.

Scarron and Dassoucy are very funny writers, deserving a place in the tradition that extends from Jean Lemaire de Belges and Marot to La Fontaine, Voltaire, and Musset: *l'art de causer en vers*. They wield the light octosyllabic couplet with brio, achieving comic effect with an economy of means that never appears forced or malicious. Their verse gives an impression of unquenchable vitality, of spontaneity and nonchalance. Thus, working from a classical source, suppressing passages of no interest to their contemporaries or which provide little scope for comedy, and adding developments of their own, the greatest of these poets do not merely parody a text. They grant it an authentic new life in the modern world on their own terms.

It has been suggested that mock-epic is a denial of the heroic, that it can exist only in a time of decadence, when true epic has become impossible. In my opinion, this is not the case; on the contrary, burlesque usually pays tribute to the literary monument it parodies, appearing alongside of the most genuine manifestations of a differing esthetic. It is a fact that great masters of the comic also tried their hand at the 'real thing.' Bracciolini wrote *La Croce racquistata* (1605, 1611) as well as *Lo Scherno degli Dei* (1618); Lope de Vega composed epics in the style of Ariosto (*La hermosura de Angélica*, 1602) and Tasso (*Jerusalén conquistada*, 1609) as well as *La Gatomaquía* (1634). Pope composed *The Rape of the Lock* (1712, 1714), then devoted years to translating Homer (1715–20, 1725–6), and Voltaire wrote *La Henriade* (1728), then devoted years to *La Pucelle* (1762, 1773). Most significantly for the context of French burlesque, Brébeuf published his translation of the *Pharsalia* (1654–5), then travestied the first book of his own author and his own translation (1656). The wave of travesty hit France at the very time Saint-Amant, Le Moyne, Chapelain, Scudéry, and Desmarets were elaborating their formal epics. The *poème heroïque* and the burlesque epic coexisted in the 1640s and 1650s, in an amazing period of artistic creativity, which also saw the flowering of preciosity, baroque religious lyrics, heroic romance, tragi-comedy, and several of Corneille's greatest dramatic masterpieces.

On the other hand, it is true that only the seventeenth century and part of the eighteenth provided the requisite conditions for widespread epic travesty. In the Middle Ages and in the modern period some writers indeed viewed the masters of Antiquity with good-humored irony (Jean de Meun and Guillaume de Machaut; Giraudoux and Anouilh), but their publics were neither sufficiently grounded in the classics nor sufficiently obsessed with classical doings to permit full-fledged parody or pastiche. Only in the age of Lalli and Scarron do we find a relatively sizable audience of well-educated people, an elite grounded in a common culture based on Latin school-texts, with a keen sense of genre and literary norms. Theirs was an age of imitation and of convention, also of 'modernist' revolt, for people were sufficiently independent to laugh at the classics yet sufficiently close to the Renaissance also to love and honor them. Finally, it was a time of wit and paradox, of fashion and refinement, in which literature was a major subject of discussion, taken seriously, yet, like the rest of life, considered to be a social game.

The idea for France's greatest mock-epic was conceived in a drawing-room. Nicolas Boileau (1636–1711) was a member of the private Academy that met regularly in the home of Guillaume de Lamoignon, Premier Président du Parlement. According to the author's own testimony (the 'Avis au lecteur' of 1674 and of 1683) and from other sources, we know that one evening an animated discussion took place concerning the theory of epic. Boileau defended the position he was to uphold in *L'Art poétique*, that, like the *Iliad*, modern epics ought to contain a very simple plot ('peu de matière,' p. 1005). Someone, probably Lamoignon himself, recalled a humorous dispute ('un differend assez leger,' p. 189) that had recently (July– August 1667) torn apart the Sainte-Chapelle, and he laughingly challenged the critic-theoretician to compose a heroic poem on this *peu de matière*. Boileau no less laughingly accepted the challenge. He read passages of the work to Lamoignon and his friends, who reacted with enthusiasm. In 1674 he published Cantos 1–4 of *Le Lutrin*, and the entire poem (six Cantos) in 1683.[3]

Although *Le Lutrin* develops a vein of parody to be found throughout Boileau's opus, it is also true that the author of *L'Art poétique* consistently attacks the burlesque poets, the use of low style in respectable verse, and the juxtaposition of *sermo gravis* and *sermo humilis*. In the ninth of his *Réflexions critiques sur Longin*, for example, after quoting Longinus – '*Les mots bas sont comme autant de marques honteuses qui flétrissent l'expression*' – he declares: 'Il n'y a rien qui avilisse davantage un discours que les mots bas. On souffrira plutost, generalement parlant, une pensée basse exprimée en termes nobles, que la pensée la plus noble exprimée en termes bas' (p. 532).

There is, however, no major inconsistency in Boileau's stance. He and his great adversary Perrault are aware of two kinds of burlesque: one, which can be called thematic parody, where the contents remain true to the sublime while the form or style is lowered (Scarron, Dassoucy); the other, stylistic pastiche, in which a truly elegant, refined style is used to recount 'low' matter (Boileau himself). In the one, to quote Boileau, 'Didon et Enée parloient comme des Harangeres et des Crocheteurs'; whereas, in his poem, 'une Horlogere et un Horloger parlent comme Didon et Enée' (p. 1006). The man who became the Regent of Parnassus despised the burlesque vogue of the 1640s. He also believed that a more elegant, witty mock-epic was possible, one full of humor but which would not violate linguistic or social decorum. Although he was influenced by *la Secchia rapita*,

Tassoni's mixed style, containing travesty as well as high comic, is closer to Pulci, Ariosto, Saint-Amant, and, for that matter, the *Roman de Renard*, than it is to *Le Lutrin*. Boileau's claim to originality ('un Burlesque nouveau') is not unfounded. *Le Lutrin* is the first poem in France which deliberately and exclusively magnifies a trivial subject on an ambitious scale, the first mock-epic, in contrast to the more traditional form of burlesque travesty. It is this originality, and Boileau's greatness as an artist, that explain the success of *Le Lutrin* in France and abroad, especially in England where the poem was translated more than once and gave rise to Dryden's *Mac Flecknoe* (1682), Garth's *The Dispensary* (1699), and Pope's *The Rape of the Lock* (1712, 1714), and had a lesser but nonetheless sizable influence on Pope's masterpiece, *The Dunciad* (1728, 1743).

In one respect at least, *Le Lutrin* resembles Dante's *Commedia* and Villon's *Testament*. As with Dante and Villon, Boileau's is a restricted, provincial world created for a public as familiar with the immediate historical 'crisis' as was the author himself. Therefore, to understand *Le Lutrin*, modern readers have to be aware of events in the year 1667 that were known to the Lamoignon circle and became the basis for Boileau's narrative: Claude Auvry, Trésorier of the Sainte-Chapelle (the Prelate), had been quarreling over a long period of time with his canons and especially with their leader, Jacques Barrin, the Chanter; on 31 July, supported by the chaplains, Auvry had a lectern placed before Barrin's choir stall; Barrin and the other canons removed the lectern by force; both sides then went to court over the issue, which was arbitrated by Guillaume de Lamoignon, Boileau's patron. Boileau heard of the incident either from his favorite nephew, Gilles Dongois, a canon in the Chapel since 1663, or from Lamoignon.[4] Much of the pleasure for Boileau's public no doubt came from the fact that the principals in *Le Lutrin* all correspond to real people, Boileau's friends and acquaintances on the Ile de la Cité. They also probably enjoyed those episodes where the poet consciously deformed reality, which he did sufficiently to claim in the *Avis* that his work was largely fictional.

Thus, despite the most assiduous recent scholarship, there is a quality of local color, of complicity between the author and his public, that we will never be able to grasp in its entirety. However, granted that *Le Lutrin* reflects and deforms contemporary reality, it also is a work of art with more universal claims. While poking fun at some of his neighbors in the Sainte-Chapelle, Boileau also creates a work of literary satire directed against social classes and professional callings.

It is obvious, given the subject of *Le Lutrin*, that Boileau reserves his sharpest jibes for the clergy. They are mocked for a series of failings which, appropriately, can be assimilated to several of the capital sins.

*Gula.* The Prelate is so terrified by a bad dream that he places lunch in jeopardy:

> Le prudent Gilotin, son Aumônier fidele ...
> Luy montre le peril: Que midi va sonner:
> Qu'il va faire, s'il sort, refroidir le disner.
>     'Quelle fureur, dit-il, quel aveugle caprice,
> Quand le disner est prest, vous appelle à l'Office? ...
> Est-ce pour travailler que vous estes Prélat? ...
> Reprenez vos esprits, et souvenez-vous bien,
> Qu'un disner réchauffé ne valut jamais rien.'    (Canto 1: p. 193)

'Pleins de vin et d'audace' (p. 202), the wig-maker and his cohorts (two chaplains) set out to place a lectern in the chapel. And the next day the canons, who normally spend their evenings in cabarets, can be awakened only by a call for food in the refectory. Throughout the poem food and wine are used to bribe canons and priests, to encourage them to war. Boileau parodies the epic councils in Homer and Virgil with gluttonous clerical banquets. These voracious council-scenes, comically inappropriate in epic, represent actions particularly sinful for men of the cloth, who should partake of spiritual food, but who, instead, are degraded by the flesh and by too close an association with the kitchen (Curtius's *Küchenhumor*).

*Acedia.* Throughout his opus Boileau upholds the virtue of hard work, especially with regard to artistic creativity ('Discours au Roy,' *Satire 2*, *Epistre* 11, *Art Poétique*). In his *Réflexions critiques sur Longin* he praises the ancient moral purity and vigor in Homer, contrasting them with the Asianic softness that has since debased those golden times. We are not surprised to find in Canto 1 of *Le Lutrin* the pink, fat Prelate, swollen-faced in bed, having slept from breakfast to lunch:

> La Jeunesse en sa fleur brille sur son visage:
> Son menton sur son sein descend à double étage:
> Et son corps ramassé dans sa courte grosseur,
> Fait gemir les coussins sous sa molle épaisseur.    (Canto 1: p. 192)

And, once the crisis of the lectern is resolved, he proceeds to sleep from lunch to dinner. In Canto 4 when the Chanter would like to wake up his colleagues, two friends point out that this is impossible: how can a mere mortal make canons rise from their beds when, for thirty years now, the chapel bells have failed (p. 208)? Traditionally, *acedia* is an especially great temptation to men of the contemplative life, but, as Boileau intimates, these canons suffer not from Saturnian melancholia but from simple fleshly indolence. Food and wine, the stomach, the bed, creature comforts in general – Bakhtin's 'material bodily lower stratum' – this is the reality of their lives. And it is the imposition of the flesh, the juxtaposition of the reality of Parisian canons' epicurean existence with the spiritual ideal they are expected to uphold, that generates humor.

*Superbia* and *Invidia*. Boileau's mock-epic war revolves around a quarrel over prerogatives: who has the right to place a lectern in the Sainte-Chapelle and who is to bless the congregation, the Prelate or the Chanter? The Prelate is obsessed with making the sign of the cross, a privilege of his (Claude Auvry's) former state as Bishop of Coutances; the Chanter dreads the Prelate's benediction, while at the same time he seeks to exercise the latter's privileges in his absence. These men will do anything, will destroy the world, in order that each may maintain his rights. As Sidrac exhorts the Prelate:

> Pour soûtenir tes droits, que le Ciel authorise,
> Abisme tout plûtost, c'est l'esprit de l'Eglise.
> C'est par là qu'un Prelat signale sa vigueur.    (Canto 1: p. 195)

In spite of the external splendor and ceremonial of their lives, these churchmen live an existence of petty cabal, of plot and counterplot over trifles. And the whole neighborhood becomes involved. In a sort of ecclesiastical class struggle, the Prelate and the chaplains join forces against the canons; a burgher from outside the walls is drawn in, followed by President Lamoignon. In the end both sides are humiliated; their most energetic efforts lead only to total loss of prerogative when they must turn to an arbiter, and they become the laughing-stock of Paris.

*Ira.* The allegorical figure Discorde is associated with monks in the *Orlando furioso*, Boileau's immediate source. In *Le Lutrin*, Discorde soars from a Franciscan monastery to a convent of Minims, her habitual haunts, furious that one church in France resists her. And soon the Sainte-Chapelle also comes under her sway, two factions squaring off and indulging in physical violence. It is inappropriate that clergymen, devoted to the spiritual life, should exchange blows. The situation is rendered even more comic by the fact that these 'saints Guerriers' (p. 212) allied in 'pieuses ligues' (p. 194), who try to act like epic heroes, like warriors, give battle so ineptly that their clerical nature shows through. The night-invaders scatter like schoolboys caught smoking (Canto 3). And when they and their enemies finally do engage in arms (Canto 5), they prove to be gouty old men capable only of tossing at each other works of literature. In this absurd Battle of the Books, this parody on a literary dispute, no one is injured, and 'ce Prelat terrible' (p. 191) obtains victory by making the sign of the cross over his adversaries, forcing them to kneel. Boileau paints in mock-heroic terms the Prelate's feat in benediction ('l'insulte sacré,' p. 217), how the epic hero, remembering his old powers, overthrows an army with his right hand.

That clergymen are guilty of the most crass ignorance, although not a mortal sin, is nonetheless subject to comic reproach in the only profession where culture and learning are presupposed, deemed responsible for *translatio studii*. According to Boileau, the *translatio* never reached Saint Louis's chapel, even though a bookshop is located near the main entrance. In Canto 4 the canons discuss what to do about the lectern. An old pedant, Alain, so learned that he even knows the Latin of Thomas à Kempis (!), takes the floor. 'Ce sçavant Canoniste' (p. 210) suggests that the erection of a lectern in the chapel derives from a Jansenist plot: the Jansenists have perchance discovered in Saint Augustine that a desk-precedent was set by Saint Louis. And he proposes that the canons return to the books in order to refute their adversaries. Evrard, the specialist in wine and strong blows, intervenes, admitting that he reads the Bible as much as the Koran, but at least he knows the sources of the chapter's income and that they should waste no more time reading or talking but act at once to remove the hated desk:

> 'Vingt muids rangez chez moy font ma Bibliotheque.
> En plaçant un Pupitre on croit nous rabbaisser,
> Mon bras seul sans Latin sçaura le renverser.
> Que m'importe qu'Arnaud me condamne ou m'approuve?
> J'abbats ce qui me nuit par tout où je le trouve.
> C'est là mon sentiment. A quoy bon tant d'apprests?
> Du reste déjeûnons, Messieurs, et beuvons frai.'    (Canto 4: p. 211)

In this scene Boileau mocks the proud, money-conscious ignorance of the one canon as much as the pretentious pedantry of the other. Evrard's materialism does not befit one of God's servants, although it is perhaps to be expected in an allegedly degenerate age. (In Canto 6 Piété rails against these modern times when indolence, vice, and ambition infest the Church, and money buys tiaras and mitres.) We must not forget, however, that, despite his faults, Evrard is authentically materialistic and lucid in his ignorance. Furthermore, for all his pretentiousness, Alain is no less unlettered than his colleague. Thomas à Kempis's *Imitatio Christi* is a devotional work written in simple medieval Latin, and only a consummate fool could be unaware that Augustine lived seven full centuries before Louis ix.

Next to the Sainte-Chapelle lies the Palais de Justice. In *Le Lutrin* the evils of the law are embodied in one of the Prelate's followers, the old chaplain Sidrac. This worthy proclaims that although perhaps clergymen

spend their time praying in the provinces, in Paris they plead before tribu-
nals (Canto 1); for years he himself has defended the honor of the Church
against all monsters of the Law (Canto 3); and in Canto 5 he consults the
sybil Chicane, imploring her to answer him, an old friend who has served
her his entire lifetime and poured ink onto her altar for decades. Significantly, these cowardly chaplains and canons are accustomed to fighting with
paper and ink; no less significantly, Boileau depicts the Palais de Justice in
mock-epic terms, as an infernal grotto, a demonic temple, the cave of a
monster, inhabited by an idol, a devourer associated with lions, serpents,
and owls and surrounded by horrid allegories: Disette, Famine, les Cha-
grins, and Ruine. It is blasphemous for clergymen to bow down before
such a false god, a true calf of gold, whom Sidrac wishes to bribe. And the
chaplains are justly punished for their sin, for the oracle gives them perfi-
dious advice (p. 214), true and yet false, which, wrongly interpreted, spurs
them on to destruction.

   Boileau's canons relish some pleasures of the flesh – eating and drinking,
for example. His two burghers, the wig-maker and his wife, named Didier
and Anne *Delamour*, indulge in that other aspect of the 'material bodily
lower stratum': sex. Boileau depicts conjugal passion discreetly yet with
sensuous allusions to kisses, caresses, and the bed:

> 'Au nom de nos baisers jadis si pleins de charmes;
> Si mon cœur de tout temps facile à tes desirs
> N'a jamais d'un moment differé tes plaisirs;
> Si pour te prodiguer mes plus tendres caresses
> Je n'ay point exigé ni sermens ni promesses;
> Si toi seul à mon lit enfin eus toûjours part,
> Differe au moins d'un jour ce funeste départ.'    (Canto 2: p. 197)

Perhaps this *fabliau*-type love is considered funny in and of itself, proper
only for base, ill-bred people incapable of appreciating the refinements of
seventeenth-century *fin' amor*. In the wig-maker's case Boileau undermines
the relationship still further by revealing that the winds of passion blow
from one side only: the wife's. Delamour desired her in the past, but that
was before they wed: I didn't want to marry you and become your slave,
he says; if I had my way, I would still be free! (p. 198). Thus the best of love
is reserved for a state of unsanctified fornication, a mortal sin as much for
burghers as for canons. In a passage suppressed from the 1683 edition and
thereafter, Boileau has Renomée proclaim that even now, in marriage, the
wig-maker continues to fornicate, that is he deceives Anne with another
woman (p. 1010, note 'c'). And, of course, he and his wife relive their old
adulterous amours in speech, and thus fall into sin again. Anne grants that it

would be excusable for him to quit her bed if he were making a wig, to earn money. Sex and lucre are both deemed more important than her husband's concerns. She is selfish and petty, yet given how ridiculous the war of the lectern turns out to be, less foolish than Delamour, who thinks he is committing great deeds for a prelate, the Church, and heaven (p. 198). For, if Anne is capable of Carthaginian passion, her spouse is hardly the most worthy embodiment of Roman reason, and his sense of duty is wasted on a trifle. It is absurd for burghers to try to lead the heroic life, as if they were Condé or Turenne, and they are doubly absurd to expend their heroism on a quarrel over the lectern.

The twelfth-century *Roman de Renard* undermines institutions and classes – the nobles, the king, the clergy, feudal law – and two of the most fashionable literary genres of the day: *chanson de geste* and *roman courtois*. In much the same way, in the age of Louis xiv Boileau mocks real people, social forces, and books. He deforms contemporary reality, viewing it from the perspective of a literary convention, and deflates literary ideals by juxtaposing them to the tawdry reality of ordinary people living in seventeenth-century Paris. Unlike that of Scarron and Dassoucy, his parody is not limited to any one classic, however pre-eminent; instead, he borrows traits from epics ancient and modern and from contemporary tragedy. *Le Lutrin* undercuts grand sentiments wherever they are to be found: in Homer, Virgil, Tasso, Chapelain, Scudéry, Corneille, and Racine. Boileau begins with a mock proposition ('Je chante les combats, et ce Prelat terrible ...') and invocation; he writes in an appropriately elevated, chaste style, with occasional Homeric similes; and he tells of a full-fledged, miniature War of Troy, 'un second Ilion' (p. 222). More than one of Curtius's topics finds a place here, *in risu*: something never said before, inexpressibility, *fortitudo et sapientia*, the book as symbol, poetry as perpetuation and entertainment, and brevity as a stylistic ideal. Part of the charm for well-educated readers comes from recognizing traditional epic motifs when they appear in the most unexpected places (a form of comic intertextuality), from Boileau's ingenuity at disguising his canons and chaplains in classical dress. Council scenes take place at the refectory table, where imprecation barely triumphs over the call of the stomach. Epic heroes are reduced to the level of types in Roman comedy: the parasite (the Prelate), the *senex iratus* (the Chanter), the pedant (Alain), and the churl (Evrard). The wise counselor, say Achates or the aged Nestor, is transformed into a *dolosus servus* or *gracioso*: a valet ('le zelé Gilotin,' p. 194; 'le vigilant Girot,' p. 206) and an old habitué of law courts. The voyage to the Underworld, to consult a sacred oracle in a no less sacred grotto (*Odyssey* 11, *Aeneid* 6), is reduced to a tour of the Palais de Justice. And the heroes are assailed by monsters, by hideous shadow-figures from the Other

World, which turn out to be an owl (a delightful reincarnation of the Bird of Athene) and the lectern itself, when, in the form of an oneiric dragon, it terrifies the sleeping Chanter (Canto 4). Although stout men undertake a night sortie (as in the *Iliad*, the *Aeneid*, the *Orlando furioso*, and the *Gerusalemme liberata*), they are armed with saw, hammer, and nails, their purpose is to move a lectern, and they are routed by the screeching of an owl. Finally, a pitched battle does occur, next to Barbin's bookshop, where the only casualties are felled with weighty romances or tomes on canon law and put to sleep by the esthetically soporific verse of Louis Le Laboureur. Thus the *fortitudo et sapientia* of ancient epic ceases to function in a modern non-aristocratic world; thus *pius Aeneas* is re-embodied in selfish, materialistic clerics obsessed with the most petty of ecclesiastical prerogatives.

Boileau's relation to, and reaction against, an earlier literary tradition will answer scholars who criticize him for having created thin, stereotyped characters. On the one hand, he perhaps did so intentionally, to demonstrate that the heroes of Le Moyne, Scudéry, Chapelain, and Desmarets lack credibility. In addition, from a Bergsonian perspective, it would be disastrous for a comic writer to depict characters other than as stereotypes, for he must prevent the public from feeling sympathy for, or identifying with, them. However, to some extent each camp does manifest a coherent psychology. The lazy, genteel Prelate, seconded by the prudent Gilotin and old Sidrac, embody decadent *sapientia* (according to the system of humors, an excess of phlegm), whereas the more anxious, insecure Chanter and the violent, free-drinking Evrard represent a parody of *fortitudo* (an excess of choler). Evrard and his canons would have routed the chaplains but for the Prelate's crafty blessing. Be this as it may, the characters on both sides are alike in their petty egocentric obsessions and in that, given the grandiloquent language they employ and the heroic deeds they propose to wage, they are all inauthentic beings acting perpetually in bad faith.

Although an epic should treat spiritual matters, the quest for a New Troy, for example, Boileau's trivial characters are embroiled in the most insignificant, materialistic of situations. Furthermore, men of the cloth, of the first Estate, should eschew worldly temptations in favor of God's service; yet they do just the opposite. This juxtaposition of the physical and the spiritual generates humor. Hence a pattern of soft, luxurious, sensuous imagery – the pink, fat Prelate lying in his feather-bed or the 'embonpoint des Chanoines' and 'vermillion des Moines' at Cîteaux (p. 199); pâtés, soup, and wine; darkness and the quiet of the alcove; and the soporific volumes by Le Laboureur and the light one by Quinault. War develops inside the walls of the Sainte-Chapelle, in this concrete, sensuous world of food, intimacy, and everyday reality. Characters are obsessed not only with honors but with physical objects, specifically the lectern itself, the title-piece of Boileau's poem. The *lutrin* is, so to speak, the fulcrum on which the action turns, because the characters concentrate their energies on it rather than on the true causes of their quarreling, for which the lectern is only a pretext, indeed a symptom. Like the Chanter's baton and the Prelate's mitre, it becomes a false, absurd mediator for power. Finally, books serve as missiles in a mock-war rather than as works of art or compendia of knowledge. Boileau satirizes bad contemporary writings by concretizing their esthetic weakness, by taking literally certain metaphoric qualities – heaviness, superficiality – he claims they possess.

The law courts and the chapel are separated in space. Between them, contiguous to the Sainte-Chapelle, lies Barbin's shop, the point of contact between the two opposing sides. Yet, paradoxically, although these ignorant canons and chaplains are in constant proximity to books, they never consult them. Nor should they, for the available reading matter is trash that sees the light of day for the first time in Canto 5 and is good only to serve in a farcical brawl:

> O que d'Ecrits obscurs, de Livres ignorez
> Furent en ce grand jour de la poudre tirez!
> Vous en fustes tirez, Almerinde et Simandre:
> Et toy, rebut du peuple, inconnu Caloandre,
> Dans ton repos, dit-on, saisi par Gaillerbois,
> Tu vis le jour alors pour la premiere fois.   (Canto 5: p. 215)

The battle scene has one useful purpose: to purge Barbin's shop of the worst that the book trade spews forth, just as one goal of Boileau's satirical epic and of his opus as a whole is to purge the literary taste of his day. Additional irony is generated by the fact that it is Barbin who, in association, published *Le Lutrin*!

In similar fashion, although the Prelate and the Chanter are obsessed with a lectern, an object that exists to aid verbal delivery during holy service, neither man speaks to the other in the course of the poem. The adversaries do not communicate other than by hurling missiles. Even within the two camps viable exchange proves to be difficult: the wig-maker and his wife speak at cross-purposes, and the Chanter, who finds almost superhuman obstacles to waking up the canons, is obviously incapable of marshalling them. The failure of traditional epic rhetoric is exemplified when these pitiable characters are persuaded to do what ought not to be done, against all rules of basic common sense. In this light perhaps the most significant act of 'communication' is the enigma pronounced by Chicane, a false oracle which serves only to deceive (Canto 5).

Although the canons do not speak to the Prelate, they most certainly behold him and his blessing; and it is the sight of the lectern, first in the Chanter's dream, then in waking reality, that drives him wild. However, the Chanter's rage derives not from the fact that the lectern will be seen, but that he will not, that is, that he will be hidden behind it, viewed only by God: 'Inconnu dans l'Eglise, ignoré dans ce lieu, / Je ne pourai donc plus estre vû que de Dieu?' (p. 208). And the canons seek desperately to escape from the Prelate's blessing. For years the lectern lay buried in the sacristy; now it is brought out; but, after Ariste's arbitration, it will be hidden again. Bad books stay indoors, unread in a dark bookshop, while Chicane lurks in her grotto, far from the light of day. It is thus epistemologically and morally proper for these characters to act at night. In the darkness the wig-maker and his wife discourse or make love, canons drink in cabarets, and the lectern is put into its place. Only in a moment of crisis do clerics rise in the early morning, causing, in mock-epic terms, the Dawn to recoil before unknown faces! (p. 212). Given Boileau's general exaltation of light as an esthetic, moral, religious, and critical force,[5] we can readily understand the implied criticism he makes of these people of the shadows.

In spite of the quarreling generated in the first five cantos of *Le Lutrin*, Boileau's ecclesiastical conflict is resolved in Canto 6, and the poem ends on a happy, moral note. The war between the chaplains and the canons is ended, peace is restored to the Sainte-Chapelle, and, although the times are recognized to be corrupt, Thémis guarantees the integrity of the Church:

> Envain de tes Sujets l'ardeur est ralentie,
> D'un ciment éternel ton Eglise est bastie,
> Et jamais de l'Enfer les noirs frémissemens
> N'en sçauroient ébranler les fermes fondemens.    (Canto 6: p. 220)

Boileau's comedy ends happily: the 'humorous,' obstructing society is purged and rendered healthy, presumably transformed into a congenial one; rigid individuals give way before a more resilient, vital, humane civilization.

From the beginning to the end of his career Boileau proclaims the necessity of order in public life and exalts Louis xiv as the image of France, a monarch who embellishes the modern age.[6] In *Le Lutrin* Louis is praised for his martial energy (in contrast to bygone *rois fainéants*) and for having reformed the Church. He is a demigod, responsible for the glory of his century; and the country, its Church, its literature all strive for one goal: to illustrate *his* glory. Indeed, in these new, unheroic times, the sun-king remains the only true hero: all revolves around him.[7]

Now King Louis's delegate in the world of the Sainte-Chapelle, the arbiter who establishes peace and justice, is Ariste, who becomes the hero (or hero-surrogate) of *Le Lutrin*. An 'homme d'un sçavoir étonnant' (p. 189), this embodiment of *sapientia* commits an intellectual exploit ('art tout-puissant,' p. 221) in the tradition of Solomon to reconcile the two adversaries. Through him, Piété and Thémis overcome the impiety and chicanery that dominated the action up to the moment of his intervention. Furthermore, unlike the Sainte-Chapelle's decadent clerics, Ariste lives in the real world. As devout as they ought to be, he has a 'pieté ... fort gaye' (p. 190) and is, therefore, capable of appreciating mock-epic. This 'fameux Heros' (p. 191) and 'Homme incomparable' (p. 220) stands for the author's patron, Guillaume de Lamoignon, who embodies forces of civilization bettering France and the Church under Louis xiv. And Lamoignon has also contributed to the betterment of the poet Despréaux. As close a relationship exists between the Narrator (implied author) and Ariste as between the Boileau and Lamoignon who really lived in the seventeenth century. Boileau praises Lamoignon-Ariste generously and, in the last canto, this personage outside the action becomes the hero. Unlike the *Aeneid, Le Lutrin* is a modern poem telling a modern story; in a world of fools, of dupers and dupes, there is no place for Aeneas, but a Maecenas can deflate ridiculous *milites gloriosi* who think they are Aeneases. Since the modern poet is the contemporary of his hero and patron, by making this latter individual the protagonist of a mock-epic Boileau renews the tradition of panegyric as well as of the heroic.

True communication does occur finally in *Le Lutrin*. In Canto 6 Piété speaks to Thémis and to Ariste, whereupon the latter makes peace between the Prelate and the Chanter and presumably causes them to address each other. Unlike others, Ariste is not a casuist who creates discord with language. The implied author, on the other hand, apparently succeeds no better than his comic characters. He appeals to his muse and to Ariste, claiming that he is not capable of ending the poem properly, that to describe the feats of such a hero (Ariste) is beyond his powers. Literally speechless, he urges Ariste to conclude the story himself:

> Parle donc: c'est à Toy d'éclaircir ces merveilles ...
>      Aussi-bien, quelque ardeur qui m'inspire,
> Quand je songe au Heros qui me reste à décrire,
> Qu'il faut parler de Toy, mon Esprit éperdu
> Demeure sans parole, interdit, confondu.    (Canto 6: pp. 221–2)

This self-deprecation serves to undermine a traditional motif: that of the author of epic, the Ronsardian *vates*. An example of Curtius's 'inexpressibility,' it is also a means for winning the reader's sympathy according to the principles of *captatio benevolentiae*. Boileau intervenes obtrusively in the story not out of real humility but in order to serve as a bridge between Ariste and the public, to establish his authority, and to mold the implied reader's norms and beliefs. He is the charming, ironic, self-conscious master behind the scenes, who keeps us informed and connives with us against his own characters. The satirist must hold the reader's attention, win his sympathy, and disarm potential criticism. Undermining the dignified tradition of epic-bard is appropriate in mock-heroic; pointing attention to himself or to his narrative *persona* reinforces his presence in the story and reminds us of his authorial stance in the *Satires* and *Epistres*: *l'ami du vrai*, an honest man, clumsy but fearless, a poet unfit for the sublime but driven to tell the truth to a corrupt world, endowed by the gods with a gift for satire.[8] That this pose is as conventional, as artificial (cf. Horace, Juvenal, Régnier) as any other takes nothing away from its effectiveness. Generations of readers have accepted Boileau's pseudo-autobiographical declarations, which permit the Narrator to associate himself with Ariste and with civilizing forces in society. His presence helps to create a detached yet sympathetic and humane tone for the poem as a whole.

The best communication takes place between the mock-author and Ariste, and between the mock-author and his public. By assimilating his hero to his patron, Boileau fuses epic action and the action of writing an epic. In this comic poem written on poetry, it is particularly appropriate that the writer should end his work ironically with an avowal of creative impotence. But he is not impotent, nor is his poem a failure. This 'bagatelle' (p. 189), 'un Ouvrage de pure plaisanterie' (p. 190), is more truthful and esthetically more beautiful than the weighty tomes employed in the Battle of the Books. Ultimately, the triumph of *Le Lutrin* is one of parody and pastiche of language; and it is through writing, through the book, that Boileau maintains his friendship with Ariste, proves his esthetic theories to be correct,[9] and creates a work of art. After all, mock-epic is by definition a genre which presupposes another genre for its very existence; it is literature parodying and pastiching literature. Relating to literary norms, it is successful only in an age when the reader's awareness is at its peak.

Boileau has the gift of arousing passion in his readers. He is one of the most adulated and condemned of the great French classics; no one remains indifferent to him; and each age interprets him confidently in its own image. Nowadays, we no longer accept the myth of Boileau the classic rule-giver, the Regent of Parnassus. But other myths – the man of sincerity, the realist – have endured. I discussed the sincerity-motif earlier in some remarks on narrative technique. The question of realism is more complex. *Le Lutrin* does reflect, more than any other poem treated in this book, contemporary events, current problems, and live, historically verifiable characters. Unlike the authors of *geste*, Chrétien de Troyes, Guillaume de Lorris, Ronsard, Saint-Amant, and Le Moyne, Boileau does examine questions of money, the law, and petty, bureaucratic prestige; his people

are of the low or lower-middle classes, whether in the ecclesiastical or lay
hierarchy; they act within precise calendar time and a no less precise
geographically delineated space (an urban environment); their names and
titles are, for the most part, eminently plausible within a contemporary
French context. Boileau evokes concrete reality, a sense of things, of property, of the external world, depicting intracultural tensions centered in
seventeenth-century Paris. His is a modern, prosaic, problematic world
inhabited by unheroic characters of the lower orders. But he treats these
beings and their problems in comic fashion, refusing to take them seriously,
or, instead, succeeds in creating a comic effect because he pretends to take
them seriously. Since the 'world' of the chaplains and canons is reflected
through the artificially literary lens of mock-epic, it is deformed beyond
recognition and so much distance is established that for modern readers *Le
Lutrin* appears to be less 'realistic' than, say, *Raoul de Cambrai* or *Les
Tragiques*. Similarly, the most realistic of the *Satires*, focusing upon a dinner
party or the noises of Paris, are conscious adaptations of Horace, Juvenal,
and Régnier. In the seventeenth century the *Kreatürlich* simply cannot be
treated in the sublime style; we have to await the fiction of Balzac and
Zola for it to accede to the honors of *sermo gravis*.

Boileau portrays a degraded, reified world, in which not only have false
values – prestige, hierarchy – usurped a position of choice, but a physical
object, the lectern, becomes the focus for life in the community, the
mediator to happiness and glory. Writing for a high bourgeois, even aristocratic public, Boileau undermines clerics and the petty bourgeoisie. Yet
his society still contains sufficient homogeneity and moral certitude for him
to proclaim the functioning (with Ariste and King Louis) of a superior
scale of values. This traditional ethos is upheld in an active, indeed militant
way.

Boileau's petty world is set against an ideal, its excesses contrasted to an
inherent classical *aurea mediocritas*. The author delights in his little world
yet is aware of its flaws. He proclaims the triumph of tradition and authority. The end of *Le Lutrin* brings about the desired victory, and a synthesis
of urbanity, piety, and justice. These more universal values provide unity
and depth to what might otherwise have been merely a *Virgile travesty* of
the court. Thus Boileau's wit, his studied illusion of negligence and even
inexpressibility, mask an eminently serious concern, and the seemingly
commonplace happy ending and apparently trite moral remarks give expression to a serious classical ideal. He unmasks man's flawed, unheroic nature
and indicates how it can be, if not improved, at least rendered tolerable
through appropriate political and esthetic control.

*Le Lutrin*, a splendid comic text, succeeding where Scarron's and Dassoucy's travesties ultimately failed, manifests fun, gratuitous wit, and intel-

lectual play and is an exquisite esthetic construction. Highly civilized mock-heroic works such as *Le Lutrin* or *The Rape of the Lock* form the appropriate epic for the late neoclassical and rococo periods, self-conscious eras lacking genuine heroism. They illustrate what we have come to recognize as the literary crisis of Louis XIV's reign.[10] Treating private instead of public concerns, undermining heroic, national, and religious ideals, concerned with concrete everyday reality, they are hallmarks of a new, more modern epoch. And Boileau succeeded in writing a better, more 'classical' epic on his trivial subject than Desmarets and Chapelain were able to write on the exploits of Clovis and Joan of Arc. His wit and grace contribute to the elaboration of a veritable jewel of society poetry, *dulce* and *utile*, succeeding admirably in both domains.

With his romantic and symbolist prejudices, the modern reader often denies the name of poet to Boileau and the men of his generation. We insist upon criteria generally absent from French letters between 1660 and 1820: concrete, striking imagery; individuality of voice; the illusion of an authentic, subjective experience or sentiment; and divergence of poetic speech from other kinds of discourse. However, this is a recent tradition in the history of civilization, absent not only from European Classicism but also, to a greater or lesser extent, from the early literatures of China, Japan, India, Arabia, and Persia. In France and England of the late seventeenth and eighteenth centuries is to be found a different kind of poetry, one closer to prose or to the refined style of elegant, worldly conversation, based on convention, decorum, taste, and judgment, and receiving much of its effect from metaphysical wit. Its hallmarks are impersonality, abstraction, normalcy in syntax, rhyme, and meter, intellectual and esthetic clarity, and a chaste diction, varying according to genre and mode but avoiding at all costs paradox, extravagance, and literary impropriety. In French literature both styles or modes are to be found in abundance: the 'romantic' verse of Villon, Scève, d'Aubigné, Le Moyne, the symbolists, and, in our day, Perse, Char, and Bonnefoy; and the more 'classical' tradition of the trouvères, Chrétien de Troyes, Guillaume de Lorris, Guillaume de Machaut, Charles d'Orléans, Marot, La Fontaine, Chénier, and, in the twentieth century, Supervielle and Prévert. Although for some moderns Boileau's verse may be harder to appreciate than, say, Mallarmé's, it is no less truly poetical. It is time we modified our definitions of poetry in order to take into account all modes and all traditions.

## Chapter Twelve

# 🕊 VOLTAIRE

The eighteenth century – age of the Rococo and of the Enlightenment – represents, for Western Europe at least, a nadir in serious epic. The language of Spenser and Milton produced Glover's *Leonidas* (1737) and Wilkie's *Epigoniad* (1757); the language of Ariosto, Tasso, and Marino, comparable mediocrities. Only in Germany, with Klopstock's *Messias* (1748–73), do we find a resurgence of the long, sublime poem, in the line of du Bartas and Milton; Klopstock has to be considered a precursor of German Classicism and perhaps an exemplar of what nowadays is designated Pre-Romanticism. Disdain for the heroic is manifest in the *Encyclopédie*, which contains a short article ('Le Héros') by Louis de Jaucourt: Jaucourt assimilates his subject to the warrior, rating him lower than truly great men – rulers or civilizers. Significantly, no article on the hero or the heroic is to be found in Voltaire's *Dictionnaire philosophique*; the Sage of Ferney downgrades some epic protagonists of the past, such as Samson, and ignores others, such as Achilles, Hercules, Theseus, and Ulysses. The men of the Enlightenment, including Voltaire, tended to denigrate war and war-making and to sap the reputation of famous conquerors, the principal exceptions being present-day autocrats (Frederick the Great, Catherine the Great) to whom they offered copious adulation.[1]

This attitude did not prevent Voltaire from including in the same *Dictionnaire philosophique* a serious, well-thought-out article entitled 'l'Epopée.' An incapacity to live the old ideals prevented no one from speculating on the nature of, and writing versions of, epic. Indeed, despite repeated failures, the prestige of the genre remained high, and people ever awaited the appearance of a Gallic Virgil. As in the two preceding centuries, the heroic poem kept the place of honor in theoretical treatises. In more practical terms, although in quantitative decline from the 1650s and 1660s, thirty-six verse epics were published in the course of the century; some in the line of *Paradise Lost* and Voltaire's own *Henriade*; some treating the discovery and exploration of the Americas; and some of an encyclopedic, scientific bent. Another fourteen 'epics in prose' were derived for the most part from Fénelon's *Télémaque*. To these we must add quite a few ambitious works, in prose and verse, which were not completed, and a series of important translations of the great classical texts: in France, Houdar de la Motte's *Iliad*, Marmontel's *Pharsalia*, and *Aeneids* by Segrais and Desfontaines; in England, successful versions of the *Iliad* and *Odyssey* by both Pope and Cowper. It is no doubt also appropriate to include under the category of the long sublime poem works of sacred didacticism such as Louis Racine's *La Grâce* (1720) and *La Religion* (1742), and Bernis's *La Religion vengée* (1795); and works of secular didacticism such as Saint-Lambert's *Les Saisons* (1769), Roucher's *Les Mois* (1779), and a series of descriptive poems by the Abbé Delille. The didactic texts are largely innovative. However, those in the heroic, narrative vein perpetuate the seventeenth-century neoclassical model, with emphasis on civic morality, the abundant use of allegory, and striving for an elegant, refined style. Although they manifest some freedom of imagination and a limited experimentation in depicting the supernatural, we judge almost all of them to be failures.[2]

The notable exceptions are, of course, Voltaire's own works. It is to be expected that the François-Marie Arouet (1694–1778) who dominated his century in its major literary and philosophical endeavors should also have striven to make a mark in the genre that Dryden called 'the greatest Work which the Soul of Man is capable to perform.'[3] Voltaire's *Essay upon the Epick Poetry of the European Nations* in its many editions, French and English, his articles for the *Dictionnaire philosophique* and the *Questions sur l'Encyclopédie*, and his offhand remarks in *Candide*, *Essai sur les mœurs*, and the correspondence make him one of the leading authorities on the subject. *La Henriade* (1728)[4] was the most influential heroic poem of the age; in spite of its failings, it is also the best in France and the only one in all of Latin and Anglo-Saxon Europe comparable in quality to Klopstock's *Messias*.

At the age of twenty-two, François-Marie Arouet began work on his heroic poem (1716). Influenced by the last phase of the Querelle des Anciens et Modernes, inspired by the counsel of the Abbé du Bos, whose *Réflexions critiques sur la poésie et la peinture* appeared in 1719 (completed in 1733), young Voltaire, while adhering to the conventions of neoclassical epic, was attracted to a modern, patriotic subject: the life of King Henry IV. Voltaire's version stressed royal legitimacy and national unity, criticized seditious lords and a hypocritical clergy, and exalted the ideal of political independence from Spain and Rome through an alliance with England. Although this by no means coincidental support of the policies of Philippe d'Orléans succeeded in assuring the Regent's approbation (1721), the poem failed to pass censure. A clandestine edition of *La Ligue* was published in Rouen in 1723; it contained 3,200 lines divided into nine books. In the ensuing years Voltaire worked hard, polishing his epic, adding a tenth book (Book 6 in subsequent editions) and over 1,100 lines. In 1726 he went to England, his aim to sell the poem on Henry IV. Assisted by a splendid publicity campaign, including two treatises purportedly composed in English (*Essay upon the Epick Poetry*; *Essay upon the Civil Wars*), and by the flagrantly pro-British sentiments that had been introduced into the work, it was published in London in 1728, under a new title, *La Henriade*, to universal acclaim. Sixty editions appeared during Voltaire's lifetime, and the poem was translated into practically all European tongues and praised to the skies by leading writers of the day: Vauvenargues, Prévost, Marmontel, Baculard d'Arnaud, Diderot, d'Alembert, Buffon, Gilbert, Condorcet; it was imitated by quite a few poetasters with heroic ambitions, and even endured the tribute of parody (cf. chapter eleven, pp. 259–60). Only in the second half of the century, when people began to ask from poetry more imagination and emotion than young Voltaire was prepared to give, did some critics suspect that *La Henriade* might be less than a masterpiece.

Even with du Bos's encouragement, it was an act of daring for Voltaire to choose as the protagonist of an epic a modern hero, dead for only one century. However, with unerring flair he correctly chose the right man, a national figure benefitting from all the prestige of Le Moyne's Saint Louis but unencumbered with the latter's out-of-date piety, one who saved France at a critical moment in his country's history and ushered in the Splendid Century. Thus Voltaire refuses to evoke a romantic, semi-mythical past. Already in the guise of a historian, he cites authorities in footnotes, is skeptical with regard to the supernatural, and indicates special concern for social background.[5] The future chronicler of Charles XII and Louis XIV and philosopher of *Essai sur les mœurs* shrewdly analyzes the psychology of the Parisian rabble at the end of the sixteenth century and the Machiavellian reasons that caused Catherine de' Medici to spare Henry of Navarre during the Saint Bartholomew's Day massacre. These are concrete historical battles he recounts, their outcome determined by men's wills and by the strong right arms of seasoned veterans, not by the miraculous interventions of Pallas Athene or Saint Michael. Henry is depicted as a great fighter indeed, but, over and above this, a great man, a *politique* in the line of Michel de l'Hospital, a far-seeing statesman and a human being, compassionate, just, and devoted to his people. This Fénelonian type embodies a new epic morality inconceivable in the worlds of Homer, Virgil, and Tasso. Although King Henry resembles Aeneas in his seeking to avoid strife, Voltaire's anti-militarism and his hatred for rebellious feudal barons, for the tyranny of the League, strike a new, humanitarian note. Queen Elizabeth is a great monarch because she has brought England peace, and Henry's most noteworthy quality is his refusal to destroy the enemy – his own people. In addition, Voltaire had already come to hate *l'infâme*. The dominant idea of *La Henriade*, the theme around which the narrative turns from beginning to end, is opposition to religious fanaticism in general, and the Roman Catholic Church in particular, because sectarian spirit is the greatest cause of war. Hence, the emotional reaction unleashed by the Saint Bartholomew's Day massacre, Jacques Clément's act of regicide, and the Black Mass celebrated by members of the League; hence also, lessons of tolerance and mutual trust, that men are brothers, all cults contain a measure of truth, and just people, regardless of affiliation, can hope to be saved. It is in the name of tolerance as well as peace that Henry pardons his enemies, proving to be so clement a victor. And it is appropriate, in this first poem of the Enlightenment, that Voltaire adopts traditional Christian light-imagery to his own purposes: thus the bright rays of Vérité and God's or Henry's sun and lightning destroy the leaguers' altars and the obscurity of outworn creeds.

The man who was to write *Candide* and *l'Ingénu* cannot tell a story badly. Although a historical epic patterned on the *Aeneid* and the *Liberata* does not provide the ideal context, Voltaire's narrative is rapid and seldom loses the reader's interest. He is at his best in the formal portrait. The strength and weaknesses of each personage – his courage or poltroonery, integrity or ruse, grandeur or baseness – are revealed in slashing, witty antitheses. This is, of course, a carryover from French Classicism. The author of *La Mort de César*, *Mérope*, and *Rome sauvée* was also at home in stoical, neo-Roman speeches of defiance: Bussy's effort to break the will of Parlement (Book 4), Potier's refusal to name a new king (Book 6), or d'Aumale's stubbornness in the face of defeat (Book 9). Whether or not Voltaire succeeded in integrating portraits, speeches, and narrative, whether or not he brought off 'great scenes,' is another matter. I am not particularly impressed by the Saint Bartholomew's Day massacre (Book 2). Unlike the majority of critics, I find it artificial and derivative; in contrast to d'Aubigné's handling of the material, Voltaire's imitation of French classical tragedy leaves me cold. On the other hand, the confrontation between Parlement and League in Book 4 and the rampant famine and cannibalism of Book 9 are more expressive. But, in my opinion, Voltaire's powers are in full display with the murder of Henry III. Profiting from a lucidity and sensitivity born from hatred, he probes into the psychology of the Catholic assassin, Jacques Clément, an austere, solitary, and obsessed personage who has been worked upon by others and who, unaware of what he is doing, commits a monstrous crime and goes happily to his doom.

Some contemporaries pointed out flaws in *La Henriade*: the poem is too short, the ending is abrupt, the author handles epic 'machinery' badly, he has written history not poetry, his work lacks imagination and an exciting plot, and the characters are wooden. Curiously, Voltaire himself, in the *Essay upon the Epick Poetry*, accuses Homer of failing to interest the reader in his characters, a criticism which generations of scholars have applied with far more justification to *La Henriade*. Like Petrarch's *Africa* and, to some extent, Ronsard's *Franciade*, Voltaire's poem is good in individual scenes, portraits, and descriptions – the classical set-piece – and it also manifests proportion with regard to overall narrative structure. All three poets fail, however, in the domains that ultimately determine our esthetic response: the hero, King Henry IV, carries no mythical, poetic aura; the supernatural, whether pagan, Christian, or allegorical, serves only an ornamental function; and the story, however well told, does not hold together. In other words, Chateaubriand was correct in observing that whereas Voltaire is a man of reason, the epic genre demands the gift of poetry. It is true, Voltaire had historical ambitions but was not capable of appreciating or resurrecting the truly picturesque, 'exotic' aspects of the past; nor did he succeed in making the age of Montaigne and d'Aubigné live anew. Although Henry of Navarre is idealized beyond credibility, his is only the stylized grandeur of an eighteenth-century benevolent despot. No idea or sentiment, neither loyalty to the crown nor tolerance, is rendered concrete in poetic terms. *La Henriade* lacks the enthusiasm, warmth, and sensitivity of Virgil and Tasso, the amplitude and quasi-mystic sublimity we have come to expect from neoclassical epic.

It is also possible to maintain that Voltaire's innovations with regard to the heroic poem, his notion of a modern epic with a modern hero (the *honnête homme*) and a modern *pietas* based on pity not piety, are admirable, that it is the academic form, the external detail carrying over from Louis XIV's century, which ruin the total effect.[6] While this may indeed be true, the failure of *La Henriade* cannot be ascribed only to the imitation of classical models. Camoens, Tasso, Saint-Amant, Le Moyne, and Milton imitated also. Unlike his forebears, however, Voltaire was unable to imprint his own personality on *La Henriade*; he did not know how to follow the conventions and free himself from their shackles at the same time. His characters are but the palest shadows of the old archetypes, and his plot merely repeats in mechanical fashion older, more magnificent wars on the plains of Troy, Latium, and Jerusalem. The love-anguish of Dido and Aeneas, or of Rinaldo and Armida, degenerates into a ridiculous pastiche when the God of Love forces Henry to forget the Siege of Paris in the arms of Gabrielle d'Estrées; and when, defying all laws of credibility, Voltaire has Henry of Navarre travel to England and recount the Saint Bartholomew's Day massacre to Queen Elizabeth, he does so, we fear, only because, even in this particular, Henry's career has to correspond to those of Odysseus and Aeneas.

Voltaire's *Henriade* is pre-eminently, ostentatiously a work of youth, the creation of a bookworm, who compiled an epic construct from his wide and more or less successfully assimilated reading. As a gifted pupil of the Jesuits, young Arouet resolved to become famous by writing the long-awaited French epic; following the dictates of his own pragmatic temperament, he gave the public exactly what it wanted: a structured, decorous neoclassical artifact with just enough innovation to pique the reader's curiosity without shocking his expectations. Handling the rules with the adroitness of a man twice his age, he perpetrated the illusion that his poem was truly in the Virgilian mode yet also intellectually and esthetically up to date. Skirting carefully between the Scylla of the Ancients and the Charybdis of the Moderns, Voltaire recognized the flaws in conventional epic machinery as he felt obliged to exploit them.

One of the finest manifestations of the eighteenth-century spirit is the problematic hero, a man of less than noble blood, who struggles with his environment in a new, exciting way. Such an 'unheroic hero' developed fully in the novel; there was a place for Gil Blas, Jacob, Saint-Preux, and Jacques le Fataliste in fictional prose; but fictional verse, bound by convention and decorum, could not express the new world view. Similarly, the spirit of the Enlightenment moved toward establishing a more truthful representation of modern life. Such 'truth' became possible in the Romantic period with epics devoted to domestic affairs or the inner life (*Hermann und Dorothea*, *The Prelude*, *Jocelyn*), but in Voltaire's day, with the long poem still committed to recounting martial events situated in the past, historical authenticity served only to undermine poetry. Voltaire's text, with its nobility and harmony of diction, flowing, elegant versification, force, grandiloquence, and pungent, biting satire, deserved a place of honor in the eighteenth century. Yet *La Henriade* is a failure. From the vantage-point of history, it appears quite small indeed when placed beside *Moyse sauvé* or *Saint Louis*, on the one side, or *Jocelyn* and *La Légende des Siècles*, on the other. And, despite our most sympathetic rationalizing, that is the final, unanswerable verdict.

In the age of Louis xv as in the Splendid Century, mock-epic plays an important role on the literary scene; for the parody of classical epos is often a more genuine artistic endeavor than serious heroic poems of the same period. We read Boileau, not Chapelain, Scudéry, or even Le Moyne; we read Pope's *Rape of the Lock* and *Dunciad*, not Glover's *Leonidas* or Wilkie's *Epigoniad*. In Germany the leading poet of the times proves to be not Klopstock but Wieland, master of the light touch and an ironic, witty

humanism, author of superbly fashioned long poems in the French and
Italian mode, the best of which are *Musarion* (1768), *Der neue Amadis*
(1771), and *Oberon* (1780): this latter, incidentally, is the finest modern
reworking of the *Huon de Bordeaux* story. In France Gresset's *Ver-Vert*
(1734) continues the tradition of *Le Lutrin*. This delightful piece (714
decasyllables) recounts the exploits and amours of a parrot, adulated by
Visitandine nuns. The anticlerical, antifeminist satire is exquisite, the theme
of language and communication treated with sophistication. Gresset's
text is supremely witty, yet I consider it to be equaled, indeed surpassed, by
a far more ambitious work – from the author of *La Henriade*! For thirty
years Voltaire worked on a long comic narrative treating the story of Joan of
Arc, a parody on Chapelain in the style of Ariosto. Although *La Pucelle
d'Orléans* was acclaimed by some of the most eminent public figures of the
age – Frederick the Great, Catherine the Great, and the kings of Poland,
Sweden, and Denmark, not to speak of Diderot, young La Harpe, Condorcet, Parini, Burns, and Mickiewicz – since the eighteenth century the
official French intellectual establishment has allowed it to fall into oblivion.
The poem was simply too bawdy, too blasphemous, too flippant toward
national myths for even the skeptics of the Third Republic to tolerate (Lanson's 'La froideur de cette polissonnerie étirée en vingt et un chants'[7] is
typical). But *La Pucelle* has recently been re-edited and is now attracting the
attention of scholars.[8] Time is ripe for a revaluation of what I consider to
be a true masterpiece.

Voltaire's comic epic was begun under circumstances comparable to
those which launched Boileau into writing *Le Lutrin*. Not long after the
publication of *La Henriade*, around 1730, Voltaire dined at the Hôtel of
the duc de Richelieu. Conversation having turned to Chapelain's *Pucelle*
(1656), the panegyrist of Henry the Great expressed scorn concerning
Chapelain's subject, the deeds of an illiterate peasant girl. When challenged
to improve upon Chapelain, Voltaire insisted that one could do so only in
the comic vein. And so he did. *La Pucelle* became his life's work. For thirty
years and more it was his pride, the joy of his idle moments, and his only
consistent relaxation. The major periods of composition extended from 1730
to 1735 and from 1759 to 1761, but at other times Voltaire returned to his
mock-epic, changing, polishing, inventing new episodes for the return of
old heroes. For, in the tradition of Ariosto, although the plot allegedly
focuses on Joan's career from Domremy to Orléans (including, as 'principal
subplot,' the parallel erotic career of Agnes Sorel, the king's mistress), in
fact *La Pucelle* encompasses an incredible variety of characters and incidents, and a wide range of satirical themes. Over the years manuscript
copies were sent to his friends, stolen, or copied against his will. The
history of the diffusion of these texts itself resembles a novel, replete with

comic misunderstanding and dangerous adventures. Suffice it to say, a
number of fraudulent copies (and, later, editions) were made public, containing explicit sexuality as well as criticism of the reigning monarch. Voltaire repudiated these travesties and sought to have them suppressed;
however, some contemporaries accused him of having composed and distributed them himself. Tension heightened in 1755 and 1756 when pirate
editions of *La Pucelle* were actually printed, placing the putative author
in danger of prison or exile. However, Voltaire weathered the storm and in
1762 published his own 'official' edition in Geneva (in twenty cantos), an
additional canto appearing in 1773.

Although *La Pucelle* is patterned after the *Orlando furioso*, Voltaire
differs from Ariosto in that his scenes of war are never beautiful in and of
themselves. As in *Candide*, *l'Histoire de Charles XII*, or, for that matter,
*La Henriade*, war is shown to be an act of folly that degrades all who take
part in it, the victors as well as the vanquished, the participants as well as
innocent bystanders. And the beauty of young love, a natural alternative to
war or clerical hypocrisy, is rendered all the more touching because almost
invariably it is exterminated by these monstrous forces that man unleashes
upon himself.

To the extent that war is waged by French and English armies on behalf of
their respective nations, national spirit is held up to ridicule. Among the
French notables besieged in Orléans (Canto 1) we find Louvet, a pompous,
pedantic cuckold; Richemont, a blasphemer; and La Trimouille, a tender
lover and good Catholic – that is, a 'Paillard dévot' (1: 297). A native of
Poitou, he is given to boasting, and this supposedly typical *miles gloriosus*
from the provinces is soundly thrashed in battle by John Chandos. The
French troops are guilty of foolhardiness when they rush out of Orléans
in quest of the enemy and are promptly ambushed (Canto 4). Most of all,
these light-hearted, light-headed Gauls are committed to the erotic life,
and their prowess suffers from it. When Saint Denis descends from heaven
in quest of a maiden, Richemont mocks him, observing that there are
probably no more virgins left in all of France:

> Quand il s'agit de sauver une ville,
> Un pucelage est une arme inutile.
> Pourquoi d'ailleurs le prendre en ce pays? ...
> Chez les Français, hélas, il n'en est plus,
> Tous nos moutiers sont à sec là dessus.
> Nos franc-archers, nos officiers, nos princes
> Ont dès longtemps dégarni les provinces.
> Ils ont tous fait, en dépit de vos saints,
> Plus de bâtards encor que d'orphelins.    (Canto 1: 344–6, 350–5)

It is not an accident that Bonifoux, Charles's confessor, experiences a vision of various popes and practically all the kings of France who were or will be guilty of the sin of *luxuria* (Canto 13). And Charles's Gallic lechery proves to be his undoing. Not only does he fail to observe his martial obligations ('et le roi très chrétien / Baisant Agnès, et ne songeant à rien,' 1: 209–10); in addition, Agnes Sorel is seduced or raped repeatedly, almost always by the English, and thus the King of France, 'Charlot,' is cuckolded by his enemies.

The cuckolders are not treated any better than the cuckold, however. Although Voltaire laughs at the French, he also mocks their hereditary enemy, the English (for alleged stupidity, brutality, drunkenness, and a penchant for sodomy), and his poem treats in passing cowardly, bigoted Italians. The author of *La Pucelle* is against all nationalism and all exclusive patriotic sentiment. He sets the French against the English in order to mock both, each serving as a foil for the other. And he brings about the desired result through a process of anachronism, projecting eighteenth-century stereotypes (the proud, stoical Englishman; the superficial, elegant, amorous Frenchman) onto a relatively distant past when such presumably sophisticated national traits could not, from Voltaire's perspective, yet have existed.

Such characters are mocked because they kill each other needlessly, that is, belong to the only social class committed to war professionally: the nobility. Voltaire ridicules a pretentious aristocratic class presumed superior in nature to other men but in fact prone to quite common human failings: the sins of pride, envy, anger, sloth, and above all lust. The gallant pretensions of the aristocracy are shown to be hollow, a mere sham for exercising brutality and sadism.

In addition, it is these feudal knights and ladies, greedy, cruel, and debauched, who are committed to the conventions of chivalry, to the high ideals of romance. As in *Don Quixote*, an outdated literary tradition serves to corrupt the poor mortals foolish enough to believe in it. Therefore, we laugh at Agnes, whose desperate efforts to remain faithful to Charles are doomed once she has fallen into enemy hands; at Charles, who indulges in tender melancholy while others enjoy his beloved; at La Trimouille and Arundel, knights from France and England respectively, whose mistresses are kidnapped while they fight a duel to decide which one is the more beautiful. The discrepancy between the ideal and the actual, between illusion and reality, is never so blatant as with these chivalrous characters from legend who find themselves placed in a most unlegendary world of medieval savagery.

Readers who expect that the eternal enemy of *l'infâme* reserves his most crushing blows for the Church will not be disappointed. One weapon in

Voltaire's arsenal is to portray earthly clerics or heavenly saints actively indulging in martial and erotic activities proper enough in a degenerate aristocracy but most inappropriate for those who claim to imitate Christ. Near Orléans Voltaire locates a convent of nuns; in the best tradition of Boccaccio and La Fontaine, the abbess has introduced her lover inside the walls, and when Agnes Sorel flees to the convent in quest of calm and penitence, the bogus Sœur Besogne satisfies his needs on her body. In *La Pucelle* we find, in addition to other worthies, a gallery of monks, perhaps the most vivid characters in the poem: Grisbourdon, a Franciscan friar, graduate of the Devil's own seminary, guilty of two attempted rapes and sundry acts of fornication and sodomy; Dom Bonifoux, Charles VII's personal confessor, who gazes upon the rump of John Chandos's page with perhaps unconscious homosexual longing and faints from pleasure upon dreaming of famous adulterers in history; and Frère Lourdis, 'un prieur engraissé d'ignorance' (3: 46), who considers the Palais de Sottise to be his home convent and is permitted to roam the British camp, for he is nothing but

> un rustre, un imbécile,
> Un moine épais, excrément de couvent,
> Qu'il [Talbot] avait fait fesser publiquement.    (Canto 21: 194–6)

In Book 3 of *l'Art poétique* Boileau forbids *merveilleux chrétien*. On esthetic grounds at least, his leading eighteenth-century disciple wholeheartedly agrees. That is why the supernatural in *La Henriade* is, for the most part, relegated to allegorical figures such as Politique and Fanatisme. And, for the same reason, Voltaire introduces a panoply of the Christian supernatural into his mock-epic, because for him it is laughable in essence and because exploitation of such themes will help undermine *l'infâme* and augment the comic quality of his poem. The plot of *La Pucelle* revolves around an absurdly minor war between two insignificant Christian armies, in which God's heaven and Satan's hell take far too active an interest.[9] Indeed, unlike the monks, the celestial hosts are guilty more of *ira* than *luxuria*, of indulging in *militia* rather than *amor*: the quarrel in heaven between Saint Denis and Saint George (in the line of Tassoni), one supporting the French contingent, the other the English, constitutes one comic high point in the epic. The two saints, each manifesting appropriate French or English national traits, both guilty of non-Christian, Homeric or Virgilian loyalty to their devotees on earth, attack each other verbally, exchanging insults, then physically, severing each other's members in a duel, only to have them restored, 'Tant les saints ont la chair ferme et dodue' (11: 369). Since the Homeric gods (and Christian saints) are immortal, any such theomachy is inevitably inconclusive and absurd. When, in Canto 16, their dispute flares to the surface a second time, it is resolved by a poetry contest. Saint Peter awards the crown to Denis, for the latter employs the same flattery and hypocrisy that succeed in an earthly court. Lord Byron was inspired by these passages when he wrote *The Vision of Judgment*. Voltaire employs basically the same comic techniques as Jean de Meun. Like the personified allegories in *Le Roman de la Rose*, Voltaire's saints are deemed serious, truly virtuous figures; by simply reinforcing the concrete sensual failings they manifest in real life, by juxtaposing their human conduct and purportedly saint-like attributes, he makes them appear ridiculous. This juxtaposition is reinforced on the stylistic level when in Canto 1 Saint Denis arrives in Orléans ('Odeur de saint se sentait à la ronde,' 286), introduces himself: 'Je suis Denis, et saint de mon métier' (315), and is addressed as 'Monsieur le saint' (340); or when, in Canto 9, Voltaire tells of Saint Mary Magdalene, 'la sainte aventurière' (224), who 'se fessa longtemps par pénitence' (208) and 'servit le ciel étant sur le retour' (204).

Mary Magdalene is held up to ridicule as a Catholic saint and as a woman. Whether or not Voltaire was personally a misogynist does not concern us here; it is true, however, that, like Jean de Meun, he uses motifs of traditional antifeminism for comic purposes, and women in *La Pucelle* are undermined as a class. Not that the author paints them in exclusively dark colors; Dorothée and Rosamore, loved by La Trimouille and Arundel respectively, are fundamentally praiseworthy, both partaking of stereotypes from conventional Italianate epic – the damsel in distress, and the *femme forte*. However, Voltaire mocks our tendency to create such stock characters, to elaborate feminine ideals in matters such as love and war. And, by so doing, he dehumanizes these ladies (who never were anything but stereotypes anyway), making it impossible for us to conceive of them in the same terms we imagine his male characters – as real people.

In a more complex way this is also the case for the heroines, Agnes Sorel and Joan of Arc. In Chapelain's *Pucelle* Agnes was Joan's enemy; here she becomes a pleasant, good-natured slut. In the tradition of the *fabliaux*, the *Decameron*, and La Fontaine's *Contes*, the purported reality of female insatiability is ironically contrasted to the male ideal of purity. Deeply in love with Charles, her king and lover, Agnes is separated from him for less than forty-eight hours and, therefore, cuckolds him a good six times. Whether she is raped by a disgusting chaplain or joyfully gives herself to Monrose (the page with the attractive rump) or engineers a fusion of the two (Sœur Besogne), the result is the same. Agnes is obsessed with remaining faithful to King Charles, she swears fidelity again and again, and, mechanically, inevitably, succumbs to every man who crosses her path; this is the kind of behavior which, according to Bergson, provokes laughter. Continually defiled, learning and forgetting nothing, she serves as a perfect 'antitype' to the hero in eighteenth-century novels, for whom sexual initiation is one among many stages on the road to knowledge, culture, and worldly civility. True, Charles is as much a fool as anyone for believing in Agnes and for manifesting concern over whether she is virtuous or not. Yet the basic fault is that of woman, the frail vessel, treated like a sexual object by men because that is all she is. Agnes is no more capable of virtue than the nun who mourned a despoiler of her convent, charitably forgiving him his sin: 'Hélas, hélas, nul ne fut plus coupable' (11: 416).

Curiously, this is also true of Joan of Arc. On the one hand, the author undermines a traditional French myth that presumes to transform a woman into a *miles Christi*. She rides an ass, not a horse; in a joust with Chandos she is flung off her mount, falls to the ground, and faints away:

> Son quadrupède un haut le corps lui fit,
> Qui dans le pré Jeanne d'Arc étendit
> Sun son beau dos, sur sa cuisse gentille,
> Et comme il faut que tombe toute fille.   (Canto 13: 234–7)

It is true that for most of the poem Joan remains chaste; her invincible virginity contrasts strikingly with Agnes's no less invincible promiscuity. However, does Voltaire not proclaim that both are ridiculous, the one serving to undercut the other? Furthermore, even Joan of Arc has a sexual role to play. Once again Voltaire parodies Chapelain, who foolishly gave his heroine suitors (Dunois and d'Alençon) and had God render her beautiful in order to attract men to the cause: 'Et dans tout son aspect et tous ses mouvements / Met un nouvel amas de saints enchantements.' Since the poet has Joan finally yield to blandishment and lose her virginity, he places Dorothée, Rosamore, the raped nun, Agnes, and Joan in the same category. They are women, therefore it is ridiculous for them to become Amazons; therefore they are promiscuous, eager for seduction or rape, and deserve both. Incapable of the highest ideals in love or war, they commit foolish, inauthentic acts at the behest of men, who are consummate fools to sentimentalize the fair sex and place them in situations they cannot cope with.

Voltaire capitalizes on the comic potentialities inherent in juxtaposing the martial and the erotic. By so doing, he parodies the ambivalent relationship between *militia* and *amor* which characterizes the romance tradition in Western literature. In writers as disparate as Chrétien de Troyes and Tasso, Spenser and Pierre Le Moyne, love inspires yet undermines heroic deeds, and the martial life both exalts and competes with the call of Eros. A wide range of nuance is available to practitioners of the theme. However,

in Voltaire's ironic world the brutality of war intrudes upon the amorous
life, and the selfishness of primeval lust debases chivalry. Thus, war is
seen as a perversion of sex, and sex is a perversion of war, with each individual treating the Other solely as an object, a prize to be seized, awarded, or
exchanged. On the one hand, love is generally conceived in terms of violence, and people use brute force to satisfy it. On the other hand, military
engagements are determined by sexual as well as martial combat; that is,
warriors seek erotic as well as martial victory – the most striking manifestation of this being the almost obsessive recurrence of rape. Joan of Arc is
almost raped three times (twice by Grisbourdon and a muleteer, once by
Chandos); Agnes Sorel is violated four times (by Chandos, by an English
chaplain, by Sœur Besogne, by an English captain); Rosamore is molested
once (by a bandit); and the comic high point in libidinal activity proves to be
a mass rape of a convent by the English army. In another episode, Chandos challenges a French champion to a duel (both military and sexual), the
winner authorized to enjoy one of the three girls riding with the French
contingent:

> Ça, combattons; je veux que la fortune
> Décide ici qui sait le mieux de nous
> Mettre à plaisir ses ennemis dessous,
> Frapper d'estoc et pointer de sa lance.
> Que de vous tous le plus ferme s'avance,
> Qu'on entre en lice, et celui qui vaincra
> L'une des trois à son aise tiendra.   (Canto 13: 163–9)

He defeats Joan of Arc herself and would have deflowered her on the spot
had not Saint Denis reversed the course of this 'war' by rendering Chandos impotent:

> Telle une fleur des feux du jour séchée,
> La tête basse et la tige penchée,
> Demande en vain les humides vapeurs
> Qui lui rendaient la vie et les couleurs.
> Voilà comment le bon Denis arrête
> Le fier Anglais dans ses droits de conquête ...
> [Jeanne] lui dit: tu n'es pas invincible,
> Tu vois qu'ici dans le plus grand combat,
> Dieu t'abandonne et ton cheval s'abat.   (Canto 13: 420–5, 429–31)

The fact that Charles VII is cuckolded almost exclusively by Englishmen
contributes to his humiliation as a warrior and as a national leader. Indeed,
phallic activity almost decides the outcome of the war when the Englishman

Talbot seduces the Frenchman Louvet's wife, for the surrender of her
person was to precede the fall of Orléans. On the other hand, Joan of Arc
punishes English rapists, killing them on the bodies of the nuns they
deflower (*bellum vincit amorem*), a true *Liebestod* in which *la petite mort*
and real death coincide and, as Voltaire gleefully points out, the rapists'
souls go to hell in ecstasy:

> Pourfendant l'un alors qu'il commençait,
> Dépêchant l'autre alors qu'il finissait
> Et moissonnant la cohorte félonne;
> Si que chacun fut percé sur sa nonne,
> Et perdant l'âme au fort de son désir,
> Allait au diable en mourant de plaisir.    (Canto 11: 151–6)

On this occasion, Warton is mortally wounded in the loins, allowing the
nuns to remark how appropriate it is: 'Qu'on soit puni par où l'on a péché'
(11: 410). A long tradition in literature associates the military and the
erotic, and depicts the seduction of a girl, and the sexual act itself, in terms
of laying siege, pricking a lance, or riding a mare (cf. Ovid's 'Militiae
species amor est'). Another convention depicts combat between warriors in
terms applicable to lovers. Voltaire creates humor by taking these analogies or metaphors literally and by juxtaposing in concrete terms two normally separated human activities.

Ironically, the author of *La Henriade* imitates Chapelain by entitling his
poem *La Pucelle*, rather than, say, *Jeanne d'Arc* or *Orléans délivrée*.
Quite unlike Chapelain, however, he chooses to take the title literally, to
make Joan's maidenhead the central issue of the conflict, a burlesque
arch-image, like Boileau's lectern, around which the action of the poem
turns. Parodying a commonly held medieval notion that virginity possesses magical powers (the myth of the unicorn, or the story embodied in
Hartmann von Aue's *Der arme Heinrich*), Voltaire makes the battle for
Orléans and the future of France depend on whether or not Joan maintains
her chastity. Saint Denis comes to her as the angel Gabriel brought tidings
to Mary. In one of the funniest scenes in eighteenth-century letters, Joan
receives her brevet of virginity before the court (Canto 2). From then on,
Voltaire declares, she keeps the keys to Orléans under her skirt (1: 93–4; 20:
51–2), and Satan's only hope is to have Joan deflowered, whether by
Chandos or by Joan's own mount, her donkey. As the Narrator declares in
Canto 2, to win out over fools (specifically the English) you have to make
them believe you possess divine power. Since both sides in a medieval war
are assumed to be foolish, Frère Lourdis has only to cry: 'Anglais! elle est
pucelle!' (21: 462), and the invaders flee in panic, even though by that time
Joan has become Dunois's mistress. Thus Voltaire mocks both heaven

and earth for taking Joan's purity seriously (although he points out, in an ironic barb, that it is indeed miraculous for an earthy peasant girl to remain chaste for an entire year) and for persisting in this belief once it is lost. Not only is sexual love debased, employed as a weapon in battle; a particular part of the human anatomy, the maidenhead, is reified and treated as a prize, an object of value or of barter. The girl is desired not for herself nor even for the pleasure she can give but for strictly external reasons. Her sexual organs become the object of mediation for victory, the only mediation possible in this savage parody on heroism and romance.

As it does for other writers of his century – Montesquieu, Marivaux, Crébillon fils, Diderot, Sade – for Voltaire the body exists. His characters are subject to appetite, for food and sex. Whatever the situation, whoever the partners, love is concretized in the sex act, but, and it is important, such erotic activity is subject to laughter, which deflates the pretensions of the individuals involved. This is the only way, I believe, we can interpret Voltaire's predilection for the nude body. Joan of Arc paints the *fleur de lis* on the rump of a boy named Monrose, and when Charles VII views the latter nude in a closet, he assumes the image to be of diabolical origin. Similarly, the sorcerer Hermaphrodix leads Joan and Dunois naked to their execution, thus permitting the two national heroes of France to ogle each other's charms; when set free, Joan rushes off to battle naked and fights a portion of the war in that state. There is no particular reason in the story line why La Trimouille and Arundel should duel with their clothes off, or why, in a Varient to Canto 14, a French contingent, temporarily insane, should strip down and 'swim' nude on the grass. In *La Pucelle* Voltaire is obsessed with nakedness; the nude body recurs as often as scenes of rape or the appearance of loathsome monks. Nudity, of course, emphasizes the physical, a bodily presence that authors of romance choose to ignore. The artificial pride of these knights and warrior-saints in shining armor is irrevocably shattered when they are rendered equal, in the flesh, to a muledriver or a peasant. Stripping off armor, and clothes, points to the reality of life behind the literary mask, indeed symbolizes the unmasking which is central to Voltaire's craft. In Bergsonian terms, nudity provokes laughter because, in our civilization, it has become the natural thing for people to wear clothes; thus for Voltaire's characters to go about their day's activities in the nude is the ultimate in comic rigidity. Such rigidity is not entirely inappropriate in what Voltaire considers to be a barbaric age, however. Is not the author of *Le Mondain* laughing at a bygone time, a supposed Golden Age falsely exalted by some nostalgic moderns? From his perspective, the Christian Middle Ages, unlike classical Antiquity, were as primitive as the Garden of Eden, and the innocent nakedness of Adam and Even projected onto Joan of Arc proves to be an absurdity.

Voltaire does not stop here. More than other comic poets, more than

Horace and Juvenal, Jean de Meun and Boileau, he dehumanizes his naked characters, reducing them (sometimes literally) to the level of animals. English wolves violate French lambs, or they mount French nuns by force as if they were breaking horses, as does the Chaplain to Agnes Sorel, 'piquant sa monture difficile.' Joan of Arc, herself, possessing all twenty-four teeth and a 'large bec,' is depicted as a healthy beast and examined as such, like a horse at a country fair, before being granted her brevet of virginity. She is truly an animal-like child of nature. The mule-driver is transformed into a mule, and vice versa, without his or anyone else's particularly noticing the difference:

> Le muletier en son mulet caché,
> Bât sur le dos, crut gagner au marché,
> Et du vilain, l'âme terrestre et crasse
> A peine vit qu'elle eût changé de place.    (Canto 2: 263–6)

A naked Joan of Arc mounts this creature and rides him (whipped on by Saint Denis) into battle:

> Jeanne répond: faquin, je te fais grâce;
> Dans ton vil sang de fange tout chargé,
> Ce fer divin ne sera point plongé.
> Végète encor, et que ta lourde masse
> Ait à l'instant l'honneur de me porter:
> Je ne te puis en mulet translater.
> Mais ne m'importe ici de ta figure,
> Homme ou mulet, tu seras ma monture.
> Dunois m'a pris l'âne qui fut pour moi,
> Et je prétends le retrouver en toi;
> Ça, qu'on se courbe ...    (Canto 6: 92–102)

Significantly, she and the muleteer are the only prominent peasants in the world of *La Pucelle*. He represents his class as a man, she as a woman. They share the same traits: physical grossness, stupidity, ignorance, brute force. Whether Joan likes it or not, the mule-driver is her alter ego. Therefore, her scorn for him and her chastity appear all the more absurd, all the more artificially imposed on history, given the reality of his comportment. That he should be her enemy in sexual jousting, or her literal support in battle, is satirically appropriate, given the reality of her social status. And the fact that her martial successes are dependent on him shatters her glory as a Christian *bellatrix*. As for the mule-driver, in the tradition of Marot and La Fontaine he shares the base animal proclivities, including an indiscriminate, insatiable libidinal drive, of his mules; in Voltaire's comic world the two 'species' are identical. And Joan's superiority over the muleteer and his mule lies solely in the fact that she rides them; that is, she is on top and they on the bottom.

Joan's flying donkey also allows her to mount him, and like the mule-driver, dreams of a more active, truly sexual role, mounting her. This parody of Astolfo's hippogriff in the *Orlando furioso* ('Dieu soit loué, voici venir mon âne,' 5: 228) is expressly handed over to the warrior-saint. In normal, earthly terms, it is fitting for a woman, and especially a peasant-girl, to ride a donkey or a mule, not a stallion. Similarly, the donkey, a peaceful, humble animal, is associated with Christian tradition: Balaam and Christ both rode on the back of an ass. By endowing such a beast with wits, by assimilating him to Pegasus, the author slashes at Joan, a peasant and a woman, who claims to be a national hero. For Voltaire, the ass represents all that is absurd in the Christian religion and in the Joan of Arc legend: he is the epitome of sentimental, hypocritical humility. Furthermore, the protagonist of *festa asinorum*, he is the image of simplicity, that is, stupidity; he is truly 'le céleste baudet.' When we are informed that this absurd flying donkey conceives for Joan 'une discrète flamme' (13: 279), the satire becomes irresistible. Condemned to chastity and supporting his vows better than Adam (and better than most monks) only because there are no 'she-asses' in paradise, our Pegasus with the long ears (20: 77) literally becomes possessed of the devil upon contact with his new saintly mistress and, a winged serpent in the Eden of medieval France ( *pace* Milton), because of his very animalness almost seduces Joan. At this point, Voltaire gives us famous examples of bestiality in Greek myth (Leda, Pasiphaë, Ganymede) which ironically legitimize the new Christian myth he is in the process of inventing. In a suppressed version of the last canto the ass convinces Joan with an obscene gesture (a caress?) and deflowers (or sodomizes) her; in the official version he is stopped in time – only, however, by the sudden appearance of Dunois. Since in either case Joan proves to be guilty of the same sins as Eve, she is forced down to the level of the despised muleteer, and a real animal succeeds where the false one (the muleteer) had failed.

In this pseudo-medieval universe the individual is subject to chance or to arbitrary acts that derive from superior force. No justification can be found to explain meaningless, accidental events. *Sottise* rules a world made up totally of knaves and fools, tricksters and brutes. People are driven only by vanity and an appetite for food, money, sex, and power. As a result, sensual vice proves to be more powerful and authentic than virtue, and virtuous people are inevitably punished for their efforts. Happiness thrives in inverse proportion to morality, or is again the result of chance. If, that is, such a thing as morality exists, for the Agnes Sorels of this world connive with their own rapists, and seduction is but a mask for sensual complicity based upon hypocrisy or simple bad faith. On the one hand, we are not expected to blame the complicity, since, from Voltaire's perspective, Eros is good, a natural manifestation of the human condition, and a life force to be protected from the death instincts unleashed by war, nationalism, chivalry, and the Church. On the other hand, we cannot but laugh at the blindness of these characters, their non-awareness, non-lucidity, and total absence of concern for the existence of Others as subjects, not objects, and for the community as a whole. Joan of Arc is symbolically as well as literally asleep when Grisbourdon or a muleteer seeks to ravish her; the entire *dramatis personae* go insane inside Hermaphrodix's castle (Canto 14), a form of madness which concretizes the sundry obsessions that have been seizing them throughout the poem.

Among the traits Voltaire borrowed from the *Orlando furioso* is a particular kind of narrative structure. In Voltaire, as in Ariosto, we find the ultimate comic version of the interlacing process developed by Chrétien de Troyes and the *Lancelot-Grail Prose Cycle* – the major characteristics being multiple narrative lines, authorial interventions, rapid tempo, brusque shifting of scenes, and digressions. Although some of the interventions and digressions appear to be well motivated, most are quite gratuitous and willfully defy the traditon of a neoclassical epic. The world of Joan, Dunois, and Agnes in its very telling is shown to be syncopated, disjointed, upside-down; the characters are stereotypes, incapable of other than mechanical, burlesque actions; and conventional laws of time and space are abolished. As in Boileau, as in Jean de Meun and Guillaume de Machaut, this emphasis on the artificial nature of the plot and the distancing inherent in Voltairean satire create an early version of *Verfremdungseffekt*, reminding us that we are dealing with literature not reality, with a comic work of art that destroys the illusion of art in order to force us back to reality. Therefore, although *La Pucelle* is basically an *Er-Erzählung*, we find nonetheless the interventions of a narrator and his allusions to a mock-source, the Abbé Tritême (who corresponds to Archbishop Turpin in the *Furioso*), and the mock-preface by one Apuleius Risorius, OSB. For all his alleged dependence on a burlesque author or source, the omniscient Ariostian Narrator exerts absolute control over his story, shaping it at will, treating it as God treats the cosmos, and playing the role of a witty, urbane, epicurean moralist for whom the only unforgivable sin is to bore the no less urbane implied reader. Reader and author both contrast stridently with what we have ascertained to be naïve, clumsy characters. Furthermore, in the preface and elsewhere, especially in Voltaire's correspondence, the book *La Pucelle* becomes a literary character in its own right and is proclaimed to be as pure and virginal, or as subject to rape, as the Maid of Orléans herself.

Of course, the book is not a girl, but then, intimates Voltaire, Joan of Arc was not really a great general. The book is virginal only in its title, or because it has not yet gone to press; similarly, are we not told that Joan's life, sexual and otherwise, is either a sham or insignificant, of little interest to serious historians? Both virginities are artificial, foolish impositions on the reader, each serving as a foil for the other.

Like Scarron and Boileau, like all writers of mock-epic, Voltaire deflates literature as well as 'real life.' *La Pucelle d'Orléans* undercuts the various traits regularly associated with heroism and romance and the more specific epic motifs: a host of scenes, characters, and images to be found in Homer, Virgil, Honoré d'Urfé, Milton, Fénelon, Voltaire's own *Henriade* and *Temple du Goût*, and, most of all, Tasso and Chapelain. Joan and Agnes are 'anti-heroes' in the full modern sense of the term, perhaps even more so than Candide and the Huron. However, unlike his predecessors, Voltaire has in mind a particular comic model and therefore imitates Ariosto (and, to a lesser extent, Tassoni and Boileau) even more than he undercuts serious epic. Thus, any given motif derives from, and evokes to the cultivated reader, sources both sublime and ridiculous, serves as parody and travesty at the same time. For example, the timid, fleeing Agnes Sorel serves as a variation on both Angelica and Erminia, and the arrogance of Chandos has precedents in Rodomonte and Argante. For this very reason *La Pucelle* must not be considered a mere pastiche of the *Furioso*. Unlike Ariosto, Voltaire comes at the end rather than at the beginning of a rich period of national culture. Consciously aware of his heritage, he lovingly exalts some aspects of it (Ariosto, La Fontaine) while deriding others (Tasso and Chapelain). And that which he loves is recast in a new form. He delights in demystifying a comic motif in Ariosto, exploring the reality of rape or the nefarious consequences of wearing a mask; and he scrutinizes aspects of life – sodomy, pillage – largely absent from Ariosto's world, the true conditions of existence in a distant past and hardly more glorious present. Thus, although he retains the Italian's understanding and witty, humane refinement, Voltaire's vision of woman, of chivalry, of the Middle Ages and its Church are far different from Ariosto's. He uses the great Italian and honors him, but for his own purposes, to create his own, uniquely Voltairean vision of the world. *La Pucelle* embodies a new concept of epic, and its maker transforms Ariosto to the same extent that the latter originally transformed Boiardo and early medieval romance.

In a preamble to Canto 13 the implied author appeals to Ariosto's indulgence and, therefore, indirectly, also to his implied readers:

> Protège-moi contre ces durs esprits,
> Frondeurs pesants de mes légers écrits.

Si quelquefois l'innocent badinage
Vient en riant égayer mon ouvrage,
Quand il le faut je suis très sérieux.
Mais je voudrais n'être point ennuyeux.    (Canto 13: 27–32)

*La Pucelle* is, of course, a masterpiece of civilized eroticism, elegance, charm, wit, persiflage, and aristocratic sheen. The play element succeeds on all levels and with all themes, from the sublime-heroic to the low-bawdy. Indeed, certain traits – eroticism, fragmentation, formal irregularity, parody, the mock-heroic, irreverence for the past, ludic skepticism, and an overall aristocratic, amoral, apparently frivolous tone – make Voltaire's epic, along with Marivaux's theater, *The Rape of the Lock*, and *Oberon*, perfect examplars of the rococo style in literature.[10] Yet, and in this Voltaire is perhaps more complex than Marivaux and Pope, *La Pucelle* is a poem of Enlightenment as well. We must not forget that it was published three years after *Candide*, one year before the *Traité sur la Tolérance*, two years before the *Dictionnaire philosophique*. Voltaire's rhetorical stance must not blind us to the more militant aspects of his work, to the extent to which *innocent badinage* enhances his universe and serves as a vehicle for one of the most daring books of its age. The poem expresses very well its author's commitment to a modern, secular, man-oriented universe, to the rehabilitating of man's passions and instincts against life-killing authorities, whether Church, State, or History.

  *La Pucelle d'Orléans* is one of the great hedonist works of the hedonist eighteenth century. This bit of amusement speaks out for life over death, for freedom over the constraint of institutions and false dogma, for laughter over pompousness. In it we find the keenness of intellect, the choler, the verve, passion, and impetuousness that characterize Voltaire as a writer and a man.[11] Yet, as always, his *saeva indignatio* is performed in the most graceful and elegant of styles, overflowing with wit, fantasy, frivolity, and joy. Like *Candide*, *La Pucelle* is a microcosm of Voltaire's opus as a whole. Among the best products of the Enlightenment, it speaks to us with the same pungency today.

  A case can be made that, whereas *La Henriade* failed both as art and ideology, *La Pucelle* proves to be *the* great rococo-Enlightenment epic. Each age produces the books and ideas appropriate to itself. Surely Voltaire, in his way, maintains and renews the commitment, the militancy of a Turold or a d'Aubigné; the great nay-sayer proclaims his heresies with passionate fire and the skill of consummate art. The very religious concerns inherent in baroque epic (du Bartas, d'Aubigné, Saint-Amant, Le Moyne), even in Ronsard's *Hymnes* and *Discours*, are perpetuated upside-down in the mock-poems of Boileau, Gresset, and Voltaire. Thus the author of *Le*

*Dictionnaire philosophique* participates in and concludes the evolution of the long poem since the Renaissance. And, because his heroism lies in the realm of ideas, he anticipates there, as in so many other domains, the orientation of the modern world. Yet, when a genre can achieve its highest, most authentic state only in the guise of parody, it is truly time for a change. There will be a modern epic but in a new form, unrecognizable to Ronsard and Boileau, even to Voltaire himself.

Chapter Thirteen

# ❧ LAMARTINE

It is a truism that the coming of Romanticism involves a shift in literary consciousness no less striking than the Renaissance. The cliché that in the modern world, especially the nineteenth century, the novel replaces the old epic is only partly correct, however. For, in the major Western European literatures – in England, Germany, and especially France – the new current marks at the same time as the triumph of the novel a return to the sublime, to long narratives in verse – in a word, to epos, which is recognized, if only by specialists, as one of the most representative genres, perhaps the hallmark, of French Romanticism.[1] The most important harbingers of the new style were Chénier and Chateaubriand. The creator of 'La Jeune Tarentine' and 'Néaere' also projected two long poems, *l'Amérique* and *Hermès*, which would have celebrated the discoveries of science and exploration and provided a vision of man's progress over the ages, with the author himself, a modern Lucretius, playing the role of artist, inventor, and prophet. Although these works survive only in fragments, Chénier's example was to serve as a model for subsequent writers. Chateaubriand defended the claims of Christian epos in *Le Génie du Christianisme* (Part 2, Book 1), then proceeded to compose narratives in the sublime style, conceived as epics in prose: *Les Martyrs* (1809) and *Les Natchez* (1826). Although these books are considered nowadays to be failures, they had an immeasurable influence upon Lamartine's generation. It can be said that, in the epic as well as in sentimental religiosity, most of the great writers of the first half of the nineteenth century are descendants of Chateaubriand.

Under the heady influence of the Revolution and Empire heroic poems flourished; with the seemingly more prosaic Restoration and July Monarchy they flourished even more. Twenty such works mark the first decade of the century, over forty the second decade, and, from 1820 on, the number of verse and prose narratives purporting to be epic is legion. The period extending from 1800 to 1860 represents quantitatively the summum of epic production in France, eclipsing by far the Middle Ages and the Baroque. All possible subjects and modes are represented: mock-heroic in the style of

Voltaire and Parny; burlesque and satire; didactic, scientific, and philosophical poems; works in the 'troubadour' mode or in the style of Ossian;
poems treating classical Greek subjects or the Bible; and, above all, national,
patriotic texts. We find more than one *Franciade*, *Clovis*, *Caroléide*, and
*Philippide*, and in the period from 1830 to 1860 nine evocations of Joan of
Arc and twenty treating the French Revolution. It is surely not coincidental that the term 'romantic' is etymologically related to medieval narrative in
the long form. That the vast majority of these artifacts are esthetically
worthless ought to surprise no one: they prove to be no more and no less so
than the majority of seventeenth-century plays and twentieth-century
novels. More significant is the fact that today a certain number of them are
recognized as possessing artistic value, and that two modes, two forms of
romantic epic, bore fruit, proving that the age was capable of producing
masterpieces of the highest order in all literary domains.

The most important of these modes is one that has been called the Epic of
Humanity. Scholars have included in the *épopée humanitaire* prose works
by Ballanche (*Antigone*, 1814; *Orphée*, 1827; *La Vision d'Hébal*, 1831),
Quinet (*Merlin l'enchanteur*, 1860), and Ludovic de Cailleux (*Le Monde
antédiluvien*, 1845); Quinet's drama *Ahasvérus*, 1833; and narratives in
verse by Lamartine (*Jocelyn*, 1836; *La Chute d'un Ange*, 1838), Quinet
(*Napoléon*, 1836; *Prométhée*, 1838; *Les Esclaves*, 1853), Soumet (*La Divine
Epopée*, 1840), Laprade (*Eleusis*, 1841; *Psyché*, 1841), and, of course,
Hugo (*La Légende des Siècles*, *La Fin de Satan*, and *Dieu*; see chapter
fifteen). These books share a concern for man's evolution over the ages,
depicting in one form or another the history of civilization, our slow march
toward progress, and a vision, cosmic and apocalyptic, of humanity in the
universe. They also share a religious orientation. The supernatural and
divine providence are no longer conceived to be literary ornament: on the
contrary, Ballanche, Quinet, Lamartine, Soumet, Laprade, and Hugo seek
out mysteries and reveal arcane truths. In their works, *Gesta Dei per
homines*, mankind, the universe, even Satan shall be redeemed. These writers are optimists, preaching a synthetic total view of history, with the
divine presence ever hovering over man's destiny. And, reacting against bad
neoclassical texts of the 1820s, they repudiate the old canons, accepting as
epic works long or short, written in verse or prose, conceived as a unity or a
series of episodes. In fact, the preferred format is an endless, organic
opus, an anatomy incorporating existing genres and forms. What counts is
the poem's spirit and message. Even so, in the 1830s and 1840s, first
Lamartine and then Soumet and Laprade do publish *épopées humanitaires*
which are also 'true epics,' not perhaps based upon the *Aeneid* or the
*Liberata* but nonetheless long narrative poems in verse conceived to perpetuate the 'modern epic' tradition of Dante, Milton, and Klopstock.

A second mode, neglected by scholars, is what I choose to call the *épopée intime*. The notion of a private or domestic epic, paradoxical as it may sound to French ears, is a truism in German and even English studies. Its manifestations, French and European, could form the subject of a book. It is basically narrative poetry treating the lives of humble people in their daily concerns. Generally situated in the provinces, these stories contrast the purportedly idyllic existence of country folk with the cares of the great outside that impinge on them through war and revolution. They are sentimental, conservative, escapist, and committed to the primacy of love. Theirs is a tiny world within a world yet paradoxically one containing universal significance and in which a new kind of heroism is deemed possible. Whereas, for the period of Romanticism, the epic of humanity is predominantly a French phenomenon (notable exceptions being Shelley's *Queen Mab*, 1813, *The Revolt of Islam*, 1818, and *Prometheus Unbound*, 1820; and Lenau's *Savonarola*, 1837, and *Die Albigenser*, 1842), the intimate or rustic poem has a truly European dimension. It is to be found in the Anglo-Saxon countries, primarily with Wordsworth (in many of his shorter works and in *The Prelude*, 1805, and *The Excursion*, 1814), Shelley (*Rosalind and Helen*, 1819), Longfellow (*Evangeline*, 1847, and *The Courtship of Miles Standish*, 1858), and Tennyson (*Enoch Arden*, 1864); and in Germany, with Voss (*Luise*, 1795), Goethe (*Hermann und Dorothea*, 1797), Mörike (*Die Idylle vom Bodensee*, 1846), and Hebbel (*Mutter und Kind*, 1859); its finest manifestation is perhaps Mickiewicz's *Pan Tadeusz* (1834). Lamartine's *Jocelyn* (1836) adheres to this convention less artificially, I think, than to the epic of humanity; other notable French examples are Brizeux's *Marie* (1831) and *Les Bretons* (1845), and Laprade's *Pernette* (1868); in Occitan we find, of course, Mistral's *Mirèio* (1859), followed, in a different style, by *Calendau* (1867), *Nerto* (1884), and *Lou Pouèmo dóu Rose* (1897).

Fame as an elegiac poet, who created deeply spiritual lyrics, both erotic and religious, did not suffice to bring fulfillment to Alphonse de Lamartine (1790–1869). The author of 'Le Lac' and 'Novissima Verba' considered these and his other shorter texts to be a mere pastime, the products of an idle moment, useful for attracting public attention. Like so many of his predecessors on Parnassus – Ronsard, d'Aubigné, Saint-Amant, and Voltaire – Lamartine believed that a poet achieves immortality only by taking the epic path, that epic alone is worthy of man's noblest efforts in the world of art. And as a critic he is best known for claiming (falsely, it appears) to have heralded the coming of Mistral – in the *Cours familier de littérature* (fortieth *Entretien*, 1859). From 1813 to 1820 he worked sporadically on a *Clovis*, two fragments of its first canto appearing under a different guise in *Nouvelles Méditations Poétiques* (1823). In the meantime, on 20 January 1821, in Italy, Lamartine was struck by an 'illumination,' which resulted in his decision to follow in Dante's footsteps by composing a long epic in the new style. The plan for *Les Visions* was elaborated in 1823, and, for the next six years, the young writer devoted to it the time he could spare from other projects. Influenced strongly by the apocryphal Book of Enoch, Byron's *Heaven and Earth* (1822), and Moore's *The Loves of the Angels* (1823), *Les Visions* was to recount how, in Biblical times, shortly before the Flood, an angel, having fallen in love with a mortal woman, expresses a desire to assume human status. God grants the angel's wish but condemns him to die and be reborn on earth one hundred times, reliving his fall, until, through successive stages of expiation, he acquires the courage to spurn temptation and thus win back immortality. He will then be redeemed, and he and his soul mate ascend spiritually to God. In this work we recognize Ballanche's theory of palingenesis, or man's evolution through successive reincarnations or metempsychoses and his reintegration into the original pristine state through a series of ordeals and expiations. Some twelve or seventeen 'visions,' each an epic in its own right, each recounting an episode in the angel's career, one of his myriad lives, were projected. However, Lamartine only succeeded in completing two cantos located near the end of time, shortly before Judgment Day, and two other cantos belonging to the Eighth Vision, *Les Chevaliers*, a poem treating a medieval subject and conceived in the 'troubadour style.' Although his vision of the end of the world is quite powerful, and his conception of a gigantic super-epic, in the Sanskrit tradition, worthy of our admiration, Lamartine's plan was simply too vast for any Western poet to bring to fruition. Like *Clovis*, it reposes in the graveyard of artistic good intentions.

Then in November 1831, basking in the triumph of *Harmonies Poétiques et Religieuses*, Lamartine conceived of a poem in two cantos, a melodramatic idyll modelled upon *Paul et Virginie*, the hero to be a country priest. As his project expanded, the author realized that it could fit into the cadre of *Les Visions*. Indeed, he had never entirely abandoned the super-epic; his voyage to the Holy Land in 1832 and 1833 was undertaken primarily to provide background material for the Biblical 'visions.' Meanwhile, for five years he worked steadily on the *poemetto*, publishing it in 1836 under the title *Jocelyn*. It had become a respectable book of over eight thousand lines. As a result of *Jocelyn*'s resounding success with the public, Lamartine immediately set to work on another episode of *Les Visions*, which was to recount the actual temptation, fall, and first life of the angel Eloïm-Cédar on earth. During a period of ten months he composed some twelve thousand lines and published *La Chute d'un Ange* early in 1838. These two 'episodes' represent Lamartine's contribution to the epic mode in France.

Of the two, I choose to concentrate on *Jocelyn*.[2] My reasons are based on practical considerations (limitations of space) and on the importance of the

*épopée intime* as a nineteenth-century literary phenomenon heretofore
somewhat neglected. *Jocelyn* diverges from the other long poems I have
studied in this book. Representation of intimate, everyday doings, within
an idyllic love-format, is to be found in the Middle Ages – in romances by
Jean Renart, for example, and in the love-allegories extending from Guillaume de Lorris to Machaut, Froissart, and Christine de Pisan – as well as in
a more recent pastoral tradition: one thinks of Saint-Amant's *Moyse sauvé*,
La Fontaine's *Adonis*, and rustic poems in the eighteenth century. Nonetheless, Lamartine's is the first *épopée intime* in a Romance tongue, the first
totally humble, intimate text to claim the form and title, the glory and
responsibility, of being epic. In the course of this chapter the reader will
see how Lamartine gives his poem a traditionally epic character, integrating
epos and the idyllic mode.

What an outrageous phenomenon it is, from the perspective of Ronsard or
Boileau! The protagonist is a poor country priest, the narrative is his own
story, told by himself, a 'Journal trouvé chez un curé de village.' The
peripetias are of the most down-to-earth, unheroic kind. Deciding to
sacrifice his worldly heritage in order that his sister may marry, a boy enters
the seminary. He escapes from the Terror by fleeing to the mountains
where he falls in love with Laurence, the daughter of another refugee. Their
idyll is broken when Jocelyn accepts ordination. The remainder of the
poem recounts the young man's experiences as a priest in a mountain village,
a trip to Paris accompanying his sister (where he beholds Laurence), and
his administering the last rites to his mother, Laurence, and a weaver, the
latter a victim of the plague. Like Wordsworth, Lamartine is concerned
with the life of a private individual; the characters in his rustic, bourgeois
tale are a widow, a country priest, a servant, peasants, and urban workers.
He writes for all men but about simple, everyday things in the lives of little
people, events treated in both the sentimental and tragic modes. By taking
the life of his protagonist seriously, Lamartine makes the destiny of the
individual meaningful, but by idealizing him and his surroundings, he
avoids the critical realism we find in the novels of Balzac and Stendhal.

Jocelyn's diary opens with a dance and festival, celebrating the renewal
of the year in springtime, a May Day which coincides with the protagonist's
sixteenth birthday and marks his first experience of love: 'Car, je le sens
ce soir, mon âme n'est qu'amour!' (p. 580). This latter force is depicted as a
sentiment condoned by the community, and humble country people are
shown leading lives of beauty and integrity, enhanced by the weight of
tradition.

For a time Jocelyn only witnesses the love of others: his sister and her
husband, for example, or two mountain shepherds. But when Eros descends
upon him, it comes with a vengeance: Jocelyn and Laurence are one of the

great tragic couples in French literature, on a par with Tristan and Iseut,
Lancelot and Guinevere, des Grieux and Manon, Saint-Preux and Julie, and
Marcel and Albertine. In *Jocelyn*, as in *La Chute d'un Ange*, his novels,
and so many of his finest lyrics, Lamartine adheres to the conventions of *fin'
amor*. The woman is a figure of light, an angel to be adored, her eyes and
hair shining upon her suitor's darkness:

> Il semble, à cette forme où tout est luxe et grâce,
> Que cet être céleste est né d'une autre race
> Et n'a rien de commun avec ceux d'ici-bas ...
> Plus son sourire est tendre et son regard m'est doux,
> Plus je sens le besoin de tomber à genoux,
> De consacrer mon cœur en lui rendant hommage,
> Et d'adorer mon Dieu dans ce divin ouvrage.
>
> (Epoch 3: p. 630; Epoch 4: p. 664)

Even though his love is menaced by obstacles and the inevitable passing of
time, it is the most deeply satisfying condition to which a man can aspire.
The discovery of one's anima, one's *âme-sœur* – 'cet autre soi-même ...
l'autre part de moi-même' (pp. 623, 624) – is an extraordinary privilege, and
the love of such a woman makes one a better person and raises one's soul
to God. Since an Elvire, a Julie (in *Raphaël*), or a Laurence serves as an
intercessor, a religious *mediatrix*, one attains immortality by being joined
to her in heaven. Indeed, as a result of earthly separation, the beloved is
metamorphosed into a purely spiritual force. Fulfillment is attained through
renunciation and regeneration, a *Liebestod* transformed into art. Lamartine
departs from the tradition, however, in that his characters never indulge
in fornication or adultery. Laurence and Jocelyn avoid physical intimacies;
the latter remains a virgin for his entire lifetime. Furthermore, their passion is doomed because it cannot achieve fruition in marriage and the birth
of children; or, perhaps on the contrary, Lamartine condemns it because
it does not result in wedlock and issue. In contrast, the happy couples in
*Jocelyn*, whose loves serve as foils to the main intrigue – the protagonist's
father and mother, his sister and brother-in-law, shepherds, farmers, weav-
ers – all appear in a family situation. Lamartine's social ideal is clearly the
rural family working together. And it is the atmosphere of the home – the
world of *La Vigne et la Maison* – that gives *Jocelyn* much of its charm.

For the most part, the action takes place in the Alps, a mountainous
setting which had become fashionable in the late eighteenth and early
nineteenth centuries, largely owing to the influence of Rousseau, Senancour,
Delille, and Byron.[3] Nonetheless, such a décor, with its discreet yet
explicit local color, is new to the French epic. In *Jocelyn* the Alps, far from

the madding crowd, separated from corrupt cities both horizontally and vertically, provide solitude. The author's treatment of the mountain paradise is unusually complex, containing a variety of conventions and motifs. One of them is the *locus amœnus*, the idyllic garden spot conducive to the flowering of love, a paradise or Arcadia inhabited by amorous shepherds: here Lamartine was most directly influenced by Tasso, Fénelon, Bernardin de Saint-Pierre, and Chateaubriand. Another is the erotic grotto, hidden from the outside world, defended by a triple barrier: this Grotte des Aigles adheres to a more immediate epic tradition, in the line of Homer, Virgil, and the masters of the Renaissance. The grotto especially, associated with dripping water and a mountain lake[4] (images of purity, baptism, and secular grace), evokes a maternal refuge, an Eden constructed by God in nature, which becomes a home for lonely people thrust into exile. In the second half of the poem these two motifs are undermined by, yet also synthesized in, Jocelyn's mountain presbytery at Valneige. There, in a celibate state, he nonetheless dines on the same bread, wine, milk, honey, fruit, and grapes as Daphnis and Chloe or, for that matter, Saint-Amant's Elisaph and Marie, and finds the same protection from a cruel world, the same womb-like refuge, as in the Grotte des Aigles. Indeed, this pervasiveness of nature contributes greatly to the 'message' of Lamartine's poem. God's true temple stands in the open air, where all is sparkle, light, bursting, and blowing, in an animistic, naturally fecund universe. We can even say that, in nature, man is initiated, attains an 'I-Thou' relationship with other people and with God, in an otherwise 'I-It' world.

The reality of Paris and of nearby provincial cities and the presence of forces from outside that impinge upon Lamartine's happy lovers remind us that an idyll is idyllic only in contrast to, and in contact with, the 'real world.' The pastoral mode takes shape as an imagined refuge, a wish-fulfillment décor for lovers or poets who seek happiness, innocence, wisdom, and good love, all without nagging responsibilities – far from urban centers, which in fact do not permit Eden to remain inviolate. Although natural disasters can also undermine the bucolic, the conflicts that corrode Lamartine's universe are of human origin, the result of people congregating in society. First of all, as with Jean de Meun, mankind suffers from gold, from a money economy in which prestige and even happiness are based upon possessions. Not only this, but exploitation gives rise to violence, war, and civil strife. Because of the French Revolution Jocelyn is chased from the seminary, his bishop is executed, and Laurence's father is murdered by soldiers. Although, but for the Terror, Laurence and Jocelyn would never have met, it also brings about their separation and the death of two fine men; the Revolutionary-Bonapartist mentality is partly responsible for the degradation of Paris, which becomes an armed camp, a forest of muskets, a city

where people are metamorphosed into algae, and for the moral degradation of Laurence, who dwells there as a kept woman. Like so many writers
of his and the previous century (Rousseau, Vigny, Baudelaire, and others),
Lamartine envisages the capital as a place of alienation, an inferno, yet a
place where the future of mankind will be determined. He assimilates
Paris to decadent Biblical cities such as Sodom, Babel, and Babylon (cf. the
demonic metropolis in *La Chute d'un Ange*), yet he also rejects pre-
romantic Arcadian pastoral in favor of a more modern, true-to-life vision of
the countryside as a region with roots based upon concrete traditions (as
do Wordsworth, Balzac, Goethe, and Turgenev). *Jocelyn* manifests a tragic
modern sense of reality in which events concerning humble people are
based upon contemporary or near-contemporary history and treated in the
most serious manner: an innovation in literature and a hallmark of the
romantic period.

The city versus the country, revolution and military strife versus love
and the family – these are the issues of conflict. On the one hand, a masculine realm of commerce and war, of urban society; on the other, a feminine world of home, of idyllic love in a natural refuge graced by a lake and a
grotto. The tension between these opposing forces gives rise to melodrama,
to extraordinary events that would normally be out of place in the lives of
quiet, humble folk.

As a result, Jocelyn's private career corresponds (as displacement, in
Frye's sense of the term) to the life of all heroes, and his adventures can be
considered a low-mimetic version of the archetypal quest pattern to be
found in almost every poem treated in this book. Forced by circumstances beyond his control, he quits everyday existence in favor of a life of
adventure in exile, a road of trials. Accepting the aid of an older guide, a
creature of nature, he traverses a series of mountain barriers into a sort of
Other World far from the eyes of mortal man. There, in this return to the
womb, at the point of epiphany, in paradise, he encounters a maiden whom
he worships as an angel or goddess. At his moment of greatest happiness,
however, life takes another turn: like Aeneas, like Yvain, like Rinaldo, like
Télémaque, the youth discovers existence to be hollow. Through an act of
ascetic renunciation, he abandons the maiden (metamorphosed into a temptress), accepts guidance from a supremely powerful father-figure who also
serves as his antagonist, and proceeds to embark upon a new series of
adventures. He again climbs past mountain barriers, expiates sin through a
series of ordeals, this time resists the woman's temptation, and learns to
love, serve, and guide his people. Now his life is directed in accordance with
the dictates of society. In the end he becomes a spiritual father, a teacher
and sage; he dies in an aura of sanctity, having attained apotheosis in heaven,
master of both worlds. In his career he has crossed more than one threshold

and undergone more than one rite of passage: separation from family, love, ordination, and death.

Of particular significance is the fact that, for the first time since Chrétien de Troyes and Guillaume de Lorris, an epic hero's quest takes place within: his combat is spiritual rather than physical in nature. We find the typically romantic sequence of ordeal, expiation, and initiation (Ballanche, Quinet, Laprade, Hugo). Jocelyn twice sacrifices erotic happiness, in the process learning to devote himself to his fellow men and to God. The moment of initiation – the sacrament of ordination – occurs in the very center of the poem, Epoch 5, separating the realms of secular and sacred love, and marking the principal stage in Jocelyn's pilgrimage.[5] Although he progresses from the outer world to an inner realm, paradoxically the *homo viator* finds fulfillment in a modern, realistic, and authentic rural setting (the *vita activa*) before arriving at a *unio mystica* with Laurence and God. To some extent, his quest conforms to the pattern of the Orphic poet-seer, the fundamental archetypal personage in the romantic period.[6]

A major concern in medieval and baroque epic, religion is no less central to works composed by Chateaubriand, Ballanche, Quinet, Soumet, Laprade, Hugo, and, of course, the author of *Harmonies Poétiques et Religieuses. Jocelyn*, however, turns out to be the only major epic in French in which the protagonist is an ordained priest. Christian faith not only plays its usual role of recalling a warrior to duty, away from dalliance with a temptress; as in *La Chanson de Roland* and *Les Tragiques*, it is central to the plot and to the poem's doctrinal line. Throughout the poem individuals are assimilated to Christ, become Christ-figures imitating his Passion. Jocelyn especially drinks from the Messiah's cup, teaches his flock by parables, and, accompanied by shepherds, retreats into solitude (his desert, his Mount of Olives), then returns to the city where he offers the ultimate sacrifice to God. In his own words:

> Ô Christ! j'ai comme toi sué mon agonie
> Dans ces trois doubles nuits d'horreur et d'insomnie!
> Oh! Pourquoi cette voix dans mon Gethsémani
> Ne me dit-elle pas aussi ... tout est fini! ...
> Dieu me sèvre à jamais du lait de ses délices.
> Eh! bien, j'épuiserai la coupe des supplices;
> Dans les vases fêlés où l'homme boit ses pleurs,
> Avec lui, je boirai ses gouttes de douleurs.   (Epoch 5: pp. 686, 687)

Sacrifice and regeneration through suffering is a favorite theme of Chateaubriand, Ballanche, and Lamartine himself, in all his novels: *Graziella, Raphaël, Geneviève, Le Tailleur de pierres de Saint-Point, Fior d'Aliza,* and

*Antoniella*. Having fallen from a formerly privileged state, having been separated from a happy childhood, a rural home, the love of woman, only by imitating Christ can Lamartine's characters hope to recover their lost paradise and be reintegrated into a world of joy. What can be more heroic than to follow in the footsteps of the God-man who, like Moses, Theseus, and Hercules, came from obscure beginnings, underwent exile, temptation, and humiliation, was martyred but then won rebirth, salvation, apotheosis with the Father, and epiphany?

To imitate Christ, one must learn to bear his Cross. A weaver bears his wife's coffin on his back for three days, seeking a priest to perform the last rites, then Jocelyn and the man transport it up into the Alps; this is the weaver's and, presumably, Jocelyn's Calvary. Significantly, the widower constructed the coffin from his own bed-boards, an act of charity anticipated by Jocelyn under other circumstances. And the latter's mother fainted away on the bed in which her husband died. Thus, Lamartine assimilates the bed, the coffin, and the cross; the womb and the tomb; birth, death, and rebirth. It is also true that Jocelyn's faith has been upheld by a real crucifix – one which received a kiss from the mouth of his dying father, which he shared with Laurence in the mountains, which was bathed in the dying bishop's blood, which hangs on the wall of his cottage at Valneige, and which, after his death, is bequeathed to the Narrator along with the diary that constitutes the poem *Jocelyn*. No less symbolic are the five rocks arranged in the shape of a cross by the protagonist over Laurence's father's grave at la Grotte des Aigles, where the lovers will also one day be buried. This site constitutes a sanction and a covenant governing their lives. Where man lives and loves he will die, and where he takes his daily rest he will ultimately repose; for death can lead to eternal redemption.

Finally, Jocelyn himself is a living rood, a tree of life. In the 'Epilogue' the Narrator refers to him as a splendid oak who grew to maturity, in spite of suffering, in spite of an axe that penetrated the bark to his inner heart. Similarly, a bush rises into the roof of Jocelyn's home; it cannot be separated from the cottage without the structure crumbling and the plant being killed. This imagery, which reinforces Lamartine's conception of benevolent nature, can be assimilated to Christian motifs of the Tree of Life, the Tree of Jesse, and, of course, the Holy Rood. Jocelyn as a tree provides sustenance, protection, and hope to his flock, while he himself benefits from Christian doctrine. He bears a cross and is a cross, imitates Christ and becomes Christ, for the sake of his parishioners (as a priest) and for his own salvation.

The nuptial cup of the Song of Songs has been metamorphosed into Christ's chalice of blood and bile. Jocelyn, the bishop, and the weaver all imitate Christ by drinking from his cup. Furthermore, during the Revolu-

tion much blood is shed, and people weep bitter tears. Water plays a
special role in *Jocelyn* in terms of Christian ritual. For with the holy water of
baptism, the wine of the Mass, the anointing of ordination and of extreme
unction, the Christian dies and is reborn, a *homo novus* in Christ. In addition to the usual death-rebirth experiences, one pattern especially stands
out: on the very same day that the bishop takes the Eucharist, that is,
perishes spiritually and is reborn in Christ, Jocelyn is ordained a priest,
that is, he dies to the world and is resuscitated as Christ's deputy in the
Church; the bishop is literally dismembered only to relive in heaven; and
finally France is resurrected from the tomb of Revolution, its joy restored
thanks to the sacrifice of this holy scapegoat.

Most critics have assumed *Jocelyn* to be a profoundly religious poem that
glorifies a country priest who keeps his faith and even succeeds in redeeming the Fallen Woman, his temptress. From this vantage-point, it narrates
the slow progression toward sainthood of a highly sensitive devout young
man, his evolution from romantic love to the maturity of a clerical calling. In
addition, on a symbolic level, the protagonist represents the modern
Church that must make sacrifices for the good of society, and, as we have
seen, Christ himself, for each and every vicar of Christ, a Christ-figure
serving Mass, must forsake individual love (*concupiscentia*) for the love of
many (*caritas*), one soul for the collective soul of the Church to be led
back to God:

> Dites plutôt qu'à l'homme il étend sa famille:
> Les pauvres sont pour lui mère, enfants, femme et fille.
> Le Christ met dans son cœur son immense amitié;
> Tout ce qui souffre et pleure est à lui par pitié.    (Epoch 1: p. 584)

Such indeed is an appropriate lesson from a writer who devoted his lifetime *ad majorem Dei gloriam*, who, for most of his public, was the official,
consecrated Catholic poet.

However, if in 1836 eight out of ten readers assumed that *Jocelyn* was a
Catholic poem, they and subsequent generations were moved above all
by a sentimental love story, by a melodrama in which two ideally mated
young people are separated forever by circumstances beyond their control. We must not allow neat literary-historical assertions to convince us that
all romantic epics preach optimism and progress. Furthermore, it is a
literary-historical fact that *Jocelyn* was placed on the *Index librorum pro-
hibitorum* (22 September 1836) and that many influential Catholics were
scandalized by the poem, as they were by *Le Voyage en Orient* (1834)
and *La Chute d'un Ange* (1838), also placed on the *Index*. Although
Lamartine sought God all his life, by December 1832 he ceased to be a

believing, submissive Catholic, and his religion resembles the Deism of
Voltaire, Rousseau, Bernardin de Saint-Pierre, and Swedenborg. It is from
this perspective that we can appreciate certain romantic and pre-romantic
anti-Catholic motifs, such as the evil bishop and the seminarist in love, and
the central increment of the plot: the pathos of a sensitive young man,
predestined to love and marriage yet forced to abandon life's dearest delights
by the interference of a bishop and his Church, perhaps by God – for at
one time or another, even the divinity is reproached for the misery inflicted
on Jocelyn and his beloved. The rights of the heart to love and happiness, as
opposed to the social or religious code, is a great theme in early nineteenth-
century literature, starting with Madame de Staël (*Delphine*, 1802; *Cor-
inne*, 1807) and continuing unabated to the publication of Hugo's prose
romances (*Les Misérables*, 1862; *Les Travailleurs de la Mer*, 1867).[7]

As I see it, the problem is not whether Lamartine favors religion over love
or love over religion. This is Jocelyn's story (he is the title figure), recounted
in his voice from his point of view, whether as a protagonist or witness,
the lone exceptions a 'Prologue' and 'Epilogue' ascribed to a young disciple, a Narrator who loves the priest and manipulates the reader on his
behalf. Because of the diary format chosen by Lamartine, the protagonist
expresses all the lyricism and passion of which his soul is capable, on the
spot, without time for reflection or distancing. Indeed, the seeming authenticity of his voice is guaranteed by the fact that he does not write for a
public, that these pages of a diary are tossed into the attic. We are moved
by his ardor; he is participant, sufferer, visionary, and poet all in one.
Therefore, the implied reader identifies with his amorous longings and
with his religious commitment, each in turn. How can he be expected to
choose between them? Does not the author himself refuse to take sides?

I shall go further. I believe that Lamartine's sense of ambiguity extends to
Jocelyn himself, that, in spite of the immediacy of the narrative mode, we
are expected, while sympathizing and even identifying with the young man,
also to judge him. No doubts are permitted of his success as a priest; but
the youth's attainments as a lover and a man are another question altogether.
Jocelyn is, in many respects, a typical romantic hero. Subject to melancholia and paralysis of the will, hypersensitive, egocentric, introspective, often
withdrawn into himself, yet capable of the greatest leaps of passion and
self-sacrifice, he embodies *le mal du siècle*; he is a younger brother to Saint-
Preux, Paul, René, Obermann, Adolphe, Joseph Delorme, and Antony,
as well as to the heroes created by Byron, Shelley, and Keats. The Romantics never set their protagonists on pedestals to be adored; they delve into
them, scrutinizing their 'myths' with no less lucidity than did writers in the
centuries of Chrétien de Troyes and Racine.[8]

Standing back from Jocelyn, we observe that one of his most notable traits is an incapacity to make active decisions that will change his destiny. This passivity is accompanied by a propensity to witness life instead of living it, to be a spectator to others' happiness instead of an actor of his own. Thus (to note but the most significant examples), the young man silently spies on his mother and Julie talking of dowries, on Laurence reacting to the news of his ordination, on Laurence in Paris, on Laurence on her deathbed, and on the affectionate intimacy of three couples: Julie and her husband, two shepherds, and two farm laborers.

Along with his passivity and an inclination to voyeurism, we find that, brought up without a father, the youth has an almost pathological attachment to his mother, his alter ego whom he adores like a goddess. And he sacrifices all hope for natural, socially acceptable love with a woman for the sake of his sister, Julie. Mother, sister, and beloved are closely associated in his thoughts, and the youth wallows in tenderness for all three of them. Finally, he administers extreme unction to his mother and to Laurence, in the same terms and with identically passionate tenderness.

I consider it significant that Jocelyn also projects his affection for women onto the land, onto geographical locations associated with the women he loves. Forced to leave home, he embraces the earth more even than his mother and collects moss and soil to take with him. During the Terror he falls into a rage upon hearing that his mother has been exiled and his house burned:

> A ma soif de vengeance ou plutôt de justice
> Je ferais de mes jours cent fois le sacrifice,
> Je me consacrerais pour punir ces bourreaux,
> Deux poignards dans les mains, à des dieux infernaux,
> Et j'irais, de ce toit vengeant chaque parcelle,
> D'une goutte de sang payer chaque étincelle!    (Epoch 2: p. 600)

And later, when informed that the family home now belongs to another, this disciple of Christ assimilates his anguish to that of a husband discovering he has lost his wife to another man. Jocelyn also loves his mountain grotto in the same terms as Laurence, and, as an alternative to his mother's home, finds satisfaction in the dark, silent, womb-like refuge of the seminary.

Finally, it is a fact that the youth's most sincere, most authentic and passionate love is nourished for a full fourteen months during which he believes Laurence to be a boy. There is no overt homosexual behavior on Jocelyn's part, far from it; but under the socially acceptable category of friendship, he does adore his companion like an angel; his affection for her is as deep as one human being's can possibly be for another, and he is quite aware of her physical beauty:

Par moment, quand sur moi son visage rayonne,
La splendeur de son front m'éblouit et m'étonne;
Je ne puis soutenir l'éclat de sa beauté ...    (Epoch 3: p. 625)

This forbidden, seemingly homosexual passion was one manifestation of romantic sensibility that Lamartine introduced into his epic to please the public. Disguise and subsequent change of sex had a long tradition in romantic literature, in authors read and loved by Lamartine – d'Urfé, Prévost, Ossian, Goethe, and Byron – and he was to exploit the theme in *Raphaël* and *Fior d'Aliza*, as well as in *Jocelyn*.

The result of all this is a series of erotic situations in which the protagonist loves his mother, his sister, Laurence as a boy, Laurence as a girl, his old home, his grotto in the mountains – and on each occasion desire is thwarted, obstacles oppose its consummation. And well they might, considering that Jocelyn's passion so consistently takes on the form of tabu, whether it be the Oedipal stage, incest, homosexuality, or the breaking of priestly vows. Since the young cleric always becomes involved in forbidden relationships, is he therefore incapable of playing a more active, virile role when the possibility of a mature libido transferal presents itself? Or is it because he is a passive individual, a spectator and not an actor in life, that he unconsciously chooses love-objects he is doomed to lose? Whatever the answer, Jocelyn's relationship with Laurence definitely corresponds to the pattern of his life as a whole: he envisages her in the same terms as his mother and sister and, therefore, feels guilt and remorse as if his love for her were a form of incest. Indeed, his desire to enjoy freedom and love outside the law, to place spontaneous passion over reason, ends in disaster. Although the young man acts like a father to Laurence, calling her his child, she proves to be more mature and authentic than he, more virile than her feminized suitor. As if to prove the point, at a key moment in the narrative the bishop sends for one of his 'children,' and Jocelyn, who in the poem has never had a living father, comes running. Acting with the wrath of a jealous God, of God the Father, the prelate castigates the seminarist's sinful passion for a weaker vessel, a mere woman, and drums it out of him, referring to it in the following terms: 'honteux et ridicule piège ... sacrilège ... crime ... Mauvais fruit du loisir et de la solitude ... Risible enfantillage et des sens et du cœur ... de folles amours ... déshonneur ... votre infâme amour' (pp. 675, 676, 678). Jocelyn was guilty of forbidden curiosity when he gazed upon Laurence's naked breasts in the mountains. Now the rebellious Oedipal son is punished for his sin by symbolic mutilation or impotence and condemned to abstinence for the rest of his life. And, like so many other epic heroes, he accepts the dictates of the Father-figure, the superego principle of reason and law, thrusting away the Mother-Temptress. He takes the Father's side against the Mother and against himself, repudiating those feminine, sensuous, emotion-oriented aspects of his psyche that he now, as a defense mechanism, represses or projects onto the Mother. Although this paternal surrogate acts with all the rage of a shadow-figure, a demon adversary, the hero masochistically yields to him and accepts his values. Indeed, the seminarist has found a double, who conveniently embodies his own latent rejection of woman and provides the sanction for abandoning her, and on whom he can blame his own failings. It will come as no surprise that the bishop's insults turn out to be prophetic, that the virgin girl is metamorphosed into a courtesan, whom Jocelyn then can virtuously pity and redeem. In his consciousness as in the story (the record of his consciousness), she has never been a woman, only a tabu maiden and whore. In this poem, as in so many other works, Lamartine compensates for the protagonist's sense of tabu by having him either indulge in narcissistic contemplation or retaliate by projecting onto the beloved his own guilt and punishing her, making her suffer and wallowing in her suffering. Jocelyn chooses Jupiter over the Titans but pays a terrible price for it.

From this perspective, we can perhaps account for certain patterns of imagery in *Jocelyn*, spatial patterns especially. Erotic passion is associated with light, fresh air, joy, and radiant self-fulfillment in the Alps, whereas Jocelyn's priestly vocation and his encounter with the Father are located in seminaries, ecclesiastical retreats, and prisons – demonic temples, cold, dark, damp, with the moral as well as physical characteristics of stone. Paradoxically, it is in the mountains, with Laurence, far from the seminary, that Jocelyn experiences an evanescent, dissolving space. For this is truly a 'high place,' sacred like Mount Sinai or the Mount of Olives in the Bible, a point of Epiphany between heaven and earth. The two are fused, and space radiates with divine force; in the Alps Jocelyn's spirit soars to God, free from gross material cares. He undergoes spiritual flight, conscious of God and the cosmos, in a state of ecstasy. Here also he experiences a sense of pulsation, in time and space, all joy and song, his inner being responding to God's harmony, the universe vibrating in unison with his soul: *Coeli enarrant gloriam Dei*. Indifferent to the physical décor that surrounds him, Jocelyn experiences a *räumliche Expansionserlebnis*, a pre-natal *ozeanisches Gefühl* that permits his soul to yearn for the Almighty and ultimately to partake of a divine, absolute *nunc stans*. However, since he cannot grasp God or does so only for tiny instants, he abandons infinite space and time for more concrete settings, for protection in an intimate, enclosed, narrow, shady décor, a refuge such as la Grotte des Aigles or a mountain valley.[9] Hence also the ultimate return to the womb and to imagery of death, associated with the paternal superego. And it is here that the young hero perhaps comes closest to God: by delving into himself, into his deepest inner receptacle, his unconscious, he is enabled paradoxically to expand his soul and rise from within to the divinity, to know true love and the life-in-death of the spirit.

To arrive at such states of spiritual communion, Jocelyn is separated from his fellow men – from family, Laurence, his bishop, his parishioners – and reduced to solitude, a loneliness harder to endure than Adam's after the Fall. Some of the loveliest passages in the epic concern the young priest's affection for his dog, the only friend (except, later on, the Narrator) God permits him to keep:

> Me pardonnerez-vous, vous qui n'avez sur terre
> Pas même cet ami du pauvre solitaire? ...
> Ô pauvre et seul ami, viens, lui dis-je, aimons-nous!
> Car partout où Dieu mit deux cœurs, s'aimer est doux!
> (Epoch 9: p. 735)

Lamartine proclaims that suffering and isolation are the necessary prerequisites for spiritual visionary power. As in Wordsworth, all the major characters are solitaries, including the protagonist. However, Jocelyn is not permitted to remain in any one place for long. Indeed, as a questing hero (see above, pp. 305–6), he moves back and forth throughout the poem. The wanderer or *homo viator* as hero and the life of man as a voyage or pilgrimage are universal literary archetypes revived in the romantic period by the author of *Childe Harold*. For Lamartine, as for Byron, man is born to the Eden of heaven or an earthly childhood but then exiled to the reality of our mortal life, and he spends the rest of his days wandering to and fro seeking vainly to return home ('Milly ou la Terre natale,' 'Le Retour,' *La Vigne et la Maison*), to recover his lost paradise. Similarly, mankind travels through history like a caravan, in accordance with God's will. Jocelyn will eventually find contentment in his grotto, but in the afterworld, in death not life, in a realm of pure light where space and time cease to exist.

No less complex, no less ambivalent is Lamartine's attitude toward poetry, language, and the act of verbal communication. Jocelyn is a relatively literate country priest, who has been moved by Ossian and Bernardin de Saint-Pierre in addition to Thomas à Kempis and the Bible. Yet, during the two most happy, fulfilling periods in his life, he reads nothing, is proud to exist far from the world of letters. In the seminary he has not written in his diary for six years; his life is quiet and contented; he holds God's hand, not a pen; may all his life be such a blank page, he cries!

> Aussi, blanche est la page où je notai mes jours.
> Qu'aurais-je écrit? ...
> Ah! grâce aux passions que mon cœur se retranche,
> Puisse toute ma vie être une page blanche!   (Epoch 2: p. 591)

And in the Alps he peruses no books, only the face and soul of Laurence, finer reading matter than any other:

Ah! c'est assez pour moi de lire dans un cœur ...
Aussi je ne lis plus. Moi lire? Eh! quel poème
Egalerait jamais la voix de ce qu'on aime?    (Epoch 4: p. 647)

Still, on this very occasion, he and Laurence become poets, spontaneously singing hymns to God. And Lamartine's protagonist does find the time to write letters to his mother and sister, to compose two poems, 'Stances à Laurence' and a lyrical defense of the Church, and, above all, to keep his diary. We must not forget that, but for the 'Prologue' and 'Epilogue,' the entire epic is ascribed to the priest, is alleged to be a transcription of the diary he bequeathed, along with his Bible, to the Narrator. These pages, beaten by wind and rain, gnawed by rats or torn to kindle fires, are the outpouring of a sensitive soul. They also stand as an intense, powerful work of art. Because of them Jocelyn as a literary character has the right to be considered an author, an example of the romantic myth of the poet: a writer who is also an honest human being, his opus the spontaneous, artless projection of his soul. Jocelyn creates as well as acts, is a poet as well as a lover; indeed it is as a writer (and priest and lover) that he appeals to our sympathy: as *sacer vates*, a solitary visionary and leader, misunderstood by society but able to see beyond other men, worthy of initiation into the divine mysteries. Thus *Jocelyn* joins other works by Lamartine, such as *La Mort de Socrate*, *Les Chevaliers*, *Raphaël*, 'À Némésis,' 'Le Génie dans l'obscurité,' in defense of art and the artist or in which the protagonist is a poet. And, because he is an ordained priest, Jocelyn the poetical diarist provides an example of the *sacerdoce poétique* typical of the romantic period,[10] for he is a Catholic martyr of the Terror who yearns for both Laurence and God, for secular and sacred love, in much the same terms, and who, as priest, lover, and diarist, embodies the best of mankind.

From Jocelyn's point of view, his deepest, most valid esthetic experiences occur not when he writes his diary but during moments of spiritual ecstasy. The universe throbs with poetry, God's soul and his own pulsating together. The young man's prayer is both verse and music, and his truest poetry the yearning of his soul for God. A secondary process involves his transferal of the divine 'harmonies' to others. He teaches Laurence, the peasants and shepherds in his village, children, and the most gifted of these, the youth from outside who is to become the Narrator, his literary heir and the editor of his diary. As a teacher of children, Jocelyn resembles his spiritual brothers depicted in *Graziella* and *Raphaël*; as a guide to his people, he resembles Ballanche's Orpheus, Lamartine's Socrates and Adonaï, and Hugo's

Victor Hugo. The modern epic hero makes men better by teaching; he does
for his contemporaries what Hercules and Theseus did for the Ancients,
but through words – that is, he becomes a creator and civilizer without
arms.

Paradoxically, however, the priest-poet fails to communicate verbally
with Laurence. At their first encounter, the girl's dying father places their
relationship under the sign of silence and mystery:

> Enfin quand le regard s'éteignit dans ses yeux,
> Il posa sur sa bouche un doigt mystérieux,
> Et d'un reste de voix nommant encor Laurence,
> Il mourut en faisant le geste du silence!    (Epoch 3: p. 619)

Needless to say, on several occasions verbal exchange between them is
hindered or, if it does take place, leads to misunderstanding. Significantly,
such failures occur after the first mystery is resolved, after Jocelyn has
discovered that his companion is a girl and therefore that their relationship is
a sexual one with overtones of sin and tabu. And when they meet in Paris,
after Laurence has become a 'fallen woman,' not one word is exchanged. On
the contrary, from the beginning their finest communication, before and
after the fall, occurs on a totally different level, one which corresponds to
the technique of *sous-conversation* in the French New Novel. Jocelyn
tells us that no speech is necessary between Laurence and himself, for theirs
is a perfect wedding of souls, and indeed they communicate with eye
contact, posture, facial expression, gestures, and the flow of tears. Such body
language is a standard trait in French Romanticism, especially in the work
of Lamartine, and is to be found in *La Chute d'un Ange, Raphaël, Gra-*
*ziella*, and the lyrics, where it is shown to be the mark of soul mates in
love. It may also correspond to the ineffable muteness in contemporary
melodrama, the notion that truly virtuous and innocent people have recourse
to a code less coarse than speech, truly a primal language.[11] In sum, Jocelyn's greatness as a poet, priest, and lover resides not in verbal dexterity
but in his soul, in sympathetic vibrations from his heart.

Modern scholarship has come to recognize in Alphonse de Lamartine a child
of the eighteenth century, not a revolutionary apostle of Romanticism. In
matters of language, meter, style, and form, in the use of tropes and rhetoric, he was the disciple of Saint-Lambert, Bertin, Delille, Parny, and the
author of *Zaïre* and *Mérope*, just as, in the realm of ideas, he followed in the
wake of the *philosophes*. One canon of eighteenth-century poetics he
adopted with enthusiasm: the notion of literary decorum and a hierarchy of
genres. Like Wordsworth he was familiar with the idea of epic, its tradi-

tion in the West and the necessity for a poet to succeed in this the greatest, most serious of literary kinds. Unfortunately, in his day no commonly held, living myth existed to provide the material for epic, and, in any case, the martial code of Homer and Virgil, or of the *chansons de geste*, ran counter to Lamartine's gifts as an artist. However, since by the 1830s the rules of the neoclassical heroic poem no longer held absolute sway, the bard of Milly could choose to sing of more bucolic, intimate matters and in the first-person mode of pseudo-autobiography. Thus he acquired the liberty to combine public and private concerns, to intersperse a lyric voice in verse narrative, to juxtapose pathos and ethos, the lofty and the familiar, high style and middle or low subject-matter. In so doing he created the first great French long poem in the nineteenth century.

*Jocelyn* has been criticized for a variety of reasons, both by Lamartine's contemporaries and in our own day. That this verse melodrama is neither the *Aeneid* nor *Madame Bovary* and was not meant to be is a fact clearly recognized by the twenty-four thousand people who purchased copies in the first month after publication and the hundreds of thousands, even millions, who have read the poem over the succeeding century and a half, making it Lamartine's most popular book except for *Graziella*. His masterwork proves to be a finely constructed narrative whole, based upon the rules of composition and rhetoric, yet also contains those very qualities that appeal to the popular spirit: pathos, tears, melodrama, power, anguish, suffering, the modes of heroism and of pity. And, from a modern perspective, it appears as a uniquely personal work of art, ambivalent and ambiguous, in which a tortured soul seeks answers that never come, and we scrutinize to the depths of his being his anguish and his human failing: intense psychological insight inserted into a pastoral-romance frame. It is Jocelyn's poem, and in the tortured complexity of Jocelyn's soul, in this seemingly un-Lamartinian anguish, greatness lies. Taken in its totality, *Jocelyn* is an extraordinarily varied work – pseudo-autobiography, idyll, *Bildungsroman*, sermon, prayer, oracle, diary, lyric, and epic – and a startlingly original creation by one of the most versatile masters of French Romanticism: a man who created three new subgenres in French verse: the Meditation, the Harmony, and the familiar epic.

It is obvious that quite a few of the traits I have discovered in *Jocelyn* are to be identified as hallmarks of the romantic movement. In addition, we also find a quality of intimacy, in the home, garden, and family, of idyllic realism, gentle melancholy, and non-militant resignation, of loyalty to the establishment and the upholding of a doctrine of *Ora et labora*, of *Sammeln und Hegen*. These are among the salient traits of a literary movement in German-speaking lands – *Biedermeier* – which may have been of more general, European import than has been heretofore recognized.[12]

Traits of *Biedermeier* are to be found in many French writers of the day, such as Brizeux, Gautier, and Sainte-Beuve, as well as in poems by Hugo, Musset, and Lamartine. Personally, I consider a further scrutiny of the *Biedermeier* phenomenon in its European dimensions to be one way of appreciating the tradition of rustic epic in nineteenth-century France.

Lamartine provided one solution to the problem that his generation of poets took more seriously than we generally realize: how is epic possible, given the absence of a common ideology and the pervasiveness of a modern, prosaic environment, a totally problematic world? His answer was to create an unheroic protagonist who was nonetheless epic, that is, a problematic hero of the spirit (an ordained priest) whose struggles occur in an inner realm; and who acts in a contemporary setting which nonetheless, because of its location (the country, the Alps), provides for its home-bound, bourgeois public a modicum of distance, even the exotic. This is a new sort of hero: a man of peace, a civilizer, in his way an artist, and, for all the benefits he brings to society, a solitary. The long poem turns inward, its story the heart of a gifted individual: hence the lyrical quality of much of Lamartine's text, the lyrics interspersed in the narrative whole (as with Scott, Byron, and Coleridge, among others), and the subjective, even fragmented form which the poem adopts. A case can be made that, in the tradition of Guillaume de Lorris and Guillaume de Machaut, Lamartine takes a lyric speaker or *persona*, in his case an 'elegiac self,'[13] and makes of him a protagonist of epic-romance. In a world without faith, the quest for faith, man's arrival at knowledge, and belief itself become the subject of epic. In this way the romantic poet overcomes the gap between epic and lyric, grants his inspired vision scope and intensity, and renews the centuries-old tradition of the heroic long poem.

Chapter Fourteen

#  VIGNY

Chateaubriand called for a new epic in France, indicating what form it should take. In the 1830s and 1840s his summons was answered by Lamartine and by a host of respectable, though perhaps less talented writers, in the line of Quinet, Brizeux, Laprade, and Soumet. The question of the long poem was by no means resolved, however, nor were the 'epic of humanity' and the 'intimate epic' to satisfy the nineteenth century's quest for the sublime style. For many writers of the age, epos was associated with outdated, anachronistic heroics, perpetrated in the old days by Chapelain and Voltaire and more recently by a mass of neoclassical hacks who littered the presses of the Empire and the Restoration, while the new romantic epic often suffered from sentimentality, historical untruth, and a weak, enervating style. For these individuals, since the long poem could not cope with the demands of the modern temper, other modes would have to be explored. One possibility was the philosophical epic (Ballanche) or the philosophical, Faustian drama (Quinet), both in prose. Another lay in short narrative poems, brief epics, whether taken singly or arranged in a sequence.

In the days of Saint-Amant and Le Moyne, the word *poème* meant epic. Then, in the late eighteenth and early nineteenth centuries, short *poëmes* were composed on subjects taken from the Bible, Antiquity, or the Middle Ages: they exhibited the usual epic devices and were recognized to be a compact variation of the genre. André Chénier's opus, published for the first time in 1819, made a strong impression upon the early Romantics. In particular, *L'Aveugle*, *Le Mendiant*, and *Le Malade* set a model for the *Kurzepos*. In the 1820s, influenced by Chénier and Lord Byron, Lamartine wrote *La Mort de Socrate* (1823) and *Le Dernier Chant du pèlerinage d'Harold* (1825), and Vigny published the various editions of his *Poëmes Antiques et Modernes* (1822, 1826, 1829). In 1835 Creuzé de Lesser presented his theory of the *Odéide* or sequence of poems on the same subject. Meanwhile, secondary figures such as Edouard d'Anglemont, Aubry, Auguste Barbier, and Laurent-Pichat were working more or less in the style of Vigny. Then, during the first decade of the Second Empire, there appeared collections of brief epics meant to rival or surpass Chénier and Vigny: Leconte de Lisle's *Poèmes antiques* (1852), Laprade's *Idylles héroïques* (1858), Hugo's *Légende des Siècles* (1859), Leconte's *Poèmes barbares* (1862), and finally in 1864 the posthumous edition of Vigny's *Destinées*. In the second half of the century the *Kurzepos* predominates, in the hands of Leconte de Lisle, Banville, Coppée, Catulle Mendès, Léon Dierx, André de Guerne, and Sully Prudhomme; it remains the most important manifestation of the sublime style up to Péguy and Claudel.

Prior to the publication of *La Légende des Siècles* the leading master of brief epic was Alfred de Vigny (1797–1863). In the 'Préface' to his *Etudes françaises et étrangères* (1828), Emile Deschamps assigns first place to Hugo in the lyric, to Lamartine in the elegy, and to Vigny in the epic. According to Deschamps, 'M. Alfred de Vigny, un des premiers, a senti que la vieille épopée était devenue presqu' impossible en vers, et principalement en vers français, avec tout l'attirail du merveilleux; il a senti que les *Martyrs* sont la seule épopée qui puisse être lue de nos jours, parce qu'elle est en prose …; et à l'exemple de Lord Byron, il a su renfermer la poésie dans des compositions d'une moyenne étendue et toutes inventées; il a su être grand sans être long' (p. 13). Vigny refers to himself as a *moraliste épique* or *génie épique*, and in the 1837 'Préface' to his collection declares: 'Le seul mérite qu'on n'ait jamais disputé à ces compositions, c'est d'avoir devancé en France toutes celles de ce genre, dans lesquelles une pensée philosophique est mise en scène sous une forme Epique ou Dramatique.'[1] In essence, he modernizes the heroic poem, shortening it and eliminating the marvelous. He also reacts against the largely didactic, descriptive long poem in the line of Saint-Lambert, Roucher, and Delille. Furthermore, by refusing the subjectivism, ecstasy, and claim to a highly sensitive personal vision typical of his contemporaries, he retains a quality of third-person objectivity and a fascination for narrative inherent in the epic tradition. Infatuation with ideas and a claim to philosophical profundity are typically romantic traits; Vigny thus responds to Quinet's request that modern epos be speculative or philosophical, in contrast to the heroic (Homer) and the theological (Dante) modes of the past. For him, the *poëme* acquires the dignity of the old epic and also presents a message to humanity.[2]

Vigny's earliest long poem, *Héléna* (1822), a Byronic tale treating the Greek uprising, proved to be a failure and was suppressed from later collections of his verse. For a decade after 1815 he envisaged long, epic-type poems treating Susanna and the Elders, the Last Judgment, and Satan, even a Christian theogony. Ultimately, these projects were never completed, but they did provide the inspiration for two of his finest poems, both called 'mysteries' (under the influence of Byron): *Eloa* and *Le Déluge*.

*Eloa ou la Sœur des anges,*[3] a *mystère* of some 778 lines, composed in 1823 and published the following year, develops themes dear to the romantic temperament: the seduction of an angel, woman as redeemer, Satan the handsome rebel, and the fatality of love. Vigny exploits the vogue of Satan, portraying him as a tender, beautiful, melancholic youth, purportedly a friend and benefactor of mankind, and as a 'fated being,' doomed to destroy himself and those he loves. The Devil willfully seduces Eloa, but in the process, for an instant, comes to care for her and experiences remorse, only to reaffirm his will to conquer. Vigny also scrutinizes Eloa's character, delving into the psychology of compassion. Indeed, with some justification, he makes a claim for originality, for having launched the literary motif of a female angel, born on earth, a more compassionate, more 'human' embodiment of God's ministry than was possible in the past. Although the divinity created her, and Eloa's tenderness evokes a sense of maternal paradise and innocence, although her 'feminine' purity and spontaneity are presumed superior to man's nature, nonetheless her behavior, the manifestation of her pity, leads to weakness and the fall. Is God himself responsible for the presence of evil in his cosmos, for the seduction of an angel that he could easily have prevented? Or are love and compassion to be condemned for blinding Eloa to reality, both human and divine? Perhaps, like many another early Romantic, including Lamartine, Vigny was unable to break with the Church and support Satan as a rebel-hero, yet was no less unwilling to condemn him as a monster or laugh at him as a grotesque. Hence this fascinatingly ambivalent poem in which the Fiend loves and suffers remorse, and in which the redeeming angel shares her seducer's boredom with heaven and his moral guilt. Hence also a sense of universality, derived from the fact that Eloa's fate parallels that of Eve in the Garden of Eden, that this 'sister to the angels' evokes the mother of mankind, for her destiny is that of the race as a whole.

Spatially, Eloa's heaven, a refuge, a feminine world of lushness and splendor, is set in opposition to Satan's inferno, home of darkness, captivity, and pain. Paradise contains community and harmony; hell, loneliness and silence. Paradise lies above, hell below. For whatever reasons, Eloa refuses the stasis of her celestial refuge. She begins by quitting the sacred place in the center of the universe, by daring to visit an intermediate outlying region where angels fear to tread. This more or less horizontal mobility manifests a form of disobedience and discontent; it concretizes her inner solitude, thus anticipates the more striking descent which will ensue when Satan carries her down with him to be his slave forever. It is appropriate that this winged female angel is compared to a bird: dove, partridge, and hummingbird, beautiful yet frail, a delicate creature of the spirit given to love, she is foredoomed by her very nature to wander and eventually become lost.

The upper paradise is a realm of pure light, sparkling with gold and precious gems, reflecting the colors of the prism, redolent with the odor of flowers. Its transparent softness and grace – a myriad of whites, blues, pinks, and golds – contrast with the harsh scarlet, gold, and black incarnate in Satan.[4] Thus Eloa embodies pure, innocent light, whereas Satan stands for death and the darkness of the pit. He even delivers a speech in praise of the night, of intimacy in the dark:

> 'Es-tu venue, avec quelques Anges des cieux,
> Admirer de mes nuits le cours délicieux?
> As-tu vu leurs trésors? Sais-tu quelles merveilles
> Des Anges ténébreux accompagnent les veilles?'    (p. 22)

However, this paradoxically beautiful fallen angel, himself dazzled by Eloa's sheen, once was Lucifer the light-bearer, and he is not above evoking light-imagery (love equals the union of two flames or of the dawn and the setting moon) in order to seduce her, or even assuming the pose of a white bird, the swan. Furthermore, Eloa's shimmering brilliance proves to be flawed, is corrupted upon contact with the darkness or false light of the pit. Born from God's gaze upon one of Christ's tears shed over the death of Lazarus, she weeps over Satan's misery upon hearing his speech and seeing him cry. In her case the hard will of heaven's treasure (gold, gems) is metamorphosed into feminine water; tears of pity and weakness are her emblem. They shine in light yet cause her undoing. Satan, on the other hand, is on the verge of sincerely weeping, so eager to shed 'larmes des humains,' but holds back in time. Instead he cries falsely, hypocritically. Thus his darkness and the cruel light of his will triumph over the fluid evanescence embodied in God's bird of pity.

It has been claimed that *Eloa* depicts less a metaphysical drama of good versus evil than the spectacle of mystic eroticism, a drama of the senses. There can be no doubt that, under the influence of Byron, Moore, Chénier, Parny, and 'Monk' Lewis, Vigny created an atmosphere of sensuousness, where the flowers of heaven and Satan's languorous beauty contribute equally to Eloa's seduction. Themes of defiling, of defloration, are exploited. The angel's innocence is troubled, and unaccustomed desires give battle for her soul, as she is fascinated by sensuous reverie, as her nascent sensuality leads to disobedience and a kind of liberation. Yet Eloa chooses to fall because of Satan's words; it is his speech, his verbal skills, that destroy her. And he not only seduces this one angel but has succeeded in deceiving generations of Vigny's readers. It is an error to presume that the Devil is a true friend of man who pities persecuted lovers and slaves, and/or that Vigny the author agrees with him, taking the side of darkness against God's light. Satan the sympathetic rebel and friend to mankind is evoked only from his own perspective, in his own voice. Vigny ascribes to him a resoundingly humanitarian speech, because in Satan's mouth it serves to seduce Eloa, to render him interesting in her eyes and weaken her resistance to his blandishments. His real attitude toward humankind we shall never know, but, given the sadistic brutality with which he treats the earth-born angel, now become his slave, whom he loved and to whom he offered companionship and sharing, we have the right to question the good faith of his words.

I propose that Vigny's poem treats in magnificent fashion the relationship between two beings and the problems of communication that arise between them. At first fellow angels warn Eloa against Satan, an imprudent act of pedagogy that only fans the flames of her curiosity and awakens her sympathy. When she meets the fallen light-bearer, he begins by speaking. He is the first creature who relates to her in a meaningful way. Yet everything he says is false, and the purpose of his words is to seduce. When she finally replies, when Satan's monologues are transferred into a dialogue, her defeat has been half consummated. Yet this is not a true exchange: Eloa tells the truth while Satan continues to lie. They only communicate authentically in the end, in the last ten lines of the poem, after the fall, when it is too late and both figures are doomed:

'Où me conduisez-vous, bel Ange? – Viens toujours.
– Que votre voix est triste, et quel sombre discours!
N'est-ce pas Eloa qui soulève ta chaîne?
J'ai cru t'avoir sauvé. – Non, c'est moi qui t'entraîne.
– Si nous sommes unis, peu m'importe en quel lieu!
Nomme-moi donc encore ou ta Sœur ou ton Dieu!
– J'enlève mon esclave et je tiens ma victime.
– Tu paraissais si bon! Oh! qu'ai-je fait? – Un crime.
– Seras-tu plus heureux du moins, est-tu content?
– Plus triste que jamais. – Qui donc es-tu? – Satan.'    (pp. 30–1)

What renders their drama so complex is the fact that a second facet of communication or non-communication, as the case may be, occurs on a different level, one of non-verbal body language (see chapter thirteen, p. 315). Eloa would like to help the Devil, but, since he suffers most from sterile rage at the beauty and goodness of heaven, her presence increases his misery instead of alleviating it. Satan lowers his eyes before addressing her, either, says Vigny, because he comprehends the force of his gaze or perhaps because he might otherwise reveal to her his secret, inner thoughts (p. 20). In fact, later, his gaze will conquer her and compel her to remain. At a particular moment in the dialogue, Satan, like Choderlos's Valmont, is persuaded by his own rhetoric; he does fall in love with Eloa and is on the point of yielding to her and to God. He experiences regrets, remorse, and despair, he realizes her truth and wishes to cry human tears. As a result of this battle within his soul, for the first time a natural look appears on his face, *douleur convulsive* (p. 29), and his authentic anguish is communicated to Eloa. She, however, fails to decipher the code: at the very moment when Satan is closest to her, she recoils. She had taken his hypocritical blandishments literally at face value and cannot now cope with or interpret correctly genuine affection. Meanwhile, Satan, far more lucid than she and a greater master of body language, having discovered her error, is enabled to subdue his own weakness. He effaces love from his heart, replaces the mask, and becomes authentically himself again: an inauthentic liar. Appearing to her as she unconsciously wishes him to, the fallen Lucifer weeps false tears that then evoke genuine ones in his prey. Although, like Lamartine, Vigny assumes that the most truly passionate Eros expresses itself in *sous-conversation* (cf. *Cinq-Mars* and *Chatterton*), here the language of vision succeeds no better than that of the mouth. Eye contact, tears, and speech prevaricate: reality turns out to be illusion, and illusion reality. Eloa is unable to distinguish between genuine and false tears, between authentic rage and a lying melancholia. Perhaps then she falls as a result of her own blindness, and is responsible for her damnation.

Be this as it may, the irony of the poem centers on these problems of communication and the fact that the alleged benefactor of lovers and slaves ceases to cherish his beloved, indeed returns her affection by making her a slave. Eloa the Elect (according to Chateaubriand's comment on Klopstock's *Messias*, known to Vigny) has apparently been elected to fall. The relationship between two creatures in love leads to damnation, their companionship to hell. Yet the author is fascinated by the psychology of his characters, by the way they interrelate, by the way each strives to manipulate, to master the other. In this, perhaps his most starkly pessimistic work, Vigny expresses a sense of disillusionment over the 'human' and 'angelic' conditions in a cosmos where such punishment is meted out to Eloa, and to Satan also, for daring to love, to feel pity, to join with another, and above all to think.

Although in *Eloa* God is noticeable by his absence, the heroine may or may not be guilty of transgression: the question is unanswered. In Vigny's second 'mystery,' *Le Déluge*, and in the splendid poem, *La Prison* (composed in 1821), God's absence clearly points to the innocence of mankind vis-à-vis the divinity. *La Prison*[5] is based upon the legend of the Man in the Iron Mask. An old Monk is led inside a dungeon, in order to administer extreme unction to one of the captives. This individual, presumably a twin brother to Louis xɪv, has, but for a brief period of escape, spent his lifetime incarcerated, a metallic mask riveted to his face. The Prisoner proclaims his innocence in the face of God and king; he cries out against metaphysical injustice. Since his only fault is to have been born a member of the human race, he repudiates a God who permits a lifetime of such suffering: 'Il est un Dieu? J'ai pourtant bien souffert!' (p. 71). He refuses the Monk's absolution, claiming that no heavenly reward can possibly undo his misery on earth, and that, in any case, he has no knowledge of better conditions. He goes to his death in a state of delirium and rebellion, breaking his arm against the cell wall. Neither salvation nor the existence of an afterlife is assured; the Monk speaks of a just, beneficent God but, quite possibly, is mistaken. Thus Vigny undermines the deity who dares to judge us and permit our misery.

In this poem, the imagery evokes masculine power. The mask is iron, rusted by the captive's tears: 'Mes larmes ont rouillé mon masque de torture' (p. 74). It evokes the dehumanization inflicted upon a wretch whose facial features have never existed for others. This outer, artificial, false visage is eternally static, just as stone walls render the Prisoner immobile. With splendid manipulation of narrative point of view, Vigny shows us the prison through the Monk's consciousness; we discover it, enter into its confines, are terrified by it, as he is. The poet demystifies a nascent romantic myth: that the prison is a refuge that provides healthy solitude and encourages its inmate on the road to poetry and spiritual transcendence.[6] The jail symbolizes life, man's existential situation, is a setting of anxiety and terror, where one religious has already disappeared and where our Monk, although possessing greater freedom of action than the Prisoner, is rendered immobile all night long at the dying man's side and, in any case, also risks death and stasis. In the end the captive retreats into a harsher, still more confining dungeon – his coffin; while the Monk leans over the dead man's face in terror and perhaps soon is to join him in the grave. For both individuals there is 'no exit.' We comprehend Vigny's archetypal demonic universe: poisoned, repugnant air; muddy, dank, serpentine corridors; the weight of chains; creaking noises; and cold stone walls.[7] This is the maze, the prison, the tomb, an inferno with torture and pain, under the auspices of a wicked God, in which a scapegoat is sacrificed in the presence of a monk. It is also Vigny's portrait of an inner hell, where the child is deserted and love refused, where corrupt, sadistic power is unleashed upon the innocent.

The Prisoner is a captive in life and in death. Born a prince of the blood, he has spent his entire mortal span as a slave. Yet the Monk, God's servant, therefore the willing slave of a benevolent autocrat, is no more a master than his interlocutor. A bit of a coward (with good reason), he fears

for his own safety in this demonic place; he too is, at least symbolically, a
captive and in danger. And he has suffered in life, his flesh macerated by a
hairshirt. When the Monk offers the Prisoner freedom in heaven, the
latter demurs, proclaiming that surely chains await him there also: 'A moi!
je n'en veux pas; j'y trouverais des chaînes' (p. 76). Then, although we are
told that the poor wretch attains freedom in death, since the mask follows
him into the tomb, even there he is bound, a captive to his destiny. The
mask is his prison. From Vigny's perspective, it is only by refusing the
Monk's ministry, by rebelling against God and against his deputy, his
alter ego, that the Prisoner can arrive at a form of poetic freedom, an agnostic spirituality, the only kind Alfred de Vigny knows.

One aspect of the Monk's slavery derives from impaired vision. Led
through the maze to the captive's cell blindfolded, his first speech is a
plaint that he cannot see! Once in the Prisoner's presence, the Monk's blind-
fold is removed, but still he never beholds his penitent's face beneath the
mask, even in death. This stage of relative physical blindness corresponds to
his spiritual blindness, that is, his trust in a beneficent deity. Although the
Prisoner also has problems seeing and in a moment of delirium fails to
recognize the Monk, for most of the poem he perceives the world lucidly.
Furthermore, a martyr to an evil God, never permitted to live a normal life,
nonetheless he is the actor in this drama, and the Monk a mere observer,
lacking the perspicacity of those other spectators, the Black Doctor in *Stello*
and the narrator of *Servitude et Grandeur Militaires*. Louis xiv's brother
is authentically open to reality and full of insight, capable of facing the world
as it is. Nonetheless, both men remain in shadows, within a dungeon.
Their darkness corresponds to that of *La Colère de Samson*, *Le Mont des
Oliviers*, and *La Mort du Loup* – symbolizing a state of metaphysical
anguish, a world without God where man must grope his way alone.

The two men also fail to communicate with each other and with the
outside world. At first the Prisoner states that he will listen to the Monk,
that he will not disdain friendly human voices:

> Hélas! malgré ma haine,
> J'écoute votre voix, c'est une voix humaine:
> J'étais né pour l'entendre ...
> Jamais je ne connus cette rare parole
> Qu'on appelle amitié, qui, dit-on, vous console ...
> Et pourtant, lorsqu'un mot m'arriva moins sévère,
> Il ne fut pas perdu pour mon cœur solitaire.   (p. 70)

The Monk, who received no answers from the guards to his queries, will
speak to the dying prince. A dialogue thus is launched, but the captive

refuses the priest's message, will not accept the spirit of his exhortation. Solitude has been the man's lot throughout the span of his years: he has no past, no future; he has never lived:

> Des péchés tant proscrits, où toujours l'on succombe,
> Aucun n'a séparé mon berceau de ma tombe;
> Seul, toujours seul, par l'âge et la douleur vaincu,
> Je meurs tout chargé d'ans, et je n'ai pas vécu …
> Je n'eus point d'avenir et n'ai point de passé … (p. 73)

He declares that since men's voices were refused to him in life, he in turn shall refuse the voice of God. Although urged to speak one word of prayer, he refuses, for one old monk is not a sufficient mediator between himself and the Almighty; the Monk is literally too little and too late. Furthermore, in the course of their dialogue, the Prisoner falls into delirium. He ceases to recognize his interlocutor or to understand the latter's speech; his own remarks wander irrationally. Thus, even this form of communication breaks down. And well it might: the Prisoner is dying, and his unmerited end after a lifetime of undeserved captivity refutes the Monk's naïve Christian faith. The captive ceases talking to die, thus, like Christ and the wolf (*Le Mont des Oliviers*, *La Mort du Loup*), answering with silence the silence of a distant, indifferent creator.

If all great narrative poetry treats, in some sense, an initiation or rite of passage, in the majority of Vigny's works the passage and initiation are over the threshold of death. It is on the point of expiring that Moses, the wolf, Christ, and the heroes of *Le Déluge* and *La Bouteille à la mer* must each come to terms with God's silence. And Vigny's heroes face death without hope of a subsequent rebirth; the shadow-monster they defy is God himself. The old epic motif of an Olympian adversary (in Homer, Virgil, Camoens) is transformed in the modern world: here the Christian divinity himself is shown to be hostile or indifferent, so that coming to terms with one's mortality becomes a far more anguishing experience than it was for Gilgamesh, Achilles, and Beowulf. In *La Prison* the Prisoner and the Monk, both old, both broken by life, face together the anguish of mortality. The issue is rendered all the more poignant by the fact that the two men, doubles, the innocent captive and the Christian ascetic, have never lived, that, incarcerated in their respective dungeon and monastic cell, each has inhabited the tomb before the fateful day when they meet for the first and last time. At any rate, Vigny chooses man's pitiful, dogged, despairing existence over God's heaven. The Prisoner goes to his end in revolt. Lacking a past, unsure of a future that he renounces in advance, his anguished yet vitally lucid present measures itself against the eternal present of God's infinity. And Vigny's readers, imitating the Monk, can only gasp with admiration and wonder.

The city of Paris was to become one of the leading motifs in nineteenth-century letters, highlighted in the works of Balzac, Michelet, Hugo, Nerval, Baudelaire, Flaubert, and Zola, to name only the most eminent. Scholars estimate that the vogue was launched in 1831 by two poems, both crucial for later developments of the theme: Barbier's *La Cuve* and Vigny's *Paris*. *Paris*[8] is one of two 'elevations' (defined as meditative or philosophical poems treating contemporary social problems, rising from mundane matters to the divine) that Vigny completed out of the ten or so he planned to write. Made up largely of a dialogue between two characters, whom we can designate as the Speaker (a Parisian) and his interlocutor, a Traveler, it treats in poetic terms the present reality of the capital and its future. Paris is viewed as a passive décor, speculated upon by these two active spirits. That one of the spectators should be a voyager from foreign parts is an original contribution of Vigny to the development of the Paris-theme. And, although the poem contains little direct allusion to the 1830 Revolution, it can be fully understood only with reference to those momentous days that toppled the French royal House for the second time in less than half a century.[9]

The Speaker and the Traveler look down on Paris from a height, probably one of the towers of Notre-Dame (cf. comparable panoramas in Nerval and Hugo) or perhaps Montmartre (other possibilities are the Tour Saint-Jacques and the Vendôme Column). This location is a point of epiphany, an intermediary realm between men and the gods, appropriate for poet-seers in quest of truths denied to their fellow mortals. The Speaker shares glory and anguish with several other of Vigny's characters: Moses on Mount Sinai, Emmanuel on Mount Ararat, and Christ on the Mount of Olives, who all benefit from increased vision but suffer from loneliness, isolated from the crowd beneath and the silent divinity above, looking up to the one and down upon the others.

Immobile in the center of the maze (as in *La Prison* and *Les Destinées*), they behold Paris, which stretches about them in the form of a circle. Such a concave landscape pervades Vigny's opus, whether in the form of an inferno or a refuge. Hard minds at the center probe images scattered out toward the circumference.[10] Indeed, Vigny compares the city to a wheel, more specifically to the circular moving parts of a vehicle or a clock. Paris is itself the wheel or the axle of a wheel, which turns the entire world, a machine attached to and moving other machines. These figures recall the traditional Wheel of Fortune and the four wheels of the Prophet Ezekiel. On the one hand, Vigny's city is credited with power, and his clock-imagery reinforces the notion of progress, of duration, in harmony with, even determined by, Paris. Yet we are also expected to recognize the menace inherent in modern life, in science and technology, in the 1789 and 1830 revolutions, depicted in terms of machinery, inhuman in its ruthless, truly Fortuna-like motion.

The poem is set at night, in a black, sinister, man-made world (with white walls, the whited sepulchres of Scripture), lacking the qualities of organic nature. And Paris is compared to a furnace or crucible:

> Le vertige parfois est prophétique. Il fait
> Qu'une Fournaise ardente éblouit ta paupière.
> C'est la Fournaise aussi que tu vois. Sa lumière
> Teint de rouge les bords du ciel noir et profond.    (p. 111)

The source of the image, of course, is the Burning Fiery Furnace of the Bible, in which Nebuchadnezzar fails to vanquish Daniel's supporters. Thus the diabolic furnace, with circles of fire and accompanying lava flow, corresponds to a hellish black city, a threat to mankind through violence and atheism. This is evil red and black, the fire, blood, and night that haunt Vigny's imagination, along with accessory 'demonic' motifs: avenging deities, wasteland, tower, maze, serpent, and death. In the spirit of Dante, the Inferno is observed from a height by a pilgrim and his guide. On the other hand, however, Vigny also alludes to Paris as the City of Light (illuminated in the evening by recently installed gas lamps), a modern, secular Jerusalem. This forge or crucible generates Promethean fire – new ideas, for flames of revolution clear away archaic institutions. And its light evokes creative minds ('des Esprits, / Grands ouvriers d'une œuvre et sans nom et sans prix,' p. 111), who work at their lamps by night, the philosophers of the Enlightenment and thinkers in Vigny's own day, contemporary lay equivalents to the Prophets of Israel, who succeed in making Paris the center of a world-axis and a pillar of fire leading beleaguered peoples toward a spiritual Promised Land.

Vigny's judgment on the metropolis is ambivalent, as complex as his psychological presentations of Eloa and Satan. To the extent that Paris is demonic, a modern Dantean City of Dis, the threat of apocalypse, of divine judgment, appropriately waits in the offing. We are told that the volcano will one day destroy itself, leaving only a flat plain and ashes in its wake. And a black cloud or rock or millstone in the sky will come to crush the impious place, and an exterminating angel will destroy it:

> Mais je crains bien pour elle et pour vous, car voilà
> Quelque chose de noir, de lourd, de vaste, là,

Au plus haut point du ciel, où ne sauraient atteindre
Les feux dont l'horizon ne cesse de se teindre;
Et je crois entrevoir ce rocher ténébreux
Qu'annoncèrent jadis les prophètes hébreux.  (p. 114)

Thus, in Vigny, as in Lamartine and Hugo, modern Paris is also assimilated
to decadent, antediluvian centers, such as Babel and Sodom. Yet, aside
from the question of punishment, Paris will end one day, says the Traveler,
for all men and cities have an allotted span: as in *La Prison*, death comes
inevitably. Here the motif of the Angel of Doom joins the imagery of clocks
and machines. A watch marks time, interprets and even creates the time
without which it has no reason to exist and because of which it too shall
perish. One day all machines shall break down and all clocks stop. And
the very motion of the watch forces us to conceive of destiny, of the inexor-
able march of time and of death. This horrifying, paradoxical end of all
things was often expressed by the Romantics as the fall of Paris: by Lamartine (in *Les Visions*), Slowacki, Hugo, and Quinet, among others.

From another perspective, of course, Paris is not the City of Dis but a
holy place, a center of the world-maze, an Eden for intellectuals, created
by God for the benefit of mankind. It resembles the wheel of Ezekiel, its
tower is a cathedral, its flames give forth light and truth, the spark of life,
and contribute to alchemical rebirth. Paris is good fire, its adversaries are
black. After the City of Light is extinguished, darkness will prevail over
the face of the earth. Therefore, whether we deem the capital to be good or
evil (and it no doubt partakes of both categories), it is both powerful and
unique. Since the Speaker tells us that the exterminating angel will destroy
the metropolis, with reverence, on his knees, we should revere the dust
and ashes that will remain after the apocalypse. The spirit of God was here,
inhabiting this place, he declares, and no one knows what will succeed
Paris after its passing. It is appropriate that the city of spiritual light be
discussed by intellectuals, and that with this agnostic affirmation of doubt
and of the dignity of man, Vigny terminates his meditation and his myth.

Unlike Lamartine and Hugo, Vigny exhibits more than a little misogyny.
Often in his work a charming, fickle, weak woman inspires a superior
man who affords her protection. Sensuous, seductive females appear in the
early poems as well as in *Cinq-Mars* and the minor comedy *Quitte pour
la peur*. It is perhaps not coincidental that one of the two Shakespearean
plays Vigny chose to translate was *Othello*. However, the work which
has carried Vigny's message to posterity is *La Colère de Samson*,[11] written in
1839 and published posthumously in 1864. In this poem Samson, fully
aware that Delilah has betrayed him, weary of her lying and treachery,

allows himself to be blinded by the Philistines, but not before having denounced womankind and God, who permits such a betrayal of man's idealism. According to Samson, man is good and woman evil; the former, by his very nature, loves and gives; the latter deceives and takes. Delilah is the examplar of all females, who are inherently impure, defiled, and given to fraud. Thus woman's actions undermine God's pattern in the universe, are an offense to him and to nature. Although Vigny's portrayal of Delilah of course was partly derived from his own antifeminist imagination and from the end of his affair with Marie Dorval, it can be assimilated to a number of nineteenth-century portrayals of fatal women, Lilith-Ishtar figures that Mario Praz ranges under the heading *La Belle Dame sans Merci.*[12] In this category he includes Salammbô, Carmen, Salome, and characters in Barbey d'Aurevilly, Louÿs, Sue, and Huysmans as well as Swinburne and d'Annunzio. The fact that the sadistic female is a type prevalent in the second half of the century indicates how progressive in sensibility Vigny was, closer to, say, Baudelaire and Mallarmé than to his immediate contemporaries.

Vigny exults in an exotic Biblical world, redolent with local color of the East. He evokes fire, wind, and the desert, sensuousness under a tent in hot climates, voluptuous odors, cushions, soft whispers, the sheen of jewelry, and the temptress's warm, round body and flowing hair. The tent ought to serve as a place of happy solitude, a languorous refuge conducive to love. This is Bachelardian intimate space, a Durandian world of the feminine. Delilah is compared to a leopard and a gazelle in a climate of lions. Her sensual, animal nature is underscored by allusions to her lovely feet as she crouches before Samson. But does she possess human feet? Vigny also compares her to a viper, and she is said to slither like a snake. Resembling Richelieu in *Cinq-Mars* and Robespierre in *Stello*, the Philistine woman is cold and calculating, a gilded serpent covered with jewels who betrays for money and power or simply because it is in her nature to do so, a castrating figure who recalls the reptilian arch-traitor Satan in the Garden of Eden. This is Delilah the Fatal Woman, descendant of Ishtar and Eve, sister of Circe and Calypso, comparable to modern epic temptresses as well: Alcina, Armida, Duessa, Acrasia, and Chateaubriand's Velléda. Adhering to the old Christian archetype and to the tradition of Virgil, Tasso, and the *chanson de geste*, Delilah represents passion, unawareness, immaturity, lightness, and weakness, whereas Samson stands for reason, lucidity, paternal maturity, stolid weight, and strength. However, since she crouches down next to Samson's legs, her arms around him, binding him, since he is seated like the dog-faced Egyptian god Anubis worshiped by Pagans, since he yields to her and serves her lust −

L'une est grande et superbe, et l'autre est à ses pieds:
C'est Dalila, l'esclave, et ses bras sont liés
Aux genoux réunis du maître jeune et grave
Dont la force divine obéit à l'esclave.    (p. 143)

– we realize that, whether because of her, God, or his own nature, he also
has been reduced to physical passion and the irrational, he too has been
dehumanized. It is a fact that they make love after Samson discovers
Delilah's treachery. In this feminine world, the Hebrew yields to the flesh,
and for the primeval fault he is punished.

In an early prose draft for *La Colère de Samson*, Vigny imagined a long
dialogue between the lovers, which he later suppressed. In the final poetic
version they never communicate verbally. In fact, the absence of interchange
is greater in their case perhaps than in any of Vigny's other poems. For
Delilah is not an Israelite, and she does not speak Hebrew. She understands
not one word of Samson's chant:

Lui, murmure ce chant funèbre et douloureux
Prononcé dans la gorge avec des mots hébreux.
Elle ne comprend pas la parole étrangère ...    (p. 143)

(In *La Mort du Loup* more effective exchange occurs between beings of
different species, the Speaker and the wolf!) Their only rapport is physical.
They have reached an understanding on the lowest of planes. As a result,
when the war of the sexes breaks out between them, they are strangers, each
treating the other as an object. Furthermore, separated from the people,
isolated by a tent in the desert, they belong to no community, and only
interact with the cowardly soldiers that take Samson prisoner. The latter
calls out to God, his protest reinforced by the implied author (in Vigny's
own voice), but, as in *Moïse*, *Le Déluge*, *La Prison*, and *Le Mont des
Oliviers*, the Almighty does not answer. In his place we hear the Philistine
idol Dagon, an ironic parody of the divinity, and of Samson as well, who
can only groan and thus echo the Hebrew murmuring in his throat.

Similarly, although aware of Delilah's machinations, Samson cannot or
will not act to change the course of events, and at the poem's end he is
blinded by the Philistines. From a Freudian perspective, blindness here
represents mutilation, the punishment for breaking a sexual tabu. He who at
first kept awake during Delilah's unconscious sleep now loses his sight,
while she gazes upon him in his misery. He submits to the same darkness we
find in *La Prison*, *Le Mont des Oliviers*, and *La Mort du Loup*. The
embodiment of *fortitudo*, Samson proves to be extraordinarily weak yet,

paradoxically, a disillusioned, chastened example of male *sapientia*, one who can accept anguish and the absence of God. Of course, Delilah is afraid of him even in chains, content that he cannot behold her –

> Dalila, pâle prostituée,
> Couronnée, adorée et reine du repas,
> Mais tremblante et disant: '*Il ne me verra pas!*'    (p. 146)

– and the mock-author queries whether heaven and earth are happy to gaze upon the Hebrew's vengeance; but it is more a pious wish than a reference to reality. In this world of feminine heat and ruse, where woman's values triumph, Samson sees but is powerless to act just as no one but the mock-author is capable of communicating with others. Samson and Delilah are alone, each surrounded by a wall, unable to pierce it effectively, immobile and inactive, lacking genuine human warmth and even love, depicted only in terms of *post coitum* satiety.

In the course of the poem the protagonists change places. Their transformation in quality of vision corresponds to an exchange of status. Samson the hero, seated like an Egyptian god and possessing godlike powers, is rendered a slave of the Philistines, whereas the slave Delilah, sleeping at Samson's feet, pressed down by chains of jewelry, comes to dominate her master. Yet, just as he remains more lucid, more authentically aware, than she, even after he has lost physical sight, I believe that Samson remains spiritually a master vis-à-vis the terrified woman who hovers about him, dreading his now impotent glance. Scholars have criticized him for being a weakling, incapable of love and of self-control. According to them, he is at fault for having believed that his strength comes from his hair and for having yielded to Delilah; he would then be an anti-hero not to be imitated, differing totally from the other figures in Vigny's pantheon: the wolf, the sea-captain, and Christ. In my opinion, on the contrary, it is significant that in contrast to the Biblical source-narrative where Delilah seduces Samson, here he is fully aware of her plot and willfully allows himself to be captured. He does so not out of weakness or ignorance but as an act of heroic resignation, in authentic 'good faith.' He had believed in passion, as other Vigny heroes believe in power, authority, and responsibility. Since his ideal proves to be hollow, since womankind is not worthy of the devotion man accords her, Samson, unlike those other all-but-invulnerable heroes – Achilles and Siegfried – chooses to fall. He knows full well that his powers come from love, not his hair; he chooses to renounce it and physical strength both in favor of higher spiritual mastery, signified by language, by the song he delivers in Hebrew, the sacred language that

Delilah cannot speak, a protest of rage which shall reach the ears of the
implied author and his public, if not of God.

Not a well-known poem, *Wanda*[13] is, in my opinion, one of Vigny's most
powerful works and, in spite of the strophic form, especially sublime and
'epic' in character. Composed, all but the last stanzas, in 1847, published in
*Les Destinées* (1864), it is based upon an incident in contemporary Russian history, the sufferings of the Troubetskoï family after the failure of the
Decembrist Uprising of 1825. The Narrator allegedly meets Wanda at a
ball. The latter tells the story of her sister (the Princess), who chose to take
her children and spend over twenty years with her husband imprisoned in
Siberia.

Vigny is concerned with the plight of the noble classes, who, from his
perspective, embody the spirit of freedom and an impulse for social reform
but are crushed by a tyrant, the cruel, autocratic Czar of all the Russias,
just as in *La Prison* the Man in the Iron Mask is persecuted by Louis xiv (cf.,
for a similar pattern, his novels *Cinq-Mars* and *Stello*). Thus the poet
renews a tradition of epic illustrated by medieval singers of *geste* and, from
another perspective, the Huguenot d'Aubigné. The Princess and her husband, born to lead others, are reduced literally to slavery: he carries ball and
chains, while she accompanies him, trudging through the snow. He cuts
ice or labors in the mines; she spins. Indeed, the Russian people, Slavs, given
over to serfdom, are associated by their very name with slavery. The Czar
is symbolized by a great axe, the image of savagery and violence in *La
Sauvage*. As distant, as pitiless as the divinity in *La Prison* and *Le Mont
des Oliviers*, he plays the role of a vengeful father-god, crushing the Princess
and her children who are guilty of no transgression other than the
Byronic one, that is of being members of the human race. The Princess is
humiliated as well as punished, as if the devotion she manifests to her
family is itself a crime.

In striking contrast to the frame-setting, the gay Parisian ball where
Wanda tells her story, the central action takes place in an exotic Oriental
décor, quite different from the Palestine of *Samson* and from the various
'Turqueries' in *Les Orientales*, the tales of Musset, Gautier, and Mérimée,
or, for that matter, Vigny's own *Héléna*. True, the poem contains some
typically 'Byzantine' motifs: crucifix, ring, axes, and jewelry. Above all, we
find the horror of a Russian winter, characterized by snow, cold, whiteness, and silence. Vigny alludes to the gates of hell and to the Dantean figure
Ugolino. This inferno is a prison and a maze, with violence and torturers,
a world of the living dead, where the Princess is unknown and the Prince has
lost his rank. Most terrifying of all is the suspense, since a mother requests

that her children be taught to read, and ten years elapse before the Czar deigns to reply – in the negative:

> 'Un esclave a besoin d'un marteau, non d'un livre:
> La lecture est fatale à ceux-là qui, pour vivre,
> Doivent avoir bon bras pour gagner un bon pain.'     (p. 166)

Before leaving for Siberia, the Princess gives her family jewels to Wanda; the sight of these gems at a Parisian ball years later causes the Narrator to question Wanda and thus is at the origin of his (and our) knowledge of the story. However, although the Princess abandons physical gems, she preserves spiritual ones, her children. And, to the extent that she does sacrifice them, she is impelled by the finest of motives – loyalty to her husband, to the honor of her family and class, and to the cause of freedom. She and her husband form an 'epic couple,' a modern variation on an old motif, to be found in Homer, the Guillaume Cycle of *chansons de geste*, Chrétien de Troyes, Tasso, Le Moyne, even Milton and Lamartine. Theirs is an example of Roman fortitude, appropriate in the Russian Empire, the Third Rome. Ironically, however, the children do not survive, at least spiritually (they cannot read), whereas the jewels live on to reveal their story to the implied author and his public. Blood-red rubies and black pearls at the ball evoke the blood of the Princess's offspring, their value as young, innocent, human creatures. In Vigny's world the ruby and pearl, like the diamond, mummy, and bottle, are images of poetry, of the preciousness of the mind ( *La Maison du Berger, La Bouteille à la mer, L'Esprit pur, Daphné*). In contrast to Siberian snow, these stones shine with the power of the will, the Princess's will, and with the flame of life. They embody a feminine treasure, the best that a non-cruel, non-violent world can give, a spiritual force that will not yield to the Czar's masculine physical inferno. For this wife and mother so loves her husband that she sacrifices all for him, providing him with the comfort that men seek. The total opposite of a Delilah, she takes to Siberia only a hammer (for her husband to work), a needle (for her to work), and their children – their responsibility, love, and hope. Her sacrifice and her devotion, her maternal innocence, render human interaction possible in a world of snow and axes.

The revolt of the masses, the smiting of Russia's second axe, is alluded to as a portentous future possibility. In the present, however, in reply to the Czar's silence, Wanda speaks to the Narrator, and the Narrator speaks to his implied readers. All presumably condemn the Czar in their hearts. In the final strophes, written ten years after the poem proper, we discover that the Princess is avenged. Russia has lost the Crimean War, and Czar Nicholas dies in rage. This 'little father' of the Russian people was responsible for the

spiritual death of children and for destroying the maternal principle inherent in the Princess and her family. Then, in a denouement of pure Oedipal
wish-fulfillment, the evil father is crushed down as a result of the good
offices of the innocent mother-victim. For, we are told, the Princess held
God's scales in heaven, and, because of her, they fell against the Czar.
Like the goddess Astraea beloved of Ronsard or the allegorical figures in
medieval mystery plays, this Russian *mulier fortis*, close to God, embodies his justice and mercy. The wife and the martyr could have forgiven
the Czar, we are told, but the mother never:

>                – On dit que la balance immense
> Du Seigneur a paru quand la foudre a tonné.
> – La sainte la tenait flottante dans l'espace.
> L'Epouse, la Martyre a peut-être fait grâce,
> Dieu du ciel! – Mais la Mère a-t-elle pardonné?    (p. 170)

The Czar committed his greatest crime against children and, because of
them, against the human spirit. In contrast, like the Eva of *La Maison du
Berger*, the Princess is a consoling woman and a symbol of intelligence. For
Vigny, the book is sacred, symbolic of the highest attainments possible to
humankind. The mute, non-communicative Czar, who denies the spirit,
who renders his silent people slaves (the Slavs), will be defeated by God,
the Word, from whom comes the breath of life, for whom is etched an
eternal Book of Judgment (p. 168), and by Vigny the poet, who defies
and undoes his adversary through an act of the imagination, *esprit pur* – the
writing of this poem.

Scholarly clichés, the myths to be found in literary manuals, often do an
author injustice. We have seen how limited are prevalent estimates of Voltaire, author of *Candide*, and Lamartine, author of 'Le Lac,' as if both
men had not succeeded in other areas, including the long poem. In contrast,
Vigny's opus, in verse and in prose, has been accepted into the French
literary canon in its entirety. However, he suffers from a myth he himself
helped to propagate: that he is a thinker, a man concerned largely with
ideas, a deep philosophical writer for whom doctrine precedes poetry both
chronologically and ontologically. In fact, Vigny's ideas are vague, simplis-
tic, and far from original. He is a poet, not a philosopher; his verse is
grounded in neoclassical conventions of myth and allegory, and in the
Enlightenment tradition of elegant, subtle anti-Christianity. His opus does
not embody a consistent philosophical system, and it is doubtful that the
order of poems in *Les Destinées*, for example, corresponds to a conscious
plan on the author's part, an evolution from despair to hope or from

pessimism to a precarious *sagesse* and acceptance of life. Vigny leaves us
with a series of independent lyrico-narrative poems, fragments if you
will, each a unique drama of anguish and hope, each with its own mood,
tone, and 'world.'

It is true, however, that, as in the case of Ronsard, Vigny's brief narratives
successfully make a claim for being epic. They contain most of the time-
honored characteristics of heroic poetry: gravity of tone, grandeur of
imagery, nostalgia for a fallen past and hope for the future, the reincarnation
of old heroes of myth (Moses, Samson, Satan, Christ, the Man in the Iron
Mask), the presence of a leader or hero who embodies the ideal of his age,
the assertion of individuality and of the ultimate metaphysical significance
of life, plus high seriousness, breadth, inclusiveness, transcendence, control,
structure, an abiding significance, universal values, and the sublime style.
Vigny even reacts against certain aspects of romance which, dating back to
Tasso and, before him, to Chrétien de Troyes and late *chanson de geste*,
had adulterated the pure 'heroic' spirit. Thus he denies the happy prison or
garden and reasserts the old Homeric, Virgilian, Turoldian dominance of
man over woman, reason over passion, and duty over sensual indulgence.
True, *Poëmes Antiques et Modernes* and *Les Destinées* do not manifest
the spirit of optimism, humanitarianism, and religiosity to be found in most
epics of the romantic period. But, in my opinion, pessimism and the
absence of a happy ending do not suffice to deny Vigny a place in the canon.
His voice, and Leconte de Lisle's, belong to epic as do those of *Raoul de
Cambrai* and *Garin le Lorrain* in the twelfth century, or d'Aubigné in the
sixteenth: for the tragic sense of life, like the comic and, for that matter,
the romantic, can develop inside a traditional heroic framework.

This tragic insight is one of Vigny's contributions to the modern epic.
In reaction to the pervading optimism of the century, he gives vent to
disillusionment. In his universe an inner and outer destiny weighs heavily
on men, who live immobile in bondage or exile. Mother-figures are fickle
and deceptive, fatal women, and the Father a tyrant, the dispenser of evil
laws. Communication fails to provide otherwise lucid heroes with answers
to their questions: man cannot act because, isolated, in the dark, he is
prevented from knowing. A problematic hero, he seeks authentic values in a
degraded world. He does not defend the order of his age but attacks it: he
rebels against his society and against God.[14]

Alfred de Vigny is the first French romantic poet with a fully elaborated demonic vision, complete with a metallic or stone-like décor, black
sky, machinery, bondage instruments (net, collar, chains), perverted Eros,
alienation, a sinister, absent deity, and the determination of men's lives by
games (chess, dice, cards) and Fortuna's wheel. People are either innocent
victims who suffer at God's hands or lucid, courageous advocates who

accuse him. Given the divinity's silence, man has no choice but to proceed alone, to survive even in a state of metaphysical anguish. At the center of his adventure is a rite of passage, the death-experience, which is not followed by rebirth. His characters (Moses, Emmanuel, the Prisoner, Christ, Samson, the wolf, the sea-captain) endure the anguish of perishing without hope of reunion with the Godhead.

They partake of romantic myths: Prometheus, Cain, Christ the rebel, and the fatal superman. Their author exhibits the same conservative, aristocratic scorn for a bourgeois age and for the values it promulgates that we find in Byron, Stendhal, Musset, and Gautier. Neither men nor gods, torn between freedom and bondage, heaven and earth, these heroes are alone, isolated on mountaintops and towers or in the center of a maze. They are scapegoats immolated to the all-powerful, lacking hubris or a tragic flaw but nonetheless cast down, their fall a portent to others. With the Romantics the old hierarchy has been upended. Vigny's world is man- not God-centered. Lower nature is valued over a now distant, unattainable paradise, and the author's sympathy reaches out to the rebel, for modern heroism to be found within his dark soul, not in the light of the stars.

Along with Nerval, Vigny is in some ways the most modern of the Romantics. Before Nerval, Baudelaire, Leconte de Lisle, and Lautréamont, he stands chronologically as perhaps the first metaphysical rebel of the age. His authenticity and torment in the act of being, his corroding lucidity, and his dense, demanding style are closer to Baudelaire and Valéry than to his immediate contemporaries. And his attitude toward poetry curiously anticipates the spirit of literature in our day.[15] The theme of art and the artist is central to much of his work: *La Maison du Berger*, *La Flûte*, *L'Esprit pur*; *Cinq-Mars*, *Stello*, and *Chatterton*. The poet, like the soldier and the aristocrat, stands forth as one of the great alienated heroes of modern times. Symbolic of the work of art and the artist's calling are the crystal mummy (*Daphné*) covered with hieroglyphs, the thick, impenetrable bottle containing a message or discovery (*La Bouteille à la mer*), and the pearl (*Wanda*). These sharp, precious, durable creations evoke purity, refuge, and a magic transformation of brute matter. Thus, in spite of some negative art-imagery (God's book in *Les Destinées*), Vigny elaborates his cult of Pure Spirit. Winged Eloa can be redeemed, and the winged Destinies overcome, by this esthetic Holy Ghost that shall bring the Word to man through the mediation of a poet-prophet-priest. It is here, in his refuge, at the end of an *itinerarium mentis ad spiritum*, that man's only hope for inner contentment and attainment of wisdom lies. Art alone can vanquish time, space, and the malevolent deity who wages war against us all.

Chapter Fifteen

 # HUGO

It is appropriate that the apex of nineteenth-century epic be associated with Victor Hugo (1802–85), a writer who dominates his century in much the same way that Voltaire did his. A case can be made that Hugo's genius is truly epic, and that sublime traits appear in almost everything he wrote. His lyrics swell into the heroic, throughout his career, but especially in the philosophical and apocalyptic sections of *Les Contemplations* (1856) and the series of poems devoted to the figure of Napoleon Bonaparte, which extend from 1829 (*Lui*, in *Les Orientales*) to 1877 (*Le retour de l'Empereur*, 1840, included in *La Légende des Siècles*, second series). In addition, *Les Burgraves* (1843) stands as an example of sublime drama, *Châtiments* (1853) as sublime satire, and all of his novels, without exception, partake of the mode of sublime romance. For all that, scholars quite rightly consider that the summit of epic in Hugo's career occurs with his exile to the Channel Islands, covering roughly the years 1852–60. During this period he composed and published *Châtiments*, *Les Contemplations*, and *La Légende des Siècles*, first series (1859). He also wrote many 'petites épopées' that were later gathered into the second and third versions of *La Légende des Siècles*; the poems published in his lifetime under the titles *Le Pape* (1878), *La Pitié suprême* (1879), *Religions et Religion* (1880), *L'Ane* (1880), and *La Révolution* in *Les Quatre Vents de l'Esprit* (1881); and the long apocalyptic fragments that appeared posthumously as *La Fin de Satan* (1886) and *Dieu* (1891).

Faced with the most extraordinary epic production by any one author in the Western tradition, I find it difficult to treat Hugo within the confines of a single chapter. Therefore, I shall limit myself to the first series of *La Légende des Siècles* and *La Fin de Satan*. Thus at least I shall be able to touch upon Hugo's achievement in the *Kurzepos* and the *Grossepos*, in both the historical and apocalyptic modes. The master's other long poems (*Le Pape*, *La Pitié suprême*, and so on) are not of the same high quality, although they tower over the achievements of most other nineteenth-century versifiers. The same can be said for the second and third series of *La*

*Légende des Siècles*, which, in spite of individual high points (*La Vision d'où est sorti ce livre, Les Trois Cent, Montfaucon, L'Aigle du Casque*), contain dull patches and repeat motifs elaborated in the first series. In any case, I agree with scholars who maintain that *La Légende des Siècles* was published in three distinct versions and ought to be considered as three successive works of art – not to be arbitrarily fused into a single corpus, lacking focus and a clear chronological or thematic pattern. Viewed from this perspective, the first series is a complete, coherent text in its own right, maintaining a more consistently narrative quality and epic tone than the other two. As for *Dieu*, I shall neglect this splendid quest for the Godhead simply out of considerations of space and time.

I do wish to raise one further point. The criticism of Hugo's opus in general, and his sublime verse in particular, is so rich, so thorough, that any overall analysis on my part would prove to be banal. My best chance to say something original is to return to the text. Therefore, I shall concentrate on four of the individual 'legends,' and follow this with a reading of *La Fin de Satan*, reserving for the end synthetic remarks on the two works as a whole.

A few of the 'little epics' that form *La Légende des Siècles* were written before the fall of Louis-Philippe, as far back as 1846, and the forthcoming collection was announced in 1853. However, during the last two years of exile in Jersey (1854–5) Hugo concentrated on *La Fin de Satan* and *Dieu* (in addition to *Les Contemplations*). In the spring of 1854 he ceased work on *La Fin de Satan*, perhaps in order to complete *Les Contemplations*, perhaps because the Tables (28 April 1854) ordered him to do so. In 1856, now installed at Guernsey, Hugo abandoned *Dieu* in favor of a massive effort on *La Légende des Siècles*, either because he could not resolve the philosophical and artistic problems that *Dieu* posed, or under the pressure of his editor, Hetzel, who convinced the Magus that his public was more receptive to narrative poems in the style of *Le Revenant* (*Les Contemplations*) than to the apocalyptic or philosophical style of *La Fin de Satan* and *Dieu*. At any rate, from October 1857 to May 1859 he labored almost exclusively on his 'petites épopées' and published the first series in 1859, with a preface that also speaks of *La Fin de Satan* and *Dieu*, claiming that all three poems, taken together, would form an epic of humanity in its totality. In 1877 and 1883, incorporating some new poems as well as those left over from his creative surge in the 1850s, Hugo published two new series of *La Légende des Siècles*. However, although he returned to *La Fin de Satan* in 1859–60, neither it nor *Dieu* was completed; they only saw the light of day after the author's death, in 1886 and 1891 respectively.[1]

Like *La Conscience*, also in *La Légende des Siècles*, like *Lucrèce Borgia* and *Les Burgraves*, *Le Parricide*[2] tells the story of an assassin. King Kanut,

Danish national hero of the Middle Ages, was a good man, a leader, warrior, and lawgiver; but because once in his early youth, long ago, he killed his father and thus arrived at power through a murder, because all his admirable deeds were brought about through an act of parricide, he is accorded neither peace nor honor in the afterlife. While on the march to God's kingdom, the Dane discovers that his shroud of snow is being defiled by a rain of blood; torn by guilt and remorse, he wanders indefinitely. This man, equal to Caesar, is held responsible for his acts as are the meanest of his subjects. His is a story of punishment, of the vengeance God metes out to the evil-doer. Thus the individual who, unlike Cain, does not flee from God but actively seeks him is brought down, and the tyrant is felled. But in his fall he cuts a splendid figure, and in his tragic grandeur he contributes to the gallery of fatal romantic supermen: Vautrin, Moïse, Rolla, Monte-Cristo, Bonaparte, and above all, the mythical hero he resembles so closely – Ahasvérus, the Wandering Jew.

Hugo elaborates a pattern of demonic imagery to illustrate his tale of judgment and vengeance. Kanut's is a world of darkness and night, where the blackness of his surroundings, the shadows that surround him, reflect his growing sense of guilt:

> Il entra, par delà l'Islande et la Norvège,
> Seul dans le grand silence et dans la grande nuit;
> Derrière lui le monde obscur s'évanouit;
> Il se trouva, lui, spectre, âme, roi sans royaume,
> Nu, face à face avec l'immensité fantôme;
> Il vit l'infini, porche horrible et reculant
> Où l'éclair, quand il entre, expire triste et lent,
> L'ombre, hydre dont les nuits sont les pâles vertèbres,
> L'informe se mouvant dans le noir, les Ténèbres;
> Là, pas d'astre; et pourtant on ne sait quel regard
> Tombe de ce chaos immobile et hagard;
> Pour tout bruit, le frisson lugubre que fait l'onde
> De l'obscurité, sourde, effarée et profonde ...    (pp. 470–1)

The snow of the Scandinavian North, colored white, normally suggests purity and innocence, but since it is icy cold and forms Kanut's shroud, it evokes overtones of death, solitude, and remorse. Furthermore, the soft rain of blood that turns the shroud from white to red or black symbolizes Kanut's guilt and is the act of condemnation, for red is the color of passion and violence, and these are either drops of the old king's blood that Kanut shed years before or tears of blood. In this scene of Gothic horror, in a world of stone – feudal castles, mountains, menhirs, tombs, a stone coffin –

the great king who conquers hard earth, who rises from his own grave, falls victim to snow, darkness, and blood.

Surrounded by shadows, Kanut sees little or nothing. He tries to gaze upon the external world, to find his way, but to no avail. Similarly, he attempts a dialogue with Mount Savo, but the mountain cannot answer his question satisfactorily. He encounters no one else in his peregrinations, thus is unable to communicate. In the central section of the poem Kanut is in utter solitude, in a world without light and sound. His only contact with reality turns out to be the tactile sensation of the falling raindrops. Symbolically, the murderer's punishment fits his crime, is the manifestation of a *lex talionis*. He who slew his senile, demented, and therefore unconscious father with a physical blow, in the dark ('l'aveugle immense,' p. 469), without witnesses, is now punished by a suddenly renewed consciousness of his father's blood, in the dark, alone. It is also true that Kanut's senses can no longer cope with the external world, for he exists as if in a state of hallucination, in anguish and terror. This is a splendid example of the fantastic mode that was to play so important a role in nineteenth-century fiction as well as in poetry and the theater.

The hallucination creates distortions in space and time. This dead man's shade, liberated from the tomb, exists in a dream-world. He sets out on a quest for heaven, for a place where he will be granted repose. It is the last rite of passage for the old warrior, an experience in which he is separated from his own kind yet hopes to be integrated into a finer community. And, in the best epic tradition, Kanut's adventure entails a long, solitary voyage to the Other World, to a kind of Hades, in search of a precious object or boon, an ordeal in which not everyone can hope to succeed. However, it slowly becomes apparent to Kanut and to the reader that the traditional pattern has been undermined. The sacred mountain is located at the beginning of the voyage, not the end. No helpful guide appears to succor the wanderer. In fact, it is possible that this ironically successful dragon-killer fails to cross the first threshold. Nor does he enter the sacred space, the temple or fortress that he seeks. Upon arriving at heaven, Kanut finds the portals closed and dares not advance. Uncharted, boundless, intangible space becomes for him a prison, and his wandering is a metaphor for inner chaos and solitude; as with Cain and Jean Valjean, as with René, Obermann, and Ahasvérus, his quest is transformed into flight and his seeking to punishment.

Temporally, Victor Hugo makes us aware of disparity, of a paradoxical asymmetry, between the eternal, boundless dream-time of Kanut's wandering and the highly precise, minute fragments of duration measured by the drops of blood falling onto his shroud. One falls at a time, in a syncopated yet increasing rhythm, that reflects Kanut's nightmare-like anguish.

They slowly but surely destroy Kanut and all he represents, breaking his psyche into fragments, as drops of water carve out the Gavarnie Circus in *Dieu*.[3] Symbolically, this seemingly insignificant rain, the result of one act committed years previously, is capable of negating the feats of an entire lifetime. A similar paradox governs the relationship between *Erzählzeit* and *erzählte Zeit* as narrative technique. Hugo devotes six lines to the murder, thirty-five lines to Kanut's successful reign, and the entire remainder of the poem to 'unofficial history,' his post-mortem experiences, the expiation. Thus the reality of historical time is reversed; the telling of the story itself indicates the ethical importance of deeds envisaged in accordance with a divine sense of duration, in contradiction to man's limited notions of chronology.

Kanut is a particular kind of murderer, a parricide, his 'classification' underscored in the poem's title. He slays his father and, in secular life, replaces him, becomes a father to his people in turn. His story would appear to be a successful working out of the Oedipal fantasy, with love for the woman displaced onto the kingdom and onto a successful political career. However, guilt and remorse, repressed far from the rational light of day, return to the surface at night, in the afterlife. Kanut sets out in quest of God. For the dead man, God ought to be a refuge and a paternal surrogate, and the quester seeks guidance from an ancestor, another father-surrogate, the old mountain Savo. It is, therefore, significant that Savo cannot give him useful information and that Kanut never finds the Almighty at all. Indeed, the tears of blood that fall on his shroud may come from God's own eyes: 'qui donc pleurait ces larmes formidables? / L'infini' (p. 472). Jung defined religion as an aggressive reaffirmation of the Father-imago. In *Le Parricide* the divinity, the ultimate father and superego (cf. *La Conscience* and *L'Aigle du Casque*), replaces Kanut's progenitor and punishes the son for parricide, forcing him to flee in the night. The man who 'looked upon' his sire is metaphorically blinded. Like Ahasvérus, who spat upon Christ, Kanut's crime was against the Fathers, and his punishment is to wander rootless for eternity.

Kanut resembles Hugo's Cain and the Wandering Jew in both crime and punishment. For all his greatness, however, the Nordic warrior falls to a lower state than either of his analogues. For, unlike them, he had literally forgotten his transgression. Just as the old king was slain while unconscious ('Lui-même n'en sait rien,' p. 469), so Kanut loses all memory of the deed. Supernatural vengeance works to render the murderer's shade lucid, to force him to become aware of his guilt. And the drops of rain that slowly awaken Kanut's psyche remind us of the impenetrable, unbroken gaze of God's eye in *La Conscience*. Kanut's quest for God is transformed into flight, and the man of destiny, the outcast, wends his way forever

in a chartless prison of inner space and time. He never crosses the
threshold, he dies but is never reborn; in a just, lawful, father-oriented
cosmos this is the punishment for one who promulgated laws for others but
himself broke them and who took life from the sire who gave it to him.

*Le Jour des Rois*,[4] 860 AD, set in the Spanish Pyrenees, although recounting
an event that occurred one-and-a-half centuries before Kanut's death,
treats the same period of history as *Le Parricide*: the early feudal epoch,
which marks the end of what once was called the Dark Ages. We find an
atmosphere of war and violence, of sadism and horror. Instead of King
Kanut, alone in his solitude, Hugo tells of a group of predatory feudal
lords, working in tacit connivance. These are not the romantic, admirably
portrayed bandits of Scott and Byron; no Karl Moor or Götz von Berli-
chingen here. They are tyrants, sadistic fiends who despoil the poor, who
rebel against no earthly man, since the world around them is subject to
their power. They enjoy to the fullest the Sadian pleasures of destruction
and transgression. For, in this reified universe, the people of the plains,
slaves and victims, offer tribute in exchange for life; when tribute is lacking,
the masters, their executioners, seize, pillage, and destroy – they take life.
Crime serves as mediator between two groups of men, and between the
barons and happiness or fulfillment. And they commit this blasphemy,
defiling God's creation, on the Day of Epiphany, the Day of Kings.

Opposed to the pillagers we find one man, an idiot-beggar infected
with vermin or leprosy. Although this dehumanized creature, compared to a
worm and to a larva, is totally alienated from society, he plays the role of
Greek chorus and *Deus vindex*; low as he is, the basest of slaves, he judges
the masters. This beggar with a noble soul, a commonplace in the romantic era, is an anti-hero in the tradition of the Spanish pícaro, the man of low
class who eventually comes to possess truth that others lack. And he helps
to propagate a message of social justice and respect for the dignity of the
common man, ideals we associate with George Sand, Lamennais, Michelet, and, above all, Hugo himself, author of *Le Mendiant*, *Les Pauvres
Gens*, *L'Ane*, *Les Misérables*, and *L'Homme qui rit*.

*Le Jour des Rois* evokes Attila's scourge, the sword of battle, and the
rope of the scaffold. But the arch-image dominating the poem (in contrast
to the snow of *Le Parricide*) is fire, the flames of cities that the kings burn.
We see the sky aflame in the morning from sunrise, aflame in the evening
from the lords' evil deeds. The reflection of the sunset on the mountains
symbolizes blood shed by these mountain men:

> Et, reflet du couchant, ou bien de l'attentat,
> La chaîne des vieux monts, funeste et vaste bouge,

> Apparaissait, dans l'ombre horrible, toute rouge;
> On eût dit que, tandis qu'en bas on triomphait,
> Quelque archange vengeur de la plaine avait fait
> Remonter tout ce sang au front de la montagne.    (pp. 491–2)

Here, as in *Raoul de Cambrai* and *Les Tragiques*, fire symbolizes animal passion, the sadistic, demonic nature of the kings when they unleash death and destruction on all around them.

Whereas the hero of *Le Parricide* wandered aimlessly in space, seeking a displaced center, in *Le Jour des Rois* the kings move in a most precise manner, on the periphery of a circle, destroying four cities at the four compass points: Vich, Girone, Lumbier, and Teruel. Meanwhile, in the middle of the plain crouches the beggar, in a mock-sacred spot which nonetheless is the symbolic center for the poem. At the Crassus bridge, so low he is unseen by people, the beggar gazes upon and judges others; from there we view the scene, from his point of view. It is at this bridge that the brigands commit the sacrilege of slaying innocent people in flight. As we saw in chapter thirteen, in the romantic period mountains represent a sacred locus, close to nature and God, where free men contemplate eternal mysteries. This is the case in the works of Byron and Lamartine (especially *Jocelyn*), of Mickiewicz, Slowacki, and Pushkin, and in several episodes from *La Légende des Siècles* (*Le Régiment du baron Madruce*, *Désintéressement*, *Welf, castellan d'Osbor*). However, the descent and return of the lords becomes a horrible parody on the romantic quest, as Hugo and others conceived of it.

These sharp, jagged mountains are set in opposition to the plains. In contrast to the usual romance archetypes, evil descends from on high. The mountain men represent masculine will-to-power; with their pikes they ride down to the plains to kill and burn. Significantly, the cities on the flatland open their gates; theirs is a more passive, feminine décor, where women are raped in convents, where books are destroyed by sharp instruments and fire. The wicked King Gesufal chooses Teruel to kiss, and his embrace is mortal:

> Le roi du mont Jaxa, Gesufal le Cruel,
> Pour son baiser terrible a choisi Teruel;
> Il vient d'en approcher ses deux lèvres funèbres,
> Et Teruel se tord dans un flot de ténèbres.    (p. 488)

Just as the people of the cities are humiliated and injured, so also the beggar remains motionless, on a bridge covered with blood, as if he had been mutilated or violated by the predatory barons. Since these masters, these fathers, turn out to be evil, however, the beggar curses them, appealing symbolically over their heads to God the Father, who will mete out justice. Indeed, his voice as a prophet is assimilated to God's, just as his leprous body is analogous to Christ's.

The lowest of the low, dressed in rags, suffering from hideous skin diseases, the beggar embodies the medieval notion of the leper: on the one hand, a sinning mortal justly punished by God for his transgressions, yet, on the other, perhaps also an unusually gifted man, chosen by God for special favor, for the boon of his ordeal. This leper, an outcast from society, society's scapegoat, denounces the fact that his own sacrifice will not suffice to preserve the community. Himself beyond the human pale, he witnesses what happens to others. Enduring pain and deformity, he becomes a seer, a prophet. In typically Hugolian fashion he gazes upon the events of that day; he contemplates, deciphers, and unveils; as with the Almighty, power resides in his eye, not his hands. And he speaks out to curse the villains; he communicates with the implied reader, and, presumably, with God; for his voice is the only lucid, authentic speech in the poem. He is the immobile seer, the magus in the center who judges and, in his way, punishes. Technically an idiot, he benefits from *sancta stultitia*; he plays the role of fool and scapegoat but also that of prophet and judge, *agroikos* and *eiron*. As prophet, he castigates as well as predicts. And as a symbolic rebel, a poor, ugly creature who in his way triumphs, he reminds us not only of Hugo's toad and donkey, his peasants and fishermen, but also of those great Prometheus-figures in *La Légende des Siècles* who denounce Olympus: the Satyr, and Phtos the Titan.

The day is Epiphany, when the three Wise Men, Kings of the East, brought gifts to Christ in a manger; here four evil kings seize money from the people, pillage the land, and then return to their lairs, unaware of the Christ-figure in their midst: 'Ils vont fêtant le jour des rois, car c'est leur jour' (p. 490). But he is aware of them. In a powerfully grotesque finale, he curses the predators, comparing them to the lice that dwell in his own rags, on his body. This juxtaposition of the grotesque and the tragic, the tragic ending in grotesque, recalls *L'Expiation* in *Châtiments*; it corresponds to Hugo's notion of drama as a modern literary mode, as defined in the *Préface de Cromwell* and *William Shakespeare*. The beggar that became a worm and a larva transforms these proud robber-princes into lice, his lice; he who had been dehumanized dehumanizes in turn; and these masters become the lowest of slaves, lower than the beggar himself. As in d'Aubigné vile creatures are evoked in order to create a sense of cosmic justice. Of course, the socio-political situation is overturned only in a metaphorical sense, given that the beggar's revenge is merely verbal. Yet, in a poem, a verbal construct, this suffices, indeed is most appropriate. Although the kings are men of the sword, who rape nuns, the readers of books, they are cursed by a passive, immobile creature whose only human trait is to pray in Latin, whose only weapon is his tongue. Thus a suffering, tortured leper-figure, deformed image of Christ, a true *pauperus*, speaks out and, like Christ, defies evil men on the Day of Epiphany. The Word indeed triumphs over Satan, and the spirit over flesh.

Victor Hugo situates *Eviradnus*[5] centuries later, at the end of the Middle Ages. To depict this more courtly age, Hugo provides us with a plot closer to Arthurian romance than to *chanson de geste*. *Eviradnus* recounts one episode in the life of a knight-errant, a *preux* (p. 511) who roams the world in quest of adventure, to right wrongs and institute justice and chivalry. The old paladin discovers that the Emperor of Germany and the King of Poland seek to despoil the orphan marquise Mahaud of her lands. He defends her from their schemes and slays them in combat. Hugo's plot is by no means only medieval, however. The tyrant who (with the aid of a treacherous confidant) persecutes an innocent maiden is a theme in much of the best pre-romantic literature (Richardson, Diderot, Laclos, Sade, Restif, Goethe), as well as in Gothic romance and nineteenth-century melodrama. Hugo then embellished this conventional narrative line with appropriate motifs: abandoned castle, storm, philter, dagger, night vigil, disguises, infernal pact, secret dungeon, and purported ghosts. And the story is located in what for the Romantics was *the* medieval land: Germany (cf. Hugo's own *Le Rhin*, 1842, and *Les Burgraves*, 1843).[6] Since this is the first tale in *La Légende des Siècles* to manifest an atmosphere of wooing and courtly gallantry, a case can be made that the lady Mahaud is as much the protagonist of the action as Eviradnus himself. Furthermore, Hugo's poem is enriched with touches of humor and truculence, and with a quality of intimacy, of fantasy, joy, laughter, and caprice that provide relaxation from the apocalyptic.[7] *Eviradnus* is one of the most complex works in the entire *Légende des Siècles*.

Nonetheless, the dominant tone is one of terror, of horror and the demonic. As with King Kanut and the brigands of Spain, might alone makes right, and the two monarchs who swore a pact with Satan are sadistic fiends, associated with the claw, the talon, and the beak. However, whereas the previous poems are situated in the open air, here evil is concentrated within an enclosed space, a treacherous Gothic maze. This is Corbus, an abandoned castle, an arch-image which dominates the poem. Hugo depicts Corbus as a living being, associated with war and endowed with attendant gargoyles and monsters, statues and demons that come alive. In summer the castle is attacked by lichens and plants but in winter triumphs over her enemies, joyful during stormy weather. Within is to be found a weird dining hall (built over a pit) which contains the usual Hugolian demonic appurtenances: reptiles, larvae, spiders, and rows of men carved in stone or metal. The enclosed space of Corbus, where Mahaud must spend the night in the company of her enemies, is an example of the prison motif so prevalent in Hugo's works, especially *Le Dernier Jour d'un condamné*, *Notre-Dame de Paris*, *Les Misérables*, *La Fin de Satan*, and *Quatrevingt-treize*.[8] Social evil is committed in this place, a medieval analogue to the Bastille, by spiritual ancestors of the Bourbon and Bonaparte lines. And inside the prison, this concrete manifestation of a harsh, mineralized world, creatures swarm, statues move, and spiders crawl; the walls themselves become viscous, crack, ooze, and disintegrate; and people are threatened by a paw, a tentacle, a snake, the slipping away of mud, and the smothering of the walls themselves.

Within the tower a death-rebirth experience is ritualized. Each new marquis must sleep in the company of his ancestors, must spend the night in their castle, near their tombs, and endure a vision, before being led out the next morning to freedom, glory, and power. Unfortunately, the two monarchs who accompany Mahaud are followers of Satan, possessed of a death-instinct. These minions of Thanatos, who would rather kill the girl than rape her, manifest horror of life-giving forces. However, rebirth will succeed to life, owing to Eviradnus's exertions. In this world of decreasing generations, he represents Mahaud's animus, a wise counselor and friend who punishes the shadow-figures, a good grandfather-surrogate à la Victor Hugo who protects the child, the orphan, from her evil stepfather-surrogates, the predatory monarchs. His is the watching eye; a Christian Samson, he stands for justice and order, he is a superego fit to repel the lawless, passion-ridden id embodied in the two kings. It is not inappropriate that this knight takes the place of a suit of armor in the dining hall and that, like a man of stone, he comes to life in order to pass judgment on evil-doers (cf. *Hernani*, *Le Rhin*, *Les Burgraves*, *Notre-Dame de Paris*, *Les Misérables*, *Les Quatre Vents de l'Esprit*, and, in *La Légende*, *La Paternité*). And, by substituting himself for one of Mahaud's forefather's suits of armor, Eviradnus symbolically becomes a father in the royal line. Knights-errant are superior to paladins in that they actively right wrongs, seeking out victims everywhere in order to succor them. Seven feet tall and with white hair, seventy years old yet made of steel, this old man with the heart of a young boy (Hugo reverses the *puer senex* motif) proves the appropriate sun-hero to defeat the dragon-figure and deliver the maiden. With the dawn, she awakens to a new day, escorted by her savior.

Mahaud is the victim of deception. Her enemies disguise themselves as minstrels in order to destroy her. She then unwittingly insults them, rendering her death all the more certain. Nevertheless, the two manipulators are deceived in turn by Eviradnus, who also enters into disguise, masking himself as the ghost of one of Mahaud's ancestors. Mahaud was unable to distinguish appearance from reality since she believed the monarchs to be friends; yet they also are the victims of illusion, terrified by Eviradnus, convinced that he is a specter, a statue come to life, or Satan himself. The reader is not taken in, however. Although Hugo relishes the aura of mystery of Corbus, he makes the reader privy to the secrets of his plot. And, just before the end, Eviradnus, who has succeeded in unmasking the traitors, rips off his own mask and identifies himself. He who had seen and heard them, unseen and unheard, authentically places himself on their level and triumphs in the open:

> – 'Princes, votre façon d'être lâches me gêne.
> Je suis homme et non spectre. Allons, debout! mon bras
> Est le bras d'un vivant; il ne me convient pas
> De faire une autre peur que celle où j'ai coutume.
> Je suis Eviradnus.'    (p. 535)

It is significant that this is one poem where art and language are viewed negatively. Frescos on the walls of the dining hall and artistic helmets contribute to the demonic mood of the place. The two kings pretend to be a musician and a poet, Joss and Zéno; they learned their arts from Satan (p. 527); they perform a lovely but false, inauthentic love song for Mahaud. These men, who are praised by court sycophants in Italian sonnets, deliver speeches in order to trick her. Whereas they are verbally oriented, articulate leaders, at first Eviradnus says little. But he listens and sees. He overhears one word of theirs in the forest and deciphers the plot. From then on, he keeps silent yet acts, witnessing their lying speeches. Only in the end does he communicate with them and to Mahaud herself. But, even here, he retains the mask, keeping secret from Mahaud the risks she ran in the course of her slumber. For when she wakens the following morning, he says only: 'Madame ... avez-vous bien dormi?' Thus, for all his chivalry, Eviradnus is to some extent a primitive, a 'strong silent type.' He represents the old medieval virtues in contrast to a more recent, civilized, and decadent Renaissance-oriented tyranny. It is only in the modern age, in Victor Hugo's century, that heroism can be totally allied to artistic endeavors, when the poet-magus himself becomes a hero.

*La Rose de l'Infante*[9] is one of the few individual legends to have been acclaimed upon the publication of the first series in 1859. In this poem Hugo exploits the Spanish décor he employed in *Le Jour des Rois* and *Le petit roi de Galice*, as well as in *Hernani* and *Ruy Blas*. Romantic Spain, land of

noble hidalgos, decadent Moors, and insolent pícaros, of dignity, passion, and violence, was an obsession for Hugo as for many of his contemporaries; witness Musset's *Contes d'Espagne et d'Italie* (1830), Gautier's
*España* (1845), and Mérimée's *Carmen* (1845), to cite the most famous
examples.[10] *La Rose de l'Infante* resembles *Eviradnus* in that the action is
limited to an enclosed space; it differs from *Le Jour des Rois*, *Le petit roi
de Galice*, and *Eviradnus* in that the setting does not exude predominantly
connotations of the demonic. Hugo's Infanta and her governess converse
in the Gardens of Aranjuez. These utterly civilized surroundings evoke
shimmering imagery of light, Renaissance urbanity, and courtliness. We
find allusions to gentle fauna – swans, peacocks, does, and fawns – and to
roses, which recall the bucolic mode of so many Hugolian lyrics. This is a
world of freshness, beauty, serenity, and majesty, of flowers, childlike
innocence, and the nostalgia of childhood lost. As with Guillaume de
Lorris, the garden is a *locus amœnus*, a sacred spot, its beauty and purity
embodied in a fountain at the center.

The two most important figures in the garden, representative of both
loveliness and evanescence, are the Infanta and the rose she holds in her
hand: these are the title figures of the poem:

> La douce enfant sourit, ne faisant autre chose
> Que de vivre et d'avoir dans la main une rose,
> Et d'être là devant le ciel, parmi les fleurs.   (p. 604)

As in *Le Roman de la Rose* the flower is assimilated to the girl herself, is
the girl: it is also associated with the Armada, thus with Spain, a refined,
aristocratic nation. The Infanta embodies femininity and culture; her name
is Marie; she inhabits an enclosed garden; she stands for Catholic Spain. A
virgin heroine, a very little girl dressed in white, she recalls the Virgin
Mary and Kore or Gretchen, innocent figures of beauty in springtime. She is
one of many who grace Hugo's world, who culminate in the Léopoldine
of *Les Contemplations* and the Jeanne of *L'Art d'être grand-père* (1877).
Her fragility, her meekness are the appropriate thematic dominants in this
high-art version of romantic pastoral.

One aspect of the pastoral is its evanescence, the fact that injustice can
corrode its values so easily. The Gothic horror of *Eviradnus* does indeed
make an appearance in this refined, Renaissance décor. For within the
garden, behind the fountain, lies Philip II's palace, and behind the windows
lurks the king's shadow. Philip is depicted as a fanatic, a tyrant like
Xerxes (cf. *Les Trois Cent* in *La Légende*, second series); a monster associated with phantoms, torture, death, night, owls, the sphinx, and Satan
clad in black, he does not speak or smile. In contrast to the world of the

Infanta – to her rose, garden, light, jewels, innocence, beauty, goodness, and weakness – we find, contiguous to it, the king's prison, blackness, shadow, remorse, ugliness, evil, and strength.

King Philip, the evil father, seeks to become God. He wishes to seize the planet and attain mastery over all men. Indeed, as the governess explains to the Infanta, kings such as he do master the earth and more than the earth – three of the four elements that make up the cosmos. They command the land, the sea, and those destructive forces of war embodied in fire. But the fourth element, the air, is not subject to man's wishes. Indeed, the wind that blows the Infanta's rose into the basin, destroying it, and that destroys her father's armada, that stirs up the waters of the fountain and ocean, comes from the sky, from heaven, is an instrument in the hands of God. The ultimate father-judge denies the claims of a mere earthly pretender, destroying Philip's pretensions with his breath, that image of divine justice and phallic power, the *verbum Dei* that cows the impotent monarch lurking passively in his palace and his innocent but no less passive daughter.

We are expected to distinguish between the princess and her blood-thirsty sire. Yet they are of one family, caste, and nation. The Infanta needs the rose to mediate between herself and happiness; King Philip uses the armada in a comparable manner. Such mediation is both groundless and unrealistic. The loss of the rose represents the end of innocence for the Infanta, a symbolic violation and initiation into reality, away from the walls of her garden. Will this also be the case for her father when the invasion of England fails? The girl gazes ahead of her, sees nothing, is unaware of the wind until it strikes, and even then cannot account for her loss. Similarly, Philip, although a more lucid, wily creature, gazing out from behind his windows, does not look at his daughter; he only beholds in his mind's eye, in a daydream, the fleet setting out on a successful campaign. He lives as much in a dream-world as the Infanta, and his vision is as faulty as hers. Both father and daughter, monster and angel, have learned the habit of ruling; both take illusion for reality and reality for illusion. Significantly, neither speaks, neither seeks to communicate with the other or with the governess. In the end this latter personage does inform the Infanta of the truth that lies behind appearances: 'Madame ... tout sur terre appartient aux princes, hors le vent' (p. 608). No one tells the king. But, of course, Hugo does inform us, his public, with the poem, *La Rose de L'Infante*. Because of him we see better than the Infanta and her father. Based upon a famous painting by Velasquez, the poem is an intertext which 'contains' the painting; it is a work of art which exalts and at the same time reveals the flaws in that artistic and artificial Spanish Golden Age embodied in Velasquez and Philip II – in the rose, the young girl, and the fanatic who lurks behind the windows of his palace.

Just as Satan was perhaps the greatest cultural hero of European Romanticism, his rehabilitation, his reconciliation with God, becomes one of the dominant themes in literature during the period which extends from Byron to Hugo. During the early years French epics treating the theme of 'Satan sauvé' were written or projected by Ballanche, Vigny, Soumet, and Henri Delpech, and in the 1840s and 1850s authors as varied as Lamennais, the Abbé Constant, Proudhon, Ludovic de Cailleux, Maxime du Camp, and Quinet all meditated on how, why, and when the prince of darkness would be redeemed and, along with him, our sinful universe. Hugo's unfinished masterpiece, *La Fin de Satan* (1854, 1859–60; publ. 1886), is the finest expression of, and culminating monument to, one of the great myths of the nineteenth century; it is also his grandest artistic vision of man and the universe.[11]

Like *La Légende des Siècles*, *La Fin de Satan* includes the entire time-flow of history from Creation to Doomsday, but it treats in addition both the human and divine spheres, establishing parallelisms between secular and sacred levels of action. The theme is the fall of Satan and of man, and their travail through eons of suffering, which then leads to progress on earth and forgiveness in heaven brought about by the redeeming force of liberty. The dominant secular symbolism is embodied in the murer of Abel by Cain, that human act of rebellion corresponding to Satan's act of rebellion against God. Satan's daughter Isis-Lilith retains Cain's weapons – the nail, the wood, and the stone – and bequeaths them to mankind. From the nail is fashioned a dagger, image of war, symbol of distant Antiquity; from the wood is shaped a gibbet, image of fanaticism, symbol of the Judaeo-Christian era; and from the stone is constructed a prison, image of tyranny, symbol of modern times. For each of these three implements, corresponding to the three historical periods, a story is told; the three together reflect the nature of man and of Satan, throughout cosmic time.

Cain's gigantic nail was hammered into the form of a dagger and placed on the end of a pike by Nemrod the hunter, king of the giants. This descendant of the Titans and of Satan himself is a monster of cruelty. A warlord, he leaves in his wake mountains of corpses to be devoured by clouds of ravens. Like Satan and like the monarchs of *La Légende des Siècles*, Nemrod is not satisfied with the earthly sovereignty he has more or less legitimately acquired. Instead, he wishes to soar into the heavens to conquer God, to become God, in a sort of flying machine drawn upward by four eagles, accompanied only by his evil genius, the black eunuch Zaïm. The imagery associated with Nemrod – the flames with which he devastates the earth, his pike and dagger, his sling, his arrows, his eagles, and his flying – all connote a frenetic will to power, a spirit of rebellion and sexual aggression against the Father, in the tradition of Prometheus, Phaeton, and Oedipus.

The eagles, generally manifestations of good, as in *Ibo*, *L'Aigle du Casque*, or *Dieu*, here are assimilated to military conquest and the rule of empire: specifically, to Alexander, Hannibal, Caesar, and Napoleon. Most striking of all, however, is Nemrod's last demonic act, to shoot an arrow into the sky from his flying machine; then he falls to earth, and so does the arrow, tainted with blood:

> Un mois après, la nuit, un pâtre centenaire
> Qui songeait dans la plaine où Caïn prit Abel,
> Champ hideux d'où l'on voit le front noir de Babel,
> Vit tout à coup tomber des cieux, dans l'ombre étrange,
> Quelqu'un de monstrueux qu'il prit pour un archange;
> C'était Nemrod.
>
>               Couché sur le dos, mort, puni,
> Le noir chasseur tournait encor vers l'infini
> Sa tête aux yeux profonds que rien n'avait courbée.
>
> Auprès de lui gisait sa flèche retombée.
> La pointe, qui s'était enfoncée au ciel bleu,
> Etait teinte de sang. Avait-il blessé Dieu?   (p. 1653)

This, the ultimate in martial and sexual aggression, recalls an obsessive motif in the Hugolian corpus, God depicted as a great eye, and atheism or God's death symbolized by an empty socket or the eye gouged out. Nemrod's intention was to deny God, and, through acts of war committed by himself and his successors, for a time he succeeds.

Nemrod constructed his flying machine out of the remains of Noah's ark. However, the wood of Cain's club was reserved for those who made of it a cross to slay Jesus. Still later Torquemada reduces the cross to a stake for the executions under his auspices:

> – Torquemada, j'entends le bruit de ta cognée;
> Tes bras sont nus, ta face est de sueur baignée;
> A quoi travailles-tu seul dans ton noir sentier? –
> Torquemada répond: – Je suis le charpentier.
> Et j'ai la hache au poing dans ce monde où nous sommes.
> – Qu'est-ce donc que tu fais? – Un bûcher pour les hommes.
> – Avec quel bois? – Avec la croix de Jésus-Christ.   (p. 1718)

Since Montfaucon rises metaphorically next to Golgotha, in our Christian era Jacob could enjoy a vision of angels (victims of injustice) proceeding on a new ladder to the gibbet of religious persecution. To designate this second period in the history of man, Hugo retells with studied simplicity the story of Christ's passion, emphasizing the demonic Tree of the Rood, that is, Cain's murder weapon, horrible, deformed, and, after centuries of oblivion, still covered with Abel's blood. Hugo is well aware of the place the cross occupies in typological tradition. He associates the Holy Rood with the slaying of Abel, and Jews with Cain and Satan. However, his version of the myth is stunningly original in that he insists upon Christ's failure:[12] the prince of peace was martyred in vain and now suffers from clerical descendants of the Pharisees, his own disciples who will bring others to martyrdom in the same spirit of hatred. Instead of ending violence, Christianity feeds it anew, for the stake of the Inquisition and the gibbet of feudalism prove to be appropriate modern manifestations of the cross. Thus its meaning is deformed, and wood, image of creative life and refuge in the natural world, becomes an instrument of death, the denial of its very self.

Except for fragments, the third section, concerned with the French Revolution, was never written. Significantly, what little of this material Hugo did compose evokes the Bastille, constructed from Cain's stone weapon. Hugo depicts the fortress as a living female monster, a devourer; he also emphasizes its tomb-like nature, with windowless cells, chains, and, above all, the great clock, image of destiny. In *La Fin de Satan*, as in the epic section of *Les Quatre Vents de l'Esprit*, also devoted to 1789, the tyranny of the Ancien Régime is depicted in terms of old stone – culturally meaningful, even beautiful, but cold, cruel, and lifeless.

The dagger, the gibbet, and the dungeon are gifts to mankind from Isis-Lilith. This ghoul, who leaves sulphurous traces in her wake and who drinks blood in the forests, appears to be an evanescent form covered by a white veil; in fact a skeleton lurks inside her shroud. A figure of idolatry, fanaticism, hatred, and predestination, she is the eternal enemy of God and man. Symbolizing pure evil, she does not, truly cannot, exist, nor can she be redeemed. Based upon the legendary figure of Adam's first wife, a demon of the night and kidnapper of children, this is one incarnation of a common Hugolian figure, Arachne-Ananke: woman conceived as the Terrible Mother, the spider, the octopus. Hers is the monstrous beauty of the Medusa, the harpy, the sphinx, and of Kali, goddess of death, which was to become so fashionable in the second half of the nineteenth century.

As a figure of terror, Lilith is an appropriate daughter for Satan. Victor Hugo suppresses all of the beauty and majesty to be found in the rebel of *Paradise Lost* and in the various Byronic heroes – Harold, Cain, the Giaour, and so on – who evoked the prince of darkness for nineteenth-century man. On the contrary, Hugo returns to a Dantesque vision of Lucifer: he paints him as a monster, a formerly angelic being degraded, bestialized, transformed into the lowest of animals. The Devil is thus meta-morphosed into a giant bat, a dog that bays in the night, a goat, a serpent, a hydra, a worm, a caterpillar, a larva, a tarantula, and a spider. Metaphori-cally, this loathsome animal-figure is then associated with other incarna-tions of evil, persecutors of Christ: the hypocrite Caiaphas, who wears a shroud-like robe, thus resembling Isis-Lilith, and is depicted as a snake and a fox; or the criminal Barabbas, compared to a serpent, a specter, and a larva. In traditional Christian iconography, and in Hugo's personal my-thology, these images are associated with vices and with the qualities of hell.

Hugo's inferno is a terrifying place, again closer in inspiration to Dante than to Milton. The arch-fiend is pressed down into a tiny spot at the center of the earth, a mockery of the divine sacred apex he hoped to attain; there, cut off from the outside, smothered, 'L'antique patient de l'éternel supplice' beats his wings like a bat in a cage. In this middle of a labyrinth, comparable to the dungeon-tomb in which Cain, Esmeralda, and Gwyn-plaine are imprisoned, Satan's cage also resembles the sewers of Paris in Les Misérables. To arrive there, the prince of darkness falls into the abyss, slips into the void, a Kantian space that engulfs him, dragging him down (or up?) into a cosmic continuum with which he cannot cope. His imprison-ment also provides the appropriate backdrop for certain monstrous scenes on earth: the clouds of crows feasting on corpses and the burning plains of Nemrod's country, or Golgotha and Potter's Field, cursed, bald, sterile settings for tragedy in Christ's Jerusalem. Even Melchisedech, a just man, a prophet of the good, evokes the old Chaos, where the amorphous slides, swarms, and proliferates, where the elements are confused, where solids become viscous and fluidify – a state to which Satan has returned in his prison and is then re-enacted on earth in the days of the Flood, and more than once since.

Falling and imprisonment serve as external projections of an internal men-tal state, of the anguish and void in Satan's soul, the inferno inside his skull.[13] The great rebel suffers not from hell-fire or the traditional punitive machinery, but from solitude. His is not a condition of pride but of jealousy, of alienation from God, an Augustinian *privatio boni*, for he loves the Father but can never hope to be loved in return, to share in the *caritas* that radiates from the divinity to all creatures. When Satan fell away from God, a literal fall into the abyss, he saw the stars go out one by one. Now, in his dungeon-like cave, he is deprived of all light as of God's love: *Et nox facta est*. The rebel can never close his eyes, sleep, die, forget, or behold anything. His is a true existential hell worthy of Sartre, one where the victim creates his own pain. His torture proves to be his own lucidity, his introspection. Significantly, this angel of light who rebelled against the source of all light and who fathered a Nemrod whose goal was to put out God's eye is punished by darkness, is rendered immobile and impotent, symbolically mutilated (he is also the ancestor of Zaïm the eunuch), transformed into a larva in his hole.

But Satan's hole is a cocoon and his despair is not eternal, for the prison situation contributes to his transcendence. The captive can be redeemed, as were Claude Gueux and Jean Valjean. He is miserable, yes, but not irrevocably wicked. The arch-rebel does yearn for God, whose love is inevitably omnipotent, omniscient, and omnipresent. Satan himself discovers, then proves to God, the ontological necessity for his own redemption, which logically forms part of God's plan for the universe. As in Shelley's *Prometheus Unbound*, love conquers hate, thus establishing mastery over the cosmos; it stands at the base of intellect, power, and freedom. Since hatred and jealousy are mere manifestations of non-love, they do not exist, for the same reasons that hell and Lilith do not exist. The only possible 'final solution' for the problem of non-love is love, as is forgiveness for crime – the answer Hugo proposes in *Cromwell*, *Hernani*, *Les Burgraves*, *Les Misérables*, and *La Pitié suprême*.[14] In contrast to Zaïm, a leper, though afflicted with characteristics of rot, slime, and garbage, cherishes the fellow men who have cast him out and, prefiguring Christ, blesses them, urging God to place their suffering on his shoulders. In contrast to Sadoch, priest of Israel, who preaches the Law, Christ answers one word only: Love!

> – Toute la loi d'en haut est dans un mot: aimer ...
> Si vous aimez bien, voilà le paradis ...
> > Marchez dans la route tracée,
> Aimez ...
> Soyez doux. Aimez-vous toujours les uns les autres.
> > (pp. 1669, 1692, 1695)

His is a victory of the Holy Spirit, of the Word, of divine and human Agape, when in his 'triumph' he rides into Jerusalem on the back of an ass, under palm branches. Then Satan's descendant, like Nemrod and Zaïm an individual who takes after his ancestor, another worm, another larva, and a proven criminal, is weaned from bitterness to charity and redeemed through suffering: Barabbas, who, hurtling into Christ's cross in the darkness, comes to an understanding of solitude and death. This brutish creature is converted, this serpent is fascinated by the eye of the dove, and, like the leper, like Christ himself, he becomes a prophet and a witness to the Good.

One of the great themes of Romanticism is salvation through woman, the notion that woman's love can redeem the male sinner, although often women prove to be temptresses or figures of illusion. Vigny developed the topos of the redeeming woman in *Eloa* and *La Maison du Berger*, and Lamartine in *Jocelyn*; we also find it in Ballanche, Quinet, Soumet, and the

Abbé Constant, not to speak of Shelley's *Revolt of Islam* and *Prometheus Unbound*, Schiller's *Wallenstein* trilogy, and Goethe's *Faust*. A variation on this pattern is to be found in Hugo's works: that of the virgin daughter who redeems her old, sinning father or father-surrogate, the girl serving as mediator for her father's salvation. There are several examples of woman's love and pity in *La Fin de Satan*: the mother (Mary), the sister (Magdalene), and the wife (Lucile Desmoulins – projected but unwritten). However, most powerful of all and central to the narrative line is the role played by Liberté in redeeming her father Satan. An angel of pure light, she is set off in antithesis to her alter ego, her sister, Isis-Lilith. Indeed, having descended into the center of the earth in order to give battle to Isis, the white lady succeeds in conquering the dark lady (an allegory of liberty overcoming fatality), so that a feminine archetype of purity and goodness rather than one of terror will henceforth accompany the striving, struggling male. This is Hugo's variation on the old epic theme of the hero delivered from the clutches of a temptress (Calypso or Circe, Dido, Morgain la fée, Alcina, Armida, Acrasia) who lures him from the true path, or of the warrior maiden (Bradamante, Britomart) who rescues a beloved male hero. Satan is reborn because of a symbolic union, a sort of atonement with a feminine being like himself, the anima-figure he himself created. Nonetheless, because Liberté weeps tears over Satan, who drinks her tears and her words, who receives milk from her, the daughter-savior is symbolically transformed into a mother. It is through contact with this good mother that the creeping prisoner escapes the soft, amorphous center of the earth; she permits him to crawl out of his metaphorical womb, to transcend death through a new rebirth.

As was the case in *La Légende des Siècles*, Hugo's divinity incarnates the ultimate paternal principle, the supreme judging eye, the cosmic superego. God himself, as well as Liberté, embodies light, progress, spirit, mobility, and the airy splendor that defeat Isis-Lilith. This victory of spirit over matter and of freedom over fatality is symbolized, in Hugo's epic as in Christian tradition generally, as a triumph of the male over the female. Indeed, since Satan yearns for God's male love in a passive, seemingly feminine way, we associate him with d'Aubigné's Narrator in *Les Tragiques* and the image of the Church or the individual Christian soul yearning for Christ in the allegorized Song of Songs or the mystical poetry of Juan de la Cruz. Satan's *passio*, in Jungian terms, is a regressive reanimation of the Father-imago. God, who created Lucifer in the beginning, is recognized to be Satan's all-powerful father-judge and the embodiment of creative fecundity in the universe. In the end, Satan and God are reconciled; God blesses his son, who, because he also is a father, because he sired Liberté as well as Isis-Lilith, is worthy of standing again before him:

– Non, je ne te hais point! ...
Viens; l'ange Liberté, c'est ta fille et la mienne.
Cette paternité sublime nous unit.
L'archange ressuscite et le démon finit;
Et j'efface la nuit sinistre, et rien n'en reste.
Satan est mort; renais, ô Lucifer céleste!
Viens, monte hors de l'ombre avec l'aurore au front!　(p. 1762)[15]

According to the Apostles' Creed, Christ was crucified on Good Friday, then descended to hell, but on Easter Sunday he rose from the grave, ascending to the Father. In *La Fin de Satan* the prince of darkness descends and is forcibly imprisoned in the center of the earth. But whereas Nemrod and Zaïm fail in their efforts to soar to heaven, and Satan, given over to frenetic wandering, cannot find a home on a burning star, he eventually does break out of his prison. The larva is transformed and in the end becomes a true angel, a winged light-bearer who flies upward. This is a modern, neo-Christian version of the homecoming motif to be found in the *Odyssey*, the *Aeneid*, many *chansons de geste*, the romances of Chrétien, and the *Lusiads*. 'Chanson des Oiseaux' speaks in praise of God, liberty, and love. Significantly, Christ himself is assimilated to the Dove of Peace and to the Holy Ghost (his eye fascinates the serpent Barabbas), and Liberté is born from a feather that dropped off Satan's wing. In *La Fin de Satan*, as in *La Légende des Siècles* (*Pleine Mer – Plein Ciel*) and *Dieu*, a bird's flight is the concrete poetic metaphor for love, freedom, spiritual life, and the quest for God. Only such flight can give a measure of Hugo's conception of an open, expanding universe, and of man's capacity to master it under God's benevolent aegis.

Liberté, a light-figure with a star on her forehead, illuminates the darkness of Satan's hole, her rays eclipsing, indeed disintegrating, Isis-Lilith. At the end of time, Satan, so desperate at the stars' extinction during his early career, also partakes of light – borne by Liberté, by Christ, and presumably (in the unwritten portions) by the Enlightenment that gave rise to 1789. After all, it is Satan's word, '– Va! –' that grants Liberté permission to seize the Bastille. Brightness triumphs over darkness, good over evil. God's seeing eye has not been put out by Nemrod; even Barabbas, unseeing in the darkness, is converted by Christ's eye; and Satan, become Lucifer again, perceives God face to face, a light-bearer in harmony with his creator, the source of all whiteness, all vision.

In the 'Préface' to *La Légende des Siècles* (1859), Victor Hugo refers to *La Légende*, *La Fin de Satan*, and *Dieu* as three works forming a whole: an immense, unified epic of being: 'une sorte de poëme d'une certaine étendue

où se réverbère le problème unique, l'Etre, sous sa triple face: l'Humanité,
le Mal, l'Infini; le progressif, le relatif, l'absolu; en ce qu'on pourrait
appeler trois chants: *la Légende des Siècles, la Fin de Satan, Dieu.*' In a
sense all three works exploit an identical theme: the fall of man and his long,
slow rise to progress, forgiveness, and knowledge of God. There is no
doubt that consciously or unconsciously Hugo is at his best treating the Fall:
he relishes scenes of apocalyptic terror; he is most successful in re-enacting
Virgil's *ingens numinis horror* and Goethe's *Schaudern*. The Legend of the
Centuries becomes largely the telling of a quasi-infinite sequence of crimes;
we remember above all Satan's misery in his dungeon and the wickedness of
Nemrod, Zaïm, Sadoch, and Caiaphas (significantly, the section on the
French Revolution was never completed); and *Dieu* is structured as a pattern
of negative answers, for the Narrator will discover the Truth, if at all,
only after death.

On the other hand, Hugo's vision of the universe is far from being
pessimistic in the manner of Leconte de Lisle or Vigny. Not inherent in man
or nature, evil has been foisted on us by outside forces: Satan, Isis-Lilith,
or the gods of Olympus. Those tyrants who encourage pillage, war, and
oppression are punished. A Nemrod, a Kanut, a Philip II, the feudal
barons of Spain, and the monarchs of Germany all yield to God's justice,
embodied as an avenging knight-errant or as the force of the wind, an
eagle, a thunderclap, or an angel's sword. Of course, victims do not benefit
personally from the realization that their torturers are punished by a just
and vengeful deity. On the other hand, progress, however slow, however
intermittent, is part of God's plan for the universe. A first step is represented by the Coming of Christ, the apostle of love; a second by the Renaissance (*Le Satyre*), when the Olympians, symbols of fatalism and oppression, are overthrown. The French Revolution then marks the third and most
important stage in man's rise from the depths. It is the mother of peoples
(1789), symbolized by Lucile Desmoulins, and the goddess Liberté, not the
Virgin Mary, who redeem Eve, mother of Cain, and Satan himself. The
fall of the Bastille, an act of justice, will succeed in a way that Christ and Pan
failed, preparing a better future for mankind, so that people can physically (*Pleine Mer – Plein Ciel*) and spiritually (*Dieu*) rise to the stars. Thus
matter gives way to spirit, the shadows to pure light, and Satan, humanity, and the questing spirit of a poet are redeemed.

The Revolution of 1789 is crucial to the sense and tone of Hugo's
poetry of redemption as well as to its chronology. For Ballanche, Soumet,
Laprade, the Abbé Constant, even Lamartine, progress is largely a spiritual matter, accomplished through personal expiation. Victor Hugo partakes
of this current but also joins Quinet and Michelet in a more militant
espousal of revolution. Christ revolts against the law of Sadoch, Pan against

the laws of Olympus. Political rebels enact God's will by punishing tyrants. As we have seen, 1789 replaces the Advent of Christ as the crucial turning-point in history, and the message of the Rights of Man completes the Sermon on the Mount. In a modified secular version of *translatio imperii et studii*, Paris supplants Jerusalem, and the *Lumières* of Voltaire's and Hugo's centuries prove of greater benefit to mankind than an earlier *lumen mundi*. Finally, Satan himself, the arch-rebel, is redeemed by the principle of liberty that he and God mutually created. Hugo saves him, not in spite of himself, but because he is a rebel. This means that all of mankind, sinner and saint, master and slave, bandit and law-giver, deserves to be saved. Also, only a free man is capable of bettering himself and his fellows, and only a free man is worthy to see God. Knowledge of and reconciliation with the divinity become the ultimate goals of humanity and the culmination of history, in *La Légende des Siècles*, *La Fin de Satan*, and *Dieu*. And Victor Hugo, as Republican bard, prophet, and priest, teaches the people and both recognizes and helps shape the course of history.

These masterpieces attain a grandiose coherence, manifesting at the same time a powerfully original vision of the universe. In them we find, as one critic says, an *Iliad* of one hundred acts and an *Odyssey* of one hundred landings, as man, the eternal Ulysses, journeys to the stars.[16] That two of the poems were never completed, survive only as fragments, underscores Hugo's world view, in which mankind and the cosmos itself are perceived as ruins, crumbling words and stones, a great wall eaten away by the ravages of time, and a cosmic Tower of Babel. Hugo's opus, along with the *chansons de geste* in their final, cyclical form, is the closest Western equivalent of the *Rāmāyana* and the *Mahābhārata*. And it is Hugo who created the 'appropriate' epic of Romanticism, in which the historical, humanitarian, revolutionary, and religious calls are blended and man is depicted in his totality, in this world (past, present, future) and in the supernatural sphere as well. In *L'Art romantique* (1861) Baudelaire wrote, referring to *La Légende des Siècles*: 'Victor Hugo a créé le seul poème épique qui pût être créé par un homme de son temps pour les lecteurs de son temps.'[17] Since this outrageously modern epos is not based upon one single hero, not even Satan, but upon heroism embodied in mankind as a whole, it tells the adventure of all men, of our culture, not just one culture hero. Combining lyricism with narration, and intensity with scope, Hugo presents an inner as well as outer history of man. His is a vision of totality, of continuity in time and space, in which our world situation is made meaningful because it is bound to history and the cosmos.

For a generation now critics have proclaimed that Hugo at his best is neither the young leader of Romanticism nor the official bard of the Third Republic but the prophet, the seer in exile, the magus of the night. And, as magus, perhaps his greatest contribution to French literature has been a rehabilitation of the archetypal, apocalyptic spirit (largely dormant since the advent of Classicism) and, along with it, the creation of new myths central to the romantic and modern imagination: Notre-Dame and Quasimodo; the redeemed convict and the Parisian *gamin*; Gilliatt, his boat, and his octopus; Satan and his two daughters; Cain, Kanut, the world of feudal Spain, and the brotherhood of poor people in our time; the castle at Corbus, the gardens of the Aranjuez, the tower of Babel, and the sewers of Paris; the wall of history, and flight to the stars. Hugo's work culminates and fulfills the epic experimentation of half a century in half a dozen European nations: he created the archetypal epic of Romanticism. He succeeded in attaining the sublime style, the truly epic spirit for which modern man yearns.

## Chapter Sixteen

# ❧ SAINT-JOHN PERSE

In 1885 the Republic of France honored the remains of the octogenarian Victor Hugo with perhaps the most sumptuous state funeral in the history of letters. Such ceremonies are normally reserved for the 'classics,' for figures so enshrined that they no longer relate to life in the present. Indeed, literary values had already begun to shift in the 1850s, Hugo's most creative decade, with the publication of *Madame Bovary* and *Les Fleurs du Mal*. By the 1880s new 'isms' had replaced those of Hugo's and even Flaubert's time: impressionism, naturalism, symbolism, and the many facets of avant-garde. Although this *Belle Epoque*, these Banquet Years from 1885 to 1914,[1] were an age of exuberance and creativity in the arts, the achievements of Verlaine and Mallarmé, of Zola and Anatole France, of Huysmans and Jarry, could hardly provide a climate for epic. For a truly sublime style, for works of art in the grand manner, we have to turn to Péguy and Claudel. Great innovators in verse theater and the sublime lyric, they manifest a quality of 'epicness' comparable to that of the Ronsardian Hymn and provide an example that was not to be lost on future generations. Their influence on Saint-John Perse, Aragon, Jouve, and Emmanuel has yet to be measured. In a more traditional style, followers of Leconte de Lisle published collections of 'little epics,' for example *Les Siècles morts* by André de Guerne (in three installments: 1890, 1892, 1897), and Sully Prudhomme wrote discursive poems of a philosophical, scientific bent: *Les Destins* (1872), *La Justice* (1878), and *Le Bonheur* (1888). In the early years of the twentieth century the tradition was renewed by Henri de Régnier, Albert Samain, Verhaeren, and their disciples. A host of long poems and narrative fragments in the neoclassical vein (*l'école romane*) were produced by Fernand Gregh, André Bellesort, François-Paul Alibert, Michel de Bellomayre, Gustave Zidler, Ernest Prévost, André Berry, Paul de Nay, J.-P. Rabaté, Félix Ménétrier, Serge Barrault, Georges Duhamel, and Pierre de Nolhac – this current extending well into the 1930s. It is scarcely necessary to add that these poets, like their counterparts in England (Kipling, Davidson,

Chesterton, Noyes, and Masefield) and Germany (Hart, Dehmel, Däubler, Liliencron, Frenssen, and Ernst) were not in tune with their age. With the exceptions of Péguy and Claudel, the generations of Sully Prudhomme (awarded the first Nobel Prize for Literature in 1901) and Mallarmé and of Jarry and Apollinaire were no more conducive to literary heroism than the century of Voltaire and Marivaux – and for largely the same reasons.[2]

The various schools that have blossomed since 1914 – cubism, Dada, surrealism, existentialism, structuralism – are in essence no more oriented toward the epic spirit than was symbolism. Indeed, for all of Western Europe the Great War represented the end of a traditional way of life, a loss of innocence, with much of the best literature in the succeeding decades devoted to exploring, among other things, the demise of the heroic ideal. In Northrop Frye's terminology, ours is an age of irony, which has replaced romance, tragedy, even realism. In the specific domain of poetry most critics assume that we in the twentieth century are the direct inheritors of the late nineteenth, that Nerval, Baudelaire, Rimbaud, and Mallarmé made striking innovations in verse technique and mentality which have persisted to our own day. The post-Rimbaldian bard is especially concerned with exploring his inner world, the anguish which he alone can know; for him, poetry is a way of knowing, an arcane experience which is also an adventure in experiencing life; and although he questions the essence of language and the writing process, he also proclaims that his contact with language is unique and privileged and that poetry reflects only itself, is its only reality. All this implies a break with the past, a rejection both of rhetoric and of the enshrined literary forms, especially tragedy and epic.

To some extent, the foregoing is valid. I agree that the poetic rift was greater in the fifty years extending from 1870 to 1920 than in any comparable period in Western literature, and that Mallarmé and Valéry had as great an impact on the evolution of poetry as previous 'reformers' such as Machaut, Ronsard, Malherbe, and Hugo. However, I also believe that the importance of the symbolist revolution has been exaggerated and that the view that twentieth-century verse has only one voice is a simplification unfair to the richness and complexity of artistic creation in our time. We must also distinguish, as we do for medieval trouvères and for Ronsard, between modern poets' stated conception of poetry and what in fact they write. Although this talk of creating a new language has resulted in a modest evolution in the conventions of typography and a no less modest enrichment of the lexicon, the structure of the language – grammar, meter, and rhythm – remains the same. A Valéry and a Breton, consciously or unconsciously, employ the same rhetoric and manifest the same high moral tone as their predecessors in a tradition which begins with the troubadours and the trouvères.

It is quite true that the most important current in recent French verse springs from the analogue (and progenitor) of the High Modernist mode in England, that is, the 'Hermetic School' of Nerval, Mallarmé, and Valéry; it includes the work of Char, Bonnefoy, Dupin, Du Bouchet, and Jaccottet, to name but a few. However, other traditions in our century prove to be no less productive. Among them are cubism, Dada, and surrealism in its full range of influence; the *fantaisistes*, derived from Laforgue, including Apollinaire, who gave expression to *Esprit nouveau*, and his many disciples or those influenced by him; and the Catholic revival, the chief representatives of which, aside from Péguy and Claudel, are Milosz, Jouve, La Tour du Pin, and Emmanuel. Since World War II we find a profusion of trends; the currents mentioned above and many others, which derive from them or cut across the same literary terrain. These are concrete and spatialist verse, *lettrisme* and *spatialisme* (Isou, Garnier); a phenomenological school, sometimes called *chosisme*, obsessed with material things (Ponge, Guillevic); the *tranche d'écriture* anti-poetry of the *Tel Quel* and *Change* groups (Deguy, Pleynet, Roche, Roubaud); 'cosmic counter-humanism' (Jouve, Perse, Char); a pseudo-popular tradition (Prévert, Brassens, Vian); poetry of commitment (Aragon, Eluard); 'realists' who return to concrete simplicity, including the *Ecole de Rochefort* (Cadou, Manoll, Follain); and others.

Where does the epic fit into this scheme? For Valéry and his disciples, as for Edgar Allen Poe, the long poem is a contradiction in terms; according to them, it never existed at all, except as an imposed academic institution, and it certainly has no place in the esthetics of our century. The other movements do not call for a return to the epic nor, however, do they preach against it. The genre is by no means 'in favor' in our century; it is not one of the goals of artistic endeavor, as it was in the baroque and romantic periods. On the other hand, individual poets, committed to an esthetic, working within the norms of their group, or acting independently of Parisian circles, have written highly successful, brilliant long poems in our time: these are the post-symbolist Saint-John Perse, the Communist Aragon, the Catholic Pierre Emmanuel, and the structuralist Marcelin Pleynet. Although a time of heroism such as World War II and the Resistance helped arouse the heroic vein, in my opinion the epic production of the twentieth century is not the result of occasional, externally imposed events. Nor, of course, do contemporary epicists follow blindly in the wake of Lamartine, Hugo, Leconte de Lisle, or Régnier, any more than they imitate the *Aeneid* or *La Chanson de Roland*. Their works are inevitably of a new kind to fulfill new needs, reflecting our own unique world view. Indeed, their 'epic quest' serves, as in all other periods of literature, as one alternative open to poetic creation, one means of wrestling with the problems of our age, which a certain number of highly gifted poets will adopt, regardless of what they and we are told in the Academy.

Of the considerable output by Saint-John Perse (pseudonym for Alexis Saint-Leger Leger, 1887–1975),[3] three works deserve to be included in a book on epic: *Anabase* (1924), *Vents* (1946), and *Amers* (1957). *Vents*, written during the authors's 'exile' in the United States, fulfills André Chénier's dream of a poem dealing with the American experience, developing themes of exploration and scientific discovery on a cosmic level and in almost encyclopedic detail. Nonetheless, for reasons of space, and because *Vents* contains fewer narrative elements than either *Anabase* or *Amers* and is, in the long run, perhaps less successful as a total work of art, I have chosen not to discuss it in this chapter. The scientific-philosophical poem, in the hands of the Reclus de Molliens, Scève, du Bartas, Louis Racine, Sully Prudhomme, and Perse, is an important phenomenon in the history of French literature which in this book I have had to neglect.[4]

*Anabase*[5] was composed during the years Leger spent as a member of the French diplomatic corps in Peking (1916 – 21), set down, according to the author, in the small disused temple of Tao-Yu, on the old caravan route to the Northwest. Perse specifically denies that his poem has any direct relationship to Xenophon's *Anabasis*: he writes, '*Anabase* a pour objet le poème de la solitude dans l'action,' that is, an active synthesis of human resources, and he defines the title etymologically as 'montée en selle' and as an 'expédition vers l'intérieur' (p. 1108). The question is of some importance because *Anabase*, divided into ten cantos, with an opening and concluding *chanson*, reveals those traits of ambiguity and distortion which have become hallmarks of twentieth-century letters. The poem appears to be fragments of an epic or chronicle, a sacred text from an ancient civilization, written in, or literally translated from, the original language. A primitive nomadic society wanders over immense spaces, forms a town, yearns to move on, and does so. The exact interpretation to be given the individual cantos is quite another matter, open to dispute. I agree with those scholars who maintain that almost the entire poem is recited by a leader of the tribe in his own voice and, therefore, reflects his point of view. Consulting the various authorities who have worked on the problem and have proposed plot-analyses of *Anabase*,[6] and, where necessary, choosing between their interpretations, I propose the following synthetic scheme:

'Chanson.' A Stranger encounters the Leader, offering him and his tribe
    drugs, spiritual euphoria, new horizons, and the will to move on.
Canto 1. The Leader rejoins his tribe; he will establish a new order.
Canto 2. A sacred ritual; triumph over obstacles of sex and death.

Canto 3. Harvest time and purification rites; defiant affirmation of life
and action.
Canto 4. Founding the city.
Canto 5. Restlessness: yearning for departure and further explorations.
Canto 6. Invitation to adventure; propaganda and recruiting.
Canto 7. Decision to set out and the eve of departure.
Canto 8. The Long March resumes across the desert to the West.
Canto 9. Arrival at the threshold of a new country; *repos du guerrier.*
Canto 10. Festivities: celebration, census, leisure; the urge to set forth
again.
'Chanson.' The Leader hears of his brother the Poet.

Thus, in Cantos 1 – 5 the Leader is on the move, then builds a port-city
on an estuary; in Cantos 6 and 7 he experiences a longing to depart; and in
Cantos 8 – 10 he does set forth: this is the culmination, the anabasis itself.

Central to the poem is the notion of movement in space. *Anabase* evokes a
world of steppes and deserts extending over vast dimensions, and of great
winds blowing up the sand. Previously in *Eloges* Saint-John Perse contrasted his island paradise favorably with enclosed space, that is, a room
(four walls) within an urban environment, and he established an antithesis
between the luxurious refuge of his home and the search for new horizons
on the open sea. However, in *Anabase* both the dimensions and the call
to adventure are continental not insular. Perse's epic captures with gusto the
gallop of horses and the flow of the wind. The yearning to depart is the
dominant emotion in the poem. The Leader and his people move back and
forth from cities to the open plains. They are a tribe of nomads, full of
life, sensitive to the rumor of other provinces, open to the external world,
and themselves eager to seize it and the land which it contains. Indeed, it
can be said that this limitless space about them is given meaning, defined, by
their traversing and conquering it.

I have already said that *Anabase* gives the illusion of being a chronicle or
sacred text from an ancient civilization. Perse's tribe wanders over indefinite spaces at a no less indefinite time which we can nonetheless locate in the
distant past. Although Saint-John Perse was surely influenced by native
story-tellers in the Antilles where he grew up and although *Anabase* may
contain some allusions to the islands at the time of the Spanish conquest
in the seventeenth century,[7] the poem reflects more immediately northern
China where it was written and the steppes which Perse visited in 1920. He
evokes the plains of Central Asia, the cradle of civilization, the continent of
migrations, before missionaries and spice-traders appeared on the scene.
True, the Leader recalls traits of Alexander of Macedon, who broke horses,
founded a city, set out on a long voyage of conquest, and enjoyed King

Darius's women, yet he also reminds us of Genghis Khan, Mohammed, Cortés, and even Lawrence of Arabia.

There can be no doubt that Saint-John Perse revels in 'primitive' archetypal cultures in much the same way that he exalts his own childhood in the Caribbean (*Eloges*). He, the most rhetorical of poets, devoted much of his career to renewing the old topics of *laudatio temporis acti* and *florebat olim*. Indeed, it is an epic commonplace, from Homer and Virgil on, to exalt the *exempla maiorum*, to manifest a naïve, even reactionary nostalgia for bygone heroic doings. However, although Perse's epic deals with the past, with the history of a fictional community of the steppes, the plot also covers one chronological year in time: beginning with winter harvest in springtime, proceeding to the hot, dry period of midsummer, and ending with the renewal of the monsoon.[8] The three seasons of the Oriental year also bear a symbolic import; for we can assume that this period 'contains' the history of the tribe or even mankind as a whole. Thus a rhythm of recurrence is created, a cyclical structure of withdrawal and return. And at times visions of heroism are projected into the future, for the Stranger and the Leader are both prophets, and the story continues, open-ended, looking forward to new explorations. More than the past or the future, however, *Anabase* gives the reader an intense feeling for the here and now: although other poets resent or abolish duration, Perse accepts but then compresses it into an intense, living, sacred present. He creates this effect in part by an evocation of primitive rites that organize the everyday life of his community: the ritual of striding over the robes of the queen and her daughter, garments then borne away by the wind (Canto 2); purification rites (Canto 3); founding the city and sacrificing the body of a woman, burnt alive (Canto 4); offering the heart of a black sheep (Canto 8); and the final celebration accompanied by enumerations of trades and classes of people (Canto 10). In such a society history does not exist, and time as we know it has been abolished. Men's actions are significant not because of their intrinsic importance but in so far as they participate in transcendent being and reflect divine archetypes. Thus the founding of a city and the colonizing of new lands partake of the heavenly act of creation; the immolation of a scapegoat regenerates society because it evokes death and rebirth. This presence of ritual and of the sacred, and of an intensely present time, helps create a tone or mood of epic which no other work in French literature, except for *La Chanson de Roland*, possesses to the same degree. Saint-John Perse succeeds in concretizing the Hegelian unproblematic society which lives a meaningful, immediately comprehensible existence, all elements of which are understood as a totality, grasped as a coherent process.

To elaborate his epic 'world' Perse follows the example of such writers as d'Aubigné and Hugo: he forms patterns of imagery, opposing the 'good'

he favors and the 'evil' he abhors. Even though domestic security in Guada-
loupe is a subject of praise in *Eloges*, even though the Leader takes pleasure
in founding a city (*Anabase*, Canto 4), the obstacles that man must overcome are represented by urban stagnation. Significantly, as his correspondence shows, the diplomat Alexis Saint-Leger Leger preferred the steppes
of Mongolia and Sinkiang to life in Peking; for all his insight into Oriental
politics, he failed to comprehend the values of traditional Chinese civilization. In *Anabase* and his other poems the city represents wallowing in
*acedia*, and it is evoked in terms of dust, fat, and rot: it is a focus of impu-
rity. Perse also condemns the mentality of followers, of slaves who prefer
creature comforts and the security of a soft life to a more ascetic existence on
the steppes. Among the images he associates with the luxurious negative
state ('nos pièges au bonheur,' p. 102) are honey, trees, and the sun at high
noon.

Most of all, I believe, the author assimilates luxury, corruption, and vice
to woman and to the temptation she projects. The values of his community
are antifeminine. His male heroes – the Leader, the Stranger, and their
cohorts – stride over the outstretched lace robes of the queen and her
daughter, sullied by sweat in the armpits and which attract swarms of ants;
these robes, images of defilement, decadence, and death, are then carried
away by the sea wind like a priest cut into pieces (Canto 2). Prostitution
thrives in the new city, which imports indiscriminately cargoes of girls
and mules; the body of a girl is sacrificed; an outsider solicits for his sister
(Canto 4):

> (Un enfant triste comme la mort des singes – sœur aînée d'une
> grande beauté – nous offrait une caille dans un soulier de satin
> rose.)    (Canto 4: p. 99)

It is true that in Canto 9, after the long desert march, the Leader accepts
the advances of a conquered woman, but the offer is made in terms of
effrontery, the person in question opens her mouth to be inspected like a
saleable horse, and Perse tells us how, during the day, these girls urinate in
public:

> – et debout sur la tranche éclatante du jour, au seuil d'un grand
> pays plus chaste que la mort,
>     les filles urinaient en écartant la toile peinte de leur robe.
>                                                     (Canto 9: p. 110)

Critics have made a claim that these and other images exalt women, who
are assimilated to unrestrained natural functions. However, in *Anabase*

these functions are limited to females, we see females only in the process
of urinating, perspiring, and offering themselves to men's lust. The protagonists are exclusively male; they never engage in a serious relationship with
any woman. They may enjoy a woman at night, but, in the daytime,
when public life returns, they reassert dominance on *their* terms. As in the
early *chanson de geste* or, for that matter, Camoens's *Lusiads,* women
exist for simple, almost hygienic pleasure (*le repos du guerrier*) or as symbols
of temptation, pitfalls to be avoided; they are imported in herds or, as
individuals, sacrificed to the deity. This formulation corresponds to the
sensual yet sterile sexuality evoked in *La Gloire des Rois* and the notion,
in 'Berceuse,' that only with the sacrifice of a female baby can male legitimacy be restored. In *Anabase* women and sexual desire are associated
with creature comforts and the immobility of cities, with moisture, warmth,
and decay, with death, night-time, stars, and milk, with passion and
temptation, with defilement, with the moon and the menstrual cycle, with
the world of dreams and contemplation, melancholia, and the intellectual
life. All of these phenomena are recognized as dangerous to the heroic, virile
life of the steppes; these sisters of Ishtar, Delilah, Calypso, and Dido,
who threaten to emasculate the hero, must never be allowed to prevail.

The values that Saint-John Perse projects onto the Leader and the
Stranger are diametrically opposed to the feminine traits enumerated above.
The Leader's is a career of violence, war, and conquest – of lands and
women seized at the point of a lance. 'Un grand principe de violence com-
mandait à nos mœurs' (p. 108). He and his followers despise the stagnation
of cities, for their life is based upon movement, action, and adventure. Theirs
is a Nietzschean will to power, haughty and pitiless, the *menos* ascribed
to wrathful Achilles and fierce Roland. Superior in degree to other men and
to his environment, Perse's Leader partakes of the heroic life enshrined in
epic. Forced out of his apathy by the Stranger, a herald of adventures, he
quits his natural environment and journeys to the West, overcoming
ordeals, undergoing a quest for new experiences, accompanied by followers,
the best warriors among his people. Driven to the limits of being, the
spokesman for the tribe founds a new city and becomes master of his world
with an extraordinary freedom and joy in life.

This masculine world is embellished with imagery of a martial, dynamic
quality. In contrast to the sun and stars, Perse offers wind and lightning
blasts, God's sign of approbation, elements that purify. The Leader's favorite
animals are birds, flying creatures that call to action, images of motion,
anger, and transgression: '(L'ombre d'un grand oiseau me passe sur la face',
p. 106) (cf. *Oiseaux*); and horses, essential to the nomadic life, which in
*chanson de geste* and the American Western replace women in men's eyes,
are symbolic of the subhuman side of the psyche dominated and con-

trolled. In contrast to immobile trees and cities, we find narcotics and fields of grass, with the organic quality of seed, flowing like the sea. Blades of grass are thin, sharp, and cutting, as are the swords and lances wielded by the conquerors – masculine images that conquer matter by penetrating it. And *Anabase* depicts a world of the desert, bathed in hard yellow-golden light, a mineral setting of sharp, gleaming, crystalline sand and salt. Salt is a principal element in Perse's opus, standing for wit, spirit, desire, and life: in his last published poem, *Sécheresse*, the author praises the hot, dry season, a time of salt and thirst, a time of possibilities, creation, heresy, and transgression for an elite of 'spiritual' men. This is the salt of the intellect and of purity, of male austerity, of ascetic slimness, and of alchemical creation, characteristics of a world of masculine ordeals and martial initiation, in contrast to the female sensuality of the cities.

As in early *chansons de geste*, in place of the erotic relationship, man to woman, Perse exalts the all-male comradeship of warriors in arms: *militia* and *amicitia* replace *amor*. The most significant encounter, in the course of *Anabase*, is the friendship established between the Leader and the Stranger, a relationship which parallels that of the two protagonists of *Amitié du Prince* in *La Gloire des Rois*. At the beginning and later in the course of the narrative, the Stranger incites the tribe to set off on adventures across the desert:

> Un homme mit des baies amères dans nos mains. Etranger. Qui passait. Et voici qu'il est bruit d'autres provinces à mon gré …
> ('Chanson': p. 89)

The Leader's double or second self, the Stranger embodies the active side of his nature, the one most in harmony with the forces that reign over his community and the cosmos. Furthermore, the Stranger, a master of salt and grains, brings to the Leader products as well as news from the outside world. Indeed, he and the Leader exchange goods as well as ideas. Their commerce is of benefit to society, dependent on trade; indeed it is the principal resource and purpose of the city that the Leader founds. And this barter (from which money is excluded) is a symbolic representation of intellectual exchange between the two men, the sharp, cutting edge of words and the exaltation of the mind which are as important to them as the salt that preserves their food and the narcotic that inspires their dreams.

The *Anabase* community is genuine. Its people liberate themselves from the fetishism of women and the reification of cities ('la ville jaune, casquée d'ombre, avec ses caleçons de filles aux fenêtres,' p. 99); they are dependent upon no mediators for happiness and fulfillment other than their horses. Their will to power à la Corneille permits them to win the esteem of their fellows, to test the human condition to the ultimate. Theirs is an absolute option for life and a no less absolute refusal of mundane reality:

> Sur trois grandes saisons m'établissant avec honneur, j'augure bien du sol où j'ai fondé ma loi.
> Les armes au matin sont belles et la mer. A nos chevaux livrée la terre sans amandes
>      nous vaut ce ciel incorruptible ...
> Tant de douceur au cœur de l'homme, se peut-il qu'elle faille à trouver sa mesure? ...
> Terre arable du songe! Qui parle de bâtir? – J'ai vu la terre distribuée en de vastes espaces et ma pensée n'est point distraite du navigateur.   (Cantos 1, 7, 10: pp. 93, 105–6, 114)

The poem also involves a political stance, a series of actions whereby the Leader triumphs over mass apathy in order to orient the life of the tribe. We can understand Perse's aristocratic bias, the emphasis on 'high condition' for his protagonists. These men partake of the noble, gentle tradition of epic dating back to Turold, Virgil, and Homer; because as free spirits they set an example for the community, they are leaders in every sense of the term. And they maintain sovereignty wherever they ride. Hence the pervasive violence in *Anabase*. Perse believes in the values of a martial society, which consecrate the distinction between masters and slaves – for masters adhere to the law of manhood, salt, and motion, whereas slaves yield to womanly fat and stasis. His nomads attain a quality of splendor, of fervor and joy, that dazzles bystanders; theirs is a world of glory and achievement.

Saint-John Perse's race conquers lands, founds cities, falls into lethargy, sets off on new voyages, founds or is accepted into cities, and so forth. Since the journey takes on a cyclical quality, the Leader's triumph is called into question, remaining ever precarious. The poem's end, like the beginning, marks a pause, by no means a definitive halt. Furthermore, *Anabase* is not so much a poem of travel as of the yearning to depart; it expresses a will to conquer rather than conquest, and a taste for adventure rather than actual expeditions. Saint-John Perse, master of lyric emotion, expresses his scorn for objects and for wallowing in material security, his nostalgia for the heroic life. Despite its optimism, his text reveals a sense of anguish in solitude, the yearning that drives man to perform great deeds yet also rips apart his being.

*Anabase* is a complex work of art, which, resembling a palimpsest, can profitably be interpreted on more than one level. The Leader is a warrior-prince like Alexander or Genghis Khan; since he tells his own story in the first person, he is also a historian like Xenophon, or a 'cultivated' hero like

Odysseus and Aeneas; and since his tale assumes the form of a lyrical outburst with philosophical and mystical overtones, he becomes a sage, a
prophet-magus like Moses or Mohammed. The journey of the tribe over the
desert can refer allegorically to mankind's adventure over the centuries,
the progress of the race from early times to the present. Furthermore, we
envisage the Leader's conquest of his inner self; set adrift from the past,
thrust into a void, he learns to come to terms with the world and with his own
spiritual nature. Finally, the reader as well as the community is instructed
and initiated, coming to know joy as the poem comes into being. As the
Leader orders his world, so does Saint-John Perse the poet. Their 'anabasis'
is to the center of the self and the poem, to the nature of language. The
theme of art and the artist, the notion of the poem as a commentary on,
and metaphor for, its own creation – these are central to Saint-John Perse's
later works, *Vents* and *Amers*. Yet, already in *Anabase*, in addition to the
facts that the Leader is a prophet and user of words, that he creates song for
the people, that stories and exhortations are essential to his mission of
driving the tribe to the West, we must not forget that at the very end the
Leader speaks of his brother the Poet:

> Mais de mon frère le poète on a eu des nouvelles. Il a écrit encore
> une chose très douce. Et quelques-uns en eurent connaissance ...
> ('Chanson': p. 117)

The Leader and his brother are obviously doubles, representing two halves
of the same person. Is it not possible then that the 'thing' created by the Poet
is *Anabase* itself, the story of the Narrator, the Poet's alter ego? And that
the end of the voyage does result in one positive act: its own recounting in a
poem?

At first glance, *Amers*[9] appears to be less epic in quality than *Anabase*.
Whereas the plot of *Anabase* covers almost a full year in time and much of
the Asian continent in space, *Amers* recounts one night in a single undesig-
nated port-city. It is a sort of pageant, in which a series of characters
or groups of characters form a procession toward the main and deliver
speeches in praise of the sea. The poem itself is made up of these speeches,
delivered in turn by the Narrator or port officials and workers, by the
Master of Stars and Navigation, by tragediennes, by patrician ladies, by
the poetess, by a sybil, by young girls, by the Stranger (he stands in a boat
off the coast), by a pair of lovers, and by the Chorus. Various human
attainments – knowledge, art, power, language, religion – are invoked to
measure the ocean, and all prove inadequate, the only exception being
love, which *is* the sea, just as the sea is love.

Most of these characters declaiming hymns of praise are women, who offer themselves sexually to the ocean or to the man it will bring to them. The tragediennes proclaim, 'Ah! notre cri fut cri d'Amantes!' (p. 295); the young girls, 'Et l'homme de mer est dans nos songes. Meilleur des hommes, viens et prends! ...' (p. 317). 'Et cette fille chez les Prêtres' is as much a temple prostitute in the tradition of Babylon and Alexandria as she is a Greco-Roman Pythoness, Virgilian Sybil or Vestal. Canto 9, 'Etroits sont les vaisseaux,' is the high point of *Amers*. This elaborated encomium, of greater significance than the others, is also an epithalamium, a dialogue of passion between two lovers lying in a boat on the waters. Their dialogue, which follows the sexual act from beginning to end, is totally lacking in prudishness; it is, as more than one critic has pointed out, the most powerful manifestation of erotic verse in the West since the Song of Songs. The act of love is immediate and absolute, an intrinsic good in itself, soaring above notions of mediation or exchange. And it contains many of the traits Western man has come to associate with *fin' amor*: beauty, fatality, mystery, admiration, the sense of obstacle, transformation of the lover, and idealization of the beloved.

Thus the joy, fervor, and splendor which in Perse's other works were devoted to recollections of childhood, the virile life of the nomad, the poet in exile, or exploration and scientific progress in the Americas, here is consecrated to love. The temptress of the steppes is transformed into a virgin of the city, who yet is as passionate as her counterpart in *Anabase* and is capable of embodying traits of the mother or goddess. Woman is conceived in a positive light. The slim warrior-maidens of *Pluies* and *Vents*, the beggar-whore in *Exil*, the Lady of Race in *Neiges* – these are now fused into a group of female speakers who dominate the scene. Indeed, in this epic of love not war, masculine heroism gives way to feminine passion; the horse, the lance, and the desert are replaced by the city, the sea, and the boat; open vistas yield partially to enclosed space; and women, not men, 'deliver' the poem, envisaged from their point of view, filtered through their consciousness.

On the level of imagery, the young girls proclaim that they prefer evening to morning; the patrician ladies speak of being impregnated by the sea in a dream; and the major action of the text, the act of love between the Stranger and the Girl, occurs at night. During their epithalamium Perse associates phallic imagery with animal life (snakes, stallions, great fish), with lightning (the Stranger is a lightning flash, the Girl the waters), and with birds (the Stranger is a falcon, he is attracted to the port by a white feather on the waves, and sea-birds cast an omen). The couple make love on a narrow boat; the ocean itself is a bed of lovers; and the Girl is a narrow (virgin) boat, the Stranger her pilot, navigator, and captain. This vessel, of course, is an image of the womb, a feminine refuge, comparable to the grotto on land, a setting for death and rebirth.

However, the dominant image, the arch-image of this poem which begins with the words 'Et vous, Mers ...' (p. 259), is the sea. Thus Saint-John Perse continues the tradition of ocean poetry in modern French verse (Hugo, Rimbaud, Lautréamont, Claudel, Valéry, Supervielle). The poem's title refers to 'sea-marks,' defined as natural or artificial phenomena that mark the separation between the shore and the waters, indicating to sailors the approach of land. It has also been claimed that although this recondite definition will satisfy scholars, the average reader has a tendency to interpret the title word as 'bitterness.'[10] Here I wish to point out that great medieval poets – Thomas of England in his *Tristan et Iseut*, Chrétien de Troyes in *Cligès* – as well as the baroque Marbeuf, consciously played upon homonymous connotations inherent in the word *amer*: it could be read as the verb 'to love,' the adjective 'bitter,' and the noun 'the sea.' Even if Saint-John Perse was unfamiliar with these Old French texts, and I am willing to take his scorn for literary culture at face value, I propose that the phonology of the French language enabled him to rediscover the archetypal force inherent in the bitter sea, symbol for the bitter experience of love.

The ocean, assimilated to cosmic forces of Eros, is conceived both as a masculine and a feminine entity, as the virile Stranger who throbs back and forth, carrying the beloved (as shore or boat) with him in sexual embrace, or as the Girl lying in her bed, submitting to the lover, who, a boat, plows through her. The sea then is *the* erotic element, image of the woman's womb or of male sperm, its bitterness evoking desire and fecundity. Thus the Girl offers to slake her beloved's thirst, thus the salt-imagery of *Anabase* is assimilated to procreation in a womb. For Perse, water is never depicted as a fountain or a still pond, but in an active, violent way, as rain-storms (*Pluies*) or the ocean in splendor (*Amers*). Significantly, the poet emphasizes the sea's cyclical ebb and flow, with high and low tide, as a symbol for cosmic breath and heartbeat, sexual stimulation, and the rhythm of his poem.

For all its blatantly feminine imagery and erotic motif, *Amers* restates many of the central themes of *Anabase*. The Stranger as herald of adventures, and as conqueror and master, reappears in the guise of a mariner. The patrician ladies, who scorn a slothful, decorative existence in the palace, call for adventure on new strands with as much vehemence as the Leader in *Anabase*. Indeed, good 'Villes hautes,' seaports bustling with trade, are set in opposition to corrupt, stagnant 'Villes basses,' located far from the water. The entire poem can be considered a celebration of the ocean conceived as a denial of routine and settled life. Routine and the settled life are embodied in enclosed space, an opulent, boring, impure, inhibited, female-oriented city in opposition to which Saint-John Perse projects open spaces, violence, desire, transgression, and a virile master inherent in the waters. Furthermore, not only the patrician ladies but all who speak are aristocrats of the spirit, leaders of the community, who proceed according to rules of hierarchy and etiquette. And, in spite of the successful sexual climax in 'Etroits sont les vaisseaux,' *Amers*, like *Anabase*, reflects the tragic isolation of mankind. Lone women yearn for fulfillment from the sea, that is, from providential men who remain distant; and the two happy lovers, after climax, discover the transitoriness of passion, for the woman, bound to him by tenderness, dreads his departure, the man is conscious both of his ability to stand alone and of the solitude inherent in the human (male) condition:

> '... Solitude, ô cœur d'homme! Celle qui s'endort à mon épaule gauche sait-elle du songe tout l'abîme? Solitude et ténèbres au grand midi de l'homme ...
> Je veille seul et j'ai souci: porteur de femme et du miel de la femme ...'    (pp. 346, 348)

The eternally moving, ever-fluctuating ocean symbolizes the instability of the cosmos, the impossibility for mankind to attain a *plenum* of stability and therefore to stop the invincible flow of time.

*Amers* projects onto the world of Eros the same vision that gave life to heroism in *Anabase*; Saint-John Perse's masterwork represents one of the most successful efforts in Western literature since Chrétien de Troyes to synthesize *militia* and *amor*, to rehabilitate love in terms of epic. Thus the sex act is conceived as a duel, a gladiatorial combat, embellished with martial imagery, in which both adversaries endure *la petite mort* only to rise again. Significantly, the girls in *Amers* in no way correspond to the temptresses of *Anabase* or the Fat Queen of *Récitation à l'éloge d'une reine*. Although these virile maidens, scornful of their aging, satiated mothers, are modern analogues to the *bellatrices* in epics by Ariosto, Tasso, and Le Moyne, they are by no means deaf to the erotic call. Slim and virginal yet passionate, capable of baroque ecstasy, opened by the lover's sword, they create life anew in their wombs – with bitterness and salt. Furthermore, in spite of Saint-John Perse's exaltation of sex, his attitude toward woman has not undergone a fundamental shift since the 1920s. His women characters seek desperately for a male to remove their solitude and give a sense of meaning to their lives, to restore their femininity. The Stranger comes and offers them love, conquers them with his manhood. He is the master! The Girl gives herself to passion, enjoys her climax to the fullest, whereas her lover thinks, reflects, manipulates, using his intellect, in command of the relationship. Nonetheless, and this *is* a new departure, the Stranger does not quit the beloved after their night of love. Although he must return to the heroic life on the sea, he urges his mate, who is both noble and free, to depart with him. They will lead an existence 'de haute condition' together, renouncing the vulgarity of port and palace. In this respect Perse again unconsciously follows the example of Chrétien de Troyes. From the beginning his Stranger chooses the path that Erec and Yvain will discover after many an ordeal. Because woman makes of passion an absolute, she proves herself worthy to share the heroic life of the male: *amor* reinforces *militia*, and *militia* makes the highest flights of *amor* possible on that symbolic bed and battlefield, the flowing, eternal sea.

Saint-John Perse created an Asiatic *Anabase* based to some extent, despite his disclaimers, on Xenophon. After having devoted a series of works to his American experience, the author returned to a Greek motif with *Amers*. His long poem on Eros is structured in the form of a dithyramb or choric ode, containing an 'Invocation,' 'Strophe,' 'Chœur,' and 'Dédicace.' He joins Claudel and Jouve in a peculiarly modern endeavor (the great precursor is, of course, Hölderlin). That is, for the first time in France since Ronsard's generation, epic is embodied in the form of a sublime Attic lyric, the Dionysian hymn or Pindaric ode. In spite of Perse's oft-proclaimed scorn for our Greco-Roman heritage, in fact he had an excellent bourgeois education, which gave him a fine command of Greek, and in his youth he translated portions of the Epinician Odes. As Valery Larbaud pointed out in a letter to Fargue, dated 6 April 1911, the young Alexis Saint-Leger Leger, ignorant in modern French letters, acknowledged as master only Pindar (p. 1091). It was in Pindar, as in Nietzsche, that Saint-John Perse discovered certain touchstones of his own genius that burst forth in *Amers*: personal anonymity, the choric voice, aristocratic scorn for the crowd, masterly esthetic control, and a sense of panegyric.

The poet assimilates his text to Greek theater. He points out that the seaport can be envisaged as the hemicycle of an Attic stage, that his 'drama' recounts an action, the subject of which is the sea, and that the characters are not people of the sea but have come to praise the ocean on its shores, the *amers* (pp. 569 – 71). We also find tragic actresses and the Pythic prophetess, who play important roles, and, at the end, in the 'Dédicace,' the Man with the Golden Mask (the Stranger? the implied author?) who rips off his mask in honor of the sea (p. 385). *Amers* can be envisaged as a pageant, lyrical and dramatic, in which a circular choir delivers tirades on a circular Greek stage at the center of which is to be found a real or symbolic altar around which they march, the dividing point, the *amer*, between land and sea, between the mortal and the divine.[11]

At or near this point of epiphany, the ritual center, two people perform an action that partakes of several archetypes and recalls more than one sacred rite: the act of love. Sterility and the tabu against exogamic sex are triumphantly overcome by a union of youth and maiden, a symbolic wedding of the city and the ocean in which romance triumphs over the Waste Land. By deflowering the Girl, the Stranger performs a rite of passage, an initiation into the mysteries, after which the Girl can take her allotted place in the adult world, reborn as a woman; as in *Exil*, the beach, the shore, is a frontier area, a threshold between land and sea, childhood and the adult state, ignorance and knowledge, reality and super-reality. This initiation rite also serves as an act of purification, whereby the corrupt, sterile ways of the city are restored to innocence; an act of sacrifice, wherein sex is envisaged as immolation; and an act of fertility, a creation myth of the Ancestors, a mystery relating to the gods. The abduction of the maiden and the myth of Hierogamos, of possession by a god, are the closest Western analogues to Perse's text – where a naked Girl is ravished by a Stranger of supernatural power, by the Ocean, or by cosmic Desire, 'Toi, dieu mon hôte' (p. 337). In the language of *Amers*, he is lightning and she is the sea; she gives herself to a god from the deep, an Eros of the waters; and she herself is golden in color, the gold or bronze of an idol: 'Ton corps ... émaillé d'or ... Tu es l'idole de cuivre vierge' (pp. 332, 333). Furthermore, this individual rite is enclosed within a public, communal rite (also of initiation, purification, immolation, and fecundity), the evocation of the sea, which contains more than one element of the Catholic mass: memory, sacrifice, celebration, and communion, ending in atonement with the divinity through a form of transubstantiation. The ocean is invoked as a pagan goddess, beyond time, memory, and consciousness:

> 'Une même vague par le monde, une même vague depuis Troie ...
>   Mer de Baal, Mer de Mammon – Mer de tout âge et de tout nom;
> ô Mer d'ailleurs et de toujours ...
>   Ah! Celle toujours qui nous fut là et qui toujours nous sera là ...'
>                                   (pp. 339 – 40, 365, 371, 372)

This is the 'Mer de la transe et du délit; Mer de la fête et de l'éclat' (pp. 367, 369), an insatiable, inscrutable goddess who over the eons offers her vulva to mankind:

> Derrière nous n'est point l'épouse de sel, mais devant nous l'outrance et la luxure ... l'immense vulve convulsive aux mille crêtes ruisselantes, comme l'entraille divine elle-même un instant mise à nu.  (p. 374)

Intercourse with her is an act of violence, passion, and rape, of absolute transgression. Sacrifice and death are repudiated in a hymn to life, to divine pleasure, the powers of eternal creation. In Perse's epic the Girl's desire for the Stranger, and the passion of all men for the sea, are conceived as healthy, sensually fulfilling acts, which permit us to partake of total Being.

In this writer's 'primitive' cosmogony, the sea is the cosmic source of existence, the primeval substance beyond life and death. Since the ocean is analogous to the astral heavens, I propose that the Master of Stars and Navigation is not a mere map-reader: he is an astrologer, a seer who beholds the Cosmic Year of Pisces the Fishes, a man whose wisdom of the sea is illuminated by the light and power of the stars:

> 'L'Année dont moi je parle est la plus grande Année; la Mer où j'interroge est la plus grande Mer ...
> Ils m'ont appelé l'Obscur et j'habitais l'éclat.'    (pp. 281, 283)

The rhythm of the sea, the ebb and flow of tides, reflects the rhythm of the universe: diurnal, lunar, and annual cycles, and the astrological cycle of eons. On our planet the ocean is circular and one. The circle and the sphere are perfect forms, images of recurrence and of self-sustained being. And we are at the center of this space-time nexus, capable of appreciating it, of opening out to it as it opens to us, of envisaging its totality and partaking of its inexhaustible numen in ecstacy.

Finally, for this erotic poet of the sea, for whom writing is an erotic act, the ocean (cosmic love) sustains poetry, indeed is itself a creative force that dreams and composes verse; it is 'la Mer en nous' (p. 261) who creates *Amers*. The poetic process is conceived as man's relationship to, and possession by, the sea, that is, the mythopeic power of the imagination. The Narrator is as much a poet wondering how to create as a nomad seeking the Beyond or a priest invoking his deity. And his text, which recounts a poetic-religious ritual, forms part of that ritual. As with the winds in *Vents*, the waters come to the poet-shaman, seize, inhabit, and inspire him: he is possessed by the sea as the Girl is by the Stranger. The ocean, beyond language, cannot be expressed through speech, yet it is 'Textuelle, la Mer' (p. 295), just as language is the poetess, and we are its creation, its poem. In the structure of *Amers*, the poetess stands at the center, is an important personage in society, a mediator between man and the elements. The tragic actresses, who renounce the art of the past (their scripts are atrocious) and the men who perpetrate it (actors? writers? the public?), are eager to create in the future; for example, they seek a new lover, that is, a great new poet. And the Narrator himself, the implied author, claims to be a man of the sea, who devotes this his last, longest, and greatest work to his first and greatest love:

> ... le Chanteur du plus beau chant ...
> homme de mer, tenant propos d'homme de mer ...
> 'Mon dernier chant! mon dernier chant! et qui sera d'homme de mer ...'  (pp. 260, 264)

Saint-John Perse renews one of the oldest topics in world literature, the nautical metaphor for artistic creation, to be found in Virgil, Horace, Dante, and Spenser, among others.[12] In his world love and the emotions weigh more than does reason, and poetry more than science. It is the word, the basis of language, which names, controls, evokes, and creates reality. And, in the last analysis, the sea, the poem *Amers*, the mock-author, and his mock-public are one.

Unlike some of the poets discussed in this book (Machaut, Ronsard, Saint-Amant, Voltaire, Hugo, Aragon), Saint-John Perse cannot be deemed a spirit of protean variety. Instead, and in spite of a noticeable evolution in the scope and orientation of his work, each text from his pen traces a similar path, exploring with greater intensity the particular esthetic domain to which he has laid claim.

*Anabase*, the poems of exile, *Vents*, *Amers*, and *Chronique* all endeavor to open up new worlds for humanity, to create an allegory of the renewal of man. By reaching out to exotic regions in space and distant periods in time, Perse strives for universality, a sense of the totality of history on our planet. And, by so doing, he has created new myths, resonant with poetic overtones – the tribe of *Anabase*, the Rains, Snows, and Winds, the lovers of *Amers* – that enrich our cultural heritage. His is a quest for origins, for the kernel of reality. According to Saint-John Perse, the world is real, pulsating with frenetic, explosive life, subject to metamorphosis yet also the measure of man at his most sublime. It is worthy of praise and celebration, truly sacred, evoking rapture in the beholder, who exalts all seasons, all spaces, all kinds of men. This is a universe of order and hierarchy that nonetheless contains irrational forces; Perse deals with the struggle and triumph of the lone individual in quest of adventure, the inner exile of men who learn to overcome all obstacles including their own selves.

From the perspective of this book, Saint-John Perse is the first Frenchman, one of the first major poets in any language (cf. Carl Spitteler's *Der olympische Frühlung*), to come to grips successfully with the problem of modern epic. The traditional norms of epos demand a measure of heroism, of beauty, and of the grand style. However, for most people, the reality

of modern life implies problematic, unheroic characters, physical and
moral ugliness, and a low, demotic level of speech. The best poets in the
Anglo-Saxon tradition (Eliot, Pound, Auden) have turned to the creation
of ironic non-epics or anti-epics which evoke the sordidness of modern life
in order to undermine it. Saint-John Perse, sharing their views, con-
demning no less resolutely than they do the breakdown in contemporary
civilization, dares to create on the old esthetic lines: in opposition to
mundane life, he sings of heroism. His is a work of high seriousness with an
ample, universal vision of man, an exemplified ideal of conduct crucial to
the history of the race, and that sense of the poet's task, the 'choric' quality
we find in Virgil and *La Chanson de Roland*. And his language is as
sublime, as rich in overtones, as ceremonial and 'poetic' as any since the
classical odes of Arabia and Persia. Perse succeeds in his wager partly by
escaping from a direct encounter with contemporary life (*Anabase* and
*Amers* are projected onto a mythical plane; even *Vents* transfigures the
mundane) but also by adhering to modernism, especially in terms of form.
Perse and his friend Eliot were among the first to bring to the long poem
the esthetics of distortion, to de-emphasize or even eliminate the classical
elements of plot and narrative continuity. Thus *Anabase* and *Amers* recall
less any one hero (the Leader, the Lover) than the notion of heroism itself
functioning as leader or lover. This kind of text seeks to make history
anew, not merely recall it; to reinvigorate the reader's sensitivities and do for
modern man what the classical and medieval epics were meant to do in
their time, but in a different way.

Thus the opus Saint-John Perse elaborated over the years manifests
traits fundamental to twentieth-century art, to modernism throughout the
Western world: violence, sex, and the exotic; the reaction against technology, bourgeois culture, and the urban environment; poetry conceived as a
metaphysical adventure and a way of knowing; obsession with form and
the creation of a new language; fragmented composition; multipersonal,
multifocal points of view; cultural anti-humanism. Yet at the same time he
reacts against some of our most cherished clichés; for Perse is a rhetorician;
he believes in heroism and order; he repudiates political commitment; he
is an optimist; he refuses to comment on his own work or otherwise deliver
manifestos; and, above all, he dares to compose long poems. This paradox,
that his work is daring and yet acceptable, new yet appropriate, may help
explain why, in a century when only novelists and film-makers attract the
public eye, he established an extraordinary, eminently respectable fame.
True, despite his professed scorn for a formal literary career and for Paris,
Parisian culture, and the 'in' circles, Saint-John Perse carefully orches-
trated his successes, cultivating with subtle and elegant perseverance the
'right people': Valéry, Claudel, Gide, Jammes, Rivière, Fargue, and Valery

Larbaud in his youth, and, from the 1940s on, a cluster of literary lights on both sides of the Atlantic, all of whom became Alexis Saint-Leger Leger's friends. But recognition of the man's genius transcends mere personal intrigue and bourgeois charm. The list of his admirers, and their quality of judgment, is most impressive, indeed has become a touchstone in Perse studies. Spirits as diverse as Aragon and Claudel, Char and Senghor, Ghelderode and Pierre Emmanuel, Gracq and Bosquet, Bonnefoy and Deguy, have praised him, declaring his pre-eminence as a poet in our time – not to speak of the encomia from the non-Francophone world, from Hofmannsthal, Guillén, Aleixandre, Asturias, Jorge Andrade, Paz, and a host of Anglo-Saxons, while his work has been translated by Rilke, Benjamin, Ungaretti, Ion Pillat, Eliot, Robert Fitzgerald, and Dag Hammarskjöld. All currents honor the author of *Anabase* and *Amers*: Marxist, Catholic, surrealist, conservative, even the apostles of Negritude. Laureate of the Nobel Prize for Literature in 1960, Saint-John Perse is the only French poet since Claudel and Valéry to have acquired international stature plus acclaim at home.[13] There can be no doubt that his voice is unique, and that the contribution he made to French letters both fecund and enduring. The voice and contribution were devoted largely to the long poem, in a splendid, highly successful version of modern epic.

# ⚐ ARAGON

Louis Aragon (born 1897)[1] has elaborated his career out of step with Parisian modes. Neither a hermetic in the vein of Mallarmé and Valéry nor a visionary in the line of Claudel and Perse, hopelessly anachronistic or no less hopelessly ahead of his time, Aragon cannot be assimilated to the kinds of poetry that have dominated the scene for almost a century. His ideas on poetry, his subject-matter, even his verse forms differ sharply from those of the figures in view: for instance, Ponge, Michaux, Char, Bonnefoy, Pleynet, and Deguy. The fact that this person is a militant in the French Communist Party helps to explain the conspiracy of silence, or indifference, directed at him equally from the Catholic Right and the New Left. It also has to be said that the adulation he received within the Party was often bestowed without scholarly rigor and for the wrong reasons. However, the verdict of posterity is quite another matter; perhaps in the long run his Lenin Prize for Peace (1957) and Medal of the October Revolution (1972) will weigh as heavily as comparable Western honors awarded to others. I consider it by no means impossible that Aragon's shadow will lie on future histories of our age in a manner not too dissimilar to his master Hugo's in the nineteenth century.

Be this as it may, it could be predicted that, once he turned to Communism, sooner or later Aragon would take up the trumpet in imitation of the singers of *geste*, d'Aubigné, and Hugo. His novel cycle in ten volumes, 'Le Monde réel,' extending from *Les Cloches de Bâle* (1934) to *Les Communistes* (1949–51), can be considered an epic fresco in prose, in the line of Jules Romains, Duhamel, and Martin du Gard. *Front Rouge* (1931), the text which completed his break with surrealism, is a relatively brief piece in the sublime style, a striving for a modern, popular, Marxist epic in the wake of Mayakovsky, Blok, and other new Soviet poets. *Hourra l'Oural* (1934) represents a much longer effort in the same vein. Then the War came, and Aragon's contribution to the Resistance included a long epic satire, *Le Musée Grévin* (1943), based on *Les Tragiques* and *Châtiments*; and

*Brocéliande* (1942), in which contemporary reality is projected onto a legendary Celtic-Arthurian past. In the 1950s and 1960s the eternally young, ever-changing co-founder of surrealism published a series of long poems or unified poetic collections devoted to Elsa Triolet and which have been called 'Le Cycle d'Elsa.'[2] Under this heading should be included *Les Yeux et la Mémoire* (1954), *Le Roman inachevé* (1956), *Elsa* (1959), *Les Poètes* (1960), *Le Fou d'Elsa* (1963), *Il ne m'est Paris que d'Elsa* (1964), *Le Voyage de Hollande* (1964), and *Les Chambres* (1969). To choose from such an imposing mass is almost as difficult an endeavor as was the case in my chapter on Hugo. Somewhat arbitrarily, I shall discuss *Brocéliande* and *Le Fou d'Elsa*: because they represent Aragon in two eminently representative moments – as singer of the Resistance and of Elsa – and because I believe they are perhaps his greatest triumphs as a writer, two landmarks in the history of twentieth-century verse.

From 1940 to 1945, for the first time since the Wars of Religion, poetry was allied to history, and was to be found at the center of political activity.[3] The Resistance poets – Aragon, Eluard, Emmanuel, Char, Frénaud, Jouve, Masson, Supervielle, Desnos, and many others – managed in their own lives to bring about the old epic synthesis of *armas* and *letras, fortitudo* and *sapientia*. Some of them wielded or at least transported arms, and they all committed their talent to the cause, they elaborated an art which sought to win men's minds and influence history. Although the ultimate value of much of the Resistance verse has been questioned, there can be no doubt that from the appearance of Aragon's *Le Crève-Cœur* in 1941 until well after victory, poetry had attained an unprecedented stature not only with intellectuals but with masses of the French people. And, in spite of the strictures of Benjamin Péret (*Le Déshonneur des poètes*), a sufficient number of masterpieces were created, if only by the nine men cited above, to compare favorably with any other half-decade in the history of world literature. As was to be expected, given the times, a kind of epic burst forth in *Brocéliande*, in *Le Musée Grévin*, in the works of Pierre Emmanuel and Pierre Jean Jouve, especially if we bear in mind Aragon's statement: 'le sens épique dont il ne faudrait guère me pousser pour que je dise qu'il n'est pas autre chose que le nom en poésie du sens national.'[4]

*Brocéliande* (1942)[5] is a difficult poem, ambivalent, allusive, based upon a complex structure of symbolism and allegory (the technique of *contrebande*) meant to delude Vichy censors. Its 'world' is one of ugliness. Human values and poetic form are dislocated and people alienated, reified, transformed into objects. No one problematic hero is singled out because the traditional bourgeois hero cannot exist in fragmented, degraded surroundings where the mere possibility of distinguishing reality from illusion and of adhering to a valid code of norms becomes an unrealizable dream. The situation refers to France during the Second World War. In a 'complaint' of passionate anger, Aragon protests against the horrors of the Occupation and the violence that man perpetrates on his fellows, which result in young men (French soldiers and freedom-fighters in the Maquis) being cut down in the springtime of their lives. He also denounces those Frenchmen, 'les magiciens sur la montagne' (p. 337), Vichy collaborators, political Rightists, who used the people's prayer for rain to bring upon them a rain of bombs – defeat and the German Occupation? the more recent occupation of the 'zone libre'? – and 'Les enfants de la peur' (p. 349), cowards who support false gods out of fear, whose evil lies primarily in deprivation of energy. From hell he calls upon the sun to rebel against the reign of spiders (pp. 333–4). With courage, good will, and a strong heart, a subversive counter-order can replace the false, evil *Ordnung* that has been imposed on France. Despair, forgetfulness, nothingness shall be eradicated by heroism inspired by the poetic voice. And, as in a vision from the Apocalypse, on an August night fire falls from the sky and Gaul is liberated. Aragon the Communist predicts the coming of a better world which will enjoy political and artistic liberty. In place of the reified non-heroes depicted in the early cantos, he proposes not a single Messiah but the French people, an anonymous group of revolutionaries. This positing of freedom is projected into the future, however, prophesied but by no means declared to be a certainty, for the world in which we live does not provide an automatic happy ending as in books. For such a denouement, says Aragon, Frenchmen must be willing to take responsibility onto their own shoulders and act. Instead of offering prayers in exchange for rain, instead of calling upon unknown gods who may be demons, they must create flame and light on their own. No words, no priests can serve to mediate between themselves and the fulfillment they seek; on the contrary, men must assume liberty, each as an individual and together in society, without external mediation. Thus, only by means of actions that demand authenticity can the people triumph, by recognizing that their priests are figures of illusion, by coming to understand that these 'faux exorciseurs complices du démon ... charlatans' (p. 332) are enemies of Gaul, like the plague they have unleashed on the countryside. Merely eliminating foreign locusts will not suffice, says Aragon, unless a new way of life, a new identity for the nation, can be installed in place of the old, and the sky-heaven exorcised ('Le ciel exorcisé,' Canto 7). In this ultimate struggle we have no difficulty in perceiving a class war that shall supersede the nationalistic strife between France and Germany, for the latter alone is meaningless.

Although in our present environment poetry appears to be banished, Aragon explains emphatically that such is not the case:

Rien n'y palpite plus des vieilles saturnales
Ni la mare de lune où les lutins dansaient
Inutile aujourd'hui de lire le journal

Vous n'y trouverez pas les mystères français
La fée a fui sans doute au fond de la fontaine ...
Les rêves de chez nous sont mis en quarantaine

Mais le bel autrefois habite le présent
Le chèvrefeuille naît du cœur des sépultures
Et l'herbe se souvient au soir des vers luisants

Ma mémoire est un chant sans appogiatures
Un manège qui tourne avec ses chevaliers
Et le refrain qu'il moud vient du cycle d'Arthur     (Canto 1: p. 325)

The beauty and heroism of the past live on, projected into the present, and past archetypes help people to survive today's crises. Perhaps the most striking aspect of *Brocéliande* is the fact that Aragon's fable of contemporary reality is filtered through a series of images borrowed from France's medieval heritage, specifically Arthurian romance. The tenor of allegory refers to the contemporary world, and the vehicle to medieval Celtic legend. Thus emerges a militant twentieth-century *Romance of the Rose*, in which Vichy collaborators, the German occupation, and resistance fighters are represented by obscurantist priests, a plague of locusts, and Merlins imprisoned inside trees. Among the specifically medieval motifs are tapestries, roses, the honeysuckle, a fountain, a nightingale, a unicorn, a giant ogre, the *gaite de la tor*, King Arthur, and Merlin. And several medieval poets are referred to directly or by allusion: the author of *Huon de Bordeaux*, Arnaut de Mareuil, Thibaut de Champagne, Marie de France, and Dante. In *Les Croisés* and *Absent de Paris*, Aragon had previously denounced contemporary abuses under the guise of a historical meditation on Eleanor of Aquitaine, Philip the Fair, and Charles the Simple. This modern 'contraband' corresponds to the medieval technique of *trobar clus*, employed by the Occitan troubadours, including Arnaut Daniel of Ribérac. Since Aragon himself was demobilized at Ribérac in 1940 and since he was aware that Arnaut receives greater praise than all other modern poets in Dante's *Commedia* and is the only personage there who speaks a language other than Italian, it is appropriate that, for Aragon as for Dante, Arnaut stands as an honored forebear, a founder of modern Western culture in general and of our love ethos based upon *fin' amor* in particular. According to Aragon, the songs of Occitania and the epics and romances of North-

ern France offer an example of medieval, Christian, French chivalry that
compares favorably both with the sterile decadence into which France fell in
the 1940s and the no less sterile propaganda of Germanic heroism propagated by the Nazis. The Communist poet informs his public that medieval
heroism (and culture) is of French not Germanic origin, and that it is
based upon *cortesie*, upon respect for woman, again in contrast to the barbaric male-oriented sadism of the Germans. That France is personified by
Marianne and as a noun is accorded the feminine gender, that the motherland was delivered long ago by Joan of Arc, and that Communist and
Jewish girls are tortured by the Nazis add to the fervor of his neo-medieval
feminism. Furthermore, these concepts are expressed through language in
works of literature, and the modern literary tradition was created by France
in the eleventh and twelfth centuries. Since French-European culture
came into being in 1150, it can be born again in 1940. In much of his war
poetry Aragon employs traditional rhyme and meter, as an act of rebellion against fashionable free verse and to make his works available to the
masses of people, but also because rhyme and meter form part of France's
cultural heritage, created by the first troubadours and trouvères. For all
these reasons, as in the old *chansons de geste*, legend becomes history and
history is transformed into legend, for past, present, and future are fused in
an intensely passionate duration, here and now:

> Je te reprends Légende et j'en ferai l'Histoire
>
> Avenir qui ressemble aux lignes de nos mains    (Canto 7: p. 350)

From a critical perspective, it becomes apparent that certain aspects of life
under the Occupation (solitude, alienation, demonic masters or intruders)
and the solutions proposed by Aragon (heroism, adventure, the quest for
a new identity, for a more communal, ritualized mode of existence, and for a
mode of literature close to the popular mentality) are congruent with the
myth he chose to elaborate.

Following the example of medieval grail romances and their modern
interpreters, especially T.S. Eliot, Aragon creates a pattern of demonic
imagery the center of which is an arid Waste Land. People wander among
bones and are attacked by locusts; in high summer, a time of pestilence, the
world is an oven; torrid, dry rocks crack and are assimilated to men's
hearts:

> Que l'eau du ciel mette en déroute
> La poussière de nos cheveux
> Et la sécheresse que broute
> Un bétail brûlé ...

Le monde est un four
Où la pierre aspire aux pas de la lune
Où la pierre éclate au genou du soleil
Où la pierre est comme un cœur dans la main terrible de l'enfant
Et qu'est-ce que je pourrais dire alors de mon malheureux cœur
     d'homme    (Canto 2: pp. 327–8)

In this anti-pastoral desert, a modern Inferno of cowardice and inauthenticity, burnt animals seek to feed in vain, and the only flocks are human
herds led astray by Vichy priests. Within the Waste Land is to be found the
forest of Brocéliande, ever a place of mystery and the imagination (cf.
*Gilgamesh*, Virgil, *Huon de Bordeaux*, Chrétien, Tasso, Spenser), realm of
the Mothers, of the unconscious, where the hero participates in adventures,
but which in Aragon's poem bears connotations of terror in place of light
fantasy. In our century the *selva oscura* ought to be a refuge for the Resistance, but instead men are held captive inside trees, and both plants and
men cut down by *d'atroces bûcherons* (p. 339). This typically surrealist
fusion of human beings and the green world, evoked in *terza rima*, recalls
Canto 13 of Dante's *Inferno*, the forest of suicide which, in Aragon's
hands, has become a forest of Nazi-Vichy execution. Like the universe of
*Anabase*, that of *Brocéliande* is a rocklike masculine world of power, but
one lacking heroism and glory; it is closed unto itself, distorted, dehumanized, and profoundly ugly. In the tradition of Eliot, there are sickly animals
(sickness and the plague are motifs applied regularly to the Occupation
in Resistance poetry), a child plays with a celluloid swan, and frustrated,
cowardly people in felt hats sweat in prayer and imbibe watered-down drinks.
The sun in the sky becomes a balloon or a pet, a dog shown in fairs and held
on a leash, and also is metamorphosed into Absalom hanging by his hair,
caught up in barbed wire. Furthermore, prayer is answered in demonic
terms. Storm clouds, evoking passion and violence, cover the heavens,
but, instead of life-giving fluid, they pour down hail or, as clouds of locusts,
unleash upon France the scriptural Plagues of Egypt. Here Aragon alludes
to German war planes, especially the Stuka dive-bomber – and his imagery
is of claws, teeth, and other cutting implements, flies, lepers, dragons,
and monsters. Druids' prayers only serve to render the hard, mutilating
texture of the Waste Land worse; in this parody of a Grail cult Attis is
castrated and Osiris dismembered without improvement in the world order.

   One cure for the sickness of *Brocéliande* is through water. Each year a
prayer for rain is said at the fountain of Bellenton. And, in the course of a
moving, eloquent discourse, water imagery is evoked; rain, tears, wine
(French champagne), and music:

Qu'il pleuve une tempête de pluie avec la générosité du fer
Des gouttes larges à noyer l'amertume ancienne

Des gouttes si proches l'une de l'autre qu'on ne puisse distinguer
    entre elles ces flèches du ciel
Crible crible ô pluie aux mains torrentielles
Pluie aux doigts de musique
Pluie à la bonne odeur de mousse et de mort
Crible les champs envahis dans ton peigne liquide
Fais couler ton cristal dans les sillons bleus où bouillait
L'esprit parasitaire des liserons
Ah pleus pluie ah pleus à pleins bords dans la coupe des horizons
Champagne de mon beau nuage boisson des jours de fête
Chère pluie à mon visage aussi douce qu'à ma terre

(Canto 2: pp. 329–30)

It is obvious that this prayer and the spring itself (which recalls the fountain in Chrétien de Troyes's *Yvain*) evoke purity, baptism, nourishment,
and regeneration, are the ultimate component in a Grail-fertility rite which
contributes to the renewal of life in springtime. They also depict water as a
feminine element, an image of woman. The forest itself is portrayed in
erotic terms, as a 'brune et blonde entre nos bras' (p. 326). And, in Canto 5,
the author has young resistance fighters cry out the name of France the
Mother associated with Marie de France and the Virgin Mary.

However, the text of the poem informs us that the appeal for rain and
the religious rites of which it forms a part do not bring about the sought-
after regeneration. Yet Aragon does not lose hope. In Canto 3 he calls
upon the sun to rebel, from hell he summons fire. Then, in Canto 6, in an
extraordinary *Walpurgisnacht* scene, shooting stars descend from heaven,
and in an Apocalyptic vision light, enlightenment, and liberty triumph over
darkness, the sleeping giant is slain, and arrows and swords contribute to
the midsummer harvest. In spite of Aragon's claims to feminism and to the
exaltation of woman in all his writings, I submit that in *Brocéliande*, the
war-epic, metaphorically at least male triumphs over female. Light from
heaven is associated with the Holy Spirit and the Apocalypse, with divine,
virile, creative power. At the moment of epiphany a harvest is gathered
and the Waste Land redeemed, through fire not water, by Solomon not
Isis. Sorcerers and their rain cult, associated with the earth, fountains,
passivity, intellectual torpor, and physical well-being, give way to the
young heroes of the Maquis, assimilated to the sky, the sun, an active existence, consciousness, and heroic self-sacrifice. Life triumphs over death,
transcendence over bestiality, and a new order, a Communist logos, over the
passions, chaos, and plague unleashed by the dragon.

Rebirth conquers death. The young men imprisoned inside trees are cut
down but will rise from the grave or be succeeded by others, to liberate
Mother France and remove the 'enchantments.' In Cantos 5 and 6 bark is

cloven and flowers torn apart, the earth reawakens and the sky is rent asunder, as if in a Caesarian birth. Young soldiers succeed where the old Druids failed, because they are capable of siring a new land with their blood and because it is they (and the Narrator) who can insult the divine Father – the sun – and prod him out of his torpor to bring about a shower of fire, metaphoric seed. Similarly, in other poems of the Resistance years, *La Rose et le Réséda* and *Elégie* for instance, France's rebirth occurs when the blood of fallen soldiers waters new plants and is transformed into wine.

Unlike most of the other war pieces, however, *Brocéliande* associates the death-rebirth archetype not only with a medieval theme – the Celtic fertility cult – but also with Orpheus and with the figure that centuries of Christian apologists claimed he had foreshadowed: the living Christ. The Narrator calls for a liberator, be it Christ, Orpheus, a medieval knight, or the People:

> Est-ce la nuit du Christ est-ce la nuit d'Orphée
> Qu'importe qu'on lui donne un nom de préférence
> Celui qui ressuscite est un enfant des fées    (Canto 3: p. 332)

The oppressed masses endure a plague of locusts and call for a redeemer who will come at Easter. Young rebels seek their elders' birthright in the tradition of Jacob and Esau, whereas their adversary, a centurion, wishes to throttle a nightingale (traditionally, the poet of the divine, the bird who glorifies and partakes of the Messiah's passion) singing on the sepulchre. These martyrs, Christ-figures, are imprisoned in trees on which is carved INRI: the trees – that is, their gibbets or the stakes on which they are shot – are assimilated to the Holy Rood:

> Le temps torride étreint l'arbre étrangement triste
> Tord ses bras végétaux au-dessus de l'étang
> Et des chaînes d'oiseaux chargent ce chêne-Christ ...
>
> Il erre par ici d'atroces bûcherons
> Il est sous le couvert des haches toujours prêtes
> Ah sera-t-il trop tard quand nous reconnaîtrons
>
> Le martyre secret dans la mort indiscrète
> Et notre propre chair et notre propre sang
> Pour jeter au bourreau le grand cri qui l'arrête
>
> Lire lorsque la nuit sur la forêt descend
> L'INRI d'une défaite à son front de ramures
> Et l'arbre porte alors l'écriteau du croissant    (Canto 5: pp. 339–40)

In their agony they cry out the Mother's name: is it the *patrie*, or 'Mary' the name of God's mother and of France's first medieval poetess, Marie de France, or both at the same time? Like Christ, they will be reborn in divine fire and their tombs, borrowed from a Dantean inferno, will be transformed into trees of knowledge and eternal life. Aragon posits a cosmic cycle: life yields to death, which in turn yields to resurrection and a better world: on the levels of the seasons, the annual harvest, the career of man, and the ebb and flow of nations, of social forces, of cultures, and of gods.

Although rebirth is brought about in answer to supplication, it must never be forgotten that *Brocéliande* recounts two rituals: a prayer for rain and an invective directed to the sun. The first, beautiful, moving, calling for a benediction, brings a plague of locusts; the other, sarcastic, insulting, quasi-insane, results in a victorious shower of stars. Aragon follows d'Aubigné in underscoring the perils involved in the use of language: the fact that speech can be distorted by evil people for the wrong purposes. He had already introduced the theme in *Les Voyageurs de l'impériale*, where the alienated intellectual Pierre Mercadier is set in opposition to a more creative, committed artist, Blaise d'Ambérieux; later he was to develop it with brio in *La Mise à mort*, *Blanche ou l'oubli*, and *Théâtre/Roman*. In addition to the two prayers, Aragon makes us aware of good speech, of patriotic commitment embodied in works of art. He does this with the image of the nightingale, the medieval bird of love and a metaphor for the poet in the troubadour songs and in Marie de France's *Laüstic*: in Canto 3 a centurion seeks to kill the nightingale; in Canto 6 the Narrator identifies with the little creature,[6] who will sing of that liberation night of love:

> Une clarté d'apocalypse embrasera le noir silence
> Quand au scandale des taillis le rossignol
> Lance
> L'étincelle de chant qui répond au ciel incendié de son signal
> Ah que je vive assez pour être ce chanteur    (Canto 6: p. 346)

And he does it through the personal, obtrusive intervention of a mock-author. This Narrator, Aragon's *persona*, tells us that the victims of Nazi oppression call on him not to forget them; although perhaps he will not live to see the great night (yet he so longs to do so), he will sing of it like the nightingale and commemorate it like the watchman in a medieval *alba*. Then in Canto 7 he calls on the people to make themselves free, and he declares that by him, through poetry, legend will be transformed into history.

The Narrator is introduced to ensure an aura of authenticity, the same truth claim we find in Guillaume de Lorris, Guillaume de Machaut, d'Aubigné, and Lamartine. Furthermore, in this Celtic, Arthurian world he replaces Merlin, predicts the future, and, a prophet also in the Biblical sense,

a witness as well as seer, indulges in satirical excoriation of his people.
Because of speech, because of the role of poetry in the class struggle, we are
reminded that heroism is embodied in *sapientia* as well as *fortitudo*. The
Narrator contributes to the good fight as much as do resistance fighters.
Since one cause of the sterility that has fallen on the land is the misuse of
speech, since the names of dying warriors are hidden, murmured only by the
shadows, it is up to the Narrator, a French poet, distinguishing himself
from magicians and sorcerers, distancing himself from timid masses of sup-
pliants, to commemorate the young men's names and to tell the truth
about his age, to use language properly in the service of art and reality. It is
he then who makes the medieval past relive in the present (Canto 1), who
juxtaposes Dante's *terza rima* and the free verse of the twentieth century;
for a nation cannot be denied its heritage, and only by recognizing a great
culture in the past (in this case, the Middle Ages) and associating it with a
message from the present (radio broadcasts from London, Canto 7) can
people be made aware of what they have lost. Like his beloved forebear,
Victor Hugo, master of realism in poetry, Aragon urges Frenchmen in
the direction of a new destiny.[7] Thus the implied reader, as he progresses
through the text, will come to separate truth from falsehood and also
discover its symbolic meaning, even participate in it himself. Aragon writes
story and history for his public; it is the reader's duty to relive both in his
own life.

Like *Brocéliande*, *Le Fou d'Elsa, poème*, Aragon's most successful effort of
the 1960s in the domain of the long poem, evokes the medieval past,
specifically the fall of Granada in 1492; and it is concerned with a political
issue, whether a people can preserve its culture when subject to invasion
and occupation.[8] However, *Le Fou d'Elsa* differs strikingly from most of
Aragon's war poetry and from the *Hourra l'Oural* tradition in one fundamental respect: this work, published in 1963, presents a dominant, all-
encompassing theme, the exaltation of Elsa Triolet. According to *Le Fou
d'Elsa*, an old Andalusian bard Kéis Ibn-Amir an-Nadjdî, having read the
Persian romance *Medjnoûn et Leïlâ*, imitates the Persian hero by becoming enamored of an inaccessible lady, then goes insane and loses his
name. This mad Andalusian love-poet, whom Aragon calls the Fool, 'le
Medjnoûn,' was in the early 1490s approximately as old as his creator Louis
Aragon in the early 1960s: he is clearly a projection, an alter ego, of
Aragon. And the Persian 'Leïlâ' can be assimilated phonemically and symbolically to 'Ella,' Elsa Triolet's name in the 1920s, and to the third-person
feminine pronoun in the French language, *elle*. In fact, the Fool, Aragon's
*persona*, a fictional character of the fifteenth century, is said to adore
the real Elsa Triolet, a historical personage of our century, the author's
own wife.

The Fool is first mentioned in the story as one whom a group of young thugs pelt with stones because his notion of love is so different from theirs (p. 50). And in the course of the poem Aragon sets him off against a myriad of other characters, each representing a competing erotic doctrine. Like the Fool, Aragon is proud of the 'scandal' that he has created: an impossible, unbelievable, and totally unacceptable love, ridiculed by his society. This is the author's version of medieval *fin' amor*, celebrated by the troubadours and trouvères, Chrétien de Troyes, and Guillaume de Lorris, which some specialists believe to have originated in Moslem Spain, exactly where Aragon locates his story. In *Le Fou d'Elsa* the modern Elsa Triolet is celebrated in the same terms as the medieval *domna* and her more recent successors, Guinevere, Beatrice, Laura, Délie, Cassandre, Hélène, Elvire, and others: she is muse, mother, teacher, and goddess to her adoring poet-lover, who, crushed by an invincible inferiority complex, masochistically reveres her without hope of reward. Her image mediates between him and the outside world, she is the foundation-stone of his existence, and his only duty in life is to sing her praises. Like so many of Aragon's other heroines – Mirabelle in *Anicet*, Catherine and Clara in *Les Cloches de Bâle*, Carlotta in *Les Beaux Quartiers*, Bérénice in *Aurélien*, Cécile in *Les Communistes*, Fougère in *La Mise à mort*, and Blanche in *Blanche ou l'oubli* – she is Woman, *das Ewig-Weibliche*, an anima-figure that dominates the poet and the universe – lover and sister, mother and friend, Demeter, Aphrodite, Sophia, and Mary all in one.

At the center of medieval *fin' amor* is to be found the notion of obstacle. Because of the obstacle, desire is rendered ever pure, encouraging the suitor to accomplish great deeds in order to be worthy of his beloved, never allowing his passion to degenerate into routine. In *Le Fou d'Elsa* Aragon constructs the greatest of obstacles: the Fool indulges truly in an *amor de lonh*, for a Russian-Frankish lady whom he has never seen, since (this is the scandal!) she lives in the twentieth century, over four hundred years after his own death. The reign of the couple, happy in marriage, is also destined for a distant future: the 'Medjnoûn' can only envisage these events from his present, which is, to him, a miserable past – he will never know the future, will never behold Elsa, they will not grow old together.

Aragon's insights into *fin' amor* prove to be deeper than this somewhat artificial construction would indicate. After all, the Fool is a fictional projection of Louis Aragon the writer; even were our Andalusian protagonist to inhabit the same space and time as Elsa (as does Aragon), the obstacle would remain, whether the author wishes it or not. Indeed, the Fool writes poems about Elsa located temporally in the future, in which he (that is, Aragon) and she dwell in separate rooms or in which, even when they lie together in the same bed, by falling asleep she escapes from him into the Other World where he cannot follow. The obstacle, Aragon tells us,

is an eternal condition between people lucid enough to recognize its existence; although we succeed in loving the Other, we can never know her
completely or fuse our nature with hers. Thus we are made aware that
each and every person, in his daily life, creates the Other in his own image
yet must face up to the intolerable Otherness of that individual who, an
object to us, remains a subject to himself and treats us as an object. Furthermore, this realization of the ontological nature of Eros explains the role of
jealousy both in *Le Fou d'Elsa* and in Aragon's other works, especially the
1959 collection *Elsa*. For the Fool-Aragon resents not only Elsa's dreams,
when she is asleep, but also her waking memories of men and places she
knew before having met him, and the literary characters that she as a
novelist has created without him, which he fears to be more alive than his
own. His jealousy, which derives from the lover's failure to communicate
totally with the beloved and from his realization that the failure is absolute,
is a striking modern parallel to the medieval *Zelotypia* promulgated by
Andreas Capellanus, which is a constituent trait of *fin' amor* in the courtly
world.

Because of the obstacle, because of jealousy, and because of his lucid,
authentic recognition of both states, the Fool goes mad. Not only is he
judged insane by the inhabitants of Granada because his love appears to
them so outlandish, but also he literally becomes the 'fou d'Elsa,' her
'Medjnoûn.' The medieval passion which rendered Lancelot mad and caused
Tristan to simulate insanity coincides with twentieth-century *fin' amor*,
the *amour fou* of Breton and the surrealists.[9] Furthermore, the Andalusian
poet is truly Elsa's fool, that is, her jester as well as her madman. As a
jester, as the sacred fool of his society, Aragon's hero partakes of wisdom as
well as folly. Madder than the mad, he is also wiser than the wise, a
*sapiens amator* in whom irrationality undermines the false order based upon
reason and custom. And, as a sacred fool, he also is the recipient of supernatural visions, a poet, seer, and prophet, an outsider to society (incapable
of marriage) who then becomes its scapegoat.

Since the jester may also serve as a priest, one facet of the Fool's madness
is mysticism, an ecstatic possession that can be assimilated to the Sufi
tradition in Islam. The Fool considers his room to be a monastic cell, where
he prays. However, this secular devotee does not believe in God. His
own Elsa poems and his copy of Jāmī's *Medjnoûn et Leïlâ* are sacred texts,
replacing the Koran; his mosque is the image of Elsa's body, who then
becomes God to him:

> Je t'ai donné la place réservée à Dieu que le poème
> A tout jamais surmonte les litanies
> Je t'ai placée en plein jour sur la pierre votive

Et désormais c'est de toi qu'est toute dévotion
Tout murmure de pèlerin tout agenouillement de la croyance
Tout cri de l'agonisant

Je t'ai donné la place du scandale qui n'a point de fin    (p. 242)

It is no wonder that the Fool is arrested for idolatry, blasphemy, and in-
citing to heresy, that is, for adoring a flesh and blood woman or, even
worse, a non-existent one in place of Allah. Once again, Aragon bases his
notion of love on medieval *fin' amor*. For, whatever its origins (and some
scholars posit that it was derived in part from the Marian cult, commenta-
ries on the Song of Songs, or liturgical hymns), *fin' amor* evolved as a kind
of secular heresy, its imagery based upon that of the Church as well as feudal
law. In this way can be explained why the troubadour 'adores' his Lady, and
Lancelot adores Guinevere; why 'priests of love' such as Guilhem in
*Flamenca* or Guillaume the Narrator in *Le Voir Dit* serve the cult of Amor,
just as the Fool does in fifteenth-century Spain, and his creator in twentieth-
century France.

Among Aragon's most startling contributions to the theory of Eros are
the following: the Fool is not a youth, the physical embodiment of *jovens*,
but a seventy-year-old man, yet 'nurtured' by Elsa as if he were the
young Lancelot; although he and his beloved are destined never to meet,
their ideal is not an adulterous tryst à la Lancelot and Guinevere, Tristan and
Iseut, or Paolo and Francesca, but a freely chosen, monogamous marriage, a relationship based upon equality and mutual trust, containing moments of ecstasy but nonetheless meant to survive over time. These notions
are central to the author's vision of Communist humanism, in which love
and society act in harmony; there is no place in his world for inauthenticity,
deception, and courtly manipulation. To a large extent Aragon also repudiates the traditional conventions of heroism. The wise old man, master,
teacher, and enlightener, the Nestor, Naimes, and Merlin figure, plays
the central role in place of an Achilles, Roland, or Yvain. He is the modern
hero, an artist, an intellectual,[10] projected onto the medieval past. War
only serves to mutilate *amor de lonh*. Amorous and martial activities are
supportive in *chanson de geste* and *roman courtois*, definitely not in Aragon's opus. Significantly, as in *La Roman de la Rose* (Part 1), imagery of
enclosed space – the Fool's room, Elsa's room in her future life, Boabdil's
palace gardens, the Fool's prison cell, a gypsy grotto in which he has a vision
of the future – forms a pattern of intimacy, of refuge (even the prison), in
opposition to the open space of medieval epic. They are feminine images –
of repose, protection, revery, solitude, a private universe which evokes
the nuptial bed and the mother-beloved's womb – in a poem which pro-

claims woman's right to a place in society and urges man to make love, not war, and exalt Eros in place of Thanatos.

Yet the forces of Thanatos do invade the Fool's world. The Castilian thrust from the outside and a corrupt, exploitative government on the inside ultimately destroy not only the old man but also his dream of a world in which *fin' amor* can exist. For to celebrate woman as he and Aragon do is scandalous in a feudal or a capitalist society, and the Fool's love songs, symbols of the old Arabic culture, become 'resistance poems' to the invader. Furthermore, moved by the sufferings of his people, the Fool composes verses of war as well as of desire: he attacks God for allowing Granada to fall. In this respect he anticipates the precepts of Louis Aragon the author, who, in the famous lyric *Il n'y a pas d'amour heureux* (*La Diane française*) and in his novels, insists that a couple's happiness is impossible as long as society itself remains corrupt and the masses of the people are oppressed.

The problem of political anguish is concentrated as much on Boabdil, King Mohammed IX of Granada, as on the Fool. Boabdil, the leader of his country, responsible for its destiny, is perhaps the only man fully aware of the Spanish threat. Obsessed with being the last ruler of his line, he can neither renounce the old regime nor accept the new one which will inevitably take its place. In a curious twist of irony, Louis Aragon, one of the most vehement opponents of Sartrean existentialism, has created an existential hero. Modern in his lucidity, in his disillusion with politics, and in his tragic solitude, Boabdil becomes an alienated outsider in the midst of his own court. No less fascinating is the relationship established between him and the Fool. The monarch loves his capital with the same longing, fidelity, and hopelessness that the jester manifests toward Elsa. Phallic imagery is employed to portray the attachment not only of Boabdil but also of King Ferdinand and of a Castilian spy for the lush, semi-tropical Islamic city:

> Mais vertige de ta beauté quand j'ouvre ta ceinture d'arbres
> Je trahis mon maître et la Croix dans tes cours d'ombrage et de
>     marbre
> Je perds le Dieu de mon baptême à l'eau fraîche de tes vergers ...
> Moi c'est une façon de langueur qui corrompt l'air de ma narine
> Mon ombre n'est plus sur mes pas mon cœur n'est plus dans ma
>     poitrine ...
> Et je frémis comme l'incestueux dans les bras de sa mère
>
> (pp. 37–8)

Boabdil also indulges in a hopeless passion for his mother Aïcha. He seeks incest with the queen in order, by committing a great sin, somehow to justify his fall. Yet, since Aïcha is Boabdil's 'miroir bien-aimé,' since she once gave him power and life, it can be posited that she is a double of

Elsa, and Boabdil a double of the Fool. The alienated *homme double,*
divided against himself, is a recurrent theme in Aragon's work, as are
'double-heroes,' the most striking examples being the Barbentane brothers,
Edmond and Armand, in *Les Beaux Quartiers,* the split personalities
Alfred-Anthoine in *La Mise à mort,* and the seventy-year-old author and
forty-year-old actor in *Théâtre/Roman.* In *Le Fou d'Elsa* Boabdil and the
Fool enter into a son-father relationship. The king, who had been cast
off and almost murdered by his own father (and therefore rejoices in his
self-created Oedipal situation), seeks a surrogate father in the 'Medjnoûn,'
who nonetheless rejects him for political reasons. These two men, embodying the traditional duo of King and Captain in epic (Agamemnon and Achilles, Charlemagne and Roland, Guillaume and Vivien, Goffredo and Rinaldo), are separated by an unbridgeable generation gap that is also ideological. It is as if Aragon had projected the Fool's anxieties onto his master,
who, young, powerful, and sexually pleasing, nonetheless is less content
than the old poet, the meanest of subjects.

The specifically epic quality of *Le Fou d'Elsa* lies in the slow, steady
Spanish victory over the Saracens, described metaphorically as a demonic
game of chess. Aragon tells us of the horrors of war. His imagery is of
fire: the Spanish use cannons for the first time at Rondah in 1485, and, later
in the campaign, by burning and pillaging, offer a fireworks display to the
Virgin each night. Once in control of Granada they will burn innocent
people at the stake as they are wont to do throughout the Peninsula. In
contrast to their role as a celestial, liberating force in *Brocéliande,* here
flames are almost exclusively a demonic motif, image of violence and
fanaticism.

One can say, however, that as in *Brocéliande,* the greatest danger to
society is to be found within. The Granada of the 1490s provides us with
an unscrupulous Grand Vizier, groups of notables, and a whirling dervish,
all of whom submit to Spanish conquest, justifying it as God's will, or,
even worse, conspire actively with the enemy. Since their chief dread is
social change, that is, a rebellion from the lower classes of Granada, they
do not hesitate to divert the attention of the masses by ascribing defeat to the
presence of heretics, traitors, and Jews within the city and then instigate
pogroms as their only response to Castilian aggression. The dominant image
is the prison, a dark smothering hole where the innocent and the guilty,
cut off from each other, are tossed like crickets into a child's jar:

> Les prisonniers comme des cigales qu'un enfant mit dans une jarre
> Une grosse pierre dessus tête à tête avec la soif et la faim
> Est-ce un bruit d'élytres qu'ils font ou leurs souffles au fin fond du
>     puisard
> Oubliés sans doute oubliés liés pliés sur cette faim sans fin

> C'est que là-haut sans doute les gardiens autre chose aujourd'hui
> les ronge   (p. 247)

As is obvious from the preceding analyses, Aragon adopts a Marxist perspective to scrutinize the waning of the Middle Ages, to investigate the political, social, and economic fabric of Andalusian society and prove that the notions of class struggle and dialectical materialism are valid in the distant past. Boabdil, for all his courage and lucidity, is condemned as a sterile esthete. Even Aïcha had to reject her son's incestuous advances with the command: 'Grenade vous attend mon fils allez régner' (p. 153). The king of Granada corresponds to Pierre Mercadier, hero of *Les Voyageurs de l'impériale*, perhaps the most alienated of Aragon's *hommes doubles*, an intellectual who dies in a bordello with the word 'politique' on his lips. True commitment, on the other hand, is embodied in the Fool, who seeks to form a couple with Elsa and who, aware of the flow of history, contests religious myths, whether Islamic or Christian, in order to proclaim Aragon's own Marxist humanism: the belief that the individual is free and responsible for his acts, that the future of man is man, and that free people of the future are willing to act in defiance of the present, in order to bring about a better, non-alienated world.

For this to take place, a sense of community is essential. This is perhaps the reason why Aragon takes such care in depicting the city of Granada. The city plays the same role as in *chansons de geste*, an object to be won and a symbol of the hero's victory and position in the social hierarchy. This Andalusian society is one of high culture, rich with poetry, music, and the arts; it also contains a bewildering variety of trades and activities, burgeoning with vitality. Above all, Granada represents a world of tolerance and peace, in contrast to the violent fanaticism that threatens it from the North. It is a land where all peoples – Muslims, Jews, gypsies, *conversos*, and *viejos Catolicos* – can live in harmony. Here is a true melting pot in which those who practice different faiths, because they are Andalusians, resemble each other more closely than they do their co-religionists across the mountains and seas.

Nor must we forget that, despite the absence of overt political allusions, *Le Fou d'Elsa* was composed during the most intense phase of the War for Algerian Independence. The divided loyalties and the sense of frustration over an impossible situation reflect Louis Aragon's own sufferings in the 1950s: thus the struggle for Algerian independence is superimposed onto this medieval tale. The brutality of French colonialism in the twentieth century and the alleged cultural backwardness of the Arabs call upon Aragon to invoke another age when Catholic, Latin, Occidental invaders were no less brutal but the civilization of Islam was superior to their own, was indeed a civilization which helped create their own. We are made aware of lost possibilities, of the tragedy that Islam was never permitted to flourish in Western Europe. And, by superimposing the 1490s on the 1950s (and on France in the 1940s), Aragon presents history from the losers' point of view; our egocentric Western prejudices are broken down, and we discover vaster horizons, a truly cosmopolitan world. Aragon rejects the traditional epic notion (cf. the *Aeneid* and the *Gerusalemme liberata* as well as the *Song of Roland* and the *Guillaume Cycle*) of a bright, rational, creative, masculine West opposed by a dark, sensuous, passive, effeminate East. Here the Eastern city is the sacred center threatened by barbaric forces, archetype of rational light ('Cette Grenade appelée vie'), which becomes a symbol of love and hope, a refuge for exiles, a community represented by the pomegranate fruit ('grenade' in French), image of fertility and the richness of artistic creation.

Like Rencesvals in *La Chanson de Roland*, Granada is located at a focal point in space, between West and East, Europe and Africa; and its fall is situated at a temporal focal point, separating the Middle Ages from the modern world. The year 1492 stands as one of the watersheds in history, the end of an old epoch for Christianity as well as Islam, and the beginning of a new one. According to Aragon, Arabic culture dies because there is no future tense in its language, whereas the Spanish, barbarous as they are, are capable of speaking in the future. The Fool shares Boabdil's temporal anguish. The young king is distressed by the notion of 'les derniers jours,' by the fatality that dooms his city and his line, the public death that has been wished upon his world, *Urbs antiqua ruit* ... And the old poet suffers anxiety from aging in solitude and the prospect of dying. Both men are conscious of the old age of the year, the city, poetry, love, and life.

However, unlike Boabdil, the Fool and Christopher Columbus, who appears in the story, resolutely opt for the future: for a New World in space (Columbus) and in time (the Fool), better than the old, a veritable *translatio imperii et studii* of the first magnitude. Thus the Fool learns to speak in the future tense and, as a prophet, proclaims quite a few of Aragon's favorite ideas. He even evolves a philosophy of time. Anticipating (in 1492) certain Bergsonian concepts, he distinguishes between objective, historical chronology and an inner movement that shifts as a person ages, between a realistic, absolute clock time and dialectical, relative duration of consciousness, both of which are related to space. Not only does the poet tell us about the past and present from a Marxist perspective but time and space are related in Einsteinian terms as well.

Aragon's vision corresponds to that of modern historians, who distinguish several times, the various temporal rhythms (human life, agriculture, political events) that make up an era. In addition, we find 'interference' between the present and the past, as when an I-narrator or implied author from the future (our present) questions and comments on historical events from before his age. Because of him and because of willed anachronism, instead of the past explaining the present, it is the present (the past's future) that explains and justifies the past.

This willed, temporal relativity renders any event in the past coequal with other events which either precede or follow it chronologically. The result is a pattern of relationships, both intellectual and esthetic, that resembles the Christian typological interpretation of history, so crucial for our understanding of medieval and Renaissance epics, *La Chanson de Roland*, *Les Tragiques*, and *Moyse sauvé* especially. The struggle between a Spanish army and the Arabic state of Granada not only 'prefigures' the twentieth-century struggle between a French colonial regime and the Algerian people; it also reflects the Nazi occupation of France in the 1940s, the Phalangist rebellion against the Spanish Republic in the 1930s, Western invasions of the Soviet Union, first in 1919 and again in 1941, and even French repression of the Huguenots under the Ancien Régime. In reading *Le Fou d'Elsa* we must keep in mind these levels of meaning, the various historical *signifiés* to which a particular *signifiant* refers, and we must be prepared to shift back and forth in history with the Fool and Aragon. Like Picasso's space, Aragon's time loses all sense of linear objectivity, so that the reader must reconsider the very nature of time and history.

This is so because under normal circumstances history is written by winners, never by losers, and winners lie in order to further their own propagandistic schemes. This was the case with epic legends in the early Middle Ages; so it has been ever since. Writers such as Chateaubriand, Washington Irving, and Barrès naïvely accept the Spanish side of the story. According to them, the last king of Granada was a cowardly boy, *el rey chico*: enemy historians have even robbed him of his name! It is only by consulting original source materials, by relying upon the most gifted and impartial of modern scholars, by caring to view events from the perspective of the losers, and by lying, that is, by writing a work of fiction, an epic poem, that Aragon can arrive at a truth far more accurate than the contents of the allegedly objective tomes we read in libraries.

On the one hand he upholds the modern Communist (and traditionally medieval) notion that it is the poet's duty to impart the knowledge that he possesses. As in *Brocéliande*, poetry is to be used as a weapon. In addition, Aragon underscores the cultural vitality of medieval Andalusia. His poem begins with 'La Bourse aux rimes': we are told how poets discuss their art and practice it publicly in a manner that Western society reserves for sport and commerce. Theirs is a new, profane culture, comparable to the secular world of medieval France commemorated in *Brocéliande*. These people have turned away from the Koran to speculate in lay terms on free will and happiness. Their ideas are spilled on the ground, says the poet, but will nourish progress in the future:

> Ecoute et retiens bien que nous sommes toujours
> Au temps où la vérité ne peut se répandre que comme l'eau du
>     bocal se perdant sur la terre
> Viennent les jours où le sol la boive pour des moissons merveilleuses
> Et qu'il n'y ait plus qu'une classe d'esprits aptes à tout connaître
>
> (p. 171)

There can be no doubt that, like so many other modern writers, Louis Aragon is conscious of the emptiness of speech, the vainglory of artistic creation, and the failure of humans to communicate meaningfully. Yet it is equally true that the Fool is a poet, and that his poetry, a mirror of words, serves as the only mediation between himself and Elsa. This is a story of the artist as lover and of the lover as artist, and it is as a writer that the Fool, in his divine frenzy, his *furor poeticus*, has the right to teach his disciple Zaïd, the citizens of Granada, and us. A key portion of *Le Fou d'Elsa* is devoted to the Fool's own *diwân*, a collection of love poems in praise of Elsa. Nor is the Fool the only artist to appear in Aragon's story. The great Persian master, Jāmī, is present, at least indirectly, with his version of *Medjnoûn et Leïlâ*; in the Spanish camp are found Fernando Rojas, author of *La Celestina*, and the Burgundian Jean Molinet. Near the end of his life, in the throes of a vision into the future, the Fool perceives his spiritual heirs, the great writers who will set foot in Granada: Juan de la Cruz, Chateaubriand, and Lorca, among others. And finally poets, painters, and literary figures who have been meaningful to him in life come to escort him to the grave.

Scholars have praised Aragon for his extraordinary command of Arabic literature and culture, for the erudition which he displays in recreating so faithfully the medieval Andalusian world.[11] I consider it even more significant that this scholarly feat also adheres to the norms of contemporary French fiction, specifically the New Novel. The first part of *Le Fou d'Elsa* reveals how the poem came into being, explains its origin and composition, and comments on the *chant liminaire* which it encloses. Later prose passages interpret, often ironically, the Fool's amorous and martial lyrics. Indeed, *Le Fou d'Elsa* as a whole can be considered an elaborate commentary on the Fool's *diwân* contained within it. Thus Aragon's masterwork recounts its own genesis and provides its own criticism; it is, in the line of the *razos*, *vidas*, *La Vita Nuova*, and Machaut's *Le Voir Dit* as of *Les Faux-monnayeurs* and so much recent fiction, including the author's own

last three novels, a poem by a poet about a poet writing poetry about
poetry.

Furthermore, *Le Fou d'Elsa* wrestles with the most immediate contemporary questions: who is able to write: the Fool? Aragon? later Spanish
poets? – for whom: Elsa? Zaïd? Boabdil? the people? – in order to speak of
what: love? class struggle? patriotism? culture? This 'poème/roman,' which
reverberates with literature, with allusions to many of the great cultural
figures of the past and present, also evokes two works of art which serve as
*mises en abyme* in our modern sense of the term: Jāmī's romance *Medjnoûn et Leïlâ*, and *La Celestina*, recited by Fernando Rojas to a select
audience of courtiers. What Aragon himself refers to as 'collage'[12] can be
assimilated to the post-structuralist notion of intertextuality: the poet 'recuperates' and revitalizes world culture – the Song of Songs, Nīzāmī, Jāmī,
Molinet, Rojas, Juan de la Cruz, Lorca, for that matter Mikhail Svetlov
and Elsa Triolet – by integrating them into his own work.

Thus he proves in the fabric of his text, in his most immediate concerns
as a writer, that the Middle Ages and the twentieth century do relate to each
other, are connected esthetically as well as historically, and that by making these connections manifest we can understand the past and create for
ourselves in the present a dynamic, meaningful culture and way of life.

Aragon has been accused of making himself ridiculous or, at least, of bad
taste, a heinous sin for the Parisian literary bourgeoisie. I suppose, from its
perspective, he is guilty as charged, as were Jean de Meun, d'Aubigné, the
Voltaire of *La Pucelle*, Hugo, and most of the other epicists treated in this
book. The bard of Elsa represents a return to Romanticism, with its sense
of commitment, grandeur, philosophical meditation, personal confession,
and sentiment. Tolerated in a Vigny or Nerval, Romanticism is found
objectionable in one of our contemporaries. Furthermore, like an *enfant du
siècle*, Aragon does not hesitate to flaunt decorum for the sheer fun of it.
Since Parisian, bourgeois culture is largely neoclassical or neo-realist,
today's rebel in the world of art has two alternatives open to him: to reject
culture altogether (this has been the option of some Maoist-Trotskyite fringe
groups); or to promulgate an all-inclusive, truly universal Frenchness that
includes the Middle Ages, the high Baroque, and the most strikingly contemporary – a tradition in which *chansons de geste*, d'Aubigné, *nouveau
roman*, and new criticism meet and are as literary, as 'French,' as Molière,
Racine, Voltaire, Flaubert, Bandelaire, and Mallarmé. This has been the
choice of Aragon, who is always at the center of things, exalting, denying, challenging, renewing. Like Picasso, he keeps contradicting himself;
like Picasso, he has been at the forefront of modern movements throughout the century. By virtually creating surrealism, by helping launch the

Marxist style of the 1930s and the poetry of Resistance, and since 1956 by adhering enthusiastically to the precepts of the New Novel, Aragon breaks barriers and claims new domains for the realm of art. In the long run perhaps the coteries are out of step, not he; and it may well be, as more and more critics are coming to realize, that he and Breton are the children of our century, not Valéry, not even Sartre.

The problem of continuity in his opus has been obfuscated by politics. Professional anti-Communists insist on a break in Aragon's career between his surrealist and communist periods, the latter representing unmitigated decadence. Friends within the Party have emphasized the concept of evolution, the novels of socialist realism serving to fulfill the earlier, incomplete manner of surrealism.[13] It is also open to question whether the new style of Le Fou d'Elsa and Blanche ou l'oubli represents a post-Stalinist return to the artistic innovation of the 1920s, or, on the contrary, is the natural outgrowth of socialist realism, or is even a dialectical synthesis of the two earlier trends. Personally, I believe that just as the novels of 'Le Monde réel' series and the war poems cannot be accounted for without Aragon's prior achievement as the friend and disciple of Breton, so too the masterpieces of his later years, in verse and in prose, are incomprehensible if we fail to recognize in this man not only a great surrealist but also a great Marxist, the Gorky and Mayakovsky of his nation. Certain surrealist-communist attitudes – exaltation of the concrete, 'real' world; rebellion against a reified society; the quest for liberty, to create society anew for all men; and a commitment to revitalize France's cultural heritage – make up the intellectual foundation of Aragon's opus. And art for him, as a Communist, has to be more than a commodity to amuse a satiated bourgeoisie and thus increase its alienation; on the contrary, it is the writer's duty to face up to the problems of history and the play of socio-economic forces, to work for mankind's liberation by increasing knowledge and decreasing lethargy.

At least three times Aragon has turned to the epic in verse (in contrast to the lyric and prose fiction) as the appropriate mode in which to express his vision of man: in the 1930s (Hourra l'Oural); during the War, in the struggle against Nazi domination (the brief epic Brocéliande); and in the 1960s with his most grandiose evocation of the past, which also comments on issues of our own age (East vs West) and is his most sublime offering to his domna, Elsa Triolet (the encyclopedic, all-encompassing Fou d'Elsa). These are his reponse, his epic solution to the problems of our time: solitude in society, cultural alienation, ignorance of the past, and loss of hope in the future. In his poems a new hero (the poet, the masses, the nation) struggles in the present, fully aware of the past and future, and by so doing renews the past and creates the future. More than any other writer of our time, Aragon is obsessed with history and culture, with that sense of continuity which unites the past to the present and both to the future. He has proved that it is possible to write successful epic in our time and to base it upon a medieval theme. *Brocéliande* and *Le Fou d'Elsa* are intellectually satisfying, emotionally moving poems, as 'relevant' as *Raoul de Cambrai* and *Girard de Roussillon* were for the public of the twelfth century; they have a message, psychology, imagery, and structure that transcend national and linguistic boundaries, that are of universal value. *Le Fou d'Elsa* is considered by some to be Aragon's masterwork and one of the finest poems to have appeared since the Second World War.

Although Aragon is no doubt the greatest living poet working in his line, following the path he has chosen with the comrades who have chosen him, he is not the only one, nor should we consider his work to be an anomaly. In the socialist camp, which now makes up a good portion of the globe, the Aragon-Eluard-Neruda-Mayakovsky-Brecht approach to art is the dominant mode by far. Third World poets like Césaire, Damas, Senghor, Diop, Glissant, and Tchicaya U Tam'si prove to be as close to the author of *Le Paysan de Paris*, *Hourra l'Oural*, and *Le Musée Grévin* as to Valéry and Char, not to speak of experimenters associated with *Tel Quel* and *Change*. At poetry conferences throughout the world political commitment is either extolled or at least tolerated, and participants often arrive at a consensus that *poésie engagée* should not be rejected out of hand.[14] On the contrary, all great verse is deemed great for the same reasons, for greatness can descend upon a politically engaged writer as easily as upon the esthete in his tower; indeed, when a committed person turns out to be an artist, it is because of, not in spite of, his commitment. There are many mansions in the House of the Lord ...*

*Louis Aragon died on 24 December 1982, an event which, comparable to the passing of Sartre and Barthes three years previously, gave rise to animated debate, to that public 'defense and illustration' of literature which is one of the glories of modern French culture. I regret that, *A Muse for Heroes* now in an advanced stage of production, it was not feasible to make the appropriate revisions within this chapter.

## Chapter Eighteen

# ❧ PIERRE EMMANUEL

In 1941, Pierre Seghers published his first complete book as editor of a press, a work of poetry entitled *Tombeau d'Orphée* by an unknown writer in his twenties, Pierre Emmanuel (pseudonym for Noël Mathieu, born 1916). Immediately Emmanuel became famous: his volume, the literary event of the year, achieved a success comparable to Aragon's *Le Crève-Cœur*. As one of the Resistance Poets his collections, *Combats avec tes défenseurs*, *Jour de Colère*, and *La Liberté guide nos pas*, as well as *Le Poète et son Christ*, associated him in the popular mind with Aragon, Eluard, and Desnos. Since the War Emmanuel's career, despite his stance on the 'other side,' has to some degree curiously paralleled Aragon's: return to a relatively tranquil way of life as a writer; the elaboration, over a thirty-year span, of a vast, complex opus, including ventures in the long poem: *Sodome* (1944), *Babel* (1951), *Jacob* (1970), *Sophia* (1973), and *Tu* (1978); and acclaim, as evidenced by the Grand Prix de Poésie de l'Académie Française (1962), reception into the Académie Française (1969), and appointment to head the Presidential Commission for Reform of French teaching in the schools (1970).[1]

Despite having taken the same road for parts of their respective careers, despite a common admiration for d'Aubigné and Hugo which has led to similar experiments in constructing modern epic, the two men do differ strikingly in doctrinal and esthetic matters, not to speak of the texture of their verse. It is not especially useful, in a critical sense, to label Pierre Emmanuel a Catholic poet, any more than it is to designate Aragon a Communist poet, or Saint-John Perse a post-symbolist, neo-pagan, Creole poet. Nonetheless, Emmanuel has been influenced by certain figures – Calvin, Pascal, Kierkegaard, Baudelaire, Bloy, Jouve, Barth, Marcel – who helped orient his mind into channels foreign to the mainstream of French verse since the high Baroque. To this extent he does share common ethical and metaphysical concerns with a group of writers – La Tour du Pin, Masson, Cayrol, Jaccottet, Grosjean, Renard, Estang, Le Quintrec, and Oster

– who, whether or not they form a 'Catholic school,' do embody one of the most significant trends in post-war verse. Besides, being now in his sixties, he is treated by many as a grand old man of letters in the line of Claudel, Gide, and Mauriac, but – nineteen years younger than Aragon, almost a third of a century younger than Saint-John Perse – Emmanuel embodies a newer current in the arts. The authors he loves – Jouve, Novalis, Hölderlin, Rilke, Kierkegaard – are guiding lights for the more sensitive among our contemporaries, of the older and more recent generations. His poetic texture, of extreme density combined with rhetorical élan, of fragmentation conceived within a total structure, and his concern for both moral commitment and artistic integrity are representative of post-war trends throughout the West. It is unusually difficult to characterize the evolution of his opus, one of extraordinary range and by no means complete; yet I detect oscillation between the long poem and collections of brief lyrics, between the elaboration of a myth-oriented, often politically militant, technically difficult verse (treating the themes of Orpheus, Christ, and the mad poet Hölderlin, for example) and inner meditations in a much simpler, frankly elegiac form. Although these trends do overlap, a claim can be made that the mythical, epic, committed poet of the forties shifted to a very different style in the 1950s and early 1960s, only to revert to a synthesis of the two earlier stances in *Jacob* and *Sophia*. Be this as it may, I have chosen to discuss the two works I consider most appropriate, given the subject of this book: *Tombeau d'Orphée* (1941), Emmanuel's most famous poem from the early years, a passionately lyrical book, his equivalent, in the private sphere, to *Brocéliande*; and *Babel* (1951), his most consistently narrative, and perhaps most coherently successful, text in the epic mode of *Le Fou d'Elsa*.

The dominant theme of *Tombeau d'Orphée*[2] is Thanatos. Cultivating Rilke's obsession with death-life or death as part of life, Pierre Emmanuel emphasizes that Orpheus's trip to the underworld is an act of suicide, for in order to enter Hades he must literally perish in his own flesh. The passing of Eurydice brings upon our protagonist a sense of alienation, an imbalance in his being, a feeling of void and disintegration. In addition, when he arrives in Hades, his wife appears before him, nude and severe, demented, with the threat of vengeance emanating from her, as if she had been transformed into Persephone or Hecate, become a queen of hell about to visit eternal torment upon the intruder. Orpheus's quest is assimilated to the Freudian death-instinct and to the deepest, most secretive drives of the unconscious.

In this poem of death, the title of which evokes a tomb, one pattern of imagery derives from the earth. Both Orpheus and Eurydice are portrayed in metaphors of decomposition, the rot and disintegration of their bodies corresponding to the soft earth of the grave that encloses them. In this sense, the earth itself is transformed into a gigantic womb-grave, a soft, porous, image of fetid intimacy and garbage-like physicality. We are also shown bodies reduced to ashes or Orpheus tortured by thirst and by arid rock, the desert that engulfs him. Most of all, however, Pierre Emmanuel depicts the underworld in terms of stone, as a true city of the dead, a cemetery of tombs or a sequence of mausoleums. The inhabitants, including Orpheus, become petrified, are themselves rocks, or they wander about enclosed in prison-like crypts. Emmanuel is fascinated by this process of petrification, in which, owing to a gradual paralysis of the outer world and of the self, the individual is brought, through his own will, to a state of living death, of non-being. It is a process of dehumanization associated with modern life – machines, advanced technology, logic – and with man's reaction to such a life – uniformity, resignation, and boredom. Stone is the evil within us, a Medusa which causes us to accept, even relish, solitude and immobility. It is our refusal of grace. Usually in the literary tradition hard earth is conceived as a masculine image of the will; in *Tombeau d'Orphée*, however, as in Le Moyne's *Saint Louis*, this stone has been carved out to form an evil temple, city, and prison. It has been feminized, and the petrification process is associated with a Medusa-complex emanating from Eurydice. Like the dream-city of Tsoar in Pierre Emmanuel's *Sodome*, Eurydice's mausoleum-city evokes sleep, memory, shadows, and the depths of the unconscious – versions of death for the rational male animus embodied in Orpheus.

Here as elsewhere in Pierre Emmanuel's work, we find the Speaker digging out a grotto or vault in the earth, burrowing and drilling. Similarly, Orpheus's body, expiring, turning to stone or lead, drops into the pit. This plunging, thrusting activity on his part often is envisaged in terms of sadism, as acts of violence directed against death or against Eurydice herself. Thus, become stone and a dagger, Orpheus rapes death (pp. 33–4), and Eurydice appears before him with mutilated breasts (p. 85). He remembers having slain her and enjoys the pleasure of killing for the sake of knowledge, since the blade can only know itself through the death of the Other (p. 81). It appears that, symbolically in Orpheus's conscience (the present) and perhaps in physical reality (the past), he was responsible for Eurydice's death and that, come to Hades (again in the present), he slays her anew with a male dagger. When they made love, each thundered and slew the other; now this mortal exchange recurs in the grave:

Que je tremblais quand tu me pris Que j'étais belle
comme je convoitais ton Ame! je hâtais
l'incroyable dénouement de la naissance

Père
Pourtant j'ai foudroyé ton corps comme la pierre
seule foudroie
avec la face résonnant comme un tambour   (p. 47)

Pierre Emmanuel's subtle use of verb tenses makes it impossible for the reader to ascertain whether a particular action or relation of an action (intercourse, murder, even speech) takes place in present reality, in past reality, in a dream, or in the memory of a dream or of reality. The general outline of the myth is clear; the details of interpretation are left intentionally ambivalent. At any rate, whether in past or present, dream or reality, the one serves as torturer and the other as victim – in turn. For Emmanuel tells us that Eurydice retaliates, that, when Orpheus comes to rescue her, she kills him and is responsible for his perishing. She also is associated with sharp instruments, with tooth-imagery. These images are, of course, a poetic representation of the *vagina dentata*, given that Eurydice embodies the characteristics of the Jungian Terrible Mother, an Ishtar, Hecate, and Kali figure, image of the castrating woman. As such, she prefigures the maenads Orpheus will encounter after his return to earth, female lovers of the tomb, naked, cutting, who will violate him, the hunted stag (p. 108), and loving him, deliver him to infernal hatred.

As is obvious from the preceding analysis, one facet of the poem is, in the author's own terms, 'une incantation érotique, la liturgie d'un irréalisable amour' (p. 16). Lover and beloved committed murder in the past by inflicting sexual ecstasy. She learns the science symbolized 'par le couteau d'un sexe mâle' (p. 76). He remembers having penetrated her, killed her, with the male blade (p. 81). Then in the present Orpheus penetrates, violates soft earth to arrive at Eurydice and, once there, rapes her in the grave. His desire to bring her back from hell is portrayed in erotic terms, for his death on her behalf and her perishing a second time in his presence are assimilated to climax in the act of love. In this respect, Pierre Emmanuel elaborates upon Rilke's injunction to his Orpheus: 'Sei immer tot in Eurydike.' However, he also follows Jouve in underscoring the ambivalence of the love-hate relationship and the nature of sexual aggression, the fact that, parted from the beloved, unable to transfer his affection to another love-object, turning in upon himself, the individual perceives tenderness shifting to hatred and resentment. It is clear that, in *Tombeau d'Orphée*, when Orpheus desires Eurydice she remains cool and distant, even spurns his advances, and when she longs to retain him in the tomb, he scorns her. Although he realizes that the only way that he can ever truly possess Eurydice is to slay her, thus terminating her consciousness, in fact even beyond the grave her consciousness, her will, her Self remain impervious to his own. Along with Jouve, Pierre Emmanuel exploits the association of Eros and Thanatos, the fact that the sexual climax implies a release of tension and annihilation of consciousness, *la petite mort*, comparable to death, and that sadism and violence are projections of frustrated desire, if not of the death-instinct itself, onto the outside world.

Eurydice reproaches Orpheus for seeking to take her away from God. According to her, his love, which disturbs her in the grave, is an insult, a scandal. She *is* Death; she hates him. He, in turn, begs God's forgiveness for having desired her and therefore placed a woman before the divinity. Because, in him, his passion was greater even than the Almighty, sobs Orpheus, he shall be damned. And he begs to be delivered from her, to slay her a second time:

> O tue-la de nouveau Seigneur!
>                pénètre-la
> du feu sauvage de l'inceste,
> délivre-moi de la Femme que j'ai criée
> d'entre les morts! ...
>
> Mais Toi terrible destinée Mère de dieu
> Toi passion farouche! Tu m'inscris
> dans ma mort et le délire de Ton sexe,
> j'appelle en vain à dieu!
>
>                J'aime et je suis damné
> la tête en bas je crie mon dieu dans les sépulcres.    (p. 51)

These examples tell us something of the tone of *Tombeau d'Orphée*, of the extent to which Pierre Emmanuel retains one aspect of the Orpheus myth in Antiquity, the notion of transgression, of a ritual crime or sin punished by the woman's death and by the man's failure to bring her back. The crime is physical sex, and only by renouncing it can humankind hope for salvation. Emmanuel shares Jouve's obsession with original sin, with that concrete evil associated with the body, for man, because of his carnal instincts, because of his fallen libido, has transformed himself into a monster. In addition, following the old Christian tradition and epic convention of duty versus passion, the poet assimilates the male to pure reason in spirit, the female to a life of flesh. Eurydice is accompanied by imagery of darkness, enclosure, petrification, reptilia, and insanity, traits that man, ashamed of his own desires, projects onto his scapegoat-partner.

This state of guilt, as well as his separation from Eurydice, creates in the hero a sentiment of Rilkean *Weltangst*. The death of the beloved, and

Orpheus's own death, appear to him as a weight (a stone) oppressing him from all sides and as a sense of nothingness, of void – the denial of existence Jouve evoked with the term *nada*. He is tortured by his failure to communicate with the Other, to establish an *Ich-Du* relationship, and she reproaches him with not relating to her as a person but as an object, with being engrossed in his subjective vision of her. A Hyperion without his Diotima, a Magdalene forbidden contact with her Christ, Pierre Emmanuel's Orpheus must struggle to find being within his own unconscious.

One road to the attainment of being, which, however, proves to be illusory, is to fuse with Eurydice or to be metamorphosed into her. Here the poet introduces one of his favorite myths, a Christian version of Plato's androgyne. According to Emmanuel (the theme is developed most fully in *Sodome*), only Adam enjoyed primal unity, before the creation of Eve; since the Fall we have desperately sought to deny our partial nature, to re-become one in Eden. Orpheus asleep discovers himself to be a woman or, loving himself in Eurydice, both male and female he becomes her. In *Tombeau d'Orphée* as in *Sodome*, the myth is a version of homosexual reverie, especially appropriate since the Ovidian version of the Orpheus story will have him introduce pederasty in Thrace and be slain by the maenads because of his sexual orientation. Orpheus-Everyman also recognizes that death, the unconscious, and the irrational (the bases for his anima) form part of himself and that a rigid distinction between flesh and spirit is impossible. Indeed, we can interpret Orpheus and Eurydice as the two fundamental aspects of the psyche – male artistic creativity and female formless matter – that each of us desperately strives to integrate in the Self. The Speaker imagines man and woman as a god, loving and hating itself (pp. 76–7) or as a statue that has self-intercourse. However, Pierre Emmanuel proclaims with fervor that such desires are both narcissistic and incestuous; and that to seek primal unity outside of God, to seek being apart from Being, is doomed to failure and can only compound our sense of *nada*. The Almighty intentionally separated the sexes – for his own glory and for ours. Because of man's anguished consciousness of separation, he is opened to God and to change; his wound thus urges him to strive for a more valid, authentic unity in Being.

Despite the avowedly pagan quality of the Orpheus myth, the Christian God, giver of being, plays a crucial role in Pierre Emmanuel's text. Orpheus appeals to him again and again, as a listener, a 'narratee' of crucial importance to the reader and to Eurydice herself. As the god of the underworld and as our savior, as Pluto and Christ, he appears in the grave with lover and beloved, he is ever a third figure between them. Eros, in the Claudelian and Jouvian sense, is perceived to be a road to the absolute, and God's love for man, embodied in the incarnation, in Christ's passion, offers us heavenly nuptials, Jouve's *Noces* in the tradition of the Song of Songs and Juan de la Cruz.[3] Thus, Christ-Pluto competes with Orpheus for Eurydice's favors and, in a development on the homosexual reverie discussed above, also enters into competition with the wife for the husband. In perhaps the most startling 'fiction' in Pierre Emmanuel's entire opus, the dead Orpheus seeks to embrace Eurydice but attains climax with Christ instead (pp. 36–7). He then renounces the girl, giving her to Christ, who becomes her lover while he the loser looks on in sexual ecstasy:

> Qu'importe: elle perdue toujours, elle adorable
> absence! il l'a livrée au ténébreux époux
> pour le sang noir d'une journée d'amour: Orphée la couche
> entre les bras du jeune Christ – et vus d'en-haut
> il les aime, et jouit de sa mort qui les crée
> il jouit! de les voir noués et ruisselants
> d'infamie et de gloire, et morts! la bien-aimée
> qui n'est plus sienne, en son amant d'ivoire ...   (p. 38)

Furthermore, as a result of this union accomplished in Orpheus's presence, the latter prays that Eurydice, impregnated with divine seed, may give birth to the poet himself; and so it shall be:

> 'Seigneur
> qui es couché sur le mont de ma mort
> engendre à cette femme un enfant de blasphème
> de certitude et de pardon qui serait moi
> de nouveau, dans les pins tranquilles et les vignes
> chaudes et l'opulent automne de la Mort.'
> 　　　　　　　　　　　　　　　　　... Le pur poète
> né du Christ et de l'aimée
> dans la fruition d'une aube effroyable ...   (pp. 39, 117)

Eurydice the tomb is metamorphosed into Eurydice the womb. As a mother-figure, she parallels Sarah in *Sodome*, Rachel in *Jacob*, Mary in *Sophia*, and, above all, the Adulterous Wife and Mary Magdalene in *Le Poète et son Christ*. Like her Greek counterpart, the Magdalene symbolizes sin and death, has intercourse with a dead Christ who, perishing in her, resurrects as she herself is transformed into the Virgin Mary. This is Pierre Emmanuel's paradoxical exaltation of cosmic Eros and redemption of the whore, of fallen, irrational woman. Were Adam to deny Eve, he would deny himself. Although Orpheus created Eurydice, he is also born from her, for women represent the creative matrix, the *anima mundi*, without which a virile God and virile men cannot exist. However, Orpheus must learn to replace the pleasure principle by the reality principle, to renounce the Mother in order to complete his own individuation process as an adult. To conquer hell he must come to terms with the Mother-imago and with his own Shadow as subjects not objects, integrating into his personality those seemingly hostile external projections of himself. In the end, as in the works of Jouve, the mother-figure takes onto herself guilt, sin, and death, leaving the son free to develop in an aura of renewed purity. Her death (her embrace of Christ) is necessary for his integration into adult society and his development as an artist.

That Pierre Emmanuel was influenced by Freud ought to surprise no reader of *Tombeau d'Orphée*. The headings of certain poetic subdivisions ('Mémoire,' 'Sommeil') indicate how much the narrating *persona*'s experience is that of the unconscious expressed through dream-imagery, latent desires projected onto dream-characters who are extensions of the Self. God-Christ-Pluto plays the paternal role, standing in judgment over Orpheus and Eurydice, children defiled by a version of incest-tabu. For, by loving Eurydice on earth, Orpheus defied the Oedipal father-God (p. 28). Given the paradoxical nature of the Christian incarnation, God becomes flesh and thus not only the Father but also Orpheus's equal, a double sharing his glory and his shame, his spirit and his lust. Indeed, he is a projection of Orpheus the poet, freed from contradictions and anguish. In the grave father and son are rivals for Eurydice's carnal embrace, and the abyss, a bull or a God, stands before the opened female corpse (p. 60). Orpheus has the choice of rejecting the paternal imago or of identifying with him. He chooses the latter option. He takes the father's side, is assimilated to him, gives him the coveted woman, and participates in their joy: the ego renounces the claims of the id (Eurydice) and submits to the superego (Christ). By identifying with the mother, he even succeeds in embracing the father. And, having thus, in one sense, renounced desire, he chooses to perish in God in order that he be reintegrated into life. And so he is, reborn from the mother and the father, become a child in Christ, a member of the restored archetypal family. Like Christ, he dies and resurrects on the third day.

The rivalry between Orpheus and Christ is transcended, largely through acts of sexual and spiritual mediation, as is the parallel competition between Orpheus and Eurydice. Only when Christ himself possesses the woman is her husband able to attain ecstasy, spiritual and erotic; thus, through the Other, Eurydice, he possesses Christ, and through the All-Other, Christ, he enjoys the woman. It is because of Orpheus's good offices, his stubborn, absolute commitment, that Eurydice also is redeemed – in Christ and himself. Alone the lover fails to bring back (resurrect) his beloved or even to escape in his own person. Christ then is the indispensable go-between because, by taking our sins on his shoulders, by torturing himself on our cross, he mediates for us with his father. Furthermore, according to Pierre Emmanuel, since Christ became a man, he requires our intervention in turn and will have fully resurrected only when each one of us has borne his cross in turn. God needs our freedom and our chaos just as we need him. The ultimate in mediation is thus to *become* the mediator, just as the essence of the Christian life is to be reborn spiritually, to become Christ, *in imitatione Christi.*

Rebirth occurs through the medium of blood and salt water, the feminine, menstrual, foetal element, and the image of male semen. According to Emmanuel, the blood of the poet and of Christ is associated with a tear that Orpheus hopes to call forth from Eurydice's dead eye; and a tear from Orpheus, the poet's own salt, shall be metamorphosed into reinvigorating dew (p. 55; also, 'de pleurs celés: rosée des morts,' p. 75), and, along with shed, sacred blood, bring about transfiguration: 'l'hosanna final est Sang réconcilié' (p. 87). Orpheus's head is tossed into the sea, where it will remain intact, immortal; one drop of dew restores his dead soul. The fluid element impregnated with salt conquers stone, nullifies female petrification, and waters ashes within the grave so that they give birth to a new phoenix. This blood symbolizes the wine of the Eucharist, the golden shower of Jupiter, rain from heaven, and the holy water of baptism.

Pierre Emmanuel adheres to the traditional archetype, the myth of Orpheus as it has developed over the ages, from archaic Greece to Rome (Virgil and Ovid), through the Middle Ages and Renaissance up to modern times.[4] The Orpheus story is probably the most distinctive theme in poetry of the last two hundred years, and *Tombeau d'Orphée* one of the most recent links in a chain that includes works by Goethe, Hölderlin, Novalis, and Hoffmann; Ballanche, Nerval, Rimbaud, Valéry, and Rilke; Segalen, Cocteau, Anouilh, Jouve, and Durry. Like so many other embodiments of the myth, Emmanuel's protagonist is a prophet and seer, drawn to the absolute, subject to divine possession, a magus who explores the world of dreams and the night, an enchanter enchanted by himself, a shaman who seeks and to some extent obtains power over Hades. He descends into the depths of his own unconscious, an inner world perceived through the eyes of the soul, and there discovers mysteries, secrets of the universe which he can reveal to others. This active hero undertakes a quest, a journey into the abyss, the Other World, where he endures sexual ordeals and finally succeeds in rites of passage resulting in rebirth and return from the maze; yet, because of his transgression, the ultimate boon is denied him, and the tragic element in his quest, the sacrifice and loss, remain ever present.

The son of Calliope and priest of Dionysus and Apollo purportedly invented the lyre, allied poetry to music, indeed gave poetry to the world when he opened the gates of hell and tamed savage beasts with his voice. Similarly, in Pierre Emmanuel's text, the hero's tomb is a hymn to song, the triumphant shout of Orpheus the poet. This man committed the ultimate blasphemy through speech; he killed his love, allowed her to die, or willfully abandoned her to the god of the underworld, in order to be free to create. He becomes a poet because she is dead (cf. Rilke, Segalen, Jouve), deceiving her ruse through song (p. 46), his spirit reborn in verse. Indeed, the ultimate masculine affront to, and triumph over, the female principle embodied in Eurydice as well as in the maenads is this commitment to the spiritual life, the world of art. Orpheus performs, all things yield before him, death expires, and open wounds sing his name. Given life by the Word, he lives as a poet. And when he finally perishes, when his severed head is tossed into the sea, it rises and sings:

> Adieu
> la tombe est engloutie sous les cheveux
> et la main agrippée au soleil se détache
> il tombe
>         Seul le chef tranché sort de la mer
> et chante
>
> Apollon qu'il te soit sur les eaux rouges un temple.   (pp. 109–10)

Finally, Emmanuel rejoins one of the oldest traditions of French epic by consciously or unconsciously conforming to the allegorical interpretation of the Orpheus myth so prevalent in the Middle Ages and Renaissance, the most important manifestation of which is the fourteenth-century *Ovide moralisé*. As we have seen, Emmanuel's hero, like his medieval forebear, symbolizes reason, man's rational faculty, whereas Eurydice symbolizes the passions and vices, specifically carnal *concupiscentia*. Since the lower part of human nature, the specifically feminine, is seduced by Satan, by an obsession with *temporalia*, man's soul can be saved only by renouncing earthly desires and rising alone to God. The poetic seer is also a Christ-figure, an Orpheus-Christus, the good shepherd who harrows hell in order to lead his flock, his bride the Church, up to the stars. For three days Emmanuel's protagonist lies in the grave, embraced by the beloved only to be reborn of God. Like Christ, he forbids the beloved (Eurydice, the Magdalene) to touch him; like Christ, he is associated with an iconography of blood, wounds, thorns, the spear, and the Veronica. His tomb, like the Rock of Peter, becomes the foundation for a new faith; his dismemberment and ritual sacrifice grant renewal to himself and others; and his blood becomes the ink from which shall be written a new sacred book of judgment on nature and the world. The Speaker's poetic consciousness seeks to become Christ, while retaining the sins of man and woman within him. His failure, if failure there be, is Orpheus's and mankind's, the impossibility of perfect union with God, face to face, in this mortal life.

Pierre Emmanuel's vast opus is coherent, the same themes, images, and obsessions reappearing in collections separated by years, even decades. It is not surprising that several concerns of *Tombeau d'Orphée* are treated again in *Babel.*[5] In this Biblical fresco, telling of the rise and fall of a demonic city under the aegis of its master, the King or Prince, the religious problem is central. God needs us as much as we need him, hence he has created humans free, granting them the autonomy to hate their maker, to strive to equal him, and thus to recommit the Fall. Man accepts the challenge and does fall. Although the Prince is guilty of hubris in seeking to be God in the solitary joy of his own power, he builds on the void of men. He shares with them the temptation of fanaticism, the impulse to raze all that has gone before. Having forgotten the Almighty, they search for being apart from Being and eternity without Christ, wish to build something earthly that will endure after they have passed away. It is clear that, according to Pierre Emmanuel, the guilty faculty is reason or abstraction, for the Prince constructs 'la Tour d'intelligence' (pp. 103, 111) according to the rules of geometry, and Babel is made of light, glass, and spirit (Vigny's *esprit pur*) – that is, of transparent reason. On another occasion, the author declares that Babel represents contemporary society: specifically, bureaucrats, graphs, machines, and our idolatry of efficiency and the work ethos.[6] I believe that Emmanuel condemns the modern style in its essence, the mentality which has triumphed in the West since the middle of the nineteenth century manifest in the myth of progress, the dependence upon technology, the consideration of quantity as a good in and of itself, the preference of dynamism to stasis, the sacrifice of the present and past for the future, and the abandonment of the notion of free will to the idols of progress and science.[7] Behind this façade of intellect, we find anguish, a sense of void torturing those men aware that since our secular culture can no longer believe in heaven or hell and since we cannot create our own gods, we are doomed instead to invent a hell and Satan here on earth. In contrast to these lucid ones, many other people of Babel, for most of their lives guilty of Sartrean bad faith, complacent in death (like Lot's wife in *Sodome* or Eurydice in *Tombeau d'Orphée*), stand beyond the pale. Following Léon Bloy, Bernanos, and Dante, Pierre Emmanuel despises above all Pharisees and Laodiceans. For all his monstrosity, the tyrant at least believes in God, if only to vanquish him, and frees his people from indifference by subjecting them to pain. This sadist is closer to the Messiah than they are because by hating God he desires his love, by torturing the masses he hurts himself, and by wounding Christ he becomes him.

Since, as in *Tombeau d'Orphée*, the erotic and religious domains are assimilated, indeed fused, the spiritual sickness of the Babel-people is directly reflected in their unhealthy private lives. Like *Sodome*, like the city of the dead in *Tombeau d'Orphée*, Babel is depicted as a prostitute, as the epitome of depraved female sexuality. Certain kinds of women give men the salt they crave, but their inscrutable blue eyes are fixed elsewhere. The men have intercourse in order to equal god but in fact embrace only the city itself, image of Thanatos; virgin for every customer, such women are never truly possessed. How can it be otherwise, since they and Babel prove to be death? Although the Prince does permit this kind of sex, at least metaphorically, on another level he denies carnal relations altogether. Demonic female sentinels, sterile virgins, are posted on the walls; Thanatos is substituted for Eros; and masochistic, castrated masses of people, trans-formed into unisexual creatures, produce stones for building and rub against them, or find their only love-partner in the King. The sterility of Sodom and Babel is contrasted to the rich, teeming cosmic maternity of Sarah (*Sodome*), Rachel (*Jacob*), and Mary (*Sophia*). Since the tyrant forbids love, woman becomes a door onto eternity; therefore, one solution to the Babel problem is a renewal of healthy sexuality, of the Eros of creation that can overcome pride and hate. He who knows how to love will be saved:

> Je te laisse, dit Dieu. Tu es heureux. Je te laisse car tu es certain.
> Toi, premier sauvé de Babel, non par vertu singulière
> Mais simplement parce que tu aimes.    (p. 228)

The individual responsible for having made Babel is the King, who came to power because of the others' fear of the dark. This shadow-figure is the embodiment of masculine will. It is he, sole mediator, who forbids sex to the masses, who have become slaves and children in his hands. This *durus pater*, an evil superego, stands as the demonic counterpart to the benevolent God of the Dead in *Tombeau d'Orphée* and also serves as an alter ego to the Shepherd (one of his early victims), Christ, and God, with whom he struggles for the soul of Babel. His hands are white, he has never tortured, for his slaves do the dirty work for him; indeed, the people of Babel wound each other in his name, creating a state of complicity between the master and his slaves, the torturer and his victims.

The King's personal creation is the Tower of Babel, a symbol of collective sin and depredation, an urban Waste Land, the image of the city assimi-lated, as in Jouve's *Kyrie*, to the Old Testament Sodom, Babylon, and Nineveh. Pierre Emmanuel develops the scriptural myth of pastoral, nomadic innocence following upon the Flood, then posits that evil returned to the world with the construction of cities: people first built houses of dried mud and crawled into them, happy like the beasts. Thus, in Christian terms, Emmanuel elaborates a demonic parody of the city as anagogic archetype, the heavenly Jerusalem where a universal chorus sings the praises of the Creator; and he joins Saint-John Perse, René Char, and other poets who rebel against the myth of Paris, that exaltation of the metropolis which became so dominant a theme in nineteenth-century verse, especially with Hugo, and was perpetuated in more recent times by Apollinaire, Fargue, J. Romains, the surrealists (especially Aragon), and Prévert. A case can be made that the demystification of the city (Baudelaire, Verhaeren, Bely, Dos Passos, Döblin, Eliot, Lorca) is one of the most pervasive literary themes of our time.[8]

As in *Tombeau d'Orphée*, a city is constructed of stone. The king himself is like a rock or a metallic idol, whom the people adore and, by so doing, petrify God. They also are petrified, are ordered like stones for work, and the tower (a Medusa that has turned them into stone) is constructed upon their rocklike bodies. In this way men are transformed into the living dead, into stone creatures reminiscent of science fiction or tales of terror. And the city itself is portrayed as a kingdom of walls (therefore a prison) rising so high that people cease to be aware of its existence. The master encloses, his slaves are enclosed. The 'happy prison'[9] is another romantic motif repudiated by Pierre Emmanuel. This hard earth, of course, symbolizes the Prince's own sadistic, ferocious virility, his will to power and delight in struggle, his law and death – and the same pride and ferocity within the people, who have created the tyrant and made it possible for him to reign.

In the world of Babel, machines, become sufficient unto themselves, assume authority over men. Devouring, castrating monsters, they crush people's bodies, which, having lost their teeth, are reduced to a state resembling larvae. Struggling to construct the city, laborers resemble armies of ants, as their feet become embedded in the stone and mortar, their sweat fusing them to the masonry:

> Des colonnes
> De fourmis à l'assaut secrètent la sueur
> Qui lie en un seul corps les hommes et les pierres.
> Les premiers rangs pétrifiés donnent appui
> Vers la hauteur à ceux qui suivent ...   (p. 103)

Indeed, the masses and their persecutor come to resemble machines or lower forms of animal life. Eunuch priests, in the form of vampires, suck

Christ's blood, or as bats and vultures perch on his (the eagle's) tomb
(p. 248). Emmanuel depicts the King as a wild beast that devours men,
a giant stomach, and we also hear of a python with a grain of sand for a
brain, for whom the whole inner earth is its egg, nourishing as its issue a
race of automatons who devour it. This combination of machine-sadism
and oral-anal cannibalism creates an unusually powerful nightmare, a
mood of terror. Not since d'Aubigné and Le Moyne have we found such
a plethora of garbage and rot imagery, such luxuriance of metaphor that
evokes the demonic. Pierre Emmanuel exploits a truly baroque imagination
in his effort to portray the Apocalypse of his own – that is, our – age.

For all its evils, the city nonetheless houses a community of men, bound
together for good or ill. The victims are a conglomeration of Others
forced into human contact, whereas the tyrant's glory and his ultimate dis-
comfort derive from the fact that he lives and will die alone, the last
insect:

> C'est moi, le Roi qui fis creuser par mes armées
> La terre en un sépulcre à ma taille, et voici
> Que je suis le dernier insecte de ma race
> Ce scarabée craquant de sécheresse au fort
> De la torride solitude: mes jointures
> Souffrent ce sourd effort immobile, la mort.   (p. 304)

His sin is to exalt individualism to the detriment of love. Does he not also
suffer from that greatest of modern sins and claims to glory – ennui?[10] Following Léon Bloy, Emmanuel adheres to the Christian tradition that
views all members of the community united in Christ's blood and forming
his body, the Church. We can find God together only by building a
Church of human beings that will dissolve the rocks of pride and hate.

These humans, the persecuted of Babel, are little people, the pauperi to
whom Christ promised the kingdom of heaven. Since they cannot escape the
prison, cannot go to the Savior, he comes to them. Banished from the
city, kept out by the Prince's walls, he sneaks in with a convoy of captive
slaves, his kind of people, declaring elsewhere that he walks not on water
but with mankind in the world, with the rabble for whom a Messe des
Ténèbres is sung and a proletarian eucharistic sacrifice is offered:

> Seigneur! J'ai ramassé ton pain dans le ruisseau,
> Jeté par quelque mauvais pauvre: la famine
> Du monde est toute dans ce pain. Le pus, et l'eau
> Des pleurs, le sang honteux versé dans les sentines
>
> Voilà le vin du sacrifice: toute soif
> A déposé son sel au creux de l'écuelle,

Et la chair de ma paume est à vif, où Tu bois
La déréliction brûlante de mes veines.   (p. 231)

The story of Babel is presumed to occur in the heart of Asia thousands
of years ago. But, as Pierre Emmanuel himself points out, it bears his personal witness to the horrors of Nazism and Stalinism (p. 17). It is not
difficult for the reader to locate in a contemporary setting camps where
victims are incinerated or perish from the cold; I presume that the false
nomads (p. 56), poets and actors, those 'Menteurs du Prince' (p. 114) and
'Parleurs de paroles' (p. 253) who twist words not stone, refer to post-
war Parisian literary cliques, especially the Existentialists or the Communist
group, and that the Lazarus who dances God's death and calls himself the
conscience of the world, a spiritual seducer gone insane, evokes a line of
thinkers Emmanuel considers unusually pernicious: Voltaire, Nietzsche,
Sartre, and Aragon. These are the new priests bearing mountains of paper
who, with a Red Flag, betray the people. The Biblical calf of gold, the
money-changers in the temple, and Judas's thirty pieces of silver are images
that evoke our horror of exploitation and tyranny, whether of the Right
or the Left.

Pierre Emmanuel's vision of history can be enriched by a typological
reading of a kind valid for all of his works, including *Tombeau d'Orphée*.
Thus Babel and its ruler correspond to, indeed represent tropologically,
the Paris, London, Berlin, and Moscow of our age and the Hitler and Stalin
who raise monuments of pride against God. The tyrant prefigures on an
allegorical level Herod, Pilate, and Satan, masters of that demonic Jerusalem
against which Christ, the good shepherd, must eternally bear witness.
And on an anagogic plane, Christ and Antichrist shall struggle for control of
the cosmos and of men's souls, in the last days before the disintegration of
all we know. It is only in this typological sense that we can interpret correctly the roles of the Shepherd, who stands as a sacrificial Christ-figure, and
of today's martyrs, who, postfiguring Christ and the prophet Daniel, cry
out from their burning fiery furnaces. In the line of Agrippa d'Aubigné,
Pierre Emmanuel's Speaker (the *Récitant*) awaits God's sun and trumpet,
the Second Coming of the Eternal Judge. And, as in Bloy and Bernanos, we
are reminded that the cycle of Christ's incarnation, crucifixion, and resurrection recurs eternally, that we are contemporary with all men and with the
Messiah – for, in him, the past, present, and future are immediate and
simultaneous. Bound together with the quick and the dead in God's great
chain of being, by striking any man we strike his son, for each one of us is
torturer and victim, Satan and Christ, at all times.

However, in spite of references to God's avenging fire and sword,
unlike his Biblical predecessor the poet does not have Satan vanquished
in battle by an apocalyptic Michael or Christ. It is significant that the

divinity does not employ his super-weapons. Babel falls, yes, but in calm and joy. As love bursts forth in men's hearts, as people breathe, the tower collapses sweetly, and trees grow from its walls (p. 300). The field of 'positive imagery' in Pierre Emmanuel's text, his answer to the tyrant, is conceived largely in a bucolic, pastoral vein. Before the rise of Babel, he tells us of innocent lovemaking, the earth pregnant with seed, a harvest, fishing, orchards, gardens, and an eagle's flight. After decadence has set in, our reminder of the lost Golden Age and our hope for the future are embodied in the Shepherd, who offers the Prince grapes, water, and milk. The face of the earth is Christ's own, says Pierre Emmanuel, who adapts for his purposes the animism we find in Goethe and Hölderlin.

As in *Tombeau d'Orphée*, blood and water withstand the menace of rocks. Christ's bodily fluid cures burning wounds; our human rebellion is depicted as blood bursting forth from stone (cf. the miracle of the rock performed by Moses at Bethel); and the fountain beneath the earth will prevail against the King. Furthermore, this maternal, pacific fluid (in opposition to the King's bellicose maleness) nourishes growing things, specifically seeds in the earth. Although men, miserable slaves, made from clay, become earth as they are pressed into it, the return to the womb is a death-rebirth experience: man is fecund, and, as seed, he renews himself spiritually as well as physically. Our words and memories are grains that sprout in the cracks of Babel's walls and eventually grow into forests of trees that crack the idol.

In Pierre Emmanuel's world seed develops into trees or wheat, which is then metamorphosed into bread. The bread is, of course, Christ's body in the sacrament of the Eucharist and, at the same time, an image of our everyday social activity, man's communion with other men, the *panem nostrum quotidianum* which is our nurture, fecundity, and right to life. Therefore, declares the Shepherd, God's Word is grain and bread (p. 139). Since the tree is an image of Christ and his Cross, blood flows from the Shepherd and his rood, and this Christ-figure speaks to God like the trunk of an elm. Whereas in *Sodome* no vegetation is to be found, here a people of Lazaruses, metamorphosed into dead plants, will become green again. The tree fuses masculine and feminine aspects of the human condition – it is phallic yet at the same time provides nourishment and refuge, serves as a home for others as well as a creative force in its own right, and, an image of androgynous fecundity, also stands for wisdom and life. It is a figure for modern man: harried, passive, silent, it survives by plunging its roots deep into the earth and deriving new life from the sap. And, physically bound to the soil, to the reality of nature, its branches rise to the skies. Man is that which grows to God, says Emmanuel, in a Christian version of Rilke's 'und in mir wächst der Baum.'

This positive aspect of verticality is reinforced by the flight of birds.
Man will offer a dove to God; the flight of an eagle is heard by the divinity
along with the growth of seeds; and, in one of the most beautiful passages
in *Babel*, man's ship, the Church, in spite of himself, shall be borne on an
eagle's wings:

> Nous
> Qui n'avons plus assez de foi pour cimenter
> Deux pierres en ton Nom qui n'est plus qu'une idole
> Nous bâtissons de flamme atroce et de refus
> De feu grégeois brûlant la barque de l'Apôtre
> Une Eglise, une nef dont la voile et le vent
> Seront l'aigle qui s'ouvre aux futurs comme un Livre.
> Nous ne le lirons pas, qu'importe? Il nous suffit
> Que l'aigle monte de nos cendres et se tienne
> Comme un miroir devant ta Face, illuminant
> Ta gloire d'un éclat qui la nie et l'avive
> Concentrant ton amour que son cœur réfléchit
> Jusques au cœur de ton absence à forme d'homme,
> Abîme de ta mort, creuset de ton Esprit!   (p. 250)

We are reminded of the role assigned to the pentecostal Dove in Emmanuel's
collection of war poetry, *La Liberté guide nos pas*. The dove and the eagle
are both birds of God, the one evoking the Holy Spirit, the Church, and the
human soul, the other the Gospel according to John and Christ himself,
for, like Christ, the legendary eagle is a king in his realm and is reborn in the
flames of the sun. With both trees and birds the poet expresses his yearning for a truly spiritual, natural existence, one that will counter the verticality of Babel, which, in fact, thrusts down, not up. For in the end, the
tyrant encounters Satan in place of God.

I should like to emphasize that Pierre Emmanuel's bucolic imagery is
one of the most recent embodiments of an archetype that goes back to the
Bible and to Virgil's Fourth Eclogue: the notion of a Shepherd-Savior
who shall redeem mankind. Like T.S. Eliot, Emmanuel compares the modern world to a Waste Land and calls for its conversion to fertility: according to the poet, nature is qualitatively superior to culture, especially when
the latter implies twentieth-century industrial technology. Man desperately longs to return to a natural life. If he can anchor himself in nature he will
also find God, for simple things – bread, wine, trees, birds – contain the
cosmos: they are close to God, alive in their own right, the only basis for
faith and poetry. Although, in his yearning for the sacred to become
manifest in everyday life, Pierre Emmanuel has been influenced by Rilke's

*Dinglichkeit*, he also joins one of the most meaningful currents in post-war French verse, represented by Jean Follain and René-Guy Cadou, who make insignificant everyday concerns live through art and add a new dimension to poetry by basing it on objects.

In addition to 'objects,' Pierre Emmanuel is obsessed with 'le problème du langage ... la question capitale.'[11] He has written that the greatest sin committed by Hitler and Vichy was to corrupt speech. In spite of dialogue, the Shepherd fails to communicate with his Prince; although people cry out in pain or prayer from burning furnaces, who but God listens to them? Alas! truth, resembling crystal, is easily broken, and prophets keep silent in horror. In this they differ from the articulate false prophets who use speech all the time but whom God curses. One of the new poets is made to 'play' on his own veins, for man's body is now stretched like a harp (p. 115). And the King himself tempts the Shepherd (as Satan tempted Christ in the wilderness), offering him the office of pontiff or poet-laureate.

It is nonetheless true that the tyrant can only speak to himself, in soliloquy, and that the redeeming Christ-figure[12] is a shepherd who exercises his traditional pastoral calling: the gifts of poetry and music. On the heights he measures grains of wheat, birds, and stars (that is, words) with his flute; alone, disobedient, he plays his instrument, singing the praises of God. The flute thus becomes a symbol of resistance. Although the Prince tries to drown the Shepherd's song and does have him executed ('Le dernier chanteur est mort,' p. 146), he cannot drown the stars. The memory of *la parole quotidienne* lives on in people's hearts, one day to flourish anew: man will himself become a shepherd of sacrifice, singing on the mountaintop, sharing God's breath and spirit. And song will take the form of prayer. At first humans cannot speak at all, can only babble inarticulately; later they achieve the strength of protest – this is the *Messe des Ténèbres* and *Hymne des Témoins*; finally, in a better, newer existence, they will have assimilated the Word and will be capable of praising God *in excelsis*, as their ultimate reason for being. In this, as in all other activities, man imitates God the maker (*Deus artifax*), the potter who on the sixth day modelled his human creation and with Christ's body and blood molds us anew, softens our stone, grants us rebirth every time we take communion in the Mass.

In a very real sense the Shepherd's successor turns out to be the Reciter (*le Récitant*). There are three major non-collective characters in the poem: the Shepherd (a figure of Christ), the Prince (a figure of Satan or Antichrist), and the Reciter (a figure of mankind). This latter personage is an anonymous voice reflecting on the story of Babel, one who has lived it in his flesh: he is a *persona* of Pierre Emmanuel the implied author and a symbol for Every Man, Any Man, or the inner self, that human entity able to resist the King's persecution. The Reciter's interventions, which form a counterpoint to the more lyrical effusions, are couched technically in prose. They contribute an epic tone to the poem, give it chronological order and a narrative framework, but also provide complexity: the events of *Babel* are interpreted through an ironic and often consciously anachronistic prism, for although the Reciter is alleged to be a contemporary witness who lived and wrote in those Biblical days, he also has a specifically twentieth-century consciousness. In contrast to the divinely sanctioned lyrical passages, his is a limited, delegated, lesser voice, which appeals directly to the implied reader. At first the Reciter merely survives, physically and spiritually: 'ils sont morts, et je suis vivant ...' He records the history of the city as an observer; although suffering from the tyrant, he remains as passive as the others, his only distinguishing qualities being an acute sensitivity and lucidity which they lack. He plays the role of *eiron*, an ironic commentator on the events he has endured. But then he discovers a forbidden book: the Hebrew Bible. And this sacred text devours him as a furrow devours a seed of wheat; he becomes a letter in Scripture:

> Celui qui ouvre une fois le Livre, le Livre se referme sur lui. Le Livre le mange comme le sillon le grain de blé: le Livre le porte en germe pour en être à son tour mangé.
>
> Je devins une lettre de ce Livre ... Je la devins sans m'en douter, ne pensant plus aux paroles du Livre. Même je voulais oublier que je l'eusse jamais ouvert. Mais le Livre en forme de Colombe était inscrit dans l'iris de mes yeux: mes cils suivaient le battement de ses ailes.  (p. 174)

Although he is arrested and tortured, the Book sustains his life. Thus in the course of the narrative he becomes a person, develops into a spiritual human being, a *witness* in the Christian sense – just as we the readers discover him to be one. Of course, the Reciter's evolution corresponds to, reflects, and anticipates that of the Babel people as a whole. As he comes to use *paroles quotidiennes*, so will they. Yet he is singled out as an artist, as one who suffers and sings. It is his duty, as a poet, to work on his fellow citizens, his public, to enlarge their poetic and religious vision and thus make speech meaningful to them. In the tradition of Ronsard and d'Aubigné, of Hölderlin and Hugo, he is to serve his fellows by replacing the Shepherd, by mediating between them and divine mysteries and thus leading them to God. His is no longer a solitary adventure, in the line of Orpheus, but a public trust, for language itself, the cause of man's fall (Satan's seductive speech, Adam's and Eve's sins of the mouth), can also be a road to salvation. We can and must return to that pre-Babelian 'verger de langage pour tous' (p. 39). Since the Fall, people have been cut off from the Word

and from everyday things: but poets such as Pierre Emmanuel can point the
way to reintegration in being, and to that All-Other who is God. Unity
will then be restored to the world, oneness in Christ that can replace the
fragmentation, linguistic and spiritual, manifest throughout history, represented by the myth of Babel and by our condition as men on earth.

More perhaps than any other living writer, Pierre Emmanuel is tortured by
the problem of God's absence, by the impossibility for modern man to
communicate with the divinity. And he has devoted his career to finding
God or the possibility of God, to rendering him visible to the reading
public, or simply to making the public aware of his absence and of their own
desperate, perhaps unconscious, need for him. In what he believes to be a
decadent age, lacking spiritual values, lacking a sense of ritual and community, such a quest assumes heroic proportions, a fact which may explain
why Pierre Emmanuel has sought inspiration in the great myths of the past –
Orpheus, Christ, Babel, Sodom, and Jacob – or exploited new ones
partly of his own invention, such as the mad poet Hölderlin or Sophia, the
feminine principle of creation. In his critical writings the author explains
that, for him, the great poetry of the future will be a poetry of symbols that
will close the gap between the human and the divine and provide a solution to the crisis of knowledge in our time, for 'Est poète celui qui pense
symboliquement.'[3]
    Such an attitude toward the creative process implies that Emmanuel,
although his politics are far from the traditional Left in France, joins all
committed intellectuals in concern for the social environment and a denial of
alienation in the artist. Christians, Communists, and Existentialists repudiate the notion so dear to Mallarmé and Valéry that the work of art points
only to itself and that the writer's sole duty is to write, that indeed he
must avoid contamination with the public. For Emmanuel, the artist is to
serve his fellow men, to point out the positive spiritual values lacking in
their lives. And poetry itself, the modern embodiment of the Word, must be
brought back to the people, must serve as a link between the artist and the
community; otherwise its very reason for being is corrupted. Such a relationship between the writer and his public further implies that the work of art
itself is not merely an esthetic object, however beautiful; on the contrary,
Pierre Emmanuel adheres to the medieval, Renaissance, and romantic notion
that it is didactic as well as decorative, *utile* as well as *dulce*, a way of
knowing and experiencing life.
    The knowledge attained by the poet is both psychological and cosmic,
his quest the same. Emmanuel's works, in both prose and verse, are characterized by an extraordinary lucidity, by a constant striving for the truth
about himself, ever in a spirit of anguish. Like Jouve, he brings to ancient

myth the insights of our twentieth-century Freudian age. It is in this will
to authenticity that he and his characters – Orpheus, Eurydice, the Reciter,
the Shepherd, the King – join the mainstream of French verse since Nerval and Baudelaire. At the same time, however, Emmanuel's *personae* plumb
the depths of the human condition in a more universal sense. According
to Alain Bosquet, an artist of a totally different temperament, Pierre
Emmanuel is the most powerful poet of his generation.[14] A plethora of epic
themes – the birth of the hero, the hero as demigod, the villain guilty of
hubris, the visit to the Underworld, the quest for the father, temptation by
woman, duty versus love, authorial intervention from a wise mock-
author – are not only given new life but make up the structure of his opus.
The myths of Orpheus, Christ, Sodom, Babel, Jacob, and Sophia breathe
faith, fire, and anger, a telluric vociferation. Pierre Emmanuel seeks to say
the unsayable, to scale heights not yet attained by man. His is a truly
sublime style, a voice that celebrates the heroism of Christian martyrs over
the ages and of that small, unalienated community that today dares to
speak and to survive in defiance of tyrants. This is a poetry that, whatever its
theme, is redolent of Hölderlin's *tremendum* and *das Heilige*, that seeks
transcendence, Baudelaire's *cri vers la hauteur*. Given the importance of the
Christian tradition in the French epic – in the *Song of Roland*, other
*chansons de geste*, and grail romances; in the baroque period in such poets as
d'Aubigné, Saint-Amant, and Le Moyne; as a dislocated, heretical, but
still vital force in Lamartine and Hugo; and as the subject for mock-epic in
Boileau and Voltaire – as the creator of a new form of Christian epic
Pierre Emmanuel connects with and renews the cultural past of his nation as
does perhaps no other living writer. It is appropriate then that with the
works of this master our book come to a close.

# Conclusion

Above all others, the Middle Ages is the period when the long poem blossomed in France. For three centuries a flood of epics, romances, and allegories burst forth on the soil of Gaul that were to provide themes, characters, stories, and generic models for the rest of Europe. *Artes poeticae* concerned with the vernacular – especially Raimon Vidal's *Razos de Trobar* and Dante's *De Vulgari Eloquentia* – testify to Northern French mastery in narrative verse, prose, and certain lyrical forms in contrast to the Occitan tradition in other genres of the lyric, including, of course, the *canso*. Although the truly aristocratic literary kinds, that is, those practiced by writers of gentle birth, were the *grand chant courtois* and the prose chronicle, it is the long narrative in verse which corresponds to Virgilian epos and adheres to the contemporary ideal of *sermo gravis* proclaimed in treatises on rhetoric: a style and a mode of literature that treat with decorum of noble personages engaged in heroic enterprises. Three genres bore this tradition through the medieval period: the *chanson de geste*, its most active production extending roughly from 1100 to 1230 or 1250; the *roman courtois*, from 1150 to 1300; and the *dit amoureux*, from 1200 on into the fifteenth century. Although each kind follows upon the preceding, romance succeeding to epic and allegory to romance, for a time they co-existed, competing for favor and perhaps appealing to different sectors of the literary public in much the same way that the neo-realistic novel and the New Novel do today. And during this entire age, the long poem was the dominant literary form not only in terms of quantity but also quality: the number of masterpieces in all three genres is striking.

The *chanson de geste* is perhaps derived from a mode of story-telling comparable to the 'oral epic' practiced today in various parts of the world, especially Yugoslavia and Central Asia. *The Song of Roland*, perhaps the earliest and surely one of the greatest of *chansons*, preserves a quality of lyricism from this earlier, pre-literary stage. In the *Roland* and in early *chansons de geste* generally we find traits of lofty, archaic, stylized diction, syntactic parataxis, dignity, monumentality, and structural compartmentalization. The *Roland* is *the* Christian epic, burning with the faith of the Crusades, redolent with Christian archetypal imagery and typological patterns, timeless and God-oriented. Yet it is also a song of war, joying in the lust of battle, scrutinizing the quality of heroism, and it is a political poem concerned with crucial problems of the age, the capacity of the feudal system to deal with the cataclysms that threaten individuals and society as a whole. In later *chansons de geste* these qualities of lyricism, of monumentality, even of an absolute Christian faith are lost. But the later poems elaborate other themes and motifs. The epics of the Guillaume Cycle (which I have not discussed in this book) examine the problem of the feudal clan, evoking the joys and sufferings of frontier barons who have to resist Saracen encroachment without the king's help, dependent upon their own resources. The Epics of Revolt, one of the greatest of which is *Raoul de Cambrai*, treat with acumen and a quality of realism political issues within France, especially the tragedy of the feudal baron caught up in an unjust system, given no occasion to exercise his manly virtues, persecuted by a tyrant yet forced to come to terms with the system. A final group of songs, represented by *Huon de Bordeaux*, turn to a world of escape, in fact become romances, for their heroes perform deeds of heroism in a fabulous Orient; and, in *Huon*, the archetypes of romance are accompanied by an element of humor and irony. The *chanson de geste* has developed into a complex genre capable of commenting on, and laughing at, itself.

Courtly romance is both more and less 'realistic' than the old epic. On the one hand, like the *Huon de Bordeaux*-type poems (which they surely influenced), the romances, represented in the twelfth century by the *Romans de Tristan* of Béroul and Thomas and by the five long narratives of Chrétien de Troyes, turn away from national history and immediate feudal problems. A lone knight, a Lancelot or an Yvain, undergoes adventures, rites, and ordeals, a symbolic initiation, in an Arthurian Other World setting. A new quality of poetry, of 'faerie,' enters into French literature for the first time. It is also true that the theme of pilgrimage or the quest on the part of a lone knight allows the poet to engage in a deeper psychological analysis than was possible in *chansons de geste*. A Chrétien or a Thomas is concerned with the inner self of his protagonist, with his life as an individual. And with *her* life, with the concerns of women – a Guinevere, a Laudine, a Lunette, and an Iseut – as well as those of men. Love has become an object of scrutiny in fiction: it inspires deeds of heroism, allowing for a more complex pattern of interpersonal relationships. Furthermore, the romance opens up vistas in a social as well as an individual sphere: we are told of the world of the court, the mores of an elite society. Chrétien treats the problem of reconciling love and marriage or love and heroism (*Yvain*), the possibility of making *fin' amor* viable in 'real life' (*Lancelot*); to do so, he juxtaposes, indeed integrates, the Other World with contemporary, twelfth-century France. With all this there comes a sense of freshness, of joy, of reawakening to life and love quite unique in world literature.

The allegorical narrative or *dit amoureux* represents a further turning inward, another step in the direction set by courtly romance. Guillaume de Lorris's *Roman de la Rose* portrays an inner quest wherein formal martial activity disappears, and the hero struggles with personified abstractions that are often aspects of his psyche. The subject of the plot is his initiation to love. This is a world of introspection; perhaps never before the age of Proust has psychological analysis been carried so far. Yet, maintaining the romance tradition of his age, Guillaume evokes evanescent beauty in an Other World setting, indeed develops patterns of archetypal imagery more consciously and overtly than Chrétien himself. And, exploiting a dream-vision frame, he capitalizes on the numen inherent when psychic redemption and integration occur in a *locus amœnus* with the aid of a sacred authority-figure. All this is transformed by Jean de Meun who, in his continuation of the *Roman*, abandons the delicate allegorical equilibrium, the poetry, and the exemplary *fin' amor* of his predecessor in favor of a strident, sarcastic demystification of romance. Although Jean proposes an ideal of universal copulation for the purposes of reproducing the species, he is no less interested in unmasking the hypocrisy of *fin' amor* and in teaching us the truth of the human condition. He exposes the human comedy in all its richness, governed by duplicity and manipulation; the exploitation of man by woman and of woman by man; and the place in our lives occupied by material concerns. His is the pre-eminent 'anti-romance' of the Middle Ages, a secular 'anatomy' in which the entire world is held up to scrutiny. Then, in the following century, Guillaume de Machaut refines the example of both masters. In some of his works (*Le Dit dou Lÿon, La Fonteinne amoureuse*) he renews the dream-vision topos of poetry and beauty in a garden of delight; in others (*Le Jugement dou Roy de Navarre, Le Voir Dit*) he ridicules *fin' amor*, undermining the conventions of love-allegory. Most of all, perhaps, Machaut elaborates the possibilities inherent in the *Ich-Erzählung*, mocking with sophisticated irony his own implied *persona* as narrator and lover-hero; in this he anticipates some of the most exciting subsequent developments in the history of fiction.

The three hundred years that extend from the Renaissance to the end of the Enlightenment represent a break with the medieval tradition of epos. On the one hand, the long poem had ceased to be the dominant form for artistic expression. The analogues of Chrétien de Troyes and Jean de Meun in this age – Rabelais, Cervantes, or Fielding – wrote in prose. Even within the domain of the muses, first the lyric, then verse tragedy occupied the center of the stage, as it were, leaving other genres in the wings. This does not mean that poets did not yearn after success in epic. On the contrary, under the influence of the Greco-Latin classics, they placed the Virgilian *poëme heroïque* at the apex of the hierarchy and sought to imitate it, to make it live again in their own age. Reverence for Antiquity and, at the same time, desire to prove the Moderns equal to the Ancients; pride in their vernacular tongues; patriotism, and the will to praise the origins of the nation or of the reigning House; a sense of Christian responsibility; the desire to promulgate the education of princes – these are some of the forces that moved poets to invoke the heroic muse. Renaissance epics were conceived as anti-romances or super-romances, with a Christian, pagan, or allegorical supernatural substituted for the old enchantments, and modern and classical Reason for the old popular story-telling. Unfortunately, forced onto a Procrustean bed of theory, endeavoring to imitate in every detail Virgil or Tasso, many of the Renaissance-Baroque-Classical-Enlightenment epicists failed in their quest. They were not able to make theoretical prescriptions live in a vital, modern work of art, to create organically, in harmony with the aspirations of their society. Among the most noteworthy examples in the French tradition are Ronsard and Voltaire, each the greatest poet of his century, each of whom sought renown in an epic poem (*La Franciade*; *La Henriade*) that the majority of scholars today consider to be, at best, mediocre.

Nevertheless, the shortcomings of the Renaissance epic ought not to be exaggerated. Failures there were, as in the Middle Ages and the modern period, yet we judge the courtly romance by the triumphs of a Béroul, a Chrétien, and a Jean Renart, not by the vastly more numerous texts read today only by a handful of scholars. Similarly, the critic should esteem the Renaissance for innovation and originality when they do occur. In spite of the stress on critical theory in those days (comparable to our own), with the best of poets a discrepancy soon developed between theory and practice. The force of literary creation was too strong to be smoothed by classical precept. The masters of epic rarely challenged the authority of the Ancients but ignored them or rationalized their own innovations. And great poems were written in new ways, considered to be imperfect by critics, but quite acceptable to the reader, then and now. Ronsard himself, although his *Franciade* did not satisfy expectations, proved in any case to be the finest practitioner of the sublime style in his generation and century. The *Hymnes* are splendid cosmic, mythological poems that combine learning, a reconstitution of Greek myth, and patterns of sublime imagery; the *Discours* are passionately satirical invectives that plumb the apocalyptic and the demonic in a new way, that launch a kind of committed, political verse. These are the appropriate forerunners of the nineteenth-century *Kurzepos*. However, the high point of the epic occurred during the baroque period. Agrippa d'Aubigné continued the tradition of Ronsard's *Discours*, offering a thunderous response to the Catholic poet of Catholic princes. *Les Tragiques* is a splendid modern epic treating of contemporary times, yet, typologically, including all of sacred and secular history; the protagonists are the Protestant people and d'Aubigné the implied author; the theme is the triumph of a God of Love and his servants over cruel adversaries. Pierre Le Moyne, probably without ever having known d'Aubigné's work, proposed a final Catholic solution to the religious question: *Saint Louis* is a militant epic of the Counter-Reformation. Based upon French national history and developing patterns of imagery to be found in *Les Tragiques*, Le Moyne wrote a *poëme heroïque* in the Tassian style, recounting the total, absolute triumph over Saracen adversaries of the Church Militant united with the House of France. Le Moyne's work contrasts sharply with Saint-Amant's *Moyse sauvé*, a curiously eclectic yet original treatment of the story of Moses in the bullrushes, which elaborates a pastoral motif within a typological vision of history. All three epics reject the relatively simple, linear mode of story-telling to be found in the Greco-Roman and medieval epos in favor of a more complex, convoluted narrative technique; they also have in common the religious militancy we associate with the Reformation and the Catholic Renaissance. Whether the faith espoused is that of passive endurance (d'Aubigné) or self-confident will to power (Le Moyne), whether the subject forms part of sacred (Saint-Amant) or profane (Le Moyne) history, the Christian theme predominates; both *figura* and allegory form an intellectual frame of reference more pervasive even than in the Middle Ages.

The period from 1670 up to the Romantic revolution is weak in formal epic. Although elegance, refinement, and wit are not favorable to manifestations of the sublime, yet this period made a major contribution to the development of the long poem in France: it created and perfected the mock-epic. Given the religious motif so prevalent in the Baroque, it is perhaps not coincidental that the four greatest neoclassical *poëmes heroï-comiques* (Boileau's *Le Lutrin*; Gresset's *Ver-Vert*; Voltaire's *La Pucelle*; Parny's *La Guerre des Dieux*) contain elements of anticlerical satire. Boileau's poem is a charming, witty caricature of Virgilian and French epos that also derides those vices presumed inherent in Parisian canons and chaplains: gluttony, sloth, envy, anger, ignorance, and pride of position. Voltaire's work is of greater scope. A parody on neoclassical epos à la Boileau, it also salutes Ariosto's *Orlando furioso*; *La Pucelle* is a delightfully brisk narrative in its own right as well as mordant satire. And Voltaire's comments on the human condition open out to include the War of the Sexes and the myths of French national history. He demystifies beliefs concerning love, war, and national honor, creating a world of the imagination based on sex and violence, reification and bestiality, obsession with the body, and staccato, syncopated motion. How ironic that whereas this man failed in *La Henriade*, in *La Pucelle* he composed the satirical epic of the rococo Enlightenment and, in an extraordinary conjunction of the centuries, recaptured much of the spirit of Jean de Meun's *Roman de la Rose*!

In France as in England, the first half of the nineteenth century represents a renewal of epic activity. Continuity with the classical tradition was maintained. The leading romantic poets and many secondary ones, conscious of the formal epic conventions, either reacted against them or sought to renew them on their own terms. For Lamartine and Vigny, the epic was as pre-eminent a genre, as lofty in the esthetic hierarchy, as in the days of Ronsard or Boileau. Yet, while continuing to respect classical values, they no longer imitated the Ancients in detail. On the contrary, possessed with new Germanic or native French models (Milton, Klopstock, Fénelon), they realized that the best way to become Virgil was to be themselves. And, despite theoretical obstacles, despite a number of semi-failures, the success of the Romantics in the domain of the long poem, even when their efforts survive only as fragments, cannot be denied. This was one of the great 'epic periods' in the history of French literature.

Lamartine's ambition was to compose a gargantuan series of poems that would recount the evolution of a human soul and of mankind over the centuries. The most successful of these 'Visions,' *Jocelyn*, also partakes of the pastoral mode, indeed is one of the most striking domestic idylls of the time. Lamartine romanticizes modern life by exploiting the rustic vein (a semi-'exotic' portrayal of the Alps) and at the same time probes into the human soul, exploring problems both erotic and metaphysical that beset a young seminarist. Torn between love and duty, Jocelyn's psyche exhibits symptoms of neurosis quite modern in flavor, fascinating to a twentieth-century reader. Alfred de Vigny chose a different medium, the brief epic, for works which he labeled simply *poëmes*. These are mystical or philosophical texts written in a dense, lofty style, reminiscent of Ronsard's *Hymnes*. They exploit symbolic patterns of imagery to illustrate Vigny's major concerns: the injustice of God to man, the tyranny of kings toward their subjects, the inability of human beings either to communicate with each other or to achieve happiness. Finally, Victor Hugo brought to a culmination the epic activity of his generation. Of his three major projects in this line, two remained incomplete. *Dieu* is a philosophical-didactic meditation that can be considered a theistic response to the questioning of Lamartine and Vigny. *La Fin de Satan* and *La Légende des Siècles* are *épopées*

*humanitaires* in the tradition of Lamartine, the second conceived as a sequence of brief epics in the spirit of Vigny and Leconte de Lisle. Hugo
brought to the French epic a sense of vast dimensions, of historical and
cosmic vistas, that had been lost since the time of d'Aubigné; he also was
capable of a profusion of both apocalyptic and demonic imagery that gives
his works unique power. He plumbs the depths of universal misery only
to proclaim the redemption of mankind and of the fallen angel, Satan,
become again Lucifer the light-bearer.

The Romantics shared a concern for major issues, a quest for values typical of an age that no longer accepted those classical-Christian postulates that
had ruled Europe for almost two millenia. Their poetry turns inward; the
center of interest is now the poet's or his protagonist's inner life, his reaction
to the world around him; and their style is always at least semi-lyrical.
The 'unheroic hero' or a representative of mankind is the protagonist. Yet,
although traditional values are questioned, although to some extent man
creates his own self, as in an earlier age the author is aware of the divinity
and of his relationship to man. These texts are metaphysical as well as
historical; they open out to the heavens as well as backwards in time, and no
one testifies more than the agnostic Vigny to the Christological obsession
of the age.

Although the generation of Rimbaud, Verlaine, and Mallarmé witnessed a lull in the production of epos comparable to that of the fifteenth and
eighteenth centuries, in our time we find a resurgence of the sublime style
in various forms. A first step was traced by the Catholic Revival, for, in
addition to their many other virtues, Claudel's *Cinq Grandes Odes* and
*Cantate à trois voix*, along with Péguy's entire corpus, proved that Mallarmé was not the only model for the century. More recently, Saint-John
Perse, Aragon, and Pierre Emmanuel have made major contributions to the
elaboration of a modern epos: a long poem, containing both narrative and
lyrical elements, composed in the sublime style and illustrating the problems
that bedevil man in our era.

It is obvious that the epicist faces greater difficulties now than at any other
time in the history of the genre. For the last hundred years or so, since the
death of Hugo, most critics, and the public, have assumed that epos as a
literary kind is dead. The old conventions, whether of Homer, Virgil,
Tasso, Milton, or Hugo himself, are presumed to be inadequate, and the old
community of spirit non-existent. If an epic is to treat of the past, then
historical accuracy is required far beyond the powers of most imaginative
writers; such accuracy in any case would diminish the sense of poetry and
myth. And if an epicist is to treat the present, then he must portray the
tawdriness, ugliness, and corruption of modern life, a prosaic environment and unheroic characters, once again leaving no room for flights of the
imagination.

The poets of the different nations have responded each in his own way to this problem. In Russian literature Blok, Mayakovsky, and their disciples have sung with epic fervor of the Revolution and of a new socialist society, recreating in our times the commitment of medieval *geste* but employing a version of *sermo humilis*, the rough, vigorous, common speech of the new Soviet man. In the United States the most successful achievement comes from Eliot and Pound, who face the reality of society head-on, but, unlike the Russians, and unlike their compatriots Sandburg, Crane, and Williams, who exalt the modern, they write from an ironic perspective, using history and myth to undermine contemporary barbarism. The French solution, on the other hand (and the German: Spitteler, Däubler, Döblin), has been to comment on the contemporary world symbolically or allegorically by splendid, supremely poetical evocations of a mythical or historical past. Hence, Pierre Emmanuel treats Greek and Biblical myth (*Tombeau d'Orphée, Babel, Sodome, Jacob*); Aragon paints symbolic frescos taken from European history (the Celtic Middle Ages in *Brocéliande*, the Fall of Granada in *Le Fou d'Elsa*); and Saint-John Perse evokes semi-Oriental primitive societies (*Anabase, Amers*). None of these men is a skeptic; each is moved by ideals and passions: for a sensuous life of esthetic beauty (Perse); for the liberation of mankind through the class struggle (Aragon); for the salvation of mankind through union with God (Emmanuel). All three poets adhere to the style of verse launched by Rimbaud, Mallarmé, Valéry, and Apollinaire: that is, they do not hesitate to indulge in incongruous form and style, shock effects, broken syntax, obscurity, and hermeticism, and, on a thematic level, to create a sense of dehumanization, alienation, *Angst, Verfremdung*, and the grotesque.[1] For the nihilist Perse, for the Catholic Emmanuel, even for the Communist Aragon, modern epic is based not upon a common ideology but upon the quest for ideology, the challenge to find values for the individual and his community. The inner history of man, the poet-protagonist's own search, becomes the subject of epos, and the life of the spirit our modern heroism.

Like any other genre, the epic evolves over the centuries, shifting in form and content, influenced by the forces that shaped literature as a whole. From the Middle Ages to the twentieth century the long poem undergoes a more or less steady decline, not in quantity or quality but in what we may call its centrality within the tradition. During the Middle Ages, the dominant form, it received almost no critical attention whatsoever: in the vernacular, at any rate, the Medievals were creators, craftsmen aware of their heritage but unused to theorizing except in the most rudimentary or purely technical manner. From 1500 on, although epos was granted the highest position in the hierarchy and enjoyed a vast amount of critical scrutiny, the most vital energies of the writing trade were channeled into

other domains: the lyric, verse drama, even the novel. The period from
1800 to the present represents a decline first in prescriptive theory about a
particular genre (the Romantics believed in epic but not at all in epic
rules), then in the conventional hierarchy of genres, and finally in the very
notion of literary genre at all: that is, Lamartine was desperately eager to
round off his career with a triumph in epic; following Poe, Valéry felt that
the 'long poem' is impossible, a flat contradiction in terms; and members
of the *Tel Quel* and *Change* groups urge that all works of literature be
designated *textes* or *tranches d'écriture*. Hence the critical commonplace,
elaborated by Hegel and Lukács among others, that the novel, born from
the epic, succeeded to its dead parent, and therefore that prose fiction
(Fielding, Balzac, Tolstoy, Mann, Joyce) *is* the epic of the modern world.
The days of Chrétien de Troyes and Guillaume de Machaut, even of
Lamartine and Hugo, are over. A case can be made that this evolution has
been beneficial to the long poem as a purely esthetic manifestation, that
the genre suffered when adulated by critic and poet alike and has prospered
when freed from the tyranny of rules (the Middle Ages, the Baroque,
Romanticism), even from the tyranny of readers (the twentieth century).
For, during the great periods of epic success, authors were free to invent
the kind of stories and characters they wanted, to juxtapose high, middle,
and low styles, to strive for credibility of plot and concreteness of
imagery, and to indulge in the ideological venture that most suited them,
including the slow but sure rise of a kind of 'realism' that in the modern
world has triumphed over other literary modes.

If the evolution of the long poem over the last four hundred years
involves a loosening of the vise of prescriptive theory (starting with
d'Aubigné and Saint-Amant), it also assumes a steadily increasing source of
influences, especially foreign epic models. French was the oldest, the
richest, and the most autonomous literature in the Middle Ages. Aside from
Celtic myth, poets such as Chrétien de Troyes, Guillaume de Lorris, Jean
de Meun, and Guillaume de Machaut were familiar only with Latin and
Occitan texts in addition to the French – indeed, all four were avid
readers and translators of Virgil and Ovid. With the Renaissance Homer,
Hesiod, Apollonius, and Callimachus were added to the list, as were first
Ariosto, then Tasso, Marino, and Tassoni. In time the Germanic muse
influenced French epos, first Milton, then Klopstock, finally Byron and
Shelley. The epicists of our own century range over all of world literature,
from the *griot* songs of the Caribbean (Perse) to the culture of medieval
Islam (Aragon), to a synthesis of the Old Testament, d'Aubigné, and
Hölderlin (Emmanuel). With regard both to rules and foreign models, the
French epic has evolved in the direction of freedom, of an 'opening out,'
as has, for that matter, the literary tradition in its entirety.

It is also true that over the ages the long poem has been influenced by forms and modes other than epic, especially by those dominant in a particular period. Already in the Middle Ages for both Chrétien de Troyes and Guillaume de Lorris troubadour songs fostered psychological analysis and propagated the ideology of *fin' amor*; and the *dit amoureux* was shaped by a tradition of didacticism in medieval letters. This latter trend helps explain a shift from pure narrative in early *chanson de geste* to the quasi-encyclopedic form of Jean de Meun's *Roman de la Rose*. Heroic and pastoral romance had an effect on the baroque epic: the erotic elements in Saint-Amant and Le Moyne are derived at least as much from d'Urfé, La Calprenède, and Scudéry as from Virgil and Tasso. To the extent that seventeenth-century romances were indeed considered 'epics in prose,' they provided both stimulus and competition for the *poëmes heroïques* of the 1650s.[2] Le Moyne was also influenced by the plays of Corneille, especially by the latter's notion of heroism, as an antidote to those very romances that he disapproved of but also had to come to terms with. Finally, in the modern period, it is obvious that the epic has been molded by the novel and, even more, by the lyric. Lamartine's *Jocelyn* and Aragon's *Le Fou d'Elsa* can be characterized as novels in verse; both of these poems, plus the works of Saint-John Perse, contain, indeed *are*, continuous lyrical effusions. The tendency of the twentieth-century epic is to become a collection of lyrics, counterbalanced by prosaic, distancing narrative counterpoint, a questioning and undermining of the lyrical (cf. Emmanuel's *Babel*) that is derived from prose fiction. I submit that it is to the credit of Perse, Aragon, and Emmanuel that their opus was enriched by the most vital currents of the age. Only a dead or dying genre remains pure unto itself. The strength of the long poem, from the century of *Raoul de Cambrai* and *Yvain* to our own, has been its capacity to modify its needs and goals, to adapt, to remain supple and resilient, thus to survive.

Granting that this is true and that French epicists have over the centuries been influenced by an ever-growing number of native and foreign sources, I also wish to state that poets, whether of the past or present, are not scholars, that their knowledge of literature is necessarily fluctuating and limited. Some epicists are well-read, open to a culture of world-wide proportions (Jean de Meun, Saint-Amant, Hugo, Aragon), others noticeably less so (the singers of *geste*, Boileau, Lamartine, Saint-John Perse). Furthermore, as the centuries flow past, although new works enter the literary current, old ones are lost to all but a few antiquaries or professors of literature. Even within the Middle Ages, for example, although Guillaume de Lorris was familiar with Virgil, Ovid, Chrétien de Troyes, and the troubadours, it is quite likely that the *chanson de geste* no longer formed part of his literary background. Pierre Le Moyne, Boileau, and Voltaire had a different notion of epic than did Ronsard because they loved or hated that giant Torquato Tasso; however, they were ignorant of the medieval tradition, whereas Ronsard loved *Le Roman de la Rose* and was familiar with some aspects of *chanson de geste*. Similarly, in our time epicists have at their fingertips a *Weltliteratur* of staggering richness, but, in the process, Ariosto and Tasso have lost their seminal force and, except inside Italy, become more 'obscure' than French Arthurian romance.

The development of epos in France then is shaped by two forces: archetypal cohesion within the mode, and the normal evolution of literary history, shaped and controlled by the imitation of predecessors and adherence to theoretical precepts. That is, to cite one example, if Guillaume de Lorris assimilates the woman-imago to a rose, he does so for unconscious archetypal reasons and because he had seen the woman-rose metaphor in Horace, Ovid, Tibullus, and Ausonius. The esthetics of reception elaborated by Wolfgang Iser and Hans Robert Jauss tells us that although the 'epic' or 'narrative' genre cannot be a fixed norm, it does serve as a complex of directives for the reader and for the poet himself. It is an invitation to writing within a conventional pattern that inevitably helps shape a work in progress and its interpretation by the public. Furthermore, since genres and genre expectations evolve in time, as more works are written the quantity of potential sources increases, and the normative pattern becomes more complex. Epic is not the same, the reader's and the poet's expectations of it differ, after the appearance on the scene of 'brusque mutations' such as the *Aeneid, Le Roman de la Rose, Orlando furioso, la Gerusalemme liberata, Paradise Lost,* and *La Légende des Siècles,* to cite a few noteworthy examples.

In the course of French literary history there are times when epos flowers and other times when the crop proves to be less rich: some generations produce more than one masterpiece, others none at all. Epic will dominate one period, decline in another, then be renewed in a third. The great moments are the early Middle Ages (the twelfth and thirteenth centuries), the early and high Baroque, Romanticism, and the contemporary; the fallow epochs are the late Middle Ages and early Renaissance (1400–1550), Classicism and the Enlightenment (with the exception of the comic epic), and the period including Symbolism and Naturalism, extending from the death of Hugo to the Catholic Revival and the appearance of Saint-John Perse. It is obvious that epic ebbs and flows to form some kind of cycle. Curiously, for both the Middle Ages and Renaissance-Classicism taken in its broadest sense, a similar pattern of evolution can be observed. That is, epos bursts upon the scene with an archaic or experimental work of power, idealism, and almost classical perfection (*La Chanson de Roland*; Ronsard's *Hymnes* and *Discours*). The mode then develops in two directions: 1 / toward realism, concreteness, political commitment, and formal diffuseness (*Raoul de Cambrai; Les Tragiques*); and 2 / toward concern with Eros and the theme of the quest, that is, the wish-fulfillment world of romance (*Huon de Bordeaux* and works by Chrétien de Troyes and Guillaume de Lorris; *Moyse sauvé* and *Saint Louis*). The romance element remains dominant for a time but eventually yields to a spirit that can be qualified as 'anti-romantic,' characterized by encyclopedic or didactic pretensions and social satire, which undermine the genre as a whole (Jean de Meun and Guillaume de Machaut; *Le Lutrin* and *La Pucelle*). With this extreme form of sophistication the genre peters out; the cycle is complete. It is surely not coincidental that three of the most refined, mannered periods of French literature – the ages of Charles d'Orléans, Marivaux, and Mallarmé – were the least propitious for the writing of long poems, and that a comparable evolution, from epos to romance to the didactic and the satirical, governs the great tradition of Persian letters, which, incidentally, covers approximately the same centuries as the French Middle Ages. If my analysis is correct, it could add support to the cyclical theory proposed by Focillon and others to explain the evolution of art history: a medieval sequence of romanesque, gothic, *rayonnant*, and *flamboyant* styles which correspond to the experimental, High Renaissance, mannerist, and baroque of a later epoch. Be that as it may, we do face a problem in accommodating any such structure to the literature of the last two centuries. The third great subdivision of the epic in France (1800–19—), does not conform at all to the evolution of the preceding two. The only hypothesis I can make (and I do so in the most tentative manner possible) is that Romanticism ought to be considered as the end of a Renaissance-baroque-classical-rococo curve. The romantic style would correspond to the *flamboyant* of the waning Middle Ages, Lamartine would be analogous to Charles d'Orléans, and Hugo both to Villon and the mystery plays. In that case, Saint-John Perse and his successors are launching an experimental phase, preceded in literature by Rimbaud and Mallarmé, in the fine arts by Cézanne and Picasso – and our twentieth-century art forms represent the beginnings of a totally new style that will perhaps take centuries to evolve before it becomes assimilated in the annals of literary history.

Despite this ebb and flow, what is most amazing about the evolution of long poem in France is its continuity. Although individual decades or generations can be unproductive and some are less rich than others, there is nonetheless a surge of masterpieces over the centuries, from the early Middle Ages to the present. All centuries, with the possible exception of the fifteenth, make a significant contribution. In this respect, France is unique among the European nations, and the fortunes of epos do correspond to the development of French literature as a whole: a steady, homogeneous stream of literary masterpieces launched by the *Saint-Alexis* in the middle of the eleventh century and never interrupted since.

A second observation concerns the quantity of first-rate long poems: low, compared to the number of successful comedies, novels, or collections of lyrics, yet high, given pronouncements that each nation shall be represented by one and only one epic. If we consider the hundreds of plays produced in the seventeenth century and the relatively few masterworks created by Corneille, Racine, Molière, and Rotrou; if we consider the thousands of novels published in the eighteenth and nineteenth centuries and the quite limited number of outstanding texts that extend from *Gil Blas* to *La Bête humaine* – then it can be posited that our epicists have done their job with equivalent competence. Although the number of great epics in the history of French literature is small, few are the daring souls who composed them in the first place. From the point of view of quality, the writing trade is much the same whatever one sets out to do and whatever age one does it in.

Looking back over the development of the epic in France (and over the eighteen chapters that make up this book), I find it an ordeal (in the medieval sense) to isolate the traits common to all or most long narrative poems that can be said to define the genre. The absence of unifying characteristics justifies *ex post facto* my decision to consider the long poem as a formal entity and to work from an inductive rather than a deductive frame of reference. Thus, I repeat the hypothesis sketched out in my Introduction: that the majority of definitions of epic, based upon too narrow a corpus, cannot encompass the tradition as a whole.

Such skepticism certainly is valid with regard to themes, motifs, even scenes and stock characters pervasive during the Renaissance but not necessarily so in the Middle Ages or in modern times: the voyage to the underworld, the heavenly vision, the marshalling of the troops, the enchanted garden, the storm at sea, the warrior maiden, the sorcerer, the temptress, and so on. No serious modern critic would exclude from the corpus of epic a work because it fails to include specific Virgilian motifs or even because its overall structure is not patterned after the *Aeneid* or the *Gerusalemme liberata.*

I believe that a comparable situation exists for the very heart of epic, the war-motif, which proves to be by no means as universal as most people suppose. True, the *Iliad,* the *Aeneid,* and most *chansons de geste* are songs of deeds in arms, and, at least in the Latin and French traditions, epics exalt the people, the race, and the nation. This martial pattern is an essential component in early epos that helps explain the origins of the mode. However, already in the *Odyssey,* not to speak of the *Argonautica* and Ovid's *Metamorphoses,* we find a more private, more intimate, more individual-

oriented notion of heroism, based as much upon cunning as upon brute
force. From this vantage-point, the *romans courtois* of Béroul, Thomas,
Chrétien, and Jean Renart conform to the tradition of the *Odyssey*, indeed
go farther in certain 'romance directions': analysis of the individual
psyche; the knight's personal relationship to his lady, to his king, or to
society as a whole; and a series of rites of passage in which prowess
constitutes only one among many elements to be tested. And in medieval
erotic allegory heroism in any form largely disappears from the action.
Although war reappears as a dominant theme in most Renaissance *poëmes
heroïques*, the need to integrate Christian subjects or a Christ-oriented
world view results in a series of epics in which scenes of battle and even
formal heroism are lacking: this is true, in absolute terms, for Sannazaro's
*De partu Virginis*, du Bartas's *La Sepmaine*, and Milton's *Paradise Re-
gained*, and, to some extent, for Vida's *Christias* and Saint-Amant's *Moyse
sauvé*. Since 1800, with the exception of *La Légende des Siècles*, *Anabase*,
and *Brocéliande*, all major poems either ignore heroism altogether or
propose a new kind of virile behavior that dispenses with the trade of arms.
It is also interesting to note the number of long poems in the tradition that
denounce the evils of war or of nationalism or both: *Raoul de Cambrai*,
*Girard de Roussillon*, *Garin le Lorrain*; *Les Tragiques*, Voltaire's *Pucelle*;
*Jocelyn*, *La Légende des Siècles*, *Le Fou d'Elsa*, and the collected meditations on Scripture by Pierre Emmanuel.

A theory, widespread among Germanic and some Anglo-Saxon critics and
given weight by Lukács, states that the epic corresponds to and reflects a
primitive, spontaneous mentality, derived from a heroic age that precedes
our complex, humdrum modern civilization.[3] According to Lukács, *das
Epische*, as opposed to the spirit of tragedy or of the novel, creates a world
on the human scale, its elements immediately meaningful to the literary
characters and public, with life grasped as a total process and social institutions conceived as both stable and organic. The Hellenic *Weltanschauung*,
one of harmonious unity and totality, would then contrast sharply with the
fragmented, alienated spirit of the modern West. This world view characterizes with reasonable accuracy the oldest Greek epic, the *Iliad*, and the
oldest French epic, *La Chanson de Roland*. It can also be found in certain
modern poets, specifically Pierre Le Moyne and Saint-John Perse. But the
majority of long poems scrutinized in this book manifest a complex,
fragmented world view comparable to that of Shakespearean, Racinian, or
Goethean tragedy or of the modern novel. *La Chanson de Roland* itself
is, on the political and psychological levels, a far more sophisticated, ambivalent work than, say, Auerbach would want us to believe. And those
modern epics that attain some sort of harmonious, total vision of the
world do so because their authors project, consciously (Perse) or uncon-

sciously (Le Moyne), their wish-fulfillment fantasies upon a bygone, semi-fictional Golden Age. Epos in France is as rich, as refined, as any other genre, and the notion we have been discussing derives from the Romantics, who imposed on the past a conceptual framework which tells us a great deal about them but nothing about the reality of the literature they chose to discuss.

Traits common to the majority of long poems would have to be of a different nature, dependent upon inner form or deep structure. Although not a contradiction in terms, the 'long poem' is, by its nature, a complex, ambivalent mode partaking of the narrative (or philosophical or satirical) and the lyrical at the same time. Adding 'poetry' to a narrative component means, inevitably, that certain aspects of fiction endemic to the modern novel – psychological analysis, a mimetic representation of reality – will be sacrificed to story-telling; therefore, in spite of the existence of 'novels in verse' such as *Jocelyn* or *Le Fou d'Elsa*, the epic mode will normally veer away from neo-realism toward archetypal patterns of romance. Similarly, in spite of these lyrical elements, whether they be independent poems inserted into a narrative framework (Machaut, Lamartine, Hugo, Aragon, Pierre Emmanuel) or simply a heightening of tension, a functional aspect of 'song' that contributes organically to the 'tone' of the opus as a whole (Turold, Ronsard, Saint-John Perse), epos will always shy away from the subjective, meditative, private voice in favor of a more objective, public vision. Its temper is sanguine, perhaps choleric (Ronsard, d'Aubigné, Voltaire, Hugo, Pierre Emmanuel), never lymphatic and rarely melancholic (Lamartine), or the melancholic is treated with wit and humor (Chrétien de Troyes, Machaut). Finally, the epic has always been an 'aristocratic' genre, characterized by pomp, ceremony, a festal aura, and a heightened, sublime diction, destined for an elite public: the aristocratic court of the Middle Ages and Renaissance, the only audience that literature could reach in those days; or the intellectual public of our era, the only one that persists in reading books that rhyme.

It is obvious from the critical approaches I have explored in the preceding eighteen chapters that I believe most French epics adhere in one way or another to the archetypal pattern of heroism or romance as formulated by Jung, Rank, Lord Raglan, Campbell, Baudouin, and de Vries. Some poems will concentrate upon the protagonist's miraculous birth and childhood adventures (*Moyse sauvé*, *La Chute d'un Ange*), others upon his death and apotheosis (*Tombeau d'Orphée*, *Le Fou d'Elsa*), still others upon the dream-vision which permits him to be initiated into divine mysteries (*Le Roman de la Rose*, *Les Tragiques*, *Dieu*). But in almost all cases we find a structure of withdrawal and return, of the great adventure, a road of trials and ordeals including struggle with adversaries – a rite of passage which leads to conquest of the unknown, knowledge, and attainment of sovereignty, the protagonist learning to become a man and the master of his world. This is true even when the heroic quest motif is undermined, whether in the tragic mode (*Raoul de Cambrai*, *Les Tragiques*, *La Légende des Siècles*) or in the satiric (*Huon de Bordeaux*, Jean de Meun's *Roman de la Rose*, *Le Jugement dou Roy de Navarre*, *Le Lutrin*, *La Pucelle*).

The poet's attitude toward woman is quite varied: he has the option of treating his heroine as a temptress, a sex-object in the non-pejorative sense (*le repos du guerrier*), a transmitter of courtly inspiration, a redeemer, a bride (the final reward), or a martial companion. It has been claimed that two patterns evolved in the course of Western civilization: the first, in which the divine or semi-divine authority-figure is male and the protagonist an adult, a symbolic father with respect to the women he encounters, derives from a conservative, masculine mentality, centering on deeds in arms, in which reason triumphs over passion; the second, in which the authority-figure is a woman and the hero, a child with respect to her, commits himself to the practice of Eros and, to some extent, suffers as an innocent victim, derives from the Eternal Feminine.[4] The martial tradition is, of course, exemplified in Homer, Virgil, and *chansons de geste*, the courtly in Apollonius Rhodius, Ovid, medieval romance and love-allegory. Although the masculine-oriented pattern is perhaps central to the notion of heroic epic, the feminine one serves as an alternative, heretical pole to which the epicist can turn and by which he is ever tempted. Ronsard, d'Aubigné, and Le Moyne remain faithful to the masculine formulation as do the mock-epicists Scarron, Boileau, Voltaire, and Parny; the romantic and post-romantic poets – especially Lamartine, Hugo, Aragon, and, in part, Pierre Emmanuel – proclaim the doctrine of redemption through woman and the ideal of peace not war. During the Middle Ages and various post-medieval centuries the feminine vision appears as a more 'modern,' anti-heroic alternative to the original epic scheme. This pattern, however, in no way prevents poets in an 'age of romance,' such as Jean de Meun, Vigny, and Saint-John Perse, from preferring the old virtues. And a case can be made that baroque epos as a whole, and its twentieth-century equivalent (the 'resistance epic' of Aragon and Pierre Emmanuel), stand as a conservative, public, masculine-oriented reaction against literary modes devoted to frivolity, love, and effete esthetic play.

Whether the protagonist atones with a father-god or a mother-goddess, he himself is, at least metaphorically, a hero in the Greek sense, a demigod greater in force, vision, attainments, and circumstance than other men. Limited only by mortality, even when he does not participate in the martial life, when he only dreams, loves, composes poems, and dies (cf. Guillaume de Lorris, Guillaume de Machaut, Lamartine, Aragon, Pierre Emmanuel), his existence is one of grandeur, and his non-martial activities proclaim a new, different heroism in place of the old. This does not mean that the tragic vision is absent from epos: *La Chanson de Roland* contains tragic elements, as do *Raoul de Cambrai* and many other *chansons de geste*, Ronsard's *Discours*, d'Aubigné's *Les Tragiques*, and the entire epic corpus of Lamartine, Vigny, Hugo, Leconte de Lisle, Aragon, and Pierre Emmanuel. But in most of these works, the chief exception being Lamartine, the tragic is Cornelian rather than Racinian in nature; that is, admiration surpasses pity, and the hero's destiny is truly exemplary, for even when he is a tyrant or rebel, he remains a model for men to follow. This can help to explain why, in most cases, our epicists are committed writers, promulgating high ideals. Whether they support the feudal aristocracy or the king, Catholics or Protestants, an elite or the masses, their works are also meant to be exemplary, to teach us how to live.

Finally, I should like to emphasize the fact that all the poems studied in this book, without exception, contain elements of the supernatural, and that, but for mock-epic, the marvelous is an inherent, organic ingredient in the epicist's world-view – whether or not he evokes specific neoclassical motifs such as the journey to the underworld. The theme of epic is transcendence, in both an earthly and cosmic sense. Therefore, I wish to claim that the mode or genre has a religious orientation even when specific poets happen to be agnostics or atheists, as is the case with Vigny and Aragon, who sing of the individual rebelling against God or of the masses rebelling against an earthly tyrant. It is no coincidence that the *chanson de geste* was originally a song of the crusades, allied to hagiography in its constitutive form; that the best baroque poems are Biblical or, at any rate, oriented toward a synthesis of sacred and secular history; and that since 1789 several of the leading epicists have either sought to renew the old Catholic tradition or to launch a new religion in its place.

The issues I have raised in this Conclusion – a shift in readers' expectations, in taste, and in literary culture over the centuries, as well as the continuity of epos, those traits common to the sublime spirit everywhere – have implications for the future creation and appreciation of epic. On the one hand, the French critic, when he thinks of poetry, evokes fashionable modern lyricists, not Virgil, Turold, Chrétien de Troyes, Tasso, and Lamartine. There is a Parisian, bourgeois prejudice against literary kinds dating from the past. Where else but in France could the following dialogue have purportedly taken place?

> Valéry: Connais-tu rien de plus embêtant que l'*Iliade*?
> Gide: Oui. *La Chanson de Roland.*

Yet, in a sense we are all the children of the Romantics and, perhaps even more, of the Symbolists. The vast majority of readers, including university professors, and not only in the Francophone world, express romantic or symbolist doctrine when it comes to defining the nature of poetry: all art entails precise, concrete mimesis of the external world of nature; poetry demands that the poet express his personal, emotional response to the world, that he bare his 'self'; all great art is sincere, authentic, and original; the language of verse manifests an *écart* from the language of prose, and each great writer creates his own, unique speech, different from that of all others. Meanwhile, the epic has been embalmed and entombed, classified as 'primary' and 'secondary,' and treated like archeology.[5] 'Epic spirit,' if it exists at all, is reserved for the detective story, the spy novel, science fiction, and the Western, perhaps for tales of adventure (Malraux, Saint-Exupéry, Lartéguy) and for the cinema of Eisenstein, Ford, and Welles.[6] Since Poe, Mallarmé, Valéry, and Eliot assume the long poem to be impossible, a great epic can only be a series of intense lyrics connected by patches of inferior verse, and the business of poetry is to cultivate the series not the patches. This romantic-symbolist bias certainly is dominant in our universities, in Parisian literary circles, and in the majority of reviews.

Fortunately, a minority of creative artists simply do not heed their own obituary notices. Critics can ring the death knell, but poets go on writing. And they succeed in producing highly successful long poems – because their intention is, in part, to shock the reader, to shatter his expectations, and because the chic, ultra-modern critics do not in fact possess the dictatorial power they lay claim to. More people still read Lamartine and Hugo than Mallarmé or Valéry. For political but also esthetic reasons Aragon will 'sell' better than, say, René Char and Yves Bonnefoy, great as these latter indubitably are. Furthermore, as 'modern' gives way to 'postmodern,' the symbolist esthetic à la Poe, Mallarmé, Valéry, and Eliot is itself in the process of revision in favor of a more objective, public, rhetorical stance, in both France and the Anglo-Saxon world. Eliot himself, as far back as 1949, wrote that 'the *art poétique* of which we find the germ in Poe, and which bore fruit in the work of Valéry, has gone as far as it can go.'[7]

It is true that one historical event launched an upsurge of heroic poetry in our time, the Occupation of France and the Resistance movement which it created. Both Aragon and Pierre Emmanuel were moved by those years, as was Saint-John Perse, who chose exile in the United States. The careers of all three men were to some extent shaped by this rupture in their lives and by their reactions to it. It is no less true that more than one observer of the French literary scene, including, of course, Benjamin Péret, considers the War years and the school of Resistance poetry to be an aberration, an interlude of no great importance in the development of twentieth-century letters. It will come as no surprise to the readers of this book that I do not share Péret's views concerning the 'dishonor of poets.' I wish to point out, however, that Perse and Aragon had practiced the lyrico-epic mode in the 1920s and 1930s (*Anabase, Hourra l'Oural*), that *Tombeau d'Orphée* was composed before the Fall of France, and that since the end of the war, over the last thirty years, all three masters have continued to explore the possibilities of the long poem. The holocaust of the 1940s is not a historical accident. It represents the spirit of our age as truly as the café-philoso-phizing of self-proclaimed mandarins. Surely *Brocéliande* is as repre-sentative of our century's life and letters as is *Un Coup de dés* or *Le Cimetière marin*. And surely those who denounce the absence nowadays of a collective consciousness, and thus deny the ontological possibility of epos, forget that in international Communism and the Roman Catholic Church are to be found two institutions eminently capable of inspiring heroic myth. Myth is as alive, as vibrant now as at any time since the twelfth century,[8] and whole new worlds (science, history, the holocaust) have been opened for poets to explore. Writers from Black Africa, Latin Amer-ica, and the Caribbean indulge in *sermo gravis*, proclaiming their heroism or protest in works of truly epic scope and vision. And Frenchmen are aware of other literatures and of their own cultural past as never before. Further-more, is it not significant that a younger generation of writers, not at all committed to the same causes as Aragon and Emmanuel, have created successful long poems? I am thinking especially of Marcelin Pleynet, one of the leaders of the *Tel Quel* group, author of *Comme* (1965) and *Stanze: Incantation dite au bandeau d'or I–IV* (1973). Pleynet, along with Denis Roche and others, seeks to mediate between structuralism and Maoist dialectical materialism as well as between Eros and the craft of writing. His *Stanze*, which betrays the influence of Marx, Freud, Lautréamont, Pound, Joyce, and, of course, Mao, repudiates ostentatiously our past culture including romantic and classical rhetoric. It breaks sexual, political, and syntactic tabus. Nonetheless, it is a long poem of consistent structure, tex-ture, and power, cutting across cultures and centuries, manifesting breadth and range. And while disdaining the tradition of, say, a Hugo, Pleynet does not refuse inspiration from Dante. *Stanze* and other works in the same vein perhaps indicate the direction that epos will take in the last quarter of our century. Pleynet and Sollers both point 'toward the new, lyrico-epic mode of writing ... indispensable generally at this point in history.'[9]

In our age poetry itself – all forms of verse – have been displaced by prose, and 'la crise de la poésie' has become a major topic of discussion. Nevertheless inside the Hexagon fifty thousand human beings practice the art, and a case can be made that post-war verse is as rich, as varied, as successful esthetically in France as anywhere on the globe and can bear comparison with comparable periods in the past: the time of the trouvères, the generation of the Pléiade, the high Baroque, or the age of Hugo, for example. People speak of the death of the novel, of tragedy, and of the written word in general, with much the same cogency. It has also been said that our age represents the end of literary genre altogether, because, more or less since Baudelaire and absolutely since Breton, each work of art repudiates its forebears and the kind to which it belongs and questions the very nature of literature. Whether or not this formulation is accurate, one can respond that even though the official genres of the past are gone, they have been replaced by new ones that fulfill the same function or, rather, they have been reshaped to conform to new expectations while maintaining their old function. To transgress an old literary kind makes it live, for transgression requires a sense of the law one is breaking; then a number of similar transgressions become a law (that is, a genre) in turn.[10]

It is, of course, impossible to predict the future. But since the long poem perseveres in our era, since it has been practiced by some of the greatest poets of our century, and since it today finds renewed inspiration in the Third World, I dare to presume that this literary kind will survive in our post-modern bourgeois or socialist world and will continue, seeking new forms, in the decades to come. After all, there are many options in the arts, and artists have a proclivity to investigate them all: one can conform to or protest against one's society; one can respond to chaos with chaos or with renewed order: the explosions of a Breton or the discipline of a Valéry; the heroism of Aragon or the rather different ethical stance of Céline.

The career of epic is one of the anomalies of history. It behooves the critical establishment in French studies to become aware of a tradition that has played so important a role in France over the last nine centuries. Otherwise, a unique segment of our heritage will be lost forever. And the very existence of the tradition should encourage us to revise the generally accepted literary canon. Not that I wish to denigrate highly esteemed periods of lyricism: the generation of the Pléiade or the period from Baudelaire to Valéry. However, from another perspective, specifically that of the long poem, greater attention ought to be paid to the early Middle Ages, the Baroque, Romanticism, and the Contemporary. Poets such as the singers of *geste*, Chrétien de Troyes, Guillaume de Lorris, Jean de Meun, Machaut, d'Aubigné, Saint-Amant, Le Moyne, Aragon, and Pierre Emmanuel would receive the plaudits they deserve and be included, as a matter of course, in the pantheon of French verse, which would then be immeasurably enriched. And other masters – Ronsard, Boileau, Voltaire, and Lamartine – would be appreciated as much for *Les Hymnes, Le Lutrin, La Pucelle*, and *Jocelyn* as for their sonnets, satires, prose tales, and meditations on love and nature. Their stature would also gain immeasurably.

We could also revise some clichés concerning the nature of poetry. Unity of tone cannot be applied to Jean de Meun and Hugo. The individual voice is as incongruous in the Middle Ages as in the century of Corneille and Boileau. Modern criteria of value – tension, ambiguity, irony, complexity, the *écart* – are useless in coping with just about all poets discussed in this book. It is perhaps time for us to return to some old notions: that art is knowledge and entertainment as well as expressivity; and that it is wrong to demand the same beauty from the humming-bird and the eagle, from a village in Quercy or Auvergne and New York City.[11] The experience of modern North American criticism, especially the writings of Northrop Frye, will help remind us that poets do not 'live it up,' nor do they reproduce external reality or their own experience: they read other poets and compose in verse; for literature is made up of rules, conventions, registers, common themes and motifs. The vocation of letters is handed down in the tradition of the 'clerks,' forming an unbroken historical succession and a professional brotherhood. In the last analysis, literature is based on and derived from other literature, it is an ontological whole in and of itself. Furthermore, literature reaches out across the ages, in terms of genre, mode, and tone: the *Raoul*-poet, d'Aubigné, Hugo, and Pierre Emmanuel have much in common; as do Turold, Le Moyne, and Saint-John Perse; Guillaume de Lorris, Saint-Amant, and Lamartine; or Jean de Meun and Voltaire. The fashions, the literary biases and conscious assumptions of any one age, whether it be Ronsard's, Boileau's, or our own, weigh little in the final balance. Eliot and Leavis bequeathed to England a sense of the tradition of their national poetry. In my opinion, France needs to become aware of her own, which, for largely external, non-literary reasons, she has up to now failed to obtain.

It is the ultimate purpose of my book to contribute, if only in a small way, to the elaboration of such a notion of tradition. In this I subscribe to Curtius's ideal of cultural continuity as the *exempla maiorum*, a perpetual celebration, preservation, rediscovery, and restoration of our culture.[12] The true Aristoi are kindred spirits over the ages who give the lie to barbarism, defined as the refusal of our past heritage or the denial of creativity in the present. Culture is open-ended and cumulative rather than substitutive: great works of the past are rediscovered at the same time that new ones are born. Malraux is surely correct in positing as one of the glories of our age the fact that, for the first time in the history of the globe, we are capable of appreciating esthetic beauty derived from all climes and times: Chinese bronzes and Japanese prints, Indian ragas and African drum-beats, romanesque churches and Persian mosques, and, of course, our own Western literary heritage in its entirety. Under these circumstances, we need not fear the birth of an Aquarian Eon, for our culture will survive and grow with us; man will continue to build, paint, compose, write, play, and sing – as he has always done and ever shall do.

In the last analysis, the French epicists provide no answers. Great poets never do. They only ask questions and create visions of man. Their poems of war and love, of fire and roses, illuminate the crises of their own times, and more. The crises and the visions have never died; the flames still flicker over the ages, down the centuries, and across the seas, to us today.

# Notes

Critical works are cited in shortened form. Complete reference is to be found in the Bibliography.

## INTRODUCTION

1 *Essai sur la poésie épique*, in *Œuvres complètes de Voltaire*, ed. Louis Moland, vol. 8 (Paris: Garnier, 1877), p. 363. In context, Malézieu comments negatively on the French public, not on French writers. See Saulnier, 'Voltaire, Malézieu et la tête épique.'
2 Levrault, *L'Épopée*; Citoleux, *La Voie royale de la poésie française*; Germain, *L'Art de commenter une épopée*. Simon, *Le Domaine héroïque des lettres françaises*, cannot be considered a serious work of scholarship in the modern sense. In contrast, see the various papers devoted to Greek, Roman, and French epos presented to the 1978 Congress of the Association Guillaume Budé: *Association Guillaume Budé: Actes du Xe Congrès*.
3 *Le Triomphe du héros*.
4 Greene, *The Descent from Heaven*; Pollmann, *Das Epos in den romanischen Literaturen*.
5 I consulted the most recent editions of Littré, the *Dictionnaire de l'Académie Française*, the *Grand Larousse*, the 'Grand Robert,' the *Oxford English Dictionary*, *Webster's New International Dictionary*, and six Dictionaries of Literary Terms chosen at random.
6 Useful here were Abercrombie, *The Epic*; Lewis, *A Preface to 'Paradise Lost'*; Bowra, *From Virgil to Milton*; Tillyard, *The English Epic and Its Background*; Germain, *L'Art*; McNamee, *Honor and the Epic Hero*; Greene, *Descent*; Sellier, *Le Mythe du héros ou le désir d'être Dieu*; Merchant, *The Epic*.
7 *English Epic*, and *The Epic Strain in the English Novel*.
8 This view is prevalent in the study of English literature: see Sewell, *The Orphic Voice*; Pearce, *The Continuity of American Poetry*; Lindenberger, *On Wordsworth's 'Prelude'*; Hägin, *The Epic Hero and the Decline of Heroic Poetry*; Wilkie, *Romantic Poets and Epic Tradition*; Köhring, *Die Formen des 'long poem' in der modernen amerikanischen Literatur*; Vogler, *Preludes to Vision*; *The Long Poem in the Twentieth Century*, ed. Riddel; Miller, *The American Quest for a Supreme Fiction*. For German literature, see Schueler, *The German Verse Epic in the Nineteenth and Twentieth Centuries*; and Maiworm, *Neue deutsche Epik*.

9 Views paralleling mine, arrived at from a different perspective, were presented at
   the December 1978 Modern Language Association in New York in what I
   consider to be a brilliant paper by Robert Francis Cook, 'The Search for the
   Medieval Epic,' publication forthcoming.
10 Schürr, *Das altfranzösische Epos*; Pollmann, *Epos*. See also the format of *The
   Epic in Medieval Society*, ed. Scholler.
11 On this question I recommend Ruttkowski, *Die literarischen Gattungen*;
   Guillén, *Literature as System*, chaps. 1, 4, and 9; *Die Gattungen in der Vergleichenden Literaturwissenschaft*, ed. Rüdiger; Genette, 'Genres, "types", modes.'
12 Etiemble, 'L'épopée de l'épopée'; Siciliano, *Les Chansons de geste et l'épopée*.
   Similar views are expressed by Albert Cook, *The Classic Line*.
13 Paul Robert, *Dictionnaire alphabétique et analogique de la langue française*
   (Paris: s.n.l., 'Le Robert,' 1976), 2: 592B.
14 Bynum, 'The Generic Nature of Oral Epic Poetry.'
15 Lord, 'Narrative Poetry,' p. 542; Collinder, 'On the Translation of Epics,'
   p. 327. Also Atsuhiko, 'L'épopée,' p. 199.

CHAPTER ONE

1 For general studies on the *chanson de geste* as a whole, I recommend Crosland,
   *The Old French Epic*; de Riquer, *Los cantares de gesta franceses*; and the
   major synthesis by de Combarieu, *L'Idéal humain et l'expérience morale chez les
   héros des chansons de geste*.
2 The bibliography on the oral hypothesis is immense. In my opinion, the best
   argument in favor of it remains Rychner, *La Chanson de geste*; the most
   convincing refutation, Delbouille, 'Les chansons de geste et le livre.'
3 *La Chanson de Roland*, ed. Cesare Segre, Documenti di filologia, 16 (Milan:
   Ricciardi, 1971). Also *The 'Song of Roland': An Analytical Edition*, ed. Gerard J.
   Brault, 2 vols. (University Park: Pennsylvania State Univ. Press, 1978); and
   *La Version d'Oxford*, vol. 1 of *Les Textes de la 'Chanson de Roland,'* ed. Raoul
   Mortier (Paris: La Geste Francor, 1940). Good introductions to *The Song of
   Roland* are by Le Gentil, *La Chanson de Roland*; Vance, *Reading the 'Song of
   Roland'*; and Burger, *Turold, poète de la fidélité*.
4 The most cogent presentation of this view is to be found in Auerbach, *Mimesis*,
   chapt. 5. Auerbach's interpretation does not differ markedly from that of
   Bowra, *Heroic Poetry*, on the heroic epic as a world-wide phenomenon.
5 On Ganelon's trial, consult Ruggieri, *Il processo di Gano nella 'Chanson de
   Roland'*; Halverson, 'Ganelon's Trial'; and Mickel, 'The Thirty *Pleges* for
   Ganelon.'
6 Important books of sociological criticism in this area are Waltz, *Rolandslied,
   Wilhelmslied, Alexiuslied*; Bender, *König und Vasall*; Köhler, 'Conseil des
   barons' und 'Jugement des barons'*; and Mancini, *Società feudale e ideologia nel
   'Charroi de Nîmes'*. See also, for the feudal motivation, Aebischer, 'Pour la
   défense et l'illustration de l'épisode de Baligant.'
7 Lejeune, 'Le péché de Charlemagne et la *Chanson de Roland*.'
8 See Curtius, *Europäische Literatur und lateinisches Mittelalter*, chapt. 9.
9 This point has been made by W. Mary Hackett, 'Le gant de Roland'; and Lyons,
   'More About Roland's Glove.'
10 Noyer-Weidner, 'Zur "Heidengeographie" im Rolandslied,' and 'Vom biblischen "Gottesberg" zur Symbolik des "Heidentals" im Rolandslied'; Vance,

*Reading*, chapt. 3; Brault, 'Quelques nouvelles tendances de la critique et de l'interprétation des chansons de geste.' Also Payen, 'Encore le problème de la géographie épique.'

11 On this problem, Frappier, 'Le thème de la lumière, de la *Chanson de Roland* au *Roman de la Rose*'; Noyer-Weidner, 'Farbrealität und Farbsymbolik in der "Heidengeographie" des Rolandsliedes'; and Bennett, 'Further Reflections on the Luminosity of the *Chanson de Roland*.'

12 Steinmeyer, *Untersuchungen zur allegorischen Bedeutung der Träume im altfranzösischen Rolandslied.*

13 Baudouin, *Triomphe*. For Freudian readings of the *Roland*, Vodoz, *'Roland,' un symbole*; Bloch, 'Roland and Oedipus'; Nolting-Hauff, 'Zur Psychoanalyse der Heldendichtung'; and Planche, 'Roland fils de personne.'

14 On the horn, Nichols, 'Roland's Echoing Horn'; Atkinson, 'Laisses 169–170 of the *Chanson de Roland*'; Szittya, 'The Angels and the Theme of *Fortitudo* in the *Chanson de Roland*'; Kostoroski, 'Further Echoes from Roland's Horn.'

15 Among the most important Christian readings of the text are Segre, 'Schemi narrativi nella *Chanson de Roland*'; Payen, *Le Motif du repentir dans la littérature française médiévale*, pp. 108–37; Rütten, *Symbol und Mythus im altfranzösischen Rolandslied*; Wendt, *Der Oxforder 'Roland'*; and the Introduction and Commentary (vol. 1) of Brault's edition, which incorporates the findings of a series of excellent articles. These and other scholars generally also uphold an interpretation of the *Chanson* that minimizes the protagonist's guilt; they believe Roland to be an ideal Christian warrior, who benefits from the author's and the public's total approbation.

## CHAPTER TWO

1 On this topic, see Bezzola, 'De Roland à Raoul de Cambrai,' and 'A propos de la valeur littéraire des chansons féodales.'

2 *Raoul de Cambrai, chanson de geste*, ed. Paul Meyer and Auguste Longnon, Société des Anciens Textes Français (Paris: Didot, 1882). The following books deal directly with this poem: Calin, *The Old French Epic of Revolt*; Matarasso, *Recherches historiques et littéraires sur 'Raoul de Cambrai'*; Adler, *Rückzug in epischer Parade*, chapt. 5, and *Epische Spekulanten*; Siciliano, *Chansons de geste*, pp. 395–416; de Combarieu, *L'Idéal humain*, pp. 112–21, 316–38.

3 On aspects of realism, Calin, *Epic of Revolt*, chapt. 5; Waltz, 'Spontanéité et responsabilité dans la chanson de geste'; Adler, 'Guillaume et son cercle "dans" *Raoul de Cambrai*'; Kay, 'Topography and the Relative Realism of Battle Scenes in Chansons de geste'; Bloch, *Medieval French Literature and Law*, chapt. 2.

4 Lukács, *Studies in European Realism*, p. 208.

5 On the *bachelers* and related political problems, in addition to the works cited in chapt. 1, note 6, Dessau, 'L'idée de la trahison au moyen âge et son rôle dans la motivation de quelques chansons de geste'; Duby, 'Au xııe siècle: les *jeunes* dans la société aristocratique'; Bender, 'Un aspect de la stylisation épique'; Flori, 'Qu'est-ce qu'un *bacheler*?'; Boutet, 'La politique et l'histoire dans les chansons de geste.' On *Raoul de Cambrai* in particular, Adler, *Rückzug*; Waltz, 'Spontanéité et responsabilité'; Roncaglia, 'Come si presenta oggi il problema delle canzoni di gesta,' pp. 282–5; and Pica, '*Raoul de Cambrai*.'

6 On this topos, see Curtius, *Europäische Literatur*, chapt. 5.

7 Antoine discusses the role and function of money in Old French literature from a different perspective, 'La place de l'argent dans la littérature française médiévale.'
8 See Bloomfield, 'The Problem of the Hero in the Later Medieval Period,' for an analysis of the ambivalent nature of the hero in the late Middle Ages. Among other texts, Bloomfield cites Chrétien's *Perceval*, a work contemporary with *Raoul de Cambrai*.

### CHAPTER THREE

1 *Huon de Bordeaux*, ed. Pierre Ruelle (Brussels: Presses Universitaires de Bruxelles, 1960). Recent books dealing directly with this poem are Adler, *Rückzug*, chapt. 7; Calin, *The Epic Quest*, chapt. 4; and Rossi, '*Huon de Bordeaux*' *et l'évolution du genre épique au XIIIe siècle*. I have incorporated revised material from *The Epic Quest* in this chapter.
2 *Anatomy of Criticism*, pp. 367, 151.
3 *The Hero with a Thousand Faces*, p. 30.
4 This is perhaps the major contribution of Rossi's excellent book; see '*Huon de Bordeaux*,' chapt. 5.
5 A major theme in Adler, *Rückzug*; see also Kinter and Keller, *The Sibyl*, pp. 50–2 and 61–4.
6 On the forest in medieval literature, Stauffer, *Der Wald*, esp. pp. 40–5.
7 *Anatomy*, p. 33.
8 Gerhardt, *Old Men of the Sea*.
9 For the latter, Harward, *The Dwarfs of Arthurian Romance and Celtic Tradition*.
10 Frye, *Anatomy*, p. 151; Campbell, *Hero*, p. 72.
11 We find a good existential reading of the text in Adler, *Rückzug*; see also Mealy, '*Huon de Bordeaux*.'
12 Calin, *Epic Quest*, chapt. 1.
13 Bergson, *Le Rire*, p. 39.
14 *Europäische Literatur*, excursus 4.
15 For a divergent view, Rossi, 'Loyauté et déloyauté dans *Huon de Bordeaux*,' and '*Huon de Bordeaux*,' chapt. 7.
16 For views of the *enfes* in medieval literature (apart from the question of babies and small children), Lods, 'Le thème de l'enfance dans l'épopée française'; Wolfzettel, 'Zur Stellung und Bedeutung der *Enfances* in der altfranzösischen Epik'; Colliot, 'Perspective sur la condition familiale et sociale de l'enfant dans la littérature médiévale'; de Combarieu, 'Enfance et démesure dans l'épopée médiévale française'; also Bynum, 'Themes of the Young Hero in Serbocroatian Oral Epic Tradition.' On *Huon de Bordeaux* in particular, Johnson, '*Huon de Bordeaux* et la sémantique de l'*enfes*'; see also Colliot, 'Enfants et enfance dans *Raoul de Cambrai*.'
17 Ménard, *Le Rire et le sourire dans le roman courtois en France au Moyen Age (1150–1250)*.
18 He examines a series of late *chansons* in 'Über die altfranzösische Epik II, III, IV, V.' See esp. 'II,' pp. 423–4. For theoretical considerations of the genre as a whole, I recommend Nichols, 'The Spirit of Truth'; Paquette, 'Epopée et roman'; Poirion, 'Chanson de geste ou épopée?'; and Zumthor, *Essai de poétique médiévale*, pp. 322–38 and 455–66.

CHAPTER FOUR

1 Stimulating recent articles on the problem of *chanson de geste* and courtly
romance are by Jauss, 'Chanson de geste et roman courtois au xiie siècle'; Köhler, 'Quelques observations d'ordre historico-sociologique sur les rapports
entre la chanson de geste et le roman courtois'; Pollmann, 'Von der *chanson de
geste* zum höfischen Roman in Frankreich'; Zumthor, *Essai*, pp. 352–70;
Ollier, 'Demande sociale et constitution d'un genre.' For studies on the development of the *roman courtois* as a whole, I recommend Payen, *Les Origines de
la courtoisie dans la littérature française médiévale*, vol. 2, *Le Roman*, and *Le
Roman*; Vinaver, *The Rise of Romance*; *Le Roman jusqu'à la fin du XIIIe
siècle*, ed. Frappier and Grimm; Schmolke-Hasselmann, *Der arthurische Versroman von Chrestien bis Froissart*; and, from a comparatist perspective, Stevens,
*Medieval Romance*.
2 *Le Chevalier de la Charrete*, vol. 3 of *Les Romans de Chrétien de Troyes*, ed.
Mario Roques, Les Classiques Français du Moyen Age, 86 (Paris: Champion,
1958). For good general introductions to Chrétien's opus, Hofer, *Chrétien de
Troyes*; Frappier, *Chrétien de Troyes*; Maranini, *Personaggi e immagini nell'
opera di Chrétien de Troyes*; Topsfield, *Chrétien de Troyes*. Two excellent
books have been written on the *Lancelot*: Kelly, *'Sens' and 'Conjointure' in the
'Chevalier de la Charrette'*; and Ribard, *Chrétien de Troyes, 'Le Chevalier de
la Charrette.'*
3 Jonin, 'Le vasselage de Lancelot dans le *Conte de la Charette.*'
4 Lazar, 'Lancelot et la "mulier mediatrix." '
5 Andrea Capellano, *Trattato d'amore: De amore libri tres*, ed. Salvatore Batta-
glia (Rome: Perrella, 1947), p. 32.
6 I have benefited from Köhler's major study, *Ideal und Wirklichkeit in der
höfischen Epik*; also Emmel, *Formprobleme des Artusromans und der Graldichtung*. For recent analyses of the court situation and twelfth-century ideology
in *Lancelot* and *Yvain*, Maranini, ' "Cavalleria" e "Cavalieri" nel mondo di
Chrétien de Troyes'; Payen, 'Lancelot contre Tristan'; Brand, 'Das Wirklichkeitsbild im *Lancelot* und *Yvain*'; Pasero, 'Chrétien, la realtà, l'ideologia'; Ra-
duleţ, 'Intorno al realismo cerimoniale del *Lancelot* di Chrétien de Troyes';
Marazza, 'Immaginazione poetica e realtà sociale'; Boklund, 'On the Spatial and
Cultural Characteristics of Courtly Romance'; Pioletti, 'Lettura dell' episodio
del "Chastel de Pesme-Aventure" '; and the important book by Hanning, *The
Individual in Twelfth-Century Romance*.
7 Loomis, *Arthurian Tradition and Chrétien de Troyes*, book 3.
8 Damon, 'Myth, Metaphor, and the Epic Tradition.'
9 Moller, 'The Meaning of Courtly Love'; Askew, 'Courtly Love'; Koenigsberg,
'Culture and Unconscious Fantasy.'
10 Mandel, 'Elements in the *Charrette* World.'
11 Ribard, *Chrétien de Troyes*. Without proposing a Christological allegory,
Kelly, *'Sens' and 'Conjointure,'* also emphasizes Lancelot's role as savior, as does
Rychner, 'Le sujet et la signification du *Chevalier de la charrette*,' and 'Le
prologue du *Chevalier de la charrette* et l'interprétation du roman.' In these and
two other articles Rychner effectively defends the literary coherence and integrity of the romance. A number of scholars, especially in America, now claim that
Chrétien views *fin' amor* from an ironic perspective and consciously undermines his protagonist.

12  See especially Kellermann, *Aufbaustil und Weltbild Chrestiens von Troyes im Percevalroman*; Bezzola, *Le Sens de l'aventure et de l'amour*; and Brand, *Chrétien de Troyes*.

13  *Le Chevalier au Lion (Yvain)*, vol. 4 of *Les Romans de Chrétien de Troyes*, ed. Mario Roques, Les Classiques Français du Moyen Age, 89 (Paris: Champion, 1960). For a good general introduction, Frappier, *Etude sur 'Yvain ou le Chevalier au Lion' de Chrétien de Troyes*.

14  On adventure and the theme of the quest, Auerbach, *Mimesis*, chapt. 6; Locatelli, 'L'avventura nei romanzi di Chrétien de Troyes e nei suoi imitatori'; Köhler, *Ideal und Wirklichkeit*, chapt. 3; Pfeiffer, *En route vers l'au-delà arthurien*; Ménard, 'Le chevalier errant dans la littérature arthurienne.' Also Le Goff and Vidal-Naquet, 'Lévi-Strauss en Brocéliande.' For a fascinating recent article on Chrétien's symbolism, Grigsby, 'Sign, Symbol and Metaphor.'

15  Loomis, *Arthurian Tradition*, book 4. Two books from a folklore-oriented perspective have been written on Chrétien and popular tradition: Völker, *Märchenhafte Elemente bei Chrétien de Troyes*; and Mauritz, *Der Ritter im magischen Reich*.

16  Robert G. Cook, 'The Ointment in Chrétien's *Yvain*'; Brown, 'Yvain's Sin of Neglect.'

17  *Trattato*, pp. 178–80.

18  Recent scholars tend to see humor and irony in Chrétien's romances. For especially penetrating insights, Haidu, *Aesthetic Distance in Chrétien de Troyes*, and *Lion-queue-coupée*; Ménard, *Rire*; and Green, *Irony in the Medieval Romance*.

19  Consult the recent book on Kay by Haupt, *Der Truchsess Keie im Artusroman*.

20  *Sens*. For Yvain's growth through repentance, Payen, *Motif*, pp. 385–90.


CHAPTER FIVE

1  Honig, *Dark Conceit*, p. 12; also Fletcher, *Allegory*; and Quilligan, *The Language of Allegory*.

2  For the development of medieval allegory, see the following works, which also contain penetrating analyses of *Le Roman de la Rose*: Lewis, *The Allegory of Love*; Muscatine, 'The Emergence of Psychological Allegory in Old French Romance'; Jauss, 'Entstehung und Strukturwandel der allegorischen Dichtung'; Jung, *Etudes sur le poème allégorique en France au moyen âge*; Zumthor, *Essai*, pp. 117–34 and 371–5.

3  Guillaume de Lorris and Jean de Meun, *Le Roman de la Rose*, ed. Félix Lecoy, 3 vols., Les Classiques Français du Moyen Age, 92, 95, 98 (Paris: Champion, 1965–70). Also *Le Roman de la Rose*, ed. Ernest Langlois, 5 vols., La Société des Anciens Textes Français (Paris: Didot, 1914–24). I recommend highly four book-length studies devoted to the *Roman*: Gunn, *The Mirror of Love*; Batany, *Approches du 'Roman de la Rose'*; Poirion, *Le Roman de la Rose*; Payen, *La Rose et l'utopie*.

4  On this topic, see Köhler, 'Narcisse, la Fontaine d'Amour et Guillaume de Lorris'; and Ribard, 'Introduction à une étude polysémique du *Roman de la Rose* de Guillaume de Lorris,' and 'De Chrétien de Troyes à Guillaume de Lorris.'

5  *Europäische Literatur*, chapt. 10. See also Piehler, *The Visionary Landscape*, chapt. 6; Thoss, *Studien zum 'Locus Amœnus' im Mittelalter*, pp. 115–38; and Doris Ruhe, '*Le Dieu d'Amours avec son paradis*,' pp. 101–9 and, on Jean de Meun, pp. 128–32.

6 See Badel, *'Le Roman de la Rose' au XIVe siècle.*
7 Bakhtin, *Rabelais and His World.*
8 For a sociological reading of Jean de Meun, Payen, *La Rose*; *'Le Roman de la Rose* et la notion de carrefour idéologique'; and 'Eléments idéologiques et revendications dans *le Roman de la Rose.*' Also Lepage, 'Le *Roman de la Rose* et la tradition romanesque au moyen âge'; and, on Guillaume de Lorris, Ott, '*"Armut"* und *"Reichtum"* bei Guillaume de Lorris.'
9 Patricia J. Eberle, 'The Lovers' Glass.'
10 On sexual comedy and problems of language relevant to this scene, see Calin, 'La comédie humaine chez Jean de Meun'; Hill, 'Narcissus, Pygmalion, and the Castration of Saturn'; Poirion, 'Les mots et les choses selon Jean de Meun'; Jung, 'Jean de Meun et l'allégorie'; Quilligan, 'Words and Sex'; Ineichen, 'Le discours linguistique de Jean de Meun.' For penetrating analyses of irony and satire in Jean, Tuve, *Allegorical Imagery*, chapt. 4; Fleming, *The 'Roman de la Rose'*; and Payen, 'Le comique de l'énormité.'
11 On narrative technique in Guillaume de Lorris, Strohm, 'Guillaume as Narrator and Lover in the *Roman de la Rose*'; E.B. Vitz, 'The *I* of the *Roman de la Rose*'; and Rychner, 'Le mythe de la fontaine de Narcisse dans le *Roman de la Rose* de Guillaume de Lorris'; for both sections of the poem, Nichols, 'The Rhetoric of Sincerity in the *Roman de la Rose.*'
12 One school of thought, represented by Robertson, *A Preface to Chaucer*, and Fleming, *'Roman de la Rose,'* claims that the entire *Roman* should be interpreted ironically, as a work which castigates secular passion, proposing in its place *caritas*, love of God. On the intellectual content and background of the poem, see also Piehler, *Visionary Landscape*; Economou, *The Goddess Natura in Medieval Literature*; Wetherbee, *Plantonism and Poetry in the Twelfth Century*; Nitzsche, *The Genius Figure in Antiquity and the Middle Ages.*
13 On the strongly didactic aura emanating from both sections of the *Roman* and the theme of teaching, Gunn, 'Teacher and Student in the *Roman de la Rose*'; Kanduth, 'Der Rosenroman – ein Bildungsbuch?'; Kelly, ' "Li chastiaus ... Qu'Amors prist puis par ses esforz," ' and *Medieval Imagination*, chapt. 4.
14 For the 'philosophy of plenitude' I follow entirely Gunn, *Mirror.*
15 For views on art and communication, see Poirion, 'Narcisse et Pygmalion dans le *Roman de la Rose*'; Zumthor, 'Récit et anti-récit'; Jung, 'Jean de Meun et l'allégorie,' and 'Jean de Meun et son lecteur'; Dragonetti, 'Pygmalion ou les pièges de la fiction dans le *Roman de la Rose*,' and 'Le "singe de nature" dans le *Roman de la Rose.*'
16 Hatzfeld, 'La mystique naturiste de Jean de Meung'; Scaglione, *Nature and Love in the Late Middle Ages*, pp. 33–42.

CHAPTER SIX

1 I refer, of course, to Huizinga's seminal book, translated into English as *The Waning of the Middle Ages.*
2 On Machaut's relationship to his predecessors and the literature of his age, Wimsatt, *Chaucer and the French Love Poets*; and Poirion, *Le Moyen Age II, 1300–1480.* Also Hieatt, ' "Un autre fourme." '
3 The most complete biographical and musical study of Machaut is by Machabey, *Guillaume de Machault, 130–?–1377*; for a brief, more recent volume, Reaney, *Guillaume de Machaut.* On Machaut as lyricist, Poirion, *Le Poète et le prince*; on

his narrative verse, Calin, *A Poet at the Fountain*, from which I have incorporated revised material in this chapter.

4 *Œuvres de Guillaume de Machaut*, ed. Ernest Hoepffner, Société des Anciens Textes Français, vol. 1 (Paris: Didot, 1908), pp. 137–291.

5 See also Kelly, *Medieval Imagination*, chapt. 6, who posits a serious transformation in the poet's love ethos.

6 On medieval attitudes toward the hunt, Robertson, *Preface*; Thiébaux, *The Stag of Love*; and the papers collected in *La Chasse au Moyen Age*. See also Planche, ' "Est vrais amans li drois oisiaus de proie ..." '

7 Spitzer, 'Note on the Poetic and the Empirical "I" in Medieval Authors.'

8 For Machaut's place in a tradition of plague literature dating back to Homer and the Bible, see Grimm, *Die literarische Darstellung der Pest in der Antike und in der Romania*, esp. pp. 143–54.

9 *Europäische Literatur*, chapt. 5.

10 For an excellent study of melancholia in late medieval verse, see Heger, *Die Melancholie bei den französischen Lyrikern des Spätmittelalters*, esp. pp. 70–91.

11 *Le Livre du Voir-Dit*, ed. Paulin Paris (Paris: La Société des Bibliophiles François, 1875). This defective, inadequate edition will be superseded by the new Paul Imbs version, to appear shortly in the 'Société des Anciens Textes Français' series. I also consulted with profit mss 1584 and 22545, fonds français, of the Bibliothèque Nationale.

12 'Über Guillaume de Machauts *Voir Dit*.'

13 On the relationship between letters, poems, and narrative text, Zumthor, *Essai*, pp. 310–11; Ernstpeter Ruhe, '*De Amasio ad Amasiam*,' pp. 275–85; Cerquiglini, 'Le montage des formes,' 'Pour une typologie de l'insertion,' and 'Syntaxe et syncope.'

14 Gybbon-Monypenny, 'Guillaume de Machaut's Erotic "Autobiography." ' See also Zumthor, 'Autobiographie au Moyen Age?' and, from a different perspective, Ruhe, '*De Amasio*.'

15 This has been a major thrust of recent American scholarship: Williams, 'An Author's Role in Fourteenth Century Book Production,' 'The Lady, the Lyrics and the Letters,' and 'Machaut's Self-Awareness as Author and Producer'; Oliver, 'Guillaume de Machaut'; Calin, *Poet*; and Brownlee, 'The Poetic Œuvre of Guillaume de Machaut,' and 'Transformations of the Lyric "Je." '

CHAPTER SEVEN

1 Simone, *Il Rinascimento francese*, and *Storia della storiografia letteraria francese*.

2 Joachim du Bellay, *La Deffence et Illustration de la Langue Françoyse*, ed. Henri Chamard, Société des Textes Français Modernes (Paris: Didier, 1948), pp. 45, 46–7, 107–8.

3 'Préface sur la Franciade, touchant le Poëme Heroïque' (1587), in vol. 16 of *Œuvres complètes* (see note 5 below), p. 345.

4 The bibliography on the Renaissance epic as a European phenomenon is immense. For the specifically French context, Cioranescu, 'La Pléiade et le poème épique'; Pollmann, *Épos*, pp. 127–31; Müller-Bochat, 'Die Einheit des Wissens und das Epos'; Hagiwara, *French Epic Poetry in the Sixteenth Century*; Maskell, *The Historical Epic in France, 1500–1700*; Németh, 'La raison d'être d'un genre "avorté" '; Werner, *Die Gattung des Epos nach italienischen und französischen Poetiken des 16. Jahrhunderts*; Céard, 'L'épopée en France au XVIe siècle.'

5  *La Franciade (1572)*, ed. Paul Laumonier, vol. 16 of *Œuvres complètes*, Société des Textes Français Modernes (Paris: Didier, 1950–2). I used with profit the following criticism: Silver, *Ronsard and the Hellenic Renaissance in France*, vol. 1; Stone, 'Dido and Aeneas'; Pollmann, *Epos*, pp. 127–31; Cameron, 'Ronsard and Book IV of the *Franciade*'; Hagiwara, *French Epic Poetry*, chapt. 3; Maskell, *Historical Epic*, chapt. 6; Werner, *Gattung*, pp. 203–10; Leslie, *Ronsard's Successful Epic Venture*, chapts. 1–3; and Ménager, *Ronsard*, pp. 275–316.
6  Silver, *Hellenic Renaissance*, p. 472.
7  Henri Weber, *La Création poétique au XVIe siècle en France de Maurice Scève à Agrippa d'Aubigné*, chapts. 7 and 8, and Gadoffre, *Ronsard par lui-même*, contributed to a revaluation of Ronsard as a sublime poet. More recently, the essays collected in *Ronsard the Poet*, ed. Cave; Calin, 'Ronsard's Cosmic Warfare,' from which I have incorporated revised material in this chapter; Cave, *The Cornucopian Text*, pp. 223–70; and Leslie, *Epic Venture*, chapt. 4 and Conclusion.
8  See Dassonville, 'Eléments pour une définition de l'hymne ronsardien,' and *Ronsard: Etude historique et littéraire*, vol. 3, chapt. 4; Stone, 'The Sense and Significance of Ronsard's Seasonal Hymns'; Gordon, *Ronsard et la rhétorique*; Demerson, *La Mythologie classique dans l'œuvre lyrique de la 'Pléiade'*; Albert Py, Introduction.
9  *Les Hymnes de 1555, Le Second Livre des Hymnes de 1556*, ed. Paul Laumonier, vol. 8 of *Œuvres complètes*, Société des Textes Français Modernes, 2nd ed. (Paris: Didier, 1966), pp. 150–61 and 255–93.
10  See Joukovsky-Micha, 'La Guerre des dieux et des géants chez les poètes français du XVIe siècle (1500–1585).'
11  On the importance of allegory, even typology, in Ronsard's works, Dagens, 'La théologie poétique au temps de Ronsard'; Demerson, *Mythologie*; Silver, *The Intellectual Evolution of Ronsard*, vol. 2, chapt. 11; Bellenger, 'L'allégorie dans les poèmes de style élevé de Ronsard'; Calin, 'Ronsard and the Myth of Justice.' For the idea of an 'allegorical epic' in the Renaissance, Murrin, *The Allegorical Epic*.
12  Joukovsky, *Orphée et ses disciples dans la poésie française et néolatine du XVIe siècle*, pp. 62–103, esp. 69–71.
13  *Discours des Misères et autres pièces politiques, 1562–1563*, ed. Paul Laumonier, vol. 11 of *Œuvres complètes*, Société des Textes Français Modernes, 2nd ed. (Paris: Didier, 1973), pp. 17–176. For the corresponding Protestant texts, consult *La Polémique protestante contre Ronsard*, ed. Jacques Pineaux, 2 vols., Société des Textes Français Modernes (Paris: Didier, 1973). For criticism on the *Discours*, Weber, *Création poétique*, chapt. 8; Nothnagle, 'The Drama of *Les Discours* of Ronsard'; Py, *Ronsard*, chapt. 8; Pineaux, 'Poésie et prophétisme'; Ménager, *Ronsard*, pp. 185–274; Marchal, 'De l'actualité au mythe dans les *Discours* de Ronsard.'
14  On this motif in Rabelais, Montaigne, and La Fontaine, see Lapp, *The Esthetics of Negligence*.

CHAPTER EIGHT

1  See Albert-Marie Schmidt, *La Poésie scientifique en France au seizième siècle*; Weber, *Création poétique*, chapt. 7; Müller-Bochat, 'Einheit'; Keller, *Palingène, Ronsard, Du Bartas*; *French Renaissance Scientific Poetry*, ed. Wilson. For

a comparable phenomenon in Italy, Roellenbleck, *Das epische Lehrgedicht Italiens im fünfzehnten und Sechzehnten Jahrhundert.*

2 Agrippa d'Aubigné, *Œuvres*, ed. Henri Weber, Jacques Bailbé, and Marguerite Soulié, Bibliothèque de la Pléiade (Paris: Gallimard, 1969), pp. 1–243. Also *Les Tragiques*, ed. Armand Garnier and Jean Plattard, 4 vols., Société des Textes Français Modernes (Paris: Droz, 1932).

3 A number of books have appeared in recent years devoted wholly or partly to d'Aubigné. I especially profited from, and recommend, Sauerwein, *Agrippa d'Aubigné's 'Les Tragiques'*; Weber, *Création poétique*, chapt. 9; Greene, *Descent*, chapt. 9; Bailbé, *Agrippa d'Aubigné, poète des 'Tragiques'*; Fasano, *'Les Tragiques': Un' epopea della morte*; Regosin, *The Poetry of Inspiration*; Baïche, *La Naissance du baroque français*; Soulié, *L'Inspiration biblique dans la poésie religieuse d'Agrippa d'Aubigné*; Kennedy, *Rhetorical Norms in Renaissance Literature*, pp. 151–66.

4 See Grob, *Studien zu den 'Tragiques' des Agrippa d'Aubigné.*

5 This notion is the major contribution of Sauerwein, *'Les Tragiques.'*

6 For a quite different Freudian reading of the text, Dubois, *'Les images de parenté dans Les Tragiques.'*

7 He thus renews an old epic motif, prominent in *La Chanson de Roland* and other medieval and classical texts; on this topic, see Frings, 'Europäische Heldendichtung'; and Knapp, 'Die grosse Schlacht zwischen Orient und Okzident in der abendländischen Epik.'

8 On typology during this period from a European perspective and the specifically Protestant interpretation of history, *Literary Uses of Typology from the Late Middle Ages to the Present*, ed. Miner; and Dubois, *La Conception de l'Histoire en France au XVIe siècle (1560–1610).*

9 On narrative technique and the poetic voice in Renaissance epic, Durling, *The Figure of the Poet in Renaissance Epic*; Delasanta, *The Epic Voice*; Kennedy, *Rhetorical Norms*, chapt. 3. On d'Aubigné in particular, Bensimon, 'Essai sur Agrippa d'Aubigné'; Kolstrup, 'La conception de l'homme dans les *Tragiques*'; Romani, *Impegno e retorica in Agrippa d'Aubigné*; Kennedy, *Rhetorical Norms*; and Greenberg, 'The Poetics of Trompe-l'œil.'

10 Stanzel, *Die typischen Erzählsituationen im Roman.*

11 A great deal of research has been devoted to d'Aubigné as a Calvinist and the Biblical inspiration in his work: Grob, *Studien*; Fasano, *'Les Tragiques'*; Regosin, *Poetry*, chapt. 3; Crosby, 'Prophetic Discourse in Ronsard and D'Aubigné'; Mario Richter, 'Aspetti e orientamenti della poetica protestante francese nel secolo XVI'; Soulié, *Inspiration biblique*; Forsyth, 'Le message prophétique d'Agrippa d'Aubigné.'

12 Lapp, *Esthetics*, and chapt. 7 above, pp. 186–9.

13 Bailbé, *Agrippa d'Aubigné.*

14 *Introduction à la poésie française*, p. 79.

CHAPTER NINE

1 Toinet, *Quelques Recherches autour des poèmes héroïques-épiques français du dix-septième siècle*; Marni, *Allegory in the French Heroic Poem of the Seventeenth Century*, pp. 3, 105. Other book-length studies are Duchesne, *Histoire des poëmes épiques français du XVIIe siècle*; Sayce, *The French Biblical Epic in the Seventeenth Century*; Maskell, *Historical Epic.*

2 Adam, *Histoire de la littérature française au XVIIe siècle*, vol. 2, p. 59.
3 For general studies of his life and works, see Lagny, *Le Poète Saint-Amant (1594–1661)*; and Gourier, *Etude des œuvres poétiques de Saint-Amant*.
4 Saint-Amant, *Œuvres*, vol. 5, ed. Jacques Bailbé and Jean Lagny, Société des Textes Français Modernes (Paris: Champion, 1979), pp. 1–290. I recommend the following criticism: Sayce, *French Biblical Epic*, chapt. 7; Noehte, '*Moyse Sauvé' von Saint-Amant*; Seznec, 'Saint-Amant, *le poète sauvé des eaux*'; Greene, *Descent*, chapt. 11; Genette, 'D'un récit baroque'; Hallyn, 'La matière biblique et son sens religieux dans le *Moyse Sauvé* de Saint-Amant.'
5 On this topic, Warnke, *Versions of Baroque*, chapts. 7 and 8; Stegmann, 'L'ambiguïté du concept héroïque dans la littérature morale en France sous Louis XIII'; Steadman, 'The Arming of an Archetype'; Wardropper, 'The Epic Hero Superseded.'
6 *Œuvres*, vol. 1, ed. Bailbé, Société des Textes Français Modernes (Paris: Didier, 1971), p. 20.
7 Insights into the pastoral mode and the garden in the Renaissance are provided by Giamatti, *The Earthly Paradise and the Renaissance Epic*; and Poggioli, *The Oaten Flute*.
8 For Marino's influence on the French epic, see Chauveau, 'A la recherche de la modernité en poésie (1623–1630)'; and Warman, 'Saint-Amant et la *Bella Schiava* de Marino.'
9 See *Mimesis*, chapt. 10.
10 Marni, *Allegory*, pp. 117–30; Noehte, '*Moyse Sauvé.*' Also Hallyn, 'Matière biblique'; and Couffignal, *La Lutte avec l'ange*, pp. 39–41.
11 Sayce, *French Biblical Epic*, pp. 205–6; Kurman, 'Ecphrasis in Epic Poetry.'
12 A number of articles have been devoted to this subject, in addition to a monograph by Rolfe, *Saint-Amant and the Theory of 'Ut Pictura Poesis.'*
13 See Seznec, 'Saint-Amant'; Genette, ' "L'or tombe sous le fer," ' and 'L'univers réversible'; Angeli, ' "Comique" e "illusion" nella poesia di Saint-Amant'; and Rothe, *Französische Lyrik im Zeitalter des Barock*, pp. 70–8.
14 On Saint-Amant as a learned poet, Duval, *Poesis and Poetic Tradition in the Early Works of Saint-Amant*.
15 This has been shown by Cosper, 'Saint-Amant: Pictorialism and the Devotional Style.'
16 Boileau, *Art poétique*, in *Œuvres complètes*, ed. Antoine Adam and Françoise Escal, Bibliothèque de la Pléiade (Paris: Gallimard, 1966), p. 157.
17 See Warnke, 'Baroque Transformations in the Romance Epic.'

CHAPTER TEN

1 Except for occasional lyrics in anthologies and extracts from his *Dissertation du poëme heroïque* in *Dichtungslehren der Romania aus der Zeit der Renaissance und des Barock*, ed. August Buck et al. (Frankfurt/Main: Athenäum, 1972), pp. 459–65.
2 *La Littérature de l'âge baroque en France*; *Anthologie de la poésie baroque française*; *L'Intérieur et l'extérieur*; also 'Un brelan d'oubliés.'
3 I shall quote from my copy of *Les Œuvres poétiques du P. Le Moyne* (Paris: Thomas Jolly, 1672), pp. 1–235, an edition somewhat less inaccessible than the others. For scholarship and criticism on Le Moyne, see Chérot, *Etude sur la vie et les œuvres du P. Le Moyne (1602–1671)*; Gross-Kiefer, *Le Dynamisme cosmique chez Le Moyne*; Ulriksen, 'Pierre Le Moyne – poète baroque fran-

çais' (a résumé of Aarnes, *Pierre Le Moyne: En fransk barokkdikter*); Bertaud, 'Un Jésuite au désert, le Père Le Moyne,' and *La Jalousie dans la littérature au temps de Louis XIII*, pp. 136–46; Demerson, 'Métamorphose et analogie'; Hope, 'Pierre Lemoyne's Glorious and Lofty Hymns.' On *Saint Louis* specifically, Edelman, *Attitudes of Seventeenth-Century France toward the Middle Ages*, pp. 239–45; Maskell, *Historical Epic*, pp. 120–6 and 206–7; and Calin, *Crown, Cross, and 'Fleur-de-lis,'* from which I have incorporated revised material in this chapter.

4 See Beall, *La Fortune du Tasse en France*; Cottaz, *L'Influence des théories du Tasse sur l'épopée en France*; Simpson, *Le Tasse et la littérature et l'art baroques en France*.

5 Edelman, *Attitudes*, chapt. 3.

6 On this motif in literature, Cherchi, 'Un dovere della *pietas* regia.'

7 According to Gross-Kiefer, *Dynamisme cosmique*, Le Moyne's 'false heroes,' dominated by their passions, subject to doubt and anguish, manifest a Racinian rather than a Cornelian psychology. On the heroic vein in Le Moyne's work as a whole, Gross-Kiefer, pp. 52–61, and Ulriksen, 'Pierre Le Moyne,' pp. 32–3. For seventeenth-century notions of heroism and the hero, Sutcliffe, *Guez de Balzac et son temps*, chapt. 3; Dawson, 'The Ideal Hero'; Stegmann, *L'Héroïsme cornélien*, and 'L'ambiguïté'; also Drijkoningen, 'Quelques aspects de la pompe littéraire au xviie siècle.' See also my chapter eleven, note 7.

8 *Dissertation du poëme heroïque*, in *Œuvres*, sigs. ĩ4r, ĩ4v, and õ1r, and in *Dichtungslehren der Romania*, p. 464.

9 On this subject, consult Sayce, *French Biblical Epic*, esp. pp. 78–9; Angenot, *Les Champions des femmes*; and Maclean, *Woman Triumphant*.

10 See Gross-Kiefer, *Dynamisme cosmique*, pp. 8–16; and Stegmann, *Héroïsme cornélien*, vol. 2, p. 236–7.

11 On this theme in Western epic generally, Moorman, *Kings and Captains*; and Jackson, *The Hero and the King*. On the political aspects in seventeenth-century France, Sutcliffe, *Politique et culture, 1560–1660*.

12 Warnke, *Versions*, chapt. 7.

CHAPTER ELEVEN

1 The bibliography is immense. Neglecting articles (for reasons of space), I mention the following recent books, which make a significant historical or theoretical contribution to the subject: Adam, *Histoire*, pp. 75–84; Karlernst Schmidt, *Vorstudien zur einer Geschichte des komischen Epos*, pp. 76–85; Bar, *Le Genre burlesque en France au XVIIe siècle*; Greene, *Descent*, pp. 349–53; Broich, *Studien zum komischen Epos*, chapt. 2; Giraud, *La Fable de Daphné*, pp. 301–24; von Stackelberg, *Von Rabelais bis Voltaire*, pp. 104–7, and *Literarische Rezeptionsformen*, pp. 169–75; Jump, *Burlesque*; Karrer, *Parodie, Travestie, Pastiche*; Moog-Grünewald, *Metamorphosen der 'Metamorphosen.'*

2 Quoted in *La Poésie française de 1640 à 1680*, ed. Raymond Picard, vol. 2, p. 22.

3 *Œuvres complètes*, ed. Antoine Adam and Françoise Escal, Bibliothèque de la Pléiade (Paris: Gallimard, 1966), pp. 187–222 and 1004–20; also *Œuvres complètes*, ed. Charles H. Boudhors, vol. 2 (Paris: Les Belles Lettres, 1939). For criticism on *Le Lutrin*, Broich, *Studien*, chapt. 10; H.A. Mason, 'Boileau's *Lutrin*'; Canfield, 'The Unity of Boileau's *Le Lutrin*'; Pocock, *Boileau and the Nature of Neo-Classicism*, pp. 148–52.

4 Consult Emard and Fournier, *La Sainte-Chapelle du 'Lutrin'*; for additional background material, Reed, *Claude Barbin, libraire de Paris sous le règne de Louis XIV*.

5 Beugnot, 'Boileau, une esthétique de la lumière'; also Edelman, *'L'Art poétique: "Long-temps plaire, et jamais ne lasser."'*

6 Zdrojewska, *Boileau*, chapt. 6.

7 On this topic, Fumaroli, 'Ethique et rhétorique du héros humaniste'; Magné, *Crise de la littérature française sous Louis XIV*.

8 For recent interpretations of *l'ami du vrai* and his rhetorical stance, France, *Rhetoric and Truth in France*, pp. 151–72; Tiefenbrun, 'Boileau and His Friendly Enemy'; Marmier, 'La conscience du satirique, d'Horace à Boileau.'

9 On Boileau using poetry to criticize poetry, Beugnot, 'Boileau et la distance critique'; Brody, 'Boileau et la critique poétique,' also *Boileau and Longinus*; Tocanne, 'Boileau et l'épopée d'après l'*Art Poétique*'; and Pocock, *Boileau*. For a recent sociological view on Boileau and epic, Nerlich, 'La mythologie comme arme poétique dans la lutte pour la paix.'

10 Magné, *Crise*.

CHAPTER TWELVE

1 Consult Sellier, *Mythe*, chapt. 5; and Pomeau, 'Voltaire et le héros.'

2 Taylor, Introduction to his edition of *La Henriade*; Eckart Richter, 'Zum Problem des französischen Epos im 18. Jahrhundert'; Gillet, *'Le Paradis perdu' dans la littérature française de Voltaire à Chateaubriand*, chapt. 6; Jacobs, 'Das Verstummen der Muse'; Menant, *La Chute d'Icare*, chapt. 6. On Voltaire's notion of epic, Naves, *Le Goût de Voltaire*, pp. 472–9; Taylor, Introduction, chapt. 2; Rousseau, *L'Angleterre et Voltaire*, vol. 2, pp. 509–66; and Gunny, *Voltaire and English Literature*, pp. 107–15.

3 *The Poems of John Dryden*, ed. James Kinsley (Oxford: Clarendon Press, 1958), vol. 3, p. 1003.

4 *La Henriade*, ed. O.R. Taylor, vol. 2 of *Les Œuvres complètes de Voltaire* (Geneva: Institut et Musée Voltaire, 1970). Among recent books that contain criticism on this text are Baudouin, *Triomphe*, chapt. 11; Klemperer, *Geschichte der französischen Literatur im 18. Jahrhundert*, vol. 1, pp. 47–50; Pomeau, *La Religion de Voltaire*, pp. 105–11; Besterman, *Voltaire*, chapt. 9; Wade, *The Intellectual Development of Voltaire*; Ridgway, *Voltaire and Sensibility*, pp. 149–53; Henry Meyer, *Voltaire on War and Peace*, pp. 82–6; Menant, *Chute*.

5 Brumfitt, *Voltaire, Historian*; Taylor, 'Voltaire's Apprenticeship as a Historian.'

6 Klemperer, *Geschichte*.

7 Lanson, *Voltaire*, p. 92.

8 *La Pucelle d'Orléans*, ed. Jeroom Vercruysse, vol. 7 of *Les Œuvres complètes de Voltaire* (Geneva: Institut et Musée Voltaire, 1970). See Topazio, 'Voltaire's *Pucelle*'; Marcuse, 'Schiller, Voltaire und die Jungfrau'; Josef Eberle, *Voltaires 'Pucelle'*; Besterman, *Voltaire*, chapt. 29; von Stackelberg, *Von Rabelais bis Voltaire*, pp. 332–6, and *Literarische Rezeptionsformen*, pp. 188–94; Adams, *La Femme dans les contes et les romans de Voltaire*, chapt. 5; Haydn Mason, *Voltaire*, pp. 89–108; Calin, 'Love and War,' from which I have incorporated revised material in this chapter; Russo, 'Sexual Roles and Religious Images in Voltaire's *La Pucelle*'; Gunny, *Voltaire*, pp. 136–41; and Lindner, *Voltaire und die Poetik des Epos*.

9 On 'Gods at War' as a literary motif, George deForest Lord, *Heroic Mockery*, chapt. 2.

10 For two generations German scholars have associated their own and the English eighteenth-century comic epic with the Rococo. The three most recent full-length studies are Kind, *Das Rokoko und seine Grenzen im deutschen komischen Epos des 18. Jahrhunderts*; Beeken, *Das Prinzip der Desillusionierung im komischen Epos des 18. Jahrhunderts*; Maler, *Der Held im Salon*.

11 See Delattre, *Voltaire l'impétueux*.

CHAPTER THIRTEEN

1 The definitive studies are by Hunt, *The Epic in Nineteenth-Century France*; and Cellier, *L'Epopée romantique*. Also Müller-Bochat, 'Einheit'; Huch, *Erlösungsdenken im humanitären Epos des 19. Jahrhunderts in Frankreich*; and Detalle, *Mythes, merveilleux et légendes dans la poésie française de 1840 à 1860*, part 3.

2 Lamartine, *Œuvres poétiques*, ed. Marius-François Guyard, Bibliothèque de la Pléiade (Paris: Gallimard, 1963), pp. 567–794. On *Jocelyn*, from a literary-historical perspective, consult the excellent book by Guillemin, *Le 'Jocelyn' de Lamartine*; also the Introduction to his edition of *Les Visions*. For a good modern reading of the text, from a different perspective, Orr, *'Jocelyn* et l'Histoire.'

3 Guillemin, *'Jocelyn,'* pp. 477–91; Van Tieghem, *Le Sentiment de la nature dans le préromantisme européen*, pp. 155–98; Horváth, 'The Romantic Attitude to Nature'; Lacoste-Veysseyre, *Les Alpes romantiques*.

4 On the grotto and water-imagery in Lamartine, Viallaneix, 'Les eaux lamartiniennes'; Cordier, 'Réflexions sur la description lamartinienne des grottes'; Araujo, *In Search of Eden*, chapt. 5.

5 See Pollmann, *Epos*, pp. 144–7; Hirdt, *Studien zur Metaphorik Lamartines*, pp. 151–61; Stephan, *Goldenes Zeitalter und Arkadien*, pp. 77–83.

6 On this topic, Cellier, 'Le romantisme et le mythe d'Orphée'; Hermine B. Riffaterre, *L'Orphisme dans la poésie romantique*; Juden, *Traditions orphiques et tendances mystiques dans le romantisme français (1800–1855)*. See also my chapter eighteen, note 4.

7 There is an enormous bibliography on religion in Lamartine. For the purposes of this chapter, consult Guillemin, *'Jocelyn,'* pp. 246–96; Grillet, *La Bible dans Lamartine*, chapt. 29; and Lombard, 'The Evolution of Critical Opinion on the Ordination Scene in *Jocelyn.*'

8 For a recent essay on the topic, Furst, 'The Romantic Hero.' Gaudon has demonstrated the Sadian presence in Lamartine, especially with regard to *La Chute d'un Ange*: 'Lamartine lecteur de Sade,' and 'Les infortunes de la vertu.'

9 On space and time phonomenology in Lamartine, Schlötke-Schröer, 'Das Raum-Zeiterlebnis in der französischen Frühromantik'; Poulet, *Les Métamorphoses du cercle*, chapt. 7, and *Mesure de l'instant*, chapt. 9; Steele, 'Lamartine et la poésie vitale'; Richard, *Etudes sur le romantisme*, pp. 143–59; Lefèvre, 'Le printemps alpestre de *Jocelyn* ou l'imagination lamartinienne du bonheur.'

10 Bénichou, *Le Sacre de l'écrivain, 1750–1830*. On Lamartine, pp. 171–92.

11 On this topic, consult Brooks, *The Melodramatic Imagination*.

12 See Sengle, *Biedermeierzeit*; and Remak, 'The Periodization of xixth Century German Literature in the Light of French Trends.' One of the finest insights into the mentality of the period remains Auerbach, *Mimesis*, chapts. 16 and 17.

13 The term is from Porter, *The Renaissance of the Lyric in French Romanticism*, chapt. 1.

CHAPTER FOURTEEN

1 *Œuvres complètes*, ed. Fernand Baldensperger, Bibliothèque de la Pléiade, vol. 1 (Paris: Gallimard, 1950), p. 3. The major critical study on Vigny is by Germain, *L'Imagination d'Alfred de Vigny*.
2 On the *Kurzepos* during this period and on Vigny as an epic poet, Hunt, *Epic*, chapts. 7, 10, 11, and 12; Cellier, *Epopée romantique*, pp. 61–5; Bénichou, *Sacre*, pp. 353–79; Porter, *Renaissance*, chapt. 2; Saint-Gérand, *Les Destinées d'un style*, pp. 75–85.
3 *Œuvres complètes*, vol. 1, pp. 10–31. On Satan in Vigny and the seduction of an angel motif, see Milner, *Le Diable dans la littérature française de Cazotte à Baudelaire*, chapt. 11, and 'Le sexe des anges'; and Mölk, '*Ange femme* und *donna angelo.*'
4 Consult Germain, *Imagination*, pp. 131–50; and Legrand, *La Notion de 'couleur' dans l'œuvre poétique d'Alfred de Vigny*.
5 *Œuvres complètes*, vol. 1, pp. 69–77.
6 On this topic, Brombert, *La Prison romantique*.
7 On 'demonic imagery' throughout this period and in Vigny, Houston, *The Demonic Imagination*, esp. chapt. 4. Also Nitschke, *Studien zum Schiksalsgedanken und seiner dichterischen Gestaltung bei Alfred de Vigny*; and Savage, ' "Cette Prison Nommée La Vie." '
8 *Œuvres complètes*, vol. 1, pp. 109–15. For criticism on this text, Citron, *La Poésie de Paris dans la littérature française de Rousseau à Baudelaire*, pp. 264–78; Sokolova, 'Alfred de Vigny and the July Revolution, 1830–1831'; Viallaneix, 'Vigny prophète?'
9 On the Paris-theme, Citron, *Poésie*; Minder, 'Paris in der französischen Literatur (1760–1960)'; Wolfzettel, 'Funktionswandel eines epischen Motivs.' On the related topic of machinery and technology, Janik, 'Die technische Lebenswelt in der französischen Lyrik'; on clocks and time-imagery in Vigny, Jean-Paul Weber, *Genèse de l'œuvre poétique*, pp. 33–90.
10 Important essays have been written on space and time in Vigny: Poulet, *Etudes sur le temps humain*, chapt. 13, and *Métamorphoses*, chapt. 9; Germain, *Imagination*, esp. pp. 226–51; Richard, *Romantisme*, pp. 161–76.
11 *Œuvres complètes*, vol. 1, pp. 143–6. For criticism, Doolittle, 'The Function of *La Colère de Samson* in *Les Destinées*'; Haig, 'Notes on Vigny's Composition'; Minogue, 'Paths and Feet in *Les Destinées*,' and 'The Tableau in *La Colère de Samson*'; Wolfgang Meyer, *Die Gestaltung alttestamentlicher Erzählstoffe in der Poesie der Romantik und Spätromantik in Frankreich*, pp. 192–8.
12 *La carne, la morte e il diavolo nella letteratura romantica.*
13 *Œuvres complètes*, vol. 1, pp. 163–70. For the historical background, Bikoulitch and Nikolski, 'Une correspondance de Vigny avec la comtesse Kossakovskaïa'; Cadot, 'La véritable histoire de Wanda.'
14 For recent sociological interpretations of Vigny, see Fischer, 'Alfred de Vigny und die Interpretation der Romantik'; Sokolova, 'Alfred de Vigny'; Jameson, 'L'inconscient politique.'
15 Several books treat this problem: Petroni, *Poetica e poesia d'Alfred de Vigny*; Shroder, *Icarus*, chapt. 4; Viallaneix, *Vigny par lui-même*; Doolittle, *Alfred de Vigny*.

CHAPTER FIFTEEN

1 On Hugo as a poet of epic and myth, and on the composition of his three major works in this mode, see Hunt, *Epic*, chapt. 10; Berret, '*La Légende des Siècles*' *de Victor Hugo*; Cellier, *Epopée romantique*, pp. 221–73; Albouy, *La Création mythologique chez Victor Hugo*; Pollmann, *Epos*, pp. 147–51; Grant, *The Perilous Quest*, chapt. 6; Gaudon, *Le Temps de la Contemplation*, pp. 192–275; Gugelberger, ' "Tentative vers l'idéal" '; Houston, *Victor Hugo*, chapts. 5 and 6; Detalle, *Mythes*, pp. 357–413.

2 *Œuvres complètes*, ed. Jean Massin, vol. 10 (Paris: Club Français du Livre, 1969), pp. 469–72. On *Le Parricide*, Wäber, 'Victor Hugos "Le Parricide" und das Motiv von Schuld und Bestrafung.'

3 See Butor, 'Babel en creux.'

4 *Œuvres complètes*, vol. 10, pp. 486–92.

5 *Œuvres complètes*, vol. 10, pp. 511–37.

6 On Hugo and the Middle Ages, Berret, *Le Moyen Age dans 'La Légende des Siècles' et les sources de Victor Hugo*; Zumthor, 'Le Moyen Age de Victor Hugo'; Dakyns, *The Middle Ages in French Literature, 1851–1900*, chapt. 6; Ward, *The Medievalism of Victor Hugo*, esp. chapt. 8. On Hugo and Germany, with special reference to *La Légende*, Dédéyan, *Victor Hugo et l'Allemagne (1848–1885)*, vol. 1, chapt. 8; vol. 2, chapts. 4 and 5.

7 These qualities in Hugo's work have been elucidated by Barrère, *La Fantaisie de Victor Hugo*; and Gély, *Victor Hugo, poète de l'intimité*. Also consult Jauss, '*La douceur du foyer*'; and the papers collected in *Intime, intimité, intimisme*, ed. Molho and Reboul.

8 On architectural imagery, the prison, and the demonic in Hugo, consult Mallion, *Victor Hugo et l'art architectural*; Gaudon, *Contemplation*, pp. 299–312; Houston, *Demonic Imagination*, chapt. 7; Brombert, *Prison romantique*, pp. 93–125.

9 *Œuvres complètes*, vol. 10, pp. 603–8. On *La Rose de l'Infante*, Glauser, *La Poétique de Hugo*, pp. 227–39.

10 Hoffmann, *Romantique Espagne*.

11 *Œuvres complètes*, vol. 10, pp. 1621–1786; also René Journet and Guy Robert, *Contribution aux études sur Victor Hugo, vol. 2: Le texte de 'La Fin de Satan'* (Paris: Les Belles Lettres, 1979). On Hugo's conception of Satan and for criticism of *La Fin de Satan*, see the following books: Zumthor, *Victor Hugo, poète de Satan*; Milner, *Diable*, chapt. 26; Albouy, *Création mythologique*, pp. 263–304, and *Mythes et mythologies dans la littérature française*, pp. 146–50; Meyer, *Gestaltung*, pp. 127–32.

12 For the complex, many-stranded views on Christ during the first half of the nineteenth century, Bowman, *Le Christ romantique*. Also, Detalle, 'Le Christ dans l'épopée de Victor Hugo.'

13 The 'Hugolian imagination' has been studied from a phenomenological or existentialist perspective by Béguin, *L'Ame romantique et le rêve*, chapt. 18; Poulet, *La Distance intérieure*, chapt. 6; Michael Riffaterre, 'La vision hallucinatoire chez Victor Hugo'; Moreau, 'Les deux univers de Victor Hugo'; Richard, *Romantisme*, pp. 177–99; Glauser, *Poétique*; and Raymond, *Romantisme et rêverie*, chapt. 16.

14 On this topic, Savey-Casard, *Le Crime et la peine dans l'œuvre de Victor Hugo*.

15 For various Freudian or Jungian readings of Hugo's opus as a whole, Baudouin, *Triomphe*, chapt. 15, and *Psychanalyse de Victor Hugo*; Weber, *Genèse*, pp. 91–184; Mauron, 'Les personnages de Victor Hugo'; Seebacher, 'Poétique et politique de la paternité chez Victor Hugo'; also Schor, 'Superposition of Models in *La Légende des Siècles*.'

16 Cellier, *Epopée romantique*, p. 268.

17 *Œuvres*, ed. Yves-Gérard le Dantec, Bibliothèque de la Pléiade (Paris: Gallimard, 1954), p. 1092.

## CHAPTER SIXTEEN

1 I refer to Shattuck's seminal book, *The Banquet Years*.

2 On the epic in France during this period, Citoleux, *Voie royale*, chapt. 8; Hunt, *Epic*, chapts. 11 and 12.

3 The bibliography on Perse is immense. I recommend three books in English: Knodel, *Saint-John Perse*; Galand, *Saint-John Perse*; and Little, *Saint-John Perse*. Among recent studies in French, Caillois, *Poétique de St.-John Perse*; Poulet, *Le Point de départ*, chapt. 7; Richard, *Onze études sur la poésie moderne*, chapt. 2; Caduc, *Saint-John Perse*; Favre, *Saint-John Perse*; Levillain, *Le Rituel poétique de Saint-John Perse*; Ryan, *Rituel et poésie*; Nasta, *Saint-John Perse et la découverte de l'être*.

4 On this topic, Fusil, *La Poésie scientifique de 1750 à nos jours*; Schmidt, *Poésie scientifique*.

5 *Œuvres complètes*, Bibliothèque de la Pléiade (Paris: Gallimard, 1972), pp. 85–117. For criticism specifically on this text, Weinberg, *The Limits of Symbolism*, pp. 365–419; Elbaz, *Lectures d'Anabase' de Saint-John Perse*; Pruner, *L'Esotérisme de Saint-John Perse (dans 'Anabase')*; Richard, 'A propos d'*Anabase*,' and '*Anabase*'; Henry, 'Une lecture d'*Anabase*.'

6 I profited from Fabre, 'Publication d'*Anabase*,' pp. 406–7; Eliot, Preface, p. 10; Poggioli, 'The Poetry of St.-J. Perse,' pp. 12–19; Knodel, *Perse*, p. 45; Galand, *Perse*; Henry, 'Lecture.' Other exegetes offer radically different schemas or deny a narrative component to the text.

7 Quite a few articles have appeared on the subject, and one book by Yoyo, *Saint-John Perse et le conteur*.

8 Parent, *Saint-John Perse et quelques devanciers*, pp. 197–205.

9 *Œuvres complètes*, pp. 253–385. A well-received book on *Amers* is by Henry, '*Amers' de Saint-John Perse*.

10 Blin, 'Poésie et mantique chez Saint-John Perse'; also Guicharnaud, 'Vowels of the Sea.' On sea-marks as threshold, Little, 'The Image of the Threshold in the Poetry of Saint-John Perse.'

11 On the classical Greek element in *Amers* and the theme of ritual, see Noulet, *Le Ton poétique*, pp. 185–249; Galand, *Perse*, chapt. 6; Liliane Py, 'Dionysos dans l'espace théâtral d'*Amers*'; Rieuneau, '"Langage que fut la poétesse"'; Brunel, 'L'ode pindarique au XVIe siècle et au XXe siècle'; Favre, *Perse*; Levillain, *Rituel poétique*; Ryan, *Rituel*.

12 On this topos, Curtius, *Europäische Literatur*, chapt. 7.

13 Strikingly evident in the collection *Honneur à Saint-John Perse*, ed. Paulhan, and in the notes to the Pléiade edition of the *Œuvres complètes*.

CHAPTER SEVENTEEN

1 For a general introduction to Aragon's work, I recommend Raillard, *Aragon*;
and Lecherbonnier, *Aragon*. Garaudy, *L'Itinéraire d'Aragon*, is a major contribution. Also consult Daix's recent biography, *Aragon, une vie à changer*; and
*Les Critiques de notre temps et Aragon*, ed. Lecherbonnier.
2 Lecherbonnier, *Aragon, Le 'cycle d'Elsa.'* See also Labry, 'Le poète d'Elsa.'
3 On this topic, Seghers, *La Résistance et ses poètes*; Gaucheron, *La Poésie, la
Résistance*; and the issue of *Europe* devoted to *La Poésie et la Résistance*.
4 Quoted by Lecherbonnier, *Aragon*, p. 132.
5 *L'Œuvre poétique*, vol. 9 (Paris: Livre Club Diderot, 1979), pp. 321–50. On
*Brocéliande* and the poetry of the War years, Balakian, 'The Post-Surrealism
of Aragon and Eluard'; Carmody, 'The Sources of Aragon's War Poetry,
1939–1942.'
6 See Seghers, *Résistance*, p. 232.
7 On realism and patriotism in Aragon's poetry and poetics, especially during
the War years, Garaudy, *Itinéraire*, pp. 360–76; Raillard, *Aragon*, chapt. 4;
Lecherbonnier, *Aragon*, pp. 122–42 and 236–50; Selle, 'Das Verhältnis Aragons
und Johannes R. Bechers zum nationalen Erbe,' 'Aragons Reflexionen über die
französische Lyrik (1939–1959),' and 'Aragons Realismuskonzeption im Lichte
seiner Erbetheorie.'
8 *L'Œuvre poétique*, vol. 14 (Paris: Livre Club Diderot, 1981). For criticism on
this text, Haroche, *L'Idée de l'amour dans 'Le Fou d'Elsa' et l'œuvre d'Aragon*;
Babilas, 'Louis Aragon: *Le Fou d'Elsa*'; Husson, 'Lecture du *Fou d'Elsa*';
Berque, 'Zadjal pour une Grenade possible.'
9 On Aragon, with reference to *Le Fou d'Elsa* and surrealist *amour fou*, Caws, *The
Poetry of Dada and Surrealism*, chapt. 2.
10 See Brombert, *The Intellectual Hero*, and 'The Idea of the Hero.'
11 Haroche, *Idée*; Babilas, '*Fou d'Elsa*'; Berque, 'Zadjal.'
12 Babilas, 'Le collage dans l'œuvre critique et littéraire d'Aragon.' On the theme of
the writer in *Blanche ou l'oubli*, Bougnoux, '*Blanche ou l'oubli*' *d'Aragon*;
Jakobson, 'Le métalangage d'Aragon.'
13 This is the main thrust of Garaudy, *Itinéraire*.
14 One example among many, the conference in Montreal, 6–10 September 1967,
reported in *Etudes Littéraires: Le Poète dans la société contemporaine*.

CHAPTER EIGHTEEN

1 On Pierre Emmanuel's work as a whole, see Béguin, 'Pierre Emmanuel ou le
ciel en creux'; Bosquet, *Pierre Emmanuel*; Kushner, 'L'évolution des symboles
dans la poésie de Pierre Emmanuel'; Kuster, *L'Homme et la pierre dans la
poésie moderne*, pp. 33–9; Siegrist, *Pour et contre Dieu*; Onimus, *Expérience de
la poésie*, pp. 207–29; Marissel, *Pierre Emmanuel*; Jordens, *Pierre Emmanuel*;
and, for philosophical insights, the unpublished doctoral dissertation by Vistica,
'The Poetry of Pierre Emmanuel.'
2 *Tombeau d'Orphée suivi de Hymnes orphiques* (Paris: Seghers, 1967), pp.
23–118. I recommend the following criticism on this text: Chiari, *Contemporary
French Poetry*, chapt. 4; Kushner, *Le Mythe d'Orphée dans la littérature
française contemporaine*, pp. 297–346, and 'Evolution des symboles'; Vistica,
'Poetry,' pp. 78–109; Strauss, *Descent and Return*, pp. 241–8.

3  For an excellent study on the erotic in literature and its relationship to the sacred, Perella, *The Kiss, Sacred and Profane*.

4  On this theme I have used with profit Cellier, 'Romantisme'; Sewell, *Orphic Voice*; Kushner, *Mythe*; Bays, *The Orphic Vision*; Cattaui, *Orphisme et pro-phétie chez les poètes français, 1850–1950*; Albouy, *Mythes*, pp. 187–201; Fried-man, *Orpheus in the Middle Ages*; Joukovsky, *Orphée*; Riffaterre, *Orphisme*; Juden, *Traditions orphiques*; Strauss, *Descent*; Bräkling-Gersuny, *Orpheus, der Logos-Träger*. Also, with reference to Emmanuel, Livi, 'L'un des thèmes éternels de l'imagination poétique.'

5  *Babel* (Paris: Desclée De Brouwer, 1951). For criticism on this text, Kushner, 'Evolution'; Vistica, 'Poetry,' pp. 162–203; Couffignal, *'Aux premiers jours du monde ...,'* 'note complémentaire,' pp. v–vi.

6  *L'Ouvrier de la onzième heure* (Paris: Seuil, 1953).

7  Frye, *The Modern Century*, and Steiner, *In Bluebeard's Castle*, provide bril-liant analyses of the style and the way of life Pierre Emmanuel castigates in this poem.

8  Ginestier, *Le Poète et la machine*, chapt. 3; Minder, 'Paris'; Janik, 'Technische Lebenswelt'; Bonn-Gualino, *La Rêverie terrienne et l'espace de la modernité*; Krysinski, 'Entre aliénation et utopie'; Wolfzettel, 'Funktionswandel'; Zéraffa, 'Villes démoniaques.'

9  See Brombert, *Prison romantique*.

10  On this topic in literature, Kuhn, *The Demon of Noontide*.

11  *Poésie Raison ardente* (Paris: l.u.f. and Egloff, 1948), p. 7.

12  Although the Shepherd certainly is a Christ-figure and, typologically, he pre-figures Christ, his career does not correspond sufficiently to the Messiah's for him to be designated a 'fictional transfiguration,' in the sense given the term by Ziolkowski, *Fictional Transfigurations of Jesus*.

13  *Poésie Raison ardente*, p. 128.

14  *Pierre Emmanuel*, p. 44.

CONCLUSION

1  The modern style is analyzed with especial cogency by Friedrich, *Die Struktur der modernen Lyrik von Baudelaire bis zur Gegenwart*.

2  The point is made by Wentzlaff-Eggebert, *Der französische Roman um 1625*, pp. 34–43.

3  See *Die Theorie des Romans*.

4  Frye, *The Stubborn Structure*, chapt. 9, esp. p. 158; also *The Secular Scripture*.

5  A situation denounced by Sewell, *Orphic Voice*, pp. 302–3.

6  Sellier, *Mythe*, chapt. 8; Mathé, *L'Aventure, d'Hérodote à Malraux*, chapt. 8.

7  Quoted by Lindenberger, *Wordsworth's 'Prelude,'* p. 104.

8  The main lesson, perhaps, to be drawn from Albouy, *Mythes*.

9  Robert W. Greene, *Six French Poets of Our Time*, chapt. 6, esp. p. 175. It is interesting to note that, at a recent (Dec. 1978) special session of the MLA devoted to French verse since 1968, two young poets, Claude Herviant and Vim Karenine, informed me that their own work is tending now in the direction of epic. And, from an Anglo-American perspective, see Coxe, 'The Narrative Poem.' However, for the opposite view, cf. C.A. Hackett, 'Les grandes ten-dances de la poésie française depuis 1950,' p. 202.

10  Todorov, 'The Origin of Genres.'

11 See Bradley, 'The Long Poem in the Age of Wordsworth'; and Lindenberger, *Wordsworth's 'Prelude,'* chapt. 4.
12 See his essays on Virgil and Goethe in *Kritische Essays zur europäischen Literatur.*

# Bibliography of Critical Works Cited

Aarnes, Asbjørn *Pierre Le Moyne: En fransk barokkdikter*. Oslo: Tanum, 1965
Abercrombie, Lascelles *The Epic*. New York: Doran, n.d.
Adam, Antoine *Histoire de la littérature française au XVII siècle*. Vol. 2. Paris:
    Domat, 1951
Adams, D.J. *La Femme dans les contes et les romans de Voltaire*. Paris: Nizet, 1974
Adler, Alfred *Epische Spekulanten: Versuch einer synchronen Geschichte des altfran-
    zösischen Epos*. Munich: Fink, 1975
- 'Guillaume et son cercle "dans" *Raoul de Cambrai*.' *Romania*, 93 (1972), 1–19
- *Rückzug in epischer Parade: Studien zu 'Les Quatre Fils Aymon,' 'La Chevalerie
    Ogier de Danemarche,' 'Garin le Loherenc,' 'Raoul de Cambrai,' 'Aliscans,'
    'Huon de Bordeaux.'* Frankfurt/Main: Klostermann, 1963
Aebischer, Paul 'Pour la défense et l'illustration de l'épisode de Baligant.' In
    *Mélanges de philologie romane et de littérature médiévale offerts à Ernest
    Hoepffner*. Paris: Les Belles Lettres, 1949, pp. 173–82
Albouy, Pierre *La Création mythologique chez Victor Hugo*. Paris: Corti, 1963
- *Mythes et mythologies dans la littérature française*. Paris: Colin, 1969
Angeli, Giovanna ' "Comique" e "illusion" nella poesia di Saint-Amant.' *Saggi e
    Ricerche di Letteratura Francese*, no. 10 (1969), 31–95
Angenot, Marc *Les Champions des femmes: Examen du discours sur la supériorité
    des femmes, 1400–1800*. Montreal: Presses de l'Université du Québec, 1977
Antoine, Gérald 'La place de l'argent dans la littérature française médiévale.' *Tra-
    vaux de Linguistique et de Littérature*, 16:1 (1978), 17–31
Araujo, Norman *In Search of Eden: Lamartine's Symbols of Despair and Deliv-
    erance*. Brookline: Classical Folia Editions, 1976
Askew, Melvin W. 'Courtly Love: Neurosis as Institution.' *Psychoanalytic Review*,
    52 (1965), 19–29
*Association Guillaume Budé. Actes du Xe Congrès*. Paris: Les Belles Lettres, 1980
Atkinson, James C. 'Laisses 169–170 of the *Chanson de Roland*.' *MLN*, 82
    (1967), 271–84
Atsuhiko, Yoshida 'L'épopée.' In *Littérature et genres littéraires*. Paris: Larousse,
    1978, pp. 199–214
*Atti del convegno internazionale sul tema: La poesia epica e la sua formazione*.
    Rome: Accademia nazionale dei Lincei, 1970
Auerbach, Erich *Mimesis: dargestellte Wirklichkeit in der abendländischen Lite-
    ratur*. Berne: Francke, 1946

Babilas, Wolfgang 'Le collage dans l'œuvre critique et littéraire d'Aragon.' *Revue des Sciences Humaines*, no. 151 (1973), 329–54
– 'Louis Aragon: *Le Fou d'Elsa* – eine Reflexion über Zukunft und Liebe.' *Zeitschrift für französische Sprache und Literatur*, 77 (1967), 131–54
Badel, Pierre-Yves '*Le Roman de la Rose' au XIVe siècle: Etude de la réception de l'œuvre*. Geneva: Droz, 1980
Baïche, André *La Naissance du baroque français: Poésie et image de la Pléiade à Jean de La Ceppède*. Toulouse: Université de Toulouse-Le Mirail, 1976
Bailbé, Jacques *Agrippa d'Aubigné, poète des 'Tragiques.'* Caen: Université de Caen, 1968
Bakhtin, Mikhail *Rabelais and His World*. Cambridge, Mass.: MIT Press, 1968
Balakian, Anna 'The Post-Surrealism of Aragon and Eluard.' *Yale French Studies*, no. 2 (1948), 93–102
Bar, Francis *Le Genre burlesque en France au XVIIe siècle: Etude de style*. Paris: D'Artrey, 1960
Barrère, Jean-Bertrand *La Fantaisie de Victor Hugo*. 3 vols. Paris: Corti, 1949–60
Batany, Jean *Approches du 'Roman de la Rose.'* Paris: Bordas, 1973
Baudouin, Charles *Psychanalyse de Victor Hugo*. New ed. Paris: Colin, 1972
– *Le Triomphe du héros: Etude psychanalytique sur le mythe du héros et les grandes épopées*. Paris: Plon, 1952
Bays, Gwendolyn *The Orphic Vision: Seer Poets from Novalis to Rimbaud*. Lincoln: Univ. of Nebraska Press, 1964
Beall, Chandler B. *La Fortune du Tasse en France*. Eugene: Univ. of Oregon and Modern Language Association of America, 1942
Beeken, Lüder *Das Prinzip der Desillusionierung im komischen Epos des 18. Jahrhunderts: Zur Wesenbestimmung des deutschen Rokoko*. Diss. Hamburg, 1954
Béguin, Albert *L'Ame romantique et le rêve: Essai sur le romantisme allemand et la poésie française*. Paris: Corti, 1939
– 'Pierre Emmanuel ou le ciel en creux.' In his *Poésie de la Présence de Chrétien de Troyes à Pierre Emmanuel*. Neuchâtel: La Baconnière, 1957, pp. 337–60
Bellenger, Yvonne 'L'allégorie dans les poèmes de style élevé de Ronsard.' *Cahiers de l'Association Internationale des Etudes Françaises*, no. 28 (1976), 65–80
Bender, Karl-Heinz 'Un aspect de la stylisation épique: l'exclusivisme de la haute noblesse dans les chansons de geste du XIIe siècle.' In *Société Rencesvals. IVe Congrès International. Actes et Mémoires*. Heidelberg: Winter, 1969, pp. 95–104
– *König und Vasall: Untersuchungen zur Chanson de geste des XII. Jahrhunderts*. Heidelberg: Winter, 1967
Bénichou, Paul *Le Sacre de l'écrivain, 1750–1830: Essai sur l'avènement d'un pouvoir spirituel laïque dans la France moderne*. Paris: Corti, 1973
Bennett, P.E. 'Further Reflections on the Luminosity of the *Chanson de Roland*.' *Olifant*, 4 (1976–7), 191–204
Bensimon, Marc 'Essai sur Agrippa d'Aubigné.' *Studi Francesi*, 7 (1963), 418–37
Bergson, Henri *Le Rire: Essai sur la signification du comique*. 97th ed. Paris: Presses Universitaires de France, 1950
Berque, Jacques 'Zadjal pour une Grenade possible.' *L'Arc*, no. 53 (1973), 62–7
Berret, Paul '*La Légende des Siècles' de Victor Hugo: Etude et analyse*. Paris: Mellottée, 1945

- *Le Moyen Age dans 'La Légende des Siècles' et les sources de Victor Hugo.*
  Paris: Paulin, 1911
Bertaud, Madeleine *La Jalousie dans la littérature au temps de Louis XIII: Analyse littéraire et histoire des mentalités.* Geneva: Droz, 1981
- 'Un Jésuite au désert, le Père Le Moyne.' *XVIIe Siècle*, no. 109 (1975), 51–66
Besterman, Theodore *Voltaire.* New York: Harcourt, Brace and World, 1969
Beugnot, Bernard 'Boileau et la distance critique.' *Etudes Françaises*, 5 (1969), 195–206
- 'Boileau, une esthétique de la lumière.' *Studi Francesi*, 15 (1971), 229–37
Bezzola, Reto R. 'A propos de la valeur littéraire des chansons féodales.' In *La Technique littéraire des chansons de geste: Actes du Colloque de Liège.* Paris: Les Belles Lettres, 1959, pp. 183–95
- 'De Roland à Raoul de Cambrai.' In *Mélanges de philologie romane et de littérature médiévale offerts à Ernest Hoepffner.* Paris: Les Belles Lettres, 1949, pp. 195–213
- *Le Sens de l'aventure et de l'amour (Chrétien de Troyes).* Paris: La Jeune Parque, 1947
Bikoulitch, V.B., and A.D. Nikolski 'Une correspondance de Vigny avec la comtesse Kossakovskaïa.' *Europe*, no. 589 (May 1978), 20–8
Blin, Georges 'Poésie et mantique chez Saint-John Perse.' In *Mouvements premiers: Etudes critiques offertes à Georges Poulet.* Paris: Corti, 1972, pp. 299–305
Bloch, R. Howard *Medieval French Literature and Law.* Berkeley: Univ. of California Press, 1977
- 'Roland and Oedipus: A Study of Paternity in *La Chanson de Roland*.' *French Review*, 46 (Special Issue, no. 5, Spring 1973), 3–18
Bloomfield, Morton W. 'The Problem of the Hero in the Later Medieval Period.' In *Concepts of the Hero in the Middle Ages and the Renaissance.* Ed. Norman T. Burns and Christopher J. Reagan. Albany: State Univ. of New York Press, 1975, pp. 27–48
Boklund, Karin M. 'On the Spatial and Cultural Characteristics of Courtly Romance.' *Semiotica*, 20 (1977), 1–37
Bonn-Gualino, Annette *La Rêverie terrienne et l'espace de la modernité (dans quelques romans français parus de 1967 à 1972).* Paris: Klincksieck, 1976
Bosquet, Alain *Pierre Emmanuel.* Poètes d'Aujourd'hui, 67. Paris: Seghers, 1959
Bougnoux, Daniel *'Blanche ou l'oubli' d'Aragon.* Paris: Hachette, 1973
Boutet, Dominique 'La politique et l'histoire dans les chansons de geste.' *Annales. E.S.C.*, 31 (1976), 1119–30
Bowman, Frank Paul *Le Christ romantique.* Geneva: Droz, 1973
Bowra, Sir Cecil Maurice *From Virgil to Milton.* London: Macmillan, 1945
- *Heroic Poetry.* London: Macmillan, 1952
Bradley, Andrew Cecil 'The Long Poem in the Age of Wordsworth.' In his *Oxford Lectures on Poetry.* London: Macmillan, 1909, pp. 175–205
Bräkling-Gersuny, Gabriele *Orpheus, der Logos-Träger: Eine Untersuchung zum Nachleben des antiken Mythos in der französischen Literatur des 16. Jahrhunderts.* Munich: Fink, 1975
Brand, Wolfgang *Chrétien de Troyes: Zur Dichtungstechnik seiner Romane.* Munich: Fink, 1972
- 'Das Wirklichkeitsbild im *Lancelot* und *Yvain*.' *Vox Romanica*, 33 (1974), 186–213
Brault, Gerard J. 'Quelques nouvelles tendances de la critique et de l'interprétation

des chansons de geste.' In *Société Rencesvals. VIe Congrès International. Actes.*
Aix-en-Provence: Université de Provence, 1974, pp. 13–26
– ed. *The 'Song of Roland': An Analytical Edition.* Vol. 1: *Introduction and Commentary.* University Park: Pennsylvania State Univ. Press, 1978
Brody, Jules *Boileau and Longinus.* Geneva: Droz, 1958
– 'Boileau et la critique poétique.' In *Critique et création littéraires en France au XVIIe siècle.* Colloques Internationaux du CNRS, no. 557. Paris: Editions du Centre National de la Recherche Scientifique, 1977, pp. 231–50
Broich, Ulrich *Studien zum komischen Epos: Ein Beitrag zur Deutung, Typologie und Geschichte des komischen Epos im englischen Klassizismus, 1680–1800.* Tübingen: Niemeyer, 1968
Brombert, Victor 'The Idea of the Hero.' In his ed. *The Hero in Literature.* Greenwich, Conn.: Fawcett, 1969, pp. 11–21
– *The Intellectual Hero: Studies in the French Novel, 1880–1955.* Philadelphia: Lippincott, 1961
– *La Prison romantique: Essai sur l'imaginaire.* Paris: Corti, 1975
Brooks, Peter *The Melodramatic Imagination: Balzac, Henry James, Melodrama, and the Mode of Excess.* New Haven: Yale Univ. Press, 1976
Brown, George Hardin 'Yvain's Sin of Neglect.' *Symposium,* 27 (1973), 309–21
Brownlee, Kevin 'The Poetic Œuvre of Guillaume de Machaut: The Identity of Discourse and the Discourse of Identity.' In *Machaut's World: Science and Art in the Fourteenth Century.* Ed. Madeleine Pelner Cosman and Bruce Chandler. New York: New York Academy of Sciences, 1978, pp. 219–33
– 'Transformations of the Lyric "Je": The Example of Guillaume de Machaut.' *L'Esprit Créateur,* 18 (1978), 5–18
Brumfitt, J.H. *Voltaire, Historian.* London: Oxford Univ. Press, 1958
Brunel, Pierre 'L'ode pindarique au XVIe siècle et au XXe siècle.' *Revue de Littérature Comparée,* 51 (1977), 264–71
Burger, André *Turold, poète de la fidélité: Essai d'explication de la 'Chanson de Roland.'* Geneva: Droz, 1977
Butor, Michel 'Babel en creux.' In his *Répertoire II: Etudes et conférences, 1959–1963.* Paris: Minuit, 1964, pp. 199–214
Bynum, David E. 'The Generic Nature of Oral Epic Poetry.' *Genre,* 2 (1969), 236–58
– 'Themes of the Young Hero in Serbocroatian Oral Epic Tradition.' *PMLA,* 83 (1968), 1296–303
Cadot, Michel 'La véritable histoire de Wanda.' *Europe,* no. 589 (May 1978), 84–95
Caduc, Eveline *Saint-John Perse: Connaissance et création.* Paris: Corti, 1977
Caillois, Roger *Poétique de St.-John Perse.* Paris: Gallimard, 1954
Calin, William 'La comédie humaine chez Jean de Meun.' In *Mélanges d'histoire littéraire, de linguistique et de philologie romanes offerts à Charles Rostaing.* 2 vols. Ed. Jacques De Caluwé, et al. Liège: Association des Romanistes de l'Université de Liège, 1974, pp. 101–14
– *Crown, Cross, and 'Fleur-de-lis': An Essay on Pierre Le Moyne's Baroque Epic 'Saint Louis.'* Saratoga: Anma Libri, 1977
– *The Epic Quest: Studies in Four Old French 'Chansons de Geste.'* Baltimore: Johns Hopkins Press, 1966
– 'Love and War: Comic Themes in Voltaire's *Pucelle.*' *French Forum,* 2 (1977), 34–46

- *The Old French Epic of Revolt: 'Raoul de Cambrai,' 'Renaud de Montauban,' 'Gormond et Isembard.'* Geneva: Droz, 1962
- *A Poet at the Fountain: Essays on the Narrative Verse of Guillaume de Machaut.* Lexington: Univ. Press of Kentucky, 1974
- 'Ronsard and the Myth of Justice: A Typological Interpretation of *Hymne de la Justice.' Degré Second*, no. 1 (1977), 1–11
- 'Ronsard's Cosmic Warfare: An Interpretation of his *Hymnes* and *Discours.' Symposium*, 28 (1974), 101–18
Cameron, Keith 'Ronsard and Book IV of the *Franciade.' Bibliothèque d'Humanisme et Renaissance*, 32 (1970), 395–406
Campbell, Joseph *The Hero with a Thousand Faces.* New York: Pantheon, 1949
Candelaria, Frederick H., and William C. Strange, ed. *Perspectives on Epic.* Boston: Allyn and Bacon, 1965
Canfield, J. Douglas 'The Unity of Boileau's *Le Lutrin*: The Counter-Effect of the Mock-Heroic.' *Philological Quarterly*, 53 (1974), 42–58
Carmody, Francis J. 'The Sources of Aragon's War Poetry, 1939–1942.' *Books Abroad*, 35 (1961), 330–4
Cattaui, Georges *Orphisme et prophétie chez les poètes français, 1850–1950: Hugo, Nerval, Baudelaire, Mallarmé, Rimbaud, Valéry, Claudel.* Paris: Plon, 1965
Cave, Terence *The Cornucopian Text: Problems of Writing in the French Renaissance.* Oxford: Clarendon Press, 1979
–, ed. *Ronsard the Poet.* London: Methuen, 1973
Caws, Mary Ann *The Poetry of Dada and Surrealism: Aragon, Breton, Tzara, Eluard and Desnos.* Princeton: Princeton Univ. Press, 1970
Céard, Jean 'L'épopée en France au XVIe siècle.' In *Association Guillaume Budé. Actes du Xe Congrès.* Paris: Les Belles Lettres, 1980, pp. 221–41
Cellier, Léon *L'Epopée romantique.* Paris: Presses Universitaires de France, 1954
- 'Le romantisme et le mythe d'Orphée.' *Cahiers de l'Association Internationale des Etudes Françaises*, no. 10 (1958), 138–57
Cerquiglini, Jacqueline 'Le montage des formes: l'exemple de Guillaume de Machaut.' *Perspectives Médiévales*, no. 3 (October 1977), 23–6
- 'Pour une typologie de l'insertion.' *Perspectives Médiévales*, no. 3 (October 1977), 9–14
- 'Syntaxe et syncope: langage du corps et écriture chez Guillaume de Machaut.' *Langue Française*, no. 40 (1978), 60–74
*La Chasse au Moyen Age. Actes du Colloque de Nice.* Paris: Les Belles Lettres, 1980
Chauveau, Jean-Pierre 'A la recherche de la modernité en poésie (1623–1630).' In *Le XVIIe Siècle et la recherche. Actes du 6ème Colloque de Marseille.* Marseille: Centre Méridional de Rencontres, n.d., pp. 163–8
Cherchi, Paolo 'Un dovere della *pietas* regia: l'uccisione del nemico.' *Modern Philology*, 73 (1975–6), 244–56
Chérot, Henri *Etude sur la vie et les œuvres du P. Le Moyne (1602–1671).* Paris: Picard, 1887
Chiari, Joseph *Contemporary French Poetry.* New York: Philosophical Library, 1952
Cioranescu, Alexandre 'La Pléiade et le poème épique.' In *Lumières de la Pléiade. Neuvième Stage International d'Etudes Humanistes.* Paris: Vrin, 1966, pp. 75–86
Citoleux, Marc *La Voie royale de la poésie française.* Paris: Garnier, n.d.

Citron, Pierre *La Poésie de Paris dans la littérature française de Rousseau à Baude-laire.* 2 vols. Paris: Minuit, 1961

Collinder, Björn 'On the Translation of Epics.' *Sprachkunst,* 3 (1972), 327–32

Colliot, Régine 'Enfants et enfance dans *Raoul de Cambrai.*' In *L'Enfant au Moyen-Age (Littérature et civilisation).* Aix-en Provence: CUER MA, 1980, pp. 233–52

– 'Perspective sur la condition familiale et sociale de l'enfant dans la littérature médiévale.' In *Morale pratique et vie quotidienne dans la littérature française du Moyen Age.* Aix-en-Provence: CUER MA, 1976, pp. 17–33

Combarieu, Micheline de 'Enfance et démesure dans l'épopée médiévale française.' In *L'Enfant au Moyen-Age (Littérature et civilisation).* Aix-en-Provence: CUER MA, 1980, pp. 405–56

– *L'Idéal humain et l'expérience morale chez les héros des chansons de geste, des origines à 1250.* 2 vols. Aix-en-Provence: Université de Provence, 1979

Cook, Albert *The Classic Line: A Study in Epic Poetry* Bloomington: Indiana Univ. Press, 1966

Cook, Robert Francis 'The Search for the Medieval Epic.' Comparative Studies in Medieval Literature, MLA Convention, New York. Dec. 1978

Cook, Robert G. 'The Ointment in Chrétien's *Yvain.*' *Mediaeval Studies,* 31 (1969), 338–42

Cordier, Marcel 'Réflexions sur la description lamartinienne des grottes.' *Revue des Sciences Humaines,* no. 149 (1973), 105–38

Cosper, D. Dale 'Saint-Amant: Pictorialism and the Devotional Style.' *Romance Notes,* 17 (1976–7), 286–97

Cottaz, Joseph *L'Influence des théories du Tasse sur l'épopée en France.* Paris: Italia, 1942

Couffignal, Robert *'Aux premiers jours du monde ...': La Paraphrase poétique de la 'Genèse' de Hugo à Supervielle.* Paris: Minard, 1970

– *La Lutte avec l'ange: Le récit de la 'Genèse' et sa fortune littéraire.* Toulouse: Université de Toulouse-Le Mirail, 1977

Coxe, Louis 'The Narrative Poem: Novel of the Future?' *Minnesota Review,* 3 (1962–3), 17–31

Crosby, Virginia 'Prophetic Discourse in Ronsard and D'Aubigné.' *French Review,* 45 (Special Issue, no. 3, Fall 1971), 91–100

Crosland, Jessie *The Old French Epic.* Oxford: Blackwell, 1951

Curtius, Ernst Robert *Europäische Literatur und lateinisches Mittelalter.* Berne: Francke, 1948

– *Kritische Essays zur europäischen Literatur.* Berne: Francke, 1950

– 'Über die altfranzösische Epik II, III, IV, V.' *Romanische Forschungen,* 61 (1948), 421–60; 62 (1950), 125–57 and 294–349; *Zeitschrift für romanische Philologie,* 68 (1952), 177–208

Dagens, Jean 'La théologie poétique au temps de Ronsard.' In *Atti del quinto congresso internazionale di lingue e letterature moderne.* Florence: Valmartina, 1955, pp. 147–53

Daix, Pierre *Aragon, une vie à changer.* Paris: Seuil, 1975

Dakyns, Janine R. *The Middle Ages in French Literature, 1851–1900.* London: Oxford Univ. Press, 1973

Damon, Phillip 'Myth, Metaphor, and the Epic Tradition.' *Orbis Litterarum,* 24 (1969), 85–100

Dassonville, Michel 'Eléments pour une définition de l'hymne ronsardien.' *Bibliothèque d'Humanisme et Renaissance*, 24 (1962), 58–76
– *Ronsard: Etude historique et littéraire*. Vol. 3. Geneva: Droz, 1976
Dawson, F.K. 'The Ideal Hero: A Seventeenth-Century Choice.' *Nottingham French Studies*, 4 (1965), 54–65
Debidour, Victor-Henry *Saveurs des lettres: Problèmes littéraires*. Paris: Plon, 1946
Dédéyan, Charles *Victor Hugo et l'Allemagne (1848–1885)*. 2 vols. Paris: CDU and SEDES, 1977
Delasanta, Rodney *The Epic Voice*. The Hague: Mouton, 1967
Delattre, André *Voltaire l'impétueux*. Paris: Mercure de France, 1957
Delbouille, Maurice 'Les chansons de geste et le livre.' In *La Technique littéraire des chansons de geste. Actes du Colloque de Liège*. Paris: Les Belles Lettres, 1959, pp. 295–407
Demerson, Guy 'Métamorphose et analogie: Pierre Le Moyne.' In *La Métamorphose dans la poésie baroque française et anglaise: Variations et résurgences*. Ed. Gisèle Mathieu-Castellani. Tübingen: Narr, 1980, pp. 143–58
– *La Mythologie classique dans l'œuvre lyrique de la 'Pléiade.'* Geneva: Droz, 1972
Dessau, Adalbert 'L'idée de la trahison au moyen âge et son rôle dans la motivation de quelques chansons de geste.' *Cahiers de Civilisation Médiévale*, 3 (1960), 23–6
Detalle, Anny 'Le Christ dans l'épopée de Victor Hugo.' In *Association Guillaume Budé. Actes du Xe Congrès*. Paris: Les Belles Lettres, 1980, pp. 275–8
– *Mythes, merveilleux et légendes dans la poésie française de 1840 à 1860*. Paris: Klincksieck, 1976
Doolittle, James *Alfred de Vigny*. New York: Twayne, 1967
– 'The Function of *La Colère de Samson* in *Les Destinées*.' *Modern Language Quarterly*, 18 (1957), 63–8
Dragonetti, Roger 'Pygmalion ou les pièges de la fiction dans le *Roman de la Rose*.' In *Orbis Mediaevalis: Mélanges de langue et de littérature médiévales offerts à Reto Raduolf Bezzola*. Ed. Georges Güntert, et al. Berne: Francke, 1978, pp. 89–111
– 'Le "singe de nature" dans le *Roman de la Rose*.' *Travaux de Linguistique et de Littérature*, 16:1 (1978), 149–60
Drijkoningen, F.F.J. 'Quelques aspects de la pompe littéraire au XVIIe siècle.' *Neophilologus*, 51 (1967), 364–81
Dubois, Claude-Gilbert *La Conception de l'Histoire en France au XVIe siècle (1560–1610)*. Paris: Nizet, 1977
– 'Les images de parenté dans *Les Tragiques*: essai de mythocritique.' *Europe*, no. 563 (March 1976), 27–42
Duby, Georges 'Dans la France du Nord-Ouest au XIIe siècle: les *jeunes* dans la société aristocratique.' *Annales. E.S.C.*, 19 (1964), 835–46
Duchesne, Julien *Histoire des poëmes épiques français du XVIIe siècle*. Paris: Thorin, 1870
Durling, Robert M. *The Figure of the Poet in Renaissance Epic*. Cambridge, Mass.: Harvard Univ. Press, 1965
Duval, Edwin M. *Poesis and Poetic Tradition in the Early Works of Saint-Amant: Four Essays in Contextual Reading*. York, S.C.: French Literature Publications, 1981

Eberle, Josef *Voltaires 'Pucelle': Die Geschichte eines Gedichtes*. Aschaffenburg: Gesellschaft der Bibliophilen, 1966

Eberle, Patricia J. 'The Lovers' Glass: Nature's Discourse on Optics and the Optical Design of the *Romance of the Rose*.' *University of Toronto Quarterly*, 46 (1976–7), 241–62

Economou, George D. *The Goddess Natura in Medieval Literature*. Cambridge, Mass.: Harvard Univ. Press, 1972

Edelman, Nathan *'L'Art poétique:* "Long-temps plaire, et jamais ne lasser." ' In *Studies in Seventeenth-Century French Literature Presented to Morris Bishop*. Ed. Jean-Jacques Demorest. Ithaca: Cornell Univ. Press, 1962, pp. 231–46

– *Attitudes of Seventeenth-Century France toward the Middle Ages*. New York: King's Crown Press, 1946

Elbaz, Shlomo *Lectures d'"Anabase' de Saint-John Perse: Le désert, le désir*. Lausanne: L'Age d'Homme, 1977

Eliot, Thomas Stearns, ed. and trans. *Anabasis, A Poem by St.-J. Perse*. New York: Harcourt, Brace, 1938

Emard, Paul, and Suzanne Fournier *La Sainte-Chapelle du 'Lutrin': Pourquoi et comment Boileau a composé son poème*. Geneva: Droz, 1963

Emmel, Hildegard *Formprobleme des Artusromans und der Graldichtung: Die Bedeutung des Artuskreises für das Gefüge des Romans im 12. und 13. Jahrhundert in Frankreich, Deutschland und den Niederlanden*. Berne: Francke, 1951

Etiemble, René 'L'épopée de l'épopée.' In his *Essais de littérature (vraiment) générale*. Paris: Gallimard, 1974, pp. 163–75

Fabre, Lucien 'Publication d'*Anabase*.' Repr. in *Honneur à Saint-John Perse*. Ed. Jean Paulhan. Paris: Gallimard, 1965, pp. 406–11

Fasano, Giancarlo *'Les Tragiques': Un' epopea della morte*. 2 vols. Bari: Adriatica, 1970

Favre, Yves-Alain *Saint-John Perse: Le langage et le sacré*. Paris: Corti, 1977

Fischer, Jan O. 'Alfred de Vigny und die Interpretation der Romantik.' *Beiträge zur romanischen Philologie*, 8 (1969), 82–93

Fleming, John V. *The 'Roman de la Rose': A Study in Allegory and Iconography*. Princeton: Princeton Univ. Press, 1969

Fletcher, Angus *Allegory: The Theory of a Symbolic Mode*. Ithaca: Cornell Univ. Press, 1964

Flori, Jean 'Qu'est-ce qu'un *bacheler*? Etude historique de vocabulaire dans les chansons de geste du xiie siècle.' *Romania*, 96 (1975), 289–314

Forsyth, Elliott 'Le message prophétique d'Agrippa d'Aubigné.' *Bibliothèque d'Humanisme et Renaissance*, 41 (1979), 23–39

France, Peter *Rhetoric and Truth in France: Descartes to Diderot*. Oxford: Clarendon Press, 1972

Frappier, Jean *Chrétien de Troyes, l'homme et l'œuvre*. Paris: Hatier-Boivin, 1957

– *Étude sur 'Yvain ou le Chevalier au Lion' de Chrétien de Troyes*. Paris: SEDES, 1969

– and Reinhold R. Grimm, ed. *Le Roman jusqu'à la fin du XIIIe siècle*. Vol. 4, t. 1 of *Grundriss der romanischen Literaturen des Mittelalters*. Heidelberg: Winter, 1978

– 'Le thème de la lumière, de la *Chanson de Roland* au *Roman de la Rose*.' *Cahiers de l'Association Internationale des Etudes Françaises*, no. 20 (1968), 101–24

Friedman, John Block *Orpheus in the Middle Ages*. Cambridge, Mass.: Harvard Univ. Press, 1970

Friedrich, Hugo  *Die Struktur der modernen Lyrik von Baudelaire bis zur Gegen-
wart.* Hamburg: Rowohlt, 1956
Frings, Theodor  'Europäische Heldendichtung.' *Neophilologus,* 24 (1938–9), 1–29
Frye, Northrop  *Anatomy of Criticism: Four Essays.* Princeton: Princeton Univ.
Press, 1957
– *The Modern Century.* Toronto: Oxford Univ. Press, 1967
– *The Secular Scripture: A Study of the Structure of Romance.* Cambridge, Mass.:
Harvard Univ. Press, 1976
– *The Stubborn Structure: Essays on Criticism and Society.* Ithaca: Cornell Univ.
Press, 1970
Fumaroli, Marc  'Ethique et rhétorique du héros humaniste: du Magnanime à
l'Homme de ressentiment.' *Papers on French Seventeenth Century Literature,*
nos. 4–5 (Summer 1976), 167–201
Furst, Lilian R.  'The Romantic Hero, or is he an Anti-Hero?' *Studies in the Liter-
ary Imagination,* 9:1 (1976), 53–67
Fusil, C.-A.  *La Poésie scientifique de 1750 à nos jours: Son élaboration, sa constitu-
tion.* Paris: Scientifica, 1917
Gadoffre, Gilbert  *Ronsard par lui-même.* Paris: Seuil, 1960
Galand, René  *Saint-John Perse.* New York: Twayne, 1972
Garaudy, Roger  *L'Itinéraire d'Aragon: Du surréalisme au monde réel.* Paris: Galli-
mard, 1961
Gaucheron, Jacques  *La Poésie, la Résistance: Du Front Populaire à la Libération.*
Paris: Editeurs Français Réunis, 1979
Gaudon, Jean  'Les infortunes de la vertu.' In *Lamartine: Le Livre du Centenaire.*
Ed. Paul Viallaneix. Paris: Flammarion, 1971, pp. 31–43
– 'Lamartine lecteur de Sade.' *Mercure de France,* no. 343 (Sept.–Dec. 1961),
420–38
– *Le Temps de la Contemplation: L'œuvre poétique de Victor Hugo, des 'Misères'
au 'Seuil du Gouffre' (1845–1856).* Paris: Flammarion, 1969
Gély, Claude  *Victor Hugo, poète de l'intimité.* Paris: Nizet, 1969
Genette, Gérard  'D'un récit baroque.' In his *Figures II.* Paris: Seuil, 1969, pp.
195–222
– 'Genres, "types", modes.' *Poétique,* no. 32 (1977), 389–421
– ' "L'or tombe sous le fer." ' In his *Figures I.* Paris: Seuil, 1966, pp. 29–38
– 'L'univers réversible.' In his *Figures I.* Paris: Seuil, 1966, pp. 9–20
Gerhardt, Mia I.  *Old Men of the Sea: From 'Neptunus' to Old French 'luiton', An-
cestry and Character of a Water-Spirit.* Amsterdam: Polak and Van Gennep, 1967
Germain, François  *L'Art de commenter une épopée: Etude du style épique avec
applications à la composition française.* Paris: Foucher, 1960
– *L'Imagination d'Alfred de Vigny.* Paris: Corti, 1961
Giamatti, A. Bartlett  *The Earthly Paradise and the Renaissance Epic.* Princeton:
Princeton Univ. Press, 1966
Gillet, Jean  *'Le Paradis perdu' dans la littérature française de Voltaire à Chateau-
briand.* Paris: Klincksieck, 1975
Ginestier, Paul  *Le Poète et la machine.* Paris: Nizet, 1954
Giraud, Yves F.-A.  *La Fable de Daphné: Essai sur un type de métamorphose
végétale dans la littérature et dans les arts jusqu'à la fin du XVIIe siècle.* Geneva:
Droz, 1968
Glauser, Alfred  *La Poétique de Hugo.* Paris: Nizet, 1978
Gordon, Alex L.  *Ronsard et la rhétorique.* Geneva: Droz, 1970

Gourier, Françoise *Etude des œuvres poétiques de Saint-Amant.* Geneva: Droz, 1961

Grant, Richard B. *The Perilous Quest: Image, Myth, and Prophecy in the Narratives of Victor Hugo.* Durham, N.C.: Duke Univ. Press, 1968

Green, Dennis H. *Irony in the Medieval Romance.* Cambridge, England: Cambridge Univ. Press, 1979

Greenberg, Mitchell 'The Poetics of Trompe-l'œil: d'Aubigné's "tableaux célestes."' *Neophilologus,* 63 (1979), 4–22

Greene, Robert W. *Six French Poets of Our Time: A Critical and Historical Study.* Princeton: Princeton Univ. Press, 1979

Greene, Thomas *The Descent from Heaven: A Study in Epic Continuity.* New Haven: Yale Univ. Press, 1963

Grigsby, John L. 'Sign, Symbol and Metaphor: Todorov and Chrétien de Troyes.' *L'Esprit Créateur,* 18:3 (1978), 28–40

Grillet, Claudius *La Bible dans Lamartine.* Lyon: Vitte, 1938

Grimm, Jürgen *Die literarische Darstellung der Pest in der Antike und in der Romania.* Munich: Fink, 1965

Grob, Ruth *Studien zu den 'Tragiques' des Agrippa d'Aubigné.* Zurich: Akeret, 1942

Gross-Kiefer, Esther *Le Dynamisme cosmique chez Le Moyne.* Zurich: Juris, 1968

Gugelberger, G.M. ' "Tentative vers l'idéal": Genero-periodicism and Victor Hugo's *La Légende des Siècles* (A Reconsideration of the Term "Romantic" through Genology).' *Genre,* 7 (1974), 322–41

Guicharnaud, Jacques 'Vowels of the Sea: *Amers,* by Saint-John Perse.' *Yale French Studies,* no. 21 (1958), 72–82

Guillemin, Henri *Le 'Jocelyn' de Lamartine: Etude historique et critique avec des documents inédits.* Paris: Boivin, 1936

–, ed. *Les Visions.* By Lamartine. Paris: Les Belles Lettres, 1936

Guillén, Claudio *Literature as System: Essays toward the Theory of Literary History.* Princeton: Princeton Univ. Press, 1971

Gunn, Alan M.F. *The Mirror of Love: A Reinterpretation of 'The Romance of the Rose.'* Lubbock: Texas Tech Press, 1952

– 'Teacher and Student in the *Roman de la Rose*: A Study in Archetypal Figures and Patterns.' *L'Esprit Créateur,* 2 (1962), 126–34

Gunny, Ahmad *Voltaire and English Literature: A Study of English Literary Influences on Voltaire.* Oxford: Voltaire Foundation, 1979

Gybbon-Monypenny, G.B. 'Guillaume de Machaut's Erotic "Autobiography": Precedents for the Form of the *Voir-Dit.*' In *Studies in Medieval Literature and Languages in Memory of Frederick Whitehead.* Ed. W. Rothwell et al. Manchester: Manchester Univ. Press, 1973, pp. 133–52

Hackett, C.A. 'Les grandes tendances de la poésie française depuis 1950.' *Cahiers de l'Association Internationale des Etudes Françaises,* no. 30 (1978), 195–208

Hackett, W. Mary 'Le gant de Roland.' *Romania,* 89 (1968), 253–6

Hägin, Peter *The Epic Hero and the Decline of Heroic Poetry: A Study of the Neoclassical English Epic with Special Reference to Milton's 'Paradise Lost.'* Berne: Francke, 1964

Hagiwara, Michio Peter *French Epic Poetry in the Sixteenth Century: Theory and Practice.* The Hague: Mouton, 1972

Haidu, Peter  *Aesthetic Distance in Chrétien de Troyes: Irony and Comedy in 'Cligès' and 'Perceval.'* Geneva: Droz, 1968
- *Lion-queue-coupée: L'écart symbolique chez Chrétien de Troyes.* Geneva: Droz, 1972
Haig, Stirling 'Notes on Vigny's Composition.' *Modern Language Review*, 60 (1965), 369–73
Hallyn, Fernand 'La matière biblique et son sens religieux dans le *Moyse Sauvé* de Saint-Amant.' *Romanica Gandensia*, no. 12 (1969), 73–92
Halverson, John 'Ganelon's Trial.' *Speculum*, 42 (1967), 661–9
Hanf, Georg 'Über Guillaume de Machauts *Voir Dit.*' *Zeitschrift für romanische Philologie*, 22 (1898), 145–96
Hanning, Robert W.  *The Individual in Twelfth-Century Romance.* New Haven: Yale Univ. Press, 1977
Haroche, Charles  *L'Idée de l'amour dans 'Le Fou d'Elsa' et l'œuvre d'Aragon.* Paris: Gallimard, 1966
Harward, Vernon J., Jr.  *The Dwarfs of Arthurian Romance and Celtic Tradition.* Leiden: Brill, 1958
Hatzfeld, Helmut 'La mystique naturiste de Jean de Meung.' *Wissenschaftliche Zeitschrift der Friedrich-Schiller-Universität Jena: Gesellschafts- und Sprachwissenschaftliche Reihe*, 5 (1955–6), 259–69
Haupt, Jürgen  *Der Truchsess Keie im Artusroman: Untursuchungen zur Gesellschaftsstruktur im höfischen Roman.* Berlin: Schmidt, 1971
Heger, Henrik  *Die Melancholie bei den französischen Lyrikern des Spätmittelalters.* Bonn: Romanisches Seminar der Universität Bonn, 1967
Henry, Albert  *'Amers' de Saint-John Perse: Une poésie du mouvement.* Neuchâtel: La Baconnière, 1963
- 'Une lecture d'*Anabase.*' *Cahiers Saint-John Perse*, no. 2 (1979), 35–60
Hieatt, Constance B.  ' "Un autre fourme": Guillaume de Machaut and the Dream Vision Form.' *Chaucer Review*, 14 (1979–80), 97–115
Hill, Thomas D. 'Narcissus, Pygmalion, and the Castration of Saturn: Two Mythographical Themes in the *Roman de la Rose.*' *Studies in Philology*, 71 (1974), 404–26
Hirdt, Willi  *Studien zur Metaphorik Lamartines: Die Bedeutung der Innen/Aussen-Vorstellung.* Munich: Fink, 1967
Hofer, Stefan  *Chrétien de Troyes: Leben und Werke des altfranzösischen Epikers.* Graz: Böhlau, 1954
Hoffmann, Léon-François  *Romantique Espagne: L'image de l'Espagne en France entre 1800 et 1850.* Paris: Presses Universitaires de France, 1961
Honig, Edwin  *Dark Conceit: The Making of Allegory.* Evanston: Northwestern Univ. Press, 1959
Hope, Quentin M. 'Pierre Lemoyne's Glorious and Lofty Hymns.' *L'Esprit Créateur*, 20:4 (1980), 29–39
Horváth, K. 'The Romantic Attitude to Nature.' In *European Romanticism.* Ed. I. Sötér and I. Neupokoyeva. Budapest: Akadémiai Kiadó, 1977, pp. 209–71
Houston, John Porter  *The Demonic Imagination: Style and Theme in French Romantic Poetry.* Baton Rouge: Louisiana State Univ. Press, 1969
- *Victor Hugo.* New York: Twayne, 1974
Huch, Volker  *Erlösungsdenken im humanitären Epos des 19. Jahrhunderts in Frankreich.* Wiesbaden: Steiner, 1974
Huizinga, Johan  *The Waning of the Middle Ages: A Study of the Forms of Life,*

*Thought and Art in France and the Netherlands in the XIVth and XVth Centuries.* London: Arnold, 1924

Hunt, Herbert J. *The Epic in Nineteenth-Century France: A Study in Heroic and Humanitarian Poetry from 'Les Martyrs' to 'Les Siècles Morts.'* Oxford: Blackwell, 1941

Husson, Roland 'Lecture du *Fou d'Elsa.*' *Australian Journal of French Studies,* 5 (1968), 59–83

Ineichen, Gustav 'Le discours linguistique de Jean de Meun.' *Romanistische Zeitschrift für Literaturgeschichte,* 2 (1978), 245–51

Jackson, William T.H. *The Hero and the King: An Epic Theme.* New York: Columbia Univ. Press, 1982

Jacobs, Jürgen 'Das Verstummen der Muse: Zur Geschichte der epischen Dichtungsgattungen im XVIII. Jahrhundert.' *Arcadia,* 10 (1975), 129–46

Jakobson, Roman 'Le métalangage d'Aragon.' *L'Arc,* no. 53 (1973), 79–84

Jameson, Fredric 'L'inconscient politique.' In *La Lecture sociocritique du texte romanesque.* Ed. Graham Falconer and Henri Mitterand. Toronto: Stevens, Hakkert, 1975, pp. 39–48

Janik, Dieter 'Die technische Lebenswelt in der französischen Lyrik: Erfahrungen und Ausdrucksformen.' *Romanische Forschungen,* 87 (1975), 593–616

Jauss, Hans Robert 'Chanson de geste et roman courtois au XIIe siècle (Analyse comparative du *Fierabras* et du *Bel Inconnu*).' In *Chanson de Geste und höfischer Roman. Heidelberger Kolloquium.* Heidelberg: Winter, 1963, pp. 61–77

– '*La douceur du foyer:* Lyrik des Jahres 1857 als Muster der Vermittlung sozialer Normen.' In his *Ästhetische Erfahrung und literarische Hermeneutik.* Vol. 1. Munich: Fink, 1977, pp. 343–76

– 'Entstehung und Strukturwandel der allegorischen Dichtung.' In his ed. *La Littérature didactique, allégorique et satirique.* Vol. 6, t. 1 of *Grundriss der romanischen Literaturen des Mittelalters.* Heidelberg: Winter, 1968, pp. 146–244

Johnson, Phyllis '*Huon de Bordeaux* et la sémantique de l'*enfes.*' *Zeitschrift für romanische Philologie,* 91 (1975), 69–78

Jonin, Pierre 'Le vasselage de Lancelot dans le *Conte de la Charette.*' *Moyen Age,* 58 (1952), 281–98

Jordens, Camille *Pierre Emmanuel: Introduction générale à l'œuvre.* Louvain: Universiteit Leuven, 1981

Joukovsky-Micha, Françoise 'La Guerre des dieux et des géants chez les poètes français du XVIe siècle (1500–1585).' *Bibliothèque d'Humanisme et Renaissance,* 29 (1967), 55–92

– *Orphée et ses disciples dans la poésie française et néolatine du XVIe siècle.* Geneva: Droz, 1970

Juden, Brian *Traditions orphiques et tendances mystiques dans le romantisme français (1800–1855).* Paris: Klincksieck, 1971

Jump, John D. *Burlesque.* London: Methuen, 1972

Jung, Marc-René *Etudes sur le poème allégorique en France au moyen âge.* Berne: Francke, 1971

– 'Jean de Meun et l'allégorie.' *Cahiers de l'Association Internationale des Etudes Françaises,* 28 (1976), 21–36

– 'Jean de Meun et son lecteur.' *Romanistische Zeitschrift für Literaturgeschichte,* 2 (1978), 241–4

Kanduth, Erika 'Der Rosenroman – ein Bildungsbuch?' *Zeitschrift für romanische Philologie,* 86 (1970), 509–24

Karrer, Wolfgang  *Parodie, Travestie, Pastiche.* Munich: Fink, 1977

Kay, H.S.  'Topography and the Relative Realism of Battle Scenes in Chansons de geste.' *Olifant,* 4 (1976–7), 259–78

Keller, Luzius  *Palingène, Ronsard, Du Bartas: Trois études sur la poésie cosmologique de la Renaissance.* Berne: Francke, 1974

Kellermann, Wilhelm  *Aufbaustil und Weltbild Chrestiens von Troyes im Percevalroman.* Halle/Saale: Niemeyer, 1936

Kelly, Douglas  ' "Li chastiaus ... Qu'Amors prist puis par ses esforz": The Conclusion of Guillaume de Lorris' *Rose.'* In *A Medieval French Miscellany: Papers of the 1970 Kansas Conference on Medieval French Literature.* Ed. Norris J. Lacy. Lawrence: Univ. of Kansas Publications, 1972, pp. 61–78

– *Medieval Imagination: Rhetoric and the Poetry of Courtly Love.* Madison: Univ. of Wisconsin Press, 1978

– *'Sens' and 'Conjointure' in the 'Chevalier de la Charrette.'* The Hague: Mouton, 1966

Kennedy, William J.  *Rhetorical Norms in Renaissance Literature.* New Haven: Yale Univ. Press, 1978

Kind, Helmut  *Das Rokoko und seine Grenzen im deutschen komischen Epos des 18. Jahrhunderts.* Diss. Halle/Saale, 1945

Kinter, William L., and Joseph R. Keller  *The Sibyl: Prophetess of Antiquity and Medieval Fay.* Philadelphia: Dorrance, 1967

Klemperer, Victor  *Geschichte der französischen Literatur im 18. Jahrhundert.* Vol. 1. Berlin: Deutscher Verlag der Wissenschaften, 1954

Knapp, F.P.  'Die grosse Schlacht zwischen Orient und Okzident in der abendländischen Epik: Ein antikes Thema in mittelalterlichem Gewand.' *Germanisch-romanische Monatsschrift,* 55 (1974), 129–52

Knodel, Arthur  *Saint-John Perse: A Study of his Poetry.* Edinburgh: Edinburgh Univ. Press, 1966

Köhler, Erich  *'Conseil des barons' und 'Jugement des barons': Epische Fatalität und Feudalrecht im altfranzösischen Rolandslied.* Heidelberg: Winter, 1968

– *Ideal und Wirklichkeit in der höfischen Epik: Studien zur Form der frühen Artus- und Graldichtung.* Tübingen: Niemeyer, 1956

– 'Narcisse, la Fontaine d'Amour et Guillaume de Lorris.' *Journal des Savants* (1963), 86–103

– 'Quelques observations d'ordre historico-sociologique sur les rapports entre la chanson de geste et le roman courtois.' In *Chanson de Geste und höfischer Roman. Heidelberger Kolloquium.* Heidelberg: Winter, 1963, pp. 21–30

Köhring, Klaus Heinrich  *Die Formen des 'long poem' in der modernen amerikanischen Literatur.* Heidelberg: Winter, 1967

Koenigsberg, Richard A.  'Culture and Unconscious Fantasy: Observations on Courtly Love.' *Psychoanalytic Review,* 54 (1967), 36–50

Kolstrup, Søren  'La conception de l'homme dans les *Tragiques.'* *Revue Romane,* 4 (1969), 20–7

Kostoroski, Emilie P.  'Further Echoes from Roland's Horn.' *Romance Notes,* 13 (1971–2), 541–4

Krysinski, Wladimir  'Entre aliénation et utopie: la ville dans la poésie moderne.' *Revue d'Esthétique,* 1977 (no. 3–4), 33–71

Kuhn, Reinhard  *The Demon of Noontide: Ennui in Western Literature.* Princeton: Princeton Univ. Press, 1976

Kurman, George  'Ecphrasis in Epic Poetry.' *Comparative Literature,* 26 (1974), 1–13

Kushner, Eva 'L'évolution des symboles dans la poésie de Pierre Emmanuel.' *Ecrits du Canada Français*, 13 (1962), 9–70
– *Le Mythe d'Orphée dans la littérature française contemporaine.* Paris: Nizet, 1961
Kuster, Otto *L'Homme et la pierre dans la poésie moderne.* Zurich: Zentralstelle der Studentenschaft, 1970
Labry, Suzanne 'Le poète d'Elsa.' *Europe*, no 454–5 (Feb.-March 1967), 130–44
Lacoste-Veysseyre, Claudine *Les Alpes romantiques: Le thème des Alpes dans la littérature française de 1800 à 1850.* 2 vols. Geneva: Slatkine, 1981
Lagny, Jean *Le Poète Saint-Amant (1594–1661): Essai sur sa vie et ses œuvres.* Paris: Nizet, 1964
Lanson, Gustave *Voltaire.* Paris: Hachette, 1906
Lapp, John C. *The Esthetics of Negligence: La Fontaine's 'Contes.'* Cambridge: Cambridge Univ. Press, 1971
Lazar, Moshé 'Lancelot et la "mulier mediatrix": La quête de soi à travers la femme.' *L'Esprit Créateur*, 9 (1969), 243–56
Lecherbonnier, Bernard *Aragon.* Paris: Bordas, 1971
– *Aragon, Le 'cycle d'Elsa': Analyse critique.* Paris: Hatier, 1974
–, ed. *Les Critiques de notre temps et Aragon.* Paris: Garnier, 1976
Lefèvre, Roger 'Le printemps alpestre de *Jocelyn* ou l'imagination lamartinienne du bonheur.' In *Lamartine: Le Livre du Centenaire.* Ed. Paul Viallaneix. Paris: Flammarion, 1971, pp. 95–106
Le Gentil, Pierre *La Chanson de Roland.* Paris: Hatier-Boivin, 1955
Le Goff, Jacques, and Pierre Vidal-Naquet 'Lévi-Strauss en Brocéliande.' *Critique*, 30 (1974), 541–71
Legrand, Yolande *La Notion de 'couleur' dans l'œuvre poétique d'Alfred de Vigny.* Bordeaux: Pechade, 1966
Lejeune, Rita 'Le péché de Charlemagne et la *Chanson de Roland.*' In *Studia Philologica: Homenaje ofrecido a Dámaso Alonso.* Vol. 2. Madrid: Gredos, 1961, pp. 339–71
Lepage, Yvan G. 'Le *Roman de la Rose* et la tradition romanesque au moyen âge.' *Etudes Littéraires*, 4 (1971), 91–106
Leslie, Bruce R. *Ronsard's Successful Epic Venture: The Epyllion.* Lexington: French Forum, 1979
Levillain, Henriette *Le Rituel poétique de Saint-John Perse.* Paris: Gallimard, 1977
Levrault, Léon *L'Epopée (évolution du genre).* Paris: Delaplane, n.d.
Levy, Gertrude R. *The Sword from the Rock: An Investigation into the Origins of Epic Literature and the Development of the Hero.* London: Faber, 1953
Lewis, Clive Staples *The Allegory of Love.* Oxford: Clarendon Press, 1936
– *A Preface to 'Paradise Lost.'* London: Oxford Univ. Press, 1942
Lindenberger, Herbert *On Wordsworth's 'Prelude.'* Princeton: Princeton Univ. Press, 1963
Lindner, Monika *Voltaire und die Poetik des Epos: Studien zur Erzähltechnik und zur Ironie in 'La Pucelle d'Orléans.'* Munich: Fink, 1980
Little, Roger 'The Image of the Threshold in the Poetry of Saint-John Perse.' *Modern Language Review*, 64 (1969), 777–92
– *Saint-John Perse.* London: Athlone Press, 1973
Livi, François 'L'un des thèmes éternels de l'imagination poétique: l'orphisme.' In *L'Imagination créatrice. Rencontre Internationale ... Poigny-la-Forêt. Actes.* Ed. Roselyne Chenu. Neuchâtel: La Baconnière, 1971, pp. 61–9

Locatelli, Rossana 'L'avventura nei romanzi di Chrétien de Troyes e nei suoi imitatori.' *ACME*, 4 (1951), 3–22

Lods, Jeanne 'Le thème de l'enfance dans l'épopée française.' *Cahiers de Civilisation Médiévale*, 3 (1960), 58–62

Lombard, Charles M. 'The Evolution of Critical Opinion on the Ordination Scene in *Jocelyn.*' *Symposium*, 10 (1956), 311–15

Loomis, Roger Sherman *Arthurian Tradition and Chrétien de Troyes.* New York: Columbia Univ. Press, 1949

Lord, Albert B 'Narrative Poetry.' In *Encyclopedia of Poetry and Poetics.* Ed. Alex Preminger. Princeton: Princeton Univ. Press, 1965, pp. 542–50

Lord, George deForest *Heroic Mockery: Variations on Epic Themes from Homer to Joyce.* Newark: Univ. of Delaware Press, 1977

Lukács, György *Studies in European Realism: A Sociological Survey of the Writings of Balzac, Stendhal, Zola, Tolstoy, Gorki, and Others.* London: Hillway, 1950

– *Die Theorie des Romans: Ein geschichtsphilosophischer Versuch über die Formen der grossen Epik.* 2nd ed. Neuwied/Rhein: Luchterhand, 1963

Lyons, Faith 'More About Roland's Glove.' In *Société Rencesvals. Proceedings of the Fifth International Conference.* Salford: Univ. of Salford, 1977, pp. 156–66

Machabey, Armand *Guillaume de Machault, 130-?–1377: La vie et l'œuvre musical.* 2 vols. Paris: Richard-Masse, 1955

Maclean, Ian *Woman Triumphant: Feminism in French Literature, 1610–1652.* Oxford: Clarendon Press, 1977

McNamee, Maurice B., sj *Honor and the Epic Hero: A Study of the Shifting Concept of Magnanimity in Philosophy and Epic Poetry.* New York: Holt, Rinehart and Winston, 1960

Magné, Bernard *Crise de la littérature française sous Louis XIV: Humanisme et nationalisme.* Paris: Champion, 1976

Maiworm, Heinrich *Neue deutsche Epik.* Berlin: Schmidt, 1968

Maler, Anselm *Der Held im Salon: Zum antiheroischen Programm deutscher Rokoko-Epik.* Tübingen: Niemeyer, 1973

Mallion, Jean *Victor Hugo et l'art architectural.* Paris: Presses Universitaires de France, 1962

Mancini, Mario *Società feudale e ideologia nel 'Charroi de Nîmes.'* Florence: Olschki, 1972

Mandel, Jerome 'Elements in the *Charrette* World: The Father-Son Relationship.' *Modern Philology*, 62 (1964–5), 97–104

Maranini, Lorenza '"Cavalleria" e "Cavalieri" nel mondo di Chrétien de Troyes.' In *Mélanges de langue et de littérature du Moyen Age et de la Renaissance offerts à Jean Frappier.* 2 vols. Geneva: Droz, 1970, pp. 737–55

– *Personaggi e immagini nell' opera di Chrétien de Troyes.* Milan: Istituto Editoriale Cisalpino, 1966

Marazza, Camillo 'Immaginazione poetica e realtà sociale: Il caso delle "Tisseuses" di Chrétien de Troyes.' *Quaderni di Lingue e Letteratura*, 1 (1976), 49–57

Marchal, Bertrand. 'De l'actualité au mythe dans les *Discours* de Ronsard.' *Information Littéraire*, 32 (1980), 208–10

Marcuse, Ludwig 'Schiller, Voltaire und die Jungfrau.' *Club Voltaire*, 2 (1965), 15–19

Marissel, André *Pierre Emmanuel: Essai.* Noisy-le-Sec: Editions de la Fraternité, 1974

Marmier, Jean 'La conscience du satirique, d'Horace à Boileau.' In *Critique et création littéraires en France au XVIIe siècle*. Colloques Internationaux du CNRS, no. 557. Paris: Editions du Centre National de la Recherche Scientifique, 1977, pp. 29–38

Marni, Archimede *Allegory in the French Heroic Poem of the Seventeenth Century*. Princeton: Princeton Univ. Press, 1936

Maskell, David *The Historical Epic in France, 1500–1700*. London: Oxford Univ. Press, 1973

Mason, H.A. 'Boileau's *Lutrin*.' *Cambridge Quarterly*, 4 (1969–70), 362–80

Mason, Haydn *Voltaire*. New York: St. Martin's Press, 1975

Matarasso, Pauline *Recherches historiques et littéraires sur 'Raoul de Cambrai.'* Paris: Nizet, 1962

Mathé, Roger *L'Aventure, d'Hérodote à Malraux*. Paris: Bordas, 1972

Maulnier, Thierry, ed. *Introduction à la poésie française*. Paris: Gallimard, 1939

Mauritz, Hans-Dieter *Der Ritter im magischen Reich: Märchenelemente im französischen Abenteuerroman des 12. und 13. Jahrhunderts*. Berne: Lang, 1974

Mauron, Charles 'Les personnages de Victor Hugo: Etude psychocritique.' In *Victor Hugo, Œuvres complètes*. Ed. Jean Massin. Vol. 2. Paris: Club Français du Livre, 1967, pp. i–xlii

Mealy, Kenneth C. '*Huon de Bordeaux*: An Examination of Generative Forces in Late Epic Diction.' *Olifant*, 2 (1974–5), 80–90

Ménager, Daniel *Ronsard: Le roi, le poète et les hommes*. Geneva: Droz, 1979

Menant, Sylvain *La Chute d'Icare: La crise de la poésie française, 1700–1750*. Geneva: Droz, 1981

Ménard, Philippe 'Le chevalier errant dans la littérature arthurienne: Recherches sur les raisons du départ et de l'errance.' In *Voyage, quête, pèlerinage dans la littérature et la civilisation médiévales. Actes du Colloque*. Aix-en-Provence: CUER MA, 1976, pp. 289–310

– *Le Rire et le sourire dans le roman courtois en France au Moyen Age (1150–1250)*. Geneva: Droz, 1969

Merchant, Paul *The Epic*. London: Methuen, 1971

Meyer, Henry *Voltaire on War and Peace*. Banbury: Voltaire Foundation, 1976

Meyer, Wolfgang *Die Gestaltung alttestamentlicher Erzählstoffe in der Poesie der Romantik und Spätromantik in Frankreich*. Munich: Fink, 1972

Mickel, Emanuel J., Jr 'The Thirty *Pleges* for Ganelon.' *Olifant*, 6 (1978–9), 293–304

Miller, James E., Jr *The American Quest for a Supreme Fiction: Whitman's Legacy in the Personal Epic*. Chicago: Univ. of Chicago Press, 1979

Milner, Max *Le Diable dans la littérature française de Cazotte à Baudelaire, 1772–1861*. 2 vols. Paris: Corti, 1960

– 'Le sexe des anges: de l'ange amoureux à l'amante angélique.' *Romantisme*, no. 11 (1976), 55–67

Minder, Robert 'Paris in der französischen Literatur (1760–1960).' In his *Dichter in der Gesellschaft: Erfahrungen mit deutscher und französischer Literatur*. Frankfurt/Main: Insel, 1966, pp. 287–339

Miner, Earl, ed. *Literary Uses of Typology from the Late Middle Ages to the Present*. Princeton: Princeton Univ. Press, 1977

Minogue, Valerie 'Paths and Feet in *Les Destinées*.' *Modern Languages*, 46 (1965), 131–9

- 'The Tableau in *La Colère de Samson*.' *Modern Language Review*, 60 (1965), 374–8
Mölk, Ulrich '*Ange femme* und *donna angelo*: Über zwei literarische Typen des weiblichen Engels.' *Romanistisches Jahrbuch*, 25 (1974), 139–53
Molho, Raphaël, and Pierre Reboul, ed. *Intime, intimité, intimisme*. Lille: Editions Universitaires, 1976
Moller, Herbert 'The Meaning of Courtly Love.' *Journal of American Folklore*, 73 (1960), 39–52
Moog-Grünewald, Maria *Metamorphosen der 'Metamorphosen': Rezeptionsarten der ovidischen Verwandlungsgeschichten in Italien und Frankreich im XVI. und XVII. Jahrhundert*. Heidelberg: Winter, 1979
Moorman, Charles *Kings and Captains: Variations on a Heroic Theme*. Lexington: Univ. Press of Kentucky, 1971
Moreau, Pierre 'Les deux univers de Victor Hugo: le visible et l'invisible.' In Victor Hugo, *Œuvres complètes*, ed. Jean Massin. Vol. 3. Paris: Club Français du Livre, 1967, pp. i–xxv
Müller-Bochat, Eberhard 'Die Einheit des Wissens und das Epos: Zur Geschichte eines utopischen Gattungsbegriffs.' *Romanistisches Jahrbuch*, 17 (1966), 58–81
Murrin, Michael *The Allegorical Epic: Essays in Its Rise and Decline*. Chicago: Univ. of Chicago Press, 1980
Muscatine, Charles 'The Emergence of Psychological Allegory in Old French Romance.' *PMLA*, 68 (1953), 1160–82
Nasta, Dan-Ion *Saint-John Perse et la découverte de l'être*. Paris: Presses Universitaires de France, 1980
Naves, Raymond *Le Goût de Voltaire*. Paris: Garnier, 1938
Németh, Jenö Újfalusi 'La raison d'être d'un genre "avorté": la théorie du poème héroïque sous l'Ancien Régime.' *Acta Romanica*, 3 (1976), 87–153
Nerlich, Michael 'La mythologie comme arme poétique dans la lutte pour la paix: Propos hérétiques sur Boileau, le poème épique et la "doctrine classique."' *Beiträge zur romanischen Philologie*, 17 (1978), 65–80
Nichols, Stephen G., Jr 'The Rhetoric of Sincerity in the *Roman de la Rose*.' In *Romance Studies in Memory of Edward Billings Ham*. Ed. Urban Tigner Holmes. Hayward: California State College, 1967, pp. 115–29
- 'Roland's Echoing Horn.' *Romance Notes*, 5 (1963–4), 78–84
- 'The Spirit of Truth: Epic Modes in Medieval Literature.' *New Literary History*, 1 (1969–70), 365–86
Nitschke, Uwe *Studien zum Schiksalsgedanken und seiner dichterischen Gestaltung bei Alfred de Vigny*. Hamburg: Romanisches Seminar der Universität Hamburg, 1969
Nitzsche, Jane Chance *The Genius Figure in Antiquity and the Middle Ages*. New York: Columbia Univ. Press, 1975
Noehte, Simone '*Moyse Sauvé' von Saint-Amant: Ein Beitrag zu Konzeption und Stil des christlichen Epos in Frankreich um die Mitte des 17. Jahrhunderts*. Diss. Frankfurt/Main, 1962
Nolting-Hauff, Ilse 'Zur Psychoanalyse der Heldendichtung: Das Rolandslied und die einfache Form "Sage."' *Poetica*, 10 (1978), 429–68
Nothnagle, John T. 'The Drama of *Les Discours* of Ronsard.' *L'Esprit Créateur*, 10 (1970), 117–24
Noulet, Emilie *Le Ton poétique: Mallarmé, Verlaine, Corbière, Rimbaud, Valéry, Saint-John Perse*. Paris: Corti, 1971

Noyer-Weidner, Alfred 'Farbrealität und Farbsymbolik in der "Heidengeographie" des Rolandsliedes.' *Romanische Forschungen*, 81 (1969), 22–59
– 'Vom biblischen "Gottesberg" zur Symbolik des "Heidentals" im Rolandslied.' *Zeitschrift für französische Sprache und Literatur*, 81 (1971), 13–66
– 'Zur "Heidengeographie" im Rolandslied.' In *Verba et Vocabula: Ernst Gamillscheg zum 80. Geburtstag*. Ed. Helmut Stimm and Julius Wilhelm. Munich: Fink, 1968, pp. 379–404
Oliver, Dennis 'Guillaume de Machaut: "Art poétique/Art d'amour."' *Sub-Stance*, no. 4 (Fall 1972), 45–50
Ollier, Marie-Louise 'Demande sociale et constitution d'un "genre": la situation dans la France du xɪɪe siècle.' *Mosaic*, 8:4 (1975), 207–16
Onimus, Jean *Expérience de la poésie: Saint-John Perse, Henri Michaux, René Char, Guillevic, Jean Tardieu, Jean Follain, Pierre Emmanuel*. Paris: Desclée De Brouwer, 1973
Orr, Linda '*Jocelyn* et l'Histoire, ou le texte parjure.' *Romantisme*, no. 19 (1978), 41–55
Ott, Karl August '"*Armut*" und "*Reichtum*" bei Guillaume de Lorris.' In *Beiträge zum romanischen Mittelalter*. Ed. Kurt Baldinger. Tübingen: Niemeyer, 1977, pp. 282–305
Paquette, Jean-Marcel 'Epopée et roman: continuité ou discontinuité?' *Etudes Littéraires*, 4 (1971), 9–38
Parent, Monique *Saint-John Perse et quelques devanciers: Etudes sur le poème en prose*. Paris: Klincksieck, 1960
Pasero, Nicolò 'Chrétien, la realtà, l'ideologia: ancora sul "Chastel de Pesme-Aventure" (*Yvain*, vv. 5179 ss.).' In *Studi in ricordo di Guido Favati*. Genoa: Tilgher, 1975, pp. 145–69
Paulhan, Jean, ed. *Honneur à Saint-John Perse: Hommages et témoignages littéraires*. Paris: Gallimard, 1965
Payen, Jean-Charles 'Le comique de l'énormité: goliardisme et provocation dans le *Roman de la Rose*.' *L'Esprit Créateur*, 16 (1976), 46–60
– 'Eléments idéologiques et revendications dans le *Roman de la Rose*.' In *Littérature et société au Moyen Age. Actes du Colloque des 5 et 6 mai 1978*. Ed. Danielle Buschinger. Université de Picardie: Centre d'Etudes Médiévales, n.d., pp. 285–304
– 'Encore le problème de la géographie épique.' In *Société Rencesvals. IVe Congrès International. Actes et Mémoires*. Heidelberg: Winter, 1969, pp. 261–5
– 'Lancelot contre Tristan: la conjuration d'un mythe subversif (Réflexions sur l'idéologie romanesque au Moyen Age).' In *Mélanges de langue et de littérature médiévales offerts à Pierre Le Gentil*. Paris: SEDES, 1973, pp. 617–32
– *Le Motif du repentir dans la littérature française médiévale (des origines à 1230)*. Geneva: Droz, 1967
– *Les Origines de la courtoisie dans la littérature française médiévale. Vol. 2. Le roman*. Paris: Centre de Documentation Universitaire, 1967
–, F.N.M. Diekstra, et al. *Le Roman*. Turnhout: Brepols, 1975
– '*Le Roman de la Rose* et la notion de carrefour idéologique.' *Romanistische Zeitschrift für Literaturgeschichte*, 1 (1977), 193–203
– *La Rose et l'utopie: Révolution sexuelle et communisme nostalgique chez Jean de Meung*. Paris: Editions Sociales, 1976
Pearce, Roy Harvey *The Continuity of American Poetry*. Princeton: Princeton Univ. Press, 1961

Perella, Nicolas James *The Kiss, Sacred and Profane: An Interpretative History of Kiss Symbolism and Related Religio-Erotic Themes*. Berkeley: Univ. of California Press, 1969

Petroni, Liano *Poetica e poesia d'Alfred de Vigny*. Cagliari: Università di Cagliari, 1956

Pfeiffer, Ruth *En route vers l'au-delà arthurien: Etude sur les châteaux enchantés et leurs enchantements*. Zurich: Juris, 1970

Pica, Carlo '*Raoul de Cambrai*: crisi di un sistema.' In *Studi di filologia romanza e italiana offerti a Gianfranco Folena*. Modena: STEM-Mucchi, 1980, pp. 67–77

Picard, Raymond, ed. *La Poésie française de 1640 à 1680*. Vol. 2. *Satire, Epître, Burlesque, Poésie galante*. Paris: SEDES, 1969

Piehler, Paul *The Visionary Landscape: A Study in Medieval Allegory*. London: Arnold, 1971

Pineaux, Jacques 'Poésie et prophétisme: Ronsard et Théodore de Bèze dans la querelle des *Discours*.' *Revue d'Histoire Littéraire de la France*, 78 (1978), 531–40

Pioletti, Antonio 'Lettura dell' episodio del "Chastel de Pesme-Aventure" (*Yvain*, vv. 5105–5805).' *Medioevo Romanzo*, 6 (1979), 227–46

Planche, Alice '"Est vrais amans li drois oisiaus de proie ..." Sur une image de Guillaume de Machaut.' In *Etudes de philologie romane et d'histoire littéraire offertes à Jules Horrent*. Ed. Jean Marie D'Heure and Nicoletta Cherubini. Liège: Association des Romanistes de Liège, 1980, pp. 351–60

– 'Roland fils de personne: les structures de la parenté du héros dans le manuscrit d'Oxford.' In *Charlemagne et l'épopée romane. Actes du VIIe Congrès International de la Société Rencesvals*. 2 vols. Paris: Les Belles Lettres, 1978, pp. 595–604

Pocock, Gordon *Boileau and the Nature of Neo-Classicism*. Cambridge: Cambridge Univ. Press, 1980

*La Poésie et la Résistance*. Subj. of *Europe*, no. 543–4 (July-August 1974)

*Le Poète dans la société contemporaine*. Subj. of *Etudes Littéraires*, 1:3 (Dec. 1968)

Poggioli, Renato *The Oaten Flute: Essays on Pastoral Poetry and the Pastoral Ideal*. Cambridge, Mass.: Harvard Univ. Press, 1975

– 'The Poetry of St.-J. Perse.' *Yale French Studies*, no. 2 (1948), 5–33

Poirion, Daniel 'Chanson de geste ou épopée? Remarques sur la définition d'un genre.' *Travaux de Linguistique et de Littérature*, 10:2 (1972), 7–20

– 'Les mots et les choses selon Jean de Meun.' *Information Littéraire*, 26 (1974), 7–11

– *Le Moyen Age II: 1300–1480*. Paris: Arthaud, 1971

– 'Narcisse et Pygmalion dans le *Roman de la Rose*.' In *Essays in Honor of Louis Francis Solano*. Ed. Raymond J. Cormier and Urban T. Holmes. Chapel Hill: Univ. of North Carolina Press, 1970, pp. 153–65

– *Le Poète et le prince: L'évolution du lyrisme courtois de Guillaume de Machaut à Charles d'Orléans*. Paris: Presses Universitaires de France, 1965

– *Le Roman de la Rose*. Paris: Hatier, 1973

Pollmann, Leo *Das Epos in den romanischen Literaturen: Verlust und Wandlungen*. Stuttgart: Kohlhammer, 1966

– 'Von der *chanson de geste* zum höfischen Roman in Frankreich.' *Germanisch-romanische Monatsschrift*, 47 (1966), 1–14

Pomeau, René *La Religion de Voltaire*. Paris: Nizet, 1956

– 'Voltaire et le héros.' *Revue des Sciences Humaines*, no. 64 (1951), 345–51

Porter, Laurence M.  *The Renaissance of the Lyric in French Romanticism: Elegy, 'Poëme' and Ode.* Lexington: French Forum, 1978
Poulet, Georges  *La Distance intérieure.* Vol. 2 of his *Etudes sur le temps humain.* Paris: Plon, 1952
– *Etudes sur le temps humain.* Edinburgh: Edinburgh Univ. Press, 1949
– *Mesure de l'instant.* Vol. 4 of his *Etudes sur le temps humain.* Paris: Plon, 1968
– *Les Métamorphoses du cercle.* Paris: Plon, 1961
– *Le Point de départ.* Vol. 3 of his *Etudes sur le temps humain.* Paris: Plon, 1964
Praz, Mario  *La carne, la morte e il diavolo nella letteratura romantica.* Milan: La Cultura, 1930
Pruner, Francis  *L'Esotérisme de Saint-John Perse (dans 'Anabase').* Paris: Klincksieck, 1977
Py, Albert  *Ronsard.* Paris: Desclée De Brouwer, 1972
–, ed. Ronsard, *Hymnes.* Textes Littéraires Français, 251. Geneva: Droz, 1978
Py, Liliane  'Dionysos dans l'espace théâtral d'*Amers.*' *Cahiers du 20e Siècle,* no. 7 (1976), 91–9
Quilligan, Maureen  *The Language of Allegory: Defining the Genre.* Ithaca: Cornell Univ. Press, 1979
– 'Words and Sex: The Language of Allegory in the *De planctu naturae,* the *Roman de la Rose,* and Book III of *The Faerie Queene.*' *Allegorica,* 2:1 (1977), 195–216
Raduleț, Carmen M.  'Intorno al realismo cerimoniale del *Lancelot* di Chrétien de Troyes.' *Cultura Neolatina,* 35 (1975), 9–30
Raillard, Georges  *Aragon.* Paris: Editions Universitaires, 1964
Raymond, Marcel  *Romantisme et rêverie.* Paris: Corti, 1978
Reaney, Gilbert  *Guillaume de Machaut.* London: Oxford Univ. Press, 1971
Reed, Gervais E.  *Claude Barbin, libraire de Paris sous le règne de Louis XIV.* Geneva: Droz, 1974
Regosin, Richard L.  *The Poetry of Inspiration: Agrippa d'Aubigné's 'Les Tragiques.'* Chapel Hill: Univ. of North Carolina Press, 1970
Remak, Henry H.H.  'The Periodization of XIXth Century German Literature in the Light of French Trends: A Reconsideration.' *Neohelicon,* 1:1–2 (1973), 177–94
Ribard, Jacques  *Chrétien de Troyes, 'Le Chevalier de la Charrette': Essai d'interprétation symbolique.* Paris: Nizet, 1972
– 'De Chrétien de Troyes à Guillaume de Lorris: ces quêtes qu'on dit inachevées.' In *Voyage, quête, pèlerinage dans la littérature et la civilisation médiévales. Actes du Colloque.* Aix-en-Provence: CUER MA, 1976, pp. 313–21
– 'Introduction à une étude polysémique du *Roman de la Rose* de Guillaume de Lorris.' In *Etudes de langue et de littérature du Moyen Age offertes à Félix Lecoy.* Paris: Champion, 1973, pp. 519–28
Richard, Jean-Pierre  'A propos d'*Anabase*: petite rêverie sur un titre et sur un nom.' *Information Littéraire,* 29 (1977), 70–4
– '*Anabase*: un imaginaire de l'esprit.' In *Le Lieu et la formule: Hommage à Marc Eigeldinger.* Neuchâtel: La Baconnière, 1978, pp. 216–22
– *Etudes sur le romantisme.* Paris: Seuil, 1970
– *Onze études sur la poésie moderne.* Paris: Seuil, 1964
Richter, Eckart.  'Zum Problem des französischen Epos im 18. Jahrhundert.' In *Beiträge zur französischen Aufklärung und zur spanischen Literatur: Festgabe für Werner Krauss.* Ed. Werner Bahner. Berlin: Akademie-Verlag, 1971, pp. 315–36

Richter, Mario 'Aspetti e orientamenti della poetica protestante francese nel secolo XVI.' In his *Jean de Sponde e la lingua poetica dei Protestanti nel Cinquecento.* Milan: Cisalpino-Goliardica, 1973, pp. 165–202

Riddel, Joseph N., ed. *The Long Poem in the Twentieth Century.* Subj. of *Genre,* 11:4 (1978)

Ridgway, Ronald S. *Voltaire and Sensibility.* Montreal: McGill-Queen's Univ. Press, 1973

Rieuneau, Maurice '"Langage que fut la poétesse" – la Pythie selon Saint-John Perse.' *Cahiers du 20e Siècle,* no. 7 (1976), 101–14

Riffaterre, Hermine B. *L'Orphisme dans la poésie romantique: Thèmes et style surnaturalistes.* Paris: Nizet, 1970

Riffaterre, Michael. 'La vision hallucinatoire chez Victor Hugo.' *MLN,* 78 (1963), 225–41

Riquer, Martín de *Los cantares de gesta franceses: Sus problemas, su relación con España.* Madrid: Gredos, 1952

Robertson, Durant Waite, Jr. *A Preface to Chaucer: Studies in Medieval Perspectives.* Princeton: Princeton Univ. Press, 1962

Roellenbleck, Georg *Das epische Lehrgedicht Italiens im fünfzehnten und sechzehnten Jahrhundert: Ein Beitrag zur Literaturgeschichte des Humanismus und der Renaissance.* Munich: Fink, 1975

Rolfe, Christopher D. *Saint-Amant and the Theory of 'Ut Pictura Poesis.'* London: Modern Humanities Research Association, 1972

Romani, Bruno *Impegno e retorica in Agrippa d'Aubigné.* Lecce: Milella, 1976

Roncaglia, Aurelio 'Come si presenta oggi il problema delle canzoni di gesta.' In *Atti del convegno internazionale sul tema: La poesia epica e la sua formazione.* Rome: Accademia nazionale dei Lincei, 1970, pp. 277–93

Rossi, Marguerite *'Huon de Bordeaux' et l'évolution du genre épique au XIIIe siècle.* Paris: Champion, 1975

– 'Loyauté et déloyauté dans *Huon de Bordeaux.*' In *Société Rencesvals. VIe Congrès International. Actes.* Aix-en-Provence: Université de Provence, 1974, pp. 373–87

Rothe, Arnold *Französische Lyrik im Zeitalter des Barock.* Berlin: Schmidt, 1974

Rousseau, André Michel *L'Angleterre et Voltaire.* 3 vols. Oxford: Voltaire Foundation, 1976

Rousset, Jean, ed. *Anthologie de la poésie baroque française.* 2 vols. Paris: Colin, 1961

– 'Un brelan d'oubliés.' *L'Esprit Créateur,* 1 (1961), 91–100

– *L'Intérieur et l'extérieur: Essais sur la poésie et sur le théâtre au XVIIe siècle.* Paris: Corti, 1968

– *La Littérature de l'âge baroque en France: Circé et le paon.* Paris: Corti, 1954

Rüdiger, Horst, ed. *Die Gattungen in der Vergleichenden Literaturwissenschaft.* Berlin: de Gruyter, 1974

Rütten, Raimund *Symbol und Mythus im altfranzösischen Rolandslied.* Braunschweig: Westermann, 1970

Ruggieri, Ruggero M. *Il processo di Gano nella 'Chanson de Roland.'* Florence: Sansoni, 1936

Ruhe, Doris *'Le Dieu d'Amours avec son paradis': Untersuchungen zur Mythenbildung um Amor in Spätantike und Mittelalter.* Munich: Fink, 1974

Ruhe, Ernstpeter *'De Amasio ad Amasiam': Zur Gattungsgeschichte des mittelalterlichen Liebesbriefes.* Munich: Fink, 1975

Russo, Gloria M. 'Sexual Roles and Religious Images in Voltaire's *La Pucelle.*'
*Studies on Voltaire and the Eighteenth Century*, no. 171 (1977), 31–53
Ruttkowski, Wolfgang Victor *Die literarischen Gattungen: Reflexionen über eine modifizierte Fundamentalpoetik.* Berne: Francke, 1968
Ryan, Marie-Laure *Rituel et poésie: Une lecture de Saint-John Perse.* Berne: Lang, 1977
Rychner, Jean *La Chanson de geste: Essai sur l'art épique des jongleurs.* Geneva: Droz, 1955
– 'Le mythe de la fontaine de Narcisse dans le *Roman de la Rose* de Guillaume de Lorris.' In *Le Lieu et la formule: Hommage à Marc Eigeldinger.* Neuchâtel: La Baconnière, 1978, pp. 33–46
– 'Le prologue du *Chevalier de la charrette* et l'interprétation du roman.' In *Mélanges offerts à Rita Lejeune.* 2 vols. Gembloux: Duculot, 1969, pp. 1121–35
– 'Le sujet et la signification du *Chevalier de la charrette.*' *Vox Romanica*, 27 (1968), 50–76
Saint-Gérand, Jacques-Philippe *Les Destinées d'un style: Essai sur les poèmes philosophiques de Vigny.* Paris: Minard, 1979
Sauerwein, Henry A., Jr *Agrippa d'Aubigné's 'Les Tragiques': A Study in Structure and Poetic Method.* Baltimore: Johns Hopkins Press, 1953
Saulnier, Verdun L. 'Voltaire, Malézieu et la tête épique.' In *Association Guillaume Budé. Actes du Xe Congrès.* Paris: Les Belles Lettres, 1980, pp. 195–200
Savage, Catharine '"Cette Prison Nommée La Vie": Vigny's Prison Metaphor.' *Studies in Romanticism*, 9 (1970), 99–113
Savey-Casard, P. *Le Crime et la peine dans l'œuvre de Victor Hugo.* Paris: Presses Universitaires de France, 1956
Sayce, Richard A. *The French Biblical Epic in the Seventeenth Century.* Oxford: Clarendon Press, 1955
Scaglione, Aldo D. *Nature and Love in the Late Middle Ages.* Berkeley: Univ. of California Press, 1963
Schlötke-Schröer, Charlotte 'Das Raum-Zeiterlebnis in der französischen Frühromantik (Rousseau, Chateaubriand, Lamartine).' *Zeitschrift für französische Sprache und Literatur*, 67 (1956–7), 202–20
Schmidt, Albert-Marie *La Poésie scientifique en France au seizième siècle: Ronsard, Maurice Scève, Baïf, Belleau, Du Bartas, Agrippa d'Aubigné.* Paris: Michel, 1938
Schmidt, Karlernst *Vorstudien zu einer Geschichte des komischen Epos.* Halle: Niemeyer, 1953
Schmolke-Hasselmann, Beate *Der arthurische Versroman von Chrestien bis Froissart: Zur Geschichte einer Gattung.* Tübingen: Niemeyer, 1980
Scholler, Harald, ed. *The Epic in Medieval Society: Aesthetic and Moral Values.* Tübingen: Niemeyer, 1977
Schor, Naomi 'Superposition of Models in *La Légende des Siècles.*' *Romanic Review*, 65 (1974), 42–51
Schueler, Heinz Jürgen *The German Verse Epic in the Nineteenth and Twentieth Centuries.* The Hague: Nijhoff, 1967
Schürr, Friedrich *Das altfranzösische Epos: Zur Stilgeschichte und inneren Form der Gotik.* Munich: Hueber, 1926
Seebacher, Jacques 'Poétique et politique de la paternité chez Victor Hugo.' In *Romantisme et politique, 1815–1851. Colloque de l'Ecole Normale Supérieure de Saint-Cloud.* Paris: Colin, 1969, pp. 110–28

Seghers, Pierre  *La Résistance et ses poètes: France, 1940–1945.* Paris: Seghers, 1974

Segre, Cesare  'Schemi narrativi nella *Chanson de Roland.*'  *Studi Francesi,* 5 (1961), 277–83

Selle, Irene  'Aragons Realismuskonzeption im Lichte seiner Erbetheorie.'  *Beiträge zur romanischen Philologie,* 17 (1978), 55–8

–  'Aragons Reflexionen über die französische Lyrik (1939–1959).'  *Beiträge zur romanischen Philologie,* 14 (1975), 15–35; 15 (1976), 73–90

–  'Das Verhältnis Aragons und Johannes R. Bechers zum nationalen Erbe.'  *Beiträge zur romanischen Philologie,* 13 (1974), 175–85

Sellier, Philippe  *Le Mythe du héros ou le désir d'être Dieu.* Paris: Bordas, 1970

Sengle, Friedrich  *Biedermeierzeit: Deutsche Literatur im Spannungsfeld zwischen Restauration und Revolution, 1815–1848.* 2 vols. Stuttgart: Metzler, 1971–2

Sewell, Elizabeth  *The Orphic Voice: Poetry and Natural History.* New Haven: Yale Univ. Press, 1960

Seznec, Alain  'Saint-Amant, le poète sauvé des eaux.'  In *Studies in Seventeenth-Century French Literature Presented to Morris Bishop.* Ed. Jean-Jacques Demorest. Ithaca: Cornell Univ. Press, 1962, pp. 35–64

Shattuck, Roger  *The Banquet Years: The Arts in France, 1885–1918: Alfred Jarry, Henri Rousseau, Erik Satie, Guillaume Apollinaire.* New York: Harcourt, Brace, 1958

Shroder, Maurice Z.  *Icarus: The Image of the Artist in French Romanticism.* Cambridge, Mass.: Harvard Univ. Press, 1961

Siciliano, Italo  *Les Chansons de geste et l'épopée: Mythes, histoire, poèmes.* Turin: Società Editrice Internazionale, 1968

Siegrist, Sven E.  *Pour et contre Dieu: Pierre Emmanuel ou la poésie de l'approche; L'expérience du manque et de l'antériorité potentielle.* Neuchâtel: La Baconnière, 1971

Silver, Isidore  *The Intellectual Evolution of Ronsard.* Vol. 2. *Ronsard's General Theory of Poetry.* St Louis: Washington Univ. Press, 1973

–  *Ronsard and the Hellenic Renaissance in France.* Vol. 1. *Ronsard and the Greek Epic.* St. Louis: Washington Univ. Press, 1961

Simon, Pierre-Henri  *Le Domaine héroïque des lettres françaises, Xe–XIXe siècles.* Paris: Colin, 1963

Simone, Franco  *Il Rinascimento francese: Studi e ricerche.* Turin: Società Editrice Internazionale, 1961

–  *Storia della storiografia letteraria francese: Due capitoli introduttivi.* Turin: Bottega d'Erasmo, 1969

Simpson, Joyce G.  *Le Tasse et la littérature et l'art baroques en France.* Paris: Nizet, 1962

Sokolova, T.V.  'Alfred de Vigny and the July Revolution, 1830–1831.'  *Nineteenth-Century French Studies,* 1 (1972–3), 235–51

Soulié, Marguerite  *L'Inspiration biblique dans la poésie religieuse d'Agrippa d'Aubigné.* Paris: Klincksieck, 1977

Spitzer, Leo  'Note on the Poetic and the Empirical "I" in Medieval Authors.'  *Traditio,* 4 (1946), 414–22

Stackelberg, Jürgen von  *Literarische Rezeptionsformen: Übersetzung, Supplement, Parodie.* Frankfurt/Main: Athenäum, 1972

–  *Von Rabelais bis Voltaire: Zur Geschichte des französischen Romans.* Munich: Beck, 1970

Stanzel, Franz  *Die typischen Erzählsituationen im Roman: dargestellt an 'Tom Jones,' 'Moby-Dick,' 'The Ambassadors,' 'Ulysses.'* Vienna: Braumüller, 1955

Stauffer, Marianne  *Der Wald: Zur Darstellung und Deutung der Natur im Mittelalter.* Berne: Francke, 1959

Steadman, John M.  'The Arming of an Archetype: Heroic Virtue and the Conventions of Literary Epic.' In *Concepts of the Hero in the Middle Ages and the Renaissance.* Ed. Norman T. Burns and Christopher J. Reagan. Albany: State Univ. of New York Press, 1975, pp. 147–96

Steele, A.J.  'Lamartine et la poésie vitale.' In *Secondes Journées européennes d'Etudes lamartiniennes. Actes du Congrès.* Mâcon: Comité permanent d'Etudes lamartiniennes, n.d., pp. 45–59

Stegmann, André  'L'ambiguïté du concept héroïque dans la littérature morale en France sous Louis XIII.' In *Héroïsme et création littéraire sous les règnes d'Henri IV et de Louis XIII. Colloque ... 1972. Actes.* Ed. Noémi Hepp and Georges Livet. Paris: Klincksieck, 1974, pp. 29–51

– *L'Héroïsme cornélien: Genèse et signification.* 2 vols. Paris: Colin, 1968

Steiner, George  *In Bluebeard's Castle: Some Notes towards the Redefinition of Culture.* New Haven: Yale Univ. Press, 1971

Steinmeyer, Karl-Josef  *Untersuchungen zur allegorischen Bedeutung der Träume im altfranzösischen Rolandslied.* Munich: Hueber, 1963

Stephan, Rüdiger  *Goldenes Zeitalter und Arkadien: Studien zur französischen Lyrik des ausgehenden 18. und des 19. Jahrhunderts.* Heidelberg: Winter, 1971

Stevens, John  *Medieval Romance: Themes and Approaches.* London: Hutchinson, 1973

Stone, Donald, Jr  'Dido and Aeneas: Theme and Vision in the Third Book of the *Franciade.*' *Neophilologus,* 49 (1965), 289–97

– 'The Sense and Significance of Ronsard's Seasonal Hymns.' *Symposium,* 18 (1964), 321–31

Strauss, Walter A.  *Descent and Return: The Orphic Theme in Modern Literature.* Cambridge, Mass.: Harvard Univ. Press, 1971

Strohm, Paul  'Guillaume as Narrator and Lover in the *Roman de la Rose.*' *Romanic Review,* 59 (1968), 3–9

Sutcliffe, F.E.  *Guez de Balzac et son temps: Littérature et politique.* Paris: Nizet, 1959

– *Politique et culture, 1560–1660.* Paris: Didier, 1973

Szittya, Penn R.  'The Angels and the Theme of *Fortitudo* in the *Chanson de Roland.*' *Neuphilologische Mitteilungen,* 72 (1971), 193–223

Taylor, Owen R., ed.  Voltaire, *La Henriade.* Vol. 2 of *Les Œuvres complètes de Voltaire.* Geneva: Institut et Musée Voltaire, 1970

– 'Voltaire's Apprenticeship as a Historian: *La Henriade.*' In *The Age of the Enlightenment: Studies Presented to Theodore Besterman.* Ed. W.H. Barber et al. Edinburgh: Oliver and Boyd, 1967, pp. 1–14

Thiébaux, Marcelle  *The Stag of Love: The Chase in Medieval Literature.* Ithaca: Cornell Univ. Press, 1974

Thoss, Dagmar  *Studien zum 'Locus Amœnus' im Mittelalter.* Vienna: Braumüller, 1972

Tiefenbrun, Susan W.  'Boileau and His Friendly Enemy: A Poetics of Satiric Criticism.' *MLN,* 91 (1976), 672–97

Tillyard, Eustace M.W.  *The English Epic and Its Background.* New York: Oxford Univ. Press, 1954

- *The Epic Strain in the English Novel.* London: Chatto and Windus, 1958
Tocanne, Bernard 'Boileau et l'épopée d'après l'*Art Poétique.*' In *Critique et création littéraires en France au XVIIe siècle.* Colloques Internationaux du CNRS, no. 557. Paris: Editions du Centre National de la Recherche Scientifique, 1977, pp. 203–11
Todorov, Tzvetan 'The Origin of Genres.' *New Literary History,* 8 (1976–7), 159–70
Toinet, Raymond  *Quelques Recherches autour des poèmes héroïques-épiques français du dix-septième siècle.* 2 vols. Tulle: Crauffon, 1899–1907
Topazio, Virgil W. 'Voltaire's *Pucelle:* A Study in Burlesque.' *Studies on Voltaire and the Eighteenth Century,* no. 2 (1956), 207–23
Topsfield, Leslie T. *Chrétien de Troyes: A Study of the Arthurian Romances.* Cambridge: Cambridge Univ. Press, 1981
Tuve, Rosemond *Allegorical Imagery: Some Mediaeval Books and Their Posterity.* Princeton: Princeton Univ. Press, 1966
Ulriksen, Solveig Schult 'Pierre Le Moyne – poète baroque français.' *Orbis Litterarum,* 25 (1970), 19–40
Vance, Eugene  *Reading the 'Song of Roland.'* Englewood Cliffs: Prentice-Hall, 1970
Van Tieghem, Paul  *Le Sentiment de la nature dans le préromantisme européen.* Paris: Nizet, 1960
Viallaneix, Paul 'Les eaux lamartiniennes.' In his ed. *Lamartine: Le Livre du Centenaire.* Paris: Flammarion, 1971, pp. 11–29
- *Vigny par lui-même.* Paris: Seuil, 1964
- 'Vigny prophète? Etude de *Paris.*' In *Le Réel et le texte.* Paris: Colin, 1974, pp. 197–208
Vinaver, Eugène  *The Rise of Romance.* Oxford: Clarendon Press, 1971
Vistica, Sister M. Rita Rose, SNJM 'The Poetry of Pierre Emmanuel: Incarnation in Progress.' Diss. Fordham 1965
Vitz, E.B. 'The *I* of the *Roman de la Rose.*' *Genre,* 6 (1973), 49–75
Vodoz, Jules 'Roland,' un symbole.* Paris: Champion, 1920
Völker, Wolfram  *Märchenhafte Elemente bei Chrétien de Troyes.* Bonn: Romanisches Seminar der Universität Bonn, 1972
Vogler, Thomas A. *Preludes to Vision: The Epic Venture in Blake, Wordsworth, Keats, and Hart Crane.* Berkeley: Univ. of California Press, 1971
Vries, Jan de  *Heroic Song and Heroic Legend.* Eng. tr. London: Oxford Univ. Press, 1963
Wäber, Gottfried 'Victor Hugos "Le Parricide" und das Motiv von Schuld und Bestrafung.' *Zeitschrift für französische Sprache und Literatur,* 77 (1967), 181–9
Wade, Ira O. *The Intellectual Development of Voltaire.* Princeton: Princeton Univ. Press, 1969
Waltz, Matthias *Rolandslied, Wilhelmslied, Alexiuslied: Zur Struktur und geschichtlichen Bedeutung.* Heidelberg: Winter, 1965
- 'Spontanéité et responsabilité dans la chanson de geste: *Raoul de Cambrai.*' In *Société Rencesvals. IVe Congrès International. Actes et Mémoires.* Heidelberg: Winter, 1969, pp. 194–201
Ward, Patricia A. *The Medievalism of Victor Hugo.* University Park: Pennsylvania State Univ. Press, 1975
Wardropper, Bruce W. 'The Epic Hero Superseded.' In *Concepts of the Hero in the*

492     Bibliography

*Middle Ages and the Renaissance.* Ed. Norman T. Burns and Christopher J. Reagan. Albany: State Univ. of New York Press, 1975, pp. 197–221

Warman, Stephen 'Saint-Amant et la *Bella Schiava* de Marino.' *Revue de Littérature Comparée*, 51 (1977), 528–35

Warnke, Frank J. 'Baroque Transformations in the Romance Epic.' In *Actes du VIe Congrès de l'Association Internationale de Littérature Comparée.* Stuttgart: Kunst und Wissen, 1975, pp. 531–5

– *Versions of Baroque: European Literature in the Seventeenth Century.* New Haven: Yale Univ. Press, 1972

Weber, Henri *La Création poétique au XVIe siècle en France de Maurice Scève à Agrippa d'Aubigné.* 2 vols. Paris: Nizet, 1956

Weber, Jean-Paul *Genèse de l'œuvre poétique.* Paris: Gallimard, 1960

Weinberg, Bernard *The Limits of Symbolism: Studies of Five Modern French Poets.* Chicago: Univ. of Chicago Press, 1966

Weise, Georg *L'ideale eroico del Rinascimento e le sue premesse umanistiche.* Naples: Edizioni Scientifiche Italiane, 1961

Wendt. Michael *Der Oxforder 'Roland': Heilsgeschehen und Teilidentität im 12. Jahrhundert.* Munich: Fink, 1970

Wentzlaff-Eggebert, Harald *Der französische Roman um 1625.* Munich: Fink, 1973

Werner, Klaus *Die Gattung des Epos nach italienischen und französischen Poetiken des 16. Jahrhunderts.* Frankfurt/Main: Lang, 1977

Wetherbee, Winthrop *Platonism and Poetry in the Twelfth Century: The Literary Influence of the School of Chartres.* Princeton: Princeton Univ. Press, 1972

Wilkie, Brian *Romantic Poets and Epic Tradition.* Madison: Univ. of Wisconsin Press, 1965

Williams, Sarah Jane 'An Author's Role in Fourteenth Century Book Production: Guillaume de Machaut's "livre ou je met toutes mes choses."' *Romania*, 90 (1969), 433–54

– 'The Lady, the Lyrics and the Letters.' *Early Music*, 5 (1977), 462–8

– 'Machaut's Self-Awareness as Author and Producer.' In *Machaut's World: Science and Art in the Fourteenth Century.* Ed. Madeleine Pelner Cosman and Bruce Chandler. New York: New York Academy of Sciences, 1978, pp. 189–97

Wilson, Dudley, ed. *French Renaissance Scientific Poetry.* London: Athlone Press, 1974

Wimsatt, James *Chaucer and the French Love Poets: The Literary Background of the 'Book of the Duchess.'* Chapel Hill: Univ. of North Carolina Press, 1968

Wolfzettel, Friedrich 'Funktionswandel eines epischen Motivs: Der Blick auf Paris.' *Romanistische Zeitschrift für Literaturgeschichte*, 1 (1977), 353–76

– 'Zur Stellung und Bedeutung der *Enfances* in der altfranzösischen Epik.' *Zeitschrift für französische Sprache und Literatur*, 83 (1973), 317–48; 84 (1974), 1–32

Yoyo, Emile *Saint-John Perse et le conteur.* Paris: Bordas, 1971

Yu, Anthony C., ed. *Parnassus Revisited: Modern Critical Essays on the Epic Tradition.* Chicago: American Library Association, 1973

Zdrojewska, Vera *Boileau.* Brescia: La Scuola, 1948

Zéraffa, Michel 'Villes démoniaques.' *Revue d'Esthétique*, 1977 (no. 3–4), 13–32

Ziolkowski, Theodore *Fictional Transfigurations of Jesus.* Princeton: Princeton Univ. Press, 1972

Zumthor, Paul 'Autobiographie au Moyen Age?' In his *Langue, texte, énigme*.
   Paris: Seuil, 1975, pp. 165–80
– *Essai de poétique médiévale*. Paris: Seuil, 1972
– 'Le Moyen Age de Victor Hugo.' In Victor Hugo, *Œuvres complètes*, ed. Jean
   Massin. Vol. 4. Paris: Club Français du Livre, 1967, pp. i–xxxi
– 'Récit et anti-récit: le *Roman de la Rose*.' In his *Langue, texte, énigme*. Paris:
   Seuil, 1975, pp. 249–64
– *Victor Hugo, poète de Satan*. Paris: Laffont, 1946

# Index

# UNIVERSITY OF TORONTO ROMANCE SERIES

This book
was designed by
ANTJE LINGNER
and was printed by
University of
Toronto
Press